CICERO

THE LETTERS TO HIS FRIENDS

III

CICERO

THE LETTERS TO HIS FRIENDS

III

CICERO

THE LETTERS TO HIS FRIENDS

WITH AN ENGLISH TRANSLATION BY

W. GLYNN WILLIAMS, M.A.

FORMERLY FELLOW OF ST. JOHN'S COLLEGE, CAMBRIDGE
AND HEADMASTER OF FRIARS SCHOOL, BANGOR

IN THREE VOLUMES

III
(INCLUDING THE LETTERS TO QUINTUS)

THE LETTERS TO BRUTUS

WITH AN ENGLISH TRANSLATION BY

M. CARY, D.Litt.

FORMERLY PROFESSOR OF ANCIENT HISTORY
AT THE UNIVERSITY OF LONDON

CAMBRIDGE, MASSACHUSETTS
HARVARD UNIVERSITY PRESS
LONDON
WILLIAM HEINEMANN LTD
MCMLX

First printed 1929
Revised and reprinted with additions 1954
Reprinted 1960

Printed in Great Britain

CONTENTS OF VOLUME III

	PAGE
INTRODUCTION	ix
CHRONOLOGICAL SUMMARY	xii

BOOK XIII

NOTE ON CICERO'S "LITTERAE COMMENDATICIAE"   2

LETTERS

		PAGE
I.–III.	To GAIUS MEMMIUS . . .	6
IV.–VI.	To Q. VALERIUS ORCA . . .	16
VII.	To GAIUS CLUVIUS . . .	28
VIII.	To MARCUS RUTILIUS . .	34
IX.	To P. FURIUS CRASSIPES . .	36
X.–XIV.	To M. JUNIUS BRUTUS . .	40
XV.–XVI.	To C. JULIUS CAESAR . .	52
XVII.–XXVIII.	To SERVIUS SULPICIUS RUFUS .	58
XXIX.	To L. MUNATIUS PLANCUS .	88
XXX.–XXXIX.	To MANIUS ACILIUS GLABRIO .	96
XL.	To Q. ANCHARIUS . .	110
XLI.–XLII.	To L. CULLEOLUS . .	110
XLIII.–XLIV.	To QUINTIUS GALLUS . .	114

v

CONTENTS

LETTERS		PAGE
XLV.–XLVI.	To Appuleius	118
XLVII.	To Silius	120
XLVIII.	To Sextilius Rufus	120
XLIX.	To Curius	122
L.	To Manius Acilius Glabrio	124
LI.	To P. Caesius	126
LII.	To Q. Marcius Rex	126
LIII.–LVII.	To Q. Minucius Thermus	128
LVIII.	To C. Titius Rufus	138
LIX.	To Curtius Peducaeanus	140
LX.	To C. Munatius	140
LXI.–LXV.	To P. Silius	142
LXVI.–LXXII.	To P. Servilius Isauricus	152
LXXIII.–LXXIV.	To Q. Philippus	166
LXXV.	To T. Titius	168
LXXVI.	To the Quattuorviri and Decuriones	170
LXXVII.	To P. Sulpicius Rufus	172
LXXVIII.–LXXIX.	To Aulus Allienus	174

BOOK XIV

I.–IV.	To Terentia and his family	180
V.–VI.	To Terentia and Tullia	200
VII.–XIII.	To Terentia	204

vi

CONTENTS

LETTERS   PAGE

    XIV. TO TERENTIA AND TULLIA . . 212

  XV.–XVII. TO TERENTIA 214

   XVIII. TO TERENTIA AND TULLIA . . 216

XIX.–XXIV. TO TERENTIA 218

BOOK XV

NOTE ON CICERO'S GOVERNORSHIP OF CILICIA . 225

LETTERS

  I.–II. TO THE CONSULS, PRAETORS, TRIBUNES
          OF THE PLEBS, AND SENATE . 228

  III.–IV. TO M. CATO 244

    V. THE SAME TO CICERO . . . 264

   VI. TO M. CATO 268

 VII.–VIII. TO GAIUS MARCELLUS . . . 270

   IX. TO MARCUS MARCELLUS . . . 274

  X.–XI. TO GAIUS MARCELLUS . . . 276

XII.–XIII. TO LUCIUS AEMILIUS PAULLUS . . 280

XIV.–XVIII. TO GAIUS CASSIUS LONGINUS . . 286

   XIX. THE SAME TO CICERO . . . 304

 XX.–XXI. TO TREBONIUS 308

BOOK XVI

  I.–VII. TO TIRO 316

   VIII. QUINTUS CICERO TO TIRO . . 330

  IX.–XV. TO TIRO 332

CONTENTS

LETTERS   PAGE

     XVI. Quintus Cicero to Marcus Cicero   352

  XVII.–XX. To Tiro   354

     XXI. M. Cicero Junior to Tiro.   .   362

  XXII.–XXIV. To Tiro   370

     XXV. M. Cicero Junior to Tiro.   .   376

XXVI.–XXVII. Quintus Cicero to Tiro   .   .   378

TO HIS BROTHER QUINTUS

A short Life of Quintus Tullius Cicero   .   385

BOOK I

I.–IV.   388

BOOK II

I.–XVI.   476

BOOK III

I.–IX.   546

TO BRUTUS

Preface   615

Introduction   616

LETTERS I.–XXVI.   622

Order of Letters   739

Index of Names I.   .   .   .   743

Index of Names II.   .   .   .   749

Index of Names III.   .   .   .   754

viii

INTRODUCTION

INTRODUCTION

THIS collection of Cicero's " Letters to his Friends "
was preserved and edited by his secretary Tiro. The
collection is inadequately entitled, as it includes
several letters, some of them of profound interest,
from his friends to Cicero. There are 426 letters,
divided into sixteen books, not arranged in any
sort of order,[a] chronological or otherwise, except
that letters from or to particular correspondents are
generally grouped together; the third book, for
instance, consists exclusively of letters from Cicero
to Appius Claudius Pulcher, and the eighth book of
letters from Marcus Caelius Rufus to Cicero.

The earliest letter is one from Cicero to Pompey
(x. 7) dated 62 B.C., the year after Cicero's consulship; the latest is one from him to Cassius (xii. 10)
written in 43 B.C., the year after the assassination of
Caesar, and a few months before his own.

These nineteen years from 62 to 43 B.C. cover a
period of supreme importance in the history of the
Roman Republic—a period more minutely described
and vividly illustrated in these letters, giving us as
they do the different points of view of various correspondents, than even in the " Letters to Atticus,"
written by Cicero alone.

[a] The confusion thus caused is to some extent obviated
by a summary, in chronological order, prefixed to each
volume, of the events in each year covered by the Letters.

INTRODUCTION

The Letters vary greatly in interest and style; while many of them contain matter of the highest literary or historical value—as, for instance, Cicero's explanation of his political change of front (i. 9), Sulpicius Rufus's letter of condolence to Cicero on the death of his daughter Tullia (iv. 5) and Matius's defence of his friendship for Caesar (xi. 28)—others are no more than merely formal documents.

The text is based on that of Nobbe (1849); but where there was an obvious call for emendation in that text I have not hesitated to adopt other readings, always with due acknowledgement.

Such universally accepted orthographical corrections as *cum* for *quum*, *consili* for *consilii*, and *causa* for *caussa* I have made as a matter of course.

To Tyrrell and Purser's exhaustive (it has rightly been described as " monumental ") *Commentary on the Correspondence of Cicero*[a] I have made constant reference, and owe more than I can tell; I have depended upon it, too, for the dates of the letters. Watson's *Select Letters* (with the recently revised edition by Mr. W. W. How), and Pritchard and Bernard's *Selected Letters for the use of Schools* have been of invaluable assistance to me, and I have freely consulted the admirable translations of all or some of the letters by E. S. Shuckburgh, G. E. Jeans, and S. H. Jeyes.

To all the above distinguished Ciceronians I acknowledge with gratitude my very deep indebtedness.

[a] Referred to in my notes for the sake of brevity as "Tyrrell."

INTRODUCTION

THE MANUSCRIPTS

The oldest and soundest MS. of the *Epistulae ad Familiares* is the Codex Mediceus 49. 9, now in the Laurentian Library at Florence. This is known as M. Other MSS., each giving some of the letters, are :

G, Codex Harleianus 2773, in the British Museum.
R, Codex Parisianus 17812, in the Bibliothèque Nationale.
  (G and R are closely connected, and both independent of M.)
T, Codex Turonensis 688, in the Library of Tours.
H, Codex Harleianus 2682, in the British Museum.
F, Codex Erfurtensis, now Berolinensis, 252, which closely follows H.
D, Codex Palatinus, originally at Heidelberg, now in the Vatican.

Of these M alone contains all the *Epistulae ad Familiares*, G, R, and T giving different portions of Bks. I. to VIII., and H, F, and D of Bks. IX. to XVI.

A CHRONOLOGICAL SUMMARY

OF THE PRINCIPAL EVENTS IN

THE LIFE OF CICERO

DATE B.C.

106.	Cicero is born on Jan. 3 near Arpinum.
89.	Serves under Cn. Pompeius Strabo in the Marsic War.
86.	Writes his *De inventione*.
80.	Delivers his speech *Pro Sex. Roscio Amerino*.
79-78.	Travels in Greece and Asia.
77.	Returns to Rome, and marries Terentia.
75-74.	Serves as quaestor for Lilybaeum in Sicily.
70.	Accuses Verres. First Consulship of Pompey and Crassus.
69.	Curule aedile.
66.	Praetor. Speech *Pro lege Manilia*.
64.	Elected Consul with C. Antonius Hybrida (the latter by a small majority over Catiline).

63 B.C.

§ 1. Cicero, being now consul, successfully opposes the agrarian law of the tribune P. Servilius Rullus, which was in the interests of Caesar and Crassus, and

xii

intended to check the growing power of Pompey. Caesar is elected Pontifex Maximus. Cicero carries in the Senate the proposal of a *supplicatio* of unusual length to Pompey in honour of his eastern triumphs.

§ 2. Having conciliated his colleague C. Antonius by resigning to him the governorship in 62 of the rich province of Macedonia, Cicero felt himself able in the autumn of 63 to oppose the treasonable designs of L. Sergius Catilina, of which he had full information from the spy, L. Curius. In the consular elections for 62 Catiline was again defeated. On October 21 Cicero foretold the rising of the Catilinarian Manlius in Etruria on the 27th. Martial law was proclaimed, and the conspirators failed in an attempt to seize Praeneste on November 1, and another plot to murder Cicero was exposed. But Catiline had the audacity to appear in the Senate on November 8, when Cicero so crushingly denounced him that he left Rome to take command of the insurgents in Etruria.

§ 3. Certain envoys of the Allobroges, having been approached by the conspirators to supply Catiline with cavalry, were arrested, and on the strength of incriminating letters found upon them the following five conspirators were seized and imprisoned — P. Lentulus Sura (praetor), C. Cethegus (senator), L. Statilius, P. Gabinius Cimber, and M. Caeparius ; and at a meeting of the Senate on December 5, mainly at the instance of M. Cato, though Caesar, then praetor elect, was opposed to it, a decree was carried that the five conspirators arrested should be put to death, and that same evening they were strangled under Cicero's supervision.

§ 4. On December 29 the tribune Q. Metellus Nepos vetoed Cicero's address to the people on going out of office, alleging that " he had put citizens to death without a trial"; but Cicero's declaration that he had thereby saved his country was received with applause. This Metellus was one of Pompey's officers and was probably instigated by his general, who was chagrined that Cicero, and not he, should have quelled the conspiracy.

62 B.C.

Consuls : D. Junius Silanus and L. Licinius Murena

§ 1. Catiline, making for Cisalpine Gaul with Manlius's army, is met by Metellus Celer and thrown back on the army of C. Antonius. In a battle near Pistoria the insurgents were utterly and finally defeated, and Catiline slain.

§ 2. Cicero resents Pompey's lukewarm appreciation of his services to the Republic (v. 7).

§ 3. In December P. Claudius Pulcher, commonly known as Clodius, " one of the most profligate characters of a profligate age," disguised as a female musician profaned the mysteries of the Bona Dea, which were being celebrated by Roman matrons at the house of Caesar. He was discovered and brought to trial in 61.

61 B.C.

Consuls : M. Pupius Piso and M. Valerius
Messalla Niger

§ 1. Pompey, having returned from the east and disbanded his army in the preceding December, addressed the Roman people in January of this year, but failed to create a good impression. He disapproved of the bill for Clodius's prosecution, and being distrusted by the extremists in the Senate, found himself so isolated that he made overtures to Cicero.

§ 2. The consul Pupius Piso also opposed the bill for an inquiry into Clodius's affair, but the trial ultimately came on, with the result that by means of the grossest bribery Clodius was acquitted. Cicero had given evidence cancelling an alibi put up by Clodius, who swore to be avenged upon him, and proved to be a formidable foe, owing to his family connexions, and his influence over the city populace.

60 B.C.

Consuls: L. Afranius and Q. Caecilius Metellus Celer

§ 1. Led by the consul Metellus Celer, now at enmity with Pompey for having divorced his halfsister Mucia, the Senate, by obstinately opposing Pompey's plans in Asia and grants of land to his veterans, completely alienated him, and by refusing all concessions to the *publicani* in Asia offended the *equites* from among whom the *publicani* were mainly drawn. Pompey was ultimately forced into a coalition with Caesar, who returned to Rome in June to canvass for the consulship, which by the aid of Pompey and Crassus he secured.

§ 2. The *optimates*, however, brought about by bribery the election as Caesar's colleague of

M. Calpurnius Bibulus, a staunch aristocrat, but a *fainéant* consul.

§ 3. Caesar, having effected the reconciliation of Pompey and Crassus, now invited Cicero to join them, but he preferred to retain his independence, and the coalition (incorrectly called the first triumvirate) of Caesar, Pompey, and Crassus, to which he might have belonged, was established without him.

59 B.C.

Consuls : C. Julius Caesar and M. Calpurnius Bibulus

§ 1. Caesar, having failed to carry through the Senate an agrarian law providing *inter alia* for Pompey's veterans, brought another law before the assembly of the people distributing the *ager Campanus* among those veterans, and this law was carried despite the opposition of the consul Bibulus and some of the tribunes.

§ 2. P. Vatinius, one of the most unprincipled men of the time, was a humble hireling of Caesar, and now as tribune he carried the famous Lex Vatinia, which gave Caesar the command of Cisalpine Gaul and Illyricum with three legions for five years ; and the Senate, on the motion of Pompey (now, by his marriage with Julia, Caesar's son-in-law), added Transalpine Gaul to his command, with a fourth legion.

§ 3. In March Cicero, in defending his former colleague C. Antonius, who was accused of extortion as proconsul of Macedonia, attacked the triumvirate, causing grave offence to Caesar, who immediately

xvi

retaliated by sanctioning the adoption into a plebeian family of Cicero's enemy Clodius, thus making him eligible for the tribunate, where he would be in a stronger position to wreak his vengeance on Cicero.

58 B.C.

Consuls : L. Calpurnius Piso Caesoninus and Aulus Gabinius

§ 1. Clodius, who had been elected tribune in the preceding October, having carried some very popular measures in January, further established his position in February by promulgating a law assigning to the consuls on their going out of office the provinces they most desired—Syria to Gabinius, and Macedonia with Achaia to Piso,—but he made the law contingent upon the passing of two other measures which were subsequently carried—(1) a commission giving to Cato the annexation of Cyprus, and (2) an enactment " that anyone who had put Roman citizens to death without a trial should be forbidden fire and water."

§ 2. Cicero, realizing that the enactment was aimed at himself, put on mourning and threw himself on the mercy of the people. The senators and *equites* also went into mourning, but were compelled by an edict of the consuls to dress as usual. Caesar stated in public that he thought Cicero had acted illegally in putting Lentulus Sura to death, and Pompey, on being appealed to, referred Cicero to the consuls, who had already shown their hostility. Finally Cicero, at the instance of his family and Hortensius, left Rome and went into exile at the end of March. He was immediately declared an outlaw by Clodius, and his house on the Palatine and villas at Formiae and Tusculum were pillaged and dismantled.

§ 3. Cicero went to Brundisium and thence to Thessalonica, where he sojourned for seven months at the house of his friend, the quaestor Cn. Plancius. As the year went on the situation at Rome became brighter for him ; Clodius had offended Pompey by aiding the escape from Rome of the Armenian prince Tigranes whom Pompey had captured, by defeating the consul Gabinius in a street riot, and even forcing Pompey to shut himself up in his house. Moreover, Lentulus Spinther, one of the consuls elected, was personally devoted to Cicero, and the other, Metellus Nepos, a friend of Pompey ; while among the new tribunes T. Annius Milo, T. Fadius, and P. Sestius strenuously advocated Cicero's recall. His son-in-law also, C. Calpurnius Piso, who had married Cicero's daughter Tullia in 63, and was now quaestor, exercised what influence he had in the interests of his father-in-law.

57 B.C.

Consuls : P. Cornelius Lentulus Spinther
and Q. Caecilius Metellus Nepos

§ 1. No sooner had the consul Lentulus entered into office on January 1 than he brought before the Senate, with the approval of Pompey, the question of Cicero's recall ; and despite the obstruction of two of the tribunes, the people, led by Fabricius and all the praetors (except Appius Claudius Pulcher, Clodius's brother), passed in their Assembly (the *comitia centuriata*) on January 23 a provisional decree recalling Cicero. The Senate thanked Cn. Plancius and others for sheltering Cicero in his

xviii

banishment, and summoned the Italians to vote finally for his recall in the Assembly, and the bill was carried with enthusiastic unanimity on August 4, the voters being protected from Clodius and his armed ruffians by troops under the command of Milo.

§ 2. Cicero, who had come down to Dyrrachium in the preceding autumn, now crossed over to Brundisium, where he was informed by his brother Quintus of the passing of the decree for his recall, and, after a triumphal progress homeward, re-entered Rome amid universal rejoicings on September 4.

§ 3. Later on, on the motion of Cicero, Pompey is granted the *imperium* in the form of the control of the corn supply (*curatio rei annonariae*) for five years ; and on the expiry of their terms of office Lentulus receives Cilicia, and Nepos Hither Spain, as his province.

§ 4. Ptolemy Auletes (the Flute-player), king of Egypt, father of Cleopatra, having been expelled by his subjects, comes to seek the assistance of Rome, and the Senate decrees that his restoration should be entrusted to the next governor of Cilicia, *i.e.* the then consul, Lentulus Spinther.

56 B.C.

Consuls : Cn. Cornelius Lentulus Marcellinus, who supported the optimates *and opposed the triumvirs ; and L. Marcius Philippus, who later married Atia, widow of C. Octavius, and so became the stepfather of Augustus*

§ 1. In January the question of the restoration of Ptolemy Auletes is reopened and hotly debated in the Senate, and Cicero sends Lentulus, now pro-consul of Cilicia, a full account of the voting. Pompey, though ostensibly supporting the claims of Lentulus to effect the restoration, was anxious to secure for himself a commission which would not only be highly lucrative, but would give him a fleet, an army, and a base in Egypt. Cicero felt bound to support his benefactor Lentulus, and the majority of the Senate were afraid or jealous of Pompey, when, very opportunely for them, the tribune C. Cato discovered a Sibylline oracle, forbidding the restoration of Ptolemy by anyone *cum multitudine hominum* (" with a host of men "). This is the *religio* referred to in Bk. i. 2 and 3. The wranglings in the Senate ended in no settlement, but Ptolemy was ultimately restored by A. Gabinius in 55.

§ 2. Clodius, who still lorded it in the streets of Rome, escaped being prosecuted by Milo by being elected curule aedile, and turned the tables on Milo by accusing him in February of *vis* (breach of the peace). Pompey, when defending Milo, was shouted down by Clodius's ruffians, who declared that Crassus, and not Pompey, should restore Ptolemy. This led Pompey to suspect that Crassus was aiding and abetting the rioters. The result of the trial was the closer alliance of Pompey and Milo, and the more definite support of Clodius by the extreme aristocrats—Curio, Bibulus, Favonius, and others.

§ 3. Later in February, Cicero, in defending P. Sestius, who had strongly favoured his recall, and was now accused of *vis*, made his speech (as Watson describes it) " a regular political manifesto," and converted his *interrogatio* (cross-examination) of P. Vatinius, now a witness for the prosecution, into a bitter attack upon him as the author of the Lex Vatinia in 59 (see 59 B.C., § 2). The acquittal of Sestius encouraged Cicero to hope for the restoration of the Republic, or at any rate the dissolution of the coalition, Pompey being still at feud with Crassus (§ 2) and jealous of Caesar.

§ 4. Cicero therefore, partly with a view of widening the breach between Pompey and Caesar, proposed the suspension of Caesar's law about the *ager Campanus* (see 59 B.C., § 1) on the grounds that the State could not afford any more allotments. This would not affect Pompey, whose veterans had already been provided for, whereas Caesar would be precluded from using the remaining land for his own veterans. He also saw that the repeal of the agrarian law would be followed by that of the Vatinian.

§ 5. Having therefore previously interviewed Crassus at Ravenna, Caesar took him with him to join Pompey at Luca, a town of Liguria in N. Italy; and here the coalition of 60 (see 60 B.C., § 3) was not only renewed but developed into an omnipotent triumvirate who could settle the affairs of the State at their own discretion.

§ 6. This to Cicero, the Republican, and lifelong advocate of *concordia ordinum* (" the harmony of the senatorial and equestrian orders "), was a crushing political calamity, but he had to bow to the inevitable, and the famous letter 9 in Bk. I. is his *apologia* for his change of front. Withdrawing his motion on the *ager Campanus*, he supported a motion in the Senate to provide pay for Caesar's troops and allowing him to appoint ten *legati*. This was followed by his brilliant speech *De provinciis consularibus*, practically a panegyric upon Caesar and his achievements in Gaul.

§ 7. Clodius's turbulence in 56–57 had estranged Pompey, who now leaned to the side of Milo, but the extreme *optimates* (including M. Cato, who was indebted to Clodius for a commission to settle the affairs of Cyprus in 58) showed such fulsome partiality for Clodius, that Cicero, being earnestly requested by Caesar, whom he could not now disobey, to undertake the defence of Vatinius, whom he particularly detested, adroitly converted his predicament into a means of annoying the *optimates* saying that " if *they* coquetted with one Publius (viz. Clodius), *he* would coquet with another Publius (viz. Vatinius) by way of reprisal " (i. 9. 19).

55 B.C.

Consuls (after an " interregnum " in January caused by the tribune C. Cato): Cn. Pompeius and M. Licinius Crassus, both for the second time, having been consuls together in 70

§ 1. Crassus carries his Lex Licinia for the suppression of *sodalicia* (" political combinations "). Pompey opens his new theatre with shows of unparalleled magnificence, but his wholesale slaughter of elephants disgusts not only Cicero, but the people generally.

§ 2. Cicero finishes his *De oratore*. Crassus sets out for Syria, and his departure, together with the death of Pompey's wife Julia, Caesar's daughter, put an end to even the semblance of friendship between Pompey and Caesar.

§ 3. Gabinius marches into Egypt, occupies Alexandria, and restores the ex-king Ptolemy Auletes.

xxii

54 B.C.

Consuls : L. Domitius Ahenobarbus, an optimate, who married M. Crassus's sister Porcia, and fell at Pharsalia in 48, and Appius Claudius Pulcher

§ 1. Cicero helps to secure the acquittal of his former enemy, P. Vatinius, who requited his kindness after Pharsalia and later, and at Pompey's instance defends, though unsuccessfully, his former enemy, A. Gabinius ; and also defends successfully his old friend Cn. Plancius, charged with *ambitus*, in his famous speech *Pro Plancio*.

§ 2. His brother, Q. Cicero, goes over from Pompey to Caesar as his legate, and serves him with distinction in Britain and Gaul ; and this leads to a *rapprochement* between Cicero and Caesar.

53 B.C.

Consuls, after disorder lasting till July : Cn. Domitius Calvinus and M. Valerius Messalla

Defeat and murder of M. Crassus in June, near Carrhae. Cicero is more deeply affected by the death, a little earlier, of M. Crassus's son, Publius (v. 8. 4). Cicero succeeds Crassus as augur, and supports Milo's candidature for the consulship, recommending him to C. Scribonius Curio, to whom he writes a series of letters (ii. 1-7).

52 B.C.

About the middle of January Clodius is slain near Bovillae by the retainers of Milo ; his body is buried by his supporters in the forum, when the senate-house caught fire and was destroyed ; martial law is proclaimed, and finally Pompey is made sole consul, being allowed to retain the government of Spain. Milo is accused of *vis* and condemned. He goes into exile at Massilia.

51 B.C.

Consuls : Servius Sulpicius Rufus and M. Claudius Marcellus

Cicero goes to Cilicia as proconsul, succeeding Appius Claudius, who had succeeded Lentulus in 54, and M. Calpurnius Bibulus goes to Syria. Cicero is kept fully informed of what occurs in Rome by his friend M. Caelius Rufus (Bk. VIII. of these Letters).

50 B.C.

Consuls : C. Claudius Marcellus, cousin of the consul for 51, and L. Aemilius Paullus

§ 1. Cicero, after a satisfactory tenure of office, quits his province, leaving C. Caelius Caldus, his quaestor, in charge, and reaches Rome in December. He is anxious about the honours due to his Cilician successes, having so far only had a *supplicatio* voted him, but no triumph ; he is also embarrassed about the marriage of his daughter Tullia with P. Cornelius Dolabella, who was prosecuting for treason Appius Claudius Pulcher, with whom Cicero desired a reconciliation.

§ 2. A motion in the Senate, that Caesar's candidature for the consulship should be considered in his absence, having been rejected, the tribune Scribonius Curio demands the disbanding of Pompey's army, which the Senate would have passed but for the opposition of the consul Marcellus. Curio openly declares for Caesar, whom he joins at Ravenna, thus, according to Lucan, turning the scales against the Pompeian party (*momentumque fuit mutatus Curio rerum*).

49 B.C.

Consuls: L. Cornelius Lentulus Crus and C. Claudius Marcellus, cousin of his namesake, the consul for 50, and brother of the consul for 51

The tribunes M. Antonius and Q. Cassius, accompanied by Caelius Rufus, leave Rome and join Caesar, who on January 11 crosses the Rubicon, and thereby declares war upon the Republic, and marching southwards finally besieges Pompey in Brundisium. On March 17 Pompey escapes to Dyrrachium, whither the consuls had gone with the bulk of his army on March 4. Cicero vacillates as to his future policy, but finally decides to throw in his lot with Pompey.

48 B.C.

Consuls: C. Julius Caesar (for the second time) and P. Servilius Isauricus

Cicero spends the first half of the year in Pompey's camp at Dyrrachium, where he conceives a poor opinion of Pompey's army; he is still there when he hears of the utter defeat of Pompey by Caesar near Pharsalus on August 7 and his flight to Egypt. Crossing with the Pompeians from Dyrrachium to Corcyra, Cicero is threatened with death by young Cn. Pompey for refusing to take the command as senior consul. In October he returns to Italy and settles in Brundisium.

CHRONOLOGICAL SUMMARY

47 B.C.

Consuls : Q. Fufius Calenus and P. Vatinius, but only for Oct., Nov., and Dec.

§ 1. Though allowed to remain in Italy when all other Pompeians were driven out, Cicero was not happy ; he had broken with his brother Quintus, and Terentia (he alleged) had mismanaged his financial affairs in his absence ; while Dolabella, his son-in-law, was so notoriously unfaithful to Tullia as to make a divorce inevitable.

§ 2. He was consoled, however, by a reassuring letter from Caesar in Egypt, who permitted him to retain his lictors and the title of *imperator* ; on Caesar's return Cicero met him and was cordially received, and being given leave to live wherever he liked, he chose Tusculum, so as to be near Rome.

§ 3. Dolabella, now tribune, agitating for the abolition of debts, is opposed by his colleague, Trebellius, and the ensuing riots had to be quelled by troops under M. Antonius.

§ 4. Towards the end of the year, through Caesar's influence, Q. Fufius Calenus and P. Vatinius are elected consuls.

46 B.C.

Consuls : C. Julius Caesar (third time) and M. Aemilius Lepidus

§ 1. Caesar defeats the Pompeian army under Scipio at Thapsus in Africa, and M. Cato, preferring death to slavery, commits suicide at Utica. Returning to Rome and celebrating four triumphs in August

xxvi

for his victories in Gaul, Egypt, Pontus, and Africa, Caesar is made Dictator for the year.

§ 2. Cicero's letters now show a more cheerful spirit; he had now divorced Terentia, and after a short interval married his young and wealthy ward, Publilia; the marriage, however, was an unhappy one.

§ 3. Cicero wrote this year his *Partitiones oratoriae*, *Brutus*, and *Orator*.

45 B.C.

Consul (*fourth time*) : C. Julius Caesar

§ 1. In February Tullia, shortly after her divorce from Dolabella, died in childbed. Cicero, who had loved her devotedly, refused to be comforted and sought refuge in the solitude of Astura.

§ 2. Caesar now openly aimed at monarchy, and Cicero especially resented, as an insult to the senatorial order, the election as consul for one day of Caninius Rebilus.

44 B.C.

§ 1. Caesar, now consul for the fifth time and dictator for the fourth, had already by his arrogance and ill-concealed ambition aroused the opposition of the republicans, and a conspiracy had long been maturing which culminated in his assassination on March 15 at the foot of Pompey's statue in the senate-house. By his will he adopted C. Octavius and made him his chief heir.

§ 2. On the 17th, at a meeting of the Senate in the temple of Tellus, Cicero proposed an amnesty, which the Senate passed, but at the same time ratified all Caesar's acts. After this he retired into private life for six months.

CHRONOLOGICAL SUMMARY

§ 3. He had already completed his *Tusculan Disputations* and *De natura deorum*, and during the remainder of the year composed his *De amicitia*, *De senectute*, *De officiis*, and several other works.

43 B.C.

Consuls: C. Vibius Pansa and A. Hirtius

After a series of events too complicated even to summarize here,[a] C. Octavius, by then called Octavianus, formed a triumvirate with Antony and Lepidus, who removed their chief opponents by *proscriptio*. Among the proscribed was Cicero, who was slain on December 7th, when he was approaching the end of his sixty-fourth year.

[a] A full note on the Cisalpine Campaign will be found at the beginning of Book X.

CICERO'S
LETTERS TO HIS FRIENDS
BOOKS XIII–XVI

WITH AN ENGLISH TRANSLATION BY
W. GLYNN WILLIAMS, M.A.

FORMERLY SCHOLAR OF ST. JOHN'S COLLEGE, CAMBRIDGE
AND HEADMASTER OF FRIARS SCHOOL, BANGOR

NOTE ON CICERO'S " LITTERAE COMMENDATICIAE " IN BOOK XIII

LETTERS of recommendation are to be found scattered here and there throughout Cicero's correspondence, but Book xiii. (with the single exception of *Ep.* 68, addressed to Servilius Isauricus) consists of nothing else. There are seventy-nine letters in the Book, and of these seventy-eight are commendatory of either communities or individuals.

The great bulk of them were written in 46 B.C., a few in 45, and a few in previous years. Why so many of these letters should have been written in 46 is an interesting question, on which Cicero's position at the time may throw some light.

In 47 B.C. Cicero had received a reassuring letter from Caesar (from whom he had little to hope after the battle of Pharsalia in 48), permitting him to retain his lictors and the title of *Imperator*. When Caesar landed at Tarentum about September 25, Cicero hastened to meet him, was graciously received, and allowed to choose his own place of residence ; he elected to live at Tusculum. (See Chron. Summ. for 47 B.C.)

During this and the following year Cicero was perhaps happier than he ever had been since his entry into public life. He was still on good terms with Caesar, whose generosity to himself he freely ad-

2

mitted, and who, he hoped, might yet re-establish the Republic ; he had divorced Terentia, whom he suspected of extravagance and dishonesty ; he had married his young and wealthy ward Publilia, and had not yet tired of her ; and his beloved daughter Tullia was still living. It was at this time that he composed his *Brutus* and *Orator*, and found leisure to give informal lessons in rhetoric to Hirtius and Dolabella, and his happier mood is reflected in his jocular letters to such congenial friends as Paetus (ix. 16-20).

Moreover, in 46 B.C. Cicero, with his distinguished past and his assured literary eminence (though little more than a spectator in the arena of practical politics), was probably the most widely known and influential personality, next to Caesar himself, in the Roman world. This in itself would account for the increasing numbers of those who sought his good word ; and it is reasonable to suppose that the ease of mind and freedom from anxiety he now enjoyed rendered him more responsive to such appeals.

We have thus two plausible explanations of the comparative frequency of his " Litterae Commendaticiae " in this year—the enhanced value of his recommendation, and his greater accessibility to those who applied for it.

Of letters in commendation or defence of communities there are six, viz. : *Epp.* 4, advocating the claims of Volaterrae ; 7, Concerning property owned in Gaul by Atella, a municipium of which Cicero was *patronus* ; 9, on behalf of the Bithynian Company of the *Publicani* ; 11, in defence of property owned in Gaul by his native town Arpinum ; 18 B, on behalf of the Lacedaemonians ; and 40 on behalf of the Cyprians. These letters afford convincing proof of Cicero's extraordinary public influence and authority, the variety of his interests, and the wide scope of his sympathies.

The remaining seventy-two letters are commendatory of individuals. That they should generally conform to a common type is not surprising. Those who are constantly called upon for " testimonials " know how difficult it is to avoid the repetition of certain stock phrases. Cicero indeed strives, with his usual fluency and felicity, to vary his theme, but even he fails to break the monotony of these letters, of which the following may be taken as a " skeleton " specimen :

" *A is a man to whom I am so much attached that I shall regard whatever you do for him as done for myself. I therefore entreat you with more than ordinary earnestness to do him this particular favour, and to befriend him in every other respect, so far as your integrity (honesty, sense of justice) and your high position permit of it.*" [These words recall the frequent phrase in Buckingham's letters recommending friends to Bacon when Lord Chancellor—" *So far as may stand with justice and equity.*"] Cicero goes on : " *You will find A an excellent fellow, worthy of your friendship, and most grateful for any service you may do him.*" He often, however, discounts the altruism of a letter by adding, with Pepysian candour, " *Pray make it quite clear to A that it was I who induced you to do him this kindness,*" and he sometimes attaches to a recommendation a preconcerted private mark, indicating that it is to receive particular attention.

Insipid and monotonous, however, as these letters

must appear to those who read them *en masse*, they are yet impressive evidence of Cicero's large-hearted *bonhomie*, and his unfailing readiness to do a friend, or even an acquaintance, a good turn; in short, of that *humanitas* which was one of his dominant characteristics.

M. TULLI CICERONIS EPISTULARUM
AD FAMILIARES

LIBER DECIMUS TERTIUS

I

M. CICERO S. D. C. MEMMIO

Athenis, A.U.C. 703.

1 Etsi non satis mihi constiterat, cum aliquane animi
mei molestia an potius libenter te Athenis visurus
essem, quod iniuria, quam accepisti, dolore me
afficeret, sapientia tua, qua fers iniuriam, laetitia,

ᵃ Gaius Memmius was of plebeian family, though that
family traced its origin to Trojan times and stamped the
head of Romulus on their coins. As he served as quaestor
in Spain during the war with Sertorius both before and
after 77 B.C., he must have been born before 104. In 66
he opposed the triumph of L. Lucullus, and as praetor in
58 he strenuously resisted Caesar's laws. In 57 he was
propraetor of Bithynia, where he won the title of *imperator*,
but failed, according to Catullus (x. 9-13, and xxviii.), to
promote the pecuniary interests of his staff, of whom Catullus
was one. In 54 he sought the Consulship, and was even
supported by Caesar, whose favour he again lost by dis-
closing some scandal in the election, and was himself accused
of bribery. To save himself he accused of bribery Metellus
Scipio, father-in-law of Pompey, but was forced to drop the
accusation, and went into exile at Athens. Here, by a decree

6

CICERO'S LETTERS TO HIS FRIENDS

BOOK XIII

I

CICERO GREETS GAIUS MEMMIUS [a]

Athens, June or July, 51 B.C.

THOUGH I had not quite made up my mind whether 1
I was going to meet you at Athens with a certain
feeling of distress or rather with pleasure (since,
grieved as I was at the injustice you have suffered,
I rejoiced at the philosophical spirit with which you

of the Areopagus, he obtained possession of a ruinous house,
once Epicurus's, intending to pull it down and build on
the site, but subsequently abandoned that intention. The
Epicureans at Athens wished to get the house back, but
Memmius refused to give it up, and quarrelled about it with
Patro, the head of the Epicurean Society. When Cicero
visited Athens on his way to Cilicia, Patro begged him to
get the house from Memmius, who had now gone to Mitylene.
Hence this letter, written, as Cicero tells Atticus, with care
(*accurate*).

But Memmius's chief claim to distinction is that it was
to him that Lucretius addressed his great poem *De Rerum
Natura*. Munro remarks that on all the coins of the Memmii
we find Venus crowned by Love, and this gives special point
to Lucr. i. 26-27 :

> Memmiadae nostro, quem *tu*, *dea*, tempore in omni
> omnibus ornatum voluisti excellere rebus.

7

tamen vidisse te mallem. Nam quod est molestiae,
non sane multo levius est, cum te non video ; quod esse
potuit voluptatis, certe, si vidissem te, plus fuisset.
Itaque non dubitabo dare operam, ut te videam,
cum id satis commode facere potuero. Interea,
quod per litteras et agi tecum et, ut arbitror, confici
2 potest, agam nunc. Ac te illud primum rogabo, ne
quid invitus mea causa facias ; sed id, quod mea
intelleges, tua nullam in partem multum interesse,
ita mihi des, si tibi, ut id libenter facias, ante persua-
seris. Cum Patrone Epicureo mihi omnia sunt ; nisi
quod in philosophia vehementer ab eo dissentio. Sed
et initio Romae, cum te quoque et tuos omnes obser-
vabat, me coluit in primis, et nuper, cum ea, quae
voluit, de suis commodis et praemiis consecutus est,
me habuit suorum defensorum et amicorum fere
principem ; et iam a Phaedro, qui nobis, cum pueri
essemus, antequam Philonem cognovimus, valde ut
philosophus, postea tamen, ut vir bonus et suavis et
officiosus probabatur, traditus mihi commendatusque
3 est. Is igitur Patro cum ad me Romam litteras
misisset, uti te sibi placarem peteremque, ut nescio
quid illud Epicuri parietinarum sibi concederes, nihil

bear it), for all that I should prefer to have seen you. For as far as the distress goes, it is not very much alleviated when you are out of my sight ; whereas whatever pleasure was possible would have been undoubtedly enhanced by my having seen you. I shall not hesitate, therefore, to make every effort to see you, if I can do so with any reasonable convenience. Meanwhile, whatever business can be discussed with you and, as I believe, settled by correspondence, that I will discuss here.

And first of all I shall make this request of you— 2 to do nothing for my sake against your will ; but if you perceive that what I ask is of importance to me, while of no great importance from any point of view to yourself, not to grant me even that favour unless you have previously persuaded yourself to do so with your whole heart.

With Patro the Epicurean I am in complete accord, except that I emphatically disagree with him in philosophy. But not only in the early days at Rome, while he showed deference to you too and all your friends, did he cultivate my acquaintance in a special degree, but lately also, when he realized all his wishes in the way of privileges and rewards, he regarded me as practically the leading man among his defenders and friends ; and now again he has been introduced and recommended to me by Phaedrus, of whom, when I was a boy, before I knew Philo, I entertained a high opinion as a philosopher, but afterwards as an honest, amiable, and obliging man.

This Patro, then, sent me a letter when I was at 3 Rome, asking me to make his peace with you, and beg of you to yield possession to him of some tumble-down house or other (you know it), which once belonged to

9

scripsi ad te ob eam rem, quod aedificationis tuae
consilium mea commendatione nolebam impediri.
Idem, ut veni Athenas, cum idem, ut ad te scriberem,
rogasset, ob eam causam impetravit, quod te ab-
iecisse illam aedificationem constabat inter omnes
4 amicos tuos. Quod si ita est, et si iam plane tua nihil
interest, velim, si qua offensiuncula facta est animi
tui perversitate aliquorum (novi enim gentem illam),
des te ad lenitatem, vel propter tuam summam
humanitatem vel etiam honoris mei causa. Equidem,
si quid ipse sentiam quaeris, nec cur ille tanto opere
contendat video, nec cur tu repugnes, nisi tamen
multo minus tibi concedi potest, quam illi, laborare
sine causa. Quamquam Patronis et orationem et
causam tibi cognitam esse certo scio. Honorem,
officium, testamentorum ius, Epicuri auctoritatem,
Phaedri obtestationem, sedem, domicilium, vestigia
summorum hominum, sibi tuenda esse dicit. Totam
hominis vitam rationemque, quam sequitur in philosophia, derideamus licet, si hanc eius contentionem
volumus reprehendere. Sed mehercules, quando
illi ceterisque, quos illa delectant, non valde inimici
sumus, nescio an ignoscendum sit huic, si tanto opere

---

a Probably a *clique* of Epicurean extremists.
b *i.e.*, Memmius is too important a person to be troubled
with such trifles.

Epicurus ; but I wrote nothing to you for the simple reason that I did not want your scheme of building to be interfered with by any recommendation of mine. But when he also asked me, on my arrival at Athens, to write to you to the same effect, he had his request granted to him for no other reason than because your friends were unanimously agreed that you had thrown to the winds all that building scheme of yours.

If that is so, and it is now of absolutely no im- **4** portance to you, I should like you, if your feelings have been ever so slightly hurt by the wrong-headedness of certain persons (I know that coterie *a*), to allow yourself to incline towards leniency, whether because of your own exceptional kindliness, or even as a compliment to myself.

For my part, if you ask me what my own opinion is, I fail to see either why he is so obstinately set upon it, or why you are so stoutly opposing him, except, of course, that one could far less easily allow *you* than *him* to be so needlessly troubled.*b*

And yet I am well aware that you know all about Patro's petition and the merits of his case. He avers that he must keep intact his own honour and responsibility, the sanctity of testamentary dispositions, the authority of Epicurus, the solemn injunction of Phaedrus, the residence, the domicile, the very footprints of the most illustrious men. If we are inclined to find fault with the object of his present efforts, we may as well make mock of the poor fellow's whole life and the principles he follows in philosophy. But, on my oath, since I bear no particular grudge against the great man and those others who are fascinated by such doctrines, I think perhaps that we ought to forgive Patro, if he is so much troubled ;

laborat : in quo etiamsi peccat, magis ineptiis quam
5 improbitate peccat. Sed ne plura (dicendum enim
aliquando est), Pomponium Atticum sic amo, ut
alterum fratrem. Nihil est illo mihi nec carius nec
iucundius. Is (non quo sit ex istis ; est enim omni
liberali doctrina politissimus ; sed valde diligit
Patronem, valde Phaedrum amavit) sic a me hoc
contendit, homo minime ambitiosus, minime in
rogando molestus, ut nihil umquam magis ; nec
dubitat, quin ego a te nutu hoc consequi possem,
etiam si aedificaturus esses. Nunc vero, si audierit,
te aedificationem deposuisse, neque tamen me a te
impetrasse, non te in me illiberalem, sed me in se
neglegentem putabit. Quamobrem peto a te, ut
scribas ad tuos, posse tua voluntate decretum illud
Areopagitarum, quem ὑπομνηματισμόν illi vocant,
6 tolli. Sed redeo ad prima. Prius velim tibi persuadeas, ut hoc mea causa libenter facias, quam ut
facias. Sic tamen habeto : si feceris, quod rogo,
fore mihi gratissimum.

ᵃ ὑπομνηματισμός was the recognized term for a decree of
the Areopagus, which in the time of Cicero was the chief
administrative body in Athens.

even if he is mistaken in being so, it is a mistake due
to lack of sense more than lack of morality.

But to waste no more words (I must say it sooner 5
or later), I love Pomponius Atticus as a second
brother. He is to me the dearest and most delightful man in the world. Now Atticus—not that he
is one of that lot, being a man of most refined erudi-
tion in every branch of liberal learning, but he *has*
a great esteem for Patro, and *had* a great affection
for Phaedrus—Atticus, I say, the least self-seeking
of men, and the least importunate in making requests,
entreats me to do this with as much earnestness as he
has ever evinced ; and he has no doubt that I could
get you to grant him this favour by a single nod, even
if it were still your intention to build. Now, however,
if he hears that you have abandoned that intention,
and that even so I have failed to get from you what
I want, he will not suspect you of shabbiness to me,
but me of lack of consideration for him. And that
is why I beg of you to write to your friends, saying
that with your full consent that decree of the
Areopagites, which they themselves call a *mémoire*,[a]
may be rescinded.

But I return to what I said at first. Before per- 6
suading yourself to do this at all, I would have you
persuade yourself to do it readily, as a kindness to
myself. Anyhow, let me tell you this—if you do
what I ask, it will give me the greatest pleasure.

CICERO

II

Laodiceae, (?) A.U.C. 704.

C. Aviano Evandro, qui habitat in tuo sacrario, et
ipso multum utor, et patrono eius M. Aemilio familiarissime. Peto igitur a te in maiorem modum,
quod sine tua molestia fiat, ut ei de habitatione ac-
commodes. Nam propter opera instituta multa
multorum subitum est ei remigrare Kal. Quint.
Impedior verecundia, ne te pluribus verbis rogem;
neque tamen dubito, quin, si tua nihil aut non
multum intersit, eo sis animo quo ego essem, si quid
tu me rogares. Mihi certe gratissimum feceris.

III

M. T. C. S. P. D. C. MEMMIO

Laodiceae, (?) A.U.C. 704.

A. Fufium, unum ex meis intimis, observantis-
simum studiosissimumque nostri, eruditum hominem
et summa humanitate tuaque amicitia dignissimum,
velim ita tractes, ut mihi coram recepisti. Tam
gratum mihi id erit, quam quod gratissimum. Ipsum
praeterea summo officio et summa observantia tibi
in perpetuum devinxeris.

---

^a A freedman of M. Aemilius Avianius (xiii. 27). He
was a distinguished sculptor, and Cicero had dealings with
him (vii. 23. 1).

^b Avianius was permitted by Memmius to work in the
shrine in which the Memmii celebrated their *sacra gentilicia.*

^c Nothing more is known of this man.

14

II

Laodicea, May (?), 50 B.C.

I am on intimate terms with C. Avianius Evander [a] himself, who is lodging in your family shrine, [b] and very much so with his patron M. Aemilius. I therefor beg of you, with more earnestness than usual, so far as it can be done without inconvenience to yourself, to accommodate him in the matter of his residence. For he has so many commissions on hand for a number of people that it would hurry him to have to move to his old quarters on July 1. My modesty prevents me from preferring my request at greater length, and yet I doubt not that, if it makes little or no difference to you, you will be as obliging as I should be, were you to make any request of me. At any rate you will have done me a great favour.

III

Laodicea, 50 B.C.

A. Fufius, [c] one of my most intimate friends, shows me the greatest deference and devotion. He is an accomplished man and exceedingly kind-hearted, and in every way worthy of your friendship. I should be glad if you would treat him as you promised to do when we met. That will give me as much pleasure as anything in the world. You will besides bind the man himself to you for ever by the strongest ties of obligation and respect.

15

CICERO

IV

M. T. C. S. D. Q. VALERIO Q. F. ORCAE, LEG. PROPRAET.

Romae, a.u.c. 709.

1 Cum municipibus Volaterranis mihi summa necessitudo est. Magno enim meo beneficio affecti, cumulatissime mihi gratiam rettulerunt; nam nec in
honoribus meis nec in laboribus umquam defuerunt.
Cum quibus si mihi nulla causa intercederet, tamen,
quod te vehementissime diligo, quodque me a te
plurimi fieri sentio, et monerem te et hortarer, ut
eorum fortunis consuleres, praesertim cum prope
praecipuam causam haberent ad ius obtinendum;
primum, quod Sullani temporis acerbitatem, deorum
immortalium benignitate, subterfugerunt; deinde,
quod summo studio populi Romani a me in consulatu
2 meo defensi sunt. Cum enim[1] tribuni plebis legem
iniquissimam de eorum agris promulgavissent, facile
senatui populoque Romano persuasi, ut eos cives,
quibus fortuna pepercisset, salvos esse vellent. Hanc
actionem meam C. Caesar primo suo consulatu in

[1] *Added by Victorius.*

---

[a] Orca had been praetor in 57, and supported the recall
of Cicero. In 56 he was governor of Africa (xiii. 6A. 2).
He was now one of the Land Commissioners for carrying
out Caesar's allotments of land to his veterans. This and
the following letter show the difficulties which confronted
the Commissioners.

[b] Volaterrae, in Etruria, was besieged and captured by
Sulla for having given shelter to some of those who had
been proscribed. Sulla declared their lands confiscated and
their Roman citizenship annulled, but the Roman courts

16

IV

Rome, autumn, 45 B.C.

M. T. Cicero warmly greets Q. Valerius Orca, son of Quintus, legate with rank of Praetor.

I have the closest possible connexion with the 1 townsmen of Volaterrae. Having received some considerable kindness at my hands, they have proved their gratitude to me in overflowing measure; for never once have they failed me either in my triumphs or in my troubles. And indeed, had no such relations been in existence between us, nevertheless, in view of my own warm affection for you and my appreciation of your very high esteem for me, I should both advise and exhort you to promote their best interests, especially as their claim to have their rights maintained is practically paramount, first because by the mercy of heaven they succeeded in escaping the barbarities of the days of Sulla,[b] and secondly because my defence of them in my consulship was enthusiastically applauded by the people of Rome.

For when the tribunes of the plebs [c] proposed a 2 most iniquitous law about their lands, I had no difficulty in persuading the Senate and people of Rome to be willing that those citizens, whom fortune had spared, should retain their rights. This policy of mine was heartily approved in the land-law of his first consulship by C. Caesar,[d] who freed the district and

refused to recognize the deprivation of citizenship, and the lands were never confiscated. Watson and Tyrrell.

[c] Rullus and Flavius.

[d] Caesar would favour the Volaterrans as representing the proscribed Marians.

lege agraria comprobavit agrumque Volaterranum
et oppidum omni periculo in perpetuum liberavit,
ut mihi dubium non sit, quin is, qui novas necessitudines adiungat, vetera sua beneficia conservari
velit. Quamobrem est tuae prudentiae aut sequi
eius auctoritatem, cuius sectam atque imperium
summa cum tua dignitate secutus es, aut certe illi
integram omnem causam reservare. Illud vero
dubitare non debes, quin tam grave, tam firmum,
tam honestum municipium tibi tuo summo beneficio
3 in perpetuum obligari velis. Sed haec, quae supra
scripta sunt, eo spectant, ut te horter et suadeam.
Reliqua sunt, quae pertinent ad rogandum, ut non
solum tua causa tibi consilium me dare putes, sed
etiam, quod mihi opus sit, me a te petere et rogare.
Gratissimum igitur mihi feceris, si Volaterranos
omnibus rebus integros incolumesque esse volueris.
Eorum ego domicilia, sedes, rem, fortunas, quae a
dis immortalibus et a praestantissimis in nostra
republica civibus, summo senatus populique Romani
studio, conservatae sunt, tuae fidei, iustitiae bonitati-
4 que commendo. Si pro meis pristinis opibus facultatem mihi res hoc tempore daret, ut ita defendere
possem Volaterranos, quemadmodum consuevi tueri
meos, nullum officium, nullum denique certamen, in

town of Volaterrae from any such danger for all
time ; so that I have no doubt that one who is
seeking to acquire new connexions wishes that the
privileges he granted long ago should be preserved.
For that reason it is for you, in your wisdom, either to
follow the authority of one whose party and authority
you have already, with no impairment of your high
personal position, followed, or at all events to keep the
whole case open for Caesar's decision. Of this, however, you should entertain no doubt—that it should
be your desire, by bestowing upon it the highest
favour in your power, to attach to yourself for all
time a municipality so respectable, so staunch, and
so honourable.

In what I have written above I have no other 3
object in view than to urge and persuade you. There
remains what is concerned with a personal request,
so that you may infer that I am not only offering
you advice for your own sake, but that I am also
making a petition and a request for what I have need
of myself. You will do me the greatest possible
favour therefore, if it is your pleasure to leave the
people of Volaterrae in every respect untouched and
their rights undiminished. Their domiciles and
abodes, their property and estates, preserved to
them by the immortal gods and the most eminent
members of our commonwealth—all these I commend to your honesty, sense of justice, and goodness
of heart.

Were circumstances to offer me at the present 4
moment the power, on the scale of my former resources, to protect the people of Volaterrae to the
same extent as I have always defended my own
people, there is no act of devotion, no strenuous

quo illis prodesse possem, praetermitterem. Sed
quando apud te nihilo minus hoc tempore valere me
confido, quam valuerim semper apud omnes, pro
nostra summa necessitudine parique inter nos et
mutua benevolentia abs te peto, ut ita de Volaterranis
mereare, ut existiment, eum quasi divino consilio
isti negotio praepositum esse, apud quem unum
nos, eorum perpetui defensores, plurimum valere
possemus.

V

M. T. C. S. P. D. Q. VALERIO Q. F. ORCAE, LEG. PROPRAET.

Romae, a.u.c. 709.

1 Non moleste fero eam necessitudinem, quae mihi
tecum est, notam esse quam plurimis ; neque tamen
ob eam causam (quod tu optime existimare potes)
te impedio, quo minus susceptum negotium, pro tua
fide et diligentia, ex voluntate Caesaris, qui tibi rem
magnam difficilemque commisit, gerere possis. Nam
cum multi a me petant multa, quod de tua erga me
voluntate non dubitent, non committo, ut ambitione
2 mea conturbem officium tuum.   C. Curtio ab ineunte
20

effort, I should omit, whereby I might be of service
to them. But since I am confident that I have no less
influence with you at the present moment than I
have always had with everybody, I beg of you in the name
of our very close connexion and our mutual goodwill,
so evenly balanced between us, to serve the people of
Volaterrae in such a way as to give them the impression that, as if by some divine providence, the man
who has been put at the head of the commission on
which you are now engaged is the very man of all
others with whom I, their unfailing defender, could
exercise the greatest possible influence.

V

CICERO TO VALERIUS ORCA

Rome, autumn, 45 B.C.

M. T. Cicero warmly greets Q. Valerius Orca, son
of Quintus, legate with rank of Praetor.

I have no objection to any number of people being 1
aware of the close relationship between us ; and yet I
would not for that reason (and you can best appreciate
what I say) hinder you from being able to conduct the
business you have undertaken with your usual probity
and thoroughness, and to the satisfaction of Caesar,
who has entrusted you with a commission as important as it is difficult ; for though I am besieged by
petitions from a host of men because they confidently
rely upon your goodwill towards me, I am not so
inconsiderate as to embarrass you in the performance
of your duty by any self-seeking on my own
account.

aetate familiarissime sum usus. Eius et Sullani temporis iniustissima calamitate dolui, et cum iis, qui
similem iniuriam acceperant, amissis omnibus fortunis, reditus tamen in patriam voluntate omnium
concedi videretur, adiutor incolumitatis fui. Is habet
in Volaterrano possessionem, cum in eam, tamquam
e naufragio, reliquias contulisset. Hoc autem tempore eum Caesar in senatum legit, quem ordinem
ille, ista possessione amissa, tueri vix potest. Gravissimum autem est, cum superior factus sit ordine,
inferiorem esse fortuna ; minimeque convenit, ex eo
agro, qui Caesaris iussu dividatur, eum moveri, qui
3 Caesaris beneficio senator sit. Sed mihi minus libet
multa de aequitate rei scribere, ne causa potius apud
te valuisse videar, quam gratia. Quamobrem te in
maiorem modum rogo, ut C. Curti rem meam putes
esse ; quidquid mea causa faceres, ut, id C. Curti
causa cum feceris, existimes, quod ille per me
habuerit, id me habere abs te. Hoc te vehementer
etiam atque etiam rogo.

---

* Nothing more is known of this C. Curtius.

I have been on very intimate terms with C. 2 Curtius [a] from the days of our youth. Not only did I resent his most unjust degradation in Sulla's time, but when it appeared that those who had suffered similar wrong, though they had lost all their fortunes, were yet permitted by universal consent to return to their country, I have assisted in his rehabilitation.

Now Curtius has a holding in the territory of Volaterrae into which, just as though he had been shipwrecked, he had collected all that was left to him. But just at this moment Caesar has chosen him to be a member of the Senate—a rank, which, if he loses that holding of his, he cannot easily maintain. Now it is very hard upon him that, though he has been raised higher as regards rank, he should be in a lower position as regards means ; and it is shockingly inconsistent that the very man who is a senator by Caesar's favour should be ejected from land that is being distributed by Caesar's order.

But I am less inclined to write at any length on the 3 equity of the case, for fear it should be thought that what strengthened my hands in pleading with you was not so much my personal influence as the justice of my plea. I therefore beg you, with more than usual urgency, to regard C. Curtius's affair as my own ; and in whatever you do for my sake, although you may have done it for C. Curtius's sake, to believe that any favour he obtains through me is a favour conferred upon me by yourself. This I beg of you again and again in all earnestness to do.

CICERO

VIa

M. T. C. S. P. D. Q. VALERIO Q. F. ORCAE PROCOS.

Romae, a.u.c. 698.

1 Si vales, bene est, valeo. Credo te memoria tenere,
me et coram P. Cuspio tecum locutum esse, cum
te prosequerer paludatum, et item postea pluribus
verbis tecum egisse, ut, quoscumque tibi eius necessarios commendarem, haberes eos in numero meorum
necessariorum. Id tu pro tua summa erga me benevolentia perpetuaque observantia mihi liberalissime
2 atque humanissime recepisti. Cuspius, homo in
omnes suos officiosissimus, mirifice quosdam homines
ex ista provincia tuetur et diligit, propterea quod
fuit in Africa bis cum maximis societatis negotiis
praeesset. Itaque hoc eius officium, quod adhibet
erga illos, ego mea facultate et gratia soleo, quantum
possum, adiuvare. Quare Cuspianorum omnium
commendationis causam hac tibi epistula exponendam
putavi. Reliquis epistulis tantum faciam, ut notam
apponam eam, quae mihi tecum convenit, et simul
3 significem, de numero esse Cuspi amicorum. Sed
hanc commendationem, quam his litteris consignare
volui, scito esse omnium gravissimam. Nam P.

---

^a Chronologically, this letter precedes *Epp.* 4 and 5, in
which Cicero drops the formal opening (S.V.B.E.) which he
uses here.

^b Only mentioned in this letter and in xvi. 17. 2.

^c It was customary for a magistrate to wear his *paluda-
mentum* (general's cloak) when proceeding to his province.
Cf. xv. 17. 3. Tyrrell.

^d See Preliminary Note *ad fin.*

24

VIa *a*

CICERO TO VALERIUS ORCA, PROCONSUL.

Rome, about the middle of 56 B.C.

M. T. Cicero warmly greets Q. Valerius Orca, son of Quintus, Proconsul.

If you are well, all is right ; I am well. I believe **1** it is within your recollection that I said something to you in the presence of P. Cuspius,*b* as I was escorting you when in your official uniform,*c* and that afterwards also I pleaded with you at greater length, to reckon among my own connexions any whom I might recommend to you as being his. That, consistently with your sincere affection for me and the respect you have invariably shown me, you very handsomely and courteously undertook to do for me.

Now Cuspius, a man most ready to help all those **2** associated with him, shows an amazingly benevolent interest in certain persons within your province, because he has twice been in Africa, presiding over the highly important negotiations of his society. And so I am in the habit of supporting, with such resources and influence as I can, this readiness to help which he displays towards them. I therefore thought it incumbent upon me to explain to you in this letter the reason why I recommend all the friends of Cuspius. In future letters I shall do no more than append the mark agreed upon between you and me, and indicate at the same time that it is one of Cuspius's friends.*d*

But as for the recommendation I have been willing **3** to sign in this letter, I would have you know that it is more important than any ; for Cuspius has urged me

25

CICERO

Cuspius singulari studio contendit a me, ut tibi
quam diligentissime L. Iulium commendarem. Eius
ego studio vix videor mihi satisfacere posse, si utar
verbis iis, quibus, cum diligentissime quid agimus,
uti solemus. Nova quaedam postulat, et putat me
eius generis artificium quoddam tenere. Ei ego
pollicitus sum me ex intima nostra arte depromp-
turum mirificum genus commendationis. Id quoniam assequi non possum, tu re velim efficias, ut ille
genere mearum litterarum incredibile quiddam
4 perfectum arbitretur. Id facies, si omne genus
liberalitatis, quod et ab humanitate et potestate tua
proficisci poterit, non modo re, sed etiam verbis,
vultu denique exprompseris; quae quantum in
provincia valeant, vellem expertus esses, sed tamen
suspicor. Ipsum hominem, quem tibi commendo,
perdignum esse tua amicitia, non solum, quia mihi
Cuspius dicit, credo (tametsi id satis esse debebat),
sed quia novi eius iudicium in hominibus et amicis
5 deligendis. Harum litterarum vis quanta fuerit,
propediem iudicabo, tibique, ut confido, gratias
agam. Ego, quae te velle, quaeque ad te pertinere
arbitrabor, omnia studiose diligenterque curabo.
Cura, ut valeas.

---

^a *Sc.* "te mox experturum esse."

with exceptional earnestness to recommend to you with the utmost possible particularity one L. Julius. I hardly think I can satisfy his eagerness by using such words as I usually do, even when dealing with anything most impressively. He insists upon something out of the common, and imagines that I possess a certain artistry in that style. Well, I have promised him to fetch up from the depths of my art a style of recommendation that will amaze him. Being unable to reach that standard, I should be glad if you would so act as to give him the impression that the effect of my style of letter has been something beyond all belief.

This you will do if you exhibit every form of 4 generosity which your kindness of heart and your official opportunities can suggest, not only in deed but also in word, and, let me add, even in look. How important these things are in a province, I only wish you knew by experience—I have an inkling, however, that you soon will.[a]

As to the subject of my recommendation himself, I believe him to be thoroughly worthy of your friendship, not only because Cuspius tells me so (though that ought to be enough), but also because I know Cuspius's shrewdness in estimating men and choosing his friends.

What effect this letter has produced I shall be able 5 to judge at an early date, and I feel sure I shall have to thank you. For my part, I shall attend with zeal and assiduity to whatever I think that you desire, or that effects your interests. Mind you keep well.

VIв

CICERO VALERIO S.

Romae, a.u.c. 698.

P. Cornelius, qui tibi has litteras dedit, est mihi a
P. Cuspio commendatus ; cuius causa quanto opere
cuperem deberemque, profecto ex me facile cognosti.
Vehementer te rogo, ut cures, ut ex hac commendatione mihi Cuspius quam maximas, quam primum,
quam saepissime gratias agat. Vale.

VII

M. T. C. S. P. D. CLUVIO

Romae, a.u.c. 709.

1   Cum in Galliam proficiscens pro nostra necessitudine tuaque summa in me observantia ad me
domum venisses, locutus sum tecum de agro vectigali
municipi Atellani, qui esset in Gallia ; quantoque
opere eius municipi causa laborarem, tibi ostendi.
Post tuam autem profectionem, cum et maxima res
municipi honestissimi mihique coniunctissimi, et
summum meum officium ageretur, pro tuo animo in

ᵃ Not the banker at Puteoli, who died earlier in this year
(*Att.* xiii. 46), but probably the Cluvius who was Caesar's
praefectus fabrum in Spain in the early part of this year.
    ᵇ Atella was in Campania, between Naples and Capua.
It was there that the *fabulae Atellanae* (popular farces or
Harlequinades) were first produced.
    Another instance of a Latin municipality owning property
28

VI<small>B</small>

CICERO TO VALERIUS ORCA

Rome, sometime in 56 B.C.

P. Cornelius, who delivers this letter to you, has been recommended to me by P. Cuspius ; and how much it is my desire, as it is my duty, to do for his sake, I am sure you have easily recognized from what I have said. I earnestly beg of you to see to it that the thanks I receive from Cuspius as a result of this recommendation may be as cordial, as prompt, and as frequent as possible.

VII

CICERO TO GAIUS CLUVIUS [a]

Rome, autumn, 45 B.C.

When on setting out for Gaul, in accordance with 1 our intimacy and your extreme courtesy towards myself, you visited me at my house, I spoke to you about the land in Gaul which paid rent to the municipality of Atella,[b] and I showed you how greatly distressed I was on that municipality's account. Since your departure, however, when a question arose of vital importance to that municipality, most honourable as it is and very closely connected with myself— a question too of the performance of my own duty in the highest sense,—I thought it incumbent on me, considering your extraordinary kindness to me, to

in a distant land is Arpinum, which held land in Gaul (xiii. 11. 1).

me singulari existimavi, me oportere ad te accuratius
scribere ; etsi non sum nescius, et quae temporum
ratio, et quae tua potestas sit, tibique negotium
datum esse a C. Caesare, non iudicium, praeclare
intellego. Quare a te tantum peto, quantum et te
facere posse, et libenter mea causa facturum esse
2 arbitror. Et primum velim existimes, quod res est,
municipi fortunas omnes in isto vectigali consistere ;
his autem temporibus hoc municipium maximis
oneribus pressum, summis affectum esse difficultati-
bus. Hoc etsi commune videtur esse cum multis,
tamen mihi crede singulares huic municipio calami-
tates accidisse : quas idcirco non commemoro, ne, de
miseriis meorum necessariorum conquerens, homines,
3 quos nolo, videar offendere. Itaque, nisi magnam
spem haberem, C. Caesari nos causam municipi
probaturos, non erat causa, cur a te hoc tempore
aliquid contenderem. Sed quia confido mihique
persuasi, illum et dignitatis municipi, et aequitatis,
etiam voluntatis erga se habiturum esse rationem,
ideo a te non dubitavi contendere, ut hanc causam
4 illi integram conservares. Quod etsi nihilominus a
te peterem, si nihil audivissem te tale fecisse, tamen
maiorem spem impetrandi nactus sum, posteaquam

---

a Tyrrell thinks these must be the partisans of Caesar, who
seem to have acted harshly.

write to you with greater particularity—although of course I am fully aware how you are circumstanced and how far your powers extend, and distinctly understand that what Caesar has assigned to you is not so much judicial discretion, as the transaction of a definite business. For that reason I confine myself to asking you to do what I believe you have both the power and the will to do, for my sake.

And first of all I would have you bear in mind— 2 and it is the fact—that the rent in question comprises the whole wealth of the municipality, and moreover, that as things now are, this same municipality is oppressed with very heavy burdens and involved in very serious difficulties. Although it would appear that such evils are shared with many others, still you must accept my assurance that the disasters suffered by this municipality are exceptional: and the reason I do not specify them is my fear lest by lamenting the misfortunes of those personally connected with me I should offend people I do not wish to offend.[a]

It follows that unless I had strong hopes of our 3 establishing the cause of the municipality with C. Caesar, there was no reason why I should make any such urgent request of you at the present time. But because I feel sure and have convinced myself that he will give full consideration to the fair claims of the municipality and the justice of its plea, and also to its friendliness towards himself, for that reason, I say, I have not hesitated to urge you to keep this case open for his decision.

But although, even if I had never heard of your 4 doing anything of the kind, I should none the less make this request of you, still my hope of obtaining it has been strengthened since I was told that you had

mihi dictum est, hoc idem a te Regienses impetra-
visse. Qui etsi te aliqua necessitudine attingunt,
tamen tuus amor in me sperare me cogit, te, quod
tuis necessariis tribueris, idem esse tributurum meis,
praesertim cum ego pro his unis petam, habeam
autem, qui simili causa laborent, complures necessarios. Hoc me non sine causa facere, neque aliqua
levi ambitione commotum a te contendere, etsi te
existimare arbitror, tamen mihi affirmanti credas
velim, me huic municipio debere plurimum ; nullum
umquam fuisse tempus neque honorum neque
laborum meorum, in quo non huius municipi studium
5 in me exstiterit singulare. Quapropter a te etiam
atque etiam, pro nostra summa coniunctione proque
tua in me perpetua et maxima benevolentia, maiorem
in modum peto atque contendo, ut, cum fortunas
agi eius municipi intellegas, quod sit mihi necessitudine, officiis, benevolentia coniunctissimum, id
mihi des ; quod erit huiusmodi, ut, si a Caesare, quod
speramus, impetrarimus, tuo beneficio nos id con-
secutos esse iudicemus ; sin minus, pro eo tamen id
habeamus, cum a te data sit opera, ut impetraremus.
Hoc cum mihi gratissimum feceris, tum viros optimos,
homines honestissimos eosdemque gratissimos et

---

[a] Regium Lepidi, a Roman colony on the *Via Aemilia*,
between Mutina and Parma.

[b] In other words, " if we obtain what we hope for from
Caesar, we shall give you all the credit ; if not, we shall
have instead the pleasure of knowing that you did your best,
i.e., we shall be indebted to you in either case."
32

granted the same request to the inhabitants of Regium [a] ; and although they are attached to you by a certain connexion, yet I am impelled by your affection for me to hope that you will grant those connected with me the same favour as you have granted to those connected with yourself, especially as I am pleading for these people exclusively, whereas I have several others connected with me, who are in a similar sad plight. Now, although I credit you with believing that I am not doing this without good reason, and not pressing you under the influence of some paltry spirit of self-seeking, nevertheless I should like you to believe me when I asseverate that there is no municipality to which I am more deeply indebted ; that there has never been a time either in the days of my triumph or of my trouble when the devotion shown to me by this municipality did not stand out as something wholly out of the common.

And therefore, in view of our very intimate attach- 5 ment and your affection for me, as unfailing as it is remarkable, I entreat and beseech you with more than usual urgency (since you must see that the fortunes of a municipality most closely bound to me by the ties of friendship, mutual services, and good-will, are at stake), to grant me a favour which will amount to this—I mean that, if we obtain what we hope for from Caesar, we should believe that we have secured it only by your kindness ; if we do not, then at any rate that we should have instead of that the conviction that you did *your* utmost to help us to succeed. [b]

Not only will you have given me the greatest possible pleasure by so doing, but by an inestimable service you will have laid under an everlasting obliga-

tua necessitudine dignissimos, summo beneficio in perpetuum tibi tuisque devinxeris.

VIII

M. T. C. S. P. D. M. RUTILIO

Romae, a u c. 709.

1 Cum et mihi conscius essem, quanti te facerem, et tuam erga me benevolentiam expertus essem, non dubitavi a te petere, quod mihi petendum esset. P. Sestium quanti faciam, ipse optime scio, quanti autem facere debeam, et tu et omnes homines sciunt. Is cum ex aliis te mei studiosissimum esse cognosset, petivit a me, ut ad te quam accuratissime scriberem de re C. Albini senatoris, cuius ex filia natus est L. Sestius, optimus adolescens, filius P. Sesti. Hoc idcirco scripsi, ut intellegeres, non solum me pro P. Sestio laborare debere, sed Sestium etiam pro Al-
2 binio. Res autem est haec : a M. Laberio C. Albinius praedia in aestimationem accepit, quae praedia Laberius emerat a Caesare de bonis Plotianis. Ea si dicam non esse e republica dividi, docere te

---

[a] There is no other reference in these letters to this Rutilius.

[b] Quaestor in 63, and tribune of the plebs in 57, when he strongly supported Cicero's recall ; in 56 he was accused of *vis* on account of the violence with which he had opposed P. Clodius in the preceding year, but was defended by Cicero (*Pro Sestio*) and acquitted. His son L. Sestius is the " *O beate Sesti* " in Horace's ode, i. 4.

[c] For *aestimatio* see note to ix. 16. 7.

[d] *Dividere* here, and below, =*divendere*, " to disperse by selling piecemeal," when the original ownership would disappear.

tion to yourself and yours men of excellent character, and thoroughly honourable gentlemen, who are at the same time full of gratitude, and most worthy of being connected with you.

VIII

CICERO TO MARCUS RUTILIUS [a]

Rome, autumn, 45 B.C.

Knowing in my heart how highly I valued you, 1 and having learnt by experience your friendly feeling for me, I have not hesitated to ask that of you which it was my duty to ask. How highly I value P. Sestius [b] is best known to myself; how highly I ought to do so is known both to you and to the world in general. Having been informed by others that you were my very devoted friend, he begged of me to write to you with the utmost particularity about the affair of C. Albinius the senator, whose daughter is the mother of L. Sestius, an admirable young man, son of P. Sestius. My purpose in writing you this letter was to convince you that not only is it right and proper that I should feel anxious on behalf of P. Sestius, but that he also should feel so on behalf of Albinius.

Now the circumstances are these : C. Albinius has 2 received certain estates from M. Laberius at a valuation [c]—estates which Laberius had purchased from Caesar out of the property of one Plotius. If I were to tell you that the dispersal [d] of such properties is not to the public interest, you would think that I am not so much asking a favour of you, as proffering you

CICERO

videar, non rogare. Sed tamen cum Caesar Sullanas
venditiones et assignationes ratas esse velit, quo
firmiores existimentur suae, si ea praedia dividentur,
quae ipse Caesar vendidit, quae tandem in eius
venditionibus esse poterit auctoritas ? Sed hoc quale
3 sit, tu pro tua prudentia considerabis. Ego te plane
rogo, atque ita, ut maiore studio, iustiore de causa,
magis ex animo rogare nihil possim, ut Albinio parcas,
praedia Laberiana ne attingas. Magna me affeceris
non modo laetitia, sed etiam quodammodo gloria,
si P. Sestius homini maxime necessario satisfecerit
per me, ut ego illi uni plurimum debeo. Quod ut
facias, te vehementer etiam atque etiam rogo.
Maius mihi dare beneficium nullum potes. Id mihi
intelleges esse gratissimum.

IX

M. T. C. S. P. D. CRASSIPEDI

In Cilicia, ad finem A.U.C. 703.

1 Quamquam tibi praesens commendavi, ut potui
diligentissime, socios Bithyniae, teque cum mea com-

---

^a *i.e.*, sales and allotments of property confiscated in
connexion with proscriptions of Sulla. If not "ratified,"
Caesar's title to his own estates would be invalidated, and
he would have no power to sell them.

^b The second husband of Tullia, whom he married in 56,
and divorced about 53.

^c The companies (*societates*) of *publicani* undertook State
contracts for roads, buildings, etc., but especially for the
collection of taxes. Each *societas* generally confined its

36

instruction. At all events, seeing that Caesar desires the ratification of Sulla's sales and assignments,[a] so that his own may be regarded as more secure, if those very estates which Caesar himself has sold are dispersed, what possible right of property, I ask you, can his sales carry? But you, with your usual penetration, will consider the matter in all its bearings.

I ask you frankly—and I could not do so with 3 more earnestness, in a more righteous cause, or more from my heart—to spare Albinius, and have nothing to do with the estate of Laberius. You will give me not only much pleasure, but also, in a sense, something to boast about, if it turns out that it was I who enabled P. Sestius to satisfy the claims of one so closely connected with him, as *I* owe *him* more than any other man alive. This I beg of you again and again to do. You can grant me no greater favour, and you will find that I appreciate it most highly.

IX

CICERO TO P. FURIUS CRASSIPES [b]

Cilicia, probably towards the end of 51 B.C.

Although when I met you I recommended to you 1 as particularly as I could the Bithynian company,[c] and understood that not only because of my recom-

operations to a single province, or to a particular tax (*decuma, scriptura, portoria*, etc.), though one *societas* might farm several taxes. Cicero's staunch support of the *equites* was one of the main features of his political life, and the *publicani* were drawn from the *equites*.

mendatione, tum etiam tua sponte intellexi cupere ei
societati, quibuscumque rebus posses, commodare,
tamen, cum ii, quorum res agitur, magni sua interesse arbitrarentur, me etiam per litteras declarare
tibi, qua essem erga ipsos voluntate, non dubitavi haec
2 ad te scribere. Volo enim te existimare, me, cum
universo ordini publicanorum semper libentissime
tribuerim, idque magnis eius ordinis erga me meritis
facere debuerim, tum in primis amicum esse huic
Bithynicae societati; quae societas ordine ipso et
hominum genere pars est maxima civitatis; constat
enim ex ceteris societatibus; et casu permulti sunt
in ea societate valde mihi familiares, in primisque is,
cuius praecipuum officium agitur hoc tempore, P.
Rupilius, P. F. Menenia, qui est magister in ea
3 societate. Quae cum ita sint, in maiorem modum a
te peto, Cn. Pupium, qui est in operis eius societatis,
omnibus tuis officiis atque omni liberalitate tueare,
curesque, ut eius operae (quod tibi facile factu est)
quam gratissimae sint sociis, remque et utilitatem
sociorum (cuius rei quantam potestatem quaestor
habeat, non sum ignarus) per te quam maxime
defensam et auctam velis. Id cum mihi gratissimum

ᵃ The bidding for the contract and the furnishing of
security, etc., were carried out by a *manceps* at Rome, but
the management was entrusted to an annually elected local
director (*magister*), who had charge of the accounts and
correspondence. See note *b* on *Ep.* 65. 1.

mendation, but also because that was your own inclination, you were anxious to accommodate that company in any way you could, still when those whose interests are in question thought it of paramount importance to them that I should make it plain to you by letter also how I felt towards them, I have not hesitated to write to you as I do.

I would have you believe that while it has always 2 been the greatest pleasure to me to make much of the order of *publicani* as a whole, and, considering the great services that order has rendered me, it has been my duty to do so, I am in a special sense a friend to this Bithynian company—a company which by the very fact of its connexions with the order in general, and owing to the class of men of whom it is composed, made up as it is of members of all the other companies, constitutes a most important factor in the State ; and, as it happens, a large proportion of it are on very intimate terms with myself, especially the man who at this moment occupies the position of its chief, P. Rutilius to wit, son of Publius of the Menenian tribe, who is director *a* of that company.

Such being the case, I entreat you with more than 3 usual urgency to support with every kindness and all your generosity Cn. Pupius, who is in the company's employ, and to see to it that his services (you will find it easy to do so) are as acceptable as possible to the partners, and to show your desire (and how much it is in the power of a quaestor to effect in that connexion, I am well aware) that the property and interests of those partners should prove to have been protected and enhanced as far as possible by your efforts.

feceris, tum illud tibi expertus promitto et spondeo,
te socios Bithyniae, si iis commodaris, memores esse
et gratos cogniturum.

X

CICERO M. IUNIO BRUTO S.

Romae, A.U.C. 708.

1   Cum ad te tuus quaestor, M. Varro, proficisceretur,
commendatione egere eum non putabam. Satis
enim commendatum tibi eum arbitrabar ab ipso more
maiorum, qui, ut te non fugit, hanc quaesturae coniunctionem liberorum necessitudini proximam voluit
esse. Sed cum sibi ita persuasisset ipse meas de se
accurate scriptas litteras maximum apud te pondus
habituras, a meque contenderet, ut quam diligentissime scriberem, malui facere, quod meus familiaris
2 tanti sua interesse arbitraretur. Ut igitur debere
me facere hoc intellegas, cum primum M. Terentius
in forum venit, ad amicitiam se meam contulit.
Deinde, ut se corroboravit, duae causae accesserunt,
quae meam in illum benevolentiam augerent : una,
quod versabatur in hoc studio nostro, quo etiam nunc
maxime delectamur, et cum ingenio, ut nosti, nec
sine industria ; deinde, quod mature se contulit in

---

[a] M. Brutus was now governor of Cisalpine Gaul, as will
appear from the next letter, § 1.
[b] Not the great Varro, but a man known as M. Terentius
Varro Gibba. As tribune of the plebs in 43, when the great
Varro was proscribed he was much laughed at for publishing
a notice declaring that he was not that Varro but another
(Dio Cassius, xlvii. 11. 3).

Not only will you greatly oblige *me* by so doing, but I also promise you and pledge myself as a result of my own experience, that, if you oblige them, you will find the Bithynian partners neither forgetful nor ungrateful.

X

CICERO TO M. JUNIUS BRUTUS [a]

Rome, early in 46 B.C.

When your quaestor, M. Varro,[b] was setting out to 1 join you, I did not think he required a recommendation. I considered him sufficiently recommended by the practice of our ancestors, which assumed that a quaestor's connexion with his chief closely approximated to that of a son to his father. But since he had convinced himself that a carefully written letter from me would carry the greatest weight with you and pressed me to write with the utmost particularity, I thought it better to do what my friend imagined to be of so much importance to him.

To prove to you therefore that it is my duty to do 2 this, from the moment M. Terentius entered the forum [c] he devoted himself to winning my friendship; afterwards, when he had established himself, I found two additional reasons for feeling more warmly disposed towards him ; one was that he took up the same pursuit as myself—that which even now gives me most delight—and that with ability, as you know, and with considerable industry ; the other was that at an early stage he attached himself to the companies

[c] *i.e.*, began to practise in the law-courts.

societates publicanorum, quod quidem nollem ; maximis enim damnis affectus est. Sed tamen causa
communis ordinis mihi commendatissimi fecit amicitiam nostram firmiorem. Deinde versatus in utrisque
subselliis optima et fide et fama iam ante hanc com-
mutationem reipublicae petitioni sese dedit honorem-
que honestissimum existimavit fructum laboris sui.
3 His autem temporibus a me Brundisio cum litteris
et mandatis profectus ad Caesarem est ; qua in re et
amorem eius in suscipiendo negotio perspexi, et in
conficiendo ac renuntiando fidem. Videor mihi, cum
separatim de probitate eius et moribus dicturus
fuissem, si prius causam, cur eum tanto opere diligerem, tibi exposuissem, in ipsa causa exponenda satis
etiam de probitate dixisse. Sed tamen separatim
promitto in meque recipio, fore eum tibi et voluptati
et usui. Nam et modestum hominem cognosces, et
pudentem, et a cupiditate omni remotissimum,
praeterea magni laboris summaeque industriae.
4 Neque ego haec polliceri debeo, quae tibi ipsi, cum
bene cognoris, iudicanda sunt ; sed tamen in omnibus
novis coniunctionibus interest, qualis primus aditus
sit, et qua commendatione quasi amicitiae fores
aperiantur. Quod ego his litteris efficere volui, etsi
id ipsa per se necessitudo quaesturae effecisse debet.

ᵃ Either as barrister and juryman, or as counsel for the
defence and for the prosecution.
ᵇ Brought about by Caesar's victory over the Pompeian
army at Thapsus. (See Chron. Summ. for 46 B.C.)

which manage State-contracts, and I only wish he hadn't; for he suffered very heavy losses. Be that as it may, his sharing my interest in an order I so highly esteemed tended to strengthen our friendship. Subsequently, after practising as a barrister on both benches [a] with admirable honesty and distinction, just before this transformation of public affairs [b] he became a candidate for public office, which he regarded as the most honourable fruit of his labours.

Moreover, at this crisis he has travelled from Brundisium with my letter and messages for Caesar; and in that I have had clear proof of his devotion in undertaking the business at all, and of his trustworthiness in carrying it through and reporting to me. It seems to me that, though I had intended dwelling separately on his integrity and character, if I should have fully explained to you why I was so greatly drawn to him, by giving that very explanation I should have dwelt enough upon his integrity also; but for all that I promise and pledge my word in a separate statement that he will be a source of both pleasure and profit to you. You will find him an unassuming and modest fellow, far removed from any thought of self-seeking, and I may add, hard-working and extremely industrious. **3**

Although it is no business of mine to make professions which you can verify for yourself when you have got to know him well, still in forming any new connexions it is important to consider the details of the first approach, and the value of the recommendation that throws open, so to speak, the door of friendship. That is what I wished to effect by this letter, though indeed the bond of quaestorship should have had that effect of itself. Anyhow the latter consideration **4**

CICERO

Sed tamen nihilo infirmius illud, hoc addito. Cura igitur, si me tanti facis, quanti et Varro existimat, et ipse sentio, ut quam primum intellegam, hanc meam commendationem tantum illi utilitatis attulisse, quantum et ipse sperarit nec ego dubitarim.

XI

M. T. C. S. P. D. BRUTO

Romae, a.u.c. 708.

1 Quia semper animadverti studiose te operam dare, ut ne quid meorum tibi esset ignotum, propterea non dubito, quin scias, non solum cuius municipi sim, sed etiam quam diligenter soleam meos municipes, Arpinates, tueri. Quorum quidem omnia commoda omnesque facultates, quibus et sacra conficere et sarta tecta aedium sacrarum locorumque communium tueri possint, consistunt in his vectigalibus, quae habent in provincia Gallia. Ad ea visenda pecuniasque, quae a colonis debentur, exigendas totamque rem et cognoscendam et administrandam legatos equites Romanos misimus, Q. Fufidium, Q. F., 2 M. Faucium, M. F., Q. Mamercum, Q. F. Peto a te in maiorem modum pro nostra necessitudine, ut tibi ea res curae sit, operamque des, ut per te quam commodissime negotium municipi administretur quam primumque conficiatur; ipsosque, quorum nomina

---

ᵃ See *Ep.* 7. 1 above, note *b.*

will be no whit weakened by the former. Therefore, if you value me as highly as Varro supposes, and I feel that you do, pray see to it that I have the earliest possible intelligence that this recommendation of mine has proved of as much advantage to him as he himself has hoped, and I have never doubted.

XI

CICERO TO M. BRUTUS

Rome, some time in 46 B.C.

I have always noticed that you take the greatest 1 pains to be informed of anything that concerns my interests, and I have therefore no doubt that you are aware not only to what municipality I belong, but also how conscientiously it is my habit to support my fellow-citizens, the inhabitants of Arpinum. Now it is a fact that all their income and all the means at their disposal for the maintenance of public worship and the repairs of their sacred edifices and public buildings consist in the rents they receive from their estates in the province of Gaul.[a] To visit those estates, to call in the moneys still owed by the tenants, and to investigate and arrange for the management of the whole business, we have sent a commission of Roman knights—Q. Fufidius the younger, M. Faucius the younger, and Q. Mamercus the younger.

In view of our close intimacy, I appeal to you with 2 more than ordinary urgency to charge yourself with the matter, and to do your utmost to see that the business of our town, so far as you yourself are concerned, is managed as happily, and settled as speedily, as possible, and to treat the gentlemen themselves,

45

scripsi, ut quam honorificentissime pro tua natura et
3 quam liberalissime tractes. Bonos viros ad tuam
necessitudinem adiunxeris municipiumque gratissimum beneficio tuo devinxeris ; mihi vero etiam
gratius feceris, quod cum semper tueri municipes
meos consuevi, tum hic annus praecipue ad meam
curam officiumque pertinet. Nam constituendi municipi causa hoc anno aedilem filium meum fieri volui,
et fratris filium et M. Caesium, hominem mihi
maxime necessarium ; is enim magistratus in nostro
municipio, nec alius ullus creari solet ; quos co-
honestaris, in primisque me, si res publica municipi
tuo studio, diligentia, bene administrata erit. Quod
ut facias, te vehementer etiam atque etiam rogo.

XII

M. T. C. S. P. D. BRUTO

Romae, A.U.C. 708.

1 Alia epistula communiter commendavi tibi legatos
Arpinatium, ut potui diligentissime ; hac separatim
Q. Fufidium, quocum mihi omnes necessitudines
sunt, diligentius commendo, non ut aliquid de illa

---

^a *Cf.* § 1 in the next letter.
^b Three aediles, one of whom apparently administered the
finances (*cf. Att.* xv. 15. 1), were the only regular magistrates
at Arpinum. (*Corpus Inscriptionum Latinarum*, x. 5679 and
5682, quoted by How.)

whose names I have given you, as indeed you naturally would, with all possible courtesy and generosity.

You will find that you have added some men of 3 excellent character to the list of your intimate friends, and that by your kindness you have laid under obligation a most grateful municipality, while the gratitude I shall owe you will be even greater, since not only have I always made a practice of protecting the interests of my fellow-townsmen, but this year they claim in a special degree my attention and services. The fact is that this year, with a view to putting the municipality on a sound basis, I have recommended for election my son, and also my brother's son, and M. Caesius,[a] a very intimate friend of mine, as aediles—for aediles are the magistrates, and no others, whom it is customary to elect[b] in our municipality. Now you will have done due honour to them and to myself in particular, if it turns out that the public business of the township has been, thanks to your zealous assiduity, well managed. And this is what I earnestly and again and again beg of you to do.

XII

CICERO TO M. BRUTUS

Rome, some time in 46 B.C.

In another letter I commended to you as earnestly 1 as I could the representatives of the Arpinates *in general*; in this I commend with even greater earnestness Q. Fufidius, to whom I am bound by all sorts of ties, in *particular*, not so as to detract in any

commendatione deminuam, sed ut hanc addam. Nam
et privignus est M. Caesi, mei maxime et familiaris
et necessari, et fuit in Cilicia mecum tribunus
militum ; quo in munere ita se tractavit, ut accepisse
2 ab eo beneficium viderer, non dedisse.   Est praeterea
(quod apud te valet plurimum) a nostris studiis non
abhorrens. Quare velim eum quam liberalissime
complectare operamque des, ut in ea legatione, quam
suscepit contra suum commodum, secutus auctoritatem meam, quam maxime eius excellat industria.
Vult enim, id quod optimo cuique natura tributum
est, quam maximam laudem cum a nobis, qui eum
impulimus, tum a municipio consequi ; quod ei con-
tinget, si hac mea commendatione tuum erga se
studium erit consecutus.

XIII

M. T. C. S. P. D. BRUTO

Romae, A.U.C. 708.

L. Castronius Paetus, longe princeps municipi
Lucensis, est honestus, gravis, plenus offici, bonus
plane vir et cum virtutibus, tum etiam fortuna, si
quid hoc ad rem pertinet, ornatus ; meus autem est
familiarissimus, sic prorsus, ut nostri ordinis observet

ª In Etruria.

way from my former recommendation, but so as to add this to it. He is the stepson of M. Caesius, my most intimate and familiar friend, and he was with me in Cilicia as military tribune ; and he so conducted himself in that capacity as to make me feel that I had received a kindness from him rather than conferred one.

He is, moreover—and this carries great weight 2 with you—no enemy to our favourite pursuits. And that is why I would have you welcome him as handsomely as possible, and do all you can to ensure the utmost possible success of his efforts on that commission which he has undertaken, to the detriment of his own convenience, in deference to my authority. It is his desire—and it is the natural characteristic of all good men—to win the highest possible credit, not only for me, who pressed this service upon him, but from the municipality also ; and he will succeed in doing so, if, thanks to this recommendation of mine, he enlists your enthusiastic support.

XIII

CICERO TO M. BRUTUS

Rome, some time in 46 B.C.

L. Castronius Paetus, by far the most important member of the municipality of Luca,[a] is an honourable, sterling, and most obliging man, a thoroughly good fellow, and graced not only with all the virtues, but also, if that has anything to do with the matter, with a handsome fortune. Besides he is on very familiar terms with me, so much so indeed that there

neminem diligentius. Quare ut et meum amicum
et tua dignum amicitia tibi commendo. Cui quibuscumque rebus commodaveris, tibi profecto iucundum,
mihi certe erit gratum. Vale.

XIV

M. T. C. S. P. D. BRUTO

Romae, A.U.C. 708.

1 L. Titio Strabone, equite Romano in primis
honesto et ornato, familiarissime utor. Omnia mihi
cum eo intercedunt iura summae necessitudinis.
Huic in tua provincia pecuniam debet P. Cornelius.
Ea res a Volcatio, qui Romae ius dicit, reiecta in
2 Galliam est. Peto a te hoc diligentius, quam si mea
res esset, quo est honestius de amicorum pecunia
laborare, quam de sua, ut negotium conficiendum
cures. Ipse suscipias, transigas operamque des,
quoad tibi aequum et rectum videbitur, ut quam
commodissima condicione libertus Strabonis, qui eius
rei causa missus est, negotium conficiat ad nummosque
perveniat. Id et mihi gratissimum erit, et tu ipse
L. Titium cognosces amicitia tua dignissimum. Quod
ut tibi curae sit, ut omnia solent esse, quae me velle
scis, te vehementer etiam atque etiam rogo.

---

^a L. Volcatius Tullus, who became consul in 33. This year
he was praetor at Rome.

is no member of my order to whom he pays more particular attention. I therefore commend him to you as being both my friend and worthy of your friendship ; and whatever you do to oblige him will assuredly give pleasure to yourself, and in any case be a favour to me.

XIV

CICERO TO M. BRUTUS

Rome, some time in 46 B.C.

I am on the most intimate terms with L. Titius 1 Strabo, an eminently honourable and distinguished Roman knight. There is no bond of the closest relationship that does not subsist between us. A sum of money is owing to him in your province from P. Cornelius. The *praetor urbanus* Volcatius *a* has passed on the case for trial in Gaul.

I beg of you all the more earnestly than if the case 2 were my own, in proportion as it is more a point of honour to take pains in the matter of one's friends' money than one's own, to see to it that the business is carried through. Take it on your own shoulders, settle it, and do what you can consistently with what you deem right and proper, to ensure that Strabo's freedman, who has been dispatched for the purpose, may conclude the business on the most favourable terms possible, and get at the money. Not only will that give *me* the greatest pleasure, but you yourself too will find L. Titius fully worthy of your friendship. That you should interest yourself in this matter, as you generally do in everything you know to be my wish, I earnestly beg of you again and again.

51

CICERO

XV

1 Praecilium tibi commendo unice, tui necessari,
mei familiarissimi, viri optimi filium ; quem cum
adolescentem ipsum propter eius modestiam, humanitatem, animum et amorem erga me singularem mirifice diligo, tum patrem eius re doctus intellexi et didici
mihi fuisse semper amicissimum. En, hic ille est
[de illis][1] maxime qui irridere atque obiurgare me
solitus est, quod me non tecum, praesertim cum abs
te honorificentissime invitarer, coniungerem.

> ’Αλλ’ ἐμὸν οὔ ποτε θυμὸν ἐνὶ στήθεσσιν ἔπειθεν.

Audiebam enim nostros proceres clamitantes,

> ἄλκιμος ἔσσ’, ἵνα τίς σε καὶ ὀψιγόνων εὖ εἴπῃ.
> ὣς φάτο, τὸν δ’ ἄχεος νεφέλη ἐκάλυψε μέλαινα.

2 Sed tamen iidem me consolantur ; et iam hominem
perustum inani gloria volunt incendere ; atque ita
loquuntur :

> μὴ μὰν ἀσπουδί γε καὶ ἀκλειῶς ἀπολοίμην,
> ἀλλὰ μέγα ῥέξας τι καὶ ἐσσομένοισι πυθέσθαι.

[1] *A doubtful insertion, omitted in H. Pal.*

---

[a] This letter was written within two months after Tullia's
death, and Tyrrell and Purser remark that " it has a strained
and unnatural tone of gaiety."
[b] Hom. *Od.* vii. 258.
[c] *Ib.* i. 302.
[d] *Ib.* xxiv. 315. The chieftains cried aloud to Cicero to
be brave, but a cloud of woe enveloped him—his remorse
for having ever opposed Caesar.
[e] Hom. *Il.* xxii. 304-5.

XV

CICERO GREETS C. JULIUS CAESAR, IMPERATOR

Astura, end of March, 45 B.C.[a]

I most particularly commend to you Praecilius, the 1
son of a very excellent gentleman who is your close,
and my own very intimate, friend. I am amazingly
fond of the young man himself on account of his
sobriety of conduct, his refinement, and his remarkably affectionate feeling for myself ; and his father
too, as practical experience has taught me and convinced me beyond all doubt, was always my very
sincere friend. Why, he was the man who more than
anybody used to scoff at and scold me because
I did not attach myself to you, especially when you
invited me to do so in the most complimentary terms:

But with his words never swayed he the heart that beats
    in my bosom.[b]

For I heard our chieftains crying aloud :

"Stand thou undaunted, that men e'en in ages to come
    may extol thee." [c]
So spake he, but the other a black cloud of anguish
    enveloped.[d]

But still those same men offer me comfort, and 2
even now they would set on fire a poor fellow already
scorched with the flames of a futile ambition ; and this
is the sort of thing they say :

Not without effort of mine, and not without fame, would
    I perish,
But having done such a deed as will ring through the ages
    for ever.[e]

Sed minus iam movent, ut vides. Itaque ab Homeri magniloquentia confero me ad vera praecepta Εὐριπίδου·

> μισῶ σοφιστήν ὅστις οὐχ αὑτῷ σοφός·

quem versum senex Praecilius laudat egregie, et ait, posse eumdem et ἅμα πρόσσω καὶ ὀπίσω videre, et tamen nihilominus

> αἰὲν ἀριστεύειν, καὶ ὑπείροχον ἔμμεναι ἄλλων.

3 Sed, ut redeam ad id, unde coepi, vehementer mihi gratum feceris, si hunc adolescentem humanitate tua, quae est singularis, comprehenderis, et ad id, quod ipsorum Praeciliorum causa te velle arbitror, addideris cumulum commendationis meae. Genere novo sum litterarum ad te usus, ut intellegeres, non vulgarem esse commendationem.

XVI

M. T. C. S. P. D. C. CAESARI IMP.

Romae (?), A.U.C. 709.

1 P. Crassum ex omni nobilitate adulescentem dilexi plurimum; et de eo cum ab ineunte eius aetate perbene[1] speravissem, tum praeclare[2] existimare

[1] *Schütz:* bene *Nobbe.*   [2] *Klotz:* per me *Nobbe.*

---

[a] Eur. Frag 905, ed. Nauck, p. 652.
[b] Hom. *Il.* i. 343 ; *Od.* xxiv. 452.
[c] Hom. *Il.* vi. 208 : xi. 784. Praecilius seems to have meant that a man may be a "sage," and yet attain pre-eminence in practical life.
[d] Son of the triumvir. He served with distinction as a *legatus* of Caesar in Gaul. He fell with his father at the

54

But they have less effect upon me now, as you see ; and so I turn from the grandiloquence of Homer, and betake myself to the practical precepts of Euripides :

The sage, no sage for his own ends, I loathe,[a]

a verse that Praecilius senior enthusiastically applauds, and declares that a man may be able " to see before as well as behind "[b] and yet nevertheless

Ever to prove himself best, and unrivalled to stand above others.[c]

But to return to the point with which I began : you 3 will oblige me very greatly if you extend to this young man the courtesy you possess in so remarkable a degree, and to add to what I imagine you would like to do for the sake of the Praecilii themselves the further weight of my recommendation.

I have adopted a new style of letter in writing to you, so that you may understand that this is no stereotyped recommendation.

XVI

CICERO TO JULIUS CAESAR

Rome (?), early in 45 B.C.

Out of all our nobility the young man for whom 1 I have the highest regard is P. Crassus[d] ; and while I had entertained great hopes of him from his earliest years, I began to have quite a brilliant impression of

battle of Carrhae. Cicero eulogized him in *Brut.* 282. *Cf. Fam.* v. 8. 4. His widow Cornelia afterwards became the wife of Pompey.

CICERO

coepi, eximiis[1] iudiciis, quae de eo feceras,[2] cognitis.
Eius libertum Apollonium iam tum equidem, cum
ille viveret, et magni faciebam et probabam. Erat
enim et studiosus Crassi, et ad eius optima studia
vehementer aptus; itaque ab eo admodum dilige-
2 batur. Post mortem autem Crassi eo mihi etiam
dignior visus est, quem in fidem atque amicitiam meam
reciperem, quod eos a se observandos et colendos
putabat, quos ille dilexisset et quibus carus fuisset.
Itaque et ad me in Ciliciam venit multisque in rebus
mihi magno usui fuit et fides eius et prudentia,
et, ut opinor, tibi in Alexandrino bello, quantum
studio et fidelitate consequi potuit, non defuit.
3 Quod cum speraret te quoque ita existimare, in
Hispaniam ad te, maxime ille quidem suo consilio,
sed etiam me auctore est profectus. Cui ego commendationem non sum pollicitus; non quin eam vali-
turam apud te arbitrarer, sed neque mihi egere commendatione videbatur, qui et in bello tecum fuisset,
et propter memoriam Crassi de tuis unus esset, et,
si uti commendationibus vellet, etiam per alios eum
videbam id consequi posse. Testimonium mei de
eo iudici, quod et ipse magni aestimabat, et ego
apud te valere eram expertus, ei libenter dedi.
4 Doctum igitur hominem cognovi et studiis optimis

[1] *Klotz:* ex iis *Nobbe.*
[2] *Madvig:* feceram *Nobbe.*

56

him when the highly favourable opinions you had formed of him became known to me. His freedman Apollonius I used to esteem highly and think well of, even when Crassus was alive ; for he was devoted to Crassus, and adapted himself extremely well to his highest pursuits, and was therefore much beloved by him.

After Crassus's death, however, he struck me as 2 being all the more worthy of admittance into my confidence and friendship, inasmuch as he considered it incumbent upon him to pay respect and attention to those whom Crassus had been fond of, and who had won his affection. And so he joined me in Cilicia, and his loyalty and sagacity were of material service to me in many respects, and he never failed you, I imagine, in the Alexandrine war, so far as his zeal and fidelity enabled him to do so.

And, since he hoped that you thought so too, he 3 set out to join you in Spain, mainly, it is true, by your advice, but partly also at my instance. A recommendation, however, I did not promise him—not that I supposed it would carry no weight with you, but it seemed to me that he stood in need of no recommendation at all, seeing that he had been with you during the war, and (since you could never forget Crassus) was numbered among your intimates ; and besides, if he desired to avail himself of recommendations, I saw that there were others too through whom he could get what he wanted. This testimony to my opinion of him, which he himself values highly, and which I know by experience carries weight with you, I have gladly given him.

Well then, I have found him to be a man of learning 4 and devoted to the most intellectual pursuits, and

deditum, idque a puero. Nam domi meae cum Diodoto Stoico, homine meo iudicio eruditissimo, multum a puero fuit. Nunc autem, incensus studio rerum tuarum, eas litteris Graecis mandare cupit. Posse arbitror ; valet ingenio ; habet usum ; iam pridem in eo genere studi litterarumque versatur ; satisfacere immortalitati laudum tuarum mirabiliter cupiebat. Habes opinionis meae testimonium ; sed tu hoc facilius multo, pro tua singulari prudentia, iudicabis. Et tamen, quod negaveram, commendo tibi eum. Quidquid ei commodaveris, erit id maiorem in modum gratum.

XVII

M. T. C. S. P. D. SER. SULPICIO

Romae, a.u.c. 708.

1 M'. Curius, qui Patris negotiatur, multis et magnis de causis a me diligitur. Nam et amicitia pervetus mihi cum eo est, ut primum in forum venit, instituta, et Patris cum aliquoties antea, tum proxime hoc miserrimo bello domus eius tota mihi patuit ; qua si opus fuisset, tam essem usus, quam mea. Maximum

---

a For an account of this eminent jurist and friend of Cicero see note *a* on iv. 1. 1. Sulpicius had recently been appointed Proconsul of Achaia by Caesar, *cf.* iv. 3.

b vii. 28 is a letter from Cicero to him, and vii. 29 one from him to Cicero.

that from a boy. For he was constantly at my house from his boyhood in the company of Diodotus the Stoic, in my judgment the most erudite of men. At the present moment, however, fired with enthusiastic admiration of your exploits, he desires to record them in the Greek language. I think he is competent to do so, he has great ability, he has had experience, he has been engaged for some time past in that kind of literary effort, and his eagerness to do justice to the immortal glory of your achievements is quite amazing.

Here then is the considered expression of my opinion; but such is your extraordinary penetration that you will far more easily decide the matter on your own account. And here am I, after all, doing what I said I would not do, in recommending him to you!

Whatever favour you do him will be a more than ordinary gratification to myself.

XVII

CICERO TO SERVIUS SULPICIUS RUFUS[a]

Rome, some time in 46 B.C.

I have many strong reasons for my regard for 1 Manius Curius[b] who has a banking business at Patrae. A friendship of very long standing subsists between us, which began when he first entered the Forum, and at Patrae not only on several previous occasions, but also very lately, during this most lamentable war, his house has been unreservedly thrown open to me; had there been need, I should have used it as my own.

autem mihi vinculum cum eo est quasi sanctioris
cuiusdam necessitudinis, quod est Attici nostri familiarissimus eumque unum praeter ceteros observat
2 ac diligit. Quem si tu iam forte cognosti, puto me
hoc, quod facio, facere serius. Ea est enim humanitate
et observantia, ut eum tibi iam ipsum per se commendatum putem. Quod tamen si ita est, magno
opere a te quaeso, ut ad eam voluntatem, si quam in
illum ante has meas litteras contulisti, quam maximus
3 postea commendatione cumulus accedat. Sin autem
propter verecundiam suam minus se tibi obtulit, aut
nondum eum satis habes cognitum, aut quae causa
est, cur maioris commendationis indigeat, sic tibi
eum commendo, ut neque maiore studio quemquam,
neque iustioribus de causis commendare possim.
Faciamque id, quod debent facere ii, qui religiose
et sine ambitione commendant. Spondebo enim tibi,
vel potius spondeo in meque recipio, eos esse M'.
Curii mores eamque cum probitatem, tum etiam
humanitatem, ut eum et amicitia tua, et tam accurata
commendatione, si tibi sit cognitus, dignum sis
existimaturus. Mihi certe gratissimum feceris, si
intellexero, has litteras tantum, quantum scribens
confidebam, apud te pondus habuisse.

The strongest tie that binds us however is one that I may almost call a more sacred relationship—the fact that he is a most intimate friend of my dear Atticus, whom he respects and esteems more than anybody else in the world.

If you happen to have made his acquaintance 2 already, I expect I am too late in doing what I do ; for such is his courtesy and civility, that I expect he has already been his own recommendation to you. But even if this be so, I earnestly beg you, that, whatever goodwill you may have shown him before the receipt of this letter, my recommendation, now that you have received it, may as far as possible enhance it.

If, however, his bashfulness has prevented his 3 obtruding himself upon you, or if you are not sufficiently acquainted with him, or if there be any reason for his requiring some stronger recommendation, well, then, I hereby recommend him to you so emphatically that I could not possibly recommend any man with greater enthusiasm or for sounder reasons ; and I shall do what those do who submit their recommendations conscientiously and disinterestedly, that is to say, I shall pledge my word to you, or rather give you my promise and solemn undertaking, that such is M'. Curius's character, such his integrity and his kindliness combined, that if you make his acquaintance, you will assuredly deem him worthy both of your friendship and of so elaborate a recommendation. At any rate you will have done me a great favour if I have reason to know that this letter has carried as much weight with you as I felt sure it would when I wrote it.

CICERO

XVIII

Romae, A.U.C. 708.

1 Non concedam, ut Attico nostro, quem elatum
laetitia vidi, iucundiores tuae suavissime ad eum et
humanissime scriptae litterae fuerint, quam mihi.
Nam etsi utrique nostrum prope aeque gratae erant,
tamen ego admirabar magis te, qui, si rogatus, aut
certe admonitus, liberaliter Attico respondisses[1]
(quod tamen dubium nobis, quin ita futurum fuerit,
non erat), ultro ad eum scripsisse, eique nec opinanti
voluntatem tuam tantam per litteras detulisse. De
quo non modo rogare te, ut eo studiosius mea quoque
causa facias, non debeo (nihil enim cumulatius fieri
potest, quam polliceris), sed ne gratias quidem agere,
2 quod tu et ipsius causa et tua sponte feceris. Illud
tamen dicam, mihi id, quod fecisti, esse gratissimum.
Tale enim tuum iudicium de homine eo, quem unice
diligo, non potest mihi non summe esse iucundum.
Quod cum ita sit, esse gratum necesse est. Sed
tamen, cum mihi pro coniunctione nostra vel peccare
apud te in scribendo licet, utrumque eorum, quae

---

[1] *Something, necessary to complete the sentence, has fallen
out after* respondisses, e.g., *as Lohmann suggests,* gratum
nobis fecisses.

XVIII

CICERO TO SERVIUS SULPICIUS

Rome, some time in 46 B.C.

Never shall I admit that that most charming and 1
courteous letter you wrote to him gave our friend
Atticus, who, I could see, was in an ecstasy of delight,
more pleasure than it gave myself. For though the
pleasure it gave us was about equally divided between
us, it was I who felt the greater admiration, seeing
that you, who, had you been requested or at any rate
advised to do so, would have couched your reply to
Atticus in handsome terms (and, of course, I had
never any doubt that it would have proved so),
actually wrote to him spontaneously, and laid at his
feet all your abounding goodwill through the medium
of a letter. And in this connexion not only ought I
to refrain from requesting you to write all the more
cordially because I too am interested (for nothing
that can be done would exceed the overflowing
measure of your promises), but even from thanking
you for what you had done both in Atticus's own
interest, and of your own free will.

This much, however, I will say, that what you have 2
done is most gratifying to me. For such an opinion
on your part of a man who stands alone in my
affection cannot but give me the highest degree of
pleasure ; and that being so, I cannot help but be
grateful. But anyhow, since our attachment is so
close, that I am privileged even to blunder in a letter
to you, I shall do both of the things I declared I

negavi mihi facienda esse, faciam. Nam et ad id,
quod Attici causa te ostendisti esse facturum, tantum
velim addas, quantum ex nostro amore accessionis
fieri potest, et, quod modo verebar tibi gratias agere,
nunc plane ago, teque ita existimare volo, quibuscumque officiis in Epiroticis reliquisque rebus Atticum
obstrinxeris, iisdem me tibi obligatum fore.

XIX

M. T. C. S. P. D. SER. SULPICIO

Romae, a.u.c. 708.

1 Cum Lysone Patrensi est mihi quidem hospitium
vetus, quam ego necessitudinem sancte colendam
puto, sed ea causa etiam cum aliis compluribus,
familiaritas tanta nullo cum hospite, et ea cum
officiis eius multis, tum etiam consuetudine quotidiana
sic est aucta, ut nihil sit familiaritate nostra coniunctius. Is cum Romae annum prope ita fuisset,
ut mecum viveret, etsi eramus in magna spe, te meis
litteris commendationeque diligentissime facturum
id quod fecisti, ut eius rem et fortunas absentis
tuerere, tamen, quod in unius potestate erant omnia,

---

^a Though Cicero speaks somewhat slightingly of Lyso
elsewhere (xvi. 4. 2), he seems to have had a very high
regard for him; and Lyso himself seems to have been something more than the ordinary "hotel proprietor" which
Tyrrell and Mahaffy assume him to have been.

^b *Hospes,* like the Greek ξένος, originally meant a
stranger ; then it became used for a *guest,* and finally also
for a *host,* and which of those two meanings it bears can only
be inferred from its context.

Hospitium (ξενία) is the relationship between host and
guest, for which we have no one word in English, and which
we have to render by some such paraphrase as "the ties

ought not to do. Firstly, I would have you make such
an addition to what you have already shown you are
about to do for Atticus's sake as it is possible, in view
of our mutual affection, to make ; and secondly,
though a moment ago I was afraid to thank you, I now
do so in specific terms, and I would impress this upon
you—that by whatever kind offices you put Atticus
under an obligation in dealing with affairs in Epirus
and elsewhere, for those same services shall I be
beholden to you myself.

XIX

CICERO TO SULPICIUS

Rome, some time in 46 B.C.

Between myself and Lyso of Patrae [a] are long-
standing ties of hospitality,[b] and such ties should, I
think, be religiously fostered. This is of course the
case with several others, but never have I been so
intimate with any other friend of that type ; and so
much has that intimacy been increased, not only by
many services on his part, but also by our daily intercourse, that we are on the most intimate terms in the
world. When he stayed a year at Rome, which
practically meant living at my house, although we
were in great hopes that, in view of my letter of
recommendation, you would be most assiduous in
doing what, as a matter of fact, you did—I mean in
protecting his estate and possessions—for all that,
seeing that one man [c] was all-powerful, and that

of hospitality " or " friendship based on mutual entertain-
ment."
  [c] The reference of course is to Caesar.

65

et quod Lyso fuerat in nostra causa nostrisque
praesidiis, quotidie aliquid timebamus. Effectum
tamen est et ipsius splendore et nostro reliquorumque
hospitum studio, ut omnia, quae vellemus, a Caesare
impetrarentur ; quod intelleges ex iis litteris, quas
2 Caesar ad te dedit. Nunc non modo non remittimus
tibi aliquid ex nostra commendatione, quasi adepti
iam omnia, sed eo vehementius a te contendimus,
ut Lysonem in fidem necessitudinemque tuam recipias, cuius dubia fortuna timidius tecum agebamus,
verentes, ne quid accideret eiusmodi, ut ne tu quidem
mederi posses ; explorata vero eius incolumitate,
omnia a te summo studio summaque cura peto. Quae
ne singula enumerem, totam tibi domum commendo ;
in his adulescentem filium eius, quem C. Maenius
Gemellus, cliens meus, cum in calamitate exsili sui
Patrensis civis factus esset, Patrensium legibus adop-
tavit ; ut eius ipsius hereditatis ius causamque tueare.
3 Caput illud est, ut Lysonem, quem ego virum
optimum gratissimumque cognovi, recipias in necessitudinem tuam. Quod si feceris, non dubito quin in
eo diligendo ceterisque postea commendando idem,
quod ego, sis iudici et voluntatis habiturus. Quod
cum fieri vehementer studeo, tum etiam illud vereor,
ne, si minus cumulate videbere fecisse aliquid eius
causa, me ille neglegenter scripsisse putet, non te

Lyso had been on our side and under our aegis, we were in daily dread of something happening. His own distinction, however, and the hearty support of myself and his other friends of that type have ended in our obtaining from Caesar all we wanted, as indeed you will infer from Caesar's letter to you.

In this letter not only do I make no abatement in 2 the strength of my recommendation to you, as if I had now got all I wanted, but I press you all the more earnestly to admit Lyso into your confidence and intimacy. When his fortunes were in the balance, I felt a little timid in pleading with you, fearing something so serious might happen that not even you could rectify it; but now that his civil status is assured, I beg of you in all earnestness and solicitude to carry out all my requests. To avoid a detailed list of them, I commend to you his whole family, including his young son, whom my client C. Maenius Gemellus, when in the dark days of his exile he was made a citizen of Patrae, adopted according to the laws of that town; I ask you to maintain the rights of his cause in respect of that inheritance.

The main point is that you should admit Lyso, 3 whom I have found to be a most excellent and grateful person, to your close intimacy. If you do so, I have no doubt that, in making much of him and afterwards recommending him to others, you will arrive at the same opinion and conceive the same goodwill towards him as I do. But intensely anxious as I am that this should be done, I am at the same time afraid lest if it appears that in some particular respect you have failed to display a superabundance of energy on his behalf, he may suspect *me* of not having written warmly enough, and not *you* of having forgotten me.

oblitum mei. Quanti enim me faceres, cum ex sermonibus quotidianis meis, tum ex epistulis etiam tuis
potuit cognoscere.

XX

CICERO SERVIO

Romae, A.U.C. 708.

Asclapone Patrensi, medico, utor valde familiariter,
eiusque cum consuetudo mihi iucunda fuit, tum ars
etiam, quam sum expertus in valetudine meorum ;
in qua mihi cum ipsa scientia, tum etiam fidelitate
benevolentiaque satisfecit. Hunc igitur tibi commendo, et a te peto, des operam, ut intellegat,
diligenter me scripsisse de sese, meamque commendationem usui magno sibi fuisse. Erit id mihi
vehementer gratum.

XXI

M. T. C. S. P. D. SER. SULPICIO

Romae, A.U.C. 708.

1 M. Aemilius Avianius ab ineunte adolescentia me
observavit semperque dilexit, vir cum bonus, tum
perhumanus et in omni genere offici diligendus.

---

^a He was a patron of the sculptor C. Avianius Evander
mentioned in xiii. 2, and of the C. Avianius Hammonius
mentioned in § 2 below. Freedmen generally adopted the
praenomen and *nomen* of their patron in addition to their
own, as did foreigners also when made citizens of Rome
through the influence of some great Roman.

For he must have been able to discover how highly you esteem me, not only from my daily talks, but also from your letters.

XX

CICERO TO SULPICIUS

Rome, some time in 46 B.C.

I am on very familiar terms with the physician Asclapo of Patrae, and not only has my intercourse with him been a pleasure to me, but also his skill, which I have tested in the illnesses of my household ; at those times he gave me every satisfaction by his medical knowledge, as well as by his trustworthiness and goodness of heart. I therefore recommend him to you, and I beg of you to do what you can to convince him that I have taken special care in writing about him, and that my recommendation has been of substantial service to him. It will be a great gratification to me.

XXI

CICERO TO SULPICIUS

Rome, some time in 46 B.C.

M. Aemilius Avianius [a] has always regarded me 1 with respect and esteem from his earliest youth. He is a good, and at the same time an exceedingly courteous man, and in the performance of every kind of duty worthy of esteem. If I thought he was

Quem si arbitrarer esse Sicyone, et nisi audirem, ibi
eum etiam nunc, ubi ego reliqui, Cibyrae commorari,
nihil esset necesse, plura me ad te de eo scribere.
Perficeret enim ipse profecto suis moribus suaque
humanitate, ut sine cuiusquam commendatione dili-
geretur abs te non minus, quam et a me et a ceteris
2 suis familiaribus. Sed cum illum abesse putem,
commendo tibi in maiorem modum domum eius, quae
est Sicyone, remque familiarem, maxime Gaium
Avianium Hammonium, libertum eius, quem quidem
tibi etiam suo nomine commendo. Nam cum propterea mihi est probatus, quod est in patronum suum
officio et fide singulari, tum etiam in me ipsum magna
officia contulit, mihique molestissimis temporibus ita
fideliter benevoleque praesto fuit, ut si a me manu-
missus esset. Itaque peto a te, ut eum Hammonium
et in patroni eius negotio sic tueare, ut eius pro-
curatorem, quem tibi commendo, et ipsum suo
nomine diligas, habeasque in numero tuorum. Hominem pudentem et officiosum cognosces, et dignum,
qui a te diligatur.

XXII

CICERO SERVIO S.

Romae, a.u.c. 708.

1 T. Manlium, qui negotiatur Thespiis, vehementer
diligo. Nam et semper me coluit diligentissimeque

ᵃ Situated on the river Asopus in the N.E. of the
Peloponnese.
ᵇ In Phrygia ; Cicero left him there when returning home
from Cilicia.

70

at Sicyon [a] and were not informed that he is still staying at Cibyra,[b] where I left him, there would have been no necessity for my writing to you about him at any greater length. For I feel sure that he would succeed by his own character and culture, unaided by anybody's recommendation, in winning your esteem no less than mine, and that of all his other intimate friends.

But, believing him to be away, I commend to you 2 with more than customary earnestness his family (they live in Sicyon) and his private property, and particularly Gaius Avianius Hammonius, his freedman, whom I also commend to you on his own account. For not only has he won my approval by his remarkable sense of duty and loyalty to his patron, but he has also conferred great obligations upon myself, and in the days of my greatest trouble he stood by me as faithfully and affectionately as though it were I who had manumitted him. I therefore beg of you to give that Hammonius not only your support in his patron's business, as being the agent of the man I am recommending to you, but also your regard on his own account, and put him on the list of your friends. You will find him a modest and obliging person, and worthy of your regard.

XXII

CICERO TO SULPICIUS

Rome, some time in 46 B.C.

T. Manlius, who has a banking business at Thespiae, 1 is a man I am extremely fond of; for he has always cultivated my acquaintance and shown me very

observavit, et a studiis nostris non abhorret. Accedit
eo, quod Varro Murena magno opere eius causa vult
omnia ; qui tamen existimavit, etsi suis litteris,
quibus tibi Manlium commendabat, valde confideret,
tamen mea commendatione aliquid accessionis fore.
Me quidem cum Manli familiaritas, tum Varronis
studium commovit, ut ad te quam accuratissime
2 scriberem. Gratissimum igitur mihi feceris, si huic
commendationi meae tantum tribueris, quantum cui
tribuisti plurimum, id est, si T. Manlium quam
maxime, quibuscumque rebus honeste ac pro tua
dignitate poteris, iuveris atque ornaveris, ex ip-
siusque praeterea gratissimis et humanissimis moribus
confirmo tibi, te eum, quem soles fructum a bonorum
virorum officiis exspectare, esse capturum.

XXIII

CICERO SERVIO S.

Romae, a.u.c. 708.

1   L. Cossinio, amico et tribuli tuo, valde familiariter
utor. Nam et inter nosmet ipsos vetus usus intercedit
et Atticus noster maiorem etiam mihi cum Cossinio
consuetudinem fecit. Itaque tota Cossini domus
me diligit, in primisque libertus eius, L. Cossinius

---

a A. Terentius Varro Murena, son of L. Licinius, was
adopted by A. Terentius Varro. A partisan of Pompey,
he was pardoned by Caesar. In 22 he conspired against
Augustus with Fannius Caepio, and put to death. Dio
Cassius (*Liv.* iii. 4) describes him as being offensively and
violently outspoken, and Horace appropriately addressed
to him his ode on " the golden mean " (*Od.* ii. 10).

By his adoption he became brother to Terentia, wife of
Maecenas, and also to Proculeius (Hor. *Od.* ii. 2. 5).

marked respect; and he is no enemy to our literary pursuits. I should add that Varro Murena [a] cordially wishes him well in every respect; and Varro, although he had every confidence in the letter he wrote commending Manlius to you, thought none the less that something further would be gained by a recommendation from myself; and not only my intimacy with Manlius, but my anxiety on behalf of Varro, has stimulated me to write to you with the utmost earnestness.

You will oblige me very greatly then if you attach **2** to this recommendation the highest possible importance, in other words, if you promote the interests and honour of T. Manlius as much as possible in whatever respect you can do so consistently with what is honourable and with your own high position; and, moreover, judging by the man's own very grateful and courteous character, I assure you that you will reap the reward you usually expect for services done to men of merit.

XXIII

CICERO TO SULPICIUS

Rome, some time in 46 B.C.

I am on very intimate terms with your friend and **1** fellow-tribesman, L. Cossinius; for not only is there an acquaintance of long standing between us to start with, but the bond that binds me to Cossinius has been strengthened by our friend Atticus. Consequently Cossinius's whole family is fond of me, and especially his freedman, L. Cossinius Anchialus, a

73

Anchialus, homo et patrono et patroni necessariis,
2 quo in numero ego sum, probatissimus. Hunc tibi
ita commendo, ut, si meus libertus esset, eodemque
apud me loco esset, quo est apud patronum suum,
maiore studio commendare non possem. Quare pergratum mihi feceris, si eum in amicitiam tuam
receperis, atque eum, quod sine molestia tua fiat, si
qua in re opus ei fuerit, iuveris. Id et mihi vehementer gratum erit, et tibi postea iucundum.
Hominem enim summa probitate, humanitate ob-
servantiaque cognosces.

XXIV

CICERO SERVIO S.

Romae, A.U.C. 708.

1 Cum antea capiebam ex officio meo voluptatem,
quod memineram, quam tibi diligenter Lysonem,
hospitem et familiarem meum, commendassem, tum
vero, posteaquam ex litteris eius cognovi, tibi eum
falso suspectum fuisse, vehementissime laetatus sum,
me tam diligentem in eo commendando fuisse. Ita
enim scripsit ad me, sibi meam commendationem
maximo adiumento fuisse, quod ad te delatum diceret, sese contra dignitatem tuam Romae de te loqui
solitum esse. De quo etsi pro tua facilitate et
humanitate purgatum se tibi scribit esse, tamen

ᵃ See xiii. 19.

man very highly thought of by his patron and his
patron's friends, of whom I am one. So warmly do I 2
commend him to you that if he were my own freedman and stood in the same relation to me as he does
to his patron, I could not commend him more enthusiastically. You will therefore do me a great favour if
you admit him into your friendship, and, if he needs
it in any way, give him such assistance as you can
without inconvenience to yourself. That will be both
gratifying to me and subsequently a pleasure to
yourself ; for you will find him a man of the highest
integrity, most courteous too, and most respectful.

XXIV

CICERO TO SULPICIUS

Rome, some time in 46 B.C.

I previously derived pleasure from an act of kind- 1
ness on my part, when I remembered how warmly
I had recommended to you my host and guest
and intimate friend Lyso,[a] and now that I have
gathered from his letter that he had been falsely
suspected by you, I rejoiced exceedingly that my
recommendation of him had been so warmly worded.
He told me in his letter that my recommendation
had been of the greatest assistance to him, because
(as he says) a report had reached your ears that he
had been in the habit of speaking about you at Rome
to the prejudice of your high position.

Now although he writes that, as might have been 2
expected from your good nature and kindliness, he
has cleared himself in your eyes, still in the first place,

primum, ut debeo, tibi gratias ago, cum tantum litterae meae potuerunt, ut, his lectis, omnem offensionem suspicionis, quam habueras de Lysone, deponeres ; deinde credas mihi affirmanti velim, me hoc non pro Lysone magis, quam pro omnibus scribere, hominem esse neminem, qui umquam mentionem tui sine tua summa laude fecerit. Lyso vero cum mecum prope quotidie esset unaque viveret, non solum, quia me libenter audire arbitrabatur, sed quia libentius ipse loquebatur, omnia mihi tua et facta et 3 dicta laudabat. Quapropter etsi a te ita tractatur, ut iam non desideret commendationem meam, unisque se litteris meis omnia consecutum putet, tamen a te peto in maiorem modum, ut eum etiam atque etiam tuis officiis et liberalitate complectare. Scriberem ad te, qualis vir esset, ut superioribus litteris feceram, nisi eum iam per se ipsum tibi satis esse notum arbitrarer.

XXV

CICERO SERVIO S.

Romae, a.u.c. 708.

Hegesaretus Larissaeus, magnis meis beneficiis ornatus in consulatu meo, memor et gratus fuit, meque postea diligentissime coluit. Eum tibi magno

---

^a Probably the head of the Pompeian faction in Thessaly.
^b In Thessaly.

I express my gratitude to you that my letter has had such influence with you that on perusing it you put away from you all the feeling of offence caused by the suspicion you entertained of Lyso; and secondly I would have you believe me when I asseverate that I am writing this not more on Lyso's than on every other man's behalf—that there is no man alive who has ever mentioned your name without praising you up to the skies. As for Lyso, when he was in my company almost every day and lived with me, he used to praise in my presence your every word and deed—not only because it was a pleasure to me to listen, but because it was an even greater pleasure to him to say so.

For that reason, although he is being so treated by 3 you that he no longer desires any recommendation of mine, and imagines that my single letter has enabled him to get all he wants, yet I beg of you with more than usual earnestness to show your appreciation of him by your kind services and generosity. I should write and tell you what sort of a man he is, as I did in previous letters, were I not convinced that he is by this time sufficiently well known to you on his own account.

XXV

CICERO TO SULPICIUS

Rome, some time in 46 B.C.

Hegesaretus [a] of Larissa,[b] whom I honoured with some considerable kindnesses during my consulship, has proved himself neither forgetful nor ungrateful, and has subsequently paid me marked attention. I

opere commendo, ut et hospitem meum et familiarem, et gratum hominem, et virum bonum, et principem civitatis suae, et tua necessitudine dignissimum. Pergratum mihi feceris, si dederis operam, ut is intellegat hanc meam commendationem magnum apud te pondus habuisse.

XXVI

CICERO SERVIO S.

Romae, a.u.c. 708.

1 L. Mescinius ea mecum necessitudine coniunctus est, quod mihi quaestor fuit. Sed hanc causam, quam ego, ut a maioribus accepi, semper gravem duxi, fecit virtute et humanitate sua iustiorem. Itaque eo sic utor, ut nec familiarius ullo nec libentius. Is quamquam confidere videbatur, te sua causa, quae honeste posses, libenter esse facturum, magnum esse tamen speravit apud te meas quoque litteras pondus habituras. Id cum ipse ita iudicabat, tum pro familiari consuetudine saepe ex me audierat, quam suavis esset inter nos et quanta coniunctio.

2 Peto igitur a te, tanto scilicet studio, quanto intellegis debere me petere pro homine tam mihi necessario et tam familiari, ut eius negotia, quae sunt in Achaia,

---

ᵃ L. Mescinius Rufus, one of Cicero's quaestors in Cilicia.

78

strongly recommend him to you as being a guest and
friend of mine with whom I am familiar, a grateful
fellow of excellent character, the chief man of his
State, and altogether worthy of your intimacy. You
will do me a great favour if you make a point of giving
him reason to know that this recommendation of
mine has had great weight with you.

XXVI

CICERO TO SULPICIUS

Rome, some time in 46 B.C.

The explanation of my close connexion with L. 1
Mescinius[a] is that he was my quaestor. But that
reason for intimacy, strong as I have always, in
accordance with ancestral tradition, held it to be, he
has further justified by his own merits and courtesy.
It follows that there is no one with whom I am
on more intimate terms, or with more pleasure. Now
although he appeared to be confident that you would
willingly do what you could for him, without compromising yourself, for his own sake, at the same time
he hoped that a letter from me too would have great
weight with you. Not only did he think so himself,
but he had also (such is the intimacy of our intercourse) often heard me say how delightful and how
close is my connexion with you.

I therefore entreat you with all that earnestness, 2
believe me, with which I am bound to entreat you
on behalf of one so closely connected and intimate
with me, to facilitate and expedite the business
affairs he has in Achaia (arising from the fact that he

79

ex eo, quod heres est M. Mindio, fratri suo, qui Eli[1]
negotiatus est, explices et expedias, cum iure et
potestate, quam habes, tum etiam auctoritate et
consilio tuo. Sic enim praescripsimus iis, quibus ea
negotia mandavimus, ut omnibus in rebus, quae in
aliquam controversiam vocarentur, te arbitro, et, quod
commodo tuo fieri posset, te disceptatore uterentur.
Id ut honoris mei causa suscipias, vehementer te
3 etiam atque etiam rogo. Illud praeterea, si non
alienum tua dignitate putabis esse, feceris mihi
pergratum, si qui difficiliores erunt, ut rem sine controversia confici nolint, si eos, quando cum senatore
res est, Romam reieceris. Quod quo minore dubitatione facere posses, litteras ad te a M. Lepido
consule, non quae te aliquid iuberent (neque enim
id tuae dignitatis esse arbitramur), sed quodam modo
4 quasi commendaticias sumpsimus. Scriberem, quam
id beneficium bene apud Mescinium positurus esses,
nisi et te scire confiderem et mihi peterem. Sic
enim velim existimes, non minus me de illius re
laborare, quam ipsum de sua. Sed cum illum studeo
quam facillime ad suum pervenire, tum illud laboro,
ut non minimum hac mea commendatione se consecutum arbitretur.

[1] *MSS.*, *as also in* N.D. 59: Elide *Lambinus.*

---

[a] If a Roman citizen, especially a senator, complained
against a subject or subject community, the governor could
order the latter to appear either personally or by counsel
(*ecdici*) at Rome. The transference of the case to Rome,
which entailed much expense, was a hardship to the provincials, who generally preferred to compromise.

[b] Caesar and Lepidus were consuls in 46.

is heir to his cousin M. Mindius, who was a banker at Elis) by means not only of your lawful powers but also of your weighty influence and advice. For my instructions to those to whom I entrusted those business affairs were as follows : " that in anything brought forward as admitting of any dispute they should employ you to arbitrate, and (so far as it could be done without inconveniencing you) to settle the case once for all." This I press you again and again to undertake to do in the interests of my honour.

This too is another great favour you will do me, if 3 you do not consider it incompatible with your position —that if any of those concerned are so obstinately intractable as to having the matter settled without a trial, you should refer them, since a senator is involved in the case, to Rome.[a] And to enable you to do so with the less hesitation, I have in my hands a despatch to you from the consul M. Lepidus,[b] not such as to lay any injunction upon you (that, I consider, would be inconsistent with your position) but which conveys in a sort of way what may be called a recommendation.

I should go on to tell you how sound an investment 4 you would be likely to make in doing Mescinius this favour, were not I sure that you are aware of it, and were it not that this request of mine is really a selfish one ; for I would have you believe that I am no less anxious about his interests than he is himself. But while I desire that he should come by his own with the least possible difficulty, I am also anxious to give him the impression that this recommendation of mine has not been the most negligible factor in his success.

CICERO

XXVII

CICERO SERVIO S.

Romae, A.U.C. 708.

1 Licet eodem exemplo saepius tibi huius generis
litteras mittam, cum gratias agam, quod meas commendationes tam diligenter observes (quod feci in
aliis, et faciam, ut video, saepius), sed tamen non
parcam operae, et ut vos soletis in formulis, sic ego in
2 epistulis *de eadem re alio modo.* C. Avianius igitur
Hammonius incredibiles mihi gratias per litteras
egit, et suo et Aemili Aviani, patroni sui, nomine, nec
liberalius, nec honorificentius potuisse tractari nec
se praesentem nec rem familiarem absentis patroni
sui. Id mihi cum iucundum est eorum causa, quos
tibi ego summa necessitudine et summa coniunctione
adductus commendaveram, quod M. Aemilius unus
est ex meis familiarissimis atque intimis maxime
necessarius homo et magnis meis beneficiis devinctus,
et prope omnium, qui mihi debere aliquid videntur,
gratissimus, tum multo iucundius, te esse in me tali
voluntate, ut plus prosis amicis meis, quam ego
praesens fortasse prodessem, credo, quod magis ego
dubitarem, quid illorum causa facerem, quam tu,
3 quid mea. Sed hoc non dubito, quin existimes mihi

ᵃ A formula used by lawyers, "cum ostenderent eiusdem
rei consequendae vias complures esse," "when they indicated
that there were several ways of obtaining the same result."
Brissonius, quoted by Tyrrell.

ᵇ This cognomen is added to distinguish him from the
more celebrated C. Avianius Evander. See xiii. 21. 2.

XXVII

CICERO TO SULPICIUS

Rome, some time in 46 B.C.

It is excusable to use exactly the same terms over 1
and over again in sending you letters of this kind,
thanking you for so punctiliously attending to my
recommendations ; I have done so in other cases, and
shall do so, I foresee, ever so often ; but for all that I
shall make every effort to do in my letters what you
lawyers habitually do in your *formulae*, and that is,
" *to put the same case in a different way.*" [a]

Well then, C. Avianius, I mean Hammonius,[b] has 2
in a letter to me expressed himself amazingly grateful, in his own name as well as in that of his patron
Aemilius Avianius, saying that neither he, who was
on the spot, nor the personal affairs of his patron, who
was away, could possibly have been dealt with either
more generously or with more distinguished consideration. This is a joy to me, in view of the interests
of those whom I had been induced by the closest
bonds of familiarity and fellowship to commend to
you, because M. Aemilius stands alone among all my
most intimate associates as my closest friend and
most beholden to me for considerable kindnesses, and
perhaps the most grateful of those who, I suppose,
owe me something ; but it is a far greater joy to me
that you are so well disposed towards me as to be of
more service to my friends than perhaps I should be
myself, were I on the spot, because, I imagine, I should
be in greater doubt as to what I should do in their
interests, than you as to what you should do in mine.

Of this, however, I have no doubt—that you believe 3

83

CICERO

esse gratum. Illud te rogo, ut illos quoque gratos
homines esse putes; quod ita esse tibi promitto
atque confirmo. Quare velim, quidquid habent negoti, des operam, quod commodo tuo fiat, ut te
4 obtinente Achaiam conficiant. Ego cum tuo Servio
iucundissime, coniunctissime vivo magnamque cum
ex ingenio eius singularique studio, tum ex virtute et
probitate voluptatem capio.

XXVIIIa

CICERO SERVIO S.

Romae, a.u.c. 708.

1 Etsi libenter petere a te soleo, si quid opus est
meorum cuipiam, tamen multo libentius gratias tibi
ago, cum fecisti aliquid commendatione mea, quod
semper facis. Incredibile est enim, quas mihi gratias
omnes agant, etiam mediocriter a me tibi com-
mendati, quae mihi omnia grata, sed de L. Mescinio
gratissimum. Sic enim est mecum locutus, te, ut
meas litteras legeris, statim procuratoribus suis pollicitum esse omnia; multo vero plura et maiora
fecisse. Id igitur (puto enim etiam atque etiam mihi
dicendum esse) velim existimes mihi te fecisse gratis-
2 simum. Quod quidem hoc vehementius laetor, quod
ex ipso Mescinio te video magnam capturum voluptatem. Est enim in eo cum virtus et probitas
84

me to be grateful ; and I beg of you to regard them
too as not ungrateful ; that such is the case I promise
and assure you. I would therefore have you do your
best, so far as you conveniently can, to enable them
to conclude whatever business they have on hand
while you are governor of Achaia.

I am living on delightful and most sociable terms 4
with your son Servius, whose ability and incomparable
application, not to mention his excellent character
and integrity, are a source of extreme pleasure to me.

XXVIIIa

CICERO TO SULPICIUS

Rome, some time in 46 B.C.

Although it is always a pleasure to me to make a 1
request of you, if any of my friends want anything, it
is a far greater pleasure to thank you when you have
done something on my recommendation, and you are
always doing so. For you could not believe how
cordially they all thank me, yes, even those I have
only moderately recommended ; and this is gratifying
to me in every case, but most gratifying of all in the
case of L. Mescinius ; for this is what he told me in
conversation—that as soon as ever you read my letter
you promised his agents all they wanted, but that in
number and importance your deeds went far beyond
your words. I would therefore have you believe (and
I think I ought to say so again and again) that what
you have done has been a great gratification to me.

And I rejoice at this all the more heartily because 2
I foresee that you will get a great deal of enjoyment
out of Mescinius himself ; you will find in him a man

et summum officium summaque observantia, tum
studia illa nostra, quibus antea delectabamur, nunc
etiam vivimus. Quod reliquum est, velim augeas
tua in eum beneficia omnibus rebus, quae te erunt
dignae; sed duo quidem te nominatim rogo: primum,
ut, si quid satisdandum erit, AMPLIUS EO NOMINE NON
PETI, cures, ut satisdetur fide mea; deinde, cum fere
consistat hereditas in iis rebus, quas avertit Oppia,
quae uxor Mindi fuit, adiuves, ineasque rationem,
quemadmodum ea mulier Romam perducatur. Quod
si putarit illa fore, ut opinio nostra est, negotium
conficiemus. Hoc ut assequamur, te vehementer
3 etiam atque etiam rogo. Illud, quod supra scripsi,
id in me recipio, te ea, quae fecisti Mescini causa,
quaeque feceris, ita bene collocaturum, ut ipse
iudices, homini te gratissimo, iucundissimo benigne
fecisse. Volo enim, ad id, quod mea causa fecisti,
hoc etiam accedere.

XXVIIIв

CICERO SERVIO S.

Romae, a.u.c. 708.

1 Nec Lacedaemonios dubitare arbitror, quin ipsi
sua maiorumque suorum auctoritate satis com-
mendati sint fidei et iustitiae tuae, et ego, qui te

of virtue and integrity, most willing to serve you and most respectful, and at the same time devoted to those literary pursuits which were formerly my amusement, but are now my very life. For the future I would have you even increase your favours to him in any way that is worthy of you. Two requests indeed I make of you specifically : first, that if any security has to be given " against any further claims on that score," you should see to it that I am held responsible for that security ; secondly, since his inheritance practically consists of property fraudulently appropriated by Oppia, who was the wife of Mindius, you should come to his assistance, and take steps to ensure that lady's safe-conduct to Rome. If she once realizes that it will be so, it is my opinion that the business will be settled ; and that is the object I earnestly beg of you again and again to enable us to attain.

What I wrote above I take upon myself to guar- 3 antee—that in what you have done and will do for Mescinius you will make so profitable an investment as to compel your independent conviction that the recipient of your favours is a very grateful and a very charming man. I would add this also as a sort of corollary to what you have done for me.

XXVIIIb

CICERO TO SULPICIUS

Rome, some time in 46 B.C.

I do not suppose that the Lacedaemonians are in 1 any doubt as to their having been already sufficiently recommended to your sense of loyalty and justice by their own high claims and those of their ancestors, nor

optime novissem, non dubitavi, quin tibi notissima
et iura et merita populorum essent. Itaque cum a
me peteret Philippus Lacedaemonius, ut tibi civitatem commendarem, etsi memineram, me ei civitati
omnia debere, tamen respondi, commendatione Lace-
2 daemonios apud te non egere. Itaque sic velim
existimes, me omnes Achaiae civitates arbitrari, pro
horum temporum perturbatione, felices, quod his tu
praesis ; eumdemque me ita iudicasse,[1] te, quod unus
optime nosses non nostra solum, sed etiam Graeciae
monumenta omnia, tua sponte amicum Lacedaemoniis
et esse et fore. Quare tantum a te peto, ut, cum ea
facies Lacedaemoniorum causa, quae tua fides, amplitudo, iustitia postulabit, iis,[2] si tibi videbitur,
significes, te non moleste ferre, quod intellegas ea,
quae facias, mihi quoque grata esse. Pertinet enim
ad officium meum, eos existimare, curae mihi suas res
esse. Hoc te vehementer etiam atque etiam rogo.

XXIX

M. T. C. S. D. L. PLANCO

Romae, a.u.c. 708.

1 Non dubito, quin scias, in iis necessariis, qui tibi
a patre relicti sunt, me tibi esse vel coniunctissimum,

[1] *Wesenberg* : indicare *Nobbe and* MSS.
[2] postulabit, iis *Wesenberg* : postulat ut his *Nobbe.*

[a] Plancus (for whom see note *a* on x. 1) was now serving
with Caesar in Africa.

have I myself, because I know you so very well, ever doubted that you were thoroughly acquainted with the rights and merits of nationalities. And so, when asked by Philippus, the Lacedaemonian, to recommend that state to you, although I remembered that I was under every obligation to that state, yet I replied that the Lacedaemonians stood in no need of any recommendation with you.

I would therefore have you believe that I con- 2 sider all the states of Achaia, in view of the disturbed state of the times, happy in having you for their governor, and I have, moreover, convinced myself that you, because you are better acquainted than any living man, not only with our own history, but also with the whole history of Greece, are now, and ever will be, of your own choice a friend to Lacedaemonians. For that reason I merely beg of you, when you do for the Lacedaemonians all that your conscience, dignity, and sense of justice shall demand, to convey to them, if you please, the impression that it is by no means disagreeable to you to feel that what you do will be gratifying also to myself. Indeed, it touches my sense of duty that they should be made to believe that I charge myself with their interests. This I earnestly beg of you again and again to do.

XXIX

CICERO TO L. MUNATIUS PLANCUS [a]

Rome, early in 46 b.c.

I have no doubt you are aware that among the 1 intimate friends bequeathed to you by your father,

89

non his modo causis, quae speciem habent magnae
coniunctionis, sed iis etiam, quae familiaritate et
consuetudine tenentur, quam scis mihi iucundissimam cum patre tuo et summam fuisse. Ab his
initiis noster in te amor profectus auxit paternam
necessitudinem, et eo magis, quod intellexi, ut
primum per aetatem iudicium facere potueris, quanti
quisque tibi faciendus esset, me a te in primis
coeptum esse observari, coli, diligi. Accedebat non
mediocre vinculum cum studiorum, quod ipsum est
per se grave, tum eorum studiorum earumque artium,
quae per se ipsae eos, qui voluntate eadem sunt,
2 etiam familiaritate devinciunt. Exspectare te arbitror, haec tam longe repetita principia quo spectent.
Id primum ergo habeto, non sine magna iustaque
causa hanc a me commemorationem esse factam.
C. Ateio Capitone utor familiarissime. Notae tibi
sunt varietates meorum temporum. In omni genere
et honorum et laborum meorum et animus et opera
et auctoritas et gratia, etiam res familiaris, C. Capitonis
praesto fuit et paruit et temporibus et fortunae meae.
3 Huius propinquus fuit T. Antistius; qui cum sorte
quaestor Macedoniam obtineret, neque ei successum
esset, Pompeius in eam provinciam cum exercitu

* Notorious for having published prodigies of ill omen
when Crassus was setting out for Syria; he was always an
opponent of the Triumvirs.

I am quite the most closely attached to you, not only
on such grounds as give the appearance of close
attachment, but on those also which are established
by familiarity and intercourse ; and my intercourse
with your father was, as you are aware, in the fullest
sense as agreeable as it was close. That was the
origin of my affection for you, which has enhanced
this hereditary association, and all the more so
because I realized that as soon as your years enabled
you to form an estimate as to the regard in which you
should hold each of your acquaintances, it was I who
began to be the special object of your respect,
esteem, and affection. Then there was added the
bond (no slight one), not only of common pursuits—
a bond which carries weight of itself—but also of
such pursuits and accomplishments as firmly unite
men of identical tastes in what becomes intimacy as
well.

You are curious to know, I am sure, what is the 2
drift of a preamble that stretches so far back. Well
then, let me immediately assure you that I have not
entered into this recapitulation of facts without good
and sufficient reason. I am on very intimate terms
with C. Ateius Capito.[a] The vicissitudes of my
fortunes are familiar to you. In every phase of
my career, whether distinguished or distressful, C.
Capito has ever been at hand to help me with his
courage, energy, influence, popularity, and even his
purse, and to obey the call of every crisis in my
fortunes.

He had a relative, one T. Antistius ; and when 3
this man was holding Macedonia as quaestor according to lot, and had not yet been succeeded, Pompey
arrived in that province with an army. Antistius

venit. Facere Antistius nihil potuit. Nam, si potuisset, nihil ei fuisset antiquius, quam ad Capitonem, quem ut parentem diligebat, reverti, praesertim cum sciret, quanti is Caesarem faceret semperque fecisset. Sed oppressus tantum attigit negoti, quan-
4 tum recusare non potuit. Cum signaretur argentum Apolloniae, non possum dicere eum praefuisse, neque possum negare adfuisse, sed non plus duobus an tribus mensibus. Deinde abfuit a castris ; fugit omne negotium. Hoc mihi ut testi velim credas ; meam enim ille maestitiam in illo bello videbat, mecum omnia communicabat. Itaque abdidit se in intimam Macedoniam, quo potuit longissime a castris, non modo ut non praeesset ulli negotio, sed etiam ut ne interesset quidem. Is post proelium se ad hominem necessarium, A. Plautium, in Bithyniam contulit. Ibi eum Caesar cum vidisset, nihil aspere, nihil acerbe dixit. Romam iussit venire. Ille in morbum continuo incidit, ex quo non convaluit. Aeger Corcyram venit ; ibi est mortuus. Testamento, quod Romae Paullo et Marcello consulibus fecerat, heres ex parte dimidia et tertia est Capito ; in sextante sunt ii, quorum pars, sine ulla cuiusquam querella, publica potest esse ; ea est ad HS |xxx|. Sed de hoc Caesar
5 viderit. Te, mi Plance, pro paterna necessitudine,

a Of Pharsalia in 48 B.C.   *b* *i.e.,* in 50 B.C.
c *i.e.,* 3000 *sestertia,* about £27,000.

could do nothing. Had he been able to do so, nothing would have been more to his advantage than to return to Capito, whom he loved as a father, especially as he knew how highly Capito was, and always had been, esteemed by Caesar. But, taken by surprise as he was, he only engaged in such business as he could not possible evade.

When silver was being stamped at Apollonia, I 4 cannot say that he presided over the business, nor can I deny that he was on the spot, but it could only have been for two (or was it three ?) months. After that he absented himself from the camp, and ran away from all business. I would have you take my word for this as being that of a witness, since, seeing how despondent I was during that war, he used to talk everything over with me. So he hid himself away in the heart of Macedonia, as far from the camp as he possibly could, so as to avoid not only taking a leading part in any transaction, but even taking any part in it at all. After the battle [a] he retired into Bithynia, where he joined an intimate friend of his, one A. Plautius. When Caesar saw him there, he said nothing harsh, nothing bitter, but simply ordered him to Rome. Immediately after that Antistius contracted an illness from which he never recovered. He was a sick man when he reached Corcyra, and there he died. By a will which he had made at Rome in the consulship of Paullus and Marcellus,[b] Capito was made heir to five-sixths of his estate ; those who came in for one-sixth are men whose share can be confiscated without a word of complaint from anybody ; it amounts to 3,000,000 sesterces.[c] But that is for Caesar to see to.

Now I ask you, my dear Plancus, in the name of 5

pro nostro amore, pro studiis et omni cursu nostro
totius vitae simillimo, rogo (et a te ita peto, ut maiore
cura, maiore studio nullo possim), ut hanc rem suscipias ; meam putes esse ; enitare, contendas, efficias,
ut mea commendatione, tuo studio, Caesaris beneficio, hereditatem propinqui sui C. Capito obtineat.
Omnia, quae potui in hac summa tua gratia ac
potentia a te impetrare, si petiissem, ultro te ad me
6 detulisse putabo, si hanc rem impetravero. Illud fore
tibi adiumento spero, cuius ipse Caesar esse optimus
iudex potest : semper Caesarem Capito coluit et
dilexit. Sed ipse huius rei testis est ; novi hominis
memoriam. Itaque nihil te doceo ; tantum tibi
sumito pro Capitone apud Caesarem, quantum ipsum
7 meminisse senties. Ego, quod in meipso experiri
potui, ad te deferam. In eo quantum sit ponderis,
tu videbis. Quam partem in republica causamque
defenderim, per quos homines ordinesque steterim,
quibusque munitus fuerim, non ignoras. Hoc mihi
velim credas : si quid fecerim hoc ipso in bello minus
ex Caesaris voluntate (quod intellexi[1] scire ipsum
Caesarem, me invitissimum fecisse), id fecisse aliorum

---

[1] *Tyrrell, with most editors:* intellexerim *Nobbe.*

---

[a] *i.e.*, the senatorial and the equestrian.

our hereditary connexion, our mutual affection, our common pursuits, and the close resemblance of our whole lives throughout their course (and I could not make this request with more solicitude and earnestness than I do), to account the matter mine, to spare no effort, no endeavour, and so to bring it about that through my recommendation, your own assiduity, and the kindness of Caesar, Capito may make good his claim to his relative's legacy. If I prevail upon you to do this, I shall consider that you have bestowed upon me unasked all the favours I might have prevailed upon you to grant me, had I but sought them, in this, the zenith of your popularity and power.

I hope that this fact will be of assistance to you— 6 a fact of which Caesar himself can best judge—that Capito has consistently respected and esteemed Caesar. But Caesar himself can testify to this; I know what a memory he has. I have therefore no instructions to give you; but in speaking to Caesar on Capito's behalf you must limit what you take upon yourself to say to what you perceive to be within Caesar's own recollection.

For my own part, I shall just lay before you what I 7 have been able to prove by personal experience; the significance of it you will see for yourself. What side and what cause I have always championed in politics, what individuals and what orders [a] in the State have enabled me to hold my ground, and by whom I have been protected—all that you know perfectly well. Now I would have you take my word for this—that if in this very war I did anything in the slightest degree offensive to Caesar (and I was aware that Caesar himself knew that I did so with the utmost reluctance),

consilio, hortatu, auctoritate; quod fuerim moderatior
temperatiorque, quam in ea parte quisquam, id me
fecisse maxime auctoritate Capitonis; cuius similes
si reliquos necessarios habuissem, reipublicae fortasse
8 nonnihil, mihi certe plurimum profuissem. Hanc
rem, mi Plance, si effeceris, meam de tua erga me
benevolentia spem confirmaveris, ipsum Capitonem,
gratissimum, officiosissimum, optimum virum, ad
tuam necessitudinem tuo summo beneficio adiunxeris.

XXX

M. T. C. S. P. D. ACILIO PROC.

Romae (?), a.u.c. 709.

1 L. Manlius est Sosis. Is fuit Catinensis : sed est,
una cum reliquis Neapolitanis, civis Romanus factus
decurioque Neapoli; erat enim ascriptus in id municipium ante civitatem sociis et Latinis datam. Eius
frater Catinae nuper mortuus est. Nullam omnino
arbitramur de ea hereditate controversiam eum habiturum, et est hodie in bonis. Sed, cum habet
praeterea negotia vetera in Sicilia sua, et hanc hereditatem fraternam, et omnia eius tibi commendo, in
primisque ipsum virum optimum mihique familiarissi-

ᵃ He was a *legatus* of Caesar, and was in command at
Oricum in 48. Some time between 48 and 45 (it is not clear
when) he was proconsul of Sicily. Cicero refers with gratitude to Acilius's kindness to him during his unhappy year
at Brundisium; but Acilius had reason to be grateful to
Cicero for having twice successfully defended him *de capite*
(vii. 30. 3).

ᵇ *i.e.*, before 90 B.C., when the full Roman citizenship was
offered them by L. Julius Caesar.

96

that I did by the advice and at the urgent instance of others ; but in so far as I showed more moderation and self-restraint than anybody else on that side, I did so mainly at the instance of Capito ; and had the others with whom I was closely associated been like him, I should perhaps have benefited the common-wealth to some extent, and should at any rate have benefited myself very greatly.

If you succeed in doing what I ask, my dear 8 Plancus, you will confirm my anticipations of your kindly feeling for myself, and also bind Capito, that most grateful, obliging, and excellent of men, in the bonds of friendship to yourself by your own signal good service.

XXX

CICERO TO MANIUS ACILIUS GLABRIO, PROCONSUL [a]

Rome (?), 45 B.C.

There is a certain L. Manlius Sosis.   He was for- 1 merly a citizen of Catina, but together with the other Neapolitans he was made a Roman citizen, and is in the Senate at Naples, having been enrolled in that municipality before the citizenship was granted to allies and Latins.[b]   This man's brother has lately died at Catina.   I do not think that he will find that there is any dispute about the inheritance here, and he is to-day in full possession of his goods.   But since he has besides business matters of long standing to at-tend to in his native Sicily, I commend to your notice both this inheritance from his brother, and all his interests, and in particular the man himself, as a most excellent fellow and a most intimate friend of mine,

97

CICERO

mum, his studiis litterarum doctrinaeque praeditum,
2 quibus ego maxime delector. Peto igitur abs te, ut
eum, sive aderit, sive non venerit in Siciliam, in meis
intimis maximeque necessariis scias esse, itaque tractes, ut intellegat, meam sibi commendationem magno
adiumento fuisse.

XXXI

M. T. C. S. P. D. ACILIO PROC.

Romae (?), A.U.C. 709.

1 C. Flavio, honesto et ornato equite Romano, utor
valde familiariter. Fuit enim generi mei, C. Pisonis,
pernecessarius, meque diligentissime observat et ipse
et L. Flavius, frater eius. Quapropter velim honoris
mei causa, quibus rebus honeste et pro tua dignitate
poteris, quam honorificentissime et quam liberalissime C. Flavium tractes. Id mihi sic erit gratum, ut
2 gratius esse nihil possit. Sed praeterea tibi affirmo
(neque id ambitione adductus facio, sed cum familiaritate et necessitudine, tum etiam veritate), te ex C.
Flavi officio et observantia, et praeterea splendore
atque inter suos gratia, magnam voluptatem esse
capturum. Vale.

---

[a] M. Brutus's *praefectus fabrum*, who was killed at
Philippi. It was this Flavius who suggested to Atticus that
the *equites* should raise a fund in support of the tyrannicides,
and Brutus blamed Atticus for refusing to accept the suggestion. See *Ad Brut.* i. 17. 3 and i. 6. 4.
[b] C. Piso Frugi, Tullia's first husband.

blessed too with those tastes in literature and learning which give me most pleasure.

I beg of you then to recognize that, whether he is 2
on the spot or has not yet arrived in Sicily, the man is
among my most intimate and closest associates, and
so to treat him as to give him reason to believe that
my recommendation has been of material assistance
to him.

XXXI

CICERO TO MANIUS ACILIUS GLABRIO, PROCONSUL

Rome (?), 45 B.C.

I am on very familiar terms with C. Flavius,*a* an 1
honourable and distinguished Roman knight ; for he
was a very intimate friend of my son-in-law, C. Piso,*b*
and both he himself and his brother L. Flavius
show me most marked respect. For that reason
I should like you, as a compliment to myself, to treat
C. Flavius in the most complimentary and generous
manner possible, in whatever respect you can do so
without prejudice to your honour and position. That
will give me more pleasure than anything you could
possibly do.

But I further assure you (and this I do impelled by 2
no interested motive, but by our close intimacy and
friendship, and even by truth itself) that C. Flavius's
obliging and respectful demeanour, and moreover his
distinction and popularity among his own friends, will
be a source of great pleasure to you.

CICERO

XXXII

M. T. C. S. P. D. ACILIO PROC.

Romae (?), A.U.C. 709.

1 In Halesina civitate tam lauta tamque nobili
coniunctissimos habeo et hospitio et familiaritate
M. et C. Clodios, Archagathum et Philonem. Sed
vereor ne, quia complures tibi praecipue commendo,
exaequare videar ambitione quadam commendationes
meas. Quamquam a te quidem cumulate satisfit et
2 mihi et meis omnibus. Sed velim sic existimes, hanc
familiam et hos mihi maxime esse coniunctos vetustate, officiis, benevolentia. Quamobrem peto a te
in maiorem modum, ut his omnibus in rebus, quantum
tua fides dignitasque patietur, commodes. Id si
feceris, erit mihi vehementissime gratum.

XXXIII

M. T. C. S. P. D. ACILIO PROC.

Romae (?), A.U.C. 709.

Cn. Otacilio Nasone utor familiarissime, ita prorsus,
ut illius ordinis nullo familiarius. Nam et humanitate
eius et probitate in consuetudine quotidiana magno
opere delector. Nihil iam opus est exspectare te,

---

a In the middle of the N. coast of Sicily. Having been
the first Sicilian state to join the Romans in the First Punic
War, it was favourably treated in the settlement of the island.

b *i.e.,* " I meant no reflection upon *you* in what I have just
said ; no, *you* always regard my recommendations as genuine, and respond accordingly."

c *i.e.,* the equestrian order.

XXXII

CICERO TO MANIUS ACILIUS GLABRIO, PROCONSUL

Rome (?), 45 B.C.

In the community of Halesa [a]—and a highly refined 1
and distinguished community it is—I am closely
united by bonds of both hospitality and intimacy
with the two Clodii, M. Archagathus and C. Philo.
But I am afraid that, because I am *most particularly*
recommending so many people to you, I may be
suspected of making all my recommendations equally
strong as a sort of bid for popularity—though
indeed, as far as you are concerned, both I and all my
friends are abundantly satisfied with what you do.[b]

But I would really have you believe that this 2
family, and these members of it, are very closely bound
to me by long-standing friendship, and mutual services,
and goodwill. For that reason I beg of you with
more than ordinary earnestness to do all you can
for them in every possible way, so far as your honour
and position permit. If you do so, I shall be extremely grateful.

XXXIII

CICERO TO MANIUS ACILIUS GLABRIO, PROCONSUL

Rome (?), 45 B.C.

I am on very familiar terms with Cn. Otacilius Naso
—indeed as much so as with any member of that
order.[c] I am immensely delighted both with his kindliness and his integrity in our daily intercourse. So now
there is no need for your waiting to see what words

quibus eum verbis tibi commendem, quo sic utar, ut
scripsi. Habet is in provincia tua negotia, quae
procurant liberti, Hilarus, Antigonus, Demostratus,
quos tibi negotiaque omnia Nasonis non secus commendo, ac si mea essent. Gratissimum mihi feceris,
si intellexero hanc commendationem magnum apud
te pondus habuisse.

XXXIV

M. T. C. S. P. D. ACILIO PROC.

Romae (?), A.U.C. 709.

Avitum mihi hospitium est cum Lysone, Lysonis
filio, Lilybitano, valdeque ab eo observor, cognovique
dignum et patre et avo ; est enim nobilissima familia.
Quapropter commendo tibi maiorem in modum rem
domumque eius ; magnoque opere abs te peto,
cures, ut is intellegat, meam commendationem
maximo sibi apud te et adiumento et ornamento
fuisse.

XXXV

M. T. C. S. P. D. ACILIO PROC.

Romae (?), A.U.C. 709.

1 C. Avianius Philoxenus antiquus est hospes meus,
et praeter hospitium valde etiam familiaris, quem

---

^a Cicero was quaestor of Lilybaeum in 75-74 B.C. under the
praetor Sext. Peducaeus.

^b As Philoxenus seems to have been made a Roman citizen
at Cicero's request, he should have taken the name of M.
Tullius ; but as Cicero had probably been actuated by
Avianius's advice, Philoxenus preferred to take the name of
the latter. (*Cf.* xiii. 79.)

I use in commending to you one with whom I am on such terms as I have just set down. He has some business affairs in your province which are being attended to by his freedmen, Hilarus, Antigonus, and Demostratus; and them I commend to you, and also all Naso's affairs, precisely as if they were my own. You will have gratified me extremely if I have reason to think that this recommendation of mine has had great weight with you.

XXXIV

CICERO TO MANIUS ACILIUS GLABRIO, PROCONSUL

Rome (?), 45 B.C.

I am bound by ties of hospitality, dating from the days of his grandfather, with Lyso of Lilybaeum [a]; he pays me marked attention, and I have found him worthy both of his father and of his grandfather; for he comes of a very noble family. That is why I commend him to you, and his household also, with more than ordinary earnestness, and I beg of you very particularly to give him reason to know that my recommendation has been of great assistance as well as a great compliment to him.

XXXV

CICERO TO MANIUS ACILIUS GLABRIO, PROCONSUL

Rome (?), 45 B.C.

C. Avianius Philoxenus [b] is an old friend and guest 1 of mine, and apart from the ties of hospitality, he is very intimate with me; it was as a favour to me that

103

CICERO

Caesar meo beneficio in Novocomenses rettulit.
Nomen autem Aviani secutus est, quod homine nullo
plus est usus, quam Flacco Aviano, meo, quemadmodum te scire arbitror, familiarissimo. Quae ego omnia
collegi, ut intellegeres, non vulgarem esse commen-
2 dationem hanc meam.   Peto igitur abs te, ut omnibus rebus, quod sine molestia tua facere possis, ei
commodes, habeasque in numero tuorum ; perficias-
que, ut intellegat has litteras meas magno sibi usui
fuisse.   Erit id mihi maiorem in modum gratum.

XXXVI

M. T. C. S. P. D. ACILIO PROC.

Romae (?), A.U.C. 709.

1 Cum Demetrio Mega mihi vetustum hospitium est,
familiaritas autem tanta, quanta cum Siculo nullo.
Ei Dolabella rogatu meo civitatem a Caesare impetravit : qua in re ego interfui. Itaque nunc P.
Cornelius vocatur. Cumque propter quosdam sordi-
dos homines, qui Caesaris beneficia vendebant, tabulam, in qua nomina civitate donatorum incisa essent,
revelli iussisset, eidem Dolabellae me audiente
Caesar dixit nihil esse, quod de Mega vereretur ;

ᵃ Novum Comum was a colony established by Caesar, who
regarded it as being specially under his protection.
ᵇ *i.e.*, Megas took Dolabella's name just as Philoxenus
(see the preceding letter) had taken that of Avianius, and
now called himself P. Cornelius Megas.

Caesar enrolled him among the citizens of Novum Comum.[a] He has however adopted the name of Avianius, because he was on more intimate terms with nobody than with Flaccus Avianius, who is, as I believe you are aware, a very dear friend of mine. I have put together all these details to convince you that this recommendation of mine is something out of the common.

I therefore beg of you to do all you can for him in 2 every respect, so far as you may without inconvenience to yourself, to count him as one of your friends, and to convince him without fail that this letter of mine has been of material service to him. Your doing so will give me more than ordinary pleasure.

XXXVI

CICERO TO MANIUS ACILIUS GLABRIO, PROCONSUL

Rome (?), 45 B.C.

I have ties of hospitality of long standing with 1 Demetrius Megas, and I am more intimate with him than with any other Sicilian. It was for him that Dolabella, at my request, obtained the citizenship from Caesar, and I myself took part in the transaction, so now he goes by the name of P. Cornelius.[b] And when, on account of certain disreputable persons, who used to sell his favours, Caesar gave orders that the tablet on which were engraved the names of those presented with citizenship should be torn down, Caesar assured that same Dolabella in my hearing that there was no reason why he should be appre-

2 beneficium suum in eo manere. Hoc te scire volui,
ut eum in civium Romanorum numero haberes,
ceterisque in rebus tibi eum ita commendo, ut maiore
studio neminem commendarim. Gratissimum mihi
feceris, si eum ita tractaris, ut intellegat, meam
commendationem magno sibi ornamento fuisse.

XXXVII

M. T. C. S. P. D. ACILIO PROC.

Romae (?), A.U.C. 709.

Hippiam, Philoxeni filium, Calactinum, hospitem
et necessarium meum, tibi commendo in maiorem
modum. Eius bona, quemadmodum ad me delata
res est, publice possidentur alieno nomine, contra
leges Calactinorum. Id si ita est, etiam sine mea
commendatione ab aequitate tua res ipsa impetrare
debet, ut ei subvenias. Quoquo modo autem se res
habet, peto a te, ut honoris mei causa eum expedias,
tantumque ei commodes et in hac re et in ceteris,
quantum tua fides dignitasque patietur. Id mihi
vehementer gratum erit.

---

* Καλὴ Ἀκτή on the N. coast of Sicily, east of Halesa.

hensive about Megas, adding that the favour he had
conferred upon him held good.

I was anxious that you should know this, so that you 2
might count him among the citizens of Rome, and in
all other respects I commend him to you with as much
earnestness as I have ever commended anybody.
You will give me extreme pleasure if you so treat him
as to make him feel that my recommendation has
conferred great distinction upon him.

XXXVII

CICERO TO MANIUS ACILIUS GLABRIO, PROCONSUL

Rome (?), 45 B.C.

I commend to you with more than ordinary warmth
Hippias of Calacte,[a] son of Philoxenus, as being
closely bound to me by ties of hospitality. His
property, as the matter has been reported to me, is
being held by the State, in contravention of the laws
of Calacte, on account of a debt for which he is not
responsible. If that is so, the circumstances themselves, even without any recommendation of mine,
ought to prevail upon a man with your sense of
justice to give him your assistance. But howsoever
the matter stands, I beg of you for my credit's sake
to release him from his difficulties, and to oblige him
both in this and in every other respect so far as is
compatible with your honour and position. Your
doing so will give me extreme pleasure.

CICERO

XXXVIII

M. T. C. S. P. D. ACILIO PROC.

Romae (?), A.U.C. 709.

L. Bruttius, eques Romanus, adulescens omnibus
rebus ornatus, in meis familiarissimis est meque
observat diligentissime, cuius cum patre magna mihi
fuit amicitia iam inde a quaestura mea Siciliensi.
Omnino nunc ipse Bruttius Romae mecum est ; sed
tamen domum eius et rem familiarem et procuratores
tibi sic commendo, ut maiore studio commendare
non possim. Gratissimum mihi feceris, si curaris, ut
intellegat Bruttius—id quod ei recepi—hanc meam
commendationem sibi magno adiumento fuisse.

XXXIX

M. T. C. S. P. D. ACILIO PROC.

Romae (?), A.U.C. 709.

Cum familia Titurnia necessitudo mihi intercedit
vetus, ex qua reliquus est M. Titurnius Rufus, qui
mihi omni diligentia atque officio est tuendus. Est
igitur in tua potestate, ut ille in me satis sibi praesidi
putet esse. Quapropter eum tibi commendo in
maiorem modum, et abs te peto, efficias, ut is commendationem hanc intellegat sibi magno adiumento
fuisse. Erit id mihi vehementer gratum.

---

^a See note *a* on 34 above.

XXXVIII

CICERO TO MANIUS ACILIUS GLABRIO, PROCONSUL

Rome (?), 45 B.C.

L. Bruttius, a Roman knight and in every respect a distinguished young man, is among my most intimate friends, and is most punctilious in his attentions to me ; and I have been great friends with his father ever since my Sicilian quaestorship.[a] To be sure Bruttius himself is at Rome with me, but I none the less commend to you him, his house, his estate, and his agents, with as much warmth as I could put into any recommendation. It will give me extreme pleasure if you make a point of convincing Bruttius (and I have pledged my word to him that it will be so) that this recommendation of mine has been of material assistance to him.

XXXIX

CICERO TO MANIUS ACILIUS GLABRIO, PROCONSUL

Rome (?), 45 B.C.

I have a close connexion of long standing with the Titurnian family, and the only survivor of that family is M. Titurnius Rufus, whom it is my duty to support with all the assiduity and civility I possibly can. It is within your power then to make him believe that the protection he looks for in me is adequate. For that reason I recommend him to you with more than ordinary warmth, and beg of you so to act as to convince him that this recommendation of him has been of material assistance to him. Your doing so will give me no little pleasure.

CICERO

XL

M. T. C. S. P. D. Q. ANCHARIO Q. F. PROC.

Romae, a.u.c. 699.

L. et C. Aurelios, L. filios, quibus et ipsis et patre
eorum, viro optimo, familiarissime utor, commendo
tibi maiorem in modum, adulescentes omnibus optimis artibus ornatos, meos pernecessarios, tua amicitia
dignissimos. Si ulla mea apud te commendatio valuit
—quod scio multas plurimum valuisse—haec ut
valeat, rogo. Quod si eos honorifice liberaliterque
tractaris, et tibi gratissimos optimosque adulescentes
adiunxeris, et mihi gratissimum feceris.

XLI

M. T. C. S. P. D. L. CULLEOLO

Romae, a.u.c. 695.

1 Quae fecisti L. Luccei causa, scire te plane volo
te homini gratissimo commodasse, et cum ipsi, quae
fecisti, pergrata sunt, tum Pompeius, quotiescumque
me videt (videt autem saepe), gratias tibi agit singulares. Addo etiam illud, quod tibi iucundissimum

---

a Tribune of the plebs in 59, when he opposed Caesar. He
was praetor in 56, and proconsul of Macedonia in 55.
b Tyrrell remarks that the title of proconsul does not
necessarily imply that Culleolus had been consul. It was
sometimes given to a provincial governor in command of
an army.
c This is the Lucceius whom Cicero urged to write an
account of the Catilinian conspiracy (v. 12).

110

XL

CICERO TO Q. ANCHARIUS,[a] PROCONSUL

Rome, 55 B.C.

I recommend to you with more than ordinary warmth Lucius and Gaius Aurelius, the sons of Lucius, with whom, as with their father, a most excellent man, I am exceedingly intimate ; they are young men distinguished in all the best accomplishments, very closely associated with myself, and in every way worthy of your friendship. If any recommendation of mine has ever had any influence with you—and, as to that, I know that many have had the greatest influence—I ask you to let this do so. If you treat them honourably and handsomely, you will not only win the attachment of two very grateful and excellent young men, but you will also give me the greatest possible pleasure.

XLI

CICERO TO L. CULLEOLUS, PROCONSUL [b]

Rome, 59 (?) B.C.

As regards what you have done for L. Lucceius,[c] 1 I wish you distinctly to understand that you have obliged the most grateful of men ; and while all you have done gives great pleasure to Lucceius himself, Pompey also, whenever he sees me (and he sees me often), thanks you with quite unusual warmth. This much too I may add—and I am perfectly sure you

esse certo scio, me ipsum ex tua erga Lucceium be-
2 nignitate, maxima voluptate affici. Quod superest,
quamquam mihi non est dubium, quin cum antea
nostra causa, nunc iam etiam tuae constantiae gratia,
mansurus sis in eadem ista liberalitate, tamen abs
te vehementer etiam atque etiam peto, ut ea, quae
initio ostendisti deincepsque fecisti, ad exitum augeri
et cumulari per te velis. Id et Lucceio et Pompeio
valde gratum fore, teque apud eos praeclare positu-
rum confirmo et spondeo. De republica, deque his
negotiis cogitationibusque nostris perscripseram ad
te diligenter paucis ante diebus, easque litteras
dederam pueris tuis. Vale.

XLII

M. T. C. S. P. D. L. CULLEOLO PROC.

Romae, a.u.c. 695.

1 L. Lucceius meus, homo omnium gratissimus,
mirificas tibi apud me gratias egit, cum diceret,
omnia te cumulatissime et liberalissime procuratoribus
suis pollicitum esse. Cum oratio tua tam ei grata
fuerit, quam gratam rem ipsam existimas fore, cum,
ut spero, quae pollicitus es, feceris? Omnino os-
tenderunt Bulliones, sese Lucceio Pompei arbitratu

---

[a] It appears that the inhabitants of Bullis (a town on the
coast of Illyria, S. of Apollonia) owed money to Lucceius,
and had promised to pay it, but Culleolus's official authority
would increase the prospects of its being paid.

will be delighted to hear it—that your generosity to
Lucceius is a very great pleasure to myself.

As to what remains, although I have no doubt 2
that as previously for my sake, so now on behalf of
your own consistency also you will persevere in the
same generosity, none the less I earnestly beg of you
again and again to prove your desire that the promises
you originally made, and in due course fulfilled, should
by your instrumentality be even improved upon and
brought to a completely successful issue. That this
will be highly gratifying to both Lucceius and
Pompey, and that you will be making a brilliant
investment in them, I solemnly pledge my word. As
to the political situation and the business going on
here, and our reflections thereon, I wrote to you fully
and painstakingly a few days ago, and handed the
letter to your servants. Farewell.

XLII

CICERO TO L. CULLEOLUS, PROCONSUL

Rome, 59 B.C.

My friend L. Lucceius, the most grateful of men, 1
expressed to me his amazingly cordial gratitude to
you when he told me that you had promised everything to his agents with quite unbounded generosity.
Seeing that your words gave him such pleasure,
what pleasure do you suppose your acts will give him,
when, as I hope, you have fulfilled your promises ?
The inhabitants of Bullis at all events have indicated
that they will satisfy Lucceius's claims according to
Pompey's award.[a]

2 satisfacturos. Sed vehementer opus est nobis, et
voluntatem et auctoritatem et imperium tuum accedere. Quod ut facias, te etiam atque etiam rogo.
Illudque mihi gratissimum est, quod ita sciunt Luccei
procuratores, et ita Lucceius ipse ex litteris tuis, quas
ad eum misisti, intellexit, hominis nullius apud te
auctoritatem aut gratiam valere plus, quam meam.
Id ut re experiatur, iterum et saepius te rogo.

XLIII

M. T. C. S. P. D. QUINTIO GALLO

Romae, a.u.c. 696 (?).

1 Etsi plurimis rebus spero fore, ut perspiciam, quod
tamen iampridem perspicio, me a te amari, tamen
nunc ea causa tibi datur, in qua facile declarare
possis tuam erga me benevolentiam. L. Oppius,
M. F., Philomeli negotiatur, homo mihi familiaris.
Eum tibi unice commendo, eoque magis, quod cum
ipsum diligo, tum quod negotia procurat L. Egnati
Rufi, quo ego uno equite Romano familiarissime utor,
et qui cum consuetudine quotidiana, tum officiis
2 plurimis maximisque mihi coniunctus est. Oppium
igitur praesentem ut diligas, Egnati absentis rem
ut tueare, aeque a te peto ac si mea negotia essent.

---

^a Probably a *legatus* of Marcius Philippus, who seems to
have been governor of Asia, but in what year it is not known.
  ^b See ii. 16. 7.
  ^c A town between Synnada and Iconium.
  ^d Both Marcus and Quintus Cicero had money dealings
with Egnatius. (*Att.* vii. 18. 4.)

But there is pressing need for our having the addi- 2
tional advantage of your goodwill, and of your personal
and official influence, and I beg you again and again
not to refuse us that. It is also extremely gratifying
to me that Lucceius's agents have learnt, and
Lucceius himself has inferred from the letter you
sent him, that there is nobody in the world who
carries more weight with you, or is personally more
acceptable to you, than myself. I beg you once more,
and repeatedly, to give him practical proof of that.

XLIII

CICERO TO QUINTIUS GALLUS [a]

Rome, 58 (?) B.C.

Although there are numberless circumstances in 1
which I hope I may have clear proof—and indeed I
have long since had proof enough—of your affection
for me, yet here you have a case offered you in which
you can easily make manifest your kindly feeling for
me. Lucius Oppius, [b] the son of Marcus, is a banker at
Philomelium [c] and an intimate friend of mine. I commend him to you most particularly, and all the more
because not only do I esteem him for himself, but he
is also in charge of the affairs of L. Egnatius Rufus,
a man with whom I am on more familiar terms than
with any other single Roman knight, and who is
closely associated with me both by daily intercourse
and by services as numerous as they are important.

I therefore beg of you to make much of Oppius, 2
who is with you, and to protect the interests of
Egnatius, [d] who is not, just as much as if his affairs

Velim, memoriae tuae causa, des litterarum aliquid,
quae tibi in provincia reddantur ; sed ita conscribas,
ut tum, cum eas leges, facile recordari possis huius
meae commendationis diligentiam. Hoc te vehementer etiam atque etiam rogo.

XLIV

CICERO GALLO S.

Romae, A.U.C. 696 (?).

Etsi ex tuis et ex L. Oppi, familiarissimi mei,
litteris cognovi, te memorem commendationis meae
fuisse, idque, pro tua summa erga me benevolentia
proque nostra necessitudine, minime sum admiratus,
tamen etiam atque etiam tibi L. Oppium praesentem
et L. Egnati, mei familiarissimi, absentis negotia
commendo. Tanta mihi cum eo necessitudo est
familiaritasque, ut, si mea res esset, non magis
laborarem. Quapropter gratissimum mihi feceris, si
curaris, ut is intellegat, me a te tantum amari,
quantum ipse existimo. Hoc mihi gratius facere
nihil potes. Idque ut facias, vehementer te rogo.

---

^a *Sc.* Oppius.

were my own. To assist your memory, I should be glad if you would send him[a] something in the shape of a letter to be handed back to you in the province, but please draw it up in such a way that, when you read it, you can at once recall the care I have taken in writing this recommendation. This I earnestly beg of you again and again to do.

XLIV

CICERO TO QUINTIUS GALLUS

Rome, 58 (?) B.C.

Although your own letter and that of my very dear friend L. Oppius have convinced me that you have not been forgetful of my recommendation (and I am not in the least surprised at that, considering your extremely kind feeling for me and the closeness of our connexion), still I commend to you again and again L. Oppius, who is with you, and the affairs of my very dear friend L. Egnatius, who is not. So close is my connexion and intimacy with him that I should not feel more anxious if the business were my own. That is why you will do me a very great favour if you make a point of giving him reason to know that your affection for me is as sincere as I myself believe it to be. Nothing that you can do would give me greater pleasure, and I earnestly beg of you to do so.

CICERO

XLV

Romae, A.U.C. 696 (?).

L. Egnatio uno equite Romano vel familiarissime
utor. Eius Anchialum servum negotiaque, quae
habet in Asia, tibi commendo non minore studio,
quam si rem meam commendarem. Sic enim existimes velim, mihi cum eo non modo quotidianam
consuetudinem summam intercedere, sed etiam officia
magna et mutua nostra inter nos esse. Quamobrem
etiam atque etiam a te peto, ut cures, ut intellega t
me ad te satis diligenter scripsisse. Nam de tua erga
me voluntate non dubitabat. Id ut facias, te etiam
atque etiam rogo.

XLVI

M. T. C. S. P. D. APPULEIO PROQUAESTORI

Romae, A.U.C. 696 (?).

L. Nostius Zoilus est coheres meus, heres autem
patroni sui. Ea re utrumque scripsi, ut et mihi cum
illo causam amicitiae scires esse, et hominem probum
existimares, qui patroni iudicio ornatus esset. Eum
tibi igitur sic commendo ut unum ex nostra domo.

---

a *i.e.*, to Marcius Philippus (see *Ep.* 43, note *a*).
b Zoilus was a freedman of L. Nostius, whose name he
took according to the usual practice.

XLV

CICERO TO APPULEIUS, PROQUAESTOR [a]

Rome, 58 (?) B.C.

Of all the Roman knights the one man I am most
intimate with is L. Egnatius. It is his slave
Anchialus, together with his banking business in
Asia, that I commend to you with no less warmth
than if the business I commend to you were my very
own. For I would have you believe not only that our
daily intercourse is of the closest nature, but that
we are bound together by important mutual services.
For that reason I beg of you again and again to make
a point of satisfying him that I have written to you
with no lack of careful elaboration ; for of your
goodwill towards me he has never entertained a
doubt. I ask you again and again to do so.

XLVI

CICERO TO APPULEIUS, PROQUAESTOR

Rome, 58 (?) B.C.

L. Nostius Zoilus [b] is co-heir with me, but also the
heir of his patron. My reasons for telling you these
two facts are firstly, to let you know that there are
grounds for my friendship with him, and secondly, to
convince you that he is a man of integrity, seeing that
he has been so complimented by the deliberate act
of his patron. I therefore commend him to you as
warmly as if he were of my own household. It will

119

CICERO

Valde mihi gratum erit, si curaris, ut intellegat, hanc commendationem sibi apud te magno adiumento fuisse.

XLVII

M. T. C. S. P. D. SILIO

Romae, A.U.C. 703 (?).

Quid ego tibi commendem eum quem tu ipse diligis ? Sed tamen, ut scires, eum a me non diligi solum, verum etiam amari, ob eam rem tibi haec scribo. Omnium tuorum officiorum, quae et multa et magna sunt, mihi gratissimum fuerit, si ita tractaris Egnatium, ut sentiat, et se a me, et me a te amari. Hoc te vehementer etiam atque etiam rogo. Illa nostra scilicet ceciderunt. Utamur igitur vulgari consolatione, *quid si hoc melius?* Sed haec coram. Tu fac, quod facis, ut me ames, teque amari a me scias.

XLVIII

M. T. C. S. P. D. C. SEXTILIO RUFO QUAEST.

Romae, A.U.C. 704-707.

Omnes tibi commendo Cyprios, sed magis Paphios ; quibus tu quaecumque commodaris, erunt mihi gratissima. Eoque facio libentius, ut eos tibi commendem,

---

a Probably P. Silius Nerva, propraetor of Bithynia and Pontus in 51.

b Probably some efforts of Cicero to escape from provincial government.

c Rufus seems to have been sent out to Cyprus as proquaestor by Caesar in 49. We hear of him later as commander of the fleet of Cassius in 43.

give me great pleasure if you make a point of satisfying him that my recommendation has been of
material assistance to him.

XLVII

CICERO TO SILIUS [a]

Rome, 51 (?) B.C.

Why should I commend to you a man whom you
like on your own account ? But anyhow the reason
I write thus to you is to let you know that I not only
like but even love him. Of all your services to me
(and they are many and great) what will give me
most pleasure is your so treating Egnatius as to
make him feel that I love him and you love me.
This I earnestly beg of you again and again to do.
Oh yes, those plans of ours have fallen through.[b]
Let us then comfort ourselves with the well-known
formula " Perhaps it is all for the best." But of this
when we meet. It is for you to see to it (and you do)
that you love me, and are assured that I love you.

XLVIII

CICERO TO GAIUS SEXTILIUS RUFUS, QUAESTOR [c]

Rome, between 50 and 47 B.C.

I commend to you all the inhabitants of Cyprus,
and more particularly those of Paphos, and whatever
favours you bestow upon them will be most gratifying to myself ; and I do so with all the more pleasure
—I mean commend them to you—because I think

quod et tuae laudi, cuius ego fautor sum, conducere
arbitror, cum primus in eam insulam quaestor veneris,
ea te instituere, quae sequantur alii ; quae, ut spero,
facilius consequere, si et P. Lentuli, necessari tui,
legem, et ea, quae a me constituta sunt, sequi volueris.
Quam rem tibi confido magnae laudi fore.

XLIX

CICERO S. P. D. CURIO PROC.

(Anno incerto.)

Q. Pompeius, Sext. F., multis et veteribus causis
necessitudinis mihi coniunctus est. Is, cum antea
meis commendationibus et rem et gratiam et auctoritatem suam tueri consuerit, nunc profecto, te
provinciam obtinente, meis litteris assequi debet, ut
nemini se intellegat commendatiorem umquam fuisse.
Quamobrem a te maiorem in modum peto, ut, cum
omnes meos aeque ac tuos observare, pro nostra necessitudine, debeas, hunc in primis ita in tuam fidem
recipias, ut ipse intellegat, nullam rem sibi maiori
usui aut ornamento quam meam commendationem
esse potuisse. Vale.

---

a P. Lentulus Spinther, governor of Cilicia 56–53 (i. 1. 1,
note *a*).

b When governor of Cilicia (in 51 and 52), for at that time
Cyprus was part of the province of Cilicia, and remained
so until 47, when it was handed over to Arsinoe and Ptolemy,
son of Ptolemy Auletes (Dio Cass. xiii. 35. 5).

that it will conduce to your own reputation also (which I always have at heart), if when you reach that island as its first quaestor, you set precedents for others to follow ; and this I hope you will the more easily accomplish if you decide to follow the code of your relative P. Lentulus,[a] and the regulations I instituted myself.[b] Such a policy will, I am confident, do you much credit.

XLIX

CICERO TO CURIUS[c]

(Date uncertain.)

There are many reasons of long standing for the close attachment of Q. Pompeius, son of Sextus, to myself. As in the past it is in my recommendations that he has got into the habit of finding support for his fortunes, his reputation, and influence, he certainly ought just now, when you are governor of the province, to profit by my letter so far as to be assured that there is nobody to whom he has ever been more highly commended. For that reason I beg of you with exceptional earnestness, since in view of our close association it is incumbent upon you to show my friends as much respect as your own, to admit this gentleman to your special friendship in such a way as to convince him that nothing could possibly have been of more service or more of a distinction to him than my recommendation. Farewell.

[c] See ii. 19. 2. It is not known what province he governed, or when.

123

CICERO

L

M. T. C. S. D. ACILIO PROC.

Romae (?), A.U.C. 710.

1 Sumpsi hoc mihi, pro tua in me observantia, quam
penitus perspexi, quamdiu Brundisi fuimus, ut ad te
familiariter et quasi pro meo iure scriberem, si quae
res esset de qua valde laborarem.   M'. Curius, qui
Patris negotiatur, ita mihi familiaris est, ut nihil
possit esse coniunctius.   Multa illius in me officia,
multa in illum mea, quodque maximum est, summus
2 inter nos amor et mutuus.   Quae cum ita sint, si
ullam in amicitia mea spem habes, si ea, quae in me
officia et studia Brundisi contulisti, vis mihi etiam
gratiora efficere (quamquam sunt gratissima), si me
a tuis omnibus amari vides, hoc mihi da atque largire,
ut M'. Curium sartum et tectum, ut aiunt, ab omnique
incommodo, detrimento, molestia sincerum integrum-
que conserves.   Et ipse spondeo, et omnes hoc tibi
tui pro me recipient, ex mea amicitia et ex tuo in me
officio maximum te fructum summamque voluptatem
esse capturum.

---

a See note *a* to *Ep.* 30 above.
b The stock phrase for a building in good repair.

L

CICERO TO MANIUS ACILIUS GLABRIO,[a] PROCONSUL

Rome (?), January, 44 B.C.

In view of your respect for me, of which I had con- 1
vincing proof all the time I was at Brundisium, I have
presumed so far as to address you with familiarity,
and as though I had the right to do so, if there were
anything that caused me serious anxiety.

M'. Curius, who has a banking business at Patrae,
is so intimate with me that no association could
possibly be closer. His services to me have been
many, and so have mine been to him, and (what is
most important of all) our affection for each other is
as sincere as it is mutual.

That being so, if you have anything to hope for 2
from my friendship, if you would even enhance my
gratitude, profound as it already is, for the cordial
kindnesses you heaped upon me at Brundisium, if
you observe that all your friends regard me with
affection, then I say, grant me of your bounty this one
favour—keep M'. Curius " water-tight and weather-
proof " [b] as they say, free from the slightest taint
and touch of disaster, damage, or distress. I myself
guarantee, and all your friends will pledge themselves
to you on my behalf, that you will find the combination of my friendship for you with your kindness to
me a source of immense profit and infinite pleasure
to you.

CICERO

LI

M. T. C. S. D. P. CAESIO

Romae, anno incerto.

P. Messienum, equitem Romanum, omnibus rebus
ornatum meumque perfamiliarem, tibi commendo
ea commendatione, quae potest esse diligentissima.
Peto a te et pro nostra et pro paterna amicitia, ut
eum in tuam fidem recipias eiusque rem famamque
tueare. Virum bonum tuaque amicitia dignum tibi
adiunxeris mihique gratissimum feceris.

LII

CICERO S. D. REGI

Romae, a.u.c. 708.

A. Licinius Aristoteles Melitensis antiquissimus
est hospes meus, et praeterea coniunctus magno usu
familiaritatis. Haec cum ita sint, non dubito, quin
tibi satis commendatus sit. Etenim ex multis cognosco, meam commendationem plurimum apud te
valere. Hunc ego a Caesare liberavi. Frequens
enim fuerat nobiscum, atque etiam diutius in causa
est, quam nos, commoratus, quo melius te de eo

---

a Propraetor of Sicily in 46.
b *i.e.*, the Pompeian cause.

LI

CICERO TO P. CAESIUS

Rome, date uncertain.

P. Messenius is a Roman knight, possessed of every accomplishment, and a very dear friend of mine ; I commend him to you, and my recommendation is as strong as the strongest that can be. I beg of you in the name of our own friendship and that of our fathers to admit him into your confidence, and to protect his interests and reputation. You will have won the attachment of a good man and one worthy of your friendship, and at the same time earned my most sincere gratitude.

LII

CICERO TO Q. MARCIUS REX [a]

Rome, 46 B.C.

Aulus Licinius Aristoteles of Melite is a friend of mine by virtue of very long-standing ties of hospitality, and he is moreover attached to me by constant and familiar association. Such being the case, I have no doubt that he is already sufficiently commended to you ; for I have been told by many that a recommendation from me has very great influence with you. He is the man whose freedom I secured from Caesar ; he had been associated with us on many occasions, and indeed maintained his adherence to the cause [b] even longer than I did, and I imagine you

127

existimaturum arbitror. Fac igitur, mi Rex, ut
intellegat, has sibi litteras plurimum profuisse.

LIII

CICERO THERMO PROPR. 8.

In Cilicia, ad fin. A.U.C. 703.

1   L. Genucilio Curvo iampridem utor familiarissime,
optimo viro et homine gratissimo. Eum tibi penitus
commendo atque trado ; primum, ut omnibus in
rebus ei commodes, quoad fides tua dignitasque
patietur ; (patietur autem in omnibus), nihil enim
abs te umquam, quod sit alienum tuis aut etiam suis
2 moribus, postulabit. Praecipue autem tibi commendo negotia eius, quae sunt in Hellesponto,
primum, ut obtineat id iuris in agris, quod ei Pariana
civitas decrevit et dedit, et quod semper obtinuit
sine ulla controversia ; deinde, si quid habebit cum
aliquo Hellespontio controversiae, ut in illam διοίκησιν
reicias. Sed non mihi videor, cum tibi totum hominem diligentissime commendarim, singulas ad te eius
causas perscribere debere. Summa illa sit : quidquid
offici, benefici, honoris in Genucilium contuleris, id
te existimabo in me ipsum atque in rem meam
contulisse.

ᵃ A thorough-going optimate, who was tribune of the
plebs in 62, and praetor between that year and 57. He was
governor of Asia in 51 and 50.

ᵇ A town a little E. of Lampsacus in the διοίκησις (department) of the Hellespont. It was made a colony by Augustus.

will think all the better of him for that. Be sure
then, my dear Rex, to give him the impression that
this letter has proved of invaluable service to him.

LIII

CICERO TO Q. MINUCIUS THERMUS,[a] PROPRAETOR

Cilicia, probably towards the end of 51 B.C.

I have for long been on the most intimate terms 1
with L. Genucilius Curvus, a most excellent man, and
a very grateful fellow. I commend him to you most
heartily, and I introduce him to you first of all in
order that you may serve him in every respect, so far
as your honour and position permit (and they will
permit you in every respect) ; for there is no demand
he will ever make of you that is incompatible with
your character—and, I may add, with his own.

Especially, however, do I commend to you his 2
business affairs on the Hellespont, first so that you
should ensure his maintaining those rights in regard
to land which the community of Parium [b] granted him
by decree, and which he has always maintained
without dispute ; and secondly, should he have anything in the nature of a dispute with a Hellespontian,
you should refer the matter to the above-mentioned
department. But seeing that I have commended the
man to you so very earnestly in his entirety, it does
not seem to me necessary to set out his claims
piecemeal. Let me sum up thus : whatever obligation, kindness, or honour you bestow upon Genucilius,
I shall consider you to have bestowed upon myself
and my interests.

CICERO

LIV

M. T. C. S. D. THERMO PROPR.

Laodiceae, A.U.C. 704.

Cum multa mihi grata sunt, quae tu adductus
mea commendatione fecisti, tum in primis, quod
M. Marcilium, amici atque interpretis mei filium,
liberalissime tractavisti. Venit enim Laodiceam et
tibi apud me mihique propter te gratias maximas
egit. Quare, quod reliquum est, a te peto, cum apud
gratos homines beneficium ponis, ut eo libentius his
commodes operamque des, quoad fides tua patietur,
ut socrus adulescentis rea ne fiat. Ego cum antea
studiose commendabam Marcilium, tum multo nunc
studiosius, quod in longa apparitione singularem et
prope incredibilem patris Marcili fidem, abstinentiam,
modestiamque cognovi.

LV

M. T. C. S. D. THERMO PROPR.

In Cilicia, A.U.C. 703.

1 Etsi mihi videor intellexisse, cum tecum Ephesi de
re M. Annei, legati mei, locutus sum, te ipsius causa

---

^a Nothing more is known of him.

^b It is interesting to note that Cicero had to employ
an interpreter in his province.

^c One of Cicero's *legati*, and a distinguished military
officer. The *legati* were officers who accompanied Roman
generals on their campaigns as brigadiers or aides-de-camp,
and in later times the governors of provinces also to be
employed in either a civil or a military capacity. Pompey,
when in Asia, had 15 *legati*; Cicero had 4. See Introductory
Note to this Book.

130

LIV

Laodicea, February, 50 B.C.

While I am grateful for much that you have been
induced to do by my recommendation, I am especially
so for your most generous treatment of M. Marcilius,[a]
the son of my friend and interpreter.[b] He visited me
at Laodicea and expressed the warmest gratitude
to you in my presence, and to me also because of you.
So there remains just this much—that I beg of you,
since those in whom you are investing your generosity
are a grateful set of people, to oblige them all the
more readily, and to make every effort, compatible
with your honour, to prevent the threatened prosecution of the young man's mother-in-law. While I
was previously enthusiastic in my recommendation of
him, I am now far more enthusiastic, because, during
his long spell of service as my official servant, I have
appreciated the extraordinary and almost inconceivable trustworthiness, and disinterested and unassuming character, of Marcilius's father.

LV

Cilicia, probably late in 51 B.C.

Although I seem to have gathered from our con-   1
versation at Ephesus on the matter of my legate,
M. Anneius,[c] that you were extremely anxious to

vehementer omnia velle, tamen et M. Anneium tanti
facio, ut mihi nihil putem praetermittendum, quod
illius intersit, et me a te tanti fieri puto, ut non
dubitem, quin ad tuam voluntatem magnus cumulus
accedat commendationis meae. Nam cum iam diu
diligerem M. Anneium, deque eo sic existimarem,
ut res declarat, quod ultro ei detulerim legationem,
cum multis petentibus denegassem, tum vero, posteaquam mecum in bello atque in re militari fuit, tantam
in eo virtutem, prudentiam, fidem, tantamque erga
me benevolentiam cognovi, ut hominem neminem
pluris faciam. Eum cum Sardianis habere controversiam scis ; causam tibi exposuimus Ephesi, quam
2 tu tamen coram facilius meliusque cognosces. De
reliquo mihi, mehercule, diu dubium fuit, quid ad te
potissimum scriberem. Ius enim quemadmodum
dicas, clarum et magna cum tua laude notum est.
Nobis autem in hac causa nihil aliud opus est, nisi
te ius instituto tuo dicere. Sed tamen cum me non
fugiat, quanta sit in praetore auctoritas, praesertim
ista integritate, gravitate, clementia, qua te esse inter
omnes constat, peto abs te, pro nostra coniunctissima
necessitudine plurimisque officiis paribus ac mutuis,
ut voluntate, auctoritate, studio tuo perficias, ut M.

a See Introd. Note.
b In Lydia.

further his interests in every way for his own sake,
still, so highly do I esteem M. Anneius that I think
I should omit nothing which is of importance to him,
and I think too that you esteem me highly enough to
make me feel sure that my recommendation will add
enormously to your good wishes for him. For though
my liking for M. Anneius was of long standing,
and my previous opinion of him is abundantly
proved by my having conferred upon him the post
of *legatus*,[a] without his asking for it, after refusing
it to many who did, yet, ever since he was associated
with me in the war and in military affairs, I discovered
in him such courage, sagacity. and loyalty, and such
goodwill towards myself, that there is now nobody
in the world I esteem more highly. Well, as you are
aware, he has a dispute with the people of Sardis [b];
the merits of the case I explained to you at Ephesus;
you will investigate it, however, more easily and
thoroughly in person.

For the rest, I declare to you that I have long been 2
in doubt as to just what it would be best to put in
a letter to you. Your administration of justice is
brilliant; it is a matter of common knowledge, and
greatly to your credit. In this case, however, we have
need of nothing but that you should administer
justice according to your established usage. But for
all that, since I do not forget how much influence is
vested in a praetor, especially in one of such integrity,
firmness, and leniency, as you are known by everybody
to possess, I beg of you in view of our very close association and the numberless good services we have
rendered each other with equal advantage to both,
so to manage matters by your kind feeling, influence,
and devotion. as to convince M. Anneius not only of

Anneius intellegat te et sibi amicum esse, quod non
dubitat (saepe enim mecum locutus est), et multo
amiciorem his meis litteris esse factum. In tuo toto
imperio atque provincia nihil est, quod mihi gratius
facere possis. Iam, apud ipsum gratissimum hominem atque optimum virum quam bene positurus sis
studium tuum atque officium, dubitare te non existimo.

LVI

M. T. C. S. D. THERMO PROPR.

In Cilicia, A.U.C. 703.

1 Cluvius Puteolanus valde me observat valdeque est
mihi familiaris. Is ita sibi persuadet, quod in tua
provincia negoti habeat, nisi te provinciam obtinente
meis commendationibus confecerit, id se in perditis et
desperatis habiturum. Nunc, cum mihi ab amico
officiosissimo tantum oneris imponitur, ego quoque
tibi imponam pro tuis in me summis officiis, ita tamen,
ut tibi nolim molestus esse. Μυλασεῖς et ’Αλαβανδεῖς
pecuniam Cluvio debent. Dixerat mihi Euthydemus,
cum Ephesi essem, se curaturum, ut ecdici Mylasii
Romam mitterentur. Id factum non est. Legatos
audio missos esse ; sed malo ecdicos, ut aliquid con-

ᵃ The Cluvii were a Campanian family, one of whom (*cf.*
Livy xxvi. 33. 8) supplied Roman captives with provisions
in 215. This Cluvius (M.) was a wealthy banker of Puteoli.
He made Cicero one of his heirs.

ᵇ Mylasa (or Mylassa) was an inland town of Caria, and
a free town under the Romans.

ᶜ Alabanda was also a free town in Caria.

ᵈ *Ecdici* were counsel sent by a provincial town to defend
their cause at Rome. They were generally preferred to
legati, as the latter could only make a request, whereas

your existing friendship for him—of that, as he has often told me, he has no doubt—but also of the enhancement of that friendship by this letter of mine. In the whole sphere of your official authority and of your province there is nothing you can do that would give me more pleasure. And now I do not think you can doubt how profitably you will be investing your cordial kindness in one who is himself a most grateful fellow and a very excellent man.

LVI

CICERO TO Q. MINUCIUS THERMUS, PROPRAETOR

Cilicia, probably late in 51 B.C.

Cluvius of Puteoli [a] is exceedingly devoted to me 1 and exceedingly intimate with me. He is under the conviction that he will have to reckon as lost and hopeless whatever interests he has in your province, unless he secures them through a commendatory letter from me, while you are governor of the province. Just now then, having so heavy a burden laid upon me by my most obliging friend, I too shall lay a burden upon you, counting upon the signal services you have already done me—though indeed I should be sorry to be a nuisance to you.

The people of Mylasa [b] and Alabanda [c] owe money to Cluvius. Euthydemus told me, when I was at Ephesus, that he would see that *ecdici* [d] were sent by the people of Mylasa to Rome. That was not done, and now I hear that legates have been sent, but I prefer *ecdici*, so that something definite may be done.

ecdici could plead at law, but the cost of sending them was almost prohibitive. See note *a* on *Ep. 26. 3* above.

fici possit. Quare peto a te, ut et eos et ᾽Αλαβανδεῖς
2 iubeas ecdicos Romam mittere. Praeterea Philotes
Alabandensis ὑποθήκας Cluvio dedit. Hae com-
missae sunt. Velim cures, ut aut de hypothecis
decedat easque procuratoribus Cluvi tradat aut
pecuniam solvat. Praeterea Heracleotae et Bargylietae, qui item debent, aut pecuniam solvant aut
3 fructibus suis satisfaciant. Caunii praeterea debent ;
sed aiunt se depositam pecuniam habuisse. Id velim
cognoscas ; et, si intellexeris, eos neque ex edicto
neque ex decreto depositam habuisse, des operam,
ut usurae Cluvio instituto tuo conserventur. His
de rebus eo magis laboro, quod agitur res Cn. Pompei, etiam nostri necessari ; et quod is magis etiam
mihi laborare videtur, quam ipse Cluvius ; cui satis-
factum esse a nobis valde volo. His de rebus te
vehementer etiam atque etiam rogo.

LVII

CICERO THERMO PROPR. S.

Laodiceae, a.u.c. 704.

1 Quo magis quotidie ex litteris nuntiisque bellum
magnum esse in Syria cognosco, eo vehementius a
te pro nostra necessitudine contendo, ut mihi M.
Anneium legatum primo quoque tempore remittas.

   ᵃ The inhabitants of Heraclea (also called Salbace) in
Caria.
   ᵇ Also in Caria.
   ᶜ An unhealthy town in Caria, famous for its figs.
   ᵈ An edict was in general terms, a decree more specific.
   ᵉ See note c on Ep. 55. 1 above.

And that is why I beg of you to order them, and the people of Alabanda, to send *ecdici* to Rome.

Furthermore Philotes of Alabanda has given 2 Cluvius a mortgage, and that mortgage has lapsed. I should be glad if you would see that he either surrenders the mortgaged property and hands it over to Cluvius's agent, or else pays the money ; and moreover that the people of Heraclea[a] and Bargylia,[b] who are also his debtors, should either pay him the money owed, or else satisfy his claims by allowing him a charge on their income.

The people of Caunus[c] are also in his debt but 3 they declare that they have the money lying on deposit. Please inquire into the matter, and if you arrive at the conclusion that they have not had the money deposited either by edict or by decree,[d] do your best by your ruling to secure the interest thereon for Cluvius. I am the more worried on account of all this because the interests of our friend Cn. Pompeius are at stake, and because he strikes me as being even more worried than even Cluvius himself, and I am most anxious that we should satisfy his claims. I earnestly beg of you again and again to attend to these matters.

LVII

CICERO TO Q. MINUCIUS THERMUS, PROPRAETOR

Laodicea, March, 50 B.C.

The more clearly I recognize day after day that 1 there is a great war on in Syria, the more urgently do I implore you in the name of our close association to send my legate M. Anneius[e] back to me at the first

Nam eius opera, consilio, scientia rei militaris vel maxime intellego me et rempublicam adiuvari posse. Quod nisi tanta res eius ageretur, nec ipse adduci potuisset, ut a me discederet, neque ego, ut eum a me dimitterem. Ego in Ciliciam proficisci cogito circiter Kal. Mai. Ante eam diem Anneius ad me 2 redeat oportet. Illud quod tecum et coram et per litteras diligentissime egi, id et nunc etiam atque etiam rogo curae tibi sit, ut suum negotium, quod habet cum populo Sardiano, pro causae veritate et pro sua dignitate conficiat. Intellexi ex tua oratione, cum tecum Ephesi locutus sum, te ipsius M. Annei causa omnia velle. Sed tamen sic velim existimes, te mihi nihil gratius facere posse, quam si intellexero, per te illum ipsum negotium ex sententia confecisse; idque quam primum ut efficias, te etiam atque etiam rogo.

LVIII

M. CICERO C. TITIO L. F. RUFO PR. URBANO S.

Laodiceae, a.u.c. 704.

L. Custidius est tribulis et municeps et familiaris meus. Is causam habet; quam causam ad te deferet. Commendo tibi hominem, sicuti tua fides et meus pudor postulat, tantum, ut faciles ad te aditus

138

possible opportunity. For I realize that by his activity, shrewdness, and skill in military affairs he can be of the very greatest assistance to the Republic and myself. Had not such important interests of his been at stake, neither could he himself have ever been induced to leave me, nor I to let him go. My own intention is to set out for Cilicia about May 1st. It is imperative that Anneius should rejoin me before that date.

What I most pressingly pleaded with you to do, 2 both in person and by letter, that I now beg of you again and again to do—to make it your business to enable him to conclude his negotiation with the people of Sardis in a manner befitting the justice of his case and his own position. I understood from what you said when I interviewed you at Ephesus that you were anxious to promote M. Anneius's interests in every way on his own account. But none the less I would have you believe that you can do nothing that would please me more than to convince me that he has settled his business to his own satisfaction through your instrumentality ; and I beg of you to get that done as soon as possible.

LVIII

CICERO TO C. TITIUS RUFUS, PRAETOR URBANUS

Laodicea, February, 50 B.C.

L. Custidius is a fellow-tribesman, a fellow-towns-man, and an intimate friend of mine. He has a case at law, and that case he will lay before you. I commend the man to you, but only, as your probity and my modesty demand, so far as to ask you to let him

139

CICERO

habeat ; quae aequa postulabit, ut libente te impetret ; sentiatque meam sibi amicitiam, etiam cum
longissime absim, prodesse in primis apud te.

LIX

M. T. C. C. CURTIO PEDUCAEANO, PRAETORI S. D.

Laodiceae, A.U.C. 704.

M. Fadium unice diligo, summaque mihi cum eo
consuetudo et familiaritas est pervetus. In eius con-
troversiis quid decernas, a te non peto (servabis, ut
tua fides et dignitas postulat, edictum et institutum
tuum), sed ut quam facillimos ad te aditus habeat,
quae erunt aequa, libente te impetret ; ut meam amicitiam sibi, etiam cum procul absim, prodesse sentiat,
praesertim apud te.   Hoc te vehementer etiam atque
etiam rogo.

LX

M. T. C. S. D. C. MUNATIO C. F.

Anno incerto.

1   L. Livineius Trypho est omnino L. Reguli, familiarissimi mei, libertus ; cuius calamitas etiam officio-

---

^a One of the Peducaei, adopted into the Curtian family.
^b M. Fadius Gallus, a great friend of Cicero, who ad-
dressed to him vii. 23-36.
^c The customary public announcement of a praetor on
entering office, in which he specified the rules by which he
would be guided in administering justice. Out of such
edicts was evoked an important part of the body of Roman
law.

140

have easy access to you, to grant him without reluctance his reasonable demands, and to make him feel that my friendship, even when I am very far away, is of benefit to him, especially with you.

LIX

CICERO TO CURTIUS PEDUCAEANUS,[a] PRAETOR

Laodicea, February, 50 B.C.

I am exceptionally fond of M. Fadius[b]; I have constant intercourse with him, and our intimacy is of very long standing. In his various suits I make no request as to your decisions (you will, as your credit and position demand, observe your edict[c] and your established rule of administration) but this I do ask you—to let him have as easy access to you as is possible, to grant him without reluctance such requests as are right and proper, and to make him feel that my friendship, even though I am far away, is of service to him, especially with you. That is what I beg of you again and again to do.

LX

CICERO TO C. MUNATIUS

Date uncertain.

L. Livineius Trypho is, in any case,[d] the freedman 1 of my very intimate friend L. Regulus, whose misfortune[e] makes me more ready than ever to serve him;

[d] Or, "to say the least of it," whatever other claims he may have upon me. Shuckburgh translates it "to begin with."

[e] Probably exile, but the circumstances are not known.

siorem me facit in illum. Nam benevolentior, quam
semper fui, esse non possum. Sed ego libertum eius
per se ipsum diligo ; summa enim eius erga me officia
exstiterunt his nostris temporibus, quibus facillime
benevolentiam[1] hominum et fidem perspicere potui.
2 Eum tibi ita commendo, ut homines grati et memores
bene meritos de se commendare debent. Pergratum mihi feceris, si ille intellexerit, se, quod pro
salute mea multa pericula adierit, saepe hieme
summa navigarit, pro tua erga me benevolentia
gratum etiam tibi fecisse.

LXI

M. T. C. S. D. P. SILIO PROPR.

In Cilicia, a.u.c. 703.

T. Pinnio familiarissime me usum esse, scire te
arbitror, quod quidem ille testamento declaravit,
qui me cum tutorem, tum etiam secundum heredem
instituerit. Eius filio mire studioso et erudito et
modesto pecuniam Nicaeenses grandem debent, ad
HS octogies, et, ut audio, in primis ei volunt solvere.
Pergratum igitur mihi feceris, quando non modo
reliqui tutores, qui sciunt, quanti me facias, sed
etiam puer ipse sibi persuasit, te omnia mea causa
facturum esse, si dederis operam, quoad tua fides

---

[1] *Nobbe and others have* bonam *before* benevolentiam,
*but Klotz rightly, I think, rejects it, as the collocation is
un-Ciceronian.*

---

[a] Propraetor of Bithynia and Pontus in 51. For a lawsuit
in which he was engaged see vii. 21.
[b] *i.e.*, the next heir, in the event of the first heir dying. *Cf.*
Hor. *Sat.* ii. 5. 45-50.   [c] About £70,000.

more friendly in my feeling for him than I always have
been I cannot be. But I esteem this freedman of his
for his own sake; his services to me were conspicuous
at that crisis in my life when I was able most easily to
appraise the goodwill and loyalty of my fellow-men.

I therefore commend him to you as men who are 2
grateful and not forgetful are bound to commend
those who have deserved well of them. You will
have done me a great kindness if he is led to believe
that by frequently risking his own safety for mine, and
often taking ship in the depth of winter, he did what
was acceptable to you also, since you wish me well.

LXI

CICERO TO P. SILIUS,[a] PROPRAETOR

Cilicia, probably late in 51 B.C.

I believe that you are aware that I was on very
intimate terms with T. Pinnius, and indeed he showed
that plainly by his will, since he made me not only
his trustee, but also his heir in the second degree.[b]
His son, a remarkably studious, erudite, and unassuming youth, is owed a large sum of money (about
eight million sesterces [c]), by the people of Nicaea [d];
and, according to what I hear, they are desirous of
paying him among their first creditors. You will
therefore do me a great kindness (and the other
trustees who know how highly you esteem me, as
well as the youth himself, are fully persuaded that
there is nothing you will not do for me), if you make

[a] Nicaea was one of the twelve townships into which
Bithynia was divided.

143

CICERO

dignitasque patietur, ut quam plurimum pecuniae
Pinnio solvatur Nicaeensium nomine.

LXII

M. T. C. S. D. P. SILIO PROPR.

In Cilicia, A.U.C. 703.

Et in Atili negotio te amavi (cum enim sero
venissem, tamen honestum equitem Romanum beneficio tuo conservavi), et mehercule semper sic in
animo habui, te in meo aere esse propter Lamiae
nostri coniunctionem et singularem necessitudinem.
Itaque primum tibi ago gratias, quod me omni
molestia liberas ; deinde impudentia prosequor ; sed
idem sarciam. Te enim semper sic colam et tuebor,
ut quem diligentissime. Quintum fratrem meum, si
me diligis, eo numero cura ut habeas, quo me. Ita
magnum beneficium tuum magno cumulo auxeris.

LXIII

M. T. C. S. P. D. P. SILIO PROPR.

Laodiceae, A.U.C. 704.

1   Non putavi fieri posse, ut mihi verba deessent ; sed
tamen in M. Laenio commendando desunt. Itaque

ᵃ Reading *quam plurimum pecuniae* with MH. Another
reading is *quam primum pecunia* D and Cratander, "that
the money should be paid at the earliest possible date,"
which is borne out by *in primis* above.

ᵇ It is not known what this was ; it was probably the
recovery of some heavy debt.

ᶜ *i.e.*, "entirely at my disposal," lit. "part of my own
property."   ᵈ For Lamia see xi. 16. 2 and xii. 29.

ᵉ Lit. " patch it up."   ᶠ See xiv. 4. 2.

144

every effort, so far as your integrity and position permit, to get as much of the money as possible [a] paid to Pinnius on behalf of the people of Nicaea.

LXII

CICERO TO P. SILIUS, PROPRAETOR

Cilicia, probably late in 51 B.C.

I blessed you for what you did in the business of Atilius [b] (for though I came late, I was yet able, thanks to your kindness, to save an honourable Roman knight), and as a matter of fact I have always taken it for granted that I had you " in my pocket," [c] since our friend Lamia [d] had bound us together in so peculiarly close an association. So in the first place I thank you for freeing me from all awkwardness, and then I go further in shamelessness (but I shall make it good [e]; for I shall always honour and uphold *you* more conscientiously than anybody). It is about my brother Quintus ; if you have any regard for me, see that you put him in the same category of regard as you do myself. So will you enhance your already great kindness by a great and crowning addition.

LXIII

CICERO TO P. SILIUS, PROPRAETOR

Laodicea, February, 50 B.C.

I never thought it could happen that words would 1 fail me, but they do fail me nevertheless in commending M. Laenius.[f] I shall therefore explain the matter

rem tibi exponam paucis verbis ; sed tamen, ut
plane perspicere possis voluntatem meam. Incredibile est, quanti faciamus et ego et frater meus,
qui mihi carissimus est, M. Laenium. Id fit cum
plurimis eius officiis, tum summa probitate et singulari
modestia. Eum ego a me invitissimus dimisi, cum
propter familiaritatem et consuetudinis suavitatem,
tum quod consilio eius fideli ac bono libenter utebar.
2 Sed vereor, ne iam mihi superesse verba putes, quae
dixeram defutura. Commendo tibi hominem, sicut
intellegis me, de quo ea supra scripserim, debere
commendare ; a teque vehementer etiam atque etiam
peto, ut, quod habet in tua provincia negoti, expedias,
quod tibi videbitur rectum esse, ipsi dicas. Hominem
facillimum liberalissimumque cognosces. Itaque te
rogo, ut eum solutum, liberum, confectis eius negotiis
per te, quam primum ad me remittas. Id mihi
fratique meo gratissimum feceris.

LXIV

M. T. C. S. D. P. SILIO PROPR.

In Cilicia, A.U.C. 703.

1 Nero meus mirificas apud me tibi gratias egit,
prorsus incredibiles, ut nullum honorem sibi haberi

---

a Tiberius Claudius Nero, father of the emperor Tiberius,
impeached Gabinius in 54 (*Q.F.* iii. 1. 15, and 2. 1). He
visited Cicero in Cilicia to arrange a marriage with Tullia,
but she had already become betrothed to Dolabella. Nero
afterwards married Livia Drusilla, whom he had to resign
in later life to be the wife of Augustus.

to you in a few words, and yet in such a way as to give you a clear appreciation of my friendly feeling for him. You cannot believe how highly both my brother, who is very dear to me, and myself esteem M. Laenius. It is the result not only of his numerous services to me, but also of his unimpeachable integrity, and singularly unassuming demeanour. I parted with him with the greatest reluctance, not only on account of our intimacy and the charm of our intercourse, but also because it was a pleasure to me to avail myself of his counsel, as honest as it was sound.

But I fear you will think I have a superfluity of 2 words after saying that I should run short of them. Well, I commend the man to you as heartily as I am bound to commend one of whom I have written such words as the above ; and I earnestly beg of you again and again to expedite such business as he has in your province, and to give him personally such information as you think proper. You will find him a most affable and gentlemanly fellow. And so I ask you to send him back to me as soon as you can, unembarrassed, free, and with all his business settled as far as you are concerned in it. Your doing so will greatly gratify my brother and myself.

LXIV

CICERO TO P. SILIUS, PROPRAETOR

Cilicia, probably late in 51 B.C.

My friend Nero [a] has expressed to me his gratitude 1 to you in terms of amazing, nay, absolutely unimaginable warmth, declaring that no honour could

potuisse diceret, qui a te praetermissus esset. Magnum fructum ex ipso capies ; nihil est enim illo adulescente gratius. Sed mehercule mihi quoque gratissimum fecisti ; pluris enim ex omni nobilitate neminem facio. Itaque, si ea feceris, quae ille per me tecum agi voluit, gratissimum mihi feceris. Primum de Pausania Alabandensi, sustentes rem, dum Nero veniat. Vehementer eius causa cupere eum intellexi ; itaque hoc valde te rogo. Deinde Nysaeos, quos Nero in primis habet necessarios diligentissimeque tuetur ac defendit, habeas tibi commendatissimos ; ut intellegat illa civitas, sibi in Neronis patrocinio summum esse praesidium. Strabonem Servilium tibi saepe commendavi ; nunc eo facio id impensius, quod eius causam Nero suscepit. Tantum a te petimus, ut agas eam rem, ne relinquas hominem innocentem ad alicuius tui dissimilis quaestum. Id cum gratum mihi erit, tum etiam existimabo, te humanitate tua esse usum. 2 Summa huius epistulae haec est, ut ornes omnibus rebus Neronem, sicut instituisti atque fecisti. Magnum theatrum habet ista provincia, non ut haec nostra, ad adulescentis nobilis, ingeniosi, abstinentis commendationem atque gloriam. Quare, si te fautore usus erit, sicuti profecto et utetur et usus est,

---

ª The people of Nysa in Caria.

possibly have been done him which you omitted to do
him. You will gain much by personal intercourse
with him, for that young man is the most grateful
fellow in the world. But I positively assure you that
you have done me too the greatest favour ; for there
is nobody among the aristocracy I esteem more
highly. If, therefore, you do what he wished to get
done through my pleading with you, you will have
done me the greatest possible favour. First then, as
to Pausanias of Alabanda, hold the matter open until
Nero arrives. I gathered that he was extremely
anxious to promote Pausanias's interests ; so this is
a request I strongly urge upon you. In the next place
regard the Nysaeans [a] as warmly commended to you,
for Nero regards them as his particular friends, and
supports and protects them with the utmost devotion.
Do this to make that State believe that their main
defence lies in the patronage of Nero. Strabo
Servilius I have often commended to you ; I do so
now all the more emphatically because Nero has
taken up his case. All I ask of you is to press the
business on so as not to leave an innocent man to
the mercies of some avaricious governor unlike yourself. Not only will that be a favour to me, but I
shall also consider that you have exhibited your
customary kindness.

The whole point of this letter is, that you should 2
promote Nero's honour in every respect, as indeed
you have done from the beginning. Your province,
unlike this of mine, affords a prominent stage for the
applause and glorification of a youth of high birth,
ability, and unselfish character. If, therefore, he has
the advantage of your patronage, as he assuredly
will have, and has had in the past, it will enable him

149

CICERO

amplissimas clientelas, acceptas a maioribus, confirmare poterit et beneficiis suis obligare. Hoc in
genere si eum adiuveris eo studio, quo ostendisti,
apud ipsum praeclarissime posueris, sed mihi etiam
gratissimum feceris.

LXV

M. T. C. S. D. P. SILIO PROPR.

In Cilicia, A.U.C. 703.

1 Cum P. Terentio Hispone, qui operas in scriptura
pro magistro dat, mihi summa familiaritas consuetudo-
que est, multaque et magna inter nos officia paria
et mutua intercedunt.   Eius summa existimatio
agitur in eo, ut pactiones cum civitatibus reliquis
conficiat.   Non me praeterit, nos eam rem Ephesi
expertos esse, neque ab Ephesiis ullo modo impetrare
potuisse.   Sed quoniam, quemadmodum omnes exis-
timant, et ego intellego, tua cum summa integritate,
tum singulari humanitate et mansuetudine consecutus
es, ut, libentissimis Graecis, nutu, quod velis, con-
sequare, peto a te in maiorem modum, ut honoris mei
2 causa hac laude Hisponem affici velis.   Praeterea cum

ᵃ A connexion of Cicero's through his wife Terentia.

ᵇ Such part of the *ager publicus* as could not be cultivated
was let out for grazing. It was let out by the censors to the
grazing company of the *publicani*, called *scripturarii*, from
scriptura, as the tax was called, paid by provincials for the
right of grazing, since they had to register (*scribere*) their
names and the number and kind of animals.   All such
companies of the *publicani* had a chairman at Rome (*manceps*, or *princeps societatis*), an annually elected managing
director (*magister societatis*) at Rome, and a deputy-manager
(*promagistro*) in the provinces or where the *scriptura* was
collected. Tyrrell.

150

to strengthen, and by his acts of kindness to oblige, highly influential bodies of clients bequeathed to him by his ancestors. If in this connexion you assist him with that devotion you have shown him in the past, you will have made a brilliant investment as regards the young man himself, but more than that, you will have done me too a special favour.

LXV

CICERO TO P. SILIUS, PROPRAETOR

Cilicia, probably late in 51 B.C.

P. Terentius Hispo,[a] who is employed in the 1 collection of grazing-dues as deputy-manager,[b] is a man with whom I am on the most familiar terms and in constant communication, and we have done each other many a good service with equal advantage to each of us. His reputation mainly depends upon his settling his contracts with the rest of the states. It does not slip my memory that we experienced that difficulty at Ephesus, and that we could elicit no response whatever from the Ephesians. But now that, as everybody believes and I am convinced, you have so managed matters by your perfect integrity as well as by your exceptional courtesy and gentleness that you can obtain whatever you desire by a single nod with the heartiest consent of the Greeks, I beg of you with more than ordinary earnestness, out of compliment to myself, to be good enough to let Hispo have the benefit of this praiseworthy achievement.

There is this too ; I am myself closely associated 2

151

sociis scripturae mihi summa necessitudo est, non
solum ob eam causam, quod ea societas universa
in mea fide est, sed etiam quod plerisque sociis utor
familiarissime. Ita et Hisponem meum per me or-
naris et societatem mihi coniunctiorem feceris, tuque
ipse et ex huius observantia gratissimi hominis, et
ex sociorum gratia, hominum amplissimorum, maximum fructum capies, et me summo beneficio affeceris.
Sic enim velim existimes, ex tota tua provincia
omnique isto imperio, nihil esse, quod mihi gratius
facere possis.

LXVI

M. T. C. S. D. P. SERVILIO PROPR.

Romae, a.u.c. 709.

1   A. Caecinam maxime proprium clientem familiae
vestrae non commendarem tibi, cum scirem qua fide
in tuos, qua clementia in calamitosos soleres esse, nisi
me et patris eius, quo sum familiarissime usus,
memoria, et huius fortuna ita moveret, ut hominis
omnibus mecum studiis officiisque coniunctissimi
movere debebat. A te hoc omni contentione peto,
sic, ut maiore cura, maiore animi labore petere non
possim, ut ad ea, quae tua sponte sine cuiusquam

---

a P. Servilius Vatia Isauricus, son of the Servilius who
gained the title by his victory over the pirates of Isauria in
78, was in his earlier days an aristocrat and a follower of
Cato. He was praetor in 54, and in 48 he was consul with
Caesar and opposed the revolutionary projects of Caelius
Rufus. In 46 he was governor of Asia.

b For A. Caecina see vi. 5-9.

with the partners in the grazing company, not only because I am the confidential adviser of the whole body, but also because I am on the most familiar terms with the majority of the partners. You will thus have conferred distinction on my friend Hispo at my intercession, and bound the company more closely to me, and you yourself will reap a rich reward in the respectful regard of this most grateful of men, as well as in the gratitude of partners who are men of the highest position, while you will have done me the greatest possible kindness. Indeed, I would have you believe that in the whole of your province and in the whole sphere of your imperial government there is nothing you could do that would give me greater pleasure.

LXVI

CICERO TO P. SERVILIUS ISAURICUS,[a] PROPRAETOR

Rome, probably in January, 45 B.C.

Being well aware how loyal to your friends and how merciful to those who have lost their civil rights you have always been, I should not think it necessary to commend to you A. Caecina,[b] a client in a very special sense of your own family, were it not that the memory of his father, a very intimate friend of mine, as well as his own ill-fortune, affected me in such a way as the ill-fortune of one so closely connected with me by every sort of common interest and service was bound to affect me. This is what I implore you with all possible urgency to do (and I could make no appeal with greater sincerity or more solicitude of soul) that over and above all you would do of your own

commendatione faceres in hominem tantum et talem
calamitosum, aliquem afferant cumulum meae litterae,
quo studiosius eum, quibuscumque rebus possis,
2 iuves. Quod si Romae fuisses, etiam salutem A.
Caecinae essemus (ut opinio mea fert) per te consecuti. De qua tamen magnam spem habemus, freti
clementia collegae tui. Nunc, cum tuam iustitiam
secutus tutissimum sibi portum provinciam istam
esse duxit, etiam atque etiam te rogo atque oro, ut
eum et in reliquiis veteris negotiationis colligendis
iuves, et ceteris rebus tegas atque tueare. Hoc mihi
gratius facere nihil potes.

LXVII

M. T. C. S. D. P. SERVILIO PROPR.

Romae, a.u.c. 708.

1 Ex provincia mea Ciliciensi, cui scis τρεῖς διοικήσεις
Asiaticas attributas fuisse, nullo sum familiarius usus,
quam Androne, Artemonis filio, Laodicensi, eumque
habui in ea civitate cum hospitem, tum vehementer
ad meae vitae rationem et consuetudinem accommodatum. Quem quidem multo etiam pluris postea,
quam decessi, facere coepi, quod multis rebus expertus sum gratum hominem meique memorem.

---

 a Caesar, who was Servilius's colleague, both as augur,
and in 48 as consul.
 b *Viz.* Synnada, Cibyra, and Apamea, *cf.* iii. 8. 5. διοίκησις
was an assize-district.

accord, without any extraneous recommendation, for one so eminent and so deserving, now that he is under a cloud you should allow my letter to add a sort of stimulus to your generosity, and induce you to assist him even more assiduously in whatever way you can.

Now had you been at Rome, we should have 2 actually brought about the recall of A. Caecina (as I am inclined to think) through your instrumentality. Of that, however, I am still very hopeful, because I believe in your colleague's *a* clemency. Now that, attracted by the beacon of your justice, he has decided that he can find no safer haven than your province, I ask and implore you again and again not only to help him in gathering together what is left of his old business, but also to shield and protect him in all other respects. There is nothing you can do that will give me greater pleasure.

LXVII

CICERO TO P. SERVILIUS, PROPRAETOR

Rome, some time in 46 B.C.

In all my province of Cilicia—and you are aware 1 that three Asiatic dioceses *b* have been assigned to it —I have been more intimate with nobody than with Andro of Laodicea, the son of Artemo, and in that community I found in him not only a hospitable friend, but a man extraordinarily well suited to my habitual scheme of life; though it is true that since I quitted my province I have begun to value him a great deal more highly, having had many proofs of his gratitude and unforgetfulness of what I had done for him. It

CICERO

Itaque eum Romae libentissime vidi. Non te enim fugit, qui plurimis in ista provincia benigne fecisti,
2 quam multi grati reperiantur. Haec propterea scripsi, ut et me non sine causa laborare intellegeres, et tu ipse eum dignum hospitio tuo iudicares. Feceris igitur mihi gratissimum, si ei declararis, quanti me facias, id est, si receperis eum in fidem tuam et, quibuscumque rebus honeste ac sine molestia tua poteris, adiuveris. Hoc mihi erit vehementer gratum, idque ut facias, te etiam atque etiam rogo.

LXVIII

M. T. C. S. D. P. SERVILIO ISAURICO PROC. COLLEGAE

Romae, a.u.c. 708.

1 Gratae mihi vehementer tuae litterae fuerunt, ex quibus cognovi cursus navigationum tuarum. Significabas enim memoriam tuam nostrae necessitudinis, qua mihi nihil poterat esse iucundius. Quod reliquum est, multo etiam erit gratius, si ad me de republica, id est, de statu provinciae, de institutis tuis familiariter scribes. Quae quamquam ex multis pro tua claritate audiam, tamen libentissime ex tuis

---

a *i.e.*, " how few."
b Cicero, Servilius, and Caesar were colleagues in the College of Augurs, *cf.* § 2.

156

follows that it was a great pleasure to me to see him at Rome. For you cannot have failed to notice (you who have shown generosity to such numbers of people in your province) what proportion of them are found to be grateful.[a]

I have a double object in writing thus—so that 2 you may understand that I have good reason for taking the trouble, and so that you yourself may deem the man worthy of your hospitality. You will therefore do me the greatest favour if you make it manifest to him how highly you value me—in other words, if you take him under your protection and assist him in whatever way you can consistently with your honour and convenience. That will give me extreme pleasure, and I ask you again and again to do so.

LXVIII

CICERO TO HIS COLLEAGUE [b] P. SERVILIUS, PROCONSUL

Rome, September, 46 B.C.

I was exceedingly pleased with your letter which 1 gave me the routes of your various voyagings ; for you implied thereby that you had not forgotten our close association, which was the greatest joy of my life. As to the future, it will give me even greater pleasure if you write and tell me in a friendly way all about public affairs,—in other words, about the situation in your province, and the particulars of your administration ; and although, celebrated man as you are, I shall be told all this by many others, I should like best of all to get the information out of a letter from you.

157

2 litteris cognoscam. Ego ad te, de reipublicae summa
quid sentiam, non saepe scribam, propter periculum
eiusmodi litterarum. Quid agatur autem, scribam
saepius. Sperare tamen videor, Caesari, collegae
nostro, fore curae et esse, ut habeamus aliquam
rempublicam; cuius consiliis magni referebat te
interesse. Sed si tibi utilius est, id est gloriosius,
Asiae praeesse et istam partem reipublicae male
affectam tueri, mihi quoque idem, quod tibi et laudi
3 tuae profuturum est, optatius debet esse. Ego, quae
ad tuam dignitatem pertinere arbitrabor, summo
studio diligentiaque curabo, in primisque tuebor omni
observantia clarissimum virum, patrem tuum; quod
et pro vetustate necessitudinis, et pro beneficiis
vestris, et pro dignitate ipsius facere debeo.

LXIX

M. T. C. S. D. P. SERVILIO COLLEGAE

Romae, A.U.C. 708.

1 C. Curtius Mithres est ille quidem, ut scis, libertus
Postumi, familiarissimi mei; sed me colit et observat
aeque atque illum ipsum patronum suum. Apud
eum ego sic Ephesi fui, quotiescumque fui, tamquam
domi meae; multaque acciderunt, in quibus et

---

^a Consul in 79; he gained the title of Isauricus in the
following year. See *Ep.* 66. 1 note *a* above.

For my own part, I shall not often write and tell 2
you what I think about politics in general, since a
letter of that sort has its dangers ; but about what is
actually going on, I shall write more often. In spite
of all, I am not, I think, without hope that our
colleague Caesar will be, and indeed is, anxious that
we should have a constitution worthy the name ;
and it was of great importance that you should play
your part in his deliberations. But if it is more to your
advantage, by which I mean, more to your honour
and glory, that you should be governor of Asia and
look after that part of the Republic, a part which has
suffered so cruelly, I too ought to pray preferably for
just that which is likely to be of benefit both to
yourself and to your reputation.

I shall attend with the utmost zeal and assiduity 3
to whatever I consider affects your prestige, and most
particularly shall I uphold in all reverence the dignity
of that most distinguished man, your father *a* ; and
indeed it is no less than my duty to do so, considering
our long-standing friendship, the kindnesses you have
both done me, and the honour due to your father
himself.

LXIX

CICERO TO HIS COLLEAGUE P. SERVILIUS

Rome, month uncertain, 46 B.C.

C. Curtius Mithres is, of course, as you are aware, 1
the freedman of my very dear friend Postumus, but
he has as much respect and regard for me as he has
for his patron himself. At Ephesus, whenever I
happened to be there, I was as much at home in his
house as in my own, and many things have occurred

159

benevolentiam eius erga me experirer et fidem.
Itaque si quid aut mihi, aut meorum cuipiam in Asia
opus est, ad hunc scribere consuevi, huius cum opera
et fide, tum domo et re uti, tamquam mea.   Haec ad
te eo pluribus scripsi, ut intellegeres, me non vulgari
more,[1] nec ambitiose, sed ut pro homine intimo ac
2 mihi pernecessario scribere.   Peto igitur a te, ut in
ea controversia, quam habet de fundo cum quodam
Colophonio, et in ceteris rebus, quantum fides tua
patietur, quantumque tuo commodo poteris, tantum
et honoris mei causa commodes ; etsi, ut eius modestiam cognovi, gravis tibi nulla in re erit.   Si et mea
commendatione et sua probitate assecutus erit, uti
de se bene existimes, omnia se adeptum arbitrabitur.
Ut igitur eum recipias in fidem, habeasque in numero
tuorum, te vehementer etiam atque etiam rogo.
Ego, quae te velle, quaeque ad te pertinere arbitrabor, omnia studiose diligenterque curabo.

LXX

M. T. C. S. P. D. P. SERVILIO COLLEGAE

Romae, a.u.c. 708.

Quia non est obscura tua in me benevolentia, sic
fit ut multi per me tibi velint commendari.   Ego

---

[1] *Klotz*: vulgariter *Nobbe*.

to afford me proof of his kindly feeling and loyalty towards me. And so, if either I or any of my friends want anything done in Asia, I have got into the habit of writing to him, and of availing myself of his services and devotion, and indeed of his house and purse, as though they were my own. I have written all this to you at greater length than usual in order to impress upon you that I am not writing in a conventional sort of way or with any interested motives, but simply on behalf of a man with whom I am very intimate and very closely associated.

I therefore beg of you, in the lawsuit he has on hand 2 with a certain Colophonian about some landed property, to serve his interests (and it will be a compliment to myself also) so far as you possibly can compatibly with your probity, and without trouble to yourself ; though, from what I know of his propriety of conduct, you will not find him anything of an incubus. If through my recommendation and his own integrity he succeeds in winning your good opinion, he will think that he has got all he wants. I therefore earnestly urge you again and again to take him under your wing, and count him among the number of your friends. As for myself, I shall attend devotedly and punctiliously to whatever I think you desire, or whatever concerns your interests.

LXX

CICERO TO HIS COLLEAGUE P. SERVILIUS

Rome, month uncertain, 46 B.C.

Because your friendly feeling for me is manifest to all, it naturally follows that many people desire that I should be the medium of their recommendation to

autem tribuo nonnumquam in vulgus, sed plerumque
necessariis, ut hoc tempore. Nam cum T. Ampio
Balbo mihi summa familiaritas necessitudoque est.
Eius libertum, T. Ampium Menandrum, hominem
frugi et modestum et patrono et nobis vehementer
probatum, tibi commendo maiorem in modum.
Vehementer mihi gratum feceris, si, quibuscumque
rebus sine tua molestia poteris, ei commodaris.
Quod ut facias, te vehementer etiam atque etiam
rogo.

LXXI

M. T. C. S. D. P. SERVILIO COLLEGAE

Romae, a u.c. 708.

Multos tibi commendem necesse est, quonium omnibus nota nostra necessitudo est tuaque erga me
benevolentia. Sed tamen etsi omnium causa, quos
commendo, velle debeo, tamen cum omnibus non
eadem mihi causa est. T. Agusius et comes meus
fuit illo miserrimo tempore et omnium itinerum,
navigationum, laborum, periculorum meorum socius;
neque hoc tempore discessisset a me, nisi ego ei
permisissem. Quare sic tibi eum commendo, ut
unum de meis domesticis et maxime necessariis.
Pergratum mihi feceris, si eum ita tractaris, ut
intellegat, hanc commendationem sibi magno usu
atque adiumento fuisse.

---

a The *tuba belli civilis*; see ii. 16. 3.

162

you. Now I do sometimes confer this favour indiscriminately, but I do so for the most part on my particular friends, as on the present occasion. I am extremely familiar and closely associated with T. Ampius Balbus [a] ; his freedman T. Ampius Menander, a sterling and unassuming fellow, is greatly esteemed both by his patron and myself, and I commend him to you with more than ordinary warmth. You will do me a particular favour if you serve his interests in whatever way you can without inconveniencing yourself, and I earnestly beg you again and again to do so.

LXXI

CICERO TO HIS COLLEAGUE P. SERVILIUS

Rome, month uncertain, 46 B.C.

Now that our intimacy and your goodwill towards me is a matter of common knowledge, I find myself obliged to recommend ever so many people to you. But although all whom I recommend ought to have my best wishes, I have not the same reason for such wishes in every case. T. Agusius was not only my companion during the most miserable period of my life, but also shared with me all my journeys, voyages, troubles, and dangers ; nor would he have left my side at the present time, had I not given him permission. That is the reason I recommend him to you as being one of my own household, and one of those most closely attached to me. You will do me a very great favour by so treating him as to convince him that this recommendation has been of material service and assistance to him.

CICERO

LXXII

M. T. C. S. D. P. SERVILIO COLLEGAE

Romae, a.u.c. 708.

1 Caerelliae, necessariae meae, rem, nomina, pos-
sessiones Asiaticas commendavi tibi praesens in
hortis tuis, quam potui diligentissime ; tuque mihi,
pro tua consuetudine, proque tuis in me perpetuis
maximisque officiis, omnia te facturum liberalissime
recepisti. Meminisse te id spero ; scio enim solere.
Sed tamen Caerelliae procuratores scripserunt, te
propter magnitudinem provinciae multitudinemque
negotiorum etiam atque etiam esse commonefacien-
2 dum. Peto igitur, ut memineris, te omnia, quae tua
fides pateretur, mihi cumulate recepisse. Equidem
existimo, habere te magnam facultatem (sed hoc est
tui consili et iudici) ex eo senatus consulto, quod in
heredes C. Vennoni factum est, Caerelliae commo-
dandi. Id senatus consultum tu interpretabere pro
tua sapientia. Scio enim eius ordinis auctoritatem
semper apud te magni fuisse. Quod reliquum est,
sic velim existimes, quibuscumque rebus Caerelliae
benigne feceris, mihi te gratissimum esse facturum.

---

[a] A rich and accomplished lady frequently mentioned by
Cicero in his letters to Atticus. She copied out the *De Finibus*. It appears from *Att.* xii. 51. 3 that Cicero once borrowed money from her, which Atticus considered unworthy
of his position.

[b] Tyrrell thinks this was a *senatus consultum* passed to
meet a special case in violation of the laws, another instance
of which is described in *Att.* v. 21. 12.

LXXII

CICERO TO HIS COLLEAGUE P. SERVILIUS

Rome, month uncertain, 46 B.C.

As regards the estate, investments, and Asiatic 1
possessions of my intimate friend Caerellia,[a] I commended them to you as particularly as I could when
I was with you in your pleasure-garden ; and you, in
accordance with your custom, and your unfailing and
substantial services to me, most handsomely guaranteed that you would do everything you could. I hope
you remember that ; I know you don't often forget.
But, be that as it may, Caerellia's agents have written
to me that, on account of the size of your province,
and your numerous business engagements, you have
to be reminded of that promise again and again.

I therefore beg of you to remember that you guaran- 2
teed to me that you would do everything compatible
with your honour without any reserve whatever.
Now I believe you have an excellent opportunity
(though it is a matter for your own deliberation and
judgment) of obliging Caerellia, arising out of that
decree of the Senate which was passed in reference
to the heirs of C. Vennonius.[b] In the interpretation
of that decree you will use your own wisdom. I know
that the authority of that order has always been of
importance in your eyes. As to what remains to be
done, I would have you believe that in whatever
respects you prove your kindness to Caerellia you will
do me the greatest possible favour.

LXXIII

Anno incerto.

1 Gratulor tibi, quod ex provincia salvum te ad tuos recepisti, incolumi fama et republica. Quod si Romae te vidissem, coram gratias egissem, quod tibi L. Egnatius, familiarissimus meus absens, L. Oppius
2 praesens curae fuisset. Cum Antipatro Derbete mihi non solum hospitium, verum etiam summa familiaritas intercedit. Ei te vehementer succensuisse audivi, et moleste tuli. De re nihil possum iudicare, nisi illud mihi certe persuadeo, te, talem virum, nihil temere fecisse. A te autem, pro vetere nostra necessitudine, etiam atque etiam peto, ut eius filios, qui in tua potestate sunt, mihi potissimum condones, nisi quid existimas in ea re violari existimationem tuam. Quod ego si arbitrarer, numquam te rogarem, mihique tua fama multo antiquior esset, quam illa necessitudo est. Sed mihi ita persuadeo (potest fieri, ut fallar), eam rem laudi tibi potius quam vituperationi fore. Quid fieri possit, et quid mea causa facere possis (nam, quin velis, non dubito), velim, si tibi grave non erit, certiorem me facias.

ᵃ Q. Marcius Philippus appears to have been governor of Asia, though in what year is unknown.

ᵇ Both he and L. Oppius were bankers in Philippus's province. See *Epp.* 44 and 45 above.

ᶜ Derbe was in Lycaonia. Nothing more is known of Antipater.

LXXIII

I congratulate you on your safe return from your 1 province with your reputation unimpaired and the commonwealth intact. But had I seen you at Rome, I should have thanked you in person for having shown a kindly interest in my very intimate friend, L. Egnatius,[b] who was not on the spot, and in L. Oppius, who was.

With Antipater of Derbe [c] I have ties not only of 2 mutual hospitality but also of the closest intimacy. I am told that you have been exceedingly angry with him, and it distressed me. As for the facts, I am not in a position to pass any judgment, but of this I am very sure, that being the man you are, you have done nothing without due consideration. Anyhow, in view of our long-standing association, I beg of you again and again, as a special favour to myself, to refrain from taking any action against his sons, who are at your mercy—unless of course you think that to do so involves an outrage upon your reputation. If I thought so, I should never make this request, and your fair name would weigh far more with me than the association I have mentioned. But I try to persuade myself (it is possible that I may be mistaken) that your doing so will prove a credit to you rather than a handle for abuse.

As to what can be done, and what you can do for me (of your willingness I have no doubt), I should like you, if it will be no trouble to you, to send me word.

LXXIV

M. T. C. S. D. Q. PHILIPPO PROCOS.

Romae, a.u.c. 699 (?).

Etsi non dubito, pro tua in me observantia, proque
nostra necessitudine, quin commendationem meam
memoria teneas, tamen etiam atque etiam eumdem
tibi L. Oppium, familiarem meum, praesentem,
et L. Egnati, familiarissimi mei, absentis negotia
commendo. Tanta mihi cum eo necessitudo est familiaritasque, ut, si mea res esset, non magis laborarem.
Quapropter gratissimum mihi feceris, si curaris, ut
is intellegat, me a te tantum amari, quantum ipse existimo. Hoc mihi gratius facere nihil potes. Itaque
ut facias, te vehementer rogo.

LXXV

M. T. C. S. D. T. TITIO T. F. LEGATO

Romae, a.u.c. 701.

1 Etsi non dubito, quin apud te mea commendatio prima satis valeat, tamen obsequor homini
familiarissimo, C. Avianio Flacco, cuius causa omnia
tum cupio, tum mehercule etiam debeo. De quo
et praesens tecum egi diligenter, cum tu mihi
humanissime respondisti, et scripsi ad te accurate

---

^a This Titius was a *legatus* of Pompey, when the latter was
praefectus annonae (Minister of the Corn Supply).

^b Avianius was apparently a corn-factor who had enjoyed
under Pompey certain privileges as to the time and place
for the delivery of corn, which privileges Cicero asks Titius
to enable Avianius to retain.

LXXIV

CICERO TO Q. PHILIPPUS, PROCONSUL

Rome, (?) in 55 B.C.

Although I doubt not, considering the deference
you show me and our close association, that you bear
my recommendation in mind, yet I commend to you
again and again my dear friend, that same L. Oppius
who is with you, as also the business affairs of my
dear friend, L. Egnatius, who is not. So close is my
association and intimacy with him that I could not be
more anxious if it were my own affair. On that
account you will do me the greatest favour if you
make a point of giving him the impression that your
affection for me is as sincere as I myself believe it to
be. There is nothing you can do that would please me
more ; and so I earnestly beg of you to do it.

LXXV

CICERO TO T. TITIUS, LEGATUS [a]

Rome, 53 B.C.

Although I doubt not that my first recommenda- 1
tion carries quite enough weight with you, I nevertheless accede to the request of C. Avianius Flaccus [b]
with whom I am on most intimate terms, and I wish
him every success, as indeed I am bound to do. It was
about him that I urgently pleaded with you in person,
when you replied to me with the utmost courtesy, and
in a previous letter to you I gave you full particulars ;

antea; sed putat interesse sua, me ad te quam
saepissime scribere. Quare velim mihi ignoscas, si
illius voluntati obtemperans minus videbor memi-
2 nisse constantiae tuae. A te idem illud peto, ut
de loco, quo deportet frumentum, et de tempore
Avianio commodes; quorum utrumque per eumdem me obtinuit triennium, dum Pompeius isti
negotio praefuit. Summa est, in quo mihi gratissimum facere possis, si curaris, ut Avianius, quoniam
se a me amari putat, me a te amari sciat. Erit id
mihi pergratum.

LXXVI

M. T. C. S. D. QUATT. VIRIS ET DECURIONIBUS

Romae, anno incerto.

1 Tantae mihi cum Q. Hippio causae necessitudinis
sunt, ut nihil possit esse coniunctius quam nos
inter nos sumus. Quod nisi ita esset, uterer mea
consuetudine, ut vobis nulla in re molestus essem.
Etenim vos mihi optimi testes estis, cum mihi
persuasum esset, nihil esse, quod a vobis impetrare
non possem, numquam me tamen gravem vobis esse
2 voluisse. Vehementer igitur vos etiam atque etiam
rogo, ut honoris mei causa liberalissime C. Valgium

---

^a The time and place of the delivery was of course of the
utmost importance, and Avianius seems to have been given
carte blanche in both respects.

^b That this letter is addressed to some *municipium* or
other is evident from the terms used, *IV viri* and *decuriones*, the latter being the senators of a *municipium*; but
we know no more. Tyrrell suggests that it might have been

but he imagines it to be of importance to him that I should write to you as frequently as possible. So please forgive me if in thus complying with his wishes I lead you to suspect that my recollection of your constancy is not as clear as it should be.

I also make this further request of you—to accom- 2 modate Avianius as regards both the place and the time at which he is to discharge his corn.[a] It was through me also that he secured both these privileges for a term of three years, when Pompey was in chief charge of that business. The main point is this (and you might greatly oblige me in that respect), that you should make it your object to convince Avianius, since he already assumes my affection for him, of your affection for me. That will give me great pleasure.

LXXVI

CICERO TO THE QUATTUORVIRI AND DECURIONES [b]

Rome, date uncertain.

So strong are the reasons for my association with 1 Q. Hippius that nothing could be closer than the ties which bind us. Were it not so, I should observe my usual practice and avoid giving you the slightest trouble. Indeed, you yourselves can best testify to the fact that, though I was convinced I could make no request of you which you would not grant, it has never been my wish to impose a burden upon you.

I therefore earnestly beg you again and again to 2 pay me the compliment of treating C. Valgius

Fabrateria, a restoration of Fregellae (on the Liris in Latium), under a new name.

CICERO

Hippianum tractetis, remque cum eo conficiatis, ut,
quam possessionem habet in agro Fregellano, a vobis
emptam, eam liberam et immunem habere possit.
Id si a vobis impetraro, summo me beneficio vestro
affectum arbitrabor.

LXXVII

M. T. C. S. D. P. SULPICIO IMP,

Romae, a.u.c. 708.

1   Cum his temporibus non sane in senatum venti-
tarem, tamen, ut tuas litteras legi, non existimavi
me salvo iure nostrae veteris amicitiae multorumque
inter nos officiorum facere posse, ut honori tuo
deessem. Itaque adfui, supplicationemque tibi
libenter decrevi ; nec reliquo tempore ullo aut rei
aut existimationi aut dignitati tuae deero. Atque,
hoc ut tui necessarii sciant, hoc me animo erga
te esse, velim facias eos per litteras certiores, ut,
si quid tibi opus sit, ne dubitent mihi iure suo
2 denuntiare. M. Bolanum, virum bonum et fortem
et omnibus rebus ornatum, meumque veterem
amicum, tibi magno opere commendo. Pergratum
mihi feceris, si curaris, ut is intellegat, hanc commendationem sibi magno adiumento fuisse. Ip-

---

ᵃ The son of the distinguished jurist (for whom see iv.
1. 1, note *a*). This Sulpicius was commander-in-chief of
the forces in Illyricum during 46, as Vatinius was in 45
and 43 (v. 9 *sqq.*).

ᵇ Nothing more is known of him.

172

Hippianus as handsomely as you can, and so arrange matters with him that his tenure of the estate which he holds after purchase from you in the territory of Fregellae may be free of charge and clear of obligations. If you accede to this request of mine, I shall consider that you have done me a very great kindness.

LXXVII

CICERO WITH HEARTIEST GREETINGS TO P. SULPICIUS RUFUS,[a] IMPERATOR

Rome, Autumn, 46 B.C.

Although in these days I am not very regular in 1 my attendance at the Senate, yet, after reading your letter, I did not think I could possibly fail to support your claims to honour without prejudice to our long-standing friendship and our many mutual services. That being so, I was in my place, and it gave me pleasure to vote for a *supplicatio* in your honour ; and on no occasion in the future shall I fail to support your interests, reputation, or position. Moreover, so that your relatives may be assured of this feeling I have for you, I should like you to write and tell them so, in order that, if you have any need of help, they may not hesitate to give me a clear intimation to that effect, as they have a perfect right to do.

M. Bolanus [b] is a person I warmly commend to you, 2 as being a good and gallant man, possessing every accomplishment, and an old friend of mine. You will do me a favour if you take care to make him feel that this recommendation has proved of material service to

sumque virum optimum gratissimumque cognosces.
Promitto tibi, te ex eius amicitia magnam volup-
3 tatem esse capturum. Praeterea a te peto in
maiorem modum pro nostra amicitia et pro tuo
perpetuo in me studio, ut in hac re etiam elabores :
Dionysius, servus meus, qui meam bibliothecen
multorum nummorum tractavit, cum multos libros
surripuisset nec se impune laturum putaret, aufugit.
Is est in provincia tua. Eum et M. Bolanus, familiaris
meus, et multi alii Naronae viderunt ; sed cum se
a me manumissum esse diceret, crediderunt. Hunc
tu si mihi restituendum curaris, non possum dicere,
quam mihi gratum futurum sit. Res ipsa parva, sed
animi mei dolor magnus est. Ubi sit, et quid fieri
possit, Bolanus te docebit. Ego si hominem per
te reciperaro, summo me a te beneficio affectum
arbitrabor.

LXXVIII

M. T. C. S. D. ALLIENO PROCOS.

Romae, a.u.c. 708.

1 Democritus Sicyonius non solum hospes meus est,
sed etiam, quod non multis contigit, Graecis praesertim, valde familiaris. Est enim in eo summa
probitas, summa virtus, summa in hospites liberalitas

---

a On the coast of Illyria, between Histria and Dyrrachium.
b Of Sicily. In 60 Allienus was one of Cicero's *legati* in
Asia, and in 49 was a praetor. In 43 he was a *legatus* of
Dolabella, but surrendered to Cassius. See xii. 11. 1 and
12. 1.

him. And you will find the man himself too an excellent fellow and full of gratitude. I promise you that you will get no little pleasure out of your friendship with him.

There is this too ; I beg of you more earnestly 3 than usual, in the name of our friendship and your unvarying devotion to me, to take particular pains in the following matter also : my slave Dionysius, who had the charge of my very costly library, having stolen a lot of books, and thinking that he would be punished for the theft, has absconded. He is in your province. Both my friend Bolanus and several others saw him at Narona,^a but when he declared that I had given him his freedom, they took his word for it. If you charge yourself with the business of getting him back for me, I cannot tell you how delighted I shall be. It is a small thing in itself, but my annoyance is great. Bolanus will inform you where he is, and what can be done. If you are the means of my getting the rascal back, I shall consider that you have done me a very great kindness.

LXXVIII

CICERO TO AULUS ALLIENUS, PROCONSUL ^b

Rome, month uncertain, 46 B.C.

Democritus of Sicyon is not only on hospitable 1 terms, but also (and this does not happen in many such cases, especially if they are Greeks) on very intimate terms with me ; for he is exceedingly honourable, exceedingly conscientious, and exceedingly generous

et observantia, meque praeter ceteros et colit et
observat et diligit. Eum tu non modo suorum civium,
2 verum paene Achaiae principem cognosces. Huic
ego tantummodo aditum ad tuam cognitionem
patefacio et munio ; cognitum per te ipsum, quae
tua natura est, dignum tua amicitia atque hospitio
iudicabis. Peto igitur a te, ut, his litteris lectis,
recipias eum in tuam fidem, polliceare omnia te
facturum mea causa. De reliquo, si, id quod confido,
fore dignum eum tua amicitia hospitioque cognoveris,
peto, ut eum complectare, diligas, in tuis habeas.
Erit id mihi maiorem in modum gratum. Vale.

LXXIX

M. T. C. S. P. D. ALLIENO PROCOS.

Romae, a.u.c. 708.

Et te scire arbitror, quanti fecerim C. Avianium
Flaccum, et ego ex ipso audieram, optimo et gratissimo homine, quam a te liberaliter esset tractatus.
Eius filios, dignissimos illo patre meosque necessarios, quos ego unice diligo, commendo tibi sic ut
maiore studio nullos commendare possim. C. Avia-

ª See *Epp*. 35 and 75 in this book.

and deferential in the dispensing of hospitality, and, as for myself, he venerates, respects, and esteems me more than he does anybody else. You will find him to be the chief man, not only among his fellow-citizens, but almost in the whole of Achaia.

Such is the man for whom I am merely opening the 2 door and paving the way to your acquaintance; when you know him, you will, with your innate sense of justice, pronounce him worthy of your friendship and hospitality on your own account.

I therefore beg of you, when you have perused this letter, to take him under your protection, and promise to do all you can for him for my sake. For the rest, if, as I am confident you will, you find that he is likely to be worthy of your friendship and hospitality, I beg of you to give him a hearty welcome, make much of him, and count him among your friends. That will give me more than ordinary pleasure.

LXXIX

CICERO TO A. ALLIENUS, PROCONSUL

Rome, month uncertain, 46 B.C.

I believe you know how highly I ever esteemed C. Avianius Flaccus,[a] and besides I have heard from his own lips, excellent and grateful man that he is, how generously he has been treated by you. It is his sons I now commend to you as being most worthy of such a father, and close friends of my own, of whom I am particularly fond, and there are no men I could commend to you with greater enthusiasm. C.

nius in Sicilia est. Marcus est nobiscum. Ut illius
dignitatem praesentis ornes, rem utriusque defendas
te rogo. Hoc mihi gratius in ista provincia facere
nihil potes. Idque ut facias, te vehementer etiam
atque etiam rogo. Vale.

Avianius is in Sicily, Marcus is with us. I ask you to advance the claims of the former, whom you have with you, and to protect the interests of both. There is nothing you can do in your province that would please me better, and I earnestly beg of you again and again to do so.

please me better, and I earnestly beg of you again
and again to do so.

M. TULLI CICERONIS EPISTULARUM
AD FAMILIARES

LIBER DECIMUS QUARTUS

I

**TULLIUS S. D. TERENTIAE SUAE, TULLIOLAE SUAE,
CICERONI SUO**

Incohata Thessalonicae, finita Dyrrachi, A.U.C. 696.

1 Et litteris multorum et sermone omnium perfertur
ad me, incredibilem tuam virtutem et fortitudinem
esse teque nec animi, neque corporis laboribus defati-
gari. Me miserum ! te, ista virtute, fide, probitate,
humanitate, in tantas aerumnas propter me incidisse !
Tulliolamque nostram, ex quo patre tantas voluptates
capiebat, ex eo tantos percipere luctus ! Nam quid
ego de Cicerone dicam ? qui cum primum sapere
coepit, acerbissimos dolores miseriasque percepit.
Quae si, ut tu scribis, fato facta putarem, ferrem
paullo facilius ; sed omnia sunt mea culpa commissa,
qui ab iis me amari putabam, qui invidebant, eos non

---

a All the letters in this book are from Cicero to his wife
Terentia and his family in Rome. Nothing is known of
Terentia before her marriage with Cicero. She was a
woman of sound common sense and firmness of character.
It is doubtful whether Cicero's suspicions of her extravagance

CICERO

CICERO'S LETTERS TO HIS FRIENDS

BOOK XIV

I

CICERO TO TERENTIA AND HIS FAMILY [a]

Begun at Thessalonica, finished at Dyrrachium,
Nov. 25, 58 B.C.

I am kept informed by the letters of many and the 1
conversation of everybody that your courage and
fortitude, Terentia, are beyond belief, and that you
are not exhausted by your troubles either of mind
or body. Woe is me! To think that you of all
people, virtuous, faithful, upright, and generous as
you are, should have fallen into such a morass of
misery all on my account! And that our darling
Tullia should feel that the very father who was her
greatest delight is now the source of her greatest
griefs! As to Cicero, why should I talk about *him*,
since from the very dawn of his intelligence he has
known the bitterest pangs of sorrow and misery?
Could I but imagine that all this is (as you write) the
work of destiny, I should bear it a little more easily;
but it has all been brought about by my own fault,
because I thought myself beloved by those who were

and dishonesty were justified. His letters show a gradual
waning of his affection for her, and he divorced her in 46 B.C.

181

2 sequebar, qui petebant. Quod si nostris consiliis
usi essemus, neque apud nos tantum valuisset sermo
aut stultorum amicorum aut improborum, beatissimi
viveremus. Nunc, quoniam sperare nos amici iubent,
dabo operam, ne mea valetudo tuo labori desit. Res
quanta sit, intellego, quantoque fuerit facilius manere
domi, quam redire. Sed tamen, si omnes tribunos
plebis habemus, si Lentulum tam studiosum, quam
videtur, si vero etiam Pompeium et Caesarem, non
3 est desperandum. De familia, quomodo placuisse
amicis scribis, faciemus. De loco nunc quidem iam
abiit pestilentia ; sed quamdiu fuit, me non attigit.
Plancius, homo officiosissimus, me cupit esse secum
et adhuc retinet. Ego volebam loco magis deserto
esse in Epiro, quo neque Piso[1] veniret nec milites ;
sed adhuc Plancius me retinet. Sperat posse fieri,
ut mecum in Italiam decedat. Quem ego diem si
videro et si in vestrum complexum venero ac si et vos
et me ipsum recuperaro, satis magnum mihi fructum
videbor percepisse et vestrae pietatis et meae.
4 Pisonis humanitas, virtus, amor in omnes nos tantus
est, ut nihil supra possit. Utinam ea res ei voluptati
sit ! gloriae quidem video fore. De Q. fratre nihil

---

[1] *Manutius, Drumann* : ipse *Nobbe* : Hispo *Vett.*

---

[a] He is perhaps alluding to Caesar, who had offered him
a *legatio* in his army.
[b] Consul designate for 57 B C. See i. 1. 1.
[c] Quaestor of Macedonia. Cicero never forgot his kindness
and successfully defended him when accused of *ambitus* in 54.
[d] L. Piso, father of Caesar's wife Calpurnia, consul this
year, would be coming to Macedonia as proconsul in 57.
He was one of Cicero's bitterest enemies.
[e] C. Piso, who married Cicero's daughter Tullia in 63.

jealous of me, and turned away from those who sought me.[a]

Had I but followed my own judgment, and not 2 been so unduly influenced by the talk of either misguided or unscrupulous friends, I should now be living in perfect happiness. As it is, since my friends bid me have hope, I shall do my best to prevent my health from failing to further your efforts. I quite understand how difficult the thing was, and how much easier remaining at home was than returning. However, if we can count on all the tribunes and if on Lentulus's [b] being as enthusiastic as he appears to be, if above all on Pompey and Caesar, then there is no reason to despair.

In the matter of our slaves, we shall do what you 3 say our friends think best. As to this place, the epidemic, it is true, has now passed away, but even while it lasted it did not touch me. That most obliging fellow Plancius [c] desires me to live with him and won't let me go yet. My own wish was to be in some less frequented spot in Epirus where Piso [d] and his soldiers might not come, but Plancius won't let me go yet. He hopes it may be possible for him to leave for Italy in my company. If ever I see that day, and find myself in your arms, and feel that I have regained all of you as well as myself, I shall think that both your loyalty, and mine too, have met with an adequate reward.

Piso's [e] kindness, excellence of conduct, and affec- 4 tion for us all cannot possibly be exceeded. I pray that it may be a source of pleasure to him ; that it will be a source of pride to him I feel sure. As to

He strenuously supported his father-in-law's recall from exile, but died before his return.

ego te accusavi ; sed vos, cum praesertim tam pauci
5 sitis, volui esse quam coniunctissimos. Quibus me
voluisti agere gratias, egi, et me a te certiorem factum
esse scripsi. Quod ad me, mea Terentia, scribis, te
vicum vendituram, quid, obsecro te (me miserum!)
quid futurum est ? Et, si nos premet eadem fortuna,
quid puero misero fiet ? Non queo reliqua scribere
(tanta vis lacrimarum est), neque te in eumdem fletum
adducam. Tantum scribo : si erunt in officio amici,
pecunia non deerit ; si non erunt, tu efficere tua
pecunia non poteris. Per fortunas miseras nostras,
vide, ne puerum perditum perdamus. Cui si aliquid
erit, ne egeat, mediocri virtute opus est, et mediocri
6 fortuna, ut cetera consequatur. Fac valeas et ad me
tabellarios mittas, ut sciam, quid agatur, et vos quid
agatis. Mihi omnino iam brevis exspectatio est.
Tulliolae et Ciceroni salutem dic. Valete. D. a. d.
vi. Kalendas Decembres Dyrrachi.
7 Dyrrachium veni, quod et libera civitas est, et in
me officiosa et proxima Italiae. Sed si offendet me
loci celebritas, alio me conferam et ad te scribam.

---

^a The circumstances of this disagreement are unknown.

my brother Quintus,[a] I make no charge against you, but it has ever been my wish that all of you, especially as there are so few of you, should be as closely united as possible.

I have thanked those whom you wished me to thank, and have written that you were my informant. You tell me, my dear Terentia, that you intend selling your house-property ; in that case, what, I implore you (I am sadly worried about it), what is going to happen ? And if we are dogged by the same ill-fortune, what will become of our poor boy ? I cannot write what remains to be written, so irrepressible are my tears, and I would not make you too weep as bitterly. This much I do write—that if our friends remain loyal, money will be forthcoming ; if they do not, your own money will not enable you to do what you want. In the name of our own pitiful misfortunes, beware lest we ruin our already ruined boy. With something to stave off actual want, all he needs to attain everything else is a fair share of merit, and a fair share of luck.

Be sure you keep well, and send me letter-carriers to let me know what is being done, and how you all are. In any case I have not now long to wait. Give my love to my dearest Tullia and Cicero. Good-bye. Dyrrachium, Nov. 25th.

I have come to Dyrrachium, because it is not only a free state, but devoted to me, and is also the nearest point to Italy. But if the place is too crowded for my liking, I shall betake myself elsewhere, and send you word.

CICERO

II

Thessalonicae, A.U.C. 696.

1 Noli putare me ad quemquam longiores epistolas
scribere, nisi si quis ad me plura scripsit, cui puto
rescribi oportere. Nec enim habeo, quid scribam,
nec hoc tempore quidquam difficilius facio. Ad te
vero et ad nostram Tulliolam non queo sine plurimis
lacrimis scribere. Vos enim video esse miserrimas,
quas ego beatissimas semper esse volui, idque praestare debui et, nisi tam timidi fuissemus, praestitis-
2 sem. Pisonem nostrum merito eius amo plurimum.
Eum, ut potui, per litteras cohortatus sum gratiasque
egi, ut debui. In novis tribunis plebis intellego
spem te habere. Id erit firmum, si Pompei voluntas
erit; sed Crassum tamen metuo. A te quidem
omnia fieri fortissime et amantissime video, nec
miror; sed maereo casum eiusmodi, ut tantis tuis
miseriis meae miseriae subleventur. Nam ad me P.
Valerius, homo officiosus, scripsit, id quod ego
maximo cum fletu legi, quemadmodum a Vestae ad
tabulam Valeriam ducta esses. Hem, mea lux, meum
desiderium, unde omnes opem petere solebant! te

---

^a See note *e* on *Ep.* 1. 4.

^b Terentia seems to have taken refuge on Cicero's depar-
ture in the temple of Vesta, where her half-sister Fabia was
among the Vestal Virgins.

^c It is more probable that this was a tribunal for the
administration of justice than (as some take it to be) a bank,
and that Terentia was taken there to make an affidavit about
her property which would be to Cicero's interest. If it was

186

II

Thessalonica, Oct. 5, 58 B.C.

You must never think that I write longer letters to 1
anybody unless somebody has written to me at unusual length, and I think it my duty to answer him.
For I don't know what to write, and just now there is
nothing I find greater difficulty in doing. But to
you and our darling Tullia I cannot write without a
flood of tears. I see that both of you are utterly
wretched, you, whom I have always wished to be
completely happy—a happiness it was my duty to
have secured, and I should have secured it, had I not
been so timorous.

For our friend Piso *a* I have a profound affection, 2
and it is no more than he deserves. I have done my
best to urge him on by letter, and have thanked him
as I was bound to do. I gather that you have hopes of
the new tribunes of the plebs. On that we may rely,
if we can rely on Pompey's friendliness; and yet I
have my fears of Crassus. As for yourself, I see that
you are acting in every respect most courageously
and lovingly, nor does it surprise me ; but what
saddens me is the nature of a calamity in which my
own miseries can only be alleviated at the cost of
such miseries to you. For that most obliging of
men, P. Valerius, had described in a letter to me (and
I wept bitterly as I read it) how you were haled from
the temple of Vesta *b* to the Valerian Office.*c* Alas,
light of my life, for whom I yearn, to whom all used

a bank, she must have gone there to borrow money, though
this is inconsistent with *ducta esses.*

nunc, mea Terentia, sic vexari, sic iacere in lacrimis
et sordibus! idque fieri mea culpa, qui ceteros ser-
3 vavi, ut nos periremus! Quod de domo scribis, hoc
est de area, ego vero tum denique mihi videbor
restitutus, si illa nobis erit restituta. Verum haec
non sunt in nostra manu. Illud doleo, quae impensa
facienda est, in eius partem te miseram et despoliatam
venire. Quod si conficitur negotium, omnia consequemur; sin eadem nos fortuna premet, etiamne
reliquias tuas misera proicies? Obsecro te, mea vita,
quod ad sumptum attinet, sine alios, qui possunt, si
modo volunt, sustinere, et valetudinem istam in-
firmam, si me amas, noli vexare. Nam mihi ante
oculos dies noctesque versaris. Omnes labores te
excipere video: timeo, ut sustineas. Sed video in
te esse omnia. Quare, ut id, quod speras et quod
4 agis, consequamur, servi valetudini. Ego, ad quos
scribam, nescio, nisi ad eos, qui ad me scribunt, aut
ad eos, de quibus ad me vos aliquid scribitis. Longius,
quoniam ita vobis placet, non discedam; sed velim,
quam saepissime litteras mittatis, praesertim, si quid
est firmius, quod speremus. Valete, mea desideria,
valete. A. d. III. Nonas Octobr. Thessalonica.

---

a On the day he went into exile, Cicero's house on the
Palatine was burnt down, so that nothing but the site was
left.

to look for help, to think that now, Terentia mine, you are thus harassed, thus laid low in tears and unseemly humiliation ! And to think that it is all my fault, who have saved others to perish myself !

As to what you write about our house,[a] or rather **3** its site, I assure you that I shall never feel myself fully restored until that has been restored to me. These things however are not in our hands. What distresses me is, that whatever expenditure has to be incurred, you, in your unhappy and impoverished circumstances, should be let in for part of it. Of course, if the business of my restoration is carried through, we shall get all we want ; but if we are to be dogged by the same ill-fortune as heretofore, will you, my poor wife, throw away the little that is left to you ? I implore you, my darling, as far as expense is concerned, to let others, who can if they only will, bear the burden, and do not, as you love me, tax that indifferent health of yours. Day and night you are ever before my eyes. I see you taking upon yourself all our troubles, and I fear it is too much for you. But I also see that everything depends upon you ; and for that reason, in order that we may succeed in what you are hoping and striving for, obey the dictates of health.

I know not to whom I should write, unless it is to **4** those who write to me, or to those about whom you and Tullia say anything in your letters to me. Since that is your wish, I am not going farther away ; but I should like you to send me a letter as often as possible, especially if we have any better foundation for our hopes. Good-bye, you dear ones for whom I long, good-bye. Thessalonica, Oct. 5th.

CICERO

III

TULLIUS S. D. TERENTIAE ET TULLIOLAE ET
CICERONI SUIS

Dyrrachi, A.U.C. 696.

1   Accepi ab Aristocrito tres epistulas, quas ego
lacrimis prope delevi. Conficior enim maerore, mea
Terentia, nec meae me miseriae magis excruciant,
quam tuae vestraeque. Ego autem hoc miserior
sum, quam tu, quae es miserrima, quod ipsa calamitas
communis est utriusque nostrum, sed culpa mea
propria est. Meum fuit officium vel legatione vitare[a]
periculum, vel diligentia et copiis resistere, vel cadere
fortiter. Hoc miserius, turpius, indignius nobis nihil
2 fuit. Quare cum dolore conficior, tum etiam pudore.
Pudet enim me uxori meae optimae, suavissimis
liberis virtutem et diligentiam non praestitisse.
Nam mihi[1] ante oculos dies noctesque versatur squalor
vester et maeror et infirmitas valetudinis tuae ; spes
autem salutis pertenuis ostenditur. Inimici sunt
multi, invidi paene omnes. Eicere nos magnum fuit,
excludere facile est. Sed tamen quamdiu vos eritis
in spe, non deficiam, ne omnia mea culpa cecidisse[b]
3 videantur. Ut tuto sim, quod laboras, id mihi nunc
facillimum est, quem etiam inimici volunt vivere in
his tantis miseriis. Ego tamen faciam, quae prae-

---

[1] mi *Nobbe.*

---

[a] Offered him by Caesar in 59 (*Att.* ii. 18). Cicero's
refusal to accept this well-meant offer caused Caesar great
offence. Cicero's acceptance of it would have altered the
whole course of his political life.

[b] Or, possibly, "has failed."

190

III

CICERO TO TERENTIA AND HIS FAMILY

Dyrrachium, Nov. 29th, 58 B.C.

Aristocritus has handed me three letters which I 1
have almost blotted out with my tears. I am overwhelmed with grief, my dear Terentia, and I am not
more tortured by my own miseries, than by yours
and those of my children. But, most miserable as
you are, I am more miserable than you, in that, while
my own downfall itself is common to both of us, the
fault is entirely my own. It was my duty either to
avoid danger by accepting the *legatio*,^a or to resist it
with what devotion and resources I could, or to fall
courageously. Nothing was more pitiful, more dis-
honourable, or more unworthy of myself than what
I did.

And that is why I am overcome not only by sorrow 2
but also by shame. I am ashamed of not having
given assurance of my courage and devotion to my
best of wives and my sweetest of children. Night
and day there flit before my eyes the mourning garb
and melancholy of all of you, and your own feeble
health, and slender indeed is any hope of recall that
I can see. My enemies are many, almost everybody
is jealous of me. To eject me was a big business, to
keep me out is easy. However, as long as you have
hope, I shall not falter, lest it should seem that
everything has happened ^b through my fault.

As to your anxiety that I should be personally safe, 3
that presents no difficulty at all to me just now,
when even my enemies wish me to go on living in
this hopeless misery. I shall act, however, according

191

cipis. Amicis, quibus voluisti, egi gratias, et eas litteras Dexippo dedi, meque de eorum officio scripsi a te certiorem esse factum. Pisonem nostrum mirifico esse studio in nos et officio, et ego perspicio et omnes praedicant. Di faxint, ut tali genero mihi praesenti tecum simul et cum liberis nostris frui liceat! Nunc spes reliqua est in novis tribunis plebis et in primis quidem diebus; nam si inveterarit, actum 4 est. Ea re ad te statim Aristocritum misi, ut ad me continuo initia rerum et rationem totius negoti posses scribere; etsi Dexippo quoque ita imperavi, statim ut recurreret; et ad fratrem misi, ut crebro tabellarios mitteret. Nam ego eo nomine sum Dyrrhachi hoc tempore, ut quam celerrime, quid agatur, audiam, et sum tuto; civitas enim haec semper a me defensa est. Cum inimici nostri venire dicentur, tum in 5 Epirum ibo. Quod scribis, te, si velim, ad me venturam, ego vero, cum sciam magnam partem istius oneris abs te sustineri, te istic esse volo. Si perficitis, quod agitis, me ad vos venire oportet; sin autem—: sed nihil opus est reliqua scribere. Ex primis aut summum secundis litteris tuis constituere poterimus,

to your advice. I have thanked those friends whom you desired me to thank and I have put the letters in Dexippus's hands ; and I have told him that it was you who informed me of their kindness. That our friend Piso has proved himself amazingly zealous and obliging on our behalf is very evident to me, and, besides, everybody is telling me about it. God grant that I may be privileged, together with you and our children, personally to enjoy the society of such a son-in-law ! For the time, the only hope left us is in the new tribunes of the plebs and indeed in the first days of their office ; if once the matter gets stale, it is the end of all things.

My reason for sending Aristocritus to you im- 4 mediately was to enable you to write and tell me forthwith the first formal steps taken and the general outline of the whole business ; though I gave instructions to Dexippus also to hurry back immediately, and I sent a message to my brother to despatch letter-carriers at frequent intervals. For the excuse I make for being at Dyrrachium just now is, that I may hear with the least possible delay how matters are going on, and I am in no personal danger, since this is a community I have always defended. It will be time enough to go to Epirus when the approach of my enemies is reported.

As to your suggestion that, if I wish it, you will 5 join me here, I assure you that, knowing the great proportion of this burden you are bearing on your own shoulders, my wish is that you should stay where you are. If you all succeed in your aims, it is for me to come to you ; but if you do not—well, there is no need to write the rest. Your first, or at least your second letter will give me a clue, and enable me to

quid nobis faciendum sit. Tu modo ad me velim
omnia diligentissime perscribas ; etsi magis iam rem,
quam litteras debeo exspectare. Cura, ut valeas et
ita tibi persuadeas, mihi te carius nihil esse, nec
umquam fuisse. Vale, mea Terentia, quam ego
videre videor, itaque debilitor lacrimis. Vale. Pridie
Kalendas Decembr.

IV

**TULLIUS S. P. D. TERENTIAE ET TULLIOLAE ET
CICERONI SUIS**

Brundisi, A.U.C. 696.

1 Ego minus saepe ad vos do litteras, quam possum,
propterea quod cum omnia mihi tempora sunt misera,
tum vero, cum aut scribo ad vos aut vestras lego,
conficior lacrimis, sic ut ferre non possim. Quod
utinam minus vitae cupidi fuissemus ! certe nihil,
aut non multum in vita mali vidissemus. Quod si nos
ad aliquam alicuius commodi aliquando recuperandi
spem fortuna reservavit, minus est erratum a nobis ;
sin haec mala fixa sunt, ego vero te quam primum,
mea vita, cupio videre et in tuo complexu emori,
quando neque di, quos tu castissime coluisti, neque
homines, quibus ego semper servivi, nobis gratiam
2 rettulerunt. Nos Brundisi apud M. Laenium Flaccum
dies XIII fuimus, virum optimum, qui periculum
fortunarum et capitis sui prae mea salute neglexit,

---

^a It was to this M. Laenius Flaccus that Cicero, when
governor of Cilicia, refused the post of *praefectus* on the
ground that he was a banker. Tyrrell thinks that it was
another man of the same name, but it is highly improbable

decide what I must do. All I should like you to do is to write me a full and particular account of all that happens; though indeed I ought now to be awaiting some definite action rather than a letter. Mind you keep well and assure yourself that nothing is, or ever has been, dearer to me than are you. Good-bye Terentia mine! I seem to see your very face, and so I break down and weep. Good-bye! Nov. 29th.

IV

CICERO TO TERENTIA AND HIS FAMILY

Brundisium, April 29th, 58 B.C.

Yes, I do send you a letter less often than I might, 1 because, while every hour of my life is a misery to me, yet, when I either write to you, or read a letter from any of you, I am so overcome with weeping that I cannot bear it. Would that I had been less eager to live! At any rate I should have seen no sorrow, or not much of it, in my life. But if fortune has in reserve for me any hope at all of getting back any benefit at any time, the mistake I made is not so serious; if, however, these ills can never be removed, I assure you, my dearest, that my desire is to see you as soon as possible and die in your arms, since neither the gods, whom *you* have so virtuously worshipped, nor the men, whom *I* have ever served, have shown us any gratitude.

I have been for thirteen days at Brundisium, at 2 the house of M. Laenius Flaccus,[a] an excellent man, who has shown no thought for his fortunes and civil

that there should be two men of that name in the East at the same time.

neque legis improbissimae poena deductus est, quo
minus hospiti et amicitiae ius officiumque praestaret.
Huic utinam aliquando gratiam referre possimus!
3 habebimus quidem semper. Brundisio profecti
sumus pridie Kalendas Maias. Per Macedoniam
Cyzicum petebamus. O me perditum! O afflic-
tum! quid nunc rogem te, ut venias, mulierem
aegram, et corpore et animo confectam? Non
rogem? sine te igitur sim? Opinor, sic agam; si
est spes nostri reditus, eam confirmes et rem adiuves;
sin, ut ego metuo, transactum est, quoquo modo
potes, ad me fac venias. Unum hoc scito: si te
habebo, non mihi videbor plane perisse. Sed quid
de Tulliola mea fiet? iam id vos videte; mihi deest
consilium. Sed certe, quoquo modo se res habebit,
illius misellae et matrimonio et famae serviendum
est. Quid? Cicero meus quid aget? Iste vero
sit in sinu semper et complexu meo. Non queo plura
iam scribere; impedit maeror. Tu quid egeris,
nescio; utrum aliquid teneas, an, quod metuo, plane
4 sis spoliata. Pisonem, ut scribis, spero fore semper
nostrum. De familia liberata nihil est, quod te
moveat. Primum, tuis ita promissum est, te fac-
turam esse, ut quisque esset meritus. Est autem
in officio adhuc Orpheus; praeterea magno opere

status as compared with my safety, and has not been deterred by the penalty of a most scandalous law from fulfilling the claims and duties of hospitality and friendship. I pray that I may some day be able to show my gratitude to him,—a gratitude I shall never cease to feel.

I set out from Brundisium on April 29th. I am mak- **3** ing for Cyzicus through Macedonia. Ruined, alas, and prostrate as I am, why should I now ask you to come here, you, an invalid lady, exhausted in body and mind ? Should I not ask you ? Am I then to be without you ? This, I think, is what I shall plead— if there is any hope of my return, encourage it and assist the matter ; but if, as I fear, it is over and done with, make every effort to come here in any way you can. This one thing I would have you know—if I have you, I shall not think that I am absolutely lost. But what will become of my dearest Tullia ? It is now for you to see to that ; I have no suggestion to make. But in any case, however matters turn out, we must do all we can for that poor little damsel's matrimonial settlement and reputation. Again, what will my boy Cicero do ? *He* I hope may always be in my bosom and between my arms. I cannot now write more ; grief stays my pen. How you have fared I know not,—whether you retain anything or have been, as I fear, utterly despoiled.

Piso will, as you write, always, I hope, be our **4** friend. As to the liberation of the slaves, there is nothing to upset you. In the first place yours have been promised that you will act as each of them severally deserves. Orpheus so far is doing his duty, nobody else in any marked degree. As regards the

CICERO

nemo. Ceterorum servorum ea causa est, ut, si res
a nobis abisset, liberti nostri essent, si obtinere
potuissent ; sin ad nos pertinerent, servirent, praeter-
5 quam oppido pauci. Sed haec minora sunt. Tu
quod me hortaris, ut animo sim magno et spem
habeam recuperandae salutis, id velim sit eiusmodi,
ut recte sperare possimus. Nunc, miser, quando
tuas iam litteras accipiam ? quis ad me perferet ?
quas ego exspectassem Brundisi, si esset licitum per
nautas, qui tempestatem praetermittere noluerunt.
Quod reliquum est, sustenta te, mea Terentia, ut
potes, honestissime. Viximus ;[1] floruimus ; non
vitium nostrum, sed virtus nostra nos afflixit. Peccatum est nullum, nisi quod non una animam cum
ornamentis amisimus. Sed si hoc fuit liberis nostris
gratius, nos vivere, cetera, quamquam ferenda non
sunt, feramus. Atque ego, qui te confirmo, ipse me
6 non possum. Clodium Philetaerum, quod valetudine
oculorum impediebatur, hominem fidelem, remisi.
Sallustius officio vincit omnes. Pescennius est per-
benevolus nobis ; quem semper spero tui fore obser-
vantem. Sicca dixerat, se mecum fore, sed Brundisio
discessit. Cura, quoad potes, ut valeas ; et sic
existimes, me vehementius tua miseria, quam mea
commoveri. Mea Terentia, fidissima atque optima
uxor, et mea carissima filiola, et spes reliqua nostra,
Cicero, valete. Pridie Kalendas Maias Brundisio.

[1] ut potes. Honestissime viximus *Baiter and Nobbe, and
perhaps they are right.*

[a] "Against those who might urge that the penalties of
confiscation were being thus evaded." Tyrrell.
[b] Clodius, Sallustius, and Pescennius were probably
freedmen of Cicero.
[c] A friend of Cicero's who had a villa at Vibro in Bruttium.

other slaves the arrangement is this : that if my estate passed out of my hands they were to be my freed-men, provided they could make good this claim[a]; but if the estate still remains in my hands, that they should continue to be my slaves, with the exception of an extremely small number. But these are minor points.

As to your exhorting me to be of good courage and 5 not to abandon the hope of recovering my civil rights, I could only wish that matters were such as to justify the hope. As it is, poor wretch, when shall I at last get a letter from you ? Who will bring it me ? I should have awaited one at Brundisium, had the sailors allowed it, but they did not want to miss the favourable weather. For the rest, bear up, Terentia mine, with all the dignity you can. We have lived ; we have had our day. It was not our failings, but our virtues, that laid us low ; I am guilty of no wrong, except that I did not forfeit my life when I forfeited my honours. But if our children preferred that I should live, let us bear all else, unbearable though it be. But there—I, who am encouraging you, can-not encourage myself.

That faithful fellow, Clodius Philetaerus,[b] I have 6 sent home, because he was incapacitated by a weak-ness of the eyes. Sallustius[b] takes the prize for good service. Pescennius[b] is most cordially inclined towards me, and I hope he will always be attentive to you. Sicca[c] had declared his intention of remaining with me, but he left me at Brundisium. Take as much care as possible to keep well, and always remember that your misery causes me more distress than my own. Terentia mine, the most faithful and best of wives, and my very dear little daughter and Cicero, our last remaining hope, good-bye. Brundisium, April 29th.

CICERO

V

M. T. C. S. P. D. TERENTIAE ET TULL. SUIS

Athenis, a.u.c. 704.

1 Si tu et Tullia, lux nostra, valetis, ego et sua-
vissimus Cicero valemus. Pridie Idus Octobres
Athenas venimus, cum sane adversis ventis usi essemus tardeque et incommode navigassemus. De nave
exeuntibus nobis Acastus cum litteris praesto fuit
uno et vicesimo die, sane strenue. Accepi tuas
litteras, quibus intellexi te vereri, ne superiores mihi
redditae non essent. Omnes sunt redditae diligentissimeque a te perscripta sunt omnia, idque mihi
gratissimum fuit. Neque sum admiratus hanc epistulam, quam Acastus attulit, brevem fuisse. Iam
enim me ipsum exspectas, sive nos ipsos, qui quidem
quam primum ad vos venire cupimus ; etsi, in quam
rempublicam veniamus, intellego. Cognovi enim ex
multorum amicorum litteris, quas attulit Acastus, ad
arma rem spectare, ut mihi, cum venero, dissimulare
non liceat, quid sentiam. Sed, quando subeunda
fortuna est, eo citius dabimus operam, ut veniamus,
2 quo facilius de tota re deliberemus. Tu velim, quod
commodo valetudinis tuae fiat, quam longissime
3 poteris, obviam nobis properes. De hereditate Preciana, quae quidem mihi magno dolori est (valde

---

ᵃ A slave of Cicero, often mentioned in his letters to Tiro
and Terentia.

ᵇ This may have been either the Lucius Precius of
Panormus, mentioned by Cicero in *Verr*. v. 62, or the
Precianus mentioned in *Fam*. vii. 8. 2. It appears from
auctio that Cicero had decided to dispose of the estate
bequeathed to him by selling it. Pomponius is, of course,
Atticus.

V

CICERO TO TERENTIA AND TULLIA

Athens, Oct. 16, 50 B.C.

If you and Tullia, the light of my life, are well, so 1
am I and my darling boy Cicero. We arrived at
Athens on Oct. 14th, having found the winds dead
against us and having had a slow and uncomfortable
passage. As we were disembarking Acastus [a] was
there to meet us with letters on the twenty-first day
after he started—very smart work. I got a letter
from you from which I gathered that you fear your
previous letter had not reached me. All your letters
have reached me, and you have given me a full and
most painstaking account of everything, and I am
extremely obliged to you. And as for this letter
brought by Acastus, I am not surprised at its brevity,
since you are on the look out for my, or rather, our
arrival in person ; and indeed we are anxious to get
to you as soon as possible, though I quite understand
what the public situation will be when I come. I
learn from many friends' letters brought by Acastus
that things look like war, so that, when I arrive, it
will be impossible for me to conceal my real sentiments. Anyhow, since we must face our fate, I shall
make all the more effort to hasten my arrival, so as
to have a better chance of considering the whole
situation.

I should like you, so far as you may without detri- 2
ment to your health, to come as far to meet me as
you possibly can.

As regards the legacy left by Precius,[b] which, I 3
assure you, is a sore grief to me (for I had a great

enim illum amavi), hoc velim cures : si auctio ante
meum adventum fiet, ut Pomponius aut, si is minus
poterit, Camillus nostrum negotium curet. Nos cum
salvi venerimus, reliqua per nos agemus ; sin tu iam
Roma profecta eris, tamen curabis, ut hoc ita fiat.
Nos si di adiuvabunt, circiter Idus Novembres in
Italia speramus fore. Vos, mea suavissima et optatissima Terentia et Tulliola, si nos amatis, curate ut
valeatis. Athenis, a. d. xv. Kalendas Novembr.

VI

M. T. C. S. P. D. TERENTIAE ET TULLIAE

Dyrrachi, a.u.c. 706.

Nec saepe est, cui litteras demus, nec rem habemus
ullam, quam scribere velimus. Ex tuis litteris, quas
proxime accepi, cognovi praedium nullum venire
potuisse. Quare videatis velim, quomodo satisfiat
ei, cui scitis me satisfieri velle. Quod nostra tibi
gratias agit, id ego non miror te mereri, ut ea tibi
merito tuo gratias agere possit. Pollicem, si adhuc
non est profectus, quam primum fac extrudas. Cura,
ut valeas. Idibus Quintil.

---

[a] Cicero's lawyer friend, for whom he had a high regard.
Cf. Fam. v. 20. 3. Pomponius is T. Pomponius Atticus.
[b] A servant of Cicero.

affection for him), please see that this is done—if the auction takes place before my arrival, let Pomponius, or failing him, Camillus,[a] manage the business for us. As soon as I have got safe home, I shall do what remains to be done myself; but even if you have already started from Rome you will still please see that what I have indicated is done. With heaven's help, we hope to be in Italy about Nov. 13th. My dearest and sweetest Terentia, and my darling Tullia, as you love me, take care of your health. Athens, Oct. 16th.

VI

CICERO TO TERENTIA AND TULLIA

Dyrrachium, July 15th, 48 b.c.

There is not often anybody to whom I could entrust a letter, and I have nothing that I should care to write. I learn from the letter I last received from you that no estate could be sold, so please consider, both of you, how the claims of that person are to be satisfied, who, as you both know, I am anxious should be satisfied. As to our daughter's thanking you, I am not surprised that your services are such as to enable her to thank you with good reason. If Pollex [b] has not yet started, be sure you give him a push out as soon as possible. Mind you keep well. July 15th.

203

CICERO

VII

M. T. C. S. P. D. TERENTIAE SUAE ET TULL.

Ad Formias, a.u.c. 705.

1 Omnes molestias et sollicitudines, quibus et te
miserrimam habui, id quod mihi molestissimum est,
Tulliolamque, quae nobis nostra vita dulcior est,
deposui et eieci. Quid causae autem fuerit, postridie intellexi, quam a vobis discessi—χολὴν ἄκρατον
noctu eieci. Statim ita sum levatus, ut mihi deus
aliquis medicinam fecisse videatur. Cui quidem tu
deo, quemadmodum soles, pie et caste satisfacias,
2 id est Apollini et Aesculapio. Navem spero nos
valde bonam habere; in eam simulatque conscendi,
haec scripsi. Deinde conscribam ad nostros familiares multas epistulas, quibus te et Tulliolam
nostram diligentissime commendabo. Cohortarer
vos, quo animo fortiore essetis, nisi vos fortiores
cognossem, quam quemquam virum. Et tamen
eiusmodi spero negotia esse, ut et vos istic commodissime sperem esse, et me aliquando cum similibus
3 nostri rempublicam defensurum. Tu primum valetudinem tuam velim cures ; deinde, tibi si videbitur,
villis iis utere, quae longissime aberunt a militibus.
Fundo Arpinati bene poteris uti cum familia urbana,
si annona carior fuerit. Cicero bellissimus tibi

ᵃ The words *id* . . . *Aesculapio* read like, and probably
are, a gloss on the text.
ᵇ Provisions would be cheaper in Arpinum than in Rome.

VII

CICERO TO TERENTIA AND TULLIA

Off Formiae, June 11th, 49 B.C.

All the troubles and anxieties, with which I kept 1 both you in a state of utter misery (which troubles me more than anything) and dear Tullia too, who is sweeter to us both than our very lives—all those, I say, I have put away and got rid of. What the reason was I discovered the day after I left you; it was *undiluted bile*; I got rid of it all that night. My immediate relief was such that I fancied some god or other had doctored me, and to that god I beg you to pay due tribute with piety and purity as you always do—I mean to Apollo and Aesculapius.[a]

I am confident that we have a right good ship; I 2 wrote this as soon as I had got on board. Later on I shall write a number of letters to our friends, and commend *you* and our darling Tullia to their care with all the warmth in the world. I should exhort you both to show a more courageous spirit, had I not discovered that you have more courage than any *man* of us all. Yet, after all, I trust that affairs are such that I may hope not only that you two will be extremely comfortable where you are, but also that one day I shall have men like myself at my side to defend the Republic.

As for yourself, I would have you, first of all, take 3 care of your health; in the next place, if it so please you, you will make use of those villas which will be farthest away from men-in-arms. You can conveniently occupy the farm at Arpinum with our town staff of servants, if the price of provisions has risen.[b]

salutem plurimam dicit. Etiam atque etiam vale.
D. iii. Idus Iun.

VIII

M. T. C. S. P. D. TERENTIAE

Brundisi, A.U.C. 707.

Si vales, bene est ; ego valeo. Valetudinem tuam
velim cures diligentissime. Nam mihi et scriptum
et nuntiatum est, te in febrim subito incidisse. Quod
celeriter me fecisti de Caesaris litteris certiorem,
fecisti mihi gratum. Item posthac, si quid opus erit,
si quid acciderit novi, facies ut sciam. Cura, ut
valeas. Vale. D. iv. Nonas Iun.

IX

M. T. C. S. P. D. TERENTIAE

Brundisi, A.U.C. 706.

Ad ceteras meas miserias accessit dolor e Dolabellae
valetudine et Tulliae. Omnino de omnibus rebus,
nec quid consili capiam, nec quid faciam, scio. Tu
velim tuam et Tulliae valetudinem cures. Vale.

---

a Born in 65, Cicero's son, Marcus, was now 16 years
of age.

Cicero, fine lad that he is,[a] sends you his very best love.   Again and again, good-bye.   June 11th.

VIII

CICERO TO TERENTIA

Brundisium, June 2nd, 47 B.C.

If you are in good health, all is well; so am I.   I would have you pay most particular attention to your health; for I have been told both by letter and word of mouth that you have had a sudden attack of fever. You did me a kindness in informing me so quickly of Caesar's letter.   From now on also, if there be any need, if anything new has occurred, you will please see that I am apprised of it.   Take care to keep well. Good-bye.   June 2nd.

IX

CICERO TO TERENTIA

Brundisium, probably Dec. 17th, 48 B.C.

To all my other woes must now be added the sorrow caused me by the ill-health of Dolabella and Tullia. Looking all round at everything, I don't know in the world what steps to take, or what to do.   Please take care of your own and Tullia's health.   Good-bye.

CICERO

X

M. T. C. S. P. D. TERENTIAE SUAE

Brundisi, a.u.c. 707.

Quid fieri placeret, scripsi ad Pomponium serius,
quam oportuit. Cum eo si locuta eris, intelleges,
quid fieri velim. Apertius scribi, quando ad illum
scripseram, necesse non fuit. De ea re et de ceteris
rebus quam primum velim nobis litteras mittas.
Valetudinem tuam cura diligenter. Vale. Septimo
Idus Quintil.

XI

M. T. C. S. P. D. TERENTIAE SUAE

Brundisi, a.u.c. 707.

Si vales, bene est: ego valeo. Tullia nostra venit
ad me pridie Idus Iunias ; cuius summa virtute et
singulari humanitate graviore etiam sum dolore
affectus, nostra factum esse neglegentia, ut longe alia
in fortuna esset atque eius pietas ac dignitas postulabat. Nobis erat in animo, Ciceronem ad Caesarem
mittere, et cum eo Cn. Sallustium. Si profectus erit,
faciam te certiorem. Valetudinem tuam cura diligenter. Vale. xvii. Kalendas Quintil.

---

a Otherwise unknown.

X

CICERO TO TERENTIA

Brundisium, July 9th, 47 B.C.

I wrote to tell Pomponius what my wishes were later than I should have done. When you have a talk with him, you will understand what I should like to be done. Since I have already written to him, there is no necessity to write here more openly. I should like you to send me a letter as soon as possible about that and everything else. Take particular care of your health. Good-bye. July 9th.

XI

CICERO TO TERENTIA

Brundisium, June 14th, 47 B.C.

If you are well, all is right; I am well. Our daughter Tullia joined me on June 12th. Her consummate excellence and exceptional kindliness have aggravated my regret that my own carelessness is to blame for her being in very different circumstances from what her filial affection and her position demanded. It is my intention to send Cicero to Caesar, and Cn. Sallustius [a] with him. If he sets out I shall inform you. Take particular care of your health. Good-bye. June 14th.

CICERO

XII

M. T. C. S. P. D. TERENTIAE

Brundisi, A.U.C. 706.

Quod nos in Italiam salvos venisse gaudes, perpetuo
gaudeas velim. Sed, perturbati dolore animi magnis-
que iniuriis, metuo ne id consili ceperimus, quod
non facile explicare possimus. Quare, quantum
potes, adiuva. Quid autem possis, mihi in mentem
non venit. In viam quod te des hoc tempore, nihil
est ; et longum est iter, et non tutum ; et non video,
quid prodesse possis, si veneris. Vale. D. prid.
Nonas Novemb. Brundisio.

XIII

M. T. C. S. P. D. TERENTIAE

Brundisi, A.U.C. 707.

Quod scripsi ad te proximis litteris de nuntio remit-
tendo, quae sit istius vis hoc tempore, et quae con-
citatio multitudinis, ignoro. Si metuendus iratus
est, quies tamen[1] ab illo fortasse nascetur. Totum

---

[1] quiesces : tamen *MD, followed by Tyrrell. I have
retained Nobbe's reading, as being a better order of words,
and supplying* nascetur *with a subject.*

---

[a] To Tullia's husband, Dolabella ; *nuntium remittere,*
"to send back a message" was the regular phrase for a
notice of divorce ; the technical form of the message was
tuas res tibi habeto, "keep what belongs to you," *i.e.,* "act
independently of me."

210

XII

CICERO TO TERENTIA

Brundisium, Nov. 4th, 48 B.C.

You are glad that I have arrived safe in Italy; I could wish that you may never cease to be so. But agitated as I was by anguish of mind and the cruel wrongs I had suffered, I fear I adopted a policy from which I cannot easily extricate myself. You must give me all the assistance you can. But what you can do I have no idea. That you should take to the road at this particular time is sheer nonsense. The journey is not only long, but unsafe; and I fail to see of what good you can be if you do come. Good-bye. Brundisium, Nov. 4th.

XIII

CICERO TO TERENTIA

Brundisium, July 10th, 47 B.C.

I wrote to you in my last about sending a notice of divorce [a]; well, I don't quite know what force he has behind him at the moment, and what means of rousing the populace.[b] Even if he is to be feared in his anger, he will after all perhaps take the initiative in a peaceful settlement. You will, I am sure, take a

[b] At the head of an angry mob, Dolabella would have every opportunity of wreaking his vengeance on Tullia. Dolabella was now openly favouring Caesar, and indeed acting under his orders.

iudicabis, quale sit; et quod in miserrimis rebus
minime miserum putabis, id facies. Vale. vi. Idus
Quintil.

XIV

TULLIUS TERENTIAE ET PATER TULLIOLAE DUABUS ANIMIS
SUIS ET CICERO MATRI OPTIMAE SUAVISS. SORORI
S. P. D.

Minturnis, a.u.c. 705.

1 Si vos valetis, nos valemus. Vestrum iam consilium est, non solum meum, quid sit vobis faciendum.
Si ille Romam modeste venturus est, recte in prae-
sentia domi esse potestis ; sin homo amens diripiendam Urbem daturus est, vereor, ut Dolabella ipse
satis nobis prodesse possit. Etiam illud metuo, ne
iam intercludamur, ut, cum velitis exire, non liceat.
Reliquum est, quod ipsae optime considerabitis, vestri
similes feminae sintne Romae. Si enim non sunt,
videndum est, ut honeste vos esse possitis. Quomodo quidem nunc se res habet, modo ut haec nobis
loca tenere liceat, bellissime vel mecum, vel in nostris
praediis, esse poteritis. Etiam illud verendum est,
2 ne brevi tempore fames in Urbe sit. His de rebus
velim cum Pomponio, cum Camillo, cum quibus vobis
videbitur, consideretis ; ad summam, animo forti

comprehensive view of the whole matter, and you will do what you think to be least distressing in these most distressing circumstances. Good-bye. July 10th.

XIV

CICERO TO TERENTIA AND TULLIA

Minturnae, June 23rd, 49 B.C.

Tullius sends his best love to Terentia and her father to Tullia, the two darlings of his heart, as does Cicero to his best of mothers and sweetest of sisters.

If you two are well, so are we. It lies with you 1 now, and not with me alone, to consider what we should do. If Caesar is going to enter Rome in an orderly manner, you can quite well remain at home for the present; but if in his frenzy the man is going to give up the city to plunder, I fear that even Dolabella may not be able to help us enough. I am afraid also that we may be presently cut off from you, so that when you wish to leave the city, you may not be allowed to do so. There remains the question, which nobody can discuss better than yourselves, whether ladies like you are staying in Rome. For if they are not, we must consider whether *you* can do so with any propriety. As matters now stand, provided I am allowed to retain those places of mine, you can quite nicely stay either with me, or on one of our estates. Another reason for apprehension is, that before long there may be a famine in the city.

I should like you both to consider these matters 2 with Pomponius, with Camillus, with whomever you think best ; above all be of good courage. Labienus

213

CICERO

sitis. Labienus rem meliorem fecit. Adiuvat etiam
Piso, quod ab Urbe discedit et sceleris condemnat
generum suum. Vos, meae carissimae animae, quam
saepissime ad me scribite, et vos quid agatis, et
quid istic agatur. Quintus pater et filius et Rufus
vobis salutem dicunt. Valete. VIII. Kalend. Quintil.
Minturnis.

XV

M. T. C. S. P. D. TERENTIAE SUAE

Brundisi, A.U.C. 707.

Si vales, bene est. Constitueramus, ut ad te antea
scripseram, obviam Ciceronem Caesari mittere ; sed
mutavimus consilium, quia de illius adventu nihil
audiebamus. De ceteris rebus, etsi nihil erat novi,
tamen, quid velimus et quid hoc tempore putemus
opus esse, ex Sicca poteris cognoscere. Tulliam
adhuc mecum teneo. Valetudinem tuam cura diligenter. Vale. XII. Kalendas Quintil.

XVI

M. T. C. S. P. D. TERENTIAE SUAE

Brundisi, A.U.C. 707.

Si vales, bene est ; valeo. Etsi eiusmodi tempora
nostra sunt, ut nihil habeam, quod aut a te litterarum

ª By joining the Pompeians, Labienus, Caesar's lieutenant
in Gaul, and subsequently governor of Gallia Togata
(Southern Cisalpine Gaul), had now deserted to Pompey.
He fought against Caesar at Pharsalia, in Africa, and at
Munda, where he was killed.

ᵇ L. Calpurnius Piso Caesoninus, father of Caesar's wife
Calpurnia. See note *d* on *Ep.* I. 3.

214

has improved the position.[a] Piso[b] too is helping us
by quitting the city and condemning his own son-in-
law of criminal conduct. You, the darlings of my
soul, must write to me as often as possible, and tell
me how you are and what is going on at Rome.
Quintus and his son and Rufus[c] send you their
regards. Good-bye. Minturnae, June 23rd.

XV

CICERO TO TERENTIA

Brundisium, June 19th, 47 B.C.

If you are well, all is right. I had determined, as
I wrote to you before, to send Cicero to meet Caesar,
but I have changed my intention, because I could hear
nothing about the latter's arrival. About everything
else, although there is nothing new, you will yet be
able to learn from Sicca what my wishes are and what
I think must be done at this juncture. I am still
keeping Tullia with me. Take particular care of
your health. Good-bye. June 19th.

XVI

CICERO TO TERENTIA

Brundisium, Jan. 4th, 47 B.C.

If you are well, all is right; I am well. Although
I am so circumstanced as to have nothing to look
forward to in the way of a letter from you, or to

[c] Mescinius Rufus, who had been Cicero's quaestor in
Cilicia. (See v. 19-21.)

CICERO

exspectem aut ipse ad te scribam, tamen nescio quomodo et ipse vestras litteras exspecto, et scribo ad
vos, cum habeo, qui ferat. Volumnia debuit in te
officiosior esse, quam fuit, et id ipsum, quod fecit,
potuit diligentius facere et cautius. Quamquam alia
sunt, quae magis curemus magisque doleamus, quae
me ita conficiunt, ut ii voluerunt, qui me de
mea sententia detruserunt. Cura, ut valeas. Pridie
Nonas Ianuar.

XVII

M. T. C. S. D. TERENTIAE SUAE

Brundisi, a.u c. 706.

S.v.b.e.v. Si quid haberem, quod ad te scriberem,
facerem id et pluribus verbis et saepius. Nunc
quae sint negotia, vides. Ego autem quomodo sim
affectus, ex Lepta et Trebatio poteris cognoscere.
Tu fac, ut tuam et Tulliae valetudinem cures. Vale.

XVIII

TULLIUS TERENTIAE SUAE ET PATER SUAVISS. FILIAE
TULLIOLAE, CICERO MATRI ET SORORI S. P. D.

Formiis, a.u.c. 705.

1 Considerandum vobis etiam atque etiam, animae
meae, diligenter puto, quid faciatis—Romaene sitis,

---

a Who this lady was is unknown. She may have been
the sister or daughter of P. Volumnius Eutrapelus (vii. 32).
b They had come to see Cicero at Brundisium and then
left for Rome. Q. Lepta was Cicero's *praefectus fabrum*,
"engineer-in-chief," in Cilicia. Trebatius was Cicero's
familiar friend, the young jurisconsult, so often mentioned
in his letters. *Cf.* vii. 6-22.

write to you myself, yet somehow or other I do both look forward to getting letters from you myself, and I write to you whenever I find anybody to take you a letter. Volumnia[a] ought to have been more obliging to you than she was, and to have done the little she did with more tact and caution. And yet there are other things to cause me greater anxiety and greater grief—things that distress me as much as those persons desired who forced me to abandon my original conviction. Take care to keep well. Jan. 4th.

XVII

CICERO TO TERENTIA

Brundisium, Dec. 15th, 48 B.C.

If you are well, all is right; I am well. Had I anything to write to you, I should do so, both at greater length and more frequently. The present state of affairs you can see for yourself; how they affect me, you can learn from Lepta and Trebatius.[b] Be sure you take care of your own and Tullia's health. Good-bye.

XVIII

CICERO TO TERENTIA AND TULLIA

Formiae, Jan. 22nd, 49 B.C.

Tullius sends his best love to his wife Terentia, and her father to his sweetest of daughters, his darling Tullia, as does Cicero to his mother and sister.

I think you ought carefully to consider again and again, my dearest ones, what you should do—whether

an mecum in aliquo tuto loco. Id non solum meum consilium est, sed etiam vestrum. Mihi veniunt in mentem haec : Romae vos esse tuto posse per Dolabellam, eamque rem posse nobis adiumento esse, si quae vis, aut si quae rapinae fieri coeperint. Sed rursus illud me movet, quod video, omnes bonos abesse Roma, et eos mulieres suas secum habere. Haec autem regio, in qua ego sum, nostrorum est cum oppidorum, tum etiam praediorum ; ut et multum esse mecum, et, cum abieritis, commode et
2 in nostris esse possitis. Mihi plane non satis constat adhuc, utrum sit melius. Vos videte, quid aliae faciant isto loco feminae, et ne, cum velitis, exire non liceat ; id velim diligenter etiam atque etiam vobis- cum et cum amicis consideretis. Domus ut pro- pugnacula et praesidium habeat, Philotimo dicetis. Et velim tabellarios instituatis certos, ut quotidie aliquas a vobis litteras accipiam. Maxime autem date operam, ut valeatis, si nos vultis valere. ix. Kal. Febr. Formiis.

XIX

M. T. C. S. D. TERENTIAE

Brundisi, a.u.c. 706.

In maximis meis doloribus excruciat me valetudo Tulliae nostrae. De qua nihil est, quod ad te plura

---

a By Caesar's orders. Dolabella was on Caesar's side, but would be able to help Terentia and Tullia.
b A freedman of Cicero's, not Terentia's dishonest steward.

to stay in Rome or in some place of safety with me. That is not a question for me alone, but also for you. What suggests itself to me is this—that, thanks to Dolabella, you can safely stay in Rome, and that his kindness might be of assistance to us if violence or lootings begin.[a] On the other hand I am impressed by the evidence I have that all loyalists have left Rome, and have their ladies with them. Now the district in which I am consists not only of towns devoted to me, but also of estates belonging to me, so that you could be constantly with me, and, if you went away, could be housed comfortably, and on our own property. I have not myself quite definitely 2 decided which is the better course. Please observe what other ladies of your standing are doing, and beware lest when you want to get out of Rome, you are not allowed to do so. I would have you seriously consider this again and again among yourselves and with your friends. Please tell Philotimus[b] to get the house barricaded and guarded. I would also have you establish a regular succession of letter-carriers, so that I may get some sort of a letter from you every day. But the main point is to do all you can to keep well, if you wish me to do so. Formiae, Jan. 22nd.

XIX

CICERO TO TERENTIA

Brundisium, Nov. 27th, 48 B.C.

Amid all my other overwhelming sorrows, I am kept on the rack by our dear Tullia's ill-health ; but there is no reason why I should write to you further

scribam ; tibi enim aeque magnae curae esse certo
scio. Quod me propius vultis accedere, video ita
esse faciendum. Etiam ante fecissem ; sed me multa
impediverunt, quae ne nunc quidem expedita sunt.
Sed a Pomponio exspecto litteras, quas ad me quam
primum perferendas cures velim. Da operam, ut
valeas.

XX

M. T. C. S. P. D. TERENTIAE SUAE

Venusiae, A.U.C. 707.

In Tusculanum nos venturos putamus aut Nonis
aut postridie. Ibi ut sint omnia parata. Plures enim
fortasse nobiscum erunt, et, ut arbitror, diutius ibi
commorabimur. Labrum si in balineo non est, ut
sit. Item cetera, quae sunt ad victum et ad valetudinem necessaria. Vale. Kal. Octobr. de Venusino.

XXI

M. T. C. S. P. D. TERENTIAE SUAE

Brundisi, A.U.C. 707.

Si vales, bene est ; valeo. Da operam, ut convalescas. Quod opus erit, ut res tempusque postulat,
provideas atque administres, et ad me de omnibus
rebus quam saepissime litteras mittas. Vale.

---

a This is Cicero's last letter to Terentia, whom he divorced
shortly afterwards. Curt, casual, and inconsiderate in its
vagueness, it is enough to madden any self-respecting house-
wife and hostess. As Long remarks, " A gentleman would
write a more civil letter to his housekeeper."
b The *labrum* (λούτηρ) was a large round basin raised
about three feet from the ground, in which the bathers

about it, for I am quite sure that your own anxiety is just as great. You both want me to get nearer to you, and I see that I must do so. I should have done so even before ; but I was hindered by many difficulties, which are even now unsolved. But I am waiting for a letter from Pomponius, which please take care is delivered to me as soon as possible. Do your best to keep well.

XX

CICERO TO TERENTIA [a]

Venusia, Oct. 1st, 47 B.C.

I think I shall arrive at my Tusculan villa either on the 7th inst. or on the day after. See that everything is ready there ; for perhaps I shall have several others with me, and I expect we shall stay there for some considerable time. If there is no basin [b] in the bath, see that there is one, and so with everything else necessary for everyday life and health. Goodbye. The district of Venusia, Oct. 1st.

XXI

CICERO TO TERENTIA

Brundisium, June, 47 B.C.

If you are well, all is right ; I am well. Make every effort to recover your health. Provide for and take charge of any necessary business, as time and circumstances demand, and send me letters about everything as often as possible. Good-bye.

washed themselves before they immersed themselves in the *piscina*.

CICERO

XXII

Brundisi, A.U.C. 707.

Si vales, bene est; valeo. Nos quotidie tabellarios nostros exspectamus; qui si venerint, fortasse
erimus certiores, quid nobis faciendum sit, facie-
musque te statim certiorem. Valetudinem tuam
cura diligenter. Vale. Kalendis Septemb.

XXIII

M. T. C. TERENTIAE SUAE S. P. D.

Brundisi, A.U.C. 707.

Si vales, bene est; valeo. Redditae mihi tandem
sunt a Caesare litterae satis liberales, et ipse opinione
celerius venturus esse dicitur. Cui utrum obviam
procedam, an hic eum exspectem, cum constituero,
faciam te certiorem. Tabellarios mihi velim quam
primum remittas. Valetudinem tuam cura diligenter.
Vale. D. pridie Idus Sext.

XXIV

M. T. C. S. P. D. TERENTIAE

Brundisi, A.U.C. 707.

Si vales, bene est; valeo. Nos neque de Caesaris
adventu, neque de litteris, quas Philotimus habere
dicitur, quidquam adhuc certi habemus. Si quid
erit certi, faciam te statim certiorem. Valetudinem
tuam fac ut cures. Vale. III. Idus Sextiles.

---

[a] See note *b* to *Ep.* 18 above.

XXII

CICERO TO TERENTIA

Brundisium, Sept. 1st, 47 B.C.

If you are well all is right; I am well. I am expecting letter-carriers every day, and if they arrive perhaps I shall get to know what I ought to do, and I shall let you know at once. Take particular care of your health. Good-bye. Sept. 1st.

XXIII

CICERO TO TERENTIA

Brundisium, Aug. 12th, 47 B.C.

If you are well, all is right; I am well. A letter has at last been handed me from Caesar, quite handsomely worded; and it is said that he will arrive in person more quickly than was expected. When I have made up my mind whether to go out and meet him, or wait for him here, I shall let you know. I should like you to send back my letter-carriers as soon as possible. Take particular care of your health. Good-bye. Aug. 12th.

XXIV

CICERO TO TERENTIA

Brundisium, Aug. 11th, 47 B.C.

If you are well, all is right; I am well. I have no certain information as yet either about Caesar's arrival or about the letter which Philotimus *a* is said to have in his hands. If I have such information, I shall let you know at once. Be sure you take care of your health. Good-bye. Aug. 11th.

BOOK XV

NOTE ON CICERO'S GOVERNORSHIP OF CILICIA

Cicero left Rome for Cilicia in 51 B.C. as reluctantly as Macaulay left London for India in 1834. Both were profoundly devoted to their respective mother-cities, and loved city life ; both dreaded the friend-less solitude of what they regarded as banishment in a distant land ; and both apprehended a fatal break in the continuity of their political careers at home.

Cicero arrived in Laodicea at the end of July, having with him as his *legati* [a] his brother Quintus, C. Pomptinus, M. Anneius, and L. Tullius. His province, besides Cilicia proper, included Pisidia, Pamphylia, Cyprus, Isauria, Lycaonia, and three departments (διοικήσεις) north of Taurus, the chief towns of which were Cibyra, Synnada, and Apamea.

As a civil administrator he appears to have had every desire to improve the conditions of the pro-vincials and undo the harm wrought by his pre-decessor, the " tigerish " Appius Claudius Pulcher ; but his good intentions were too often neutralized

[a] A governor's *legati*, selected by himself, but with the approval of the Senate, performed any service he thought fit to assign them, whether civil or military.

by his eagerness to support at all costs the *publicani*, who were mainly drawn from the Order to which he himself belonged, and which he consistently championed—the Order of Knights (*equester ordo*), and also by his anxiety to meet the views of his influential friends at home ; with the result that, on the civil side, his administration was no more than moderately successful, and he left the province little better than he found it.

In his military capacity, on the other hand, he showed surprising ability and resolution. Shortly after his arrival his province was threatened by an invasion of the Parthians ; but so well did his forces acquit themselves, especially on Mt. Amanus and at Pindenissus—operations described by himself in simple and lucid language—that, had he not been forestalled by Cassius, who brilliantly repulsed the Parthians at Antioch (an achievement he somewhat ill-naturedly minimizes), he might have claimed the credit of having avenged the death of Crassus at Carrhae in 53.

Moreover, all through this critical period, with little or no support from Rome, though he repeatedly appealed for it, Cicero checked all revolt in his province, and kept the feudatory and allied potentates quiet and well-disposed.

In view of these laudable achievements there is little doubt that his application for a triumph would have been granted, had it not been opposed by no less a man than M. Porcius Cato, who gives his reasons for doing so in an elaborate and highly complimentary letter (*Ep.* 5), which is, however, not without a touch of sarcasm, and Cicero's reply is a model of courtesy and self-restraint under considerable provocation.

Cato, however, did not oppose, though he refrained from voting for, a *supplicatio* to Cicero ; on the other hand, he secured a *supplicatio* of greater length (20 days) for his own incapable and worthless son-in-law, M. Calpurnius Bibulus, Governor of Syria, who (according to Cicero) " never stirred out of the well-fortified and well-provisioned town of Antioch during the whole time the Parthians were in his province." It was this, as Dr. Strachan Davidson remarks, even more than his failure to obtain a triumph, that roused Cicero's resentment and indignation.

M. TULLI CICERONIS EPISTULARUM
AD FAMILIARES

LIBER DECIMUS QUINTUS

I

M. TULLIUS CICERO, PROCOS. S. P. D. COSS.
PRAETT. TRIBB. PL. SENATUI

In Cilicia, A.U.C. 708.

1 S.v.v.b.e.e.e.q.v. Etsi mihi non dubie nuntiabatur
Parthos transisse Euphraten cum omnibus fere
suis copiis, tamen, quod arbitrabar a M. Bibulo proconsule certiora de his rebus ad vos scribi posse,
statuebam mihi non necesse esse publice scribere ea
quae de alterius provincia nuntiarentur. Postea vero
quam certissimis auctoribus, legatis, nuntiis, litteris
sum certior factus, vel quod tanta res erat, vel quod
nondum audieramus Bibulum in Syriam venisse,
vel quia administratio huius belli mihi cum Bibulo
paene est communis, quae ad me delata essent
2 scribenda ad vos putavi. Regis Antiochi Commageni

---

^a Cicero was now proconsul of Cilicia, and Bibulus of
Syria.
^b The most north-easterly district of Syria.

228

CICERO'S LETTERS TO HIS FRIENDS

BOOK XV

I

M. TULLIUS CICERO, THE PROCONSUL,[a] SENDS GREETINGS
TO THE CONSULS, PRAETORS, TRIBUNES OF THE
PLEBS AND SENATE

Near Cybistra in Cilicia, 51 B.C.

IF you are well, all is right ; I and the army are well. 1
Although I kept receiving no uncertain intelligence
that the Parthians had crossed the Euphrates with
practically all their forces, still, because I believed
that more definite despatches on these matters
could be sent to you by the proconsul Bibulus, I decided that it was not necessary for me to insert in a
public despatch what was reported about the province
of another. When, however, I was informed on the
most trustworthy authority, by envoys, messengers,
and letters—whether because of the importance of
the matter, or because I had not yet heard of Bibulus'
arrival in Syria, or owing to the fact that the conduct
of this war was almost as much in my hands as in those
of Bibulus—for anyone of these reasons I considered
it my duty to send you a despatch on what had
reached my ears.

The envoys of King Antiochus of Commagene [b] 2

CICERO

legati primi mihi nuntiarunt, Parthorum magnas
copias Euphraten transire coepisse. Quo nuntio
allato, cum essent nonnulli, qui ei regi minorem fidem
habendam putarent, statui exspectandum esse, si
quid certius afferretur. A. d. xiii. Kalendas Octobr.
cum exercitum in Ciliciam ducerem, in finibus
Lycaoniae et Cappadociae mihi litterae redditae sunt
a Tarcondimoto, qui fidelissimus socius trans Taurum
amicissimusque populi Romani existimatur; Pacorum,
Orodi, regis Parthorum, filium, cum permagno equitatu Parthico transisse Euphraten, et castra posuisse
Tybae, magnumque tumultum esse in provincia Syria
excitatum. Eodem die ab Iamblicho, phylarcho
Arabum, quem homines opinantur bene sentire ami-
cumque esse reipublicae nostrae, litterae de eisdem
3 rebus mihi redditae sunt. His rebus allatis, etsi
intellegebam socios infirme animatos esse et novarum
rerum exspectatione suspensos, sperabam tamen, eos,
ad quos iam accesseram, quique nostram mansue-
tudinem integritatemque perspexerant, amiciores
populo Romano esse factos ; Ciliciam autem firmiorem fore, si aequitatis nostrae particeps facta
esset. Et ob eam causam, et ut opprimerentur ii,
qui ex Cilicum gente in armis essent, et ut hostis is,
qui esset in Syria, sciret exercitum populi Romani

ᵃ This king, established on his throne by Pompey in 64,
reigned in Mount Amanus. He fought on the side of
Pompey at Pharsalia, and though pardoned by Caesar in 42,
fought for Cassius, and died at Actium, fighting for Antony,
in 31.
ᵇ A doughty warrior who gave much trouble to Rome in
the East ; cf. Hor. Od. iii. 6. 9.
ᶜ Son of Sampsiceramus, with whom he shared the
230

were the first to report to me that large forces of the
Parthians had begun to cross the Euphrates. On
receipt of this report, seeing that there were certain
persons who did not consider that king altogether
to be trusted, I came to the conclusion that I ought
to wait for more definite information. On the 18th
September, as I was marching my army into Cilicia, on
the frontier line between Lycaonia and Cappadocia
I received a despatch from Tarcondimotus,[a] who is regarded as our most loyal ally beyond Mount Taurus,
and the best friend of the Roman people. He reported that Pacorus,[b] son of Orodes, king of the
Parthians, had crossed the Euphrates with a very
strong force of Parthian cavalry, and pitched his
camp at Tyba, and that a serious uprising had been
stirred up in the province of Syria. On the same day I
received a despatch dealing with the same incidents
from Jamblichus,[c] the leading tribesman of the Arabs,
a man who is generally considered to be loyally disposed and friendly to our Republic.

On the receipt of this information, although I fully 3
understood that our allies had no firmly established
opinions, and were wavering in expectation of a revolution, yet I hoped that those whom I had already
approached, and who had had clear proof of my
clemency and probity, had now become more friendly
to the Roman people; and that Cilicia, moreover,
would be confirmed in its loyalty if allowed to share
the fruits of my equitable administration. For
that reason, and also with the intention of crushing
those of the Cilician people who had taken up arms
and of convincing our enemy in Syria that the army

dynasty of Emesa and Arethusa. He was put to death by
Antony just before the battle of Actium.

non modo non cedere his nuntiis allatis, sed etiam
propius accedere, exercitum ad Taurum institui
4 ducere. Sed, si quid apud vos auctoritas mea ponderis
habet, in iis praesertim rebus, quas vos audistis, ego
paene cerno, magno opere vos et hortor et moneo,
ut his provinciis serius vos quidem, quam decuit, sed
aliquando tamen consulatis. Nos quemadmodum
instructos et quibus praesidiis munitos ad tanti belli
opinionem miseritis, non estis ignari ; quod ego
negotium non stultitia obcaecatus, sed verecundia
deterritus, non recusavi. Neque enim umquam ullum
periculum tantum putavi, quod subterfugere mallem,
5 quam vestrae auctoritati obtemperare. Hoc autem
tempore res sese sic habet, ut, nisi exercitum tantum,
quantum ad maximum bellum mittere soletis, mature
in has provincias miseritis, summum periculum sit,
ne amittendae sint omnes hae provinciae, quibus
vectigalia populi Romani continentur. Quamobrem
autem in hoc provinciali delectu spem habeatis aliquam, causa nulla est. Neque multi sunt, et dif-
fugiunt, qui sunt, metu oblato ; et, quod genus hoc
militum sit, iudicavit vir fortissimus M. Bibulus in
Asia, qui, quum vos ei permisissetis delectum habere,
noluerit. Nam sociorum auxilia propter acerbitatem
atque iniurias imperi nostri aut ita imbecilla sunt, ut
non multum nos iuvare possint, aut ita alienata a

of the Roman people, so far from giving way on receiving this intelligence, was actually drawing nearer, I determined to march my army up to Mount Taurus.

But if my authority carries any weight with you 4 (especially in those matters which you know by hearsay only, whereas I have almost ocular demonstration of them), I strongly urge and advise you to take precautions for the safety of these provinces, rather later, it is true, than you should have done, but at all events before it is too late. You are well aware how poorly equipped, and how inadequately safeguarded I was when you despatched me to deal with a war that was expected to be on so great a scale; that responsibility I accepted, not because I was blindly infatuated, but because a sense of honour made me shrink from declining it. For never have I considered any danger so formidable as to desire to shirk it rather than defer to your authority.

At this juncture, however, the situation is such that, 5 unless you speedily despatch to these provinces as powerful an army as it is your practice to despatch to deal with a war of the first importance, there is every danger of our being forced to give up these provinces upon which the revenues of the Roman people depend. But you have no justification at all for basing any hopes upon a levy in this province; there are not many men, and such men as there are scatter at the first approach of danger; and in Asia that very gallant officer, M. Bibulus, has indicated his opinion of this type of soldier by declining to hold a levy when you gave him permission to do so. In fact, owing to the harshness and injustice of Roman rule, the auxiliaries among our allies are either so feeble that they cannot give us much assistance, or else so estranged

nobis, ut neque exspectandum ab iis neque com-
6 mittendum iis quidquam esse videatur. Regis Deio-
tari et voluntatem et copias, quantaecumque sunt,
nostras esse duco. Cappadocia est inanis. Reliqui
reges tyrannique neque opibus satis firmi, nec voluntate sunt. Mihi in hac paucitate militum animus certe
non deerit ; spero, ne consilium quidem. Quid
casurum sit, incertum est. Utinam saluti nostrae
consulere possimus ! Dignitati certe consulemus.

II

M. TULLIUS M. F. CICERO PROCOS. S. P. D.
COSS. PRAETT. TRIBB. PL. SENAT.

Ad Cybistra, a.u.c. 703.

1   S.v.v.b.e.e.e.q.v. Cum pridie Kalend. Sext. in provinciam venissem, neque maturius propter itinerum
et navigationum difficultatem venire potuissem,
maxime convenire officio meo, reique publicae conducere putavi, parare ea, quae ad exercitum, quaeque
ad rem militarem pertinerent. Quae cum essent a
me cura magis et diligentia quam facultate et copia
constituta, nuntiique et litterae de bello a Parthis in
provinciam Syriam illato quotidie fere afferrentur,
iter mihi faciendum per Lycaoniam et per Isauros et

from us that it looks as though we ought neither to expect anything of them nor to entrust anything to their keeping. As to the friendliness and the forces, 6 whatever their strength, of King Deiotarus, I regard them as being on our side. Cappadocia is an empty husk. The other kings and autocrats are not quite to be trusted in respect of either resources or friendliness. As to myself, numerically weak as are my military forces, I shall assuredly not be found wanting in courage, and I hope not in strategy either. What will happen nobody can tell. Pray heaven we may be able to take measures for our safety; for our honour we assuredly shall.

II

M. TULLIUS CICERO, THE PROCONSUL, SENDS GREETINGS
TO THE CONSULS, PRAETORS, TRIBUNES OF THE PLEBS
AND SENATE

Cybistra, September 21 or 22, 51 B.C.

If you are well, all is right; I and the army are 1 well. When I arrived in the province on the last day of July, having failed to arrive earlier on account of the difficulty of travelling both by land and sea, I considered it most consonant with my office and conducive to the public welfare to get ready whatever concerned the army and appertained to military affairs in general. When I had settled all that, more by careful assiduity on my part than with proper means and resources, and when I was almost daily receiving messengers and letters about the war forced upon the province of Syria by the Parthians, I thought it advisable to march my army through Lycaonia, Isauria, and

per Cappadociam arbitratus sum ; erat enim magna
suspicio, Parthos, si ex Syria egredi atque irrumpere
in meam provinciam conarentur, iter eos per Cappadociam, quod ea maxime pateret, esse facturos.
2 Itaque cum exercitu per Cappadociae partem eam,
quae cum Cilicia continens est, iter feci, castraque
ad Cybistra, quod oppidum est ad montem Taurum,
locavi, ut Artavasdes, rex Armenius, quocumque
animo esset, sciret non procul a suis finibus exercitum
populi Romani esse, et Deiotarum, fidelissimum regem
atque amicissimum reipublicae nostrae, maxime coniunctum haberem, cuius et consilio et opibus adiuvari
3 posset respublica. Quo cum in loco castra haberem
equitatumque in Ciliciam misissem, ut et meus adventus iis civitatibus, quae in ea parte essent,
nuntiatus firmiores animos omnium faceret, et ego
mature, quid ageretur in Syria, scire possem, tempus
eius tridui quod in his castris morabar in magno
4 officio et necessario mihi ponendum putavi. Cum
enim vestra auctoritas intercessisset, ut ego regem
Ariobarzanem, Eusebem et Philorhomaeum, tuerer,
eiusque regis salutem, incolumitatem, regnumque
defenderem, regi regnoque praesidio essem, ad-
iunxissetisque, salutem eius regis populo senatui-

---

* A staunch ally of Rome in the Mithridatic wars, he
was rewarded with the title of king, and the addition to his
dominions of Armenia Minor. He fought for Pompey at
Pharsalia, and was deprived by Caesar of part of his dominions, but allowed to retain his regal title. Accused in 45
by his grandson Castor of having plotted against Caesar's
life in Galatia, he was defended by Cicero in his speech
Pro Rege Deiotaro. He died at a great age in 42.
  b Ariobarzanes III., who sided with Pompey against
Caesar, but was generously treated by the latter, and

Cappadocia, as I had strong grounds for suspecting that if the Parthians tried to issue out of Syria and burst their way into my province, they would advance through Cappadocia, as offering least resistance.

I accordingly marched with my army through that 2 part of Cappadocia which adjoins Cilicia, and pitched my camp near Cybistra, a town at the foot of Mount Taurus, so as to let Artavasdes, the king of Armenia, whatever his attitude of mind might be, know that there was an army of the people of Rome not far from his frontier, and so as to have Deiotarus,[a] a most loyal king and the best of friends to our Republic, in close contact with me, so that the Republic might have the assistance of his counsel and resources.

Having encamped at this spot, and having des- 3 patched my cavalry into Cilicia, in order that the announcement of my arrival to the communities in that district might confirm them all in their loyalty, and also that I myself might have early information as to what was going on in Syria, I thought it incumbent upon me to spend the three days of my stay in that camp in the performance of an important and necessary duty.

For since you had intervened with a resolution 4 that I should protect King Ariobarzanes,[b] entitled "Eusebes" and "Philorhomaeus," and defend that monarch's personal safety and the stability of his realm, and in short, safeguard both king and kingdom, and since you had added that the security of that king was a matter of grave anxiety to the people and

opposed the Liberators, but was put to death by Cassius. The titles of Eusebes, "the Dutiful," and Philorhomaeus, "the Lover of Rome," must have been given him by the Pompeian party.

CICERO

que magnae curae esse, quod nullo umquam de rege
decretum esset a nostro ordine, existimavi, me iudicium vestrum ad regem deferre debere eique praesidium meum et fidem et diligentiam polliceri, ut,
cum salus ipsius, incolumitas regni mihi commen-
5 data esset a vobis, diceret, si quid vellet. Quae cum
essem in consilio meo cum rege locutus, initio ille
orationis suae vobis maximas, ut debuit, deinde etiam
mihi gratias egit, quod ei permagnum et perhonori-
ficum videbatur, s.p.q.r. tantae curae esse salutem
suam ; meque tantam diligentiam adhibere, ut et
mea fides et commendationis vestrae auctoritas per-
spici posset. Atque ille primo, quod mihi maximae
laetitiae fuit, ita mecum locutus est, ut nullas insidias
neque vitae suae neque regno diceret se aut intellegere fieri, aut etiam suspicari. Cum ego ei
gratulatus essem, idque me gaudere dixissem, et
tamen adulescentem essem cohortatus, ut recordare-
tur casum illum interitus paterni, et vigilanter se
tueretur, atque admonitu senatus consuleret saluti
suae, tum a me discessit in oppidum Cybistra.
6 Postero autem die cum Ariarathe, fratre suo, et cum
paternis amicis, maioribus natu, ad me in castra venit,
perturbatusque et flens, cum idem et frater faceret

shortly before Cicero arrived in the East.

238

Senate—a decree which had never been passed by our order in reference to any other king—I decided that I was bound to report your pronouncement to the king and promise him my protection and loyalty and devotion, in order that, inasmuch as his personal security and the stability of his kingdom had been entrusted by you to me, he might tell me if he wished to have anything done.

When I had explained all this to the king in 5 the presence of my council, at the beginning of his speech in reply he expressed his profound gratitude to you as in duty bound, and then to me also, because he thought it a very high and significant compliment that the Senate and people of Rome should be so keenly interested in his personal security, and that I too should show such assiduity as to make it impossible to doubt either my own sincerity or the weight of your authority. And, indeed, on this first occasion, his conversation with me was such as to convey the impression (and I was much pleased to hear it) that he neither knew of any plots being hatched against either his life or his kingdom, nor even suspected any. When I had congratulated him and assured him that I was glad of it, and had none the less urged him, young man as he was, not to forget the calamity of his father's assassination,[a] to be vigilant in self-defence and, according to the advice of the Senate, to take measures for his personal security, he left me and returned to the town of Cybistra.

On the following day, however, he visited me in my 6 camp in company with his brother Ariarathes and some elderly men, friends of his father. He was extremely agitated and in tears, as were also his brother and his friends, and fell to imploring the fulfilment of

et amici, meam fidem, vestram commendationem
implorare coepit. Cum admirarer, quid accidisset
novi, dixit ad se indicia manifestarum insidiarum
esse delata, quae essent ante adventum meum
occultata, quod ii, qui ea patefacere possent, propter
metum reticuissent ; eo autem tempore, spe mei
praesidi, complures ea, quae scirent, audacter ad se
detulisse ; in his amantissimum sui, summa pietate
praeditum, fratrem dicere ea, quae is me quoque
audiente dicebat, se sollicitatum esse, ut regnare
vellet ; id vivo fratre suo accipere non potuisse ; se
tamen ante illud tempus eam rem numquam in
medium, propter periculi metum, protulisse. Quae
cum esset locutus, monui regem, ut omnem diligentiam ad se conservandum adhiberet ; amicosque,
patris eius atque avi iudicio probatos, hortatus sum,
regis sui vitam, docti casu acerbissimo patris eius,
7 omni cura custodiaque defenderent. Cum rex a me
equitatum cohortesque de exercitu meo postularet,
etsi intellegebam, vestro senatus consulto non modo
posse me id facere, sed etiam debere, tamen, cum
respublica postularet, propter quotidianos ex Syria
nuntios, ut quam primum exercitum ad Ciliciae fines
adducerem, cumque mihi rex, patefactis iam insidiis, non egere exercitu populi Romani, sed posse
se suis opibus defendere videretur, illum cohortatus

the pledge I had given, and the trust you had imposed upon me. When I wondered what new turn things had taken, he told me " that information of a plot proved beyond doubt had been brought to his ears—information which had been concealed before my arrival because those who might have disclosed it had kept silent about it through fear ; but that now, hoping that I would protect them, several persons had boldly put this knowledge at his disposal, and that among them his brother, who was very fond of him and of a most affectionate disposition, told him (and the brother repeated the words in my hearing) that he had been worked upon to aim at the throne ; that as long as his brother was alive he could not have entertained the suggestion ; and that anyhow he had not until then given publicity to the matter because he dreaded the danger."

When he had thus spoken I advised the king to take every precaution for his own preservation, and I urged his friends, men who had won the considered approbation of his father and grandfather, to protect their king's life with all care and vigilance, warned as they had been by the very tragic fall of his father.

When the king demanded of me some cavalry and 7 cohorts out of my army, although I had no doubt that according to your decree of the Senate I not only had the power to give him them, but that it was even my duty to do so, yet, since the public interests, in view of daily messages from Syria, demanded that I should bring my army as soon as possible into the territory of Cilicia, and as it seemed to me that the king, now that the plot had been revealed, stood in no need of an army of Roman people, but could defend himself with his own resources, I urged him to learn to play

sum, ut in sua vita conservanda primum regnare
disceret ; a quibus perspexisset sibi insidias paratas,
in eos uteretur iure regio ; poena afficeret eos, quos
necesse esset ; reliquos metu liberaret ; praesidio
exercitus mei ad eorum, qui in culpa essent, timorem
potius, quam ad contentionem uteretur ; fore autem,
ut omnes, cum senatusconsultum nossent, intellege-
rent, me regi, si opus esset, ex auctoritate vestra
8 praesidio futurum. Ita confirmato illo, ex eo loco
castra movi, iter in Ciliciam facere institui, cum
hac opinione e Cappadocia discederem, ut consilio
vestro, casu incredibili ac paene divino, regem, quem
vos honorificentissime appellassetis, nullo postulante,
quemque meae fidei commendassetis, et cuius salutem
magnae vobis curae esse decrevissetis, meus adventus praesentibus insidiis liberarit. Quod ad vos
a me scribi non alienum putavi, ut intellegeretis ex
iis, quae paene acciderunt, vos multo ante, ne ea
acciderent, providisse ; eoque vos studiosius feci
certiores, quod in rege Ariobarzane ea mihi signa
videor virtutis, ingeni, fidei, benevolentiaeque erga
vos perspexisse, ut non sine causa tantam curam
diligentiamque in eius vos salutem videamini contulisse.

the part of king by first of all ensuring the preservation of his own life ; to exercise his royal rights upon those by whom he was now convinced that the plot against him had been concocted ; to punish those whom it was essential to punish, and relieve the fears of the rest ; to take advantage of the protection of my army to intimidate those who were to blame rather than to foster strife ; assuring him at the same time that all his subjects, on ascertaining the decree of the Senate, would understand that according to your resolution I should be there, if the need arose, to protect the king.

Having encouraged him so far, I struck camp from 8 there, and began my march into Cilicia, leaving Cappadocia with this impression upon my mind, that thanks to your policy, by a wonderful and almost providential accident, a king upon whom you had spontaneously and in the most complimentary manner conferred that title, a king whom you had entrusted to my protection, a king whose personal safety you had declared by your decree to be a source of serious anxiety to yourselves, has been delivered from an imminent conspiracy by my arrival on the scene. This much I thought it not irrelevant for me to write to you, so that you might gather from what has nearly happened that you had provided long before against its happening ; and I have all the more pleasure in informing you, because I believe I have discerned in King Ariobarzanes such evidence of moral worth, capacity, good faith and friendly feeling for you, as to make it seem that you have good reason for having bestowed so much care and attention upon his welfare.

CICERO

III

M. T. C. S. D. M. CATONI

In castris ad Iconium, a.u.c. 703.

1 Cum ad me legati, missi ab Antiocho Commageno, venissent in castra ad Iconium a. d. iii. Kal. Septembr., iique mihi nuntiassent, regis Parthorum filium, quocum esset nupta regis Armeniorum soror, ad Euphraten cum maximis Parthorum copiis multarumque praeterea gentium magna manu venisse, Euphratenque iam transire coepisse, dicique Armenium regem in Cappadociam impetum esse facturum, putavi, pro nostra necessitudine, me hoc ad te scri-
2 bere oportere. Publice propter duas causas nihil scripsi ; quod et ipsum Commagenum legati dicebant ad senatum statim nuntios litterasque misisse, et existimabam, M. Bibulum proconsulem, qui circiter Idus Sextiles ab Epheso in Syriam navibus profectus erat, quod secundos ventos habuisset, iam in provinciam suam pervenisse ; cuius litteris omnia certiora perlatum iri ad senatum putabam. Mihi, ut in huiusmodi re tantoque bello, maximae curae est, ut, quae copiis et opibus tenere vix possimus, ea mansuetudine et continentia nostra, sociorum fidelitate teneamus. Tu velim, ut consuesti, nos absentes diligas et defendas.

---

^a Cato had returned from Cyprus in 56, and was now in Rome.

III

CICERO TO M. CATO [a]

Camp at Iconium, August 28, 51 B.C.

Ambassadors sent to me by Antiochus of Comma- 1
gene having arrived at my camp near Iconium on the
28th August, and having reported to me that the son
of the king of the Parthians, whom the sister of the
king of the Armenians had married, had reached the
banks of the Euphrates with very large Parthian
forces and a large army of many other nations besides,
and that it was said that the Armenian king intended
making an attack upon Cappadocia, I thought that,
considering our intimate connexion, it was incumbent
upon me to send you this letter.

I sent no public despatch for two reasons, because 2
the ambassadors told me that the Commagenian himself had immediately sent messengers with a despatch
to the Senate, and because I thought that the proconsul, M. Bibulus, who had set out from Ephesus to
Syria by sea about the 13th of August, having found the
winds in his favour, had already arrived in his province,
and I supposed that his despatches would convey more
definite information on all points to the Senate. For
myself, in view of the present situation, and the
gravity of the war, my chief concern is to secure by
my leniency and moderation and by the fidelity of the
allies what I am scarcely strong enough to secure
with the forces at my disposal. I would have you, on
your part, show your regard for me and defend me,
as you have always done, in my absence.

IV

M. T. C. IMP. S. D. M. CATONI

Tarsi, A.U.C. 704.

1 Summa tua auctoritas fecit, meumque perpetuum
de tua singulari virtute iudicium, ut magni mea
interesse putarem, et res eas, quas gessissem, tibi
notas esse, et non ignorari a te, qua aequitate et
continentia tuerer socios provinciamque administra-
rem. His enim a te cognitis, arbitrabar facilius me
2 tibi, quae vellem, probaturum. Cum in provinciam
pridie Kal. Sext. venissem, et propter anni tempus
ad exercitum mihi confestim esse eundum viderem,
biduum Laodiceae fui, deinde Apameae quatriduum,
triduum Synnadis, totidem dies Philomeli. Quibus
in oppidis cum magni conventus fuissent, multas
civitates acerbissimis tributis et gravissimis usuris et
falso aere alieno liberavi. Cumque ante adventum
meum seditione quadam exercitus esset dissipatus,
quinque cohortes sine legato, sine tribuno militum,
denique etiam sine centurione ullo apud Philomelium
consedissent, reliquus exercitus esset in Lycaonia,
M. Anneio legato imperavi, ut eas quinque cohortes
ad reliquum exercitum duceret, coactoque in unum
locum exercitu, castra in Lycaonia apud Iconium
3 faceret. Quod cum ab illo diligenter esset actum,

---

[a] Laodicea was on the coast of Syria, about 50 miles
south of Antioch ; Apamea on the banks of the Maeander
in Phrygia ; Synnada in the north of Phrygia Salutaris ;
and Philomelium in Phrygia Parorius, on the borders of
Lycaonia and Pisidia, also mentioned in iii. 8. 5. 6.
[b] See the Introductory note to this Book.

IV

CICERO TO M. CATO

Tarsus, January, 50 B.C.

Your supreme influence and my own unwavering 1
opinion of your exceptional merit have given me the
impression that it is greatly to my interest not only
that you should be cognisant of my past achievements,
but also that you should not be ignorant of the fair
dealing and moderation that have characterized my
protection of our allies and my administration of this
province. For if these facts were brought to your
knowledge, I thought I should find it easier to win
your approbation of what I proposed to do.

When I entered my province on the last day of July 2
and saw that the season of the year necessitated my
joining the army without delay, I spent two days at
Laodicea, then four days at Apamea, three days at
Synnada and as many at Philomelium.[a] Having held
important assizes at all those towns, I succeeded in
delivering a large number of communities from very
harsh taxation, exorbitant interest, and fraudulent
debt-claims. And finding that, prior to my arrival,
the army had been scattered by what I may almost
call a mutiny and that five cohorts, without a *legatus*,
without a military tribune, and (would you believe it?)
without even a single centurion, had bivouacked at
Philomelium, while the rest of the army was in Lycaonia, I ordered my *legatus*, M. Anneius,[b] to bring those
five cohorts to join the rest of the army, and after con-
centrating the army in one spot, to pitch his camp at
Iconium in Lycaonia.

When he had punctiliously carried out that order, I 3

247

ego in castra a. d. vii. Kal. Septemb. veni, cum
interea superioribus diebus ex senatusconsulto et
evocatorum firmam manum, et equitatum sane
idoneum, et populorum liberorum regumque sociorum
auxilia voluntaria comparavissem. Interim cum,
exercitu lustrato, iter in Ciliciam facere coepissem,
iii. Kal. Septemb. legati, a rege Commageno ad me
missi, pertumultuose, neque tamen non vere, Parthos
4 in Syriam transisse nuntiaverunt. Quo audito, vehementer sum commotus cum de Syria, tum de mea
provincia, de reliqua denique Asia. Itaque exercitum
mihi ducendum per Cappadociae regionem eam, quae
Ciliciam attingeret, putavi. Nam si me in Ciliciam
demisissem, Ciliciam quidem ipsam propter montis
Amani naturam facile tenuissem (duo sunt enim
aditus in Ciliciam ex Syria, quorum uterque parvis
praesidiis propter angustias intercludi potest, nec est
quidquam Cilicia contra Syriam munitius) ; sed me
Cappadocia movebat, quae patet a Syria regesque
habet finitimos, qui, etiamsi sunt amici nobis, tamen
aperte Parthis inimici esse non audent. Itaque in
Cappadocia extrema non longe a Tauro apud oppidum
Cybistra castra feci, ut et Ciliciam tuerer et, Cappadociam tenens, nova finitimorum consilia impedirem.
5 Interea in hoc tanto motu tantaque exspectatione
maximi belli rex Deiotarus, cui non sine causa
plurimum semper et meo et tuo et senatus iudicio

myself arrived at the camp on Aug. 24th, having meanwhile, according to the decree of the Senate, got together during the preceding days a trustworthy body of reserves, a quite adequate corps of cavalry, and volunteer auxiliaries from the free peoples and the allied kings. Meantime, when, after reviewing the army, I had begun my march into Cilicia, on Aug. 28th some envoys sent to me by the king of Commagene reported, in a terrible state of agitation, but not without some truth, that the Parthians had crossed over into Syria.

On hearing this I was greatly disturbed about 4 Syria as well as about my province, and in short about the rest of Asia ; so I thought it necessary to march my army through that district of Cappadocia which touches on Cilicia ; for had I once descended into Cilicia, it is true that I should easily have held Cilicia itself, because of the natural advantage of Mt. Amanus—for there are two approaches to Cilicia from Syria, either of which is so narrow that it can be closed by quite a small garrison, and Cilicia is the best possible fortification against Syria—but on the other hand, I was concerned about Cappadocia, which lies open to Syria and has on its frontiers kings who, though they are secretly on friendly terms with us, yet do not dare to show overt hostility to the Parthians. I therefore encamped in the extreme south of Cappadocia, not far from Mt. Taurus, at the town of Cybistra, so as to protect Cilicia, and at the same time, by holding Cappadocia, to check any fresh designs on the part of the border tribes.

Meanwhile, amid all this commotion and excited 5 anticipation of a very serious war, King Deiotarus, to whose merits I and you and the Senate have always,

tributum est, vir cum benevolentia et fide erga
populum Romanum singulari, tum praestanti magnitudine et animi et consili, legatos ad me misit, se
cum omnibus suis copiis in mea castra esse venturum.
Cuius ego studio officioque commotus egi ei per
litteras gratias, idque ut maturaret, hortatus sum.
6 Cum autem ad Cybistra propter rationem belli
quinque dies essem moratus, regem Ariobarzanem,
cuius salutem a senatu te auctore commendatam
habebam, praesentibus insidiis necopinantem liberavi ; neque solum ei saluti fui, sed etiam curavi, ut
cum auctoritate regnaret. Metram, et eum, quem
tu diligenter mihi commendaras, Athenaeum, im-
portunitate Athenaidis exsilio multatos, in maxima
apud regem auctoritate gratiaque constitui. Cumque magnum bellum in Cappadocia concitaretur, si
sacerdos armis se, quod facturus putabatur, defenderet, adulescens et equitatu et peditatu et pecunia
paratus, ego tuto[1] iis, qui novari aliquid volebant,
perfeci, ut e regno ille discederet, rexque sine tumultu ac sine armis, omni auctoritate aulae com-
7 munita, regnum cum dignitate obtineret. Interea
cognovi multorum litteris atque nuntiis, magnas
Parthorum copias atque Arabum ad oppidum An-
tiochiam accessisse, magnumque eorum equitatum,
qui in Ciliciam transsisset, ab equitum meorum turmis

[1] ego tuto *is Tyrrell's convincing emendation* : actutum
Nobbe, et alii alia.

---

[a] The queen-mother, daughter of Mithridates the Great.
[b] The chief priest of the temple of Comana, said to have
been dedicated by Orestes to Artemis Taurica. The priest's
authority in Cappadocia was second only to that of the king.
250

and not without reason, paid the fullest tribute, a man remarkable for his friendliness and fidelity to the people of Rome, as well as for his conspicuous gallantry and sagacity—Deiotarus, I say, sent me an embassy to the effect that he would join me in my camp with all his forces. Profoundly moved by his devotion and courtesy, I expressed my gratitude to him by letter and urged him to hasten the fulfilment of his offer.

When, however, my plan of campaign compelled 6 me to stay for five days near Cybistra, I delivered King Ariobarzanes, whose safety had been entrusted to me by the Senate at your instance, from an imminent plot of which he was not aware, and I not only saved his life, but also took pains to establish his authority as king. Metras and that very Athenaeus whom you yourself had particularly commended to me, punished with banishment as they both had been by the ruthless hostility of Athenais,[a] were established by me in a position of the highest influence and favour with the king. And seeing that a serious war was being stirred up in Cappadocia in the event of the priest,[b] a young man well equipped with horse and foot and funds, defending himself with arms (and he was thought likely to do so), without compromising those who were bent upon a revolution, I contrived that the priest should leave the kingdom, and that the king without riot and without recourse to arms, and with the full authority of the court safeguarded, should remain in dignified possession of his kingdom.

Meanwhile I was informed by written and oral 7 messages from many quarters that strong forces of Parthians and Arabs had approached the town of Antioch, and that a large body of their cavalry which had crossed over into Cilicia had been cut to pieces by

et a cohorte praetoria, quae erat Epiphaneae praesidi
causa, occidione occisum. Quare cum viderem a
Cappadocia Parthorum copias aversas non longe a
finibus esse Ciliciae, quam potui maximis itineribus
ad Amanum exercitum duxi. Quo ut veni, hostem
ab Antiochia recessisse, Bibulum Antiochiae esse
cognovi ; Deiotarumque confestim, iam ad me venien-
tem cum magno et firmo equitatu et peditatu, et cum
omnibus suis copiis, certiorem feci, non videri esse
causam, cur abesset a regno, meque ad eum, si quid
novi forte accidisset, statim litteras nuntiosque mis-
8 surum esse. Cumque eo animo venissem, ut utrique
provinciae, si ita tempus ferret, subvenirem, tum id
quod iam ante statueram, vehementer interesse
utriusque provinciae, pacare Amanum et perpetuum
hostem ex eo monte tollere, agere perrexi. Cumque
me discedere ab eo monte simulassem, et alias partes
Ciliciae petere, abessemque ab Amano iter unius diei,
et castra apud Epiphaneam fecissem, a. d. quartum
Idus Octobres, cum advesperasceret, expedito exercitu ita noctu iter feci, ut a. d. tertium Idus Octobres,
cum lucisceret, in Amanum ascenderem, distributis-
que cohortibus et auxiliis, cum aliis Q. frater,
legatus, mecum simul, aliis C. Pomptinus, legatus,
reliquis M. Anneius et L. Tullius, legati, praeessent,
plerosque nec opinantes oppressimus, qui occisi capti-

---

[a] On the S.E. border of Cilicia, probably so called after
its restoration by Antiochus Epiphanes.

[b] See the Introductory note to this Book.

some squadrons of my horse and a praetorian cohort which was on garrison duty at Epiphanea.[a] Seeing therefore that the Parthian forces having been headed off from Cappadocia were not far from the frontiers of Cilicia, I marched my army, covering as much ground as I could by forced marches, to Amanus. When I got there I received the intelligence that the enemy had retired from Antioch, and that Bibulus was there ; so I informed Deiotarus, who was by this time hurrying to join me with a large and strong body of horse and foot and all his available forces, that I did not think there was any reason why he should absent himself from his kingdom, and that if perchance anything fresh occurred, I would immediately communicate with him by letter and messengers.

Having arrived with the intention of coming to the 8 aid of each of the two provinces, should circumstances necessitate it, I then proceeded to perform a task which I had some time previously decided was of paramount importance to both provinces—the pacification of Amanus and the dislodging from that mountain of a perpetual foe. Having made a feint of leaving that mount, and directing my attention to other parts of Cilicia, when I was one day's march from Amanus and had pitched my camp near Epiphanea on the 12th of October, as the evening was drawing in, with a lightly equipped army I covered so much ground by a night march that, as the dawn was breaking on the 13th, I was making my way up Amanus. When I had duly disposed my cohorts and auxiliaries, some being commanded by my brother Quintus, my *legatus*, and myself, others by C. Pomptinus, and the rest by M. Anneius and L. Tullius, all three my *legati*,[b] we surprised and crushed the greater number of them, who

que sunt, interclusi fuga. Eranam autem, quae fuit
non vici instar, sed urbis, quod erat Amani caput,
itemque Sepyram et Commorin, acriter et diu re-
pugnantes, Pomptino illam partem Amani tenente,
ex antelucano tempore usque ad horam diei decimam,
magna multitudine hostium occisa, cepimus, castella-
9 que vi[1] capta complura incendimus. His rebus ita
gestis, castra in radicibus Amani habuimus apud Aras
Alexandri quatriduum, et in reliquiis Amani de-
lendis agrisque vastandis, quae pars eius montis
meae provinciae est, id tempus omne consumpsimus.
10 Confectis his rebus, ad oppidum Eleutherocilicum
Pindenissum exercitum abduxi ; quod cum esset
altissimo et munitissimo loco, ab iisque incoleretur,
qui ne regibus quidem umquam paruissent, cum et
fugitivos reciperent, et Parthorum adventum acerrime exspectarent, ad existimationem imperi pertinere arbitratus sum comprimere eorum audaciam ;
quo facilius etiam ceterorum animi, qui alieni essent
ab imperio nostro, frangerentur. Vallo et fossa
circumdedi ; sex castellis, castrisque maximis sepsi ;
aggere, vineis, turribus oppugnavi ; ususque tor-
mentis multis, multis sagittariis, magno labore meo,
sine ulla molestia sumptuve sociorum, septimo quin-
quagesimo die rem confeci : ut, omnibus partibus

---

[1] *Madvig* : sex (vi) MSS.

---

[a] Near Issus, in the S.E. extremity of Cilicia. See ii. 10. 3.
[b] Pindenissus was a town on a spur of Mt. Amanus.

were killed or captured, being cut off from flight. Erana, moreover, which was not so much a village as a city in size, and the capital of Amanus, and also Sepyra and Commoris, though the inhabitants offered a stout and prolonged resistance from before dawn to four in the afternoon (Pomptinus occupying that part of Amanus), after a large number of the enemy had fallen, were taken by us ; and we carried by assault and set fire to several fortresses.

Having thus completed these operations, we stayed 9 in camp for four days near the Altars of Alexander,[a] and all that time we spent in effacing the last traces of Amanus, and ravaging the lands on that part of the mountain which is included in my province.

When this was finished I marched my army off to 10 Pindenissus,[b] a town of the Eleutherocilices ; and because the town was on a very elevated and strongly fortified site, and was inhabited by men who had never submitted even to the kings, and not only harboured fugitives but were also looking forward with the utmost eagerness to the coming of the Parthians, I considered it of importance to the prestige of the Empire that I should put a stop to their audacity ; and this would make it all the easier to break the spirit of all the other tribes who showed hostility to our rule.

I surrounded the town with a stockade and trench; I fenced it in with six forts and extensive encampments ; I attacked it with earthworks, mantlets, and towers, and by means of a large number of catapults and a strong force of bowmen, with no little personal exertion, without causing any trouble or expense to our allies, I completed the operation in fifty-seven days, so that when every quarter of the city had been

255

urbis disturbatis aut incensis, compulsi in potestatem
meam pervenirent. His erant finitimi pari scelere et
audacia Tebarani ; ab his, Pindenisso capto, obsides
accepi ; exercitum in hiberna dimisi. Q. fratrem
negotio praeposui, ut in vicis aut captis aut male
11 pacatis exercitus collocaretur. Nunc velim tibi sic
persuadeas, si de his rebus ad senatum relatum sit,
me existimaturum summam mihi laudem tributam, si
tu honorem meum sententia tua comprobaris. Idque,
etsi talibus de rebus gravissimos homines et rogare
solere et rogari scio, tamen admonendum potius te a
me, quam rogandum puto. Tu es enim is, qui me
tuis sententiis saepissime ornasti, qui oratione, qui
praedicatione, qui summis laudibus in senatu, in
concionibus ad caelum extulisti, cuius ego semper
tanta esse verborum pondera putavi, ut uno verbo
tuo, cum mea laude coniuncto, omnia assequi me
arbitrarer. Te denique memini, cum cuidam claris-
simo atque optimo viro supplicationem non de-
cerneres, dicere, te decreturum, si referretur ob eas
res, quas is consul in urbe gessisset. Tu idem mihi
supplicationem decrevisti togato, non ut multis, re-

<a> Distinguished senators "recorded their votes" by
making a speech, as opposed to those "*qui pedibus in
sententiam ibant.*"

<b> The consul referred to is no doubt Lentulus Spinther,
whose application for a *supplicatio* was opposed by Cato,
who said he would support it if it were on the grounds of
Lentulus's services to the State in advocating Cicero's recall
as consul in 57. See note *a* to i. 1.

either dismantled or burnt, they were driven to extremities and surrendered to me unconditionally. Their next neighbours were the inhabitants of Tebara, as ruffianly and daring as themselves ; from these, on the capture of Pindenissus, I received hostages, and then I dismissed my troops to their winter quarters. I put my brother Quintus in command, to arrange that the army should be stationed in villages that had either been taken or not completely quelled.

And now I would have you assure yourself, that, 11 should these matters be brought before the Senate, I shall consider myself the recipient of the highest possible encomium if any honour offered me meets with the approval of your vote. And as regards that, although in connexion with such matters I am well aware that even men of the greatest weight often both make and have to listen to requests, still I think that what I ought to do in your case is merely to remind you rather than address you a request. For you are the man who has so repeatedly complimented me in recording your vote,[a] who, in conversation, in public commendation, in the very high eulogies spoken in the Senate and in public meetings, has extolled me to the skies ; you are he, the weight of whose words I have ever so respected as to feel that a single word of yours, if spoken in my praise, fulfilled all my aspirations. It was you, yes, you who, when declining to vote for a *supplicatio* in honour of a certain most illustrious and excellent person, declared, I remember, that you would vote for it, if only the motion were confined to what that person had done in the city in the days of his consulship.[b] It was you also who voted for a *supplicatio* in my honour when a mere civilian, not, as in many cases "for sound administration of the

publica bene gesta, sed, ut nemini, republica con-
12 servata. Mitto, quod invidiam, quod pericula, quod
omnes meas tempestates et subieris, et multo etiam
magis, si per me licuisset, subire paratissimus fueris,
quod denique inimicum meum tuum inimicum putaris ; cuius etiam interitum, ut facile intellegerem,
mihi quantum tribueres, Milonis causa in senatu
defendenda, approbaris. A me autem haec sunt
profecta, quae ego in benefici loco non pono, sed in
veri testimoni atque iudici, ut praestantissimas tuas
virtutes non tacitus admirarer (quis enim in te id
non facit ?) sed in omnibus orationibus, sententiis
dicendis, causis agendis, omnibus scriptis, Graecis,
Latinis, omni denique varietate litterarum mearum,
te non modo iis, quos vidissemus, sed iis, de quibus
13 audissemus, omnibus anteferrem. Quaeres fortasse,
quid sit, quod ego hoc nescio quid gratulationis et
honoris a senatu tanti aestimem. Agam iam tecum
familiariter, ut est et studiis et officiis nostris mutuis
et summa amicitia dignum, et necessitudine etiam
paterna. Si quisquam fuit umquam remotus et
natura, et magis etiam, ut mihi quidem sentire
videor, ratione atque doctrina, ab inani laude et
sermonibus vulgi, ego profecto is sum. Testis est
consulatus meus, in quo, sicut in reliqua vita, fateor

---

a Clodius.

Republic," but, as in no other single case, " for having preserved the Republic."

I pass over the fact that you not only faced the un- 12 popularity, the perils, and the brunt of the storms that broke upon me, but were also perfectly ready to go even further, much further, in facing them, had I permitted it ; the fact, in short, that you regarded my enemy *a* as an enemy to yourself, and that, by pleading the cause of Milo in the Senate, you showed your approval of even that enemy's death, so that I could easily recognize your high appreciation of me. What I have done on my side however—and I do not classify it under the head of favours conferred, but under that of true testimony and deliberate opinion— amounts to this, that in my admiration of your outstanding merits (and who does not admire them ?) I have not been silent, but in all my speeches, both in the Senate and at the bar, in all my writings, Greek or Latin, in short, in all my various literary works, I have ranked you not only above all whom I ever met, but above all of whom I ever heard.

You will perhaps ask why it is that I so highly prize 13 this undefinable something in the way of congratulation and honour that I look for from the Senate. Well, I shall now talk to you in a familiar way, as befits our common tastes, our mutual good offices, our sincere friendship, and also the close intimacy of our fathers.

If ever there was a man who by natural disposition, and even more, as I seem to feel, by reasoned judgment and education, stood aloof from empty plaudits and vulgar talk, that man is assuredly myself. Witness my consulship, in the course of which, as in the rest of my life, I admit that I eagerly pursued what-

ea me studiose secutum, ex quibus vera gloria nasci
posset; ipsam quidem gloriam per se numquam putavi
expetendam. Itaque et provinciam ornatam et spem
non dubiam triumphi neglexi. Sacerdotium denique,
cum (quemadmodum te existimare arbitror) non
difficillime consequi possem, non appetivi. Idem
post iniuriam acceptam (quam tu reipublicae calamitatem semper appellas, meam non modo non calamitatem, sed etiam gloriam), studui quam ornatissima
senatus populique Romani de me iudicia intercedere.
Itaque et augur postea fieri volui, quod antea
neglexeram, et eum honorem, qui a senatu tribui
rebus bellicis solet, neglectum a me olim, nunc mihi
14 expetendum puto. Huic meae voluntati, in qua
inest aliqua vis desideri ad sanandum vulnus iniuriae,
ut faveas adiutorque sis, quod paullo ante me negaram
rogaturum, vehementer te rogo, sed ita, si non
ieiunum hoc nescio quid, quod ego gessi, et con-
temnendum videbitur, sed tale atque tantum, ut
multi, nequaquam paribus rebus, honores summos
a senatu consecuti sint. Equidem etiam mihi illud
animum advertisse videor (scis enim, quam attente
te audire soleam), te non tam res gestas, quam mores,

ᵃ *i.e.*, the augurate. Cicero might have accepted the
augurate in 59 had it been offered him, but he did not ask
for it. He was elected augur in 53, in the place of Crassus,
killed at Carrhae.
  ᵇ His banishment in 58.
  ᶜ *i.e.*, a triumph.

ever might be a source of true glory ; glory, in and for
itself, I have never thought worth the seeking. So I
shut my eyes to the lure of a province with all its
official appanages, and, by so doing, to the certain
hope of a triumph. And finally, as to the priesthood,[a]
although I might have obtained it without much
difficulty (and that I believe is your opinion also), I
never applied for it. And yet, for all that, after
the injustice I had suffered [b]—an injustice which you
always refer to as a degradation to the State, though
not only no degradation, but even an honour, to myself—I was anxious that there should follow decisions
of the Senate and Roman people regarding myself
of the most distinguished character. And so I subsequently set my heart on what I had previously
regarded with indifference—my election as augur ;
and furthermore, as to the honour [c] usually conferred
by the Senate for services in the field, though I never
troubled about it in the old days, I now think I
should make an effort to secure it.

Mingled with this aspiration of mine is a sort of in- 14
tense longing to heal the wound I suffered in the injustice done me ; and I earnestly beg of you (as a
moment ago I declared I never would) to give it your
countenance and support, but only if you think that
whatever this achievement of mine may have been, it
was not meagre and contemptible, but such in quality
and extent that many, whose exploits were by no
means comparable with mine, have obtained the
highest honours from the Senate. This too I seem to
have noticed (and you know how attentively I listen
to you), that in the award or non-award of honours, it
is not the achievements themselves that it is your
practice to keep before your eyes so much as the

CICERO

instituta, atque vitam imperatorum spectare solere
in habendis aut non habendis honoribus. Quod si in
mea causa considerabis, reperies, me exercitu im-
becillo, contra metum maximi belli, firmissimum
praesidium habuisse aequitatem et continentiam. His
ego subsidiis ea sum consecutus, quae nullis legionibus
consequi potuissem, ut ex alienissimis sociis amicissimos, ex infidelissimis firmissimos redderem,
animosque novarum rerum exspectatione suspensos
15 ad veteris imperi benevolentiam traducerem. Sed
nimis haec multa de me, praesertim ad te, a quo uno
omnium sociorum querellae audiuntur ; cognosces ex
iis, qui meis institutis se recreatos putant. Cumque
omnes uno prope consensu de me apud te ea, quae
mihi optatissima sunt, praedicabunt, tum duae maximae clientelae tuae, Cyprus insula et Cappadociae
regnum, tecum de me loquentur, puto etiam regem
Deiotarum, qui uni tibi est maxime necessarius.
Quae si etiam maiora sunt, et in omnibus saeculis
pauciores viri reperti sunt, qui suas cupiditates, quam
qui hostium copias vincerent, est profecto tuum,
cum ad res bellicas haec, quae rariora et difficiliora
sunt, genera virtutis adiunxeris, ipsas etiam illas res
16 gestas illustriores[1] et maiores putare. Extremum
illud est, ut, quasi diffidens rogationi meae, philo-

___

[1] *Manutius*: iustiores *Nobbe and* mss.

[a] He refers to his success in winning over the province by
his wisdom and moderation, which he says is something
greater than mere military success, but which, if combined
with military success, should so enhance the value of that
success as to make it worthy of a triumph.

character, principles, and everyday life of the commanders. And if you consider my case in like manner,
you will find that, weak as my army was, I found my
strongest safeguard against the threat of a most
serious war in my fair-dealing and moderation.
With these forces to aid me, I succeeded, where no
legions could have enabled me to succeed, in convert-
ing the most disaffected allies into the most devoted,
the most disloyal into the most trustworthy, and in
bringing back hearts that wavered in anticipation of a
change of rule into a feeling of friendliness for the old
régime.

But this is too much about myself, especially in 15
writing to you, the one and only man who gives ear to
the complaints of all our allies ; you will learn all
about it from those who attribute their restoration to
life to my administration. And not only will everybody almost with one consent make such remarks
about me in your hearing as are all I could pray for,
but also two of your largest client-communities, the
island of Cyprus and the kingdom of Cappadocia,
will speak to you about me ; and so too, I fancy, will
King Deiotarus, who is more attached to you than to
any man alive.

And if all this is something of greater importance,[a] and if throughout the ages fewer men have
been found who could conquer their own desires than
could conquer the enemy's forces, you are surely
bound, when you have added these rarer and more
difficult forms of moral excellence to success on the
field, to regard that very success itself as being enhanced in distinction and consequence.

My last resource is this—to send you, as if distrust- 16
ing my own appeal, a representative to plead for me—

263

CICERO

sophiam ad te allegem, qua nec mihi carior ulla umquam res in vita fuit, nec hominum generi maius a
dis munus ullum est datum. Haec igitur, quae mihi
tecum communis est, societas studiorum atque artium
nostrarum, quibus a pueritia dediti ac devincti, soli
propemodum nos philosophiam illam veram et anti-
quam, quae quibusdam oti esse ac desidiae videtur,
in forum atque in rempublicam atque in ipsam aciem
paene deduximus, tecum agit de mea laude, cui
negari a Catone fas esse non puto. Quamobrem tibi
sic persuadeas velim, si mihi tua sententia tributus
honos ex meis litteris fuerit, me sic existimaturum,
cum auctoritate tua, tum benevolentia erga me,
mihi quod maxime cupierim contigisse. Vale.

V

M. CATO S. P. D. M. T. C. IMP.

Romae, a.u.c. 704.

1 Quod et respublica me et nostra amicitia hortatur,
libenter facio, ut tuam virtutem, innocentiam, diligentiam, cognitam in maximis rebus domi togati,
armati foris pari industria administrari gaudeam.
Itaque, quod pro meo iudicio facere potui, ut innocentia consilioque tuo defensam provinciam, servatum

---

ª This letter is an answer to the last. Cato voted against
the motion for a *supplicatio* in Cicero's honour, though he
proposed a complimentary vote, and here gives his reasons
for doing so. For this and the two following letters see the
Introductory Note to this Book.

264

none other than philosophy, than which nothing in life has ever been more precious to myself, no greater boon ever bestowed by the gods upon mankind. That partnership then which we share in our pursuits and attainments, to which we have so strictly bound and devoted ourselves from boyhood that we stand practically alone in having introduced that true philosophy of the ancients, regarded by some as the hobby of the leisured and indolent, into the forum, into political life, yes, almost into the field of battle itself—that partnership, I say, now pleads with you the cause of my renown, and it is, to me, unthinkable that the plea should not be accepted by a Cato. I would, therefore, have you assure yourself of this, that if in consequence of my despatch that honour is conferred upon me by your vote, I shall consider it is due to your influence combined with your goodwill that I have been blessed with the attainment of my heart's desire. Farewell.

V

M. CATO TO CICERO [a]

Rome, end of April, 50 B.C.

It is a pleasure to me to do what both the public 1 interests and our friendship prompt me to do—to rejoice, I mean, that the courage, integrity, and energy you have already evinced as a civilian in the gravest crisis of your career at home are now being applied with equal assiduity to your military command abroad. What therefore I could conscientiously do, that I did ; that is to say, I extolled by speech and vote the integrity and judgment you have shown in protecting a

Ariobarzanis cum ipso rege regnum, sociorum
revocatam ad studium imperi nostri voluntatem,
2 sententia mea et decreto laudarem, feci. Supplicationem decretam, si tu, qua in re nihil fortuito, sed
summa tua ratione et continentia, reipublicae provisum est, dis immortalibus gratulari nos, quam tibi
referre acceptum mavis, gaudeo. Quod si triumphi
praerogativam putas supplicationem, et idcirco casum
potius, quam te laudari mavis, neque supplicationem
sequitur semper triumphus, et triumpho multo clarius
est, senatum iudicare, potius mansuetudine et innocentia imperatoris provinciam, quam vi militum aut
benignitate deorum retentam atque conservatam
3 esse ; quod ego mea sententia censebam. Atque
haec ego idcirco ad te contra consuetudinem meam
pluribus scripsi, ut, quod maxime volo, existimes me
laborare, ut tibi persuadeam me et voluisse de tua
maiestate, quod amplissimum sim arbitratus, et quod
tu maluisti, factum esse gaudere. Vale, et nos dilige,
et instituto itinere severitatem diligentiamque sociis
et reipublicae praesta.

a This is surely the bitterest sarcasm, which Cicero either
does not see, or wisely ignores. Cato plainly insinuates that
Cicero, while posing as a pious man, profoundly grateful to
the gods (for *casus* here is synonymous with *di immortales*
above), has his eye all the time on the triumph that he thinks
will follow, *i.e.*, on his own personal advancement, and
nothing else.

province, in saving the kingdom and person of King Ariobarzanes, and in winning back the hearts of our allies to an enthusiastic acceptance of our rule.

As to the *supplicatio* having been decreed, if, in a 2 matter wherein the interests of the State were secured not in any degree by chance, but by your own consummate statesmanship and self-restraint, you yourself prefer that we should render thanks to the immortal gods, rather than credit you with that success —well then I am glad of it. But if you imagine that a *supplicatio* is a sure earnest of a triumph, and if that be your reason for wishing good luck to get all the praise rather than yourself,[a] let me tell you that a triumph does not invariably follow a *supplicatio*, and that it is a much more splendid thing than any triumph to have the deliberate declaration of the Senate that the retention and preservation of the province was due to the gentle rule and probity of its commander, rather than to military force or the favour of heaven ; and that was my conviction when I recorded my vote.

Now my reason for having written to you at such 3 length in defiance of my usual practice is to induce you to believe (and I am most anxious you should) that I am making every effort to convince you of two facts—that I gave my support to that course which I considered most effectively conducive to your honour, and that at the same time I rejoice at the adoption of the course you personally preferred.

Farewell, and maintain your esteem for me, and, following the path upon which you have entered, assure to the allies and the Republic the continuance of your strict devotion to duty.

CICERO

VI

Rhodi, A.U.C. 704.

1 *Laetus sum laudari me,*

inquit Hector, opinor, apud Naevium,

abs te, pater, a laudato viro.

Ea est enim profecto iucunda laus, quae ab iis pro-
ficiscitur, qui ipsi in laude vixerunt. Ego vero vel
gratulatione litterarum tuarum, vel testimoniis sententiae dictae, nihil est, quod me non assecutum
putem. Idque mihi cum amplissimum, tum gratissimum est, te libenter amicitiae dedisse, quod liquido
veritati dares. Et, si non modo omnes, verum etiam
multi Catones essent in civitate nostra, in qua unum
exstitisse mirabile est, quem ego currum, aut quam
lauream cum tua laudatione conferrem ? Nam ad
meum sensum et ad illud sincerum ac subtile iudicium
nihil potest esse laudabilius, quam ea tua oratio, quae
2 est ad me perscripta a meis necessariis. Sed causam
meae voluntatis, non enim dicam cupiditatis, exposui
tibi superioribus litteris ; quae etiamsi parum iusta
tibi visa est, hanc tamen habet rationem, non ut
nimis concupiscendus honos, sed tamen, si deferatur
a senatu, minime aspernandus esse videatur. Spero
autem illum ordinem, pro meis ob rempublicam

---

a i.e., to a triumph.   *Cf. Ep.* 4. 14 above.

VI

Tarsus or Rhodes, about August 10, 50 b.c.

" *Right glad am I to win the praise,*" as Hector says, 1
if I am not mistaken, in Naevius, " *of one so praised as
thou, my sire* " ; for that is undoubtedly pleasant
praise which comes from those who have themselves
lived in an atmosphere of praise. Yes, I assure you,
whether because of your letter of congratulation, or
the testimony of your expression of opinion in the
Senate, I feel there is nothing left for me to attain.
And what is at once most complimentary and most
gratifying to me is, that you cheerfully conceded to
friendship what you unhesitatingly conceded to truth.
And if, I don't say everybody, but even a fair number of
folk were Catos in our state, in which the epiphany of
a single Cato is a miracle, what triumphal car or what
laurel wreath could I compare with a panegyric from
you ? For whether I regard my own feelings or the
conspicuous sincerity and penetration of your judgment, there can be no higher panegyric than that
speech of yours, a full copy of which has been sent to
me by my friends.

Now the reason of my aspiration [a] (I shall not call it a 2
passionate desire) I have explained to you in a former
letter ; and although it has struck you as being hardly
strong enough, it still has this much justification,
that while it seems that the honour is not one to be
greedily coveted, yet, if bestowed by the Senate, one
that should by no means be treated with contempt. I
hope, however, that in consideration of the labours I

269

susceptis laboribus, me non indignum honore, usitato praesertim, existimaturum. Quod si ita erit, tantum ex te peto, quod amicissime scribis, ut, cum tuo iudicio, quod amplissimum esse arbitraris, mihi tribueris, si id, quod maluero, acciderit, gaudeas. Sic enim fecisse te, et sensisse, et scripsisse video : resque ipsa declarat, tibi illum honorem nostrum supplicationis iucundum fuisse, quod scribendo adfuisti. Haec enim senatus consulta non ignoro ab amicissimis eius, cuius de honore agitur, scribi solere. Ego, ut spero, te propediem videbo ; atque utinam republica meliore, quam timeo !

VII

M. T. C. PROCOS. S. P. D. C. MARCELLO COS. DES.

Inter Iconium et Cybistra, A.U.C. 703.

Maxima sum laetitia affectus, cum audivi te consulem factum esse, eumque honorem tibi deos fortunare volo, atque a te pro tua parentisque tui dignitate administrari. Nam cum te semper amavi dilexique, tum mei amantissimum cognovi in omni varietate rerum mearum, tum patris tui pluribus beneficiis, vel defensus tristibus temporibus vel orna-

---

a Consul in 50 with Lucius Paullus. For the three Marcelli see note b on iv. 7. 6.

270

have undertaken in the public interests, that order will not deem me unworthy of such an honour, especially as its bestowal would be according to custom. If it so turns out, all I ask you to do is (to quote your very friendly words), since you have paid me what you consider the highest possible compliment by the opinion you expressed, that you should feel glad if what I have preferred comes to pass. That you have so acted, so felt, and so written, is evident to me, and the very fact of your being party to the drafting of the decree, clearly proves that the great honour done me by the *supplicatio* was a pleasure to you. For I am well aware that such decrees of the Senate are usually drafted by the greatest friends of the recipient of the honour. I shall see you, I hope, at an early date, and I pray that the political situation may then be better than I fear it will be.

VII

CICERO TO GAIUS MARCELLUS, CONSULT ELECT [a]

Between Iconium and Cybistra, early in September, 51 B.C.

I was extremely delighted to hear that you had been made consul, and I pray that heaven may prosper your office, and that you may administer it in accordance with your own and your father's honourable position. For not only have I always loved and esteemed you, but I have also found you sincerely devoted to myself through all the vicissitudes of my fortunes. Moreover, because of the repeated good services of your father, when he either defended me in the days of my gloom or honoured me in the days of

CICERO

tus secundis, et sum totus vester et esse debeo ;
cum praesertim matris tuae, gravissimae atque
optimae feminae, maiora erga salutem dignitatemque
meam studia, quam erant a muliere postulanda,
perspexerim. Quapropter a te peto in maiorem
modum, ut me absentem diligas atque defendas.

VIII

M. T. C. PROC. S. P. D. MARCELLO COLLEGAE

Inter Iconium et Cybistra, A.U.C. 703.

Marcellum tuum consulem factum, teque ea laetitia
affectum esse, quam maxime optasti. mirandum in
modum gaudeo, idque cum ipsius causa, tum quod
te omnibus secundissimis rebus dignissimum iudico,
cuius erga me singularem benevolentiam vel in labore
meo vel in honore perspexi, totam denique domum
vestram vel salutis vel dignitatis meae studiosissimam
cupidissimamque cognovi. Quare gratum mihi feceris, si uxori tuae Iuniae, gravissimae atque optimae
feminae, meis verbis eris gratulatus. A te id, quod
consuesti, peto, me absentem diligas atque defendas.

---

a Father of the C. Marcellus addressed in the preceding
letter.

my glory, I am, and I am bound to be, heart and soul at the disposal of all of you, especially as I am fully conscious of the energetic support (more than should have been demanded of any woman) given to my welfare and position by that most sterling and excellent lady, your mother. And that is my justification for entreating you with special earnestness to show your esteem for me by defending me in my absence.

VIII

CICERO TO GAIUS MARCELLUS,[a] HIS BROTHER AUGUR

Between Iconium and Cybistra, early in September, 51 B.C.

That your son Marcellus has been made consul, and that you have felt that thrill of joy for which you most devoutly prayed, is an inexpressible pleasure to me, and that not only on his own account, but because I consider that you also richly deserve all that the happiest fortune can bestow. For I have had convincing proof of your incomparable goodness of heart towards me whether in my troubles or in my triumphs; in short I have found your whole family most enthusiastic and eager in their support of my civil standing or official distinction (call it which you will). For that reason you will do me a kindness if you pass on my congratulations to that most sterling and excellent lady, your wife Junia. I beg of you to do what you always have done—to show your regard for me and defend me in my absence.

CICERO

IX

Inter Iconium et Cybistra, a.u.c. 703.

1 Te et pietatis in tuos et animi in rempublicam et
clarissimi atque optimi consulatus, C. Marcello consule facto, fructum cepisse, vehementer gaudeo. Non
dubito, quid praesentes sentiant ; nos quidem longin-
qui, et a te ipso missi in ultimas gentes, ad caelum
mehercule te tollimus verissimis ac iustissimis laudibus. Nam cum te a pueritia tua unice dilexerim,
tuque me in omni genere semper amplissimum esse
et volueris et iudicaris, tum hoc vel tuo facto, vel
populi Romani de te iudicio, multo acrius vehemen-
tiusque diligo, maximaque laetitia afficior, cum ab
hominibus prudentissimis virisque optimis, omnibus
dictis, factis, studiis, institutis, vel me tui similem
2 esse audio vel te mei. Unum vero si addis ad prae-
clarissimas res consulatus tui, ut aut mihi succedat
quam primum aliquis, aut ne quid accedat temporis
ad id, quod tu mihi et senatus consulto et lege
finisti, omnia me per te consecutum putabo. Cura
ut valeas, et me absentem diligas atque defendas.

ᵃ Marcus Marcellus, consul in 51 with Servius Sulpicius
Rufus ; he was cousin, not brother, to C. Marcellus, consul
designate for the succeeding year (50). For a further
account of the Marcelli see Indices to Vols. I and II.

ᵇ According to one of the provisions of the *Lex Pompeia
de Provinciis* the consuls were empowered to bring before
the people a *lex de Imperio* in the case of each governor,
determining the length of his tenure of office, etc.

274

IX

CICERO TO MARCUS MARCELLUS,[a] CONSUL

Between Iconium and Cybistra, early in September, 51 B.C.

I am highly delighted that by the election of Gaius 1
Marcellus to the consulship you have gathered the
fruit of your affection for your family, of your devotion
to the commonwealth, and of your own most illustrious and admirable consulship. I have no doubt as
to the sentiments of those on the spot, when I myself,
far away as I am, and despatched by yourself to the
ends of the earth, am extolling you, I vow, up to
the skies, and my praises are as sincere as they are
well deserved. For while I have had a particular
affection for you from my boyhood, and you have ever
desired, and indeed deemed me to possess the widest
influence in every direction, my affection for you has
been greatly deepened and enhanced by this achievement of yours, or shall I call it this pronouncement of
the Roman people in your favour? And I feel a thrill
of pure delight when I am told by people of uncommon shrewdness and men of the highest character
that in every word and deed, pursuit and principle, I
am like you, or you are like me (whichever you prefer).

If, however, you add to the brilliant achievements 2
of your consulship by contriving either that somebody
may succeed me at the earliest possible date, or that
no addition is made to the time you definitely fixed for
me both by a decree of the Senate and by the law,[b]—
well, then I shall consider that there is nothing you
have not enabled me to secure. Take care of your
health, and show your regard for me and defend me
in my absence.

CICERO

3 Quae mihi de Parthis nuntiata sunt, quia non putabam
a me etiam nunc scribenda esse publice, propterea
ne pro familiaritate quidem nostra volui ad te scribere ; ne, cum ad consulem scripsissem, publice
viderer scripsisse.

X

M. T. C. IMP. S. P. D. C. MARCELLO C. F. COS.

Tarsi, a.u.c. 704.

1   Quoniam id accidit, quod mihi maxime fuit optatum, ut omnium Marcellorum, Marcellinorum etiam
(mirificus enim generis ac nominis vestri fuit erga
me semper animus), quoniam ergo ita accidit, ut
omnium vestrum studio tuus consulatus satisfacere
posset, in quem meae res gestae, lausque et honos
earum potissimum incideret, peto a te id, quod
facillimum factu est, non aspernante, ut confido
senatu, ut quam honorificentissimum senatus con-
2 sultum, litteris meis recitatis, faciundum cures. Si
mihi tecum minus esset, quam est cum tuis omnibus,
allegarem ad te illos, a quibus intellegis me praecipue
diligi. Patris tui beneficia in me sunt amplissima ;
neque enim saluti meae neque honori amicior quisquam dici potest. Frater tuus quanti me faciat

---

a The Marcellini were a branch of the Marcellus family.

b What he means is, to put it shortly, that his being made
consul gives C. Marcellus an opportunity of making good all
that this devotion of his family to Cicero deserved.

Dr. Page remarks that in these unblushing requests Cicero
always veils himself in obscurity, and that this long sentence
is *deliberately embarrassed.*

As for the reports I have received about the 3
Parthians, I thought that I ought not even now to
make them the subject of a public despatch, and that
is the reason why in spite of our intimacy I did not
wish to write to you, lest, when I had written to a
consul, it might be supposed that I had written
officially.

X

CICERO TO GAIUS MARCELLUS, CONSUL

Tarsus, January, 50 B.C.

Since, as I have most earnestly desired, it has so 1
happened that the devotion of all the Marcelli, and
Marcellini *a* too (for the kindly feeling your family and
those of your name have ever shown me is something
amazing)—since, as I say, it has so happened that
the devotion you have all felt can find its full expression in your consulship because with that particular consulship my achievements and such praise and
honour as attach to them coincide *b*—for that reason I
beg of you (and it is a thing most easily done, for the
Senate, I am confident, is not likely to reject it) to see
that after the reading of my despatch, the decree of
the Senate should be drafted in the most complimentary terms possible.

Had I less to do with you than with all your folk, I 2
should commission those to present my case to you,
whom you know to be particularly attached to me.
Your father's services to me are magnificent, and no
man can be said to be a more friendly supporter of my
welfare or my public position. How highly your
brother values and has always valued me, there is no

semperque fecerit, esse hominem, qui ignoret, arbitror
neminem.   Domus tua denique tota me semper omnibus summis officiis prosecuta est.   Neque vero tu in
me diligendo cuiquam concessisti tuorum.   Quare a te
peto in maiorem modum, ut me per te quam ornatis-
simum velis esse, meamque et in supplicatione de-
cernenda, et in ceteris rebus existimationem satis
tibi esse commendatam putes.

XI

M. T. C. IMP. S. P. D. C. MARCELLO COS.

Tarsi, a.u.c. 704.

1 Quantae curae tibi meus honos fuerit, et quam
idem exstiteris consul in me ornando et amplificando,
qui fueras semper cum parentibus tuis et cum tota
domo, etsi res ipsa loquebatur, cognovi tamen ex
meorum omnium litteris.   Itaque nihil est tantum,
quod ego non tua causa debeam, facturusque sim
2 cum studiose tum libenter.   Nam magni interest,
cui debeas ; debere autem nemini malui, quam tibi,
cui me cum studia communia, beneficia paterna
tuaque iam ante coniunxerant, tum accedit mea
quidem sententia maximum vinculum, quod ita rempublicam geris atque gessisti, qua mihi carius nihil
278

man living, I believe, who does not know. In fine your whole family has never ceased to honour me with the highest favours of every kind ; nor have you yourself yielded place to any of your family in affection for me. And that is why I beg of you with no ordinary earnestness to wish me the highest possible honour as far as you are yourself concerned, and to consider that my reputation, both in the voting for a *supplicatio* and in all other matters, needs no further recommendation in your eyes.

XI

CICERO TO GAIUS MARCELLUS, CONSUL

Tarsus, July, 50 B.C.

Although the facts spoke for themselves, none the 1 less from the letters of every one of my friends I have learned fully how much pains you took about the honour done me, and how, in conferring as consul this distinction and eminence upon me, you showed yourself to be just the same as, in common with your parents and all your family, you always have been. Consequently there is no service so great that I do not owe you as a debt, and that I am not ready to discharge with as much devotion as pleasure.

For it matters greatly to whom one is indebted ; 2 but there is nobody to whom I had rather be indebted than to you, to whom I had not only been previously united by identity of tastes and your own and your father's services to me, but there exists besides what is in my opinion the strongest bond of all— the fact that your past and present administration of the Republic (to me the most precious thing in the

est, ut, quantum tibi omnes boni debeant, quo minus tantumdem ego unus debeam, non recusem. Quamobrem tibi velim hi sint exitus, quos mereris et quos fore confido. Ego, si me navigatio non morabitur, quae incurrebat in ipsos Etesias, propediem te, ut spero, videbo.

XII

M. T. C. IMP. S. P. D. L. PAULLO COS. DES.

Inter Iconium et Cybistra, A.U.C. 703.

1 Etsi mihi numquam fuit dubium, quin te populus Romanus, pro tuis summis in rempublicam meritis et pro amplissima familiae dignitate, summo studio, cunctis suffragiis consulem facturus esset, tamen incredibili laetitia sum affectus, cum id mihi nuntiatum est ; eumque honorem tibi deos fortunare volo, a teque ex tua maiorumque tuorum dignitate 2 administrari. Atque utinam praesens illum diem mihi optatissimum videre potuissem, proque tuis amplissimis erga me studiis atque beneficiis tibi operam meam studiumque navare ! Quam mihi facultatem quoniam hic necopinatus et improvisus provinciae casus eripuit, tamen, ut te consulem, rempublicam pro tua dignitate gerentem, videre possim, magno opere a te peto, ut operam des efficiasque, ne quid mihi fiat iniuriae, neve quid temporis ad meum

---

ᵃ Winds that blow from the N.W. for forty days in the Levant.

280

world) has been and is such that I do not shrink from taking upon myself alone the full amount of the debt owed you by all good citizens put together. I may therefore hope that things will result as you deserve, and as I am confident they will.

For myself, unless I am delayed on my voyage, which exactly coincides with the Etesian winds,[a] I shall see you, I hope, at an early date.

XII

CICERO TO LUCIUS AEMILIUS PAULLUS, CONSUL ELECT

Between Iconium and Cybistra, September, 51 B.C.

Although I never had any doubt that the people of 1 Rome, in consideration of your magnificent services to the Republic, and the highly influential position of your family, would elect you consul with the greatest enthusiasm and unanimity of voting, I had yet a thrill of inconceivable joy when the news reached me ; and I pray the gods to prosper your high office, and that you may administer it in a manner befitting your own and your ancestors' position.

And would that I had been able to be on the spot 2 and see that eagerly desired day, and in return for all your splendid devotion and kindness to me to render you my aid and active support ! But since that opportunity has been snatched from me by the unexpected and unforeseen incident of my provincial appointment, nevertheless, so that I may have the chance of seeing you a consul administering the Republic as befits your position, I earnestly beg of you to make every effort to prevent my suffering any injustice, or any exten-

annuum munus accedat. Quod si feceris, magnus
ad tua pristina erga me studia cumulus accedet.

XIII

M. T. C. IMP. S. P. D. L. PAULLO COS.

Tarsi, A.U.C. 704.

1 Maxime mihi fuit optatum Romae esse tecum
multas ob causas, sed praecipue, ut et in petendo, et
in gerendo consulatu meum tibi debitum studium
perspicere posses. Ac petitionis quidem tuae ratio
mihi semper fuit explorata ; sed tamen navare operam
volebam. In consulatu vero cupio equidem te minus
habere negoti ; sed moleste fero, me consulem studium tuum adulescentis perspexisse, te meum, cum
2 id aetatis sim, perspicere non posse. Sed ita, fato
nescio quo, contigisse arbitror, ut tibi ad me ornan-
dum semper detur facultas, mihi ad remunerandum
nihil suppetat praeter voluntatem. Ornasti consulatum, ornasti reditum meum. Incidit meum tempus
rerum gerendarum in ipsum consulatum tuum. Itaque
cum et tua summa amplitudo et dignitas, et meus
magnus honos magnaque existimatio postulare vi-
282

sion of time being added to my year's term of office.
If you do that, an overwhelming addition will be made
to all your previous services to me.

XIII

CICERO TO L. AEMILIUS PAULLUS, CONSUL

Tarsus, January, 50 b.c.

It has been my most earnest desire to be with you 1
in Rome for many reasons, but particularly in order
that you might have clear proof both in your candidature and in the administration of your consulship of
that devotion which I owed you. And as to your candidature, the result to my mind was always perfectly
clear ; but all the same I wished to give you my utmost
assistance. In your consulship, on the other hand, I
am, of course, anxious that you should have less
trouble than I, but I am quite distressed that, whereas I, as consul, had clear proof of your devotion when
a young man, you can have no clear proof of that on
my part, at my time of life.

But I suppose by some mysterious fate it has so 2
happened that, while you are always given the opportunity of enhancing my honour, I have nothing to fall
back upon by way of requiting you except the desire
to do so. You added distinction to my consulship,
you added distinction to my recall. My present
period of active service has happened to coincide with
the very year of your consulship. And so, although it
would seem to be demanded both by your most exalted and eminent position and by my own high office
and high reputation that I should earnestly importune

deatur, ut a te plurimis verbis contendam ac petam,
ut quam honorificentissimum senatus consultum de
meis rebus gestis faciendum cures, non audeo vehementer a te contendere, ne aut ipse tuae perpetuae
consuetudinis erga me oblitus esse videar, aut te
3 oblitum putem. Quare, ut te velle arbitror, ita
faciam, atque ab eo, quem omnes gentes sciunt de me
optime meritum, breviter petam. Si alii consules
essent, ad te potissimum, Paulle, mitterem, ut eos
mihi quam amicissimos redderes. Nunc, cum tua
summa potestas summaque auctoritas, notaque omnibus nostra necessitudo sit, vehementer te rogo, ut
et quam honorificentissime cures decernendum de
meis rebus gestis, et quam celerrime. Dignas res
esse honore et gratulatione, cognosces ex iis litteris,
quas ad te et collegam et senatum publice misi ;
omniumque mearum reliquarum rerum maximeque
existimationis meae procurationem susceptam velim
habeas. In primisque tibi curae sit, quod abs te
superioribus quoque litteris petivi, ne mihi tempus
prorogetur. Cupio te consulem videre, omniaque,
quae spero, cum absens, tum etiam praesens, te
consule assequi. Vale.

you with no economy of words to ensure that the decree of the Senate concerning my achievements should be couched in the most complimentary terms possible, yet I do not venture to lay undue stress upon my petition to you, lest I should either appear to have forgotten your habitual and uninterrupted kindness to me, or to imagine that you have forgotten it.

I shall therefore do as I believe you would have me 3 do, and use but few words in making a request of one who, as all the nations of the world are aware, has deserved extremely well of me. Were there other consuls, you are the first man, Paullus, to whom I should send, requesting you to enlist their warmest friendship on my side. As it is, seeing that you possess the highest power and influence, and that our close connexion is known to all men, I ask you in all earnestness to ensure that the decree concerning my achievements is couched in the most complimentary terms possible, yes, and as speedily as possible too. That those services are deserving of honour and congratulation you will discover from the despatch I sent in my public capacity to yourself and your colleague and the Senate; and I should be glad if you would undertake to look after all my other interests, and most especially my reputation, and particularly to see to it, as I asked you to do in a former letter also, that there is no extension of my term of office.

I am anxious to see you while you are consul, and during your consulship to secure all I hope for, not only here but at home.

CICERO

XIV

Ad aras Alexandri, A.U.C. 703.

1 M. Fadium quod mihi amicum tua commendatione
das, nullum in eo facio quaestum. Multi enim anni
sunt, cum ille in aere meo est, et a me diligitur
propter summam humanitatem et observantiam. Sed
tamen, quod ab eo te egregie diligi sensi, multo
amicior ei sum factus. Itaque quamquam profecerunt
litterae tuae, tamen aliquanto plus commendationis
apud me habuit animus ipsius erga te mihi perspectus
2 et cognitus. Sed de Fadio faciemus studiose quae
rogas ; tu multis de causis vellem me convenire
potuisses, primum, ut te, quem iamdiu plurimi facio,
tanto intervallo viderem ; deinde, ut tibi, quod feci
per litteras, possem praesens gratulari ; tum, ut, quibus de rebus vellemus, tu tuis, ego meis inter nos
communicaremus ; postremo, ut amicitia nostra, quae
summis officiis ab utroque culta est, sed longis inter-
vallis temporum interruptam consuetudinem habuit,

ᵃ Cassius had been quaestor to Crassus, after whose death
he commanded what remained of the Roman army in Syria
as *proquaestor propraetore*. *Proquaestor* was the title of
the *quaestor* of the previous year who retained his position
between the expiration of his own term of office and the
arrival of the new *quaestor*. Again, if the governor left his
province, he usually delegated his powers to the *quaestor*,
who was then entitled *quaestor* (or as here, *proquaestor*)
propraetore. He defeated the Parthians under Pacorus
before Antioch (ii. 10. 2) this year (51).

ᵇ M. Fadius Gallus, to whom Cicero addressed *Epp.* 23-26
in Bk. VII.

XIV

CICERO TO GAIUS CASSIUS LONGINUS, PROQUAESTOR OF SYRIA [a]

Arae Alexandri, near Issus, between the 14th and 15th of October, 51 B.C.

By your recommendation you present M. Fadius [b] 1 to me as a friend ; well, I gain nothing by that. As a matter of fact he has been for many years entirely at my disposal, and I have liked him for his extreme kindness and the respect he shows me. But for all that the discovery that you are extraordinarily fond of him has made me much more of a friend to him. And so, although your letter has had its effect, yet what recommends him a great deal more is that I have come fully to see and understand his kindly feelings for yourself.

But in the matter of Fadius I will do what you ask 2 with hearty goodwill ; as for yourself, I only wish for many reasons that you had been able to meet me, in the first place so that I might see you after so long an interval—you whom I have for long past valued so highly ; secondly, that I might congratulate you [c] in person as I have done by letter ; furthermore, that we might share our views about whatever matters we wished, you about your affairs, I about mine ; and lastly, that our friendship which has been fostered on either side by the most notable good services, but has had its continuity broken by long periods of interruption, might be more effectually strengthened.

[c] On his victory over Pacorus (see note a above).

3 confirmaretur vehementius. Id quoniam non accidit,
utemur bono litterarum, et eadem fere absentes,
quae, si coram essemus, consequemur. Unus scilicet
ille fructus, qui in te videndo est, percipi litteris non
potest. Alter gratulationis, est is quidem exilior,
quam si tibi teipsum intuens gratularer ; sed tamen
et feci ante, et facio nunc, tibique cum pro rerum
magnitudine, quas gessisti, tum pro opportunitate
temporis gratulor, quod te de provincia decedentem
summa laus et summa gratia provinciae prosecuta
4 est. Tertium est, ut id, quod de nostris rebus coram
communicassemus inter nos, conficiamus idem litteris.
Ego ceterarum rerum causa tibi Romam properan-
dum magno opere censeo. Nam et ea, quae reliqui,
tranquilla de te erant, et hac tua recenti victoria tanta
clarum adventum tuum fore intellego. Sed si quae
sunt onera tuorum, si tanta sunt, ut ea sustinere
possis, propera ; nihil tibi erit lautius, nihil gloriosius ;
sin maiora, considera, ne in alienissimum tempus
cadat adventus tuus. Huius rei totum consilium tuum
est. Tu enim scis, quid sustinere possis. Si potes,
laudabile atque populare est. Sin plane non potes,
5 absens hominum sermones facilius sustinebis. De me
autem idem tecum his ago litteris, quod superioribus

---

a See note *a* on *Ep.* 14 above.
b Prosecutions of his friends for extortion and other
offences, especially of his brother, Q. Cassius, who had been
quaestor to Pompey.

Since that has not come to pass, we will avail our- **3**
selves of the boon of letters, and so secure almost the
same objects in our separation as if we were together.
That one preeminent gratification, doubtless, which
consists in seeing you, cannot be enjoyed by letter ;
the other, which consists in congratulating you, is
less satisfying, it is true, than if I were to do so
with my eyes upon your face ; still I have done so
before, and I do so now, and congratulate you not only
on the magnificence of your achievements, but also on
their being so opportune in point of time, since on your
departure from your province you had the honourable
escort of its praise, as unqualified as its gratitude.

There is a third course—to carry out by correspond- **4**
ence the consultations we should have held on our respective affairs if we had met. For every other reason
also I am emphatically of opinion that you should
hasten to Rome. For the situation I left behind me
was one of complete calm as regards yourself, and
thanks to your recent victory *a* (and a glorious one it
was), I can see that your arrival will be a memorable
event. But supposing your relatives have any
burdens *b* to bear, if they are only such as you can
shoulder, hurry home ; it will be the most splendid
and glorious thing you can do. But if those burdens
are too heavy for you, pause to think, lest your
arrival may happen at a most untoward moment. On
this point the whole decision lies with you, for you
alone know what your shoulders can bear. If you have
the strength, it is a praiseworthy and popular thing to
do ; if you absolutely lack that strength, you will find
it easier to stand people's gossip if you stay away.

Now as to myself, I make the same request of you **5**
in this letter as I did in a previous one—that you

egi, ut omnes tuos nervos in eo contendas, ne quid
mihi ad hanc provinciam, quam et senatus et populus
annuam esse voluit, temporis prorogetur. Hoc a te
ita contendo, ut in eo fortunas meas positas putem.
Habes Paullum nostrum nostri cupidissimum ; est
Curio, est Furnius. Sic velim enitare, quasi in eo
6 sint mihi omnia. Extremum illud est de iis, quae
proposueram, confirmatio nostrae amicitiae ; de qua
pluribus verbis nihil opus est. Tu puer me appetisti ;
ego autem semper ornamento te mihi fore duxi.
Fuisti etiam praesidio tristissimis meis temporibus.
Accessit post tuum discessum familiaritas mihi cum
Bruto tuo maxima. Itaque in vestro ingenio et
industria mihi plurimum et suavitatis et dignitatis
constitutum puto. Id tu ut tuo studio confirmes, te
vehementer rogo, litterasque ad me et continuo
mittas, et, cum Romam veneris, quam saepissime.

XV

M. T. C. S. P. D. C. CASSIO

Brundisi, A.U.C. 707.

1 Etsi uterque nostrum, spe pacis et odio civilis
sanguinis, abesse a belli pertinacia voluit, tamen,
quoniam eius consili princeps ego fuisse videor, plus

---

should strain every nerve to prevent any prolongation of my term of office as governor of the province—a term which both the Senate and the people decreed should be for one year only. I urge this upon you so strongly that I feel all my prospects depend upon it. You have our friend Paullus on your side, a warm friend of mine, and there is Curio, and Furnius too. I pray you to make every effort just as though all I have were staked upon it.

My last point bears upon what I have already put 6 before you ; it is the strengthening of our friendship, as to which there is no need of further words. You, when a boy, sought me out, while I felt that you would always be a source of distinction to me. You were also a protection to me in the days of my deepest gloom. There came too, after your departure, my intimacy with your relative Brutus,[a] and it was of the closest. It is therefore in the ability and energy of you two that I have stored up for myself an unlimited fund of delight and distinction. I ask you in all earnestness to confirm that impression by your devotion to me, and to send me a letter not only immediately, but, on your arrival at Rome, as often as possible.

XV

CICERO TO CASSIUS

Brundisium, latter half of August, 47 B.C.

Although both of us in our hope of peace and loath- 1 ing for civil bloodshed wished to have nothing to do with the obstinate prosecution of war, still, since I seem to have taken the lead in that policy, I am

fortasse tibi praestare ipse debeo, quam a te exspectare. Etsi, ut saepe soleo mecum recordari,
sermo familiaris meus tecum, et item mecum tuus,
adduxit utrumque nostrum ad id consilium, ut uno
proelio putaremus, si non totam causam, at certe
nostrum iudicium definiri convenire. Neque quisquam hanc nostram sententiam vere umquam reprehendit, praeter eos, qui arbitrantur melius esse, deleri
omnino rempublicam, quam imminutam et debili-
tatam manere. Ego autem ex interitu eius nullam
spem scilicet mihi proponebam, ex reliquiis magnam.
2 Sed ea sunt consecuta, ut magis mirum sit, accidere
illa potuisse, quam nos non vidisse ea futura, nec,
homines cum essemus, divinare potuisse. Equidem
fateor, meam coniecturam hanc fuisse, ut, illo quasi
quodam fatali proelio facto, et victores communi
saluti consuli vellent, et victi suae ; utrumque autem
positum esse arbitrabar in celeritate victoris. Quae
si fuisset, eamdem clementiam experta esset Africa,
quam cognovit Asia, quam etiam Achaia, te, ut
opinor, ipso allegato ac deprecatore. Amissis autem
temporibus, quae plurimum valent, praesertim in
bellis civilibus, interpositus annus alios induxit, ut
victoriam sperarent, alios, ut ipsum vinci contem-
nerent. Atque horum malorum omnium culpam

---

 [a] The former by offering easy terms, the latter by laying
down their arms. Watson. The "great battle" is that of
Pharsalia in 48.
 [b] This refers to the Pompeian refugees in those countries,
many of whom had been forgiven by Caesar.

perhaps more bound to justify it to you, than to expect such justification from you. And yet, as I frequently remind myself, my observations to you and yours to me in our friendly talks led us both to this conclusion—we thought it right and proper that, if not the whole quarrel, at any rate our judgment of it, should be determined by the issue of a single battle. And not a soul has ever rightly found fault with this opinion of ours, except those who think it better that the commonwealth should be utterly destroyed than survive in an impaired and enfeebled condition. I, on the contrary, pictured to myself no hope of course in its destruction, much in any remnants that were left.

But the events which followed were such that it is 2 more of a surprise that they could have happened at all, than that we should not have seen them coming and have failed, being but human, to prognosticate them. For my part I confess that what I conjectured was this—I thought that after the great battle, fraught as it were with the issues of fate, had been fought, the victors would desire measures to be taken in the interests of the community, and the vanquished in their own ; [a] but I held that both the former and the latter depended upon the promptitude with which the victor acted. Had he shown that promptitude, Africa would have experienced the same leniency as was witnessed by Asia, yes, and by Achaia too, you yourself, as I take it, being their emissary and intercessor.[b] But those days of vital importance, especially in civil wars, having been wasted, the year that intervened tempted some to hope for victory, others to think lightly of defeat itself. And the blame for all these evils is on the shoulders of fortune.

CICERO

fortuna sustinet. Quis enim aut Alexandrini belli
tantam moram huic bello adiunctum iri, aut nescio
quem istum Pharnacem Asiae terrorem illaturum
3 putaret ? Nos tamen, in consilio pari, casu dissimili
usi sumus. Tu enim eam partem petisti, ut et consiliis
interesses, et, quod maxime curam levat, futura
animo prospicere posses. Ego, qui festinavi, ut
Caesarem in Italia viderem (sic enim arbitrabamur),
eumque multis honestissimis viris conservatis, red-
euntem ad pacem currentem, ut aiunt, incitarem,
ab illo longissime et absum et abfui. Versor autem
in gemitu Italiae, et in Urbis miserrimis querellis,
quibus aliquid opis fortasse ego pro mea, tu pro tua,
pro sua quisque parte ferre potuisset, si auctor ad-
4 fuisset. Quare velim pro tua perpetua erga me
benevolentia scribas ad me, quid videas, quid sentias,
quid exspectandum, quid agendum nobis existimes.
Magni erunt mihi tuae litterae ; atque utinam primis
illis, quas Luceria miseras, paruissem ! sine ulla enim
molestia dignitatem meam retinuissem. Vale.

ᵃ This refers to Caesar's long and doubtful struggle, in
the autumn of 48, with Arsinoe, younger sister of Ptolemy,
who was supported by the people of Alexandria.
  ᵇ Pharnaces, king of Pontus, was defeated by Caesar at
Zela in August, 47, when the latter sent his famous despatch
"*Veni, vidi, vici.*"
  ᶜ Written probably from the headquarters of Pompey at
Luceria in Apulia before he crossed over to Greece, in which
Cassius advised Cicero not to leave Italy.

For who would imagine that the war would be protracted or cause so long a delay as that caused by the Alexandrian war,[a] or that this Pharnaces,[b] whoever he may be, would intimidate Asia ?

You and I, however, though our policy was identical, 3 have found a difference in our fortunes ; for while you took a line which enabled you to share his counsels, and so being able to foresee (and that is a potent alleviation of anxiety) what was going to happen, I, who hastened to meet Caesar in Italy (for that is what I supposed) and " to spur the willing horse," as the adage has it, when, after sparing so many of our most distinguished men, he was actually returning to the ways of peace, I on the contrary, both am and have been kept utterly apart from him. I spend my life, moreover, amid the groans of Italy, and the piteous lamentations of the city ; and we might perhaps have done something to alleviate them, I in my way, you in yours, everybody in his own, if only the man in authority had been there.

I should like you, therefore, consistently with your 4 unfailing kindness to me, to write and tell me what your impressions and your feelings are, what you think we should wait for, and what you think we should do. I shall greatly value a letter from you ; and how I wish I had followed the advice contained in that first letter [c] you sent me from Luceria ! I should then have retained my position without any friction at all. Farewell.

CICERO

XVI

M. T. C. S. P. D. C. CASSIO

Romae, A.U.C. 709.

1   Puto te iam suppudere, cum haec tertia iam
epistula ante te oppresserit, quam tu scidam aut
litteram. Sed non urgeo. Longiores enim exspectabo,
vel potius exigam. Ego, si semper haberem, cui
darem, vel ternas in hora darem. Fit enim nescio
qui, ut quasi coram adesse videare, cum scribo aliquid ad te : neque id κατ᾽ εἰδώλων φαντασίας, ut dicunt
tui amici novi, qui putant etiam διανοητικὰς φαντασίας
spectris Catianis excitari (nam, ne te fugiat, Catius
Insuber, Epicureus, qui nuper est mortuus, quae ille
Gargettius, etiam ante Democritus, εἴδωλα, his spec-
2 tra nominat). His autem spectris etiamsi oculi possint
feriri, quod vel ipsa occurrunt,[1] animus qui possit,
ego non video. Doceas tu me oportebit, cum salvus
veneris, in meane potestate sit spectrum tuum, ut,
simul ac mihi collibitum sit de te cogitare, illud
occurrat ; neque solum de te, qui mihi haeres in
medullis, sed, si insulam Britanniam coepero cogitare,
3 eius εἴδωλον mihi advolabit ad pectus ? Sed haec

---

[1] quod quae velis ipsa incurrunt *Tyrrell* ; nolis velis
("*whether you wish it or not* ") ipsa accurrunt *Koch. I
retain Nobbe's reading.*

---

   [a] Literally " a letter of the alphabet."
   [b] The Epicureans, whom Cassius had recently joined.
   [c] Epicurus, who belonged to the deme of Gargettus, near
Athens.
   [d] "The Epicureans accounted for sight by supposing that
all bodies were continually giving off films or images
(εἴδωλα), which impinged upon the eye, and that produced a
"vision" (φαντασία), which in its turn struck the mind, and
became a "mental vision" (διανοητικὴ φαντασία).

XVI

CICERO TO CASSIUS

Rome, January, 45 B.C.

I expect you must be just a little ashamed of your- 1
self now that this is the third letter that has caught
you before you have sent me a single leaf or even a
line.[a] But I am not pressing you, for I shall look forward to, or rather insist upon, a longer letter. As for
myself, if I always had somebody to trust with them,
I should send you as many as three an hour. For it
somehow happens, that whenever I write anything to
you, you seem to be at my very elbow ; and that, not
by way of "*visions of images*," as your new friends [b]
term them, who believe that even "*mental visions*"
are conjured up by what Catius calls "*spectres*"
(for let me remind you that Catius the Insubrian, an
Epicurean, who died lately, gives the name of
"*spectres*" to what the famous Gargettian,[c] and
long before that Democritus, called "*images*").

But, even supposing that the *eye* can be struck by 2
these "*spectres*" because they run up against it
quite of their own accord, how the *mind* can be so
struck is more than I can see. It will be your duty to
explain to me, when you arrive here safe and sound,
whether the "*spectre*" of you is at my command to
run up against me as soon as the whim has taken me
to think about you—and not only about you, who
always occupy my inmost heart, but suppose I begin
thinking about the Isle of Britain, will the "*image*"
of that wing its way to my consciousness ? [d]

Cicero cannot understand how this second effect is produced, or why, directly he chooses to think of Cassius, the
εἴδωλον should "run up against him."

posterius. Tempto enim te, quo animo accipias. Si
enim stomachabere et moleste feres, plura dicemus
postulabimusque, ex qua αἱρέσει *vi hominibus armatis*
deiectus sis, in eam restituare. In hoc interdicto non
solet addi, *in hoc anno*. Quare si iam biennium aut
triennium est, cum virtuti nuntium remisisti, deli-
nitus illecebris voluptatis, in integro res nobis erit.
Quamquam quicum loquor ? cum uno fortissimo viro,
qui, posteaquam forum attigisti, nihil fecisti, nisi
plenissimum amplissimae dignitatis. In ista ipsa
αἱρέσει, metuo, ne plus nervorum sit, quam ego
putarim, si modo eam ut probas. Qui id tibi in
mentem venit ? inquies. Quia nihil habebam aliud,
quod scriberem. De republica enim nihil scribere
possum : neque enim, quod sentio, libet scribere.

XVII

M. T. C. S. P. D. C. CASSIO

Romae, a.u.c. 709.

1 Praeposteros habes tabellarios ; etsi me quidem
non offendunt ; sed tamen, cum a me discedunt,
flagitant litteras ; cum ad me veniunt, nullas afferunt. Atque id ipsum facerent commodius, si mihi
aliquid spati ad scribendum darent ; sed petasati

---

a " Cicero represents Cassius as having been ousted from
the Stoic philosophy by the arms of Caesar, and having
embraced the Epicurean tenets of the latter." Tyrrell.

b From which the previous words are quoted.

c The *summum bonum* of the Epicureans.

d Literally " with their travelling caps on."

But of this later on. I am only sounding you now to 3 see in what spirit you take it. For if you are angry and annoyed, I shall have more to say, and shall insist upon your being reinstated in that school of philosophy, out of which you have been ousted "*by violence and an armed force.*" *a* In this interdict of the praetor *b* the words "*within this year*" are not usually added ; so even if it is now two or three years since, bewitched by the blandishments of Pleasure,*c* you sent a notice of divorce to Virtue, I am free to act as I like. And yet to whom am I talking ? To you, the most gallant gentleman in the world, who, ever since you set foot in the forum, have done nothing but what bears every mark of the most impressive distinction. Why, in that very school you have selected I apprehend there is more vitality than I should have supposed, if only because it has your approval. "How did the whole subject occur to you ?" you will say. Because I had nothing else to write. About politics I can write nothing, for I do not care to write what I feel.

XVII

CICERO TO CASSIUS

Rome, early in January, 45 B.C.

The letter-carriers you employ are behaving pre- 1 posterously—not that they are lacking in civility to me, but, all the same, when they leave me they importune me for a letter, but when they come to me they bring no letter with them. And even so they would cause me less inconvenience if they would only allow me some reasonable time for writing ; but they come ready dressed for travelling,*d*

veniunt ; comites ad portam exspectare dicunt. Ergo
ignosces ; alteras habebis has breves ; sed exspecta
πάντα περὶ πάντων. Etsi quid ego me tibi purgo,
cum tui ad me inanes veniant, ad te cum epistulis
2 revertantur ? Nos hic (tamen ad te scribam aliquid)
P. Sullam patrem mortuum habebamus. Alii a
latronibus, alii cruditate dicebant. Populus non cura-
bat. Combustum enim esse constabat. Hoc tu pro
sapientia tua feres aequo animo. Quamquam πρό-
σωπον πόλεως amisimus. Caesarem putabant moleste
laturum, verentem, ne hasta refrixisset. Mindius
macellarius[1] et Attius pigmentarius valde gaudebant
3 se adversarium perdidisse. De Hispania novi nihil ;
sed exspectatio valde magna ; rumores tristiores, sed
ἀδέσποτοι. Pansa noster paludatus a. d. III. Kalend.
Ian. profectus est, ut quivis intellegere posset id, quod
tu nuper dubitare coepisti, τὸ καλὸν δι᾽ αὐτὸ αἱρετόν
esse. Nam quod multos miseriis levavit, et quod se
in his malis hominem praebuit, mirabilis eum virorum
4 bonorum benevolentia prosecuta est. Tu quod adhuc
Brundisi moratus es, valde probo et gaudeo ; et

---

[1] *The ingenious conjecture of Weiske and Madvig* : Marcellus MSS., *and it is true that Caesar had a friend named
Mindius Marcellus* (*Appian*, B.C. v. 102).

---

[a] Nephew of the Dictator. He was accused in 62 of
being privy to Catiline's conspiracies, but was defended by
Cicero and Hortensius and acquitted. He did a large business
in buying up the confiscated goods of Caesar's enemies,
and Cicero always speaks of him in his letters with contempt.
He must, however, have been an officer of some distinction,
as he was in joint command with Caesar himself of the right
wing at Pharsalia.

[b] Or "that he has passed through the fire," an allusion
perhaps to his having been " singed " (*cf. ambustus*) in the
law-courts.

and tell me that their mates are waiting for them at the gate. You will therefore forgive me ; this is now the second short note you will have, but you may live in hopes of *omnia de omnibus rebus*. And yet why am I excusing myself to you, when your men come to me empty-handed, and return to you with letters ?

Here (I'll send you something of a letter after all) 2 we have on our hands the death of P. Sulla senior [a] ; some say it was brigands, others indigestion. The people don't care a straw, since there is no doubt as to his cremation.[b] You, with your usual philosophy, will bear this with resignation. And yet we have lost a figure-head in the city. People think that Caesar will be annoyed because he apprehends a " slump " in his sales. Mindius the victualler and Attius the paint-seller are highly delighted at having dropped a rival bidder.[c]

There is no news about Spain, but it is very eagerly 3 awaited. There are rather depressing rumours, but they are unauthenticated. Our friend Pansa set out in military uniform on December the 29th, so that even the man in the street might grasp the fact which you had lately begun to question—that " *the good must be chosen for its own sake.*" [d] For because he relieved many of their afflictions, and because he proved his humanity amid all these disasters, he was escorted on his way by a marvellous manifestation of kindly feeling on the part of honest men. As to your 4 having stayed at Brundisium until now, I strongly approve of it and am glad of it ; and, upon my word, I

[c] They also were bidders at the auctions of proscribed goods mentioned in note *a*.

[d] Cassius had lately turned Epicurean (see the preceding letter) and therefore repudiated the Stoic dogma here quoted.

301

mehercule puto te sapienter facturum, si ἀκενόσπουδος
fueris. Nobis quidem, qui te amamus, erit gratum.
Et, amabo te, cum dabis posthac aliquid domum
litterarum, mei memineris. Ego numquam quemquam ad te, cum sciam, sine meis litteris ire patiar.

XVIII

M. T. C. S. P. D. C. CASSIO

Romae, a.u.c. 708.

1 Longior epistula fuisset, nisi eo ipso tempore petita
esset a me, cum iam iretur ad te ; longior etiam,
si φλύαρον aliquem habuisset ; nam σπουδάζειν sine
periculo vix possumus. Ridere igitur, inquis, possumus. Non mehercule facillime. Verumtamen aliam
aberrationem a molestiis nullam habemus. Ubi igitur,
inquies, philosophia ? Tua quidem iucunda, mea
molesta[1] est : pudet enim servire. Itaque facio me
2 alias res agere, ne convicium Platonis audiam. De
Hispania nihil adhuc certi, nihil omnino novi. Te
abesse, mea causa moleste fero, tua gaudeo. Sed
flagitat tabellarius. Valebis igitur, meque, ut a puero
fecisti, amabis.

---

[1] *Tyrrell has* tua quidem in culina, mea molesta est *in
his text, rejecting Manutius's in* palaestra *for* molesta ; *later
on he proposes* iucunda *for* in culina, *which, as making an
obscure passage intelligible. I have adopted.*

---

a Such as attempting to restore the free state. But Cassius
was not the man to take Cicero's advice.

b Or, as the phrase came to mean, " to be careless and
indifferent." Cicero is referring to his teaching rhetoric
and declamation to Hirtius and Dolabella, and his other
diversions in 46. See the preliminary note to Bk. XIII.

think you will act wisely if you " *shun vain pursuits.*" [a]
Certainly to me who love you, it will be a gratification, and for the future when you send home a budget
of letters, remember me, and I'll bless you. For my
own part I shall never allow anybody, if I know it, to
go to you without a letter from me.

XVIII

CICERO TO CASSIUS

Rome, towards the end of 46 B.C.

My letter would have been longer had not I been **1**
asked for it at the very moment when a post to you
was starting; longer too, had it contained some
amount of persiflage; as for speaking seriously, we
can hardly do so without risk. "Well then," you say,
" we can have a laugh." No, I positively assure you.
not very easily. And yet, that is the one and only
thing we have to distract us from our troubles. "How
about our philosophy then ?" you will say. Well,
yours is one of pleasure, but mine troubles me, because I am ashamed of being a slave. So I pretend to
busy myself with other things,[b] to prevent Plato's
emphatic reproach from ringing in my ears.[c]

There is nothing certain so far about Spain, indeed **2**
no news at all. Your absence troubles me for my own
sake, but I am very glad of it for yours. But there
goes your importunate letter-carrier. Fare you
well then, and continue to love me as you have
from a boy.

[c] Plato, *Rep.* iii. 387 B of false teaching which must not
be listened to by boys and men οὓς δεῖ ἐλευθέρους εἶναι, δουλείαν
θανάτου μᾶλλον πεφοβημένους.

CICERO

XIX

C. CASSIUS S. P. D. M. T. C.

Brundisi, A.U.C. 709.

1 S.v.b. Non mehercule in hac mea peregrinatione
quidquam libentius facio, quam scribo ad te ; videor
enim cum praesente loqui et iocari. Nec tamen hoc
usu venit propter spectra Catiana, pro quo tibi
proxima epistula tot rusticos Stoicos regeram, ut
2 Catium Athenis natum esse dicas. Pansam nostrum
secunda voluntate hominum paludatum ex Urbe
exisse, cum ipsius causa gaudeo, tum mehercule
etiam omnium nostrorum. Spero enim homines
intellecturos, quanto sit omnibus odio crudelitas, et
quanto sit amori probitas et clementia ; atque ea,
quae maxime mali petant et concupiscant, ad bonos
pervenire. Difficile est enim persuadere hominibus,
τὸ καλὸν δι' αὑτὸ αἱρετόν esse ; ἡδονήν vero et ἀταρα-
ξίαν virtute, iustitia, τῷ καλῷ parari, et verum et
probabile est. Ipse enim Epicurus, a quo omnes
Catii et Amafinii, mali verborum interpretes, profici-

---

a See *Ep.* 16 § 1 above.

b *i.e.,* "a man of education and culture," and not such
a boor after all as many of *your* Stoic friends, indifferent
translator of Greek as he may be (and this Cassius admits
at the end of § 2).

Pro quo refers to Cicero's special piece of information in
Ep. 16. 1, that Catius called εἴδωλα *spectra.* Cassius affects
to resent Cicero's sneer, and threatens to overwhelm him
with a crowd of *Stoic* boors, which will make Catius, poor
Grecian as he is, seem a very angel of light.

c See *Ep.* 17. 3. Pansa appears to have made a

334

EPISTULAE AD FAMILIARES, XV. xix.

XIX

CASSIUS TO CICERO

Brundisium, latter half of January, 45 B.C.

If you are well, all is right. I assure you that on 1
this tour of mine there is nothing that gives me more
pleasure to do than to write to you ; for I seem to be
talking and joking with you face to face. And yet that
does not come to pass because of your "*Catian
spectres*" [a] ; and, by way of retaliation for *that*, in
my next letter I shall let loose upon you such a
rabble of Stoic boors that you will proclaim Catius a
true-born Athenian.[b]

I am glad that our friend Pansa was sped on his way 2
by universal goodwill when he left the city in military
uniform,[c] and that not only on my own account, but
also, most assuredly, on that of all our friends. For I
hope that men generally will come to understand how
much all the world hates cruelty, and how much it loves
integrity and clemency, and that the blessings most
eagerly sought and coveted by the bad ultimately
find their way to the good. For it is hard to convince
men that "*the good is to be chosen for its own sake*" ;
but that "*pleasure*" and "*tranquillity of mind*" is
acquired by virtue, justice, and "*the good*," is both
true and demonstrable. Why, Epicurus himself, from
whom all the Catiuses and Amafiniuses [d] in the
world, incompetent translators of terms as they are,

journey to Caesar in Spain, to which both passages refer.
He returned, however, to Rome before he took up the
governorship of Cisalpine Gaul in March, 45.
   [d] C. Amafinius's books on Epicureanism had a great
vogue, though written in an uncouth style.

305

scuntur, dicit : οὐκ ἔστιν ἡδέως ἄνευ τοῦ καλῶς καὶ
3 δικαίως ζῆν. Itaque et Pansa, qui ἡδονήν sequitur,
virtutem retinet, et ii, qui a vobis φιλήδονοι vocantur,
sunt φιλόκαλοι καὶ φιλοδίκαιοι, omnesque virtutes et
colunt et retinent. Itaque Sulla, cuius iudicium probare debemus, cum dissentire philosophos videret,
non quaesiit, quid bonum esset, sed omnia bona
coëmit ; cuius ego mortem forti mehercules animo
tuli. Nec tamen Caesar diutius nos eum desiderare
patietur. Nam habet damnatos, quos pro illo nobis
restituat, nec ipse sectorem desiderabit, cum filium
4 viderit. Nunc, ut ad rempublicam redeam, quid in
Hispaniis geratur, rescribe. Peream, nisi sollicitus
sum, ac malo veterem et clementem dominum habere,
quam novum et crudelem experiri. Scis, Gnaeus
quam sit fatuus ; scis, quomodo crudelitatem virtutem
putet ; scis, quam se semper a nobis derisum putet.
Vereor, ne nos rustice gladio velit ἀντιμυκτηρίσαι.
Quid fiat, si me diligis, rescribe. Hui, quam velim
scire, utrum ista sollicito animo an soluto legas !
sciam enim eodem tempore, quid me facere oporteat.
Ne longior sim, vale ; me, ut facis, ama. Si Caesar
vicit, celeriter me exspecta.

---

[a] See note *a* on *Ep.* 17. 2 above.
[b] Pompey's son.

derive their origin, lays it down that "*to live a life of pleasure is impossible without living a life of virtue and justice.*"

Consequently Pansa, who follows "*pleasure*," keeps 3 his hold on virtue, and those also whom you call "*pleasure-lovers*" are "*lovers of what is good*" and "*lovers of justice*," and cultivate and keep all the virtues. And so Sulla, whose judgment we ought to accept, when he saw that the philosophers were at sixes and sevens, did not investigate the nature of "*the good*," but bought up all the *goods* there were;[a] and I frankly confess that I bore his death without flinching. Caesar, however, will not let us feel his loss too long; for he has a lot of condemned men to restore to us in his stead, nor will he himself feel the lack of someone to bid at his auctions when once he has cast his eye on Sulla junior.

And now to return to politics; please write back and 4 tell me what is being done in the two Spains. May I die if I am not full of anxiety, and I would sooner have the old and lenient master, than make trial of a new and cruel one. You know what an idiot Gnaeus[b] is; you know how he deems cruelty a virtue; you know how he thinks that we have always scoffed at him. I fear that in his boorish way he will be inclined to reply by wiping our turned-up noses with the sword. Write back as you love me, and tell me what is doing. Ah! how I should like to know whether you read all this with an anxious mind or a mind at ease! For I should know at the same time what it is my duty to do. Not to be too long-winded, I bid you farewell. Continue to love me as you do. If Caesar has conquered, look out for my speedy arrival.

307

CICERO

XX

M. T. C. S. P. D. C. TREBONIO

Romae, A.U.C. 709.

1 *Oratorem* meum (sic enim inscripsi) Sabino tuo
commendavi. Natio me hominis impulit, ut ei recte
putarem ; nisi forte, candidatorum licentia hic quoque
usus, hoc subito cognomen arripuit ; etsi modestus
eius vultus sermoque constans habere quiddam a
2 Curibus videbatur. Sed de Sabino satis. Tu, mi
Treboni, quando ad amorem meum aliquantum olei[1]
discedens addidisti, quo tolerabilius feramus igniculum desideri tui, crebris nos litteris appellato ; atque
ita, si idem fiet a nobis. Quamquam duae causae
sunt, cur tu frequentior in isto officio esse debeas,
quam nos ; primum, quod olim solebant, qui Romae
erant, ad provinciales amicos de republica scribere ;
nunc tu nobis scribas oportet. Res enim publica istic
est. Deinde, quod nos aliis officiis tibi absenti satisfacere possumus, tu nobis, nisi litteris, non video,
3 qua re alia satisfacere possis. Sed cetera scribes ad
nos postea. Nunc haec primo cupio cognoscere, iter

---

[1] *Krauss and Koch*: olim MSS.

---

[a] C. Trebonius, who in 55 proposed the law giving to
Pompey the government of Spain, and to Crassus that of
Syria, for five years.

[b] It appears that Ventidius Bassus (see note on x. 18. 3) was
about this time canvassing for the quaestorship, and falsely
assumed the name of Sabinus, and it is to this that Cicero
here refers.

[c] An ancient town of the Sabines, the birthplace of
T. Tatius and Numa Pompilius (Livy, i. 13).

308

XX

CICERO SENDS WARM GREETINGS TO TREBONIUS [a]

Rome, January (?), 45 B.C.

I have entrusted my *Orator* (for I have so en- 1
titled it) to your servant Sabinus. Considering the
man's nationality, I could not help thinking that I
was right in doing so ; unless, of course, he too has
availed himself of the licence given to candidates,
and suddenly seized upon this particular surname [b] ;
and yet his modest expression of face and the calm-
ness of his speech seems to have something derived
from Cures [c] in it. But enough about Sabinus.

You, however, my dear Trebonius, since your de- 2
parture added no little fuel to the fire of my affection
for you, to enable me the more easily to endure the intense ardency of my longing for you, be sure you ply me
with a rapid succession of letters, on the understanding that I shall do likewise. And yet there are two
reasons why you should perform that duty with more
regularity than I—firstly because in olden days it was
the custom for those who were at Rome to write about
the Republic to their friends in the provinces ; now it
is for you to write to us, for the Republic is where you
are.[d] Secondly, because while I can do you many
other services in your absence, I fail to see how you
can serve me in any other way than by writing letters.

But on all other matters you will write to me later. 3
Just now what I am anxious to know before anything

---

[d] In the person of Caesar, now in Spain. This establishes
the date of this letter.

tuum cuiusmodi sit ; ubi Brutum nostrum videris ;
quamdiu simul fueris ; deinde, cum processeris
longius, de bellicis rebus, de toto negotio, ut existimare possimus, quo statu simus. Ego tantum me
scire putabo, quantum ex tuis litteris habebo cognitum. Cura ut valeas, meque ames amore illo tuo
singulari.

XXI

M. T. C. S. P. D. C. TREBONIO

Romae, a.u.c. 708.

1   Et epistulam tuam legi libenter, et librum libentissime ; sed tamen in ea voluptate hunc accepi
dolorem, quod, cum incendisses cupiditatem meam
consuetudinis nostrae augendae (nam ad amorem
quidem nihil poterat accedere), tum discedis a nobis,
meque tanto desiderio afficis, ut unam mihi consolatio-
nem relinquas, fore ut utriusque nostrum absentis
desiderium crebris et longis epistulis leniatur. Quod
ego non modo de me tibi spondere possum, sed de
te etiam mihi. Nullam enim apud me reliquisti
2 dubitationem, quantum me amares. Nam, ut illa
omittam, quae civitate teste fecisti, cum mecum inimicitias communicasti, cum me contionibus tuis
defendisti, cum quaestor in mea atque in publica

---

^a This probably refers to his meeting with Brutus in
Cisalpine Gaul in 46.

^b A collection Trebonius had made and sent to Cicero of
" Ciceroniana," which elicited this letter of thanks.

^c " Trebonius, as quaestor in 60, had vigorously supported
the consuls, Afranius and Metellus Celer, in opposing
the tribune, C. Herennius, who brought forward a law in
favour of the transference of Clodius to the plebeians.
Who Trebonius's colleague was is not certainly known."
Tyrrell.

else is what sort of a journey you are having ; where it was you saw our friend Brutus,[a] and how long you were with him ; after that, when you have got further on your journey, write about military affairs, and indeed about the whole business, so that we can have some idea as to where we stand. I shall regard my knowledge of affairs as being in exact proportion to the information I have got from your letters.

Take care of your health, and continue to love me, as you do, with a love beyond compare.

XXI

CICERO TO TREBONIUS

Rome, towards the end of 46 B.C.

I read your letter with pleasure, and your book[b] **1** with extreme pleasure ; and yet amid all that pleasure it caused me a pang of sorrow, that when you had intensified my desire to tighten the bonds of our intimacy—to our affection, of course, no addition was possible—at that very moment you depart from me and plunge me into so deep a regret as to leave me but one single consolation—the thought that our yearning for one another in our separation may be assuaged by long and frequent letters. And that I can guarantee not only as from me to you, but also as from you to me. For you have left no shadow of doubt in my mind as to your affection for me.

For to omit what the whole state can testify to your **2** having done, when you shared my enmities with me, when you defended me in your public addresses, when as quaestor,[c] in my own, as well as the public interests,

causa consulum partes suscepisti, cum tribuno plebis
quaestor non paruisti, cui tuus praesertim collega
pareret ; ut haec recentia, quae meminero semper,
obliviscar, quae tua sollicitudo de me in armis, quae
laetitia in reditu, quae cura, qui dolor, cum ad te
curae et dolores mei perferrentur ! Brundisium denique te ad me venturum fuisse, nisi subito in Hispaniam missus esses ; ut haec igitur omittam, quae
mihi tanti aestimanda sunt, quanti vitam aestimo et
salutem meam, liber iste, quem mihi misisti, quantam
habet declarationem amoris tui ! primum, quod tibi
facetum videtur, quidquid ego dixi, quod aliis fortasse
non item ; deinde, quod illa, sive faceta sunt sive
secus,[1] fiunt, narrante te, venustissima. Quin etiam
ante, quam ad me veniatur, risus omnis paene con-
3 sumitur. Quod si in iis scribendis nihil aliud, nisi,
quod necesse fuit, de uno me tamdiu cogitavisses,
ferreus essem, si te non amarem. Cum vero ea, quae
scriptura persecutus es, sine summo amore cogitare
non potueris, non possum existimare, plus quemquam
a se ipso, quam me a te amari. Cui quidem ego amori
utinam ceteris rebus possem ! amore certe respondebo ; quo tamen ipso tibi confido futurum satis.
4 Nunc ad epistulam venio, cui copiose et suaviter
scriptae nihil est quod multa respondeam. Primum

---

[1] *Corradus, for* sic (" *so, so* ") *in the* MSS.

you sided with the consuls, when as quaestor again you refused to obey the tribune of the plebs, especially when your own colleague obeyed him—to forget all these more recent services (which I shall ever remember), what solicitude you showed for me in the war, what ecstasy in my recall, what anxiety, what grief, when my own anxieties and griefs reached your ears !—and finally the fact that you would have come to me in Brundisium, had you not been suddenly sent to Spain ;—to omit all those services then, which I am bound to value as highly as I value my own life and welfare, here is this book you have sent me ; what a revelation it is of your affection for me ! First, because whatever I have said seems brilliant to you (not so perhaps to anybody else), and secondly, because those *mots* of mine, be they brilliant or be they not, become perfectly beautiful when you are the teller. Why, even before my name is reached, people have hardly a laugh left in them.

But if this compilation proves (and it must have 3 been so) that you had been thinking of nothing else but of me, and me alone, for so long, I should indeed have a heart of stone if I did not love you. Seeing, however, that unless your affection sprang from the heart you could never have thought out what you have elaborated in writing, I cannot conceive anybody's loving himself more than you love me. And would that I could reciprocate that love in every other direction ! At any rate, as far as my love goes, I shall do so ; and after all I am confident that you will find that enough of itself.

And now I come to your letter, in which you express 4 yourself with exuberance and charm ; but there is no reason why I should write much in reply. In the first

CICERO

enim ego illas Calvo litteras misi, non plus, quam has,
quas nunc legis, existimans exituras. Aliter enim
scribimus, quod eos solos, quibus mittimus, aliter,
quod multos lecturos putamus. Deinde ingenium
eius melioribus extuli laudibus, quam tu id vere potuisse fieri putas. Primum, quod ita iudicabam ; acute
movebatur ; genus quoddam sequebatur ; in quo
iudicio lapsus, quo valebat, tamen assequebatur, quod
probaret. Multae erant et reconditae litterae ; vis
non erat. Ad eam igitur adhortabar. In excitando
autem et in acuendo plurimum valet, si laudes eum,
quem cohortere. Habes de Calvo iudicium et consilium meum—consilium, quod hortandi causa laudavi ; iudicium, quod de ingenio eius valde existimavi
5 bene. Reliquum est, ut tuam profectionem amore
prosequar, reditum spe exspectem, absentem memoria colam, omne desiderium litteris mittendis acci-
piendisque leniam. Tu velim tua in me studia et
officia multum tecum recordere, quae cum tibi liceat,
mihi nefas sit oblivisci, non modo virum bonum me
existimabis, verum etiam te a me amari plurimum
iudicabis. Vale.

---

[a] C. Licinius Macer Calvus, a distinguished orator and
poet. His most famous case was that against Vatinius, when
the latter was defended by Cicero in 54. Calvus was then only
27 years of age. His poems were classed by the ancients
with those of Catullus. He was so short in stature that
Catullus (liii. 5) says he heard him called *Salaputium
disertum*, "the eloquent Tom Thumb." Calvus himself
had no high opinion of Cicero, whom he thought *solutus et
enervis*, "sloppy and flabby," just as Cicero says of him
here that "he lacked force."

[b] I have adopted Dr. J. S. Reid's admirable rendering of
acute movebatur.

place, when I sent that letter to Calvus,[a] I had no idea that it would get abroad any more than the one you are now reading. You see, I have one way of writing what I think will be read by those only to whom I address my letter, and another way of writing what I think will be read by many. In the next place I eulogized his genius in terms of higher praise than you think could have been done with truth. To begin with, it was because I really thought so ; he was a man of keen mental activity [b]; he pursued a certain definite style, and although in that he committed an error of judgment—and yet judgment was his strong point—he none the less did capture the style of his choice. He was a man of wide and abstruse reading, but he lacked force. That is therefore what I pressed him to acquire. Now in rousing and stimulating a man's energies there is nothing more efficacious than to praise him while you urge him on. So there you have my judgment of Calvus, and my object in expressing it—my object was that I praised him with a view to encouraging him ; my judgment, that I had an exceedingly high opinion of his natural abilities.

It only remains for me to speed your departure 5 with my love, to look forward to your return with hope, to cherish your memory in your absence, and to alleviate our mutual yearnings as long as they last by the interchange of letters. On your part I should like you constantly to call to mind your acts of devotion and service to me ; and though it is open to you (it would be a crime in me) to forget them, you will have reason not only to regard me as an honest man, but also to conclude that my affection for you is of the strongest.

M. TULLI CICERONIS EPISTULARUM
AD FAMILIARES
LIBER DECIMUS SEXTUS

I

M. T. C. ET CICERO MEUS ET FR. ET FRATRIS FIL.
S. P. D. TIRONI

Inter Patras et Alyziam, A.U.C. 704.

1 Paullo facilius putavi posse me ferre desiderium
tui, sed plane non fero ; et quamquam magni ad
honorem nostrum interest, quam primum ad Urbem
me venire, tamen peccasse mihi videor, qui a te dis-
cesserim ; sed quia tua voluntas ea videbatur esse,
ut prorsus, nisi confirmato corpore, nolles navigare,
approbavi tuum consilium, neque nunc muto, si tu in
eadem es sententia. Sin autem postea quam cibum
cepisti, videris tibi posse me consequi, tuum consilium
est. Marionem ad te eo misi, ut aut tecum ad me

ᵃ Marcus Tullius Tiro was a slave of Cicero, manumitted
by him in 54 or 53. He was a man of amiable disposition
and of more than ordinary intellectual ability, and was much
beloved by his patron. He was Cicero's amanuensis and
literary assistant, and was himself an author of some reputation, among his works being a defensive biography of his
patron, a treatise on grammar, and some poetry (xvi. 18. 3).
Tiro was the chief agent in compiling and arranging Cicero's

CICERO'S LETTERS TO HIS FRIENDS

BOOK XVI

I

CICERO TO TIRO [a]

Between Patrae and Alyzia, November 3, 50 B.C.

I, Tullius, my son Cicero, and my brother and his son, send warmest greetings to Tiro.

I imagined I could bear the loss of your company 1 somewhat easily, but I simply cannot bear it ; and although it is highly important in view of my triumph that I should reach the City as soon as possible, still I think it was a mistake on my part to have left your side ; and as you seemed to be absolutely unwilling to take ship except when you had recovered your strength, I approved your decision, and I am not now changing my mind, if you are still of the same opinion. If however, after you have taken nourishment, you think you can catch me up, well, that is for you to decide. My object in sending Mario [b] to you was in order that he might join me as soon as possible and

work, and in preserving his correspondence. After Cicero's death he bought a farm near Puteoli, where, in spite of his weak health, he reached the age of 100.

[b] A slave of Cicero. *Cf. Ep.* 3. 2.

CICERO

quam primum veniret, aut, si tu morarere, statim ad
2 me rediret. Tu autem hoc tibi persuade, si commodo
valetudinis tuae fieri possit, nihil me malle, quam
te esse mecum ; si autem intelleges opus esse te
Patris convalescendi causa paullum commorari, nihil
me malle, quam te valere. Si statim navigas, nos
Leucade consequere ; sin te confirmare vis, et comites
et tempestates et navem idoneam ut habeas, diligenter videbis. Unum illud, mi Tiro, videto, si me
amas, ne te Marionis adventus et hae litterae mo-
veant. Quod valetudini tuae maxime conducet, si
feceris, maxime obtemperaris voluntati meae. Haec
pro tuo ingenio considera. Nos ita te desideramus,
ut amemus ; amor, ut valentem videamus, hortatur,
desiderium, ut quam primum. Illud igitur potius.
Cura ergo potissimum, ut valeas ; de tuis innumerabi-
libus in me officiis erit hoc gratissimum. III. Nonas
Novembres.

II

TULLIUS S. P. D. TIRONI SUO

Alyziae, A.U.C. 704.

Non queo ad te nec lubet scribere, quo animo sim
affectus ; tantum scribo, et tibi et mihi maximae
voluptati fore, si te firmum quam primum videro.

ᵃ A town on the coast of Acarnania, midway between
Astacus and Anactorium.

318

bring you with him, or else, if you made any stay, that that he might immediately return to me.

You must, however, convince yourself of this, that if 2 it can be managed without detriment to your health, nothing would please me more than to have you with me ; if, on the other hand, you feel sure that a short stay at Patrae is essential to your convalescence, that nothing would please me more than to have you well. If you take ship at once, you will catch me up at Leucas ; but if you desire to establish your health, you must see to it very carefully that you get the fellow-passengers, the weather, and the ship that exactly suit you. Be particularly mindful, my dear Tiro, as you love me, not to let Mario's arrival, and this letter, influence your plans. If you do what is most conducive to your health, you will best obey my wishes. Think it over, and use your own judgment. For myself, I long for your presence, but it is as one who loves you ; love urges " Let me see you in good health " ; longing " Let it be with all speed." The former consideration then should come first. Above everything, therefore, take care of your health ; of all your countless kindnesses to me this will be the most gratifying. Nov. 3rd.

II

CICERO TO TIRO

Alyzia,[a] November 5, 50 B.C.

I have neither the power nor the inclination to write and tell you what my feelings are ; I only tell you that the greatest pleasure either you or I can enjoy will be my seeing you in robust health as soon as may be.

Tertio die abs te ad Alyziam accesseramus. Is locus
est citra Leucadem stadia cxx. Leucade aut te
ipsum, aut tuas litteras a Marione putabam me
accepturum. Quantum me diligis, tantum fac ut
valeas, vel quantum te a me scis diligi. Nonis Novembr. Alyzia.

III

TULLIUS ET CICERO TIRONI SUO S. D. ET Q. PATER ET Q. FILIUS

Alyziae, A.U.C. 704.

1 Nos apud Alyziam, ex quo loco tibi litteras ante
dederamus, unum diem commorati sumus, quod
Quintus nos consecutus non erat. Is dies fuit Nonae
Novembr. Inde ante lucem proficiscentes, ante diem
VIII. Idus Novembr. has litteras dedimus. Tu, si nos
omnes amas et praecipue me, magistrum tuum, con-
2 firma te. Ego valde suspenso animo exspecto, primum te scilicet, deinde Marionem cum tuis litteris.
Omnes cupimus, ego in primis, quam primum te
videre, sed, mi Tiro, valentem. Quare nihil propera-
ris ; satis, quo te die videro, si valebis. Utilitatibus
tuis possum carere ; te valere, tua causa primum
volo, tum mea, mi Tiro. Vale.

We arrived at Alyzia on the third day after leaving you. The place is 120 stades on your side of Leucas. At Leucas I am expecting either to welcome yourself in person, or to receive a letter from you, brought by Mario. Let your eagerness to be well be as great as your affection for me, or (if you prefer it) as great as you know my affection for you to be. Alyzia, November 5.

III

CICERO TO TIRO

Alyzia, November 6, 50 B.C.

I, Tullius, and Cicero, and Quintus, father and son, send greetings to our Tiro.

We stayed at Alyzia—that is the place from which 1 I despatched a letter to you—for one day, because Quintus had not caught us up. That was November 5. We are despatching this letter just as we are setting out from here before dawn on November 6. As you love us all, and especially myself, who taught you, get strong again.

I am looking forward with the greatest anxiety, 2 first of all, of course, to seeing you, and in the next place to seeing Mario with a letter from you. We all desire to see you, I in particular, as soon as possible, but only, my dear Tiro, if you are well. So do not hurry at all ; it will be enough, if on the day I see you, you are well. I can dispense with the advantage of your services ; I want you to be well, my dear Tiro, first for your own sake, and then for mine. Farewell.

CICERO

IV

TULLIUS ET CICERO ET Q. FR. ET Q. FIL.
S. P. D. TIRONI S.

Leucade, a.u.c. 704.

1 Varie sum affectus tuis litteris ; valde priore pagina
perturbatus, paullum altera recreatus. Quare nunc
quidem non dubito, quin, quoad plane valeas, te
neque navigationi neque viae committas. Satis te
mature videro, si plane confirmatum videro. De
medico et tu bene existimari scribis, et ego sic audio.
Sed plane curationes eius non probo. Ius enim dandum tibi non fuit, cum κακοστόμαχος esses ; sed
tamen et ad illum scripsi accurate, et ad Lysonem.
2 Ad Curium vero, suavissimum hominem et summi
offici summaeque humanitatis, multa scripsi ; in his
etiam, ut, si tibi videretur, te ad se transferret. Lyso
enim noster, vereor, ne neglegentior sit ; primum,
quia omnes Graeci ; deinde, quod, cum a me litteras
accepisset, mihi nullas remisit. Sed eum tu laudas.
Tu igitur, quid faciendum sit, iudicabis. Illud, mi
Tiro, te rogo, sumptu ne parcas ulla in re, quod
ad valetudinem opus sit. Scripsi ad Curium, quod

---

^a His name was Asclapo (xiii. 20).
^b The hotel proprietor at Patrae. See note *a* on xiii. 19. 1.
^c Manius Curius, a money-lender at Patrae. See xiii. 17. 1.

322

IV

CICERO TO TIRO

Leucas, November 7, 50 B.C.

I, Tullius, and Cicero, and my brother Quintus and his son, send warmest greetings to their dear Tiro.

I was variously affected by your letter, being 1 seriously disturbed by the first page, but a little reassured by the second. I am now therefore in no doubt whatever that, until you are perfectly well, you should not trust yourself to any journeyings by sea or land. I shall see you quite soon enough, when I see you in robust health. About your doctor,[a] you yourself write that he is well thought of, and I am told so myself. But as for his treatment of you, I am not at all satisfied with it. For instance, you should never have been given soup, when your stomach was out of order ; anyhow, I have written to him with particular care, and also to Lyso.[b]

To Curius [c] however, that most charming, most 2 obliging and most courteous of men, I have written at great length ; among other things too, that if it be your pleasure, he should take you over into his house. For I am afraid our friend Lyso is a bit casual, first, because all Greeks are so, and secondly, because when he had had a letter from me, he sent me no letter in reply. But you speak highly of him; so you are the best judge as to what should be done. This one thing, my dear Tiro, I beg of you to do—spare no expense in any respect, if it be necessary for your health. I have written to Curius to advance you

323

CICERO

dixisses, daret. Medico ipsi puto aliquid dandum
3 esse, quo sit studiosior. Innumerabilia tua sunt in
me officia, domestica, forensia, urbana, provincialia;
in re privata, in publica, in studiis, in litteris nostris.
Omnia viceris, si, ut spero, te validum videro. Ego
puto, te bellissime, si recte erit, cum quaestore
Mescinio decursurum. Non inhumanus est, teque, ut
mihi visus est, diligit. Et cum valetudini tuae diligentissime consulueris, tum, mi Tiro, consulito navigationi. Nulla in re iam te festinare volo. Nihil laboro,
4 nisi ut salvus sis. Sic habeto, mi Tiro, neminem
esse, qui me amet, quin idem te amet; et cum tua et
mea maxime interest te valere, tum multis est curae.
Adhuc, dum mihi nullo loco deesse vis, numquam te
confirmare potuisti. Nunc te nihil impedit. Omnia
depone; corpori servi. Quantam diligentiam in valetudinem tuam contuleris, tanti me fieri a te iudicabo.
Vale, mi Tiro, vale, vale, et salve. Lepta tibi salutem
dicit et omnes. Vale. VII. Idus Novembr. Leucade.

ᵃ Mescinius Rufus, Cicero's quaestor in Cilicia, to whom
are addressed v. 19 and 20. Cicero had no high opinion of
him as quaestor, but wrote of him in complimentary terms
in xiii. 26.

ᵇ Cicero's *praefectus fabrum.* See iii. 7. 4.

whatever sum you should name. I think something should be given to the doctor himself, to quicken his interest in you.

Your services to me are past all reckoning—at 3 home, in the forum, in the City, in my province, in private as in public affairs, in my literary pursuits and performances. You will surpass them all, if I only see you, as I hope to do, in good health. If all goes well, I think you will have a perfectly charming voyage home with the quaestor Mescinius.[a] He is no churl, and he has always seemed to me to be fond of you. And when you have given the most careful consideration to your health, consider how you may best undertake a voyage. In no respect whatever would I now have you hurry yourself. My one anxiety is for your safety.

Take it as a fact, my dear Tiro, that there is nobody 4 who loves me, who does not also love you ; and while your health is of the highest importance to you and me, it is a matter of solicitude to many. So far, in your desire never to fail me anywhere, you have never been able to recover your strength. Now there is nothing to hinder you. Put everything aside ; be the slave of your body. I shall measure your esteem for me by the amount of care you bestow upon your health. Good-bye, my dear Tiro, good-bye, good-bye, and good health to you ! Lepta [b] sends you his best wishes, and so do all of us. Good-bye ! Leucas, November 7.

CICERO

V

TULLIUS ET CICERO ET Q. Q. S. P. D. TIRONI
HUMANISS. ET OPT.

Leucade,[a] A.U.C. 704.

1 Vide, quanta sit in te suavitas. Duas horas Thyrrei
fuimus. Xenomenes hospes tam te diligit, quam si
vixerit tecum. Is omnia pollicitus est, quae tibi
essent opus. Facturum puto. Mihi placebat, si
firmior esses, ut te Leucadem deportaret, ut ibi te
plane confirmares. Videbis, quid Curio, quid Lysoni,
quid medico placeat. Volebam ad te Marionem
remittere : quem, cum meliuscule tibi esset, ad me
mitteres ; sed cogitavi, unas litteras Marionem afferre
2 posse, me autem crebras exspectare. Poteris igitur,
et facies, si me diligis, ut quotidie sit Acastus in
portu. Multi erunt, quibus recte litteras dare possis,
qui ad me libenter perferant. Equidem Patras euntem neminem praetermittam. Ego omnem spem tui
diligenter curandi in Curio habeo. Nihil potest illo
fieri humanius, nihil nostri amantius. Ei te totum
trade. Malo te paullo post valentem, quam statim
imbecillum videre. Cura igitur nihil aliud, nisi ut tu

---

a In Acarnania, a little south of the Ambracian Gulf.

326

V

CICERO TO TIRO

Off Leucas, November 7, 50 B.C.

Tullius, and Cicero, and the two Quinti, send warmest greetings to that most kindly and best of men, Tiro.

See what an attractive person you are ! We have been two hours at Thyrreum.[a] Xenomenes, my host, is as fond of you as if he had been your life-companion. He has promised to do everything that you require, and I think he will do so. My view was that, should you now be stronger, he should land you in Leucas, so that you might get perfectly well there. You will see what are the views of Curius, of Lyso, and of your doctor. I wanted to send Mario back to you, so that when things are a little better with you, you should send him to me ; but I reflected that Mario could bring me but a single letter, while I was looking forward to a budget.

You can therefore, and, if you love me, you will arrange to have Acastus in attendance at the harbour every day. There will be many to whom you can properly entrust a letter, and who would deliver it to me with pleasure. For my own part I shall not pass over anybody who is going to Patrae. I put all my hopes of your being properly attended to in Curius. Nothing can be kinder or more devoted to me than he is. Put yourself entirely in his hands. I had rather see you well a little later on, than poorly in the immediate present. Let your health be your only care :

327

valeas ; cetera ego curabo. Etiam atque etiam vale.
Leucade proficiscens, VII. Idus Novembr.

VI

M. TULLIUS CIC. PATER ET FIL. ET Q. Q. S. P. D. TIRONI

Acti, A.U.C. 704.

1 Tertiam ad te hanc epistulam scripsi eodem die,
magis instituti mei tenendi causa, quia nactus eram,
cui darem, quam, quo haberem, quod scriberem.
Igitur illa ; quantum me diligis, tantum adhibe in
te diligentiae. Ad tua innumerabilia in me officia
adde hoc, quod mihi erit gratissimum omnium. Cum
valetudinis rationem, ut spero, habueris, habeto etiam
2 navigationis. In Italiam euntibus omnibus ad me
litteras dabis, ut ego euntem Patras neminem praeter-
mitto. Cura, cura te, mi Tiro ; quando non contigit,
ut simul navigares, nihil est, quod festines, nec
quidquam cures, nisi ut valeas. Etiam atque etiam
vale. VII. Idus Novembr. Actio, vesperi.

leave everything else to my care. Good-bye again and again. Just setting out from Leucas. Nov. 7th.

VI

CICERO TO TIRO

Actium, November 7 (evening), 50 B.C.

I Tullius and Cicero, and the two Quinti, send warmest greetings to Tiro.

This is the third letter I have written to you on 1 the same day, more for the sake of keeping to my established practice (having found a man to whom I may entrust it), than because I have anything to write. So I only say this : show as much regard for yourself as is your regard for me. Add this to your countless kindnesses to me, and it will be the most acceptable of them all ; when you have given full consideration to your health, as I hope you will, then give consideration to your voyage also.

Please give letters to me to all who are on their 2 way to Italy ; I never pass over anybody who is on his way to Patrae. Take care, take care of yourself, my dear Tiro. Since you were not fortunate enough to sail in my company, there is no reason why you should hurry, no reason why you should take thought for anything but your health. Again and again, good-bye ! Actium, November 7th, in the evening.

CICERO

VII

Corcyrae, A.U.C. 704.

Septimum iam diem Corcyrae tenebamur ; Quintus autem pater et filius Buthroti. Solliciti eramus de tua valetudine mirum in modum ; nec mirabamur, nihil a te litterarum. Iis enim ventis istinc navigatur, qui si essent, nos Corcyrae non sederemus. Cura igitur te et confirma et, cum commode et per valetudinem et per anni tempus navigare poteris, ad nos, amantissimos tui, veni. Nemo nos amat, qui te non diligat ; carus omnibus exspectatusque venies. Cura, ut valeas. Etiam atque etiam, Tiro noster, vale. xv. Kalend. Decembr. Corcyra.

VIII

Q. C. TIRONI S.

Formiis, A.U.C. 705.

1   Magnae nobis est sollicitudini valetudo tua. Nam, tametsi qui veniunt, ἀκίνδυνα μέν, χρονιώτερα δέ nuntiant, tamen in magna consolatione ingens inest sollicitudo, si diutius a nobis afuturus est is, cuius usum et suavitatem desiderando sentimus. Ac tamen

---

ᵃ The south-east wind, which would facilitate a crossing from Corcyra to Italy, would also bring a letter from Patrae.

330

VII

CICERO TO TIRO

Corcyra, November 16, 50 B.C.

This is the seventh day I have been held up at
Corcyra, but Quintus (father and son) at Buthrotum.
It would surprise you how anxious I am about your
health ; but I am not surprised that there is nothing
in the way of a letter from you, for ships sail from
where you are when they have just such winds as, if
they blew now, would not necessitate our lingering
at Corcyra.[a] Take care of yourself then, and get
strong, and when your health and the season of the
year enable you to sail in comfort, come to us, the
best friends you have. Nobody loves me who is not
fond of you. Dear as you are to us all, your arrival
is eagerly awaited. Take care of your health.
Again and again, Tiro mine, good-bye.

Corcyra, November 16th.

VIII

QUINTUS CICERO TO TIRO

Formiae, February 2 (?), 49 B.C.

Your health is causing us great anxiety. For 1
although those who come from you report that
your illness is not dangerous but will last some
time, yet, great as that consolation may be, it is
marred by an overwhelming anxiety, if we are to
be separated for too long a time from one whose
usefulness and charm we appreciate the better for
missing them. And yet, although my every thought

331

CICERO

quamquam videre te tota cogitatione cupio, tamen te
penitus rogo, ne te tam longae navigationi et viae per
hiemem, nisi bene firmum, committas; neve naviges,
2 nisi explorate. Vix in ipsis tectis et oppidis frigus
infirma valetudine vitatur, nedum in mari et via sit
facile abesse ab iniuria temporis.

Ψῦχος δὲ λεπτῷ χρωτὶ πολεμιώτατον,

inquit Euripides. Cui tu quantum credas, nescio.
Ego certe singulos eius versus singula testimonia
puto. Effice, si me diligis, ut valeas, et ut ad nos
firmus ac valens quam primum venias. Ama nos, et
vale. Q. F. tibi salutem dicit.

IX

M. T. ET C. ET Q. S. P. D. TIRONI

Brundisi, A.U.C. 704.

1 Nos a te, ut scis, discessimus a. d. IV. Non. Novembr.; Leucadem venimus a. d. VIII. Idus Novembr.;
a. d. VII. Actium; ibi propter tempestatem a. d. VI.
Idus morati sumus. Inde a. d. quintum Idus Corcy-
ram bellissime navigavimus. Corcyrae fuimus usque
a. d. XVI. Kalend. Decembr., tempestatibus retenti.
A. d. XV. Kalend. Decembr. in portum Corcyraeorum
ad Cassiopen stadia CXX processimus. Ibi retenti
ventis sumus usque a. d. IX. Kalendas. Interea, qui

---

^a This quotation cannot be traced.
^b A town in the north of Corcyra.

332

is a desire to see you, I beg you from my heart not to entrust yourself to so long a journey by sea and land unless you are quite strong, and not to sail at all without carefully weighing the chances.

Even in houses and towns it is difficult to avoid 2 the cold when one is in poor health ; far less easy is it to escape the cruelty of the winter weather when travelling by sea or land. And " *Cold is the tender skin's most bitter foe,*" as Euripides [a] says. How much *you* believe in him I don't know. I, at any rate, regard all his lines, one after the other, as so many declarations on oath. As you love me, make sure of your health, and of joining us as soon as possible, strong and well. Continue to love us, and good-bye. My son Quintus sends you his greeting.

IX

CICERO TO TIRO

Brundisium, November 26, 50 B.C.

I Tullius and Cicero and Quintus send warmest greetings to Tiro.

We left, as you are aware, on November 2nd. We 1 arrived at Leucas on November 6th, at Actium on the 7th. There, on account of the weather, we stayed during the 8th. From there we had a particularly nice passage on the 9th to Corcyra. We were at Corcyra until November 15th, being held up by storms. On November 16th we proceeded 120 stades to Cassiope,[b] a harbour of the Corcyreans. There we were held up by contrary winds right up to the 22nd. Meanwhile those who impatiently put to sea, and many did so, were shipwrecked.

2 cupide profecti sunt, multi naufragia fecerunt. Nos eo die cenati solvimus. Inde austro lenissimo, caelo sereno, nocte illa et die postero in Italiam ad Hydruntem ludibundi pervenimus, eodemque vento postridie (id erat a. d. VII. Kalend. Decembr.) hora quarta Brundisium venimus; eodemque tempore simul nobiscum in oppidum introiit Terentia, quae te facit plurimi. A. d. v. Kalend. Decembr. servus Cn. Planci Brundisi tandem aliquando mihi a te exspectatissimas litteras reddidit, datas Idibus Novembr., quae me molestia valde levarunt; utinam omnino liberassent! Sed tamen Asclapo medicus

3 plane confirmat, propediem te valentem fore. Nunc quid ego te horter, ut omnem diligentiam adhibeas ad convalescendum? Tuam prudentiam, temperantiam, amorem erga me novi; scio te omnia facturum, ut nobiscum quam primum sis. Sed tamen ita velim, ut ne quid properes. Symphoniam Lysonis vellem vitasses, ne in quartam hebdomada incideres. Sed quoniam pudori tuo maluisti obsequi, quam valetudini, reliqua cura. Curio misi, ut medico honos haberetur, et tibi daret, quod opus esset; me, cui iussisset, curaturum. Equum et mulum Brundisi tibi

---

a Now Otranto.

On that day, after dinner, we weighed anchor. 2 Sailing thence with a very gentle breeze from the south, and a cloudless sky, in the course of that night and the following day we reached Hydruns [a] on the coast of Italy in quite a frolicsome mood, and with the same wind on the day after (that is on November 24) at 10 a.m. we arrived at Brundisium, and at the same time, simultaneously with ourselves, Terentia entered the town ; she values you very highly. On the 26th at Brundisium the slave of Cn. Plancius at last put into my hands your most eagerly awaited letter, dated November 13th. It greatly relieved my distress ; would that it had freed me from it altogether ! But anyhow Asclapo, the doctor, declares positively that you will soon be well again.

As things now are, why should I urge you to 3 devote yourself with all possible assiduity to your convalescence ? I know your common sense, your self-restraint, and your affection for me, and I have no doubt you will move heaven and earth to join us as soon as possible. But my wish that you should do so is qualified by another—that you should not hurry yourself at all. I should have liked you to have refused to attend Lyso's musical party, for fear you might have a fourth attack of your weekly fever. But since you preferred to consider your sense of obligation rather than your health, be more careful for the future. I am sending directions to Curius that your doctor should be given a *douceur*, and that he should let you have any money you require, adding that I shall see to its repayment to any agent he may name. I am leaving a horse and a mule for you at Brundusium. I am afraid there will be

reliqui. Romae vereor, ne ex Kal. Ian. magni tu-
4 multus sint. Nos agemus omnia modice. Reliquum
est, ut te hoc rogem et a te petam, ne temere naviges.
Solent nautae festinare quaestus sui causa. Cautus
sis, mi Tiro. Mare magnum et difficile tibi restat. Si
poteris, cum Mescinio ; caute is solet navigare. Si
minus, cum honesto aliquo homine, cuius auctoritate
navicularius moveatur. In hoc omnem diligentiam si
adhibueris, teque nobis incolumem stiteris, omnia a
te habebo. Etiam atque etiam, noster Tiro, vale.
Medico, Curio, Lysoni de te scripsi diligentissime.
Vale, salve.

X

M. T. C. S. P. D. TIRONI

Cumis, a.u.c. 701 vel 700.

1   Ego vero cupio te ad me venire, sed viam timeo.
Gravissime aegrotasti ; inedia et purgationibus et vi
ipsius morbi consumptus es. Graves solent offensiones
esse ex gravibus morbis, si quae culpa commissa est.
Iam ad id biduum, quod fueris in via, dum in
Cumanum venis, accedent continuo ad reditum dies
336

serious disturbances at Rome after January 1st. As for myself, I shall act with moderation in all things.

It remains for me to request you, nay, to entreat 4 you, not to be too hasty in taking ship. Sailors are apt to hurry things with an eye to their own gain. Be cautious, my dear Tiro. You have yet a good bit of sea, and a difficult one, to cross. If you possibly can, come across with Mescinius : he is always cautious in making a voyage. Failing that, have some man of standing with you who can exercise some authority over the shipowner. If you take every precaution in this respect, and put in an appearance among us safe and sound, you will have given me all I want. Again and again, Tiro mine, good-bye. I am writing with the utmost particularity about you to your doctor, to Curius, and to Lyso. Good-bye, and good health to you.

X

CICERO TO TIRO

Cumae, April 17, 54 or 53 B.C.

Yes indeed, I am anxious that you should join me, 1 but I am afraid of your travelling. You have been very seriously ill, and you are exhausted from fasting, and taking purgatives, and the violence of the attack itself. Serious illnesses are apt to be followed by serious complications, if any mistake is made. Then, again, to the two days you will have been on the road to Cumae there will be added the five succeeding days needed for your return. I want to

CICERO

quinque. Ego in Formiano a. d. III. Kalend. esse volo.
2 Ibi te ut firmum offendam, mi Tiro, effice. Litterulae
meae, sive nostrae, tui desiderio oblanguerunt. Hac
tamen epistula, quam Acastus attulit, oculos paullum
sustulerunt. Pompeius erat apud me, cum haec
scribebam, hilare et libenter. Ei cupienti audire
nostra dixi sine te omnia mea muta esse. Tu Musis
nostris para ut operas reddas. Nostra ad diem dictam
fient. Docui enim te, fides ἔτυμον quod haberet. Fac
plane ut valeas. Nos adsumus. Vale. XIV. Kal.

XI

M. T. ET C., TERENTIA ET TULLIA, Q. FRATER ET
Q. F. S. P. D. TIRONI

Ad Urbem, A.U.C. 705.

1 Etsi opportunitatem operae tuae omnibus locis
desidero, tamen non tam mea, quam tua causa doleo,
te non valere. Sed cum in quartanam conversa vis est
morbi (sic enim scribit Curius), spero te, diligentia
adhibita, etiam firmiorem fore. Modo fac, id quod
est humanitatis tuae, ne quid aliud cures hoc tempore,
nisi ut quam commodissime convalescas. Non ignoro,
quantum ex desiderio labores, sed erunt omnia facilia,

ᵃ " Cum fit quod dicitur," " when what is said is done."
Rep. iv. 21. But in *Off.* i. 21 he fears the derivation is
durius, " a little hard to swallow."
ᵇ *i.e.,* " ready to be called upon," a term borrowed from
the law-courts.
338

be at Formiae on the 28th inst. See to it, my dear Tiro, that I find you there in robust health.

My poor little studies (or if you like, *ours*) have 2 simply pined away from longing for you. But this letter which Acastus brought me has made them lift up their eyes a little. Pompey is staying with me as I write these words ; he is in good spirits and enjoying himself. When he expresses a desire to hear something of mine, I tell him that, without you, I am altogether dumb. Please be ready to render due services to our Muses. My promise will be fulfilled on the appointed day (I have given you the etymology of the word *fides*).[a] Mind you make a complete recovery. We are " in attendance " [b] here. Good-bye ! April 17.

XI

CICERO TO TIRO

Before Rome, January 12, 49 B.C.

I Tullius and my son, Terentia, Tullia, and Quintus and his son, send warmest greetings to Tiro.

Although I miss your timely assistance at every 1 turn, yet it is not on my own account so much as on yours that your illness grieves me. But now that your violent attack has turned into a quartan fever, according to Curius's letter, I hope that with proper care you will recover your strength. Only be sure, and it is no more than your duty as a man, to give your undivided attention during these days to getting well again with all the comfort you can command. I am well aware how much you are harassed by your longing to be with us, but if you only recover your health,

si valebis. Festinare te nolo, ne nauseae molestiam
2 suscipias aeger, et periculose hieme naviges. Ego ad
Urbem accessi pridie Nonas Ianuar. Obviam mihi sic
est proditum, ut nihil potuerit fieri ornatius. Sed
incidi in ipsam flammam civilis discordiae vel potius
belli ; cui cum cuperem mederi et, ut arbitror,
possem, cupiditates certorum hominum (nam ex utra-
que parte sunt, qui pugnare cupiant) impedimento
mihi fuerunt. Omnino et ipse Caesar, amicus noster,
minaces ad senatum et acerbas litteras miserat, et erat
adhuc impudens, qui exercitum et provinciam invito
senatu teneret, et Curio meus illum incitabat. Antonius quidem noster et Q. Cassius, nulla vi expulsi,
ad Caesarem cum Curione profecti erant, postea quam
senatus consulibus, praetoribus, tribunis plebis et
nobis, qui proconsules sumus, negotium dederat, ut
curaremus, ne quid respublica detrimenti caperet.
3 Numquam maiore in periculo civitas fuit, numquam
improbi cives habuerunt paratiorem ducem. Omnino
ex hac quoque parte diligentissime comparatur. Id
fit auctoritate et studio Pompei nostri, qui Caesarem
sero coepit timere. Nobis inter has turbas senatus
tamen frequens flagitavit triumphum ; sed Lentulus
consul, quo maius suum beneficium faceret, simul
atque expedisset, quae essent necessaria de republica,

---

a See Chron. Summ. for 49 B.C.

340

all difficulties will vanish. I would not have you hurry yourself, lest you should have to suffer the agonies of sea-sickness in your feeble state, and lest a winter voyage should prove dangerous.

I approached the City on January 4. Nothing 2 could be more complimentary than the way I was met by a procession. But my arrival coincided with a very conflagration of civil discord, or rather civil war ; and though I had the eager desire, and I believe, the power, to find a remedy for it, I was thwarted by the passionate desires of certain men ; for there are those on both sides who desire to fight. To sum up, Caesar himself too, our former friend, has sent a threatening and disagreeable despatch to the Senate, and is still so insolent as to defy the Senate in retaining his army and province ; and my old friend Curio eggs him on. Our friend Antony indeed and Q. Cassius, though no violence was used in expelling them, set out in Curio's company to join Caesar, as soon as the Senate had formally charged the consuls, praetor, tribunes of the plebs, and us proconsuls with the duty of seeing that " the Republic suffered no injury."

Never was the State in greater danger ; [a] never 3 have disloyal citizens had a better prepared man at their head. On the whole very careful preparations are being made on our side also. That is due to the influence and activity of our old friend Pompey, who, now that it is too late, is beginning to be afraid of Caesar. Amid all these disturbing occurrences a full Senate none the less demanded that I should have a triumph, but Lentulus, the consul, in order to enhance the value of his own services, said that, as soon as he had despatched the necessary public

dixit se relaturum. Nos agimus nihil cupide, eoque
4 est nostra pluris auctoritas. Italiae regiones de-
scriptae sunt, quam quisque partem tueretur. Nos
Capuam sumpsimus. Haec te scire volui. Tu etiam
atque etiam cura, ut valeas, litterasque ad me mittas,
quotiescumque habebis, cui des. Etiam atque etiam
vale. D. pridie Idus Ian.

XII

M. T. C. S. P. D. TIRONI SUO

Capuae, A.U.C. 705.

1 Quo in discrimine versetur salus mea et bonorum
omnium atque universae reipublicae, ex eo scire
potes, quod domos nostras, et patriam ipsam vel
diripiendam vel inflammandam reliquimus. In eum
locum res deducta est, ut, nisi qui deus vel casus
2 aliquis subvenerit, salvi esse nequeamus. Equidem
ut veni ad Urbem, non destiti omnia et sentire et
dicere et facere, quae ad concordiam pertinerent ; sed
mirus invaserat furor non solum improbis, sed etiam
his, qui boni habentur, ut pugnare cuperent, me
clamante, nihil esse bello civili miserius. Itaque cum
Caesar amentia quadam raperetur et, oblitus nominis
atque honorum suorum, Ariminum, Pisaurum, Anco-
342

business, he would bring forward a motion on the subject. I am doing nothing in a spirit of self-aggrandizement, and my influence is by so much the more esteemed. Italy has been marked out into 4 districts, showing what part is under the charge of each of us. I have chosen Capua. That is all I wanted you to know. Again and again I beg you to take care of your health, and to send me a letter whenever you find a man to entrust with one. Again and again, good-bye. January 12.

XII

CICERO TO TIRO

Capua, January 27, 49 B.C.

The extreme peril to which my own personal safety 1 and that of all loyal citizens, and indeed that of the whole body politic is exposed, you may infer from our having abandoned our homes and our very country to either rapine or conflagration. To such a pass have things come, that unless some god, or some chance or other, comes to our aid, we cannot escape ruin.

For myself, never, since I came to the city, have I 2 ceased by thought, word, and deed, to help the cause of harmony ; but a mysterious madness had possessed not only the disloyal, but those also who are regarded as loyal, making them eager to fight, in spite of my outcries that the worst of all miseries is a civil war. Consequently, when Caesar was seized with a sort of insanity, and, forgetting his name, and the honours he held, had occupied Ariminum, Pisaurum, Ancona,

343

nam, Arretium occupavisset, Urbem reliquimus ;
quam sapienter aut quam fortiter, nihil attinet dis-
3 putare. Quo quidem in casu simus, vides. Feruntur
omnino condiciones ab illo, ut Pompeius eat in
Hispaniam ; delectus, qui sunt habiti, et praesidia
nostra dimittantur ; se ulteriorem Galliam Domitio,
citeriorem Considio Noniano (his enim obtigerunt)
traditurum ; ad consulatus petitionem se venturum ;
neque se iam velle, absente se, rationem haberi sui ;
se praesentem trinum nundinum petiturum. Accepimus condiciones ; sed ita, ut removeat praesidia
ex his locis, quae occupavit, ut sine metu de iis ipsis
4 condicionibus Romae senatus haberi possit. Id ille
si fecerit, spes est pacis non honestae ; leges enim
imponuntur. Sed quidvis est melius, quam sic esse,
ut sumus. Sin autem ille suis condicionibus stare
noluerit, bellum paratum est ; eiusmodi tamen, quod
sustinere ille non possit, praesertim cum a suis condicionibus ipse fugerit ; tantummodo ut eum inter-
cludamus, ne ad Urbem possit accedere ; quod
sperabamus fieri posse. Delectus enim magnos habebamus ; putabamusque illum metuere, si ad Urbem
ire coepisset, ne Gallias amitteret ; quas ambas habet
inimicissimas, praeter Transpadanos ; ex Hispania-

---

a L. Domitius Ahenobarbus.
b Probably the man who was praetor in 52.
c A *nundinum* being a period of eight days, three *nundina*
would be twenty-four days, the time required by law for the
professio (public declaration or manifesto) of a candidate
for office. *Trinum nundinum*, originally a gen. plur.,
came to be used (like *sestertium*) as a neuter singular, and
is here an accusative of duration of time.

344

and Arretium, we left the city; the wisdom or courage of that course it is now useless to discuss.

At any rate you see our position. These, broadly 3 speaking, are the terms Caesar offers—that Pompey should go to Spain, that the recently levied troops, and our garrisons, should be disbanded, that upon this he will surrender Northern Gaul to Domitius,[a] and Southern Gaul to Considius Nonianus [b] (for it was to them that those provinces have been allotted); that he will return to canvass for the consulship, that he no longer wishes his candidature to be admitted in his absence, and that he will be a candidate on the spot for the period covering three *nundina*.[c] These terms we have accepted, but only on condition that he withdraws his garrisons from the places he has occupied, so that the Senate may meet in Rome to discuss these same terms with no sense of apprehension.

If he does so, there is some hope of peace, though 4 not with honour; for they are orders that are laid upon us. But anything is better than that our present plight should continue. If, however, he refuses to stand by his own terms, war is ready at hand, but such a war as he could not possibly face (especially after abandoning his own conditions), if only we cut him off from all chance of approaching the city; and that we hope can be done, as we are holding levies on an extensive scale; and we believe that he is afraid, if once he begins to march upon the city, of losing the two Gauls, both of which he finds extremely hostile to him, with the exception of the Transpadani.[d] From

[a] Whose claims to the franchise had been warmly supported by Caesar, who carried them into effect when he came to Rome in April.

que sex legiones et magna auxilia, Afranio et Petreio
ducibus, habet a tergo. Videtur, si insaniet, posse
opprimi ; modo ut urbe salva ! Maximam autem
plagam accepit, quod is, qui summam auctoritatem in
illius exercitu habebat, T. Labienus, socius sceleris
esse noluit ; reliquit illum et nobiscum est ; multique
5 idem facturi esse dicuntur. Ego adhuc orae maritimae
praesum a Formiis. Nullum maius negotium suscipere volui, quo plus apud illum meae litterae co-
hortationesque ad pacem valerent. Sin autem erit
bellum, video me castris et certis legionibus prae-
futurum. Habeo etiam illam molestiam, quod Dolabella noster apud Caesarem est. Haec tibi nota esse
volui ; quae cave ne te perturbent et impediant
6 valetudinem tuam. Ego A. Varroni, quem cum
amantissimum mei cognovi, tum etiam valde tui
studiosum, diligentissime te commendavi, ut et valetudinis tuae rationem haberet et navigationis, et
totum te susciperet ac tueretur ; quem omnia facturum confido. Recepit enim, et mecum locutus est
suavissime. Tu, cum eo tempore mecum esse non
potuisti, quo ego maxime operam et fidelitatem de-
sideravi tuam, cave festines aut committas, ut aut
aeger aut hieme naviges. Numquam sero te venisse

---

[a] T. Labienus was afterwards slain at Munda.
[b] Caesar.   [c] For this Varro see note *a* on xiii. 22. 1.

the direction of Spain too he has six legions and a strong force of auxiliaries under the command of Afranius and Petreius, threatening his rear. Should he play the madman, it looks as though he might be crushed,—if only he could be, and Rome still safe ! The heaviest blow he has had, however, is that the man who held the most influential position in his army, T. Labienus,[a] has refused to associate himself with his chief's misdeeds ; he has left him and come over to us, and it is said that many others are likely to do the same.

Myself I am still in command of all the sea-coast, 5 south of Formiae ; I was disinclined to undertake any greater responsibility, so that my letters and remonstrances might carry greater weight with our friend [b] in favour of peace. If there be a war, however, I foresee that I shall be given the command of a camp and certain legions. I have this also to worry me, that my son-in-law Dolabella is in Caesar's camp. I wanted you to be apprised of all this, but take care that it does not put you out, or stand in the way of your recovery.

I have commended you very earnestly to A. Varro,[c] 6 whom I have found to be not only a very true friend to myself, but also sincerely devoted to you, asking him to interest himself in your health and voyage, and take you entirely under his charge and protection. All this I feel sure he will do ; for he guaranteed that he would, and spoke to me most charmingly. Since you could not be with me at the very time when I chiefly missed your faithful services, mind you do not hurry now, or make the mistake of sailing when you are ill, or the weather is bad. I shall never think you have come too late, if you are safe and sound when you do

putabo, si salvus veneris. Adhuc neminem videram,
qui te postea vidisset quam M. Volusius, a quo tuas
litteras accepi; quod non mirabar; neque enim meas
puto ad te litteras tanta hieme perferri. Sed da
operam, ut valeas; et, si valebis, cum recte navigari
poterit, tum naviges. Cicero meus in Formiano erat,
Terentia et Tullia Romae. Cura, ut valeas. IV.
Kalendas Febr. Capua.

XIII

M. T. C. S. P. D. TIRONI

Cumis, A.U.C. 700 vel 701.

Omnia a te data mihi putabo, si te valentem videro.
Summa cura exspectabam adventum Menandri, quem
ad te miseram. Cura, si me diligis, ut valeas et,
cum te bene confirmaris, ad nos venias. Vale. IV.
Idus April.

XIV

M. T. C. S. P. D. TIRONI

Cumis, A.U.C. 700 vel 701.

1 Andricus postridie ad me venit quam exspectaram.
Itaque habui noctem plenam timoris ac miseriae.
Tuis litteris nihilo sum factus certior, quomodo te
haberes; sed tamen sum recreatus. Ego omni de-

---

^a For Volusius see v. 20. 3.
^b Some editors read *Andrici* here; others leave *Menandri*
and read *Menander* at the beginning of the next letter.

348

come. Up to the present I have seen nobody who saw you since M. Volusius [a] did, from whose hands I received your letter, and I am not surprised at it, for I don't think my own letters to you reach their destination in such wintry weather. But do all you can to get well, and if you are well, only sail when a voyage can be made with safety. My boy Cicero is in my house at Formiae, Terentia and Tullia at Rome. Take care of your health. Capua, January 27.

XIII

CICERO TO TIRO

Cumae, April 10, 54 or 53 B.C.

I shall consider that you have done me every possible favour, if I see you in good health. I await with the greatest anxiety the arrival of Menander,[b] whom I sent to you. As you love me, take care of your health, and mind you join us when you have made a complete recovery. Good-bye. April 10th.

XIV

CICERO TO TIRO

Cumae, April 10, 54 or 53 B.C.

Andricus did not join me until the day after I expected him; so I had a night full of fear and misery. Your letter added nothing at all to my information as to your condition, but all the same it relieved me. I have nothing to amuse me, no

lectatione litterisque omnibus careo; quas ante
quam te videro, attingere non possum. Medico mer-
cedis, quantum poscet, promitti iubeto. Id scripsi
2 ad Ummium. Audio te animo angi, et medicum
dicere ex eo te laborare. Si me diligis, excita ex
somno tuas litteras humanitatemque, propter quam
mihi es carissimus. Nunc opus est te animo valere, ut
corpore possis. Id cum tua, tum mea causa facias, a
te peto. Acastum retine, quo commodius tibi mini-
stretur. Conserva te mihi; dies promissorum adest,
quem etiam repraesentabo,—si adveneris. Etiam atque etiam vale. IV. Idus hora VI.

XV

M. T. C. S. P. D. TIRONI

Cumis, A.U.C. 700 vel 701.

1   Aegypta ad me venit pridie Idus Apriles. Is etsi
mihi nuntiavit, te plane febri carere et belle habere,
tamen, quod negavit te potuisse ad me scribere,
curam mihi attulit, et eo magis, quod Hermia, quem
eodem die venire oportuerat, non venerat. Incredibili sum sollicitudine de tua valetudine; qua si me
liberaris, ego te omni cura liberabo. Plura scriberem,
si iam putarem libenter te legere posse. Ingenium
tuum, quod ego maximi facio, confer ad te mihi

ª Perhaps Cicero's *dispensator*, household steward, at
Tusculum.
ᵇ To manumit you.
ᶜ Formerly a slave, now a freedman, of Cicero.
ᵈ Probably a slave of Cicero. *Cf. Q. Fr.* i. 2. 12.

literary work on hand ; I cannot bring myself to touch it, until I see you. Please give orders that your doctor shall be promised whatever fee he asks. I am writing to that effect to Ummius.[a]

I am told that you are distressed in mind, and 2 that your doctor says that you are suffering in health as a result of it. As you love me, arouse from slumber your literary talents, and that culture which makes you so precious to me. You must now be well in mind, so as to be so in body. I beg of you to ensure this as much for my sake as for your own. Retain Acastus's services, so that you may be waited upon with greater comfort. Keep yourself safe for me ; the day of my promise [b] is at hand—indeed, I shall definitely fix it now—it will be the day you arrive. Again and again, good-bye. Noon, April 10.

XV

CICERO TO TIRO

Cumae, April 12, 54 or 53 B.C.

Aegypta [c] joined me here on April 12th. Al- 1 though he reported that you were entirely rid of your fever and were going on nicely, yet his telling me that you had been unable to write caused me some anxiety ; and all the more so, because Hermia,[d] who ought to have arrived on the same day, has not done so. You could not believe how anxious I am about your health : if you relieve me from that anxiety, I will relieve you of all your duties. I should write a longer letter if I thought you were now able to enjoy the reading of it. Concentrate your wits, of which I have the highest opinion,

tibique conservandum. Cura te etiam atque etiam
2 diligenter. Vale. Scripta iam epistula, Hermia venit.
Accepi tuam epistulam, vacillantibus litterulis ; nec
mirum, tam gravi morbo. Ego ad te Aegyptam misi,
quod nec inhumanus est et te visus est mihi diligere ;
ut is tecum esset ; et cum eo coquum, quo uterere.
Vale.

XVI

Q. C. S. P. D. M. CICERONI FRATRI

In Gallia (?), A.U.C. 700 vel 701.

1   De Tirone, mi Marce, ita te meumque Ciceronem
et meam Tulliolam tuumque filium videam, ut mihi
gratissimum fecisti, cum eum, indignum illa fortuna,
nobis amicum quam servum esse maluisti. Mihi
crede, tuis et illius litteris perlectis, exsilui gaudio.
2 Tibi et ago gratias et gratulor. Si enim mihi Stati
fidelitas est tantae voluptati, quanti esse in isto
haec eadem bona debent, additis litteris, sermonibus,
humanitate, quae sunt his ipsis commodis potiora!
Amo te omnibus equidem maximis de causis, verum
etiam propter hanc, vel quod mihi sic, ut debuisti,
352

upon keeping yourself safe for my benefit, as well
as your own. Use every care (I say it again and
again) in looking after your health. Good-bye.

P.S. Since the above was written Hermia has 2
turned up. I have got your letter, though your poor
handwriting is very shaky ; and no wonder, after
so serious an illness. I send you Aegypta to stay
with you, because he is not without culture, and is,
I believe, fond of you ; and with him a cook, for you
to make use of. Good-bye.

XVI

QUINTUS CICERO TO MARCUS CICERO

Rome, or on his way to, or in Transalpine Gaul,
54 or 53 B.C.

In the matter of Tiro, my dear Marcus, as surely 1
as I hope to see you, and my son Cicero, and my
darling Tullia, and your son, you have done what
gave me extreme pleasure, when you preferred
that he whose position was so unworthy of him
should be our friend rather than a slave. Believe me,
when I had perused your letter, and his, I jumped
for joy, and I not only thank, but I congratulate
you too.

For if Statius's faithful service is so constant a 2
pleasure to me, how inestimable should such good
qualities be in your man, when we think too of his
literary and conversational powers, and his refinement—merits which outweigh even those qualities
which minister to our personal comfort. I have every
reason, and each the strongest possible, to love you,
and I have this reason also, I mean that you sent me

353

nuntiasti. Te totum in litteris vidi. Sabini pueris
et promisi omnia, et faciam.

XVII

M. T. C. S. P. D. TIRONI

Asturae, A.U.C. 709.

Video, quid agas : tuas quoque epistulas vis referri
in volumina. Sed heus tu, qui κανών esse meorum
scriptorum soles, unde illud tam ἄκυρον, *valetudini
fideliter inserviendo* ? Unde in istum locum *fideliter*
venit ? cui verbo domicilium est proprium in officio,
migrationes in alienum multae. Nam et doctrina et
domus et ars et ager etiam *fidelis* dici potest, ut sit,
quomodo Theophrasto placet, verecunda tralatio. Sed
haec coram. Demetrius venit ad me, quo quidem
comitatu ἀφωμίλησα, satis scite.[1] Tu eum videlicet
non potuisti videre. Cras aderit ; videbis igitur.
Nam ego hinc perendie mane cogito. Valetudo tua

---

[1] *H.F.D.* : satis scis *Nobbe.*

---

[a] The news of Tiro's manumission.

[b] See xv. 20. 1.

[c] κανών = Lat. *norma*, the standard by which what is
correct is tested. ἄκυρον = "an unauthorized or obsolete
expression."

[d] Cicero's objection seems to us hypercritical : he appears
to argue that because *fidelis* implies unselfish service to others,
its application to the selfish care of one's own health is a
contradiction in terms, a confusion of the objective with the
subjective. But that *fideliter* can be used in the wider sense

the news [a] in precisely the proper way. All of you was revealed to me in your letter. I have promised Sabinus's [b] serving-men to do all they asked, and I shall do so.

XVII

Astura, July 29, 45 B.C.

I see what you are up to; you want your own letters also to be put into book form. But look you here, sir, you who love to be the "rule" [c] of *my* writings, where did you get such a solecism as "*faith-fully* ministering to your health"? How comes *fideliter* [d] to be used in such a connexion? That word's proper home is in the province of duty, though its migrations to foreign territory are frequent—for instance, learning, a house, art, or even a field, can all be called "*faithful*," provided, as Theophrastus holds, that its metaphorical application is not shockingly extravagant. But of this when we meet.

Demetrius [e] came to see me, but I was clever enough to extricate myself from that companion-ship. You evidently could not have seen him. He will be in Rome to-morrow, so you will see him then. My own intention is not to leave this place till the morning after next.

Your health is a great anxiety to me; but go on

of "thoroughly" or "conscientiously" is proved by Ovid's
"*ingenuas didicisse fideliter artes Emollit mores.*"
    [e] Perhaps this is Demetrius of Sadara, a favourite freed-man of Pompey's.   Tyrrell.

me valde sollicitat, sed inservi, et fac omnia. Tum
te mecum esse, tum mihi cumulatissime satisfacere
putato. Cuspio quod operam dedisti, mihi gratum
est. Valde enim eius causa volo. Vale.

XVIII

TULLIUS S. P. D. TIRONI

Romae, A.U.C. 709.

1   Quid igitur? non sic oportet? Equidem censeo
sic. Addendum etiam *suo*. Sed, si placet, invidia
vitetur; quam quidem ego saepe contempsi. Tibi
διαφόρησιν gaudeo profuisse. Si vero etiam Tusculanum, di boni! quanto mihi illud erit amabilius! Sed,
si me amas, quod quidem aut facis aut perbelle simulas,
quod tamen in modum procedit; sed utut[1] est, indulge
valetudini tuae, cui quidem tu adhuc, dum mihi
deservis, servisti non satis. Ea quid postulet, non
ignoras—πέψιν, ἀκοπίαν, περίπατον σύμμετρον, τρῖψιν,[2]

---

[1] *Manutius and Lambinas* : ut *Nobbe*.
[2] *HDF* : τρψιν M : *others read* τέρψιν.

---

[a] Probably the Cuspius referred to in xiii. 6*a*. 1.

[b] Cicero anticipates Tiro's objection to being addressed
without his *praenomen* (Marcus), as being too familiar and
unsuited to their respective positions. Cicero would go a step
further in familiarity and write "*Tullius Tironi suo*." For
the omission of the *praenomen* as a mark of intimacy see vii.
32. 1.

" ministering " to it, and do all you can for it. It is then you are at my side, it is then you give me the most unbounded satisfaction ; remember that.

I am thankful to you for all the assistance you have given Cuspius,[a] for I heartily wish him success. Good-bye.

XVIII

TULLIUS GREETS TIRO

Rome, late in December, 45 B.C.

Well, what of it ?[b] Should it not be so ? I think it should be so myself, and that even " *his dear* " should be added. But, since you wish it, let us avoid provoking unfavourable comment, which, I must say, I have often treated with contempt. I am delighted that the sudorifics have done you good. But if my Tusculan villa has done so too, good heavens, how much more charming the place will be to me ! But as you love me—and indeed you either do so, or make a very pretty pretence of doing so, in which, I admit, you succeed very well[c] —but however that may be, give your health fair play ; hitherto, while ministering so devotedly to me, you have not ministered to it enough. What it demands you are well aware—good digestion, avoidance of fatigue, a proper amount of walking,

---

[c] Dr. Reid translates it " which pretence, however, I must say answers your wishes," adding that *procedere in modum* denotes undisturbed rhythmical movement, hence movement in accordance with one's wishes.

CICERO

εὐλυσίαν κοιλίας. Fac bellus revertare. Non modo
2 te, sed etiam Tusculanum nostrum plus amem. Pare-
drum excita, ut hortum ipse conducat. Sic holitorem
ipsum commovebis. Helico[1] nequissimus HS ↀ
dabat, nullo aprico horto, nullo emissario, nulla ma-
ceria, nulla casa. Iste nos tanta impensa derideat?
Calface hominem, ut ego Mothonem. Itaque abundo[2]
3 coronis. De Crabra quid agatur, etsi nunc quidem
etiam nimium est aquae, tamen velim scire. Horo-
logium mittam et libros, si erit sudum. Sed tu
nullosne tecum libellos? an pangis aliquid Sophocleum? Fac opus appareat. A. Ligurius, Caesaris
familiaris, mortuus est, bonus homo et nobis amicus.
Te quando exspectemus, fac ut sciam. Cura te diligenter. Vale.

XIX

M. T. C. S. P. D. TIRONI

Tusculi, A.U.C. 709.

Exspecto tuas litteras de multis rebus, te ipsum

---

[1] Salaco *Schütz*: Helluo *Reid.*
[2] *Boot and Reid*: abutor *Tyrrell and others.*

[a] Some editors read τέρψιν, "amusement."
[b] Cicero wishes Tiro to urge one Paredrus, a market-gardener, to rent Cicero's garden, and so stir up the present gardener, who is paying a ridiculously small rent, in spite of the improvements Cicero had recently made in it.
[c] Apparently another market-gardener.
[d] The present gardener.
[e] An aqueduct extending from Tusculum to Rome, for the use of which Cicero paid a tax.

358

massage,[a] and free action of the bowels. Mind you return in fine fettle. It would make me fonder, not only of you, but of my Tusculan house.

Wake up Paredrus [b] to hire the garden for him- 2 self. Your doing so will give the present gardener a shaking-up. Why, that hopeless rascal Helico [c] used to pay me 1000 sesterces, when there was no sunny-corner, no water-drain, no wall, no garden-shed. Is he [d] to have the laugh of us, when we have gone to all that expense? Warm the fellow up, as I do Motho here, with the result that I get a glut of cut flowers.

As to the Crabra,[e] although at present we have 3 more water than we need, still I should like to know what is being done about it. I shall send you the sun-dial and the book, if we have dry weather. But about yourself, have you no light literature with you? Or are you composing something in the style of Sophocles? Let us see what you have done.

A. Ligurius,[f] the friend of Caesar, is dead—a good man and friendly disposed to me. Be sure to let me know when we are to expect you. Take particular care of yourself. Good-bye.

XIX

CICERO TO TIRO

Tusculum, early in August, 45 b.c.

I am looking forward to a letter from you on many points, but far more to seeing you in person.

[f] Mentioned in *Q. Fr.* iii. 7. 2.

multo magis. Demetrium redde nostrum, et aliud,
si quid potest boni. De Aufidiano nomine nihil te
hortor. Scio tibi curae esse. Sed confice. Et, si ob
eam rem moraris, accipio causam ; si id te non tenet,
advola. Litteras tuas valde exspecto. Vale.

XX

M. T. C. S. P. D. TIRONI

Romae, a.u.c. 709.

Sollicitat, ita vivam, me tua, mi Tiro, valetudo : sed
confido, si diligentiam, quam instituisti, adhibueris,
cito te firmum fore. Libros compone, indicem, cum
Metrodoro lubebit, quando eius arbitratu vivendum
est. Cum holitore, ut videtur. Tu potes Kalendis
spectare gladiatores, postridie redire ; et ita censeo.
Verum ut videbitur. Cura te, si me amas, diligenter.
Vale.

---

^a Who seems to have taken umbrage at Cicero's avoidance
of him.
^b Probably a citizen of Tusculum who owed Cicero money.

360

Send me back my Demetrius,[a] and send me anything else you can, if it is good. In the matter of Aufidius's[b] debt, I put no pressure upon you. I know it is an anxiety to you. But settle the business. If that is what detains you, I accept the excuse; if that is not holding you back, come here post-haste. I am eagerly awaiting a letter from you. Good-bye.

XX

CICERO TO TIRO

Rome, end of 45 B.C.

Upon my life, my dear Tiro, your health worries me; but I feel sure that if you devote that attention to it which you have begun to do, you will soon be well again. Please arrange my books and make a catalogue of them when Metrodorus[c] has no objection: since you have got to live according to his injunctions. Settle with the gardener[d] as you think proper. You can see the gladiators on January 1st, and return the next day, and that is what I think you ought to do. But just as you please. Take particular care of yourself, as you love me. Good-bye.

[c] Tiro's physician.
[d] See the last letter.

CICERO

XXI

Athenis, A.U.C. 710.

1 Cum vehementer tabellarios exspectarem quotidie,
aliquando venerunt post diem v. et xl. quam a
vobis discesserant ; quorum mihi fuit adventus
optatissimus. Nam cum maximam cepissem laetitiam ex humanissimi et carissimi patris epistula,
tum vero iucundissimae tuae litterae cumulum mihi
gaudi attulerunt. Itaque me iam non paenitebat,
intercapedinem scribendi fecisse, sed potius laetabar.
Fructum enim magnum humanitatis tuae capiebam

ᵃ Marcus the younger, Cicero's only son, was born in
65, and was thus nine years younger than his sister Tullia.
In 51 Cicero took him and his nephew Quintus with him to
Cilicia, with the excellent but irascible Dionysius as their
tutor. Writing of the boys to Atticus, Cicero says that
Quintus needs the curb, and Marcus the spur ; and this
was Marcus's characteristic through life. In 49 his father
gave him the *toga virilis* at Arpinum. He accompanied his
father to Greece, and though he was not yet 16 years old,
Pompey put him in command of a squadron of cavalry.
After Pharsalia he returned with his father to Brundisium.
In 46, through Cicero's influence, both he and his cousin
Quintus were appointed aediles at Arpinum ; and Marcus,
now 20 years old, was sent by his father to study philosophy
at Athens under Cratippus, with a handsome allowance of
something equivalent to £800 a year. Under the evil
influence of an unprincipled Greek teacher Gorgias, he
became extravagant and idle, and his father wrote per-
emptorily ordering him to have nothing more to do with
Gorgias. Marcus replied, not to his father, but to Tiro, in
this interesting and self-revealing letter, which speaks for
itself.

XXI

M. CICERO JUNIOR [a] GREETS HIS SWEETEST TIRO

Athens, August or early in September, 44 B.C.

Although I was anxiously on the look out for 1
your letter-carriers every day, they only came at
last forty-six days after they had left you, and
their arrival was most welcome to me. For though
my most kindly and well-beloved father's epistle
gave me the greatest possible pleasure, still it was
your most delightful letter that crowned my joy.
So I no longer regret having made a break in my
correspondence, but rather rejoice at it; for the
silence of my pen has brought me the rich reward

Brutus, who had made his acquaintance at Athens, made
him commander of a squadron of cavalry, in which capacity
he served with some credit against Antony. About this
time Cicero desired to see his son among the Pontifices, but
decided that he should not return to Italy unless accompanied
by Brutus; it thus fell out that he escaped the proscription,
in which perished his father, his uncle, and his cousin. He
fought at Philippi in 42, and after that battle fled to Sextus
Pompeius, who made much of him. He returned to Rome in
39 and was handsomely treated by Octavian, who in 30
made him *consul suffectus*; and it was while holding that
office that Marcus had the statues of Antony overthrown,
and carried a decree that from that day no Antonius should
bear the name of Marcus. Thus it came to pass that, in the
words of Plutarch (*Cic.* 49), " Heaven (τὸ δαιμόνιον) delivered
over to the house of Cicero the final punishment of Antony."
Some years later Marcus became proconsul of Asia, and
afterwards *legatus* of Syria.

Though he inherited some of his father's wit, Marcus was
a man of mediocre intellect and little ambition; but that
he must have possessed considerable military and administrative ability is proved by his fairly successful career.

ex silentio mearum litterarum. Vehementer igitur
gaudeo, te meam sine dubitatione accepisse excusa-
2 tionem. Gratos tibi optatosque esse, qui de me
rumores afferuntur, non dubito, mi dulcissime Tiro :
praestaboque et enitar, ut in dies magis magisque
haec nascens de me duplicetur opinio. Quare quod
polliceris, te buccinatorem fore existimationis meae,
firmo id constantique animo facias licet. Tantum
enim mihi dolorem cruciatumque attulerunt errata
aetatis meae, ut non solum animus a factis, sed
aures quoque a commemoratione abhorreant. Cuius
te sollicitudinis et doloris participem fuisse, notum
exploratumque est mihi : nec id mirum. Nam cum
omnia mea causa velles mihi successa, tum etiam
tua. Socium enim te meorum commodorum semper
3 esse volui. Quod igitur tum ex me doluisti, nunc, ut
duplicetur tuum ex me gaudium, praestabo. Crat-
ippo me, scito, non ut discipulum, sed ut filium esse
coniunctissimum. Nam cum audio illum libenter,
tum etiam propriam eius suavitatem vehementer
amplector. Sum totos dies cum eo, noctisque saepe-
numero partem. Exoro enim, ut mecum quam saepissime cenet. Hac introducta consuetudine, saepe
inscientibus nobis et cenantibus obrepit sublataque
severitate philosophiae humanissime nobiscum ioca-
tur. Quare da operam, ut hunc talem, tam iucundum,

ᵃ A philosopher of Mitylene, for whom Cicero had a high
regard. He accompanied Pompey in his flight after Pharsalia
in 48, and afterwards settled at Athens. Through Cicero's
influence he obtained from Caesar the Roman citizenship.

of your kindliness. I am, therefore, highly delighted at your unhesitating acceptance of my excuse.

That the rumours, which reach you about me, are 2 gratifying and welcome to you, I have no doubt at all, my dearest Tiro ; and I shall make every effort to guarantee that this opinion of me which is springing up more distinctly every day becomes twice as good. For that reason you may with unshaken confidence fulfil your promise of being the trumpeter of my reputation. For the errors of my youth have caused me such grief and agony that not only do my thoughts shrink from what I have done, but my very ears shrink from hearing it talked about. And that you have had your share in that anxiety and grief is well known to me as an ascertained fact ; and I am not surprised at it. For when you wished me every success on my account, you did so at the same on your own, since it has ever been my wish that you should be a partner in any prosperity of mine.

Since at that time I caused you grief, I shall 3 now guarantee that the joy I give you is double as much.

I must tell you that my close attachment to Cratippus [a] is not so much that of a pupil as that of a son. For not only do I attend his lectures with enjoyment, but I am greatly fascinated also by the charm of his personality. I spend whole days with him, and often a part of the night. Indeed I implore him to dine with me as often as possible. Now that we have become so intimate, he often strolls in upon us when we least expect him and are at dinner, and throwing to the winds all austerity as a philosopher, he bandies jokes with us in the most genial manner possible. Lay yourself out, there-

365

CICERO

4 tam excellentem virum videas quam primum. Nam
quid ego de Bruttio dicam? quem nullo tempore a
me patior discedere; cuius cum frugi severaque est
vita, tum etiam iucundissima convictio. Non est enim
seiunctus iocus a φιλολογίᾳ et quotidiana συζητήσει.
Huic ego locum in proximo conduxi, et, ut possum, ex meis angustiis illius sustento tenuitatem.
5 Praeterea declamitare Graece apud Cassium institui;
Latine autem apud Bruttium exerceri volo. Utor
familiaribus et quotidianis convictoribus, quos secum
Mitylenis Cratippus adduxit, hominibus et doctis
et illi probatissimis. Multum enim mecum est
Epicrates, princeps Atheniensium, et Leonides et
6 horum ceteri similes. Τὰ μὲν οὖν καθ᾽ ἡμᾶς τάδε. De
Gorgia autem quod mihi scribis, erat quidem ille in
quotidiana declamatione utilis; sed omnia postposui,
dummodo praeceptis patris parerem. Διαρρήδην enim
scripserat, ut eum dimitterem statim. Tergiversari
nolui, ne mea nimia σπουδή suspicionem ei aliquam
importaret. Deinde illud etiam mihi succurrebat,
7 grave esse, me de iudicio patris iudicare. Tuum
tamen studium et consilium gratum acceptumque
est mihi. Excusationem angustiarum tui temporis

---

^a We know nothing more of Bruttius.

^b It was he who sent Cicero unsatisfactory accounts of
Marcus's progress and conduct.

^c Loose liver as he was (see note on § 1), Gorgias was a
distinguished rhetorician and wrote the treatise Περὶ σχημάτων
διανοίας καὶ λέξεως of which we still possess the translation
by Rutilius Lupus.

366

fore, to win the acquaintance of such a man—so delightful and so distinguished as he is.

As to Bruttius,[a] why should I mention him at all ? 4 There is never a moment when I allow him to leave my side. He leads a simple and austere life, but at the same time he is a most delightful man to live with. For there is no ban upon merry talk in our literary discussions and our daily joint researches. I have hired lodgings for him next door, and, as far as I can, alleviate his penury out of my own narrow means.

Besides all this I have begun to practise declaim- 5 ing in Greek with Cassius ; but I like practising in Latin with Bruttius. I have as daily and intimate companions the men whom Cratippus brought with him from Mitylene—men of learning and highly esteemed by him. Epicrates, for instance, the leading man among the Athenians, is much with me, and so is Leonides,[b] and others of that stamp. So much then about myself.

As to what you write about Gorgias,[c] it is true 6 I found him useful in my practice in declamation : but I thought everything else of secondary importance, provided I obeyed my father's instructions, who had written to me in explicit terms to get rid of Gorgias at once. I did not want to temporize, for fear my making too much of the business might strike my father as somewhat suspicious ; and besides it occurred to me that it was a serious thing for me to pass judgment on the judgment of my father.

Anyhow your interest and advice is welcome and 7 acceptable to me. I accept the excuse that your

CICERO

accipio; scio enim, quam soleas esse occupatus.
Emisse te praedium vehementer gaudeo, feliciterque
tibi rem istam evenire cupio. Hoc loco me tibi
gratulari, noli mirari. Eodem enim fere loco, tu
quoque, emisse te, fecisti me certiorem. Habes.[1]
Deponendae tibi sunt urbanitates. Rusticus Romanus factus es. Quomodo ego mihi nunc ante
oculos tuum iucundissimum conspectum propono!
Videor enim videre ementem te rusticas res, cum
villico loquentem, in lacinia servantem ex mensa
secunda semina. Sed quod ad rem pertinet, me tum
tibi defuisse, aeque ac tu doleo. Sed noli dubitare,
mi Tiro, quin te sublevaturus sim, si modo fortuna
me; praesertim cum sciam, communem nobis emp-
8 tum esse istum fundum. De mandatis quod tibi
curae fuit, est mihi gratum. Sed peto a te, ut quam
celerrime mihi librarius mittatur, maxime quidem
Graecus; multum mihi enim eripitur operae in ex-
scribendis hypomnematis. Tu velim in primis cures,
ut valeas, ut una συμφιλολογεῖν possimus. Anterum
tibi commendo. Vale.

[1] rem habes *Reid* (*supposing* rem *to have been lost after*
certiorem): habes deponendae ubi sint *Graecius.*

---

[a] For this absolute use of *habere* cf. *Att.* xii. 23. 3 "habet
in Ostiensi Cotta." But see note on the text.

time is strictly limited, being well aware how busy you always are. That you have bought a farm is a great joy to me, and it is my sincere wish that the transaction may turn out happily for you. You must not be surprised at my congratulating you at this point in my letter; for it was practically at the same point in yours that you informed me of your purchase. Why, you are a land-owner! [a] You have got to drop your city ways. You have become a Roman country gentleman. How I call you up before my eyes this very moment—and a very charming picture it is! I seem to see you buying rural implements, hobnobbing with your steward, or keeping the pips after dessert in the corner of your cloak. [b] But as regards the money part of it, I am as sorry as you are that I was not forthcoming at the time. You must never doubt, however, my dear Tiro, that I shall come to your assistance, if only fortune comes to mine; especially as I know that that farm of yours was bought as our joint-investment.

For taking such trouble about my commissions, [8] I am grateful to you. But I beg of you to see that a secretary is sent me as quickly as possible—best of all a Greek; for that will relieve me of a lot of trouble in writing out lecture-notes. [c] Above all, I would have you take care of your health, so that we may have some literary talk together. I commend Anterus [d] to you. Farewell.

[b] In order to sow them.   [c] A characteristic request.
[d] The slave who brought the letter.

CICERO

XXII

TULLIUS S. P. D. TIRONI

Asturae, A.U.C. 709.

1 Spero ex tuis litteris, tibi melius esse ; cupio certe.
Cui quidem rei omni ratione cura ut inservias, et
cave suspiceris, contra meam voluntatem te facere,
quod non sis mecum. Mecum es, si te curas. Quare
malo te valetudini tuae servire, quam meis oculis et
auribus. Etsi enim et audio te et video libenter,
tamen hoc multo erit, si valebis, iucundius. Ego hic
cesso, quia ipse nihil scribo ; lego autem libentissime.
Tu istic, si quid librarii mea manu non intellegent,
monstrabis. Una omnino interpositio difficilior est,
quam ne ipse quidem facile legere soleo, de quadrimo
Catone. De triclinio cura, ut facis. Tertia aderit,
2 modo ne Publius rogatus sit. Demetrius iste numquam omnino Phalereus fuit ; sed nunc plane Billienus
est. Itaque te do vicarium. Tu eum observabis.

---

^a The story was in all probability that told of Cato
Uticensis when a boy, by Plutarch (*Cat. Min.* 2). One
Pompaedius Silo tried to induce the little Cato to influence
his uncle, Livius Drusus, to advocate the granting of the
franchise to the Italians. On the boy's refusing to do so,
Pompaedius held him out of window, and threatened to
drop him if he would not do as he was told, but the boy
remained ἀνέκπληκτος καὶ ἀδεής, "undismayed and fearless."
It is true that Cato was born in 95, and was therefore just
four years old just before the Social War of 91. This is the
story which Cicero added to his work on Cato the younger,
written in 46, but in so cramped a hand that he always
found it hard to make out what he had himself written.

^b Probably Tertia, or Tertulla, wife of Cassius, and Publius
is Dolabella ; but this is mere surmise.

XXII

CICERO TO TIRO

Astura, July 27, 45 b.c.

Your letter makes me hope that you are better; 1 that, at any rate, is what I desire. Make every thing subservient to that one object, and on no account be apprehensive that you are acting contrary to my wishes in not being at my side. You *are* at my side if you are taking care of yourself; and for that reason I had rather have you the slave of your own health than the slave of my eyes and ears. For though it is a pleasure to me to hear and see you, it will be far more delightful to do so if you are well. I am idling here, because I am not writing anything myself, but reading is a great pleasure to me. Being where you are, I am sure you will explain anything the copyists cannot make out on account of my handwriting. There is certainly one rather difficult inserted passage, which even I myself always find it hard to decipher, about Cato at the age of four.[a] About the dinner-table, please see to it, as I am sure you do. Tertia[b] will be there, provided Publius has not been asked.

That Demetrius[c] of yours was never a De- 2 metrius of Phalerum at all, but now he is an absolute Billienus. I therefore appoint you my representative. Please show him some attention. *"And*

---

[c] See *Epp.* 17. 2, and 19. Demetrius of Phalerum was a very different man — cultured and erudite. The name Demetrius suggests the Demetrius whose slave Billienus strangled Domitius at Album Intimilium. For the story see viii. 15. 2.

" Etsi," " verumtamen," " de illis "—nosti cetera. Sed tamen, si quem cum eo sermonem habueris, scribes ad me, ut mihi nascatur epistulae argumentum, et ut tuas quam longissimas litteras legam. Cura, mi Tiro, ut valeas. Hoc mihi gratius facere nihil potes. Vale.

XXIII

TULLIUS S. P. D. TIRONI SUO

Tusculi, A.U.C. 710.

1 Tu vero confice professionem, si potes. Etsi haec pecunia ex eo genere est, ut professione non egeat. Verum tamen . . . Balbus ad me scripsit, tanta se ἐπιφορᾷ oppressum, ut loqui non possit. Antonius de lege " quod egerit." Liceat modo rusticari. Ad 2 Bithynicum scripsi. De Servilio tu videris, qui senectutem non contemnis. Etsi Atticus noster, quia quondam me commoveri πανικοῖς intellexit, idem semper putat, nec videt, quibus praesidiis philosophiae septus sim ; et hercle, quod timidus ipse est, θορυβοποιεῖ. Ego tamen Antoni inveteratam sine nulla offensione amicitiam retinere sane volo, scribamque ad eum, sed

---

[a] Cicero is evidently mocking at Demetrius's *staccato* way of talking.

[b] Tyrrell thinks that this was probably the *Lex Agraria* of Lucius Antonius, passed in June of this year. The elliptical phrase *quod egerit* (sc. *id actum habebo*) = " whatever he does I shall regard as done," *i.e.* " for all I care, let him do what he likes." The phrase also occurs in the next letter.

[c] The writer of vi. 16, where see note.

[d] Servilius Isauricus, who had just died at an advanced age.

[e] *i.e.,* that I am afraid of death.

yet!" "But nevertheless!" "As for them!" You
know how he goes on.[a] Anyhow, if you have
any talk with him, please write to me, so that I
may have the germ of a theme for a letter, and
may have as long a letter as possible to read from
you. Take care of your health, my dear Tiro.
Nothing you can do will give me greater pleasure
than that. Good-bye.

XXIII

CICERO TO TIRO

Tusculum, about June 21, 44 B.C.

Yes, certainly; finish making up the tax-return 1
if you possibly can; although this particular money
is not under a heading which requires a return. But
that is as may be . . . Balbus writes that he has
had such an attack of catarrh that he has lost his
voice. As for what Antony has done about the
law, for all I care, let it stand.[b] Only let me be free
to enjoy the country. I have written to Bithynicus.[c]

About Servilius [d] you will have your own opinion 2
—you, who have a deep respect for old age. And
yet our friend Atticus, because he once noticed
that I was upset by panic, always thinks the same
of me,[e] and does not see with what safeguards of
philosophy I am hedged round; and, on my oath,
he is so timid himself, that he causes general con-
sternation. For all you say, I am very anxious to
keep up my friendship with Antony, which has
lasted so long without our falling out, and I shall
write to him, but not before I have seen you—not

373

non ante quam te videro. Nec tamen te avoco
asyngrapha ; γόνυ κνήμης. Cras exspecto Leptam
et N. . . ., ad cuius rutam pulegio mihi tui sermonis
utendum est. Vale.

XXIV

TULLIUS S. P. D. TIRONI

Arpini, a.u.c. 710.

1 Etsi mane Harpalum miseram, tamen, cum haberem, cui recte darem litteras, etsi novi nihil erat,
iisdem de rebus volui ad te saepius scribere ; non
quin confiderem diligentiae tuae, sed rei me magni-
tudo movebat. Mihi prora et puppis, ut Graecorum
proverbium est, fuit a me tui dimittendi, ut rationes
nostras explicares. Ofillio et Aurelio utique satis fiat.
A Flamma, si non potes omne, partem aliquam velim
extorqueas : in primisque, ut expedita sit pensio
Kalendis Ian. De attributione conficies. De reprae-
sentatione videbis. De domesticis rebus hactenus.

---

^a Which Cicero held.
^b Lit. " the knee is nearer home than the shin ' (γόνυ
κνήρμης ἔγγιον, Aristot. *Eth. Nic.* ix. 8. 2). *Cf.* ἀπωτέρω ἢ
γόνυ κνάμα, Theocrit. xvi. 18. The Latin equivalent is *tunica
proprior pallio*, "the coat is nearer than the cloak." *Cf.*
English "near is my shirt, but nearer is my skin." There
is a Welsh proverb very like the Greek, " *Nes elin nag
arddwrn*," "the elbow is nearer than the wrist."
^c *Cf.* vi. 18 and 19.
^d " N." probably stands for " nostrum," *i.e.*, the younger
Quintus, so spoken of by Cicero in *Att.* xv. 29. 2 also.
^e Lit. " to whose rue I must apply the pennyroyal of
your conversation."
^f Or "the Alpha and Omega" as Tyrrell renders it, and
he quotes Dio Chrys. xxxvii. p. 120 R. ὑμεῖς γὰρ ἔστε νῦν τὸ
δὴ λεγόμενον πρῷρα καὶ πρύμνα τῆς Ἑλλάδος.

that I would have you forget the payment of your bond *a* ;—"charity begins at home." *b* To-morrow I am expecting Lepta *c* and N.*d* too—and I shall have to avail myself of the sweetness of your conversation to assuage the bitterness of his.*e*

XXIV

CICERO TO TIRO

Arpinum, middle of November, 44 B.C.

Although I had sent Harpalus earlier in the day, 1 still, finding that I had a trustworthy letter-carrier, although there is nothing new, I wanted to write to you again and again on the same subjects—not that I have lost confidence in your application, but the importance of the matter makes me restless. The "stem and stern" *f* (as the Greek proverb goes) of my sending you away from me was that you might straighten out my financial affairs. It is imperative that Ofillius *g* and Aurelius *h* should have their claims satisfied. I should like you to wring out of Flamma, if not all the debt, at least some portion it ; and especially to see that the instalment *i* is cleared off on January 1st. As to the assignment of debts, make some settlement ; and please see to their paying ready money. So much for my private affairs.

g A co-heir with Cicero to the estate of Cluvius of Puteoli.
h An agent of one Montanus, who had become surety to Plancus for Flaminius Flamma, and was now obliged to meet Flamma's liabilities.
i *i.e.*, of Tullia's dowry by Dolabella.

2 De publicis omnia mihi certa ; quid Octavius, quid
Antonius : quae hominum opinio ; quid futurum
putes. Ego vix teneor, quin accurram. Sed sto[1] ;
litteras tuas exspecto ; et scito Balbum tum fuisse
Aquini, cum tibi est dictum, et postridie Hirtium.
Puto utrumque ad aquas ; sed " quod egerint."
Dolabellae procuratores fac admoneantur. Appellabis
etiam Papiam.   Vale.

XXV

CICERO FIL. S. P. D. TIRONI

Athenis, A.U.C. 710.

Etsi iusta et idonea usus es excusatione intermis-
sionis litterarum tuarum, tamen, id ne saepius facias,
rogo. Nam etsi de republica rumoribus et nuntiis
certior fio, et de sua in me voluntate semper ad me
perscribit pater, tamen de quavis minima re scripta
a te ad me epistula semper fuit gratissima. Quare
cum in primis tuas desiderem litteras, noli commit-
tere, ut excusatione potius expleas officium scribendi,
quam assiduitate epistularum.   Vale.

[1] st! *Manutius and Edd., but* sto *is obviously suggested,
I think, by the preceding words.*

---

[a] See note on the text.
[b] See note *b* on § 1 of the last letter.
[c] About the repayment of Tullia's dowry.
[d] Nothing more is known of Papia.
[e] See note at the beginning of *Ep. 21.*

On public affairs let me have every possible 2 information that can be trusted—what Octavianus, and what Antony is up to, what is generally thought, and what you suppose is going to happen. I can hardly keep myself from coming to you hot-foot. But I stand still;[a] I patiently await a letter from you ; and let me tell you that Balbus was at Aquinum on the day you were told, and Hirtius on the next day. I imagine both were going there for the waters ; but it is no business of mine![b] See that Dolabella's agents have their memories jogged.[c] Send a reminder to Papia[d] also. Good-bye.

XXV

MARCUS CICERO JUNIOR [e] TO TIRO

Athens, September or October, 44 B.C.

Although the excuse you offer for the break in your correspondence is a fair and proper one, still I beg you not to make too much of a practice of it. Although rumours and messages keep me informed about the political situation, and my father is always writing to me, and fully too, about his friendly feeling for you, for all that a letter written by you to me about anything, however trivial, has always been most welcome to me. For that reason, seeing that I miss your letters more than anything, don't make the mistake of discharging the obligations of correspondence by making excuses rather than by assiduity in letter-writing. Good-bye.

CICERO

XXVI

Romae (?), A.U.C. 710.

1   Verberavi te cogitationis tacito dumtaxat convicio, quod fasciculus alter ad me iam sine tuis litteris perlatus est. Non potes effugere huius culpae poenam, te patrono. Marcus est adhibendus; isque diu et multis lucubrationibus commentata oratione, vide ut 2 probare possit, te non peccasse. Plane te rogo, sicut olim matrem nostram facere memini, quae lagenas etiam inanes obsignabat, ne dicerentur inanes aliquae fuisse, quae furtim essent exsiccatae, sic tu, etiamsi, quod scribas, non habebis, scribito tamen, ne furtum cessationis quaesivisse videaris. Valde enim mihi semper et vera et dulcia tuis epistulis nuntiantur. Ama nos et vale.

XXVII

Romae, A.U.C. 710.

1   Mirificam mihi verberationem cessationis epistula tua[1] dedisti. Nam, quae parcius frater perscripserat,

---

[1] tua *added by Wesenberg, since* epistula *by itself cannot mean* " *by letter,*" *as* litteris *can.*

---

[a] His brother, the orator.
[b] Or, as Tyrrell translates it, "that you may not be suspected of stealing a holiday."

XXVI

Rome (?), autumn (?), 44 B.C.

I have just given you a thrashing (so far as I 1
could with the strong but inaudible language of
thought), because this is now the second packet
that has reached me without a letter from you.
That is an offence for which you cannot escape
punishment—that is, if you undertake your own
defence. No, Marcus *a* must be called in ; and when
he has spent much time and many a night elaborat-
ing his speech by lamplight, don't be so sure that
even he can prove your innocence.

I make a plain request of you ; just as in the old 2
days I remember my mother used to do—she used to
seal up her wine-jars even when she had emptied
them, so as to prevent its being said that any were
empty which had been drained of their contents by a
thief ; on the same principle, I ask you, even if you
have nothing to write, to write all the same, and so
avoid the suspicion of having tried to get a day off
by stealing it.*b* I assure you, I always find the news
in your letters as trustworthy as it is charmingly
told. Keep on loving me, and good-bye.

XXVII

Rome, late in December, 44 B.C.

You have given me in your letter a jolly good 1
thrashing for my laziness ;—for what my brother

379

CICERO

verecundia videlicet et properatione, ea tu sine assen-
tatione, ut erant, ad me scripsisti, et maxime de consulibus designatis : quos ego penitus novi libidinum
et languoris effeminatissimi animi plenos : qui nisi a
gubernaculis recesserint, maximum ab universo nau-
2 fragio periculum est.   Incredibile est, quae ego illos
scio, oppositis Gallorum castris, in aestivis fecisse,
quos ille latro, nisi aliquid firmius fuerit, societate
vitiorum deleniet.   Res est aut tribuniciis aut privatis
consiliis munienda.   Nam isti duo vix sunt digni,
quibus alteri Caesenam, alteri Cossutianarum taber-
narum fundamenta credas.   Te, ut dixi, fero oculis.[1]
Ego vos a. d. iii. Kalend. videbo, tuosque oculos,
etiamsi te veniens in medio foro videro, dissuaviabor.
Me ama.   Vale.

[1] in oculis *Tyrrell, following Ernesti.*

[a] Hirtius and Pansa : what the hot-headed Quintus says
of them here and in § 2 must be taken *cum grano salis.*   Whatever their weaknesses (and Quintus doubtlessly exaggerates
them), both fell fighting manfully for the Republic.

[b] Antony.

[c] Hirtius, with the custody of the insignificant little town
Caesena, 20 miles north-west of Ariminum, and near the
Rubicon.

[d] Pansa, with the cellars of the taverns of Cossutius (of
whom we know nothing more).

had told me in his letter with some reserve, evidently being modest about it, and also in a hurry, all that you have written to me, stating the facts without sycophancy; and particularly as regards the consuls-designate,[a] who I am absolutely assured are tainted with sensualism and a weak-mindedness that is essentially womanish; and unless they resign the helm, there is every danger of universal shipwreck.

You could never believe what I know those men 2 did in summer quarters, when the camp of the Gauls was right opposite them—men whom that scoundrel,[b] unless firmer measures are taken, will captivate by making them share in his vices. Things must be buttressed up by either the tribunes or private persons taking counsel together. For as to those two fellows, they are hardly fit to be entrusted, the one with Caesena,[c] and the other with the vaults under Cossutius's wine-shops.[d] As I said, I have you ever before my face.[e] I shall see you all on the 30th, and as for that face of yours, even if I see you in the middle of the forum on my arrival, I shall smother it with kisses. Keep on loving me. Good-bye.

[e] Lit. " eyes," here and lower down ; but a literal translation would be open to objection.

CICERO'S
LETTERS TO HIS BROTHER QUINTUS

WITH AN ENGLISH TRANSLATION BY
W. GLYNN WILLIAMS, M.A.

FORMERLY SCHOLAR OF ST. JOHN'S COLLEGE, CAMBRIDGE
AND HEADMASTER OF FRIARS SCHOOL, BANGOR

A SHORT LIFE OF QUINTUS TULLIUS CICERO

QUINTUS TULLIUS CICERO was born in 102 B.C., and was therefore four years younger than his brother Marcus, the orator. The two brothers were brought up together at Arpinum, until their father, recognizing their intellectual ability, and desiring better educational opportunities for them, moved with his family to Rome, where one of the boys' teachers was the poet Archias of Antioch.

In 67 B.C., at the age of thirty-five, Quintus became aedile, and in 62 praetor, and for the next three years governed the province of Asia as propraetor. It was during this time that Marcus wrote Book I. of his letters, *Ad Quintum Fratrem.* Returning to Rome in 58, Quintus exerted himself to procure his brother's recall from banishment, though he had enemies of his own who threatened to prosecute him for malpractices. In 56 he went to Sardinia on the staff of Pompey, who had been appointed *curator annonae,* " Minister of the Corn Supply "; and in 55 joined Caesar as his *legatus* in Gaul, where he greatly distinguished himself by gallantly resisting with one legion a vastly superior force of Gauls in the country of the Nervii. In 51 he accompanied his brother as one of his *legati* to Cilicia. When the civil war broke out in 49 he joined Pompey. After the battle of Pharsalia, Caesar, who had a high regard for him, treated him with great leniency and kindness, as indeed he did Marcus. Just at this time, when visiting Patrae in Achaia in Marcus's company, Quintus, for some reason unknown to us, developed a bitter hostility to his brother, who shortly afterwards at Brundisium intercepted a packet of Quintus's letters, addressed to various friends, full of malicious reflections upon himself, and threatening to denounce him to Caesar. So far from taking action against Quintus for his treachery, Marcus actually wrote to Caesar, absolving Quintus from any suspicion of having instigated his own opposition to Caesar, and begging of him to befriend the brother who had behaved so badly to himself. " It seems to us," as Tyrrell rightly remarks, " that this is an act of large nobleness and truly chivalrous feeling, quite startling when we remember the times in which Cicero lived "; indeed we cannot but be impressed with the more than paternal gentleness and patience with which Cicero treated his impulsive and irascible younger brother as long as they lived ; and " in death they were not divided," for Quintus, together with his son, was proscribed by the last Triumvirate (Octavian, Antony, and Lepidus) and put to death in Rome a few days before the murder of Marcus in December, 43.

Quintus was a man of ungovernable temper and harshly over-bearing in his treatment of those under his authority, but just, honest, and free from all taint of self-seeking as administrator of a province, while his gallantry as a soldier was proved beyond all question in Gaul. Apart from the unpleasant episode after Pharsalia, his attitude towards Marcus was, in the main, one of loyalty and affection. He wrote much (including four tragedies, said to have been written in sixteen days), but all that has come down to us is his *brochure* to his brother, *De petitione consulatus*. He married Pomponia, a sister of Atticus, a somewhat arrogant person. Their married life was not a happy one, and ended in his divorcing her.

M. TULLI CICERONIS
EPISTULARUM AD QUINTUM FRATREM

LIBER PRIMUS

I

M. C. S. D. Q. FRATRI

Romae, A.U.C. 694.

1   I. Etsi non dubitabam, quin hanc epistulam multi
nuntii, fama denique esset ipsa sua celeritate supera-
tura, tuque ante ab aliis auditurus esses, annum
tertium accessisse desiderio nostro, et labori tuo,
tamen existimavi a me quoque tibi huius molestiae
nuntium perferri oportere. Nam superioribus litteris, non unis, sed pluribus, cum iam ab aliis desperata
res esset, tamen ego tibi spem maturae decessionis
afferebam, non solum, ut quam diutissime sit iucunda
opinione oblectarem, sed etiam quia tanta adhibe-
batur et a nobis et a praetoribus contentio, ut rem
2 posse confici non diffiderem. Nunc quoniam ita
accidit, ut neque praetores suis opibus, neque nos
nostro studio quidquam proficere possemus, est omni-

---

^a Who was now at the beginning of his third year as pro-
praetor of Asia.

^b A vacancy in provincial government was of interest to the
praetors, one of whom might get the appointment.

388

CICERO'S LETTERS TO HIS BROTHER QUINTUS

BOOK I

I

Rome, end of 60 B.C.

I. Although I have no doubt that many a messen- 1
ger, and indeed rumour itself with its usual rapidity, is
likely to outstrip this letter, and that you are likely to
be told by others of the addition of a third year to my
longing for you, and to the period of your work, yet
I thought it right that I too should convey to you
the news of this annoying fact. For in my previous
letters, not in one, but several, though others had by
that time despaired of such a possibility, I still per-
severed in feeding you with the hope of quitting your
province at an early date, not only that I might keep
on cheering you as long as possible with an agreeable
expectation, but also because both the praetors and I
were making such strenuous efforts that I never lost
faith in the possibility of the arrangement.

As it is, since it has so happened that neither the 2
praetors *b* with all their influence, nor I with all my
zeal, have been able to do any good, it is indeed hard

no difficile non graviter id ferre ; sed tamen nostros
animos maximis in rebus et gerendis et sustinendis
exercitatos frangi et debilitari molestia non oportet.
Et quoniam ea molestissime ferre homines debent,
quae ipsorum culpa contracta sunt, est quiddam in
hac re mihi molestius ferendum, quam tibi. Factum
est enim mea culpa, contra quam tu mecum et proficiscens et per litteras egeras, ut priore anno non
succederetur. Quod ego, dum sociorum saluti con-
sulo, dum impudentiae nonnullorum negotiatorum
resisto, dum nostram gloriam tua virtute augeri
expeto, feci non sapienter, praesertim cum id com-
miserim, ut ille alter annus etiam tertium posset
3 adducere. Quod quoniam peccatum meum esse
confiteor, est sapientiae atque humanitatis tuae
curare et perficere, ut hoc, minus sapienter a me
provisum, diligentia tua corrigatur. Ac si te ipse
vehementius ad omnes partes bene audiendi excitaris,
non ut cum aliis, sed ut tecum iam ipse certes, si
omnem tuam mentem, curam, cogitationem ad excellentem omnibus in rebus laudis cupiditatem in-
citaris, mihi crede, unus annus additus labori tuo,
multorum annorum laetitiam nobis, immo vero etiam
4 posteris nostris afferet. Quapropter hoc te primum
rogo, ne contrahas ac demittas animum, neve te
obrui, tamquam fluctu, sic magnitudine negoti
sinas, contraque erigas ac resistas sive etiam ultro

---

^a The *socii* are the provincials, as opposed to the *cives*,
Romans dwelling in the province, such as *publicani* and
negotiatores.
^b Certain bankers, who out of private animosity opposed
the reappointment of Quintus, probably Paconius and
Tuscenius referred to in § 19.

not to resent it ; but, for all that, it is not right that our minds, trained as they have been in the management and maintenance of affairs of the utmost importance, should be crushed and weakened by a mere sense of annoyance. And since men ought to feel most annoyed with what has been brought about by their own fault, there is an element in this business which should cause me more annoyance than you. For it was entirely my fault—and you pleaded with me against it both on your departure and subsequently by letter—that you were not given a successor last year. And in that, in my anxiety to promote the interests of the allies,[a] and to resist the shameless policy of certain dealers,[b] and in my strong desire to see our country's glory enhanced by your excellent rule, I acted unwisely, especially since by my mistake I made it possible for that second year to bring a third also in its train.

And now that I admit that the error was mine, it 3 lies with you, in your wisdom and humanity, to see to it and ensure that this lack of wise foresight on my part is rectified by your careful administration. Indeed, if you rouse yourself in all earnestness to win golden opinions in all quarters—not in order to rival others, but to be henceforth your own rival—if you direct your whole mind, your every care and thought, into a predominating desire to be well spoken of in every respect, then, take my word for it, one single year added to your labours will bring us, and indeed those who come after us also, many a year of joy.

For that reason I beg of you, first and foremost, not 4 to let your heart shrink or sink, and not to allow yourself to be overwhelmed, as by a wave, by the greatness of your task, but, on the contrary, to lift up your

CICERO

occurras negotiis. Neque enim eiusmodi partem
reipublicae geris, in qua fortuna dominetur, sed in
qua plurimum ratio possit et diligentia. Quod si
tibi, bellum aliquod magnum et periculosum ad-
ministranti, prorogatum imperium viderem, tre-
merem animo, quod eodem tempore esse intellegerem
5 etiam fortunae potestatem in nos prorogatam. Nunc
vero ea pars tibi reipublicae commissa est, in qua aut
nullam, aut perexiguam partem fortuna tenet, et
quae mihi tota in tua virtute ac moderatione animi
posita esse videatur. Nullas, ut opinor, insidias
hostium, nullam proeli dimicationem, nullam de-
fectionem sociorum, nullam inopiam stipendi aut rei
frumentariae, nullam seditionem exercitus per-
timescimus, quae persaepe sapientissimis viris acciderunt, ut, quemadmodum gubernatores optimi vim
tempestatis, sic illi fortunae impetum superare non
possent. Tibi data est summa pax, summa tran-
quillitas ; ita tamen, ut ea dormientem gubernatorem
6 vel obruere, vigilantem etiam delectare possit. Constat enim ea provincia primum ex eo genere sociorum,
quod est ex hominum omni genere humanissimum ;
deinde ex eo genere civium, qui aut, quod publicani
sunt, nos summa necessitudine attingunt, aut, quod
ita negotiantur, ut locupletes sint, nostri consulatus
beneficio se incolumes fortunas habere arbitrantur.

---

heart and to face, or even hurry forward to meet, your responsibilities. As a matter of fact, the department of the State you are administering is not one in which fortune plays a ruling part, but one in which a reasoned policy combined with assiduity carries the greatest power; whereas if I saw that the prolongation of your government happened during your management of some great and dangerous war, I should shudder in spirit because it would be evident to me that at the same time fortune's power over us had been prolonged.

As it is, however, you have been entrusted with a 5 department of the State in which fortune holds no part, or a very insignificant one, and which, it would seem to me, depends entirely upon your own virtue and self-control. We need fear, I take it, no ambuscades of enemies, no clash of swords in battle, no revolt of allies, no lack of tribute or corn-supply, no mutiny in the army,—evils which have befallen the wisest of men, so that, just as the best of helmsmen cannot defy the violence of a tempest, neither can they defy the assault of fortune. What has been granted you is perfect peace, perfect tranquillity, with the reservation, however, that such a calm can even overwhelm the helmsman if he sleeps, while it can give him positive pleasure if he keeps awake.

For your province consists, in the first place, of that 6 type of ally *a* which of all types of humanity is the most civilized; and secondly, of that type of citizen *a* who, either because they are *publicani*, are attached to us by the closest ties, or, because their trade is such that they have amassed riches, consider that the security of the fortunes they enjoy is due to the blessing of my consulship.

7 II. At enim inter hos ipsos exsistunt graves controversiae, multae nascuntur iniuriae, magnae contentiones consequuntur. Quasi vero ego id putem,
non te aliquantum negoti sustinere. Intellego, permagnum esse negotium et maximi consili. Sed
memento, consili me hoc negotium esse magis aliquanto, quam fortunae, putare. Quid est enim
negoti, continere eos, quibus praesis, si te ipse con-
tineas ? Id autem sit magnum et difficile ceteris,
sicut est difficillimum ; tibi et fuit hoc semper
facillimum, et vero esse debuit, cuius natura talis
est, ut etiam sine doctrina videatur moderata esse
potuisse : ea autem adhibita doctrina est, quae vel
vitiosissimam naturam excolere possit. Tu cum
pecuniae, cum voluptati, cum omnium rerum cupiditati resistes, ut facis, erit, credo, periculum, ne
improbum negotiatorem, paullo cupidiorem publica-
num comprimere non possis ! Nam Graeci quidem
sic te ita viventem intuebuntur, ut quemdam ex
annalium memoria, aut etiam de caelo divinum
8 hominem esse in provinciam delapsum putent. Atque haec nunc, non ut facias, sed ut te facere et
fecisse gaudeas, scribo. Praeclarum est enim, summo
cum imperio fuisse in Asia triennium, sic ut nullum
te signum, nulla pictura, nullum vas, nulla vestis,
nullum mancipium, nulla forma cuiusquam, nulla

ᵃ *Credo* marks the statement as ironical.

II. "Ah! but," it may be objected, "among these 7 very men serious disputes arise, numerous wrongs spring up, and great conflicts are the result." As though I supposed for a moment that you had not a lot of trouble on your shoulders! I fully understand that your trouble is very great, and calls for the soundest possible judgment. But remember that, in my opinion, this trouble of yours depends far more upon judgment than upon fortune. For what trouble is it to control those whom you rule, if you control yourself? For others, I grant, that may be a great and difficult thing to do, and it is indeed most difficult; but for you it has always been the easiest thing in the world, and indeed was bound to be so, since your nature is such that I think it would have been capable of self-restraint even without education; but you have had such an education as might well ennoble the most depraved nature. While you yourself still resist money, and pleasure, and every form of desire, as you do resist them, there will, I imagine,[a] be danger of your being unable to restrain some unscrupulous trader or some rather too rapacious tax-collector! For as to the Greeks, living as you do, they will so gaze upon you as to deem you someone celebrated in their own annals, or even think that a deified mortal has dropped down from heaven into their province.

And I write thus not to make you act, but to make 8 you rejoice that you are acting, and have acted, in this way. It is a glorious thought that you should have been three years in Asia in supreme command, and not been tempted by the offer of any statue, picture, plate, garment, or slave, by any fascination of human beauty, or any pecuniary proposals—

condicio pecuniae (quibus rebus abundat ista provincia) ab summa integritate continentiaque de-
9 duxerit. Quid autem reperiri tam eximium, aut
tam expetendum potest, quam istam virtutem,
moderationem animi, temperantiam, non latere in
tenebris, neque esse abditam, sed in luce Asiae, in
oculis clarissimae provinciae, atque in auribus omnium
gentium ac nationum esse positam? non itineribus
tuis perterreri homines? non sumptu exhauriri?
non adventu commoveri? esse, quocumque veneris,
et publice et privatim maximam laetitiam, cum urbs
custodem, non tyrannum, domus hospitem, non ex-
pilatorem, recepisse videatur?

10 III. His autem in rebus iam te usus ipse profecto
erudivit, nequaquam satis esse ipsum hasce habere
virtutes, sed esse circumspiciendum diligenter, ut in
hac custodia provinciae non te unum, sed omnes
ministros imperi tui, sociis, et civibus, et reipublicae
praestare videare. Quamquam legatos habes eos,
qui ipsi per se habituri sint rationem dignitatis suae;
de quibus honore, et dignitate, et aetate praestat
Tubero, quem ego arbitror, praesertim cum scribat
historiam, multos ex suis annalibus posse deligere,
quos velit et possit imitari; Allienus autem noster
est cum animo et benevolentia, tum vero etiam
imitatione vivendi. Nam quid ego de Gratidio

---

* L. Aelius Tubero was highly esteemed for his literary
ability by Cicero, who refers to him in *Pro Plancio* as *necessarius meus.*

temptations with which that province of yours
abounds—to deviate from the path of strict integrity
and sobriety of conduct.

But what can one find so excellent or so desirable 9
as that your virtue, your restraint of passion, and
your self-control, should not lurk in the shadows or be
hidden out of sight, but set in the light of Asia, before
the eyes of a most distinguished province, to ring in
the ears of all the nations and tribes of the earth ?
That men are not trampled underfoot in your progresses, not drained by expenditure, not struck with
panic at your approach ? That, wheresoever you
come, there is an ecstasy of joy, both in public and in
private, since it would seem that the city has taken
unto herself no tyrant, but a guardian, the home no
plunderer, but a guest ?

III. In these matters, however, experience itself 10
has by this time taught you that it is by no means
sufficient to possess these virtues yourself, but that
you must keep diligent watch around you so that in
this guardianship of your province it may appear that
you are responsible to the allies, the citizens, and the
State, not for yourself alone, but for all the officials
of your government.   And yet you have as *legati* men
who are likely to consider their reputation on their
own account ; and of them, in rank, position, and age,
Tubero [a] stands first ; and I imagine, especially as he
writes history, that he can select many characters
from his own annals whom he would wish and be
able to emulate. Allienus [b] moreover is our good
friend in spirit and friendly feeling as well as in his
adaptation of himself to our rules of life. About

[b] A. Allienus, praetor in 49, and proconsul in Sicily in 46.
Fam. xiii. 78 and 79 are addressed to him.

dicam ? quem certo scio ita laborare de existimatione sua, ut propter amorem in nos fraternum etiam
11 de nostra laboret. Quaestorem habes, non tuo
iudicio delectum, sed eum, quem sors dedit. Hunc
oportet et sua sponte esse moderatum et tuis institutis ac praeceptis obtemperare. Quorum si quis
forte esset sordidior, ferres eatenus, quoad per se
neglegeret eas leges, quibus esset astrictus, non ut
ea potestate, quam tu ad dignitatem permisisses, ad
quaestum uteretur. Neque enim mihi sane placet,
praesertim cum hi mores tantum iam ad nimiam
lenitatem et ad ambitionem incubuerint, scrutari te
omnes sordes, excutere unum quemque eorum, sed,
quanta sit in quoque fides, tantum cuique com-
mittere. Atque inter hos, eos, quos tibi comites et
adiutores negotiorum publicorum dedit ipsa respublica, dumtaxat finibus his praestabis, quos ante
12 praescripsi. IV. Quos vero aut ex domesticis con-
victionibus aut ex necessariis apparitionibus tecum
esse voluisti, qui quasi ex cohorte praetoris appellari
solent, horum non modo facta, sed etiam dicta omnia
praestanda nobis sunt. Sed habes eos tecum, quos
possis recte facientes facile diligere, minus con-

---

^a M. Gratidius was a brother of Cicero's grandmother
Gratidia. If the Gratidius here mentioned was M. Gratidius's
grandson, he would be Cicero's cousin (*frater* is often used for
cousin).

^b His name is unknown.

Gratidius [a] I need say nothing ; I am well assured that he is so anxious about his own reputation that, if only out of cousinly affection for us, he is anxious about ours. Your quaestor [b] is not a man of your 11 own deliberate selection, but one assigned you by lot. He ought to be a man of instinctive self-control, and should also comply with your policy and instructions.

Among these men, should it happen that anyone could not show a clean sheet of conduct, you would put up with him so long as he defied the regulations which bound him in his private capacity only, and not to the extent of abusing for purposes of private lucre the powers you had vouchsafed him for the maintenance of his public position. For it does not at all commend itself to me (especially in view of the distinct bias of modern morality in favour of undue laxity of conduct, and even of self-seeking) that you should investigate every ugly charge; and turn every single one of the charged inside out ; no, but that you should apportion your confidence in every case to the trustworthiness of the man to whom you give it. And among all these you will be responsible for those whom the State itself has assigned to you as your *attachés* and assistants in public business, at least within the limits I have laid down above.

IV. As for those, however, whom you have chosen to 12 be about you, either in your domestic *entourage* or on your train of personal attendants, generally spoken of as a sort of " praetor's retinue," in *their* case we have to be responsible not only for their every act, but for their every word. But you have with you the kind of men whom you may easily make friends of when they act aright, and very easily check when they show

sulentes existimationi tuae, facillime coercere : a
quibus, rudis cum esses, videtur potuisse tua liberalitas decipi ; nam ut quisque est vir optimus, ita
difficillime esse alios improbos suspicatur ; nunc vero
tertius hic annus habeat integritatem eamdem,
quam superiores, cautiorem etiam ac diligentiorem.
13 Sint aures tuae eae, quae id, quod audiunt, existimentur audire, non in quas ficte et simulate quaestus
causa insusurretur. Sit anulus tuus non ut vas aliquod, sed tamquam ipse tu, non minister alienae voluntatis, sed testis tuae. Accensus sit eo etiam
numero, quo eum maiores nostri esse voluerunt ; qui
hoc non in benefici loco, sed in laboris ac muneris, non
temere nisi libertis suis deferebant, quibus illi quidem
non multo secus ac servis imperabant. Sit lictor
non suae, sed tuae lenitatis apparitor ; maioraque
praeferant fasces illi ac secures dignitatis insignia,
quam potestatis. Toti denique sit provinciae cognitum, tibi omnium, quibus praesis, salutem, liberos,
famam, fortunas esse carissimas. Denique haec
opinio sit, non modo iis, qui aliquid acceperint, sed
iis etiam, qui dederint, te inimicum (si id cognoveris)
futurum. Neque vero quisquam dabit, cum erit hoc
perspectum, nihil per eos, qui simulant se apud te
14 multum posse, abs te solere impetrari. Nec tamen

ᵃ The *accensus* was an official of low rank who attended
upon a consul, proconsul, or praetor, at Rome or abroad;
his duties were to summon parties to court, and maintain
order there. He was generally the freedman of the magistrate he served.

ᵇ This is a warning to Quintus against the undue ascendancy of his freedman Statius.

ᶜ Cicero alludes to the lictors' practice of taking bribes to
mitigate the severity of the punishment it was their duty to
inflict. Tyrrell.

too little consideration for your good name—men who might very likely have taken you in, when you were a mere novice, generous soul that you are (for the better a man is, the more difficult it is for him to suspect others of being unscrupulous), but, as it is, let the third year show the same standard of integrity as the preceding two, but even an increase in caution and in diligence.

Let your ears be such as are reputed to hear only 13 what they do hear, and not such as are open to false and interested whispers prompted by the hope of profit. Let not your signet-ring be a sort of utensil, but, as it were, your very self—not the servant of another's will, but the witness of your own. Let your beadle [a] hold the rank which he was intended to hold by our ancestors, who, regarding that post not as a lucrative sinecure but as one of work and duty, were slow to confer it upon any but their own freedmen, over whom they exercised much the same authority as over their slaves.[b] Let your lictor be the dispenser not of his own, but of your clemency,[c] and let the *fasces* and axes they carry before them be more the symbols of rank than of power. In a word, let it be recognized by the whole province that the welfare, children, reputation, and fortunes of all whom you govern are most precious to you. Finally, let it be the general impression that you will regard with disfavour not only those who have taken a bribe, but also those who have given one, if ever you get to know of it. And, as a matter of fact, there will be no giving of bribes when it is made perfectly clear that, as a rule, nothing is got out of you through the machinations of persons pretending to have great influence with you.

est haec oratio mea huiusmodi, ut te in tuos aut
durum esse nimium, aut suspiciosum velim. Nam si
quis est eorum, qui tibi bienni spatio numquam in
suspicionem avaritiae venerit, (ut ego Caesium et
Chaerippum et Labeonem et audio, et, quia cognovi, existimo,) nihil est, quod non et iis, et si quis
est alius eiusdemmodi, et committi et credi rectissime
putem. Sed si quis est, in quo iam offenderis, de
quo aliquid senseris, huic nihil credideris, nullam
15 partem existimationis tuae commiseris. V. In provincia vero ipsa, si quem es nactus, qui in tuam
familiaritatem penitus intrarit, qui nobis ante fuerit
ignotus, huic quantum credendum sit, vide ; non
quin possint multi esse provinciales viri boni, sed
hoc sperare licet, iudicare periculosum est. Multis
enim simulationum involucris tegitur, et quasi velis
quibusdam obtenditur unius cuiusque natura ; frons,
oculi, vultus persaepe mentiuntur, oratio vero saepissime. Quamobrem, qui potes reperire ex eo genere
hominum, qui pecuniae cupiditate adducti careant
his rebus omnibus, a quibus nos divulsi esse non
possumus, te autem, alienum hominem, ament ex
animo, ac non sui commodi causa simulent ? Mihi
quidem permagnum videtur ; praesertim si iidem
homines privatum non fere quemquam, praetores

---

[a] *i.e.*, the delights of life and society in Rome.

And yet by this discourse I do not mean that I 14
would have you be either unduly harsh or suspicious in
dealing with your subordinates. For if anyone of
them in the course of two years has never given you
reason to suspect him of rapacity (and I am not only
told this, but, because I know them, believe it of
Caesius and Chaerippus and Labeo), I should think
that there is nothing which might not be most
properly entrusted or confided to them, or anybody
else of the same sort. But if there is anyone whom
you have already found reason to suspect, or about
whom you may have discovered something, put no
confidence in that man, entrust him with no fraction
of your reputation.

V. In the province itself, however, if you have 15
found anyone who has become thoroughly intimate
with you without our having known him before, take
care how far you give him your confidence ; not that
many provincials may not be quite good men, but
while we may hope so, it is dangerous to be positive.
For there are many wrappings and pretences under
which each individual's nature is concealed and
overspread, so to speak, with curtains ; the brow, the
eye, and the face very often lie, but speech most
often of all. How, therefore, among that class of
men who, tempted by their greed for money, are
ready to dispense with all the amenities *a* from which
we cannot tear ourselves, how, I ask, can you
discover any who yet have a sincere affection for
you, a mere stranger, and are not simply pretending to have it in order to gain their own ends ? I
think you would find it extremely hard, especially
when those same persons show affection for hardly
anybody who is not in office, but are always at one in

semper omnes amant. Quo ex genere si quem forte
tui cognosti amantiorem (fieri enim potuit) quam
temporis, hunc vero ad tuorum numerum libenter
ascribito ; sin autem id non perspicies, nullum erit
genus in familiaritate cavendum magis, propterea
quod et omnes vias pecuniae norunt, et omnia
pecuniae causa faciunt, et, quicum victuri non sunt,
16 eius existimationi consulere non curant. Atque
etiam e Graecis ipsis diligenter cavendae sunt quaedam familiaritates, praeter hominum perpaucorum,
si qui sunt vetere Graecia digni. Isti[1] vero fallaces
sunt permulti et leves, et diuturna servitute ad
nimiam assentationem eruditi ; quos ego universos
adhiberi liberaliter, optimum quemque hospitio
amicitiaque coniungi dico oportere ; nimiae familiaritates eorum neque tam fideles sunt, (non enim audent
adversari nostris voluntatibus,) et invident non nostris
17 solum, verum etiam suis. VI. Iam qui in eiusmodi
rebus, in quibus vereor etiam ne durior sim, cautus
esse velim ac diligens, quo me animo in servos esse
censes ? quos quidem cum omnibus in locis, tum
praecipue in provinciis regere debemus. Quo de
genere multa praecipi possunt ; sed hoc et brevis-
simum est, et facillime teneri potest, ut ita se gerant

---

[1] *Tyrrell* : sic MSS.

their affection for praetors. But if you happen to have found any member of the class to be fonder of you (and it might have occurred) than of your position at the moment, by all means gladly add him to the list of your friends ; if however you are not quite certain about it, there is no class of man you will have to be more on your guard against in the matter of intimacy, for the simple reason that they are up to all the ways of making money, and stick at nothing to make it, and have no consideration for the good name of one with whom they are not going to spend their lives.

And further among the Greeks themselves there are 16 certain intimacies against which you must be strictly on your guard, except intimacy with the very few, if any, who are worthy of ancient Greece. In your province, however, there are a great many who are deceitful and unstable, and trained by a long course of servitude to show an excess of sycophancy. What I say is, that they should all of them be treated as gentlemen, but that only the best of them should be attached to you by ties of hospitality and friendship ; unrestricted intimacies with them are not so much to be trusted, for they dare not oppose our wishes, and they are jealous not only of our countrymen, but even of their own.

VI. And now, since in matters of this kind, in 17 which, though I would be merely cautious and careful, I am afraid I am somewhat too strict, what do you suppose are my sentiments in regard to slaves ? Well, it is our duty to keep them in hand everywhere, but particularly in the provinces. In this connexion a number of rules may be laid down, but the shortest as well as the easiest to remember is this—let them

in istis Asiaticis itineribus, ut si iter Appia via
faceres ; neve interesse quidquam putent, utrum
Tralles an Formias venerint. At, si quis est ex
servis egregie fidelis, sit in domesticis rebus, et
privatis ; quae res ad officium imperi tui atque ad
aliquam partem reipublicae pertinebunt, de his rebus
ne quid attingat. Multa enim, quae recte committi
servis fidelibus possunt, tamen sermonis et vitupera-
18 tionis vitandae causa committenda non sunt. Sed,
nescio quo pacto, ad praecipiendi rationem delapsa
est oratio mea, cum id mihi propositum initio non
fuisset. Quid enim ei praecipiam, quem ego in hoc
praesertim genere intellegam prudentia non esse
inferiorem quam me, usu vero etiam superiorem ?
Sed tamen si ad ea, quae faceres, auctoritas accederet
mea, tibi ipsi illa putavi fore iucundiora. Quare sint
haec fundamenta dignitatis tuae, tua primum in-
tegritas et continentia ; deinde omnium, qui tecum
sunt, pudor ; delectus in familiaritatibus, et pro-
vincialium hominum et Graecorum, percautus et
diligens ; familiae gravis et constans disciplina.
19 Quae cum honesta sint in his privatis nostris quo-
tidianisque rationibus, in tanto imperio, tam de-
pravatis moribus, tam corruptrice provincia, divina
videantur necesse est. Haec institutio atque haec

---

a A commercial town of Lydia in Asia Minor, used here of
any " out-of-the-way " foreign place, as in Juv. i. 3. 70 (" hic
Trallibus aut Alabandis ").

b See note *a* on § 2.

conduct themselves on your progresses in Asia exactly as if they were travelling by the Appian Way, and don't let them imagine that it makes any difference whether their destination is Tralles[a] or Formiae. Of course, if anyone of your slaves stands above the rest in trustworthiness, employ him in your domestic and private affairs ; but with matters belonging to your office as governor, or with any State department, —with such matters don't let him meddle. For there are many things which may quite properly be entrusted to honest slaves, but which, for all that, in order to avoid tittle-tattle and fault-finding, should not be so entrusted.

But somehow or other my discourse has dropped 18 into a scheme of instruction, though that is not what I had in view when I began. For why should I instruct one who, especially in this department, is, I well know, not inferior to myself in wisdom, and in experience my superior also ? But I thought, nevertheless, that if your actions had the additional ratification of my approval, you yourself would find a deeper satisfaction in them. Let these, therefore, be the foundations of your public position,—first of all, your own integrity and self-restraint ; secondly, the respectful treatment of those about you, an extremely cautious and careful choice, in the matter of intimacy, of both provincials[b] and Greeks, and a strict and consistent system of discipline in dealing with slaves.

Such characteristics are honourable even in our 19 private and daily business here at home ; in so important a command, where morals are so debased, and provincial life so corrupting, they must needs seem godlike. The establishment of such principles,

disciplina potest sustinere in rebus statuendis de-
cernendisque eam severitatem, qua tu in iis rebus
usus es, ex quibus nonnullas simultates cum magna
mea laetitia susceptas habemus. Nisi forte me
Paconi nescio cuius, hominis ne Graeci quidem, at
Mysii aut Phrygis potius, querellis moveri putas, aut
Tusceni, hominis furiosi ac sordidi, vocibus, cuius tu
ex impurissimis faucibus inhonestissimam cupiditatem
20 eripuisti summa cum aequitate. VII. Haec, et
cetera plena severitatis, quae statuisti in ista provincia, non facile sine summa integritate sustinere-
mus. Quare sit summa in iure dicundo severitas,
dummodo ea ne varietur gratia, sed conservetur
aequabilis. Sed tamen parvi refert abs te ipso ius
dici aequabiliter et diligenter, nisi idem ab iis fiet,
quibus tu eius muneris aliquam partem concesseris.
Ac mihi quidem videtur non sane magna varietas
esse negotiorum in administranda Asia, sed ea tota
iurisdictione maxime sustineri. In qua scientiae
praesertim provincialis ratio ipsa expedita est ; constantia est adhibenda et gravitas, quae resistat non
21 solum gratiae, verum etiam suspicioni. Adiungenda
etiam est facilitas in audiendo, lenitas in decernendo,
in satisfaciendo ac disputando diligentia. His rebus
nuper C. Octavius iucundissimus fuit, apud quem

---

^a See note *b* on § 2.
^b The father of Augustus, now praetor in Macedonia, but
the above passage refers to what he did when praetor at Rome
before he left for Macedonia.

and such discipline, may well justify that severity in the settlement and decision of affairs which you yourself have practised in certain matters, in consequence of which we have incurred several personal animosities with no little happiness to myself,—unless of course you imagine that I pay any heed to the complaints of some Paconius [a] or other, a fellow who is not even a Greek, but more of a Mysian or Phrygian, or to the ejaculations of Tuscenius,[a] a crazy fellow of the baser sort, from whose disgustingly filthy jaws you snatched the prey of his most discreditable cupidity ; and you were absolutely right.

VII. These and all the other precedents of notable 20 severity you have established in your province we should not easily justify except by the most perfect probity. For that reason be as severe as you please in administering justice, provided that your severity is not varied by partiality, but kept on the same level of consistency. However, it is of little importance that your own administration of justice is consistent and careful, unless it be so administered by those also to whom you have yielded any portion of that duty. And indeed it seems to me that there is no great variety of transactions in the government of Asia, but that the entire government mainly depends upon the administration of justice ; and, being thus limited, the theory of government itself, especially in the provinces, presents no difficulty ; you only need show such consistency and firmness as to withstand not only favouritism, but the very suspicion of it.

In addition to this there must be civility in hearing, 21 clemency in deciding, a case, and careful discrimination in the satisfactory settlement of disputes. It was by acting thus that C. Octavius [b] lately made himself

primum[1] lictor quievit, tacuit accensus, quoties quisque voluit, dixit, et quam voluit diu. Quibus ille
rebus fortasse nimis lenis videretur, nisi haec lenitas
illam severitatem tueretur. Cogebantur Sullani
homines, quae per vim et metum abstulerant,
reddere. Qui in magistratibus iniuriose decreverant,
eodem ipsis privatis erat iure parendum. Haec illius
severitas acerba videretur, nisi multis condimentis
22 humanitatis mitigaretur. Quod si haec lenitas grata
Romae est, ubi tanta arrogantia est, tam immoderata
libertas, tam infinita hominum licentia, denique tot
magistratus, tot auxilia, tanta vis populi, tanta
senatus auctoritas, quam iucunda tandem praetoris
comitas in Asia potest esse, in qua tanta multitudo
civium, tanta sociorum, tot urbes, tot civitates unius
hominis nutum intuentur? ubi nullum auxilium est,
nulla conquestio, nullus senatus, nulla contio?
Quare cum semper[2] magni hominis est, et cum ipsa
natura moderati, tum vero etiam doctrina atque opti-
marum artium studiis eruditi, sic se adhibere in tanta
potestate, ut nulla alia potestas ab iis, quibus ipse
23 praesit, desideretur. VIII. Cyrus ille a Xenophonte
non ad historiae fidem scriptus, sed ad effigiem iusti

[1] *Malaspina*: primus *mss*.
[2] *Boot*: cum permagni *M*.

---

[a] *Sullani homines* or *Sullani possessores* was the regular
term for the illegal proprietors of land confiscated by Sulla—
men who had obtained possession of the land by buying it
from the soldiers to whom it had been assigned, or encroached
on any land unassigned: for Sulla had confiscated more land
than was necessary to satisfy the soldiers.

most popular ; it was in his court, for the first time, that the lictor made no fuss, and the beadle held his tongue, while everyone spoke as often as he pleased, and as long as he pleased. It is possible that by so doing he gave one the impression of being too gentle, were it not that this very gentleness served to counteract such an instance of severity as the following : certain "men of Sulla "[a] were compelled to restore what they had carried off by violence and intimidation, and those who, when in office, had passed unjust decrees, were themselves, when private citizens, obliged to bow to the same rulings. This severity on his part might seem a bitter pill to swallow, were it not coated with the honey of many a kindness.

But if this gentleness is popular at Rome, where 22 such arrogance is to be found, such unrestricted liberty, such unbounded licence on every side, and in short, so many magistrates, so many sources of aid, such power in the people, such authority in the Senate, how welcome, I ask you, must the courteousness of a praetor be in Asia, where so vast a multitude of citizens and allies, so many cities and communities concentrate their gaze upon the nod of a single man ; where there is no succour for the oppressed, no facility for protest, no senate, no popular assembly ? It must, therefore, ever be the privilege of some great man, and a man not only instinctively self-controlled, but also refined by learning and the study of all that is best in the arts, so to conduct himself in the possession of so vast a power that the absence of any other power may never be regretted by his subjects.

VIII. The great Cyrus was portrayed by Xenophon 23 not in accord with historical truth, but as a model of

imperii ; cuius summa gravitas ab illo philosopho
cum singulari comitate coniungitur ; (quos quidem
libros non sine causa noster ille Africanus de manibus
ponere non solebat ; nullum est enim praetermissum
in his officium diligentis et moderati imperi ;) eaque,
si sic coluit ille, qui privatus futurus numquam fuit,
quonam modo retinenda sunt iis, quibus imperium
ita datum est, ut redderent, et ab his legibus datum
24 est, ad quas revertendum est ? Ac mihi quidem
videntur huc omnia esse referenda iis, qui praesunt
aliis, ut ii, qui erunt eorum in imperio, sint quam
beatissimi ; quod tibi et esse antiquissimum, et ab
initio fuisse, ut primum Asiam attigisti, constante
fama atque omnium sermone celebratum est. Est
autem non modo eius, qui sociis et civibus, sed etiam
eius, qui servis, qui mutis pecudibus praesit, eorum,
25 quibus praesit, commodis utilitatique servire. Cuius
quidem generis constare inter omnes video abs te
summam adhiberi diligentiam ; nullum aes alienum
novum contrahi civitatibus ; vetere autem magno et
gravi multas abs te esse liberatas ; urbes complures,
dirutas ac paene desertas, (in quibus unam Ioniae
nobilissimam, alteram Cariae, Samum et Halicarnas-
sum,) per te esse recreatas ; nullas esse in oppidis

just government, and the impressive dignity of his character is combined in that philosopher's description of him with a matchless courtesy; and indeed it was not without reason that our great Africanus did not often put those books out of his hands, for there is no duty belonging to a painstaking and fair-minded form of government that is omitted in them. And if Cyrus, destined as he was never to be a private citizen, so assiduously cultivated those qualities, how carefully, I ask, should they be preserved by those to whom supreme power is only given on the condition that it must be surrendered, and given too by those very laws to the observance of which those rulers must return?

And my personal opinion is, that those who govern 24 others must gauge their every act by this one test— the greatest possible happiness of the governed; and that this principle is and has been from the beginning, from the moment you set foot in Asia, of primary importance in your eyes is a fact bruited abroad by unvarying report and the conversation of all. And indeed it is the duty not only of one who governs allies and citizens, but also of one who governs slaves and dumb animals, to be himself a slave to the interests and well-being of those he governs.

And in this respect I see that there is universal 25 agreement as to the extraordinary pains you are taking; I see that no new debt is being contracted to burden the states, whereas many of them have been relieved by you of a big and heavy debt of long standing; that several cities, dismantled and almost deserted (one of them the most famous city in Ionia, the other in Caria—Samos and Halicarnassus) have been rebuilt through your instrumentality; that

seditiones, nullas discordias; provideri abs te, ut
civitates optimatium consiliis administrentur; sub-
lata Mysiae latrocinia; caedes multis locis repressas;
pacem tota provincia constitutam; neque solum illa
itinerum atque agrorum, sed multo etiam plura et
maiora oppidorum et fanorum furta et latrocinia esse
depulsa; remotam a fama et a fortunis et ab otio
locupletum illam acerbissimam ministram praetorum
avaritiae, calumniam: sumptus et tributa civitatum
ab omnibus, qui earum civitatum fines incolant,
tolerari aequabiliter; facillimos esse aditus ad te;
patere aures tuas querellis omnium, nullius inopiam
ac solitudinem, non modo illo populari accessu ac
tribunali, sed ne domo quidem et cubiculo esse
exclusam; tuo toto denique imperio nihil acerbum
esse, nihil crudele, atque omnia plena clementiae,
mansuetudinis, humanitatis.

26 IX. Quantum vero illud est beneficium tuum, quod
iniquo et gravi vectigali aedilicio, magnis nostris
simultatibus, Asiam liberasti! Enimvero, si unus
homo nobilis queritur palam, te, quod edixeris, NE
AD LUDOS PECUNIAE DECERNERENTUR, HS cc. sibi eri-
puisse, quanta tandem pecunia penderetur, si om-

---

a *i.e.*, taxation imposed by the aediles to defray the expenses
of the games.

there are no insurrections, no civil discords in the
towns ; that you are providing for the government
of the states by councils of their leading men ; that
brigandage has been exterminated in Mysia, murder
suppressed in various places, and peace established
throughout the province ; that thefts and robberies,
not only those on the highways and in the country,
but also those (and they are far more frequent and
serious) in towns and temples, have been effectually
checked ; that the good name, the possessions, and
the peace of mind of the rich has been delivered from
that most pernicious instrument of praetorian greed—
prosecution on a false charge ; that the incidence of
expenditure and taxation in the states bears in equal
proportion upon all those who dwell within the
boundaries of those states ; that it is the easiest thing
in the world to get access to you ; that your ears are
open to the complaints of all ; that no man's lack of
means or of friends has ever shut him out, nor ever
will, from approaching you, not only in public and on
the tribunal, but even in your very house and bed-
chamber ; in short, that in the whole sphere of your
command there is nothing harsh, nothing brutal, and,
look where we will, we see nothing but clemency,
gentleness, and kindness of heart.

IX. But what am I to say of the service you have 26
done us in freeing Asia from the heavy and iniquitous
tribute imposed by the aediles,ᵃ though it cost us
some bitter animosities ! For to speak plainly, if a
single man of noble rank complains without any con-
cealment that by your edict, " *that no sums of money
should be voted for the games*," you actually robbed him
of 200,000 sesterces, how much money, I should like
to know, would be paid if a grant were made to the

nium nomine, quicumque Romae ludos facerent,
quod erat iam institutum, erogaretur? Quamquam
has querellas hominum nostrorum illo consilio oppressimus, quod in Asia nescio quo modo, Romae quidem
non mediocri cum admiratione laudatur, quod, cum
ad templum monumentumque nostrum civitates
pecunias decrevissent; cumque id et pro magnis
meis meritis, et pro tuis maximis beneficiis summa
sua voluntate fecissent, nominatimque lex exciperet,
UT AD TEMPLUM MONUMENTUMQUE CAPERE LICERET;
cumque id, quod dabatur, non esset interiturum,
sed in ornamentis templi futurum, ut non mihi
potius, quam populo Romano ac dis immortalibus
datum videretur; tamen id, in quo erat dignitas,
erat lex, erat eorum, qui faciebant, voluntas, ac-
cipiendum non putavi, cum aliis de causis, tum etiam,
ut animo aequiore ferrent ii, quibus nec deberetur
27 nec liceret. Quapropter incumbe toto animo et
studio omni in eam rationem, qua adhuc usus es, ut
eos, quos tuae fidei potestatique senatus populusque
Romanus commisit et credidit, diligas, et omni
ratione tueare, ut esse quam beatissimos velis.
Quod si te sors Afris aut Hispanis aut Gallis prae-
fecisset, immanibus ac barbaris nationibus, tamen
esset humanitatis tuae, consulere eorum commodis,

account of everyone who gave games at Rome—a practice that had already become established? Anyhow our good friends had their complaints forced down their throats by what I decided to do—a decision which, however it is received in Asia, meets with no little admiration and applause at Rome—I mean that when the states had voted their contributions to a temple and monument in our honour, and though they had done so with the heartiest goodwill in view of my great deserts and your even greater services, and though the law contained a specific exception legalizing "the receipt of funds for a temple and a monument," and though the money offered was not going to be thrown away, but was to be spent on the ornamentation of a temple, so that the offer seemed to be made not so much to myself as to the people of Rome and the immortal gods,—in spite of all that I did not consider that such an offer, justified as it was by meritorious achievement, by the law, and by the goodwill of those who made it, should after all be accepted. And I did this for other reasons, but especially in order that those, in whose case such an honour was neither due nor legal, might bear their disappointment with greater resignation.

Therefore throw your whole heart and soul into the 27 policy you have hitherto adopted, treating as friends those whom the Senate and people of Rome have committed and entrusted to your honour and authority, protecting them in every possible way, and desiring their greatest possible happiness. Why, if the drawing of lots had given you the government of the Africans or the Spaniards or the Gauls, uncouth and barbarous nations, it would still be incumbent upon a man of your humane character to study their

et utilitati salutique servire. Cum vero ei generi
hominum praesimus, non modo in quo ipsa sit, sed
etiam a quo ad alios pervenisse putetur humanitas,
certe iis eam potissimum tribuere debemus, a quibus
28 accepimus. Non enim me hoc iam dicere pudebit,
praesertim in ea vita atque iis rebus gestis, in quibus
non potest residere inertiae aut levitatis ulla suspicio, nos ea, quae consecuti sumus, his studiis et
artibus esse adeptos, quae sint nobis Graeciae monumentis disciplinisque traditae. Quare praeter communem fidem, quae omnibus debetur, praeterea nos
isti hominum generi praecipue debere videmur, ut,
quorum praeceptis eruditi simus, apud eos ipsos,
29 quod ab iis didicerimus, velimus expromere. X. Atque ille quidem princeps ingeni et doctrinae, Plato,
tum denique fore beatas respublicas putavit, si aut
docti ac sapientes homines eas regere coepissent,
aut, qui regerent, omne suum studium in doctrina
ac sapientia collocassent. Hanc coniunctionem videlicet potestatis ac sapientiae saluti censuit civitatibus esse posse. Quod fortasse aliquando universae
reipublicae nostrae, nunc quidem profecto isti provinciae contigit, ut is in ea summam potestatem
haberet, cui in doctrina, cui in virtute atque humanitate percipienda plurimum a pueritia studi fuisset et
30 temporis. Quare cura, ut hic annus, qui ad laborem
tuum accessit, idem ad salutem Asiae prorogatus
esse videatur. Quoniam in te retinendo fuit Asia

---

[a] Weaknesses not unknown in the Greek character, which
Cicero claims to have avoided.
[b] *De Rep.* 473 D.

interests, and consider their welfare and security. But seeing that we are governing that race of mankind in which not only do we find real civilization, but from which it is also supposed to have spread to others, it is at any rate our duty to bestow upon them, above all things, just that which they have bestowed upon us.

For at this point, especially as my life and achieve- 28 ments leave no room for the slightest suspicion of indolence or frivolity,[a] I shall not be ashamed to assert that I am indebted for whatever I have accomplished to the arts and studies transmitted to us in the records and philosophic teachings of Greece. And that is why, over and above the common honesty due to all, yes, over and above that, it seems to me that we owe a special debt to that race of men, and that is, among those very people whose precepts have rescued us from barbarism, to be the willing exponents of the lessons we have learnt from them.

X. And indeed Plato, that foremost of men in 29 genius and learning, thought that states would only then be prosperous when learned and wise men began to rule them, or when those who ruled them devoted all their mental energies to learning and wisdom.[b] He was evidently of opinion that this combination of power and wisdom would be the salvation of states — a blessing which some day perhaps will befall our whole Republic, as it has assuredly now befallen your province, in that it has as its supreme ruler one who had from his very boyhood devoted the maximum of zeal and time to absorbing the principles of philosophy, of virtue, and of philanthropy.

See to it, then, that this year which has been added 30 to your period of work may be regarded as having been a prolongation of welfare to Asia. Since Asia

felicior, quam nos in deducendo, perfice, ut laetitia
provinciae desiderium nostrum leniatur. Etenim si
in promerendo, ut tibi tanti honores haberentur,
quanti haud scio an nemini, fuisti omnium diligentissimus, multo maiorem in his honoribus tuendis ad-
31 hibere diligentiam debes. Et quidem de isto genere
honorum quid sentirem, scripsi ad te ante. Semper
eos putavi, si vulgares essent, viles, si temporis causa
constituerentur, leves; si vero (id quod ita factum
est) meritis tuis tribuerentur, existimabam multam
tibi in his tuendis operam esse ponendam. Quare
quoniam in istis urbibus cum summo imperio et
potestate versaris, in quibus tuas virtutes consecratas
et in deorum numero collocatas vides, in omnibus
rebus, quas statues, quas decernes, quas ages, quid
tantis hominum opinionibus, tantis de te iudiciis,
tantis honoribus debeas, cogitabis. Id autem erit
eiusmodi, ut consulas omnibus, ut medeare incom-
modis hominum, provideas saluti, ut te parentem
32 Asiae et dici et haberi velis. XI. Atqui huic tuae
voluntati ac diligentiae difficultatem magnam afferunt
publicani; quibus si adversamur, ordinem de nobis optime meritum et per nos cum republica coniunctum
et a nobis et a republica diiungemus; sin autem

has been more successful in keeping her hold on
you than I have in bringing you home, so manage
matters that my own sense of loss may be lightened
by the rejoicings of the province. For if, in earning
the bestowal upon you of such honours as, I am inclined to think, have been bestowed upon no other,
you have been the most assiduous of men, far greater
is the assiduity you ought to display in justifying
those honours.

And what I feel about honours of that sort I have 31
told you in previous letters ; if given indiscriminately,
I have always thought them cheap ; if designed to
meet some difficulty of the moment, paltry ; if on
the other hand, as in this case, they were a tribute to
your deserts, I have always thought that you were
bound to take particular pains to justify them.
Therefore, now that you are engaged in a position of
supreme command and authority in cities where, as
you see, your virtues are hallowed and held up as
being nothing less than divine, well then, in all your
decisions, decrees, and official acts, you will, I am
sure, consider what you owe to the high opinions men
have of you, to their flattering judgments about you,
and to the distinguished honours conferred upon you.
And what you owe is just this—to bear in mind the
interests of all, to redress the ills of men, to provide for
their welfare, and to make it your ambition to be not
only entitled, but also esteemed, " the father of Asia."

XI. And yet to all your goodwill and devotion to 32
duty there is a serious obstacle in the *publicani* ; if
we oppose them, we shall alienate from ourselves and
from the commonwealth an order that has deserved
extremely well of us, and been brought through
our instrumentality into close association with the

omnibus in rebus obsequemur, funditus eos perire
patiemur, quorum non modo saluti, sed etiam commodis consulere debemus. Haec est una (si vere
cogitare volumus) in toto imperio tuo difficultas.
Nam esse abstinentem, continere omnes cupiditates,
suos coercere, iuris aequabilem tenere rationem,
facilem se in rebus cognoscendis, in hominibus
audiendis admittendisque praebere, praeclarum
magis est, quam difficile. Non est enim positum in
labore aliquo, sed in quadam inductione animi atque
33 voluntate. Illa causa publicanorum quantam acerbitatem afferat sociis, intelleximus ex civibus, qui nuper
in portoriis Italiae tollendis, non tam de portorio,
quam de nonnullis iniuriis portitorum querebantur.
Quare non ignoro, quid sociis accidat in ultimis terris,
cum audierim in Italia querellas civium. Hic te ita
versari, ut et publicanis satisfacias, praesertim publicis male redemptis, ac socios perire non sinas,
divinae cuiusdam virtutis esse videtur, id est, tuae.
Ac primum Graecis, id quod acerbissimum est, quod
sunt vectigales, non ita acerbum videri debet, propterea quod sine imperio populi Romani, suis institutis,
per se ipsi ita fuerunt. Nomen autem publicani

---

^a By Q. Metellus Nepos.

^b Employed by the *publicani* to collect their dues.

^c The syndicate which had bought the right to farm the
taxes of Asia had made an excessive bid for them; indeed
Cicero tells Atticus that they actually "demanded a can-
cellation of the assignment" ("ut induceretur locatio postulaverunt"), *Att.* i. 17. 9.

commonwealth; and yet, if we yield to them in everything, we shall be acquiescing in the utter ruin of
those whose security, and indeed whose interests, we
are bound to protect. This is the one outstanding
difficulty (if we would face the question honestly) in
the whole sphere of your command. For as to one's
being unselfish, curbing all one's passions, keeping
one's staff in check, maintaining a consistently uniform policy in legal proceedings, conducting oneself
with kindly courtesy in investigating cases and in
giving audience to suitors and not shutting one's door
to them,—all that is magnificent rather than difficult
to do ; for it depends not upon any strenuous exertion, but upon making up one's mind, and setting
one's will in a certain direction.

What bitterness of feeling this question of the 33
publicani causes the allies we have gathered from
those citizens who recently, on the abolition of port-
dues in Italy,[a] complained not so much of that duty
itself as of certain malpractices on the part of the
custom-officers.[b] I therefore know pretty well what
happens to allies in distant lands from the complaints
I have heard from citizens in Italy. So to conduct
yourself in this connexion as to satisfy the *publicani*,
especially when they took over the collection of taxes
at a loss,[c] and at the same time not to permit the ruin
of the allies, seems to demand a sort of divine excellence—in other words, an excellence such as yours.
Let us take the Greeks first ; their greatest grievance
is that they are subject to taxation ; but they should
not regard that as so very much of a grievance, for the
simple reason that they put themselves in that
position of their own free will by their own enactment,
quite apart from the rule of the Roman people. More-

aspernari non possunt, qui pendere ipsi vectigal sine
publicano non potuerunt, quod his aequaliter Sulla
descripserat. Non esse autem leniores in exigendis
vectigalibus Graecos, quam nostros publicanos, hinc
intellegi potest, quod Caunii[a] nuper, omnesque ex
insulis, quae erant ab Sulla Rhodiis attributae, con-
fugerunt ad senatum, nobis ut potius vectigal, quam
Rhodiis penderent. Quare nomen publicani neque
ii debent horrere, qui semper vectigales fuerunt,
neque ii aspernari, qui per se pendere vectigal non
potuerunt, neque ii recusare, qui postulaverunt.
34 Simul et illud Asia cogitet, nullam a se neque belli ex-
terni, neque discordiarum domesticarum calamitatem
abfuturam fuisse, si hoc imperio non teneretur. Id
autem imperium cum retineri sine vectigalibus nullo
modo possit, aequo animo parte aliqua suorum fruc-
tuum pacem sibi sempiternam redimat atque otium.[b]
35 XII. Quod si genus ipsum et nomen publicani non
iniquo animo sustinebunt, poterunt iis, consilio et
prudentia tua, reliqua videri mitiora. Possunt in
pactionibus faciendis non legem spectare censoriam,
sed potius commoditatem conficiendi negoti et libe-
rationem molestiae. Potes etiam tu id facere, quod[c]

---

[a] Caunus was one of the chief cities of Caria, on its south
coast, founded by the Cretans, but made subject to the
Rhodians in 300 B.C. It was unhealthily situated, but famous
for its dried figs.

[b] These words are strikingly applicable to India under
British rule.

[c] The provincials might make special arrangements, not
in strict accord with the censorian law, with the *publicani*;
they might, for instance, substitute an immediate payment
of the tax for that enjoined by the law, and thereby facilitate business, and escape the constant dunning of the tax-
farmers. Tyrrell.

over they cannot afford to disdain the name of *publicanus*, since without the aid of that *publicanus* they themselves could never have paid the assessment imposed by Sulla as a poll-tax on all alike. But that the Greek collectors are no more gentle in enforcing the payment of taxes than our own *publicani* may be inferred from the fact that the Caunians [a] and all the islands that had been made tributary by Sulla to the Rhodians quite recently fled for protection to our Senate, begging that they might pay to us rather than to the Rhodians. It follows, therefore, that neither ought those who have always been subject to the tax to shudder at the name of a *publicanus*, nor those to disdain it who have been unable to pay the tax by themselves, nor those to reject his services who have applied for them.

Let Asia at the same time bear this in mind, that 34 were she not under our government, there is no disaster in the way of either foreign war or intestine discords which she would have been likely to escape.[b] Seeing, however, that such government cannot possibly be maintained without taxes, she should not resent having to pay for perpetual peace and tranquillity with some portion at least of what her soil produces.

XII. If they will but accept without resentment 35 the mere existence of such a class, and the name *publicanus*, all else, owing to your counsel and wisdom, may possibly seem to them less oppressive. They have the power in making agreements not to regard the *lex censoria* so much as convenience in the settlement of the business and freeing themselves from annoyance.[c] You too are able to do what you

425

et fecisti egregie et facis, ut commemores, quanta
sit in publicanis dignitas, quantum nos illi ordini
debeamus, ut remoto imperio ac vi potestatis et
fascium publicanos cum Graecis gratia atque auctoritate coniungas, et ab iis, de quibus optime tu meritus
es, et qui tibi omnia debent, hoc petas, ut facilitate sua nos eam necessitudinem, quae est nobis
cum publicanis, obtinere et conservare patiantur.
36 Sed quid ego te haec hortor, quae tu non modo
facere potes tua sponte sine cuiusquam praeceptis,
sed etiam magna iam ex parte perfecisti ? Non
enim desistunt nobis agere quotidie gratias hone-
stissimae et maximae societates ; quod quidem mihi
idcirco iucundius est, quod idem faciunt Graeci.
Difficile est autem, ea, quae commodis, utilitate et
prope natura diversa sunt, voluntate coniungere.   At
ea quidem, quae supra scripta sunt, non ut te insti-
tuerem, scripsi, (neque enim prudentia tua cuiusquam praecepta desiderat,) sed me in scribendo
commemoratio tuae virtutis delectavit ; quamquam
in his litteris longior fui, quam aut vellem, aut quam
37 me putavi fore.   XIII. Unum est, quod tibi ego
praecipere non desinam, neque te patiar (quantum
in me erit) cum exceptione laudari. Omnes enim,

ª *i.e.,* of *publicani.*

have done, and are doing, in the most admirable way,—you can remind everybody of the high responsibilites imposed upon the *publicani*, and our own great indebtedness to that order, so that, waiving your official command and the might of your power with all its symbols, you may unite the *publicani* with the Greeks by means of the regard and respect they have for you personally, and entreat those Greeks whom you have so admirably served, and who owe you everything, to allow us, by showing a compliant temper, to maintain and preserve the intimate connexion which already subsists between us and the *publicani*.

But why am I thus urging you to do what you can 36 not only do on your own initiative without anybody's instructing you, but have also to a large extent succeeded in doing? For the most honourable and important companies[a] never cease expressing their gratitude to me day after day ; and that gives me all the more pleasure because the Greeks do the same. And it is no easy task to harmonize in mutual goodwill elements in respect of interests and expediency, and indeed almost intrinsically, irreconcilable.

All, however, that I have written above I have not written for the purpose of instructing you—for your good sense needs no schooling by anybody—but the rehearsal of your virtues in writing has been a pleasure to me, though I have certainly been more prolix in this letter than I could have wished to be, or ever thought I should be.

XIII. There is one lesson I shall never cease to 37 impress upon you, and (so far as in me lies) I am not going to allow your praises to be qualified by a single reservation. The fact is that all who come from your

427

qui istinc veniunt, ita de tua virtute, integritate,
humanitate commemorant, ut in tuis summis laudibus
excipiant unam iracundiam. Quod vitium cum in
hac privata quotidianaque vita levis esse animi atque
infirmi videtur, tum vero nihil est tam deforme,
quam ad summum imperium etiam acerbitatem
naturae adiungere. Quare illud non suscipiam, ut,
quae de iracundia dici solent a doctissimis hominibus,
ea tibi nunc exponam, cum et nimis longus esse
nolim, et ex multorum scriptis ea facile possis cognoscere ; illud, quod est epistulae proprium, ut is,
ad quem scribitur, de iis rebus, quas ignorat, certior
38 fiat, praetermittendum esse non puto. Sic ad nos
omnes fere deferunt, nihil, cum absit iracundia, te
fieri posse iucundius ; sed cum te alicuius im-
probitas perversitasque commoverit, sic te animo
incitari, ut ab omnibus tua desideretur humanitas.
Quare quoniam in eam rationem vitae nos non tam
cupiditas quaedam gloriae, quam res ipsa ac fortuna
deduxit, ut sempiternus sermo hominum de nobis
futurus sit, caveamus, quantum efficere et consequi
possumus, ut ne quod in nobis insigne vitium fuisse
dicatur. Neque ego hoc nunc contendo, quod
fortasse cum in omni natura, tum iam in nostra
aetate difficile est, mutare animum et, si quid est
penitus insitum moribus, id subito evellere ; sed te
illud admoneo, ut, si hoc plane vitare non potes,
quod ante occupatur animus ab iracundia, quam pro-

province, while they dwell upon your virtues, your integrity, and your kindliness, do make one reservation, and that is your irascibility. Now not only does that failing seem to betray a capricious and feeble mind, in this private and everyday life of ours, but there is nothing so repulsive as this intrusion into supreme command of acerbity of temper. I shall not therefore take upon myself to lay before you now the repeated utterances of the greatest philosophers on the subject of irascibility, as I should not like to be tedious, and you can easily discover them in many writers ; but the special purpose of a letter—the enlightenment of the recipient on matters of which he has no knowledge—that purpose, I think, should not be overlooked.

Well, what practically everybody reports of you is **38** this—that, as long as you keep your temper, they find you the pleasantest person in the world ; but when you are upset by some fellow's rascality or wrongheadedness, you become so exasperated that everybody sighs for your vanished kindliness. Therefore, since we have been brought, not so much by any kind of desire for glory as by the mere force of circumstances and by fortune, into such a position of life that men are likely to talk about us for all time, let us be careful, to the best of our ability and power, to avoid its being said of us that we had any particularly notorious failing. And I am not now urging you to do what is perhaps difficult in human nature at any time, but especially at our time of life, and that is to change one's disposition and suddenly to pluck out some evil deeply ingrained in the character ; but this much advice I do give you, that if you cannot possibly avoid it, because anger takes possession of the mind

videre ratio potuit, ne occuparetur, ut te ante compares, quotidieque meditere, resistendum esse iracundiae ; cumque ea maxime animum moveat, tum
tibi esse diligentissime linguam continendam ; quae
quidem mihi virtus non interdum minor videtur,
quam omnino non irasci. Nam illud non solum est
gravitatis, sed nonnumquam etiam lentitudinis ;
moderari vero et animo et orationi, cum sis iratus,
aut etiam tacere et tenere in sua potestate motum
animi et dolorem, etsi non est perfectae sapientiae,
39 tamen est non mediocris ingeni. Atque in hoc
genere multo te esse iam commodiorem mitiorem-
que nuntiant. Nullae tuae vehementiores animi
concitationes, nulla maledicta ad nos, nullae contumeliae perferuntur ; quae cum abhorrent a litteris, ab humanitate, tum vero contraria sunt imperio
ac dignitati. Nam si implacabiles iracundiae sint,
summa est acerbitas ; sin autem exorabiles, summa
levitas ; quae tamen (ut in malis) acerbitati ante-
40 ponenda est. XIV. Sed quoniam primus annus
habuit de hac reprehensione plurimum sermonis,
credo propterea, quod tibi hominum iniuriae, quod
avaritiae, quod insolentia praeter opinionem accide-
bat et intolerabilis videbatur, secundus autem multo
lenior, quod et consuetudo et ratio et (ut ego arbitror)
430

before reason has been able to prevent its being so possessed, in that case you should prepare yourself beforehand, and reflect daily that what you have to fight against is anger, and that when the mind is most under its influence is just the time when you should be most careful to bridle your tongue ; and indeed I sometimes think that this is as great a virtue as not feeling anger at all.   For the latter is not exclusively a sign of strength of character, but also occasionally of a phlegmatic habit of mind ; while to govern one's mind and speech when angry, or even to hold one's tongue and retain one's sway over mental perturbation and resentment, that, though not a proof of perfect wisdom, is at any rate a mark of no slight natural ability.

And even in this respect they tell me that you are 39 now far more amenable and mild. I receive no reports of any unduly violent outbursts of temper on your part, of any abusive or insulting language, which, while inconsistent with literary culture and refinement, are utterly incompatible with a position of high command. For where paroxysms of anger cannot be pacified, you will there find extreme harshness ; where they yield to remonstrances, an extremely changeable mind ; though of course the latter, as a choice of evils, is to be preferred to harshness.

XIV. But since it was in your first year that there 40 was the most talk about this subject of censure (I suppose because the cases of injustice and rapacity and the general insolence you came across took you by surprise, and struck you as intolerable), while your second year was much milder, because you improved in tolerance and mildness as the result of getting used to things and reasoning things out, and also, I do

meae quoque litterae te patientiorem lenioremque
fecerunt, tertius annus ita esse debet emendatus,
ut ne minimam quidem rem quisquam possit ullam
41 reprehendere. Ac iam hoc loco non hortatione
neque praeceptis, sed precibus tecum fraternis ago,
totum ut animum, curam, cogitationemque tuam
ponas in omnium laude undique colligenda. Quod si
in mediocri statu sermonis ac praedicationis nostrae
res essent, nihil abs te eximium, nihil praeter aliorum
consuetudinem postularetur. Nunc vero, propter
earum rerum, in quibus versati sumus, splendorem
et magnitudinem, nisi summam laudem ex ista
provincia assequimur, vix videmur summam vitu-
perationem posse vitare. Ea nostra ratio est, ut
omnes boni cum faveant, tum etiam a nobis omnem
diligentiam virtutemque et postulent et exspectent,
omnes autem improbi (quod cum his bellum suscepi-
mus sempiternum) vel minima re ad reprehendendum
42 contenti esse videantur. Quare quoniam eiusmodi
theatrum tuis virtutibus est datum, celebritate refer-
tissimum, magnitudine amplissimum, iudicio erudi-
tissimum, natura autem ita resonans, ut usque
Romam significationes vocesque referantur, contende,
quaeso, atque elabora, non modo ut his rebus dignus
fuisse, sed etiam ut illa omnia tuis artibus superasse
43 videare. XV. Et quoniam mihi casus urbanam in

believe, of reading my letters, well, then, your third year ought to be so free from blemish that nobody could possibly find the slightest fault with it.

And here I no longer plead with you by exhortation 41 and precept, but by beseeching you in brotherly fashion to devote all your mind, attention, and meditation to the winning of praise from every man's lips in every quarter. Now if our sphere of action were so limited as to elicit no more than ordinary talk and comment, nothing extraordinary, nothing beyond the common practice of others, would be demanded of you. As it is, however, owing to the splendour and magnitude of the affairs in which we have had a hand, if we fail to secure the highest praise for the administration of your province, it seems hardly possible for us to escape the bitterest vituperation. We are in such a position that all loyal men, though they support us, at the same time demand and expect of us every devotion to duty and every virtue, while all the disloyal on the other hand, since with them we are engaged in a war that knows no ending, seem to be satisfied with the most trivial pretext for censuring us.

Since, therefore, you have been assigned a theatre 42 such as this, crowded with such multitudes, so ample in its grandeur, so subtle in its criticism, and by nature possessed of such an echo that its manifestations of feeling and ejaculations reach Rome itself, for that reason, I implore you, struggle and strive with all your might, not merely to prove yourself to have been worthy of the task allotted to you, but also to prove that by the excellence of your administration you have surpassed all that has ever been achieved in Asia.

XV. And now that fortune has assigned the 43

magistratibus administrationem reipublicae, tibi pro-
vincialem dedit, si mea pars nemini cedit, fac ut
tua ceteros vincat. Simul et illud cogita, nos non
de reliqua et sperata gloria iam laborare, sed de
parta dimicare, quae quidem non tam expetenda
nobis fuit, quam tuenda est. Ac si mihi quidquam
esset abs te separatum, nihil amplius desiderarem
hoc statu, qui mihi iam partus est. Nunc vero res
sic sese habet, ut, nisi omnia tua facta atque dicta
nostris rebus istinc respondeant, ego me meis tantis
laboribus tantisque periculis, quorum tu omnium
particeps fuisti, nihil consecutum putem. Quod si,
ut amplissimum nomen consequeremur, unus praeter
ceteros adiuvisti, certe idem, ut id retineamus, praeter ceteros elaborabis. Non est tibi his solis utendum
existimationibus ac iudiciis, qui nunc sunt, hominum,
sed iis etiam, qui futuri sunt ; quamquam illorum erit
verius iudicium, obtrectatione et malevolentia libera-
44 tum. Denique illud etiam debes cogitare, non te
tibi soli gloriam quaerere ; quod si esset, tamen non
neglegeres, praesertim cum amplissimis monumentis
consecrare voluisses memoriam nominis tui ; sed
ea tibi est communicanda mecum, prodenda liberis
nostris. In qua cavendum est, ne, si neglegentior

---

^a Though Cicero does not appear to have held any
particular public office this year, his influence in the Senate
and Forum was such that he might, had he so desired, have
joined the famous coalition of Pompey, Caesar, and
Crassus. See Chron. Sum. for 60 B.C.

management of public affairs to me among the magistrates in the city,[a] and to you in a province, if I yield to no man in the part I have to play, see to it that you excel all others in yours. At the same time bear in mind that we are not now striving after a glory that remains to be won, and that we but hope to win, but fighting for a glory already ours—a glory which it was not so much our object to gain in the past, as it is to defend in the present. And indeed, if I could possess anything apart from you, I should desire nothing greater than the position which I have already won. As it is, however, the case stands thus: unless your every act and word in your province is in exact accord with my achievements, I consider that, great as have been my labours and dangers (and you have shared them all), they have brought me no gain whatever. But if it was you who helped me more than any other living man to win a highly honoured name, you will surely also exert yourself more than others to enable me to preserve that name. You must not only take the opinion and judgments of the present generation, but those also of the generations to come; though the verdict of the latter will be the more accurate because it has got rid of disparagement and malice.

Finally, you should also bear in mind that you are 44 not seeking glory for yourself alone—though even so you would not be regardless of it, especially since it has ever been your desire to hallow the memory of your name with the most magnificent memorials—but you have to share that glory with me, and bequeath it to our children. And in that connexion you must beware lest, by your undue heedlessness, you create the impression that you have not only been

fueris, non solum tibi parum consuluisse, sed etiam
45 tuis invidisse videaris. XVI. Atque haec non eo
dicuntur, ut te oratio mea dormientem excitasse, sed
potius, ut currentem incitasse videatur. Facies enim
perpetuo, quae fecisti, ut omnes aequitatem tuam,
temperantiam, severitatem integritatemque lauda·
rent. Sed me quaedam tenet, propter singularem
amorem, infinita in te aviditas gloriae ; quamquam
illud existimo, cum iam tibi Asia, sicut uni cuique
sua domus, nota esse debeat, cum ad tuam summam
prudentiam tantus usus accesserit, nihil esse, quod
ad laudem attineat, quod non tu optime perspicias
et tibi non sine cuiusquam hortatione in mentem
veniat quotidie. Sed ego, qui, cum tua lego, te
audire, et qui, cum ad te scribo, tecum loqui videor,
idcirco et tua longissima quaque epistula maxime
delector, et ipse in scribendo saepe sum longior.
46 Illud te ad extremum et oro et hortor, ut, tamquam
poetae boni et actores industrii solent, sic tu in
extrema parte et conclusione muneris ac negoti tui
diligentissimus sis, ut hic tertius annus imperi tui,
tamquam tertius actus, perfectissimus atque orna-
tissimus fuisse videatur. Id facillime facies, si me
(cui semper uni magis, quam universis, placere

neglectful of your own interests, but also to have cast an evil eye on those of your friends.

XVI. And I do not speak thus to make it appear 45 that my discourse has roused you from sleep, but rather that it has spurred you on in your career. For you will never cease to act as you have done, in such a way as to win all men's praise for your fairness, self-restraint, strictness, and integrity. Indeed, such is my extraordinary affection for you that I am possessed by a sort of insatiable desire for your glory; and yet it is my belief that since Asia ought now to be as well known to you as his own house is known to every man, and since so long an experience has now been added to the consummate wisdom you have always shown, it is my belief, I say, that there is nothing appertaining to a high reputation of which you have not the clearest apprehension, and which does not occur daily to your mind without the aid of anybody's exhortation.

But I, who seem to be listening to you whenever I read your communications, and to be talking to you whenever I write to you, for that very reason am more pleased the longer every letter of yours is, and am myself often somewhat prolix in writing to you.

I end my letter by imploring and urging you that 46 —after the fashion of good poets and hard-working actors—you should take particular pains with the last phase and *finale* of your office and employment; so that this third year of your rule may, like the third act of a play, be recognized as having been the most highly finished and brilliantly staged of the three. You will do so most easily if you imagine that I, the one man whose approbation you have ever desired

voluisti) tecum semper esse putabis et omnibus iis
rebus, quas dices ac facies, interesse. Reliquum est,
ut te orem, ut valetudini tuae, si me et tuos omnes
valere vis, diligentissime servias. Vale.

II

Romae, A.U.C. 695.

1 I. Statius ad me venit a. d. VIII. Kalend. Novembr.
Eius adventus, quod ita scripsisti, direptum iri te a
tuis, dum is abesset, molestus mihi fuit. Quod autem
exspectationem tui concursumque eum, qui erat
futurus, si una tecum decederet, neque antea visus
esset, sustulit, id mihi non incommode visum est
accidisse. Exhaustus enim est sermo hominum, et
multis emissae iam eiusmodi voces, ἀλλ᾽ αἰεί τινα
φῶτα μέγαν, quae te absente confecta esse laetor.
2 Quod autem idcirco a te missus est, mihi ut se purga-
ret, id necesse minime fuit. Primum enim numquam ille mihi fuit suspectus ; neque ego, quae ad
te de illo scripsi, scripsi meo iudicio, sed cum ratio
salusque omnium nostrum, qui ad rempublicam
accedimus, non veritate solum, sed etiam fama
niteretur, sermones ad te aliorum semper, non mea

ᵃ Statius was Quintus's freedman and secretary, whom
people suspected of undue influence over him.

ᵇ ἀλλ᾽ αἰεί τινα φῶτα μέγαν καὶ καλὸν ἐδέγμην | ἐνθάδ᾽
ἐλεύσεσθαι Hom. *Od.* ix. 513-14, "but ever it was some
mighty man and fair to look upon, whose arrival here I
awaited." They are the words of Polyphemus, who was
disappointed in Odysseus's appearance, as people at Rome
were in Statius's.

above that of the whole world, am always at your side, and taking part in everything you say or do.

It only remains for me to implore you, if you wish me and all your family to keep well, to take every possible care to keep well yourself.

II

CICERO TO HIS BROTHER QUINTUS

Rome, between October 25 and December 10, 59 B.C.

I. Statius [a] reached my house on October 25th. His arrival made me uneasy, because you wrote that during his absence you would be robbed in every direction by your domestics. But his balking the general expectation of seeing you and the eager crowding that would certainly have occurred if he left the province in your company, and nobody had ever seen him before,—that I thought to be a very fortunate incident; for all the gossip about it has run dry, and many have now done with uttering this sort of remark, " But ever it was some mighty man," [b] and I am right glad that it is all over and done with in your absence.

But as for his having been sent by you to clear 2 himself in my eyes, there was not the least necessity for that; in the first place I never suspected him, and again what I wrote to you about him was not the expression of my own judgment; when however the interests and safety of all those of us who take part in public affairs depended not on truth alone, but also on all the talk about us, I always wrote you a full account of what others were saying, and not what I

439

iudicia perscripsi. Qui quidem quam frequentes
essent et quam graves, adventu suo Statius ipse
cognovit. Etenim intervenit nonnullorum querellis,
quae apud me de illo ipso habebantur ; et sentire
potuit, sermones iniquorum in suum potissimum
3 nomen erumpere. Quod autem me maxime movere
solebat, cum audiebam, illum plus apud te posse,
quam gravitas illius aetatis et imperi prudentia
postularet,—quam multos enim mecum egisse putas,
ut se Statio commendarem ? quam multa autem
ipsum ἀφελῶς mecum in sermone ita protulisse—" *Id
mihi non placuit*," " *monui*," " *suasi*," " *deterrui*" ?
Quibus in rebus etiamsi fidelitas summa est, (quod
prorsus credo, quoniam tu ita iudicas,) tamen species
ipsa tam gratiosi liberti aut servi dignitatem habere
nullam potest,—atque hoc sic habeto, (nihil enim
nec temere dicere, nec astute reticere debeo,)
materiam omnem sermonum eorum, qui de te detra-
here velint, Statium dedisse ; antea tantum intellegi
potuisse, iratos tuae severitati esse nonnullos ; hoc
manumisso, iratis, quod loquerentur, non defuisse.
4 II. Nunc respondebo ad eas epistulas, quas mihi
reddidit L. Caesius, (cui, quoniam ita te velle intellego,
nullo loco deero,) quarum altera est de Blaudeno
Zeuxide, quem scribis certissimum matricidam tibi a

---

a A town in Mysia.

felt myself; and how sinister and general that talk was, Statius on his arrival discovered for himself. In fact he came in when some people were complaining at my house about that very thing, and could not but feel that the malevolent were venting their obloquy upon himself in particular.

But as to what used to aggravate me most when 3 told that he had more influence with you than was called for by the weight of your years and your wisdom in government—why, how many persons do you suppose have pleaded with me to recommend them to Statius? and again, how often do you suppose he himself in conversation with me has used with the utmost *naïveté* such expressions as " *I could not agree to that*," " *I lectured him*," " *I argued with him*," " *I cautioned him* " ? And although all this only proves how perfectly honest he is (and I quite believe it, since that is what you think), still the mere appearance of a freedman or slave possessing such influence cannot fail to be utterly undignified—and indeed you may take it from me (for it is my duty neither to say anything without weighing my words, nor to keep anything back in a crafty way) that all the material for the gossip of those who would disparage you has been furnished by Statius; that previously nothing more could be gathered than that certain persons were angry with you for your strictness, but that this man's manumission gave those who were angry plenty to talk about.

II. I shall now reply to the letters delivered to me 4 by L. Caesius (a man whom I shall never in any circumstances cease to serve, since I understood that to be your wish), one of which is about Zeuxis of Blaudus,[a] whom you say I particularly recommended to you, though he had most undoubtedly murdered

me intime commendari. Qua de re, et de hoc genere
toto, ne forte me in Graecos tam ambitiosum factum
esse mirere, pauca cognosce. Ego cum Graecorum
querellas nimium valere sentirem, propter hominum
ingenia ad fallendum parata, quoscumque de te
queri audivi, quacumque potui ratione placavi.
Primum Dionysopolitas, qui erant inimicissimi mei,
lenivi; quorum principem Hermippum non solum
sermone meo, sed etiam familiaritate devinxi. Ego
Apameensem Hephaestum, ego levissimum hominem,
Megaristum Antandrium, ego Niciam Smyrnaeum,
ego nugas maximas omni mea comitate sum complexus, Nymphontem etiam Colophonium. Quae
feci omnia, non quo me aut ii homines, aut tota natio
delectaret; pertaesum est levitatis, assentationis,
animorum non officiis, sed temporibus servientium.
5 Sed, ut ad Zeuxim revertar, cum is de M. Cascelli
sermone secum habito, quae tu scribis, ea ipsa
loqueretur, obstiti eius sermoni, et hominem in
familiaritatem recepi. Tua autem quae fuerit cupiditas tanta, nescio, quod scribis cupiisse te, quoniam
Smyrnae duo Mysos insuisses in culeum, simile in
superiore parte provinciae edere exemplum severitatis tuae, et idcirco Zeuxim elicere omni ratione
voluisse ; quem adductum in iudicium fortasse dimitti

ᵃ The conversation with Cascellius had evidently been
unfavourable to Quintus.

ᵇ Parricides or matricides, for whom the regular punishment was to be tied up in a sack with a dog, a cock, a snake,
and an ape, and then cast into the sea or worried by wild
beasts. Quintus wished to make an example of Zeuxis
(*certissimus matricida*) in the same way.

his mother. About this, and about the whole subject generally, pray listen to a few words of explanation, lest you should happen to be surprised at my having become so ready to make up to the Greeks. Because I felt that the complaints of the Greeks were carrying undue weight, since that nation has a natural aptitude for deceit, I used every means in my power to pacify whoever of them I was told were complaining about you. First I mollified the Dionysopolitans who were most hostile; and their chief man Hermippus I made my humble servant, not only by the way I talked to him, but also by making an intimate friend of him. I welcomed with open arms and with all the courtesy I could command Hephaestus of Apamea, that weather-cock of a fellow Megaristus of Antandros, Nicias of Smyrna, yes, and that most despicable of men also, Nymphon of Colophon. And all this I did, not because either those particular individuals or the nation as a whole had any attraction for me; no, I was heartily sick of their fickleness, their fawning, their spirit of subservience not to duty but to the advantage of the moment.

But to go back to Zeuxis. When, in describing the 5 conversation M. Cascellius had had with him, he used the very words in your letter, I put a stop to his talking,[a] and admitted the fellow into familiarity. What you meant, however, by that extraordinarily strong desire of yours I have no idea—I mean your writing that, having already sewn up in a sack two Mysians at Smyrna,[b] you desired to give a similar example of your strict discipline in the more inland part of your province, and for that purpose had been anxious to inveigle Zeuxis into the open by every means in your power. Well, if he had been brought

non oportuerat ; conquiri vero, et elici blanditiis (ut
tu scribis) ad iudicium, necesse non fuit ; eum
praesertim hominem, quem ego et ex suis civibus,
et ex multis aliis quotidie magis cognosco nobi-
6 liorem esse prope, quam civitatem suam. At enim
Graecis solis indulgeo. Quid ? L. Caecilium nonne
omni ratione placavi ? quem hominem ! qua ira !
quo spiritu ! Quem denique, praeter Tuscenium,
cuius causa sanari non potest, non mitigavi ? Ecce
supra caput homo levis ac sordidus, sed tamen
equestri censu, Catienus ; etiam is lenietur. Cuius
tu in patrem quod fuisti asperior, non reprehendo ;
certo enim scio, te fecisse cum causa. Sed quid opus
fuit eiusmodi litteris, quas ad ipsum misisti ? illum
crucem sibi ipsum constituere, ex qua tu eum ante
detraxisses ; te curaturum, in furno[1] ut combureretur,
plaudente tota provincia. Quid vero ad C. Fabium,
nescio quem ? (nam eam quoque epistulam T.
Catienus circumgestat). Renuntiari tibi Licinium
plagiarium cum suo pullo milvino tributa exigere ?
Deinde rogas Fabium, ut et patrem et filium vivos
comburat, si possit ; sin minus, ad te mittat, uti
iudicio comburantur. Hae litterae abs te per iocum
missae ad C. Fabium, si modo sunt tuae, cum leguntur,

[1] fumo *libri* : furno *Ursinus* : in furno *Wesenberg*.

a *Cf.* i. 1. 19.
b Quintus had previously forgiven Catienus for some offence
or other.
444

up for trial, perhaps it would not have been right that he should be let off; but that there should be a hue and cry for the man, and that he should be inveigled with wheedling words into court (as you yourself put it), all that was quite unnecessary, especially in the case of one who, as I learn more clearly every day from his own fellow-citizens and many others, is of a nobler character perhaps than any of his community.

But, you will say, it is to the Greeks alone that 6 I show indulgence. What? Did I not take every means to pacify L. Caecilius? And what a man he is! How passionate, how presumptuous! In short, with the exception of Tuscenius [a] (an incurable case), whom did I fail to mollify? And just see, we have our sword of Damocles in the shape of that shifty, disreputable rascal, who is yet assessed as a knight, Catienus; I shall appease even him. For having been somewhat harsh in your treatment of his father I do not blame you; I am quite sure you did not act without some good reason. But what need was there for the sort of a letter that you sent the man himself? "That the man was putting up for himself the cross from which you yourself had pulled him down on a previous occasion [b]; that you would take care to have him burnt up in a furnace amid the applause of the whole province." Why again that letter to C. Fabius, whoever he may be (for that letter also is being carried about by T. Catienus), "that the kidnapper Licinius, assisted by his chick of the old kite, is reported to you as collecting taxes," and you go on to ask Fabius to burn both father and son alive, if he can; if he can't, to send them to you to be burnt by order of the court. That letter you sent by way of a jest to C. Fabius (if indeed it is yours) conveys to

445

7 invidiosam atrocitatem verborum habent. Ac, si
omnium mearum litterarum praecepta repetes, intelleges, nihil esse a me, nisi orationis acerbitatem et
iracundiam et, si forte, raro litterarum missarum in-
diligentiam reprehensam. Quibus quidem in rebus
si apud te plus auctoritas mea, quam tua sive natura
paullo acrior, sive quaedam dulcedo iracundiae, sive
dicendi sal facetiaeque valuissent, nihil sane esset,
quod nos poeniteret. Et mediocri me dolore putas
affici, cum audiam, qua sit existimatione Vergilius,[b]
qua tuus vicinus C. Octavius? Nam si te interioribus
vicinis tuis, Ciliciensi et Syriaco,[c] anteponis, valde
magni facis. Atque is dolor est, quod cum ii, quos
nominavi, te innocentia non vincant, vincunt tamen
artificio benevolentiae colligendae, qui neque Cyrum
Xenophontis neque Agesilaum noverint; quorum
regum summo in imperio nemo umquam verbum
ullum asperius audivit. Sed haec a principio tibi
8 praecipiens, quantum profecerim, non ignoro. III.
Nunc tamen decedens (id quod mihi iam facere
videris) relinque, quaeso, quam iucundissimam
memoriam tui. Successorem habes[d] perblandum;
cetera valde illius adventu tua requirentur. In
litteris mittendis (ut saepe ad te scripsi) nimium te
exorabilem praebuisti. Tolle omnes, si potes, iniquas,[e]

---

[a] *Cf.* Hom. *Il.* xviii. 109 (χόλος) ὅστε πολὺ γλυκίων μέλιτος
καταλειβομένοιο, "(anger) which is far sweeter than dripping
honey."
[b] Vergilius and C. Octavius were governors, as propraetors,
of Sicily and Macedonia respectively.
[c] The governor of Syria was now Lentulus Marcellinus.
Who was the governor of Cilicia is not known.
[d] Perhaps C. Fabius Adrianus, but it is uncertain.
[e] *i.e.*, "requisitionary letters," of which we have an example in § 10.

the reader an impression of brutality of language that must prejudice your reputation.

Now if you recall the injunctions in any of my 7 letters, you will find that I have found fault with nothing but your bitter and angry way of talking, and possibly once or twice a lack of due caution in the letters you write. And as regards that, had my influence with you triumphed over your somewhat hasty nature, or a sort of pleasurable thrill [a] you find in anger, or your gift of pungent and sparkling speech, I should have no reason whatever for dissatisfaction. And do you suppose I am no more than slightly saddened when I hear of the high reputation of Vergilius, and of your neighbour C. Octavius [b]? If you only think yourself better than your neighbours in the interior, in Cilicia and Syria,[c] you have a mighty high standard! And what hurts me is this—that, though the men I have mentioned do not excel you in purity of conduct, they do excel you in the art of winning friends, though they know nothing about Xenophon's Cyrus, or his Agesilaus, kings from whose lips nobody ever heard a single harsh word, supreme sovereigns though they were.

But I have been lecturing you in this way from the beginning, and what effect it has had I am perfectly well aware.

III. None the less, now that you are quitting your 8 province, I entreat you to leave behind you (as indeed I think you are doing) as pleasant a memory of yourself as possible. You have as your successor [d] a man of very seductive manners; all your other characteristics will be greatly missed when he arrives. In sending out letters [e] you have shown yourself too easily worked upon. Destroy, if possible, any that

447

tolle inusitatas, tolle contrarias. Statius mihi narravit, scriptas ad te solere afferri, ab se legi, et, si iniquae sint, fieri te certiorem ; antequam vero ipse ad te venisset, nullum delectum litterarum fuisse ; ex eo esse volumina selectarum epistularum, quae
9 reprehendi solerent. Hoc de genere nihil te nunc quidem moneo. Sero est enim, ac scire potes, multa me varie diligenterque monuisse. Illud tamen, quod Theopompo mandavi, cum essem admonitus ab ipso, vide per homines amantes tui, quod est facile, ut haec genera tollantur epistularum, primum iniquarum, deinde contrariarum, tum absurde et inusitate scriptarum, postremo in aliquem contumeliosarum. Atque ego haec tam esse quam audio, non puto, et si sunt occupationibus tuis minus animadversa, nunc perspice et purga. Legi epistulam, quam ipse scripsisse Sulla nomenclator dictus est, non pro-
10 bandam ; legi nonnullas iracundas. Sed tempore ipso de epistulis. Nam cum hanc paginam tenerem, L. Flavius, praetor designatus, ad me venit, homo mihi valde familiaris. Is mihi, te ad procuratores suos litteras misisse, quae mihi visae sunt iniquissimae —ne quid de bonis, quae L. Octavi Nasonis fuissent, cui L. Flavius heres est, deminuerent ante quam

---

a A *nomenclator* ("name-caller") was a slave who attended his master, especially when canvassing, to tell him the names of those he met in the street.
b Probably the tribune who had proposed an agrarian law in 60. Tyrrell.

are inequitable, eccentric, or inconsistent with others. Statius told me that they were often brought to your house ready written, and that he read them and informed you if they contained anything inequitable; but that before he entered your service there had never been any sifting of letters, with the result that there were volumes of despatches picked out which lent themselves to adverse criticism.

In this connexion I offer you no advice now; it is 9 too late, and you must be aware that I have often advised you already in various ways and with much particularity. Still, to repeat the message I gave to Theopompus, acting on a hint he had himself given me, pray do see to it (and it is easy enough) that, through the agency of those who are really devoted to you, all letters of that kind are destroyed—first those that are inequitable, next those that are inconsistent with others, then those that are written in bad taste, and lastly those that are insulting to anyone. At the same time I do not believe that things are as bad as I am told they are; and if owing to pressure of work you have not given enough attention to certain things, now is the time to look into them and give them a winnowing. I have, for instance, read a letter alleged to have been written by your *nomenclator* [a] Sulla on his own authority, and I cannot say I like it; and I have read some that show temper. Indeed this is just the 10 moment to talk about your letters; for while this very page was under my hand, who should call upon me but L. Flavius,[b] our praetor-elect, a man on very familiar terms with me. He told me you had sent his agents a letter which struck me as most unjust, instructing them not to take anything out of the property of the late L. Octavius Naso, whom L. Flavius succeeds as

C. Fundanio pecuniam solvissent. Itemque misisse
ad Apollonidenses, ne de bonis, quae Octavi fuissent,
deminui paterentur, priusquam Fundanio debitum
solutum esset. Haec mihi verisimilia non videntur.
Sunt enim a prudentia tua remotissima. Ne de-
minuat heres ? Quid si infitiatur ? Quid si omnino
non debetur ? Quid ? praetor solet iudicare deberi ?
Quid ? ego Fundanio non cupio ? non amicus sum ?
non misericordia moveor ? Nemo magis ; sed via
iuris eiusmodi est quibusdam in rebus, ut nihil sit
loci gratiae. Atque ita mihi dicebat Flavius scriptum
in ea epistula, quam tuam esse dicebat, te aut quasi
amicis tuis gratias acturum, aut quasi inimicis in-
11 commoda laturum. Quid multa ? ferebat graviter,
id vehementer mecum querebatur, orabatque, ut ad
te quam diligentissime scriberem ; quod facio, et te
prorsus vehementer etiam atque etiam rogo, ut et
procuratoribus Flavi remittas de deminuendo, et de
Apollonidensibus, ne quid praescribas, quod contra
Flavium sit, amplius, et Flavi causa et scilicet Pompei,
facies omnia. Nolo medius fidius ex tua iniuria in
illum tibi liberalem me videri ; sed id te oro, ut tu
ipse auctoritatem et monumentum aliquod decreti

ᵃ A town in Lydia, between Pergamum and Sardis.

heir, until they had paid a certain sum of money to
C. Fundanius ; and that you had written in similar
terms to the people of Apollonis,ᵃ telling them not to
allow any deduction to be made from the estate of the
late L. Octavius Naso until a debt had been paid to
Fundanius. This does not seem to me to be at all
likely ; it is so utterly foreign to your usual cautious
behaviour. Not let the heir touch the property !
What if he denies the debt ? What if there is no debt
at all ? What ? Is it usual for the praetor to decide
whether there is a debt or not ? What ? Am I not
kindly disposed to Fundanius ? Am I not his friend ?
Do I not sincerely sympathize with him ? Nobody
more so. Yes, but in certain matters the path of
justice is so strait that there is no room in it for
favouritism. And moreover Flavius told me that the
letter (and he declared that it was yours) was so
written as to leave no doubt that you would either
express your gratitude to them as your friends, or else
make things unpleasant for them as your enemies.

To cut the story short, he was much annoyed ; he 11
complained of it to me in bitter terms, and implored
me to write to you as impressively as possible ; I am
doing so, and I ask you again and again in all earnestness to make a concession to Flavius's agents about
impairing the property, and, as regards the people of
Apollonis, to give them no further instructions in a
sense unfavourable to Flavius ; and you will, I am
sure, do all you can in the interests of Flavius, and of
course of Pompey. On my word of honour, I have
no desire that you should think me generous to him
at the cost of any injustice on your part ; but this I
do ask of you, that you should yourself leave behind
you some official declaration, or some record, in the

aut litterarum tuarum relinquas, quod sit ad Flavi
rem et ad causam accommodatum. Fert enim
graviter homo, et mei observantissimus et sui iuris
dignitatisque retinens, se apud te neque amicitia
neque iure valuisse ; et, ut opinor, Flavi aliquando
rem et Pompeius et Caesar tibi commendarunt, et
ipse ad te scripserat Flavius, et ego certe. Quare
si ulla res est, quam tibi me faciendam petente putes,
haec ea sit. Si me amas, cura, elabora, perfice, ut
Flavius et tibi et mihi quam maximas gratias agat.
Hoc te ita rogo, ut maiore studio rogare non possim.
12 IV. Quod ad me de Hermia scribis, mihi mehercule
valde etiam molestum fuit. Litteras ad te parum
fraterne conscripseram : quas oratione Diodoti,
Luculli liberti, commotus, de pactione statim quod
audieram, iracundius scripseram et revocare cupie-
bam. Huic tu epistulae, non fraterne scriptae,
13 fraterne debes ignoscere. De Censorino, Antonio,
Cassiis, Scaevola, te ab his diligi (ut scribis) vehementer gaudeo. Cetera fuerunt in eadem epistula
graviora quam vellem, — ὀρθὰν τὰν ναῦν, et ἅπαξ
θανεῖν. Maiora ista erunt ; meae obiurgationes fuerunt amoris plenissimae ; quaerunt[1] nonnulla, sed
tamen mediocria, et parva potius. Ego te numquam

---

[1] quae sunt mss. : quaerunt (?) *Tyrrell, which I have adopted.*

---

^a Probably a slave of M. Cicero.
^b The details of this incident are unknown.
^c Quintus appears to have meant " that he would keep the
ship (of office) on an even keel, or on a straight course, even if
he had to sink her," *i.e.*, " he would go down with colours
flying." The proverb was ἴσθι ὅτι ὀρθὰν τὴν ναῦν καταδύσω.
^d Aeschylus, *P. V*, 769, has κρεῖσσον γὰρ εἰσάπαξ θανεῖν | ἢ τὰς
ἀπάσας ἡμέρας πάσχειν κακῶς.
^e This is probably the meaning of *erunt*; *cf.* Juv. i. 126
quiescet, " you will find she is reposing."

form of a decree or memorandum of your own,
adapted to secure the interests of Flavius in this case.
For the poor fellow, who is most attentive to me, but
tenacious of his due rights and position, is bitterly
pained that he has had no influence with you on the
score of either friendship or justice ; and, if I am not
mistaken, both Pompey and Caesar have at some
time or other commended to your notice the interests
of Flavius, and he had written to you himself, and so
certainly had I. If there is anything, therefore, which
you think you ought to do at my request, let it be
this. As you love me, take every care and trouble
in the matter, and ensure that Flavius has reason to
express his most cordial thanks both to you and to me.
I could make no request with greater earnestness
than I do this.

IV. What you write to me about Hermias *a* has 12
been, I do assure you, a real vexation to me. I had
written you a letter not quite in a brotherly spirit, upset as I was by what Diodotus, Lucullus's freedman,
had told me, directly I had heard of the compact *b* ;
I had written it in a fit of temper, and was anxious to
recall it. Such a letter, though written in an un-
brotherly way, you ought as a brother to forgive.

As to Censorinus, Antonius, the Cassii, and 13
Scaevola, I am highly delighted that they like you as
you write they do. The rest of that same letter was
in stronger terms than I could have wished,—for
instance your " keeping the ship on an even keel " *c*
and " dying once for all." *d* Those expressions, as you
will find,*e* are needlessly vehement ; my reproaches
teemed with affection ; they only ask you for a few
things missing, and even they are of slight and indeed
negligible importance. I should never have thought

ulla in re dignum minima reprehensione putassem,
cum te sanctissime gereres, nisi inimicos multos
haberemus. Quae ad te aliqua admonitione aut
obiurgatione scripsi, scripsi propter diligentiam
cautionis meae, in qua et maneo et manebo, et, idem
14 ut facias, non desistam rogare. Attalus Hypaepenus
mecum egit, ut se ne impedires, quo minus, quod
ad Q. Publici statuam decretum est, erogaretur;
quod ego te et rogo et admoneo, ne talis viri, tamque
nostri necessari, honorem minui per te aut impediri
velis. Praeterea Aesopi tragoedi, nostri familiaris,
Licinius servus, tibi notus, aufugit. Is Athenis apud
Patronem Epicureum pro libero fuit; inde in Asiam
venit. Postea Plato quidam Sardianus, Epicureus,
qui Athenis solet esse multum, et qui tum Athenis
fuerat, cum Licinius eo venisset, cum eum fugitivum
postea esse ex Aesopi litteris cognosset, hominem
comprehendit et in custodiam Ephesi tradidit; sed
in publicam, an in pistrinum, non satis ex litteris
eius intellegere potuimus. Tu, quoquo modo potest,
quoniam Ephesi est, hominem investiges velim, summaque diligentia . . .[1] vel tecum deducas. Noli spectare, quanti homo sit; parvi enim preti est, qui tam
nihil sit[2]; sed tanto dolore Aesopus est affectus propter
servi scelus et audaciam, ut nihil ei gratius facere

---

[1] *The lacuna may be filled by some such words as* vel Romam
mittas.
[2] *Orelli:* iam nihili sit *Nobbe.*

---

[a] Hypaepa was in Lydia.
[b] Probably a Roman knight, but we know nothing more
of him.
[c] Whom Horace calls " gravis Aesopus," *Ep.* ii. 1. 82.
[d] *Cf. Fam.* xiii. 1.
[e] Where slaves were forced to grind corn.

you deserved the smallest reproof in any respect, so absolutely blameless was your conduct, were it not that we had a multitude of enemies. Whatever I have written to you in a tone of admonition and re-proof, that I have written on account of my anxious watchfulness, which I maintain and ever shall main-tain, and I shall never cease urging you to do so also.

Attalus of Hypaepa[a] has pleaded with me that 14 you should not stand in his way, and prevent the money decreed for the statue of Q. Publicius[b] being paid out of the public treasury ; and as regards that, I both request and strongly advise you not to allow any honour paid to a man of his standing, and one so closely attached to us, to be impaired or obstructed as far as you are concerned.

There is, moreover, the case of Licinius, the slave of Aesopus, the tragic actor,[c] and my friend ; you know the fellow ; well, he has run away. He posed as a freedman at Athens with Patro, the Epicurean,[d] and came from there into Asia. Later on one Plato of Sardis, an Epicurean, who spends much of his time at Athens, and happened to be there when Licinius arrived, on learning by a subsequent letter from Aesopus that he was a runaway slave, had the fellow arrested and handed over into custody at Ephesus ; but whether it was into a public prison or a private mill[e] I could not quite gather from his letter. In whatever way it is possible, since he is now at Ephesus, I should be glad if you would trace the man and be particularly careful [either to send him to Rome] or to bring him home with you. Don't stop to consider what the fellow is worth ; he is of no great value, seeing that he is a mere nobody ; but Aesopus is so grieved at his slave's criminal audacity

15 possis, quam si illum per te recuperarit. V. Nunc
ea cognosce, quae maxime exoptas. Rempublicam
funditus amisimus ; adeo ut Cato, adulescens nullius
consili, sed tamen civis Romanus et Cato, vix vivus
effugerit ; quod, cum Gabinium de ambitu vellet
postulare, neque praetores diebus aliquot adiri
possent vel potestatem sui facerent, in contionem
ascendit et Pompeium privatus dictatorem appellavit.
Propius nihil est factum, quam ut occideretur. Ex
hoc, qui sit status totius reipublicae, videre potes.
16 Nostrae tamen causae non videntur homines defuturi.
Mirandum in modum profitentur, offerunt se, polli
centur. Equidem cum spe sum maxima, tum maiore
etiam animo ; spe, superiores fore nos ; animo, ut
in hac republica ne casum quidem ullum pertimescam ;
sed tamen res sic se habet.[1] Si diem nobis Clodius
dixerit, tota Italia concurret, ut multiplicata gloria
discedamus ; sin autem vi agere conabitur, spero
fore, studiis non solum amicorum, sed etiam alie
norum, ut vi resistamus. Omnes et se et suos liberos,
amicos, clientes, libertos, servos, pecunias denique
suas pollicentur. Nostra antiqua manus bonorum
ardet studio nostri atque amore. Si qui antea aut
alieniores fuerant, aut languidiores, nunc horum

---

[1] *The arrangement of the sentence from* Equidem *to* habet
is Madvig's.

[a] C. Porcius Cato, tribune in 56.

that you could do him no greater favour than by helping him to get the man back.

V. And now let me tell you what you most desire 15 to know. The constitution is completely lost to us, —so much so that Cato,[a] a young man of no judgment, but still a citizen of Rome and a Cato, barely escaped with his life, because, when he wished to ask for leave to prosecute Gabinius for bribery, and the praetor could not be approached for several days, and granted no opportunity for an interview, he ascended the platform at a public meeting, and, in a private capacity, called Pompey a dictator. His assassination was the nearest thing that ever was. From this you may see the condition of the Republic as a whole.

And yet it seems that people are not likely to 16 desert our cause. It amazes me how they profess their loyalty, offer their services, and make promises. Indeed, high as is my hope, my courage is even higher—hope, that we shall be victorious; courage, in that, as public affairs now stand, I have no fear of even any accident. Be that as it may, this is how the matter stands : if Clodius gives notice of an action against me, the whole of Italy will rally round me, so that we shall leave the court with tenfold glory ; but if he attempts to carry things through by violence, the enthusiasm not of friends alone, but also of strangers, leads me to hope that I may oppose force to force. All men are promising to put at my disposal themselves and their children, their friends, clients, freedmen, slaves, and, to end up with, their purses. My old group of supporters is fired with enthusiasm and affection for me. If there are any who before were inclined to be either unfriendly or lukewarm,

regum odio se cum bonis coniungunt. Pompeius
omnia pollicetur et Caesar ; quibus ego ita credo, ut
nihil de mea comparatione deminuam. Tribuni
plebis designati sunt nobis amici. Consules se
optime ostendunt. Praetores habemus amicissimos
et acerrimos cives, Domitium, Nigidium, Memmium,
Lentulum ; bonos etiam alios ; sed hos singulares.
Quare magnum fac animum habeas et spem bonam.
De singulis tamen rebus, quae quotidie gerantur,
faciam te crebro certiorem.

III

M. CICERO S. D. Q. FRATRI

Thessalonicae, A.U.C. 696.

1   Mi frater, mi frater, mi frater, tune id veritus
es, ne ego iracundia aliqua adductus pueros ad te
sine litteris miserim ? aut etiam ne te videre noluerim ? Ego tibi irascerer ? tibi ego possem irasci ?
Scilicet ; tu enim me afflixisti : tui me inimici, tua
me invidia, ac non ego te misere perdidi. Meus ille
laudatus consulatus mihi te, liberos, patriam, fortunas, tibi velim ne quid eripuerit, praeter unum me.
Sed certe a te mihi omnia semper honesta et iucunda
ceciderunt ; a me tibi luctus meae calamitatis, metus

---

a i.e., the consuls elect, L. Piso and A. Gabinius.
b Praetores designatos, the praetors elect.
c F. Nigidius Figulus. See note on *Fam.* iv. 13. 1.
d See note on *Fam.* xiii. 1. 1.

their hatred of these tyrants is such that they are now joining the ranks of the loyal. Pompey makes all sorts of promises, and so does Caesar; but my belief in them does not go so far as to make me drop any of my own preparations. The tribunes designate are friendly to me; the consuls [a] are showing up excellently. Among the praetors [b] I have some very warm friends and fellow-citizens of energy in Domitius, Nigidius,[c] Memmius,[d] and Lentulus, and other sound men also, but these stand out by themselves. So have a good heart and high hopes. Anyhow I shall inform you at frequent intervals of any such particular events as may occur from day to day.

III

Brother mine, brother mine, brother mine, were you 1 really afraid that some fit of anger prompted me to send my men to you without a letter? or that I did not want to see you? *I* be angry with *you*? *Could* I be angry with you? Oh yes, to be sure, it was you who brought me low; it was your enemies, your unpopularity, that ruined me, and not I (the misery of it!) that ruined you! Yourself, my children, my country, my fortune,—that is what that highly-lauded consulship of mine has torn away from me; from you I could wish that it has torn away nothing more than myself. At any rate in you I have always found all that is honourable and pleasant; in me you have found grief for my degradation, apprehen-

459

tuae, desiderium, maeror, solitudo. Ego te videre
noluerim ? Immo vero me a te videri nolui. Non
enim vidisses fratrem tuum ; non eum, quem re-
liqueras ; non eum, quem noras ; non eum, quem
flens flentem, prosequentem proficiscens dimiseras ;
ne vestigium quidem eius, nec simulacrum, sed quam-
dam effigiem spirantis mortui. Atque utinam me
mortuum prius vidisses aut audisses ! utinam te non
solum vitae, sed etiam dignitatis meae superstitem
2 reliquissem ! Sed testor omnes deos, me hac una
voce a morte esse revocatum, quod omnes in mea
vita partem aliquam tuae vitae repositam esse dicebant. Quare peccavi scelerateque feci. Nam si
occidissem, mors ipsa meam pietatem amoremque
in te facile defenderet. Nunc commisi, ut vivo me
careres, vivo me aliis indigeres ; mea vox in domesticis periculis potissimum occideret, quae saepe alienissimis praesidio fuisset. Nam quod ad te pueri sine
litteris venerunt, quoniam vides non fuisse iracundiam causam, certe pigritia fuit, et quaedam infinita
3 vis lacrimarum et dolorum. Haec ipsa me quo fletu
putas scripsisse ? Eodem, quo te legere certo scio.
An ego possum aut non cogitare aliquando de te,
aut umquam sine lacrimis cogitare ? Cum enim te

sion of your own, yearning, mourning, abandonment.
I not want to see you ? No, it was rather that I did
not want to be seen by you. For it is not your
brother you would have seen, not him you had left
behind, not him you knew, not him you parted from
with tears on either side, when he escorted you on
your setting forth ; no, not a trace or likeness of *him*,
but something resembling one dead, but breathing.
And would that you had seen me dead, or heard of
my being so, before you went ! Would that I had
left you behind me to look back not upon my life
alone, but upon my prestige unimpaired !

But I call all the gods to witness that the one 2
argument which called me back from death was
everybody's saying that no small portion of your life
was vested in mine. And so I behaved like a fool and
a criminal. For had I died, my death in itself would
be sufficient proof of my brotherly affection for you.
As it is, I have made the mistake of depriving you of
my aid while I am yet alive, and causing you, while I
am yet alive, to need the aid of others, so that my
voice, which had so often been the salvation of the
most complete strangers, should fail of all times in
the hour of domestic danger.

As for my servants having come to you without a
letter, since you see that anger was not the reason,
it was certainly due to the numbing of my faculties,
and what I may call an overwhelming deluge of tears
and sorrows.

How do you suppose I am weeping as I write these 3
very words ? Just as you are weeping, I am sure, as
you read them. Can I for a moment cease from
thinking about you, or ever think of you without
tears ? When I miss you, is it only a brother that I

desidero, fratrem solum desidero ? Ego vero suavitate fratrem prope aequalem, obsequio filium, consilio parentem. Quid mihi sine te umquam aut tibi
sine me iucundum fuit ? Quid, quod eodem tempore desidero filiam ? qua pietate, qua modestia,
quo ingenio ? effigiem oris, sermonis, animi mei ?
Quid filium venustissimum mihique dulcissimum ?
quem ego ferus ac ferreus e complexu dimisi meo,
sapientiorem puerum quam vellem. Sentiebat enim
miser iam, quid ageretur. Quid vero tuum filium ?
quid imaginem tuam, quam meus Cicero et amabat
ut fratrem et iam ut maiorem fratrem verebatur ?
Quid, quod mulierem miserrimam, fidelissimam con-
iugem, me prosequi non sum passus, ut esset, quae
reliquias communis calamitatis, communes liberos,
4 tueretur ? Sed tamen, quoquo modo potui, scripsi,
et dedi litteras ad te Philogono, liberto tuo, quas
credo tibi postea redditas esse ; in quibus idem te
hortor et rogo, quod pueri tibi verbis meis nuntiarunt,
ut Romam protinus pergas et properes. Primum
enim te in[1] praesidio esse volui, si qui essent inimici,
quorum crudelitas nondum esset nostra calamitate
satiata. Deinde congressus nostri lamentationem
pertimui ; digressum vero non tulissem ; atque etiam
id ipsum, quod tu scribis, metuebam, ne a me
distrahi non posses. His de causis hoc maximum

---

[1] *Inserted by Madvig* : te praesidio *mss.*

miss ? No, it is one who in affection is almost a twin, in deference a son, in counsel a father. What has ever given me pleasure without your sharing it, or you without my sharing it? And what of the fact that at the same time I miss a daughter, and how affectionate a daughter, how unassuming, how talented— the very replica of myself in face, speech, and spirit? And, moreover, a son, the bonniest boy, and my very darling? Harsh and hard-hearted as I was, I put him away from my embrace, a wiser boy than I could wish ; for he already sensed what was afoot. But what of my missing your son, the image of yourself, whom my Cicero loved as a brother, and was just beginning to revere as an elder brother? What of the fact that I refused to allow that most miserable of women, my most loyal wife, to follow me into exile, so that there might be somebody to look after all that is left to us out of our common disaster, the children we have in common?

But for all that I wrote to you as best I could, 4 and gave the letter to Philogonus, your freedman, to deliver to you, and I believe that it was so delivered later on ; in it I urge and entreat you to do exactly what my slaves repeated to you as from myself—that you should proceed on your journey to Rome, and make haste about it. In the first place I wished you to be on guard, in the event of there being any enemies, whose bloodthirstiness had not even yet been glutted by my fall. In the next place I dreaded the lamentation our meeting would cause ; indeed our parting would have been more than I could bear, and I also feared the very thing you mention in your letter— that you could not tear yourself away from me. For these reasons the crowning misfortune of my not

malum, quod te non vidi, quo nihil amantissimis et
coniunctissimis fratribus acerbius ac miserius videtur
accidere potuisse, minus acerbum, minus miserum
fuit, quam fuisset cum congressio, tum vero digressio
5 nostra. Nunc, si potes, id quod ego, qui fortis tibi
semper videbar, non possum, erige te et confirma, si
qua subeunda dimicatio erit. Spero, si quid mea
spes habet auctoritatis, tibi et integritatem tuam, et
amorem in te civitatis, et aliquid etiam miseri-
cordiam nostri praesidi laturam. Sin eris ab isto
periculo vacuus, ages scilicet, si quid agi posse de
nobis putabis. De quo scribunt ad me quidem multi
multa, et se sperare demonstrant : sed ego, quid
sperem, non dispicio, cum inimici plurimum valeant,
amici partim deseruerint me, partim etiam prodide-
rint, qui in meo reditu fortasse reprehensionem sui
sceleris pertimescant. Sed ista qualia sint, tu velim
perspicias mihique declares. Ego tamen, quamdiu
tibi opus erit, si quid periculi subeundum videbis,
vivam. Diutius in hac vita esse non possum. Neque
enim tantum virium habet ulla aut prudentia aut
6 doctrina, ut tantum dolorem possit sustinere. Scio
fuisse et honestius moriendi tempus, et utilius, sed
non hoc solum, multa alia praetermisi ; quae si
queri velim praeterita, nihil agam, nisi ut augeam

<a> The prosecution for malversation in his province with
which he was threatened by Appius Claudius, nephew of
Clodius. Tyrrell.

having seen you—and it seems to me that nothing more bitter and more depressing than that could have befallen brothers so devoted to each other and so closely united—was less bitter and less depressing than would have been first our meeting, and then our parting.

And now, if you can, do what I, brave as you have always thought me, cannot do—rouse yourself and show your strength, if there be any conflict you have to face. I hope, if there are any grounds for my so hoping, that your own integrity, and the love the State bears you, and to some extent even pity for me, will prove a protection to you. But if you are free from your own particular danger,[a] you will of course do whatever you think can be done in my interests. And as to that, there are many who write long letters to me and make it plain that they have their hopes ; but I cannot discern myself what I am to hope for, seeing that my enemies are exceedingly powerful, while my friends have in some cases deserted, in others actually betrayed me, perhaps because they are terribly afraid that my recall would imply a censure upon their scandalous conduct. But as to your own troubles, I should like you to get a clear idea of them, and explain them to me. Whatever happens, as long as you have need of me, or see any danger ahead, so long shall I remain alive ; longer than that I cannot brook my present life. No wisdom, no philosophy, is strong enough to bear such a weight of woe.

That there has occurred a more honourable and more advantageous moment for dying, I am well aware ; but that is not my only sin of omission, it is but one of many ; and if I am going to bewail past opportunities, I shall do no more than aggravate your

465

dolorem tuum, indicem stultitiam meam. Illud quidem nec faciendum est, nec fieri potest, me diutius, quam aut tuum tempus aut firma spes postulabit, in tam misera tamque turpi vita commorari, ut, qui modo fratre fuerim, liberis, coniuge, copiis, genere ipso pecuniae beatissimus, dignitate, auctoritate, existimatione, gratia non inferior, quam qui umquam fuerunt amplissimi, is nunc, in hac tam afflicta perditaque fortuna, neque me neque meos lugere

7 diutius possim. Quare quid ad me scripsisti de permutatione ? quasi vero nunc me non tuae facultates sustineant. Qua in re ipsa video miser et sentio, quid sceleris admiserim, cum tu de visceribus tuis et fili tui satisfacturus sis, quibus debes, ego acceptam ex aerario pecuniam tuo nomine frustra dissiparim. Sed tamen et M. Antonio, quantum tu scripseras, et Caepioni tantumdem solutum est ; mihi ad id, quod cogito, hoc, quod habeo, satis est. Sive enim restituimur sive desperamur, nihil amplius opus est. Tu, si forte quid erit molestiae, te ad Crassum et ad

8 Calidium conferas, censeo. Quantum Hortensio credendum sit, nescio. Me summa simulatione amoris summaque assiduitate quotidiana sceleratissime insidiosissimeque tractavit, adiuncto quoque Arrio ; quorum ego consiliis, promissis, praeceptis destitutus, in hanc calamitatem incidi. Sed haec occultabis, ne

a Which chiefly consisted of large legacies left him by clients whom he had successfully defended.
b Which Quintus had offered to negotiate for Cicero in Rome, so that he might have the benefit of it at Thessalonica.
c Both were creditors of Quintus.
d M. Calidius, who as praetor in 57 supported Cicero's recall. *Cf. Fam.* viii. 4. 1 and Index II.
466

grief and divulge my own folly. But this I am not bound to do, nor can it be done—I mean my tarrying, any longer than either your needs or any trustworthy hope shall necessitate, in a life so abject and igno-minious, that I who was lately so highly blessed in brother, children, wife, and wealth, yes, in the very nature of my riches,[a] and not inferior in position, influence, reputation and popularity to any who have ever stood highest in those respects,—that I, I say, should now, in this down-trodden and desperate condition of life, be any longer able to go on lamenting my own lot and that of my family.

Why, then, did you write to me about a bill of 7 exchange[b]? As though I was not being supported as it is by your resources. And it is just there that I see and feel, alas, what a crime I have committed, seeing that you are forced to satisfy your creditors by drawing upon your own and your son's very life-blood, while I have squandered to no purpose the money I had received from the treasury on your account. Anyhow the amount you mentioned in your letter has been paid to M. Antonius, and the same amount to Caepio.[c] For myself the sum I now have in hand is sufficient for what I have in view. For whether I am restored or given up in despair, I shall need nothing more. As to yourself, if there is any trouble, you should, I think, apply to Crassus and to Calidius.[d]

How far Hortensius is to be trusted I don't know. 8 Myself, with the most misleading pretence of affec-tion and the most assiduous daily attention, he treated most atrociously and with the basest treachery, with Arrius at his side ; and it was because I was left help-less through their advice, their promises, and their directions, that I fell into this degradation. But this

quid obsint. Illud caveto (et eo puto, per Pomponium fovendum tibi esse ipsum Hortensium), ne ille versus, qui in te erat collatus, cum aedilitatem petebas, de lege Aurelia, falso testimonio confirmetur. Nihil enim tam timeo, quam ne, cum intellegant homines, quantum misericordiae nobis tuae preces et tua salus allatura sit, oppugnent te vehementius.

9 Messalam tui studiosum esse arbitror ; Pompeium etiam simulatorem puto. Sed haec utinam ne experiare ! quod precarer deos, nisi meas preces audire desissent. Verumtamen precor, ut his infinitis nostris malis contenti sint, in quibus non modo tamen nullius inest peccati infamia, sed omnis dolor est, quod optime factis poena est maxima constituta.

10 Filiam meam et tuam, Ciceronemque nostrum, quid ego, mi frater, tibi commendem ? Quin illud maereo, quod tibi non minorem dolorem illorum orbitas afferet, quam mihi. Sed, te incolumi, orbi non erunt. Reliqua, ita mihi salus aliqua detur, potestasque in patria moriendi, ut me lacrimae non sinunt scribere. Etiam Terentiam velim tueare, mihique de omnibus rebus rescribas. Sis fortis, quoad rei natura patietur. Idibus Iuniis, Thessalonica.

---

a Which gave the *iudicia* to the Senate, the *equites*, and the *tribuni aerarii.* We do not know what the epigram was, or whether Quintus really wrote it.

b Consul with M. Piso in 61.

you will keep dark for fear they do you some injury.
You must beware particularly of this—and with that
object I think you should get Pomponius to help
you to make love to Hortensius himself—that your
authorship of that epigram about the *Lex Aurelia* [a]
which was attributed to you when you were a candidate for the quaestorship, is not established by some
false testimony. There is nothing I fear so much as
this, that when people realize how much compassion
for me is likely to be excited by your supplications
combined with your acquittal, they will attack you all
the more fiercely.

I imagine that Messala [b] is devoted to you; 9
Pompey is even now, I suspect, merely affecting to be
so. But may you never have to test the truth of all
this! I should pray to the gods for that, had they
not ceased to listen to any prayers of mine. However, I do pray that they may rest content with these
endless calamities of ours—calamities in which, after
all, not only is there no dishonouring taint of wrong-
doing, but in which is concentrated all that there is of
anguish, since what was done for the best has been
visited with the heaviest penalty.

As to my daughter (who is yours), and my little 10
Cicero, why should I commend them to you, my own
brother? Not but that I grieve that their bereavement
will cause you no less sorrow than myself. But, as long
as you are safe, they will not be bereft. As for what remains to be said, as surely as I hope for some measure
of restitution, and the chance of ending my days in
my fatherland, so surely am I not allowed to write it
by my tears. Terentia also I would have you protect,
and pray reply to me on every point. Be as brave as
the nature of the case permits. Thessalonica, June 13.

CICERO

IV

M. CICERO S. D. Q. FRATRI

Thessalonicae, A.U.C. 696.

1 Amabo te, mi frater, ne, si uno meo fato et tu
et omnes mei corruistis, improbitati et sceleri meo
potius, quam imprudentiae miseriaeque assignes.
Nullum est meum peccatum, nisi quod iis credidi, a
quibus nefas putaram esse me decipi, aut etiam,
quibus ne id expedire quidem arbitrabar. Intimus,
proximus, familiarissimus quisque aut sibi pertimuit,
aut mihi invidit. Ita mihi nihil misero praeter fidem
2 amicorum, cautum meum consilium defuit. Quod si
te satis innocentia tua et misericordia hominum vin-
dicat hoc tempore a molestia, perspicis profecto, ec-
quaenam nobis spes salutis relinquatur. Nam me
Pomponius et Sestius et Piso noster adhuc Thessalonicae retinuerunt, cum longius discedere propter
nescio quos motus vetarent. Verum ego magis
exitum illorum litteris, quam spe certa exspectabam.
Nam quid sperem, potentissimo inimico, dominatione
obtrectatorum, infidelibus amicis, pluribus invidis?
3 De novis autem tribunis plebis est ille quidem in me

470

IV

CICERO TO QUINTUS

Thessalonica, early in August, 58 B.C.

I entreat you, by my love, my dear brother, do not, 1
if through my fate I alone have brought ruin upon
you and all who are mine, do not attribute it to any
criminality or guilt on my part, so much as to a pitiable
lack of foresight. I plead guilty to nothing more
than having trusted those by whom I had thought it
inconceivably base that I should be deceived, and
indeed imagined that it was not even to their own
interest. All my most intimate, my nearest, and my
dearest friends, were either panic-struck on their own
account, or were jealous of me. So I lacked nothing,
poor wretch, but fair dealing on the part of my
friends and cautious counsel on my own.

But if your own integrity and the compassion 2
generally felt for you have delivered you from per-
secution at the present juncture, you are surely in a
position to know whether there is left to me any hope
whatever of being recalled. Pomponius and Sestius
and my son-in-law Piso have so far held me back at
Thessalonica, forbidding me to go further afield on
account of some developments or other ; but it was
their letters rather than any definite hope of my own
that induced me to await the issue of those developments. For what hope have I left, with a most powerful enemy, with my detractors in supreme command,
my friends faithless, and so many envious of me ?

However, of the new tribunes, Sestius, it is true, is 3
most sincerely devoted to me, and so, I hope, are

471

officiosissimus Sestius, et, spero, Curius, Milo, Fadius,
Fabricius, sed valde adversante Clodio, qui etiam
privatus eadem manu poterit contiones concitare;
4 deinde etiam intercessor parabitur. Haec mihi
proficiscenti non proponebantur, sed saepe triduo
summa cum gloria dicebar esse rediturus. Quid
tu igitur? inquies.   Quid? multa convenerunt,
quae mentem exturbarent meam—subita defectio
Pompei, alienatio consulum, etiam praetorum, timor
publicanorum, arma. Lacrimae meorum me ad
mortem ire prohibuerunt, quod certe et ad hone-
statem et ad effugiendos intolerabiles dolores fuit
aptissimum. Sed de hoc scripsi ad te in ea epistula,
quam Phaethonti dedi. Nunc tu, quoniam in tantum
luctum et laborem detrusus es, quantum nemo umquam, si relevare potes communem casum misericordia hominum, scilicet incredibile quiddam as-
sequeris; sin plane occidimus, (me miserum!) ego
omnibus meis exitio fuero, quibus ante dedecori non
5 eram. Sed tu, ut ante ad te scripsi, perspice rem et
pertenta, et ad me, ut tempora nostra, non ut amor
tuus fert, vere perscribe. Ego vitam, quoad putabo
tua interesse, aut ad spem servandam esse, retinebo.
Tu nobis amicissimum Sestium cognosces; credo tua
causa velle Lentulum, qui erit consul. Quamquam

<hr>

^a Perhaps the M. Curius who was quaestor in 61 and
tribune of the plebs in 57. See *Fam.* xiii. 49 and Index II.
^b See *Fam.* v. 18. One of the tribunes who promoted
Cicero's recall.
^c Piso and Gabinius, who were at first, or seemed to be,
inclined to befriend Cicero, but afterwards became hostile
to him.

Curius,[a] Milo, Fadius,[b] and Fabricius; but Clodius is bitterly opposed to me, and even in his private capacity will be able to rouse the passions of public gatherings with the same old gang; and again there is this too—someone will be put up to veto the bill.

All this was not put before me as I was leaving 4 Rome, but it was repeatedly stated that I should be returning in three days' time with the greatest glory. "Why did you go, then?" you will say. Why? Well, many things occurred together to upset my mental balance—the sudden defection of Pompey, the estrangement of the consuls,[c] and of the praetors also, the timid attitude of the *publicani*, the gangs of armed roughs. The tears of my family prevented me from putting myself to death, which was certainly the course best adapted to the retention of my honour and my escape from unendurable sufferings. But I wrote to you on this point in the letter I gave Phaethon. As it is, now that you have been thrust into such a morass of grief and trouble as no man ever was before, if you, by exciting the compassion of the world, can be the means of mitigating our common misfortune, you will undoubtedly win a success of unimaginable importance; but if we are both irrevocably ruined (woe is me!), I shall prove to have brought destruction upon all my people, to whom previously I was no discredit.

But, as I wrote to you before, scrutinize and probe 5 the situation thoroughly, and report to me fully and truthfully, as our actual position and not your affection for me dictates. I shall keep my hold on life as long as I think that it is to your interest, or that it should be preserved for the possibility of hope. You will find Sestius a true friend to us, and I believe Lentulus wishes you all success, and he will be consul. And

sunt facta verbis difficiliora. Tu et quid opus sit, et
quid sit, videbis. Omnino si tuam solitudinem com-
munemque calamitatem nemo dispexerit, aut per
te confici aliquid, aut nullo modo poterit. Sin te
quoque inimici vexare coeperint, ne cessaris. Non
enim gladiis tecum, sed litibus agetur. Verum haec
absint velim. Te oro, ut ad me de omnibus rebus
scribas, et in me animi potius aut consili putes minus
esse, quam antea, amoris vero et offici non minus.

yet it is easier to talk than to act. You will see what is needful, and how things really are.

To sum up, if nobody casts a calculating eye upon your unprotected position and our common calamity, it is through you, or not at all, that something may be accomplished. But if our enemies begin to harass you as well as myself, you must be up and doing ; for their weapons against you won't be swords, but suits. However, I trust there will be none of that.

I implore you to write to me about everything, and to believe that though perhaps my courage and powers of decision are less than in the old days, there is no diminution of my love and loyalty.

M. TULLI CICERONIS
EPISTULARUM AD QUINTUM FRATREM

LIBER SECUNDUS

I

M. CICERO S. D. Q. FRATRI

Romae, A.U.C. 697.

1   Epistulam, quam legisti, mane dederam. Sed fecit
humaniter Licinius, quod ad me, misso senatu, vesperi venit, ut, si quid esset actum, ad te, si mihi
videretur, perscriberem. Senatus fuit frequentior,
quam putabamus esse posse mense Decembri sub
dies festos. Consulares nos fuimus P. Servilius, M.
Lucullus, Lepidus, Volcatius, Glabrio, duo consules
designati, praetores. Sane frequentes fuimus ;
omnino ad ducentos. Commorat exspectationem Lupus. Egit causam agri Campani sane accurate. Auditus est magno silentio. Materiam rei non ignoras.

---

  a Isauricus, consul with Appius Claudius Pulcher in 79.
  b M. Terentius Varro Lucullus, consul in 73.
  c M. Aemilius Lepidus and L. Volcatius Tullus were
consuls in 66.
  d M'. Acilius Glabrio, consul with C. Calpurnius Piso in
67.

CICERO'S LETTERS TO HIS BROTHER QUINTUS

BOOK II

I

CICERO TO QUINTUS (ON HIS WAY TO SARDINIA)

Rome, December, 57 B.C.

The letter you have just read I sent off this morn- 1
ing. But Licinius was so courteous as to visit me in
the evening after the dismissal of the Senate, so that,
if I thought good, I might write you a full account of
anything that had been done there. The Senate was
better attended than I thought possible in the month
of December so near the holidays. Of us consulars
there were P. Servilius,[a] M. Lucullus,[b] Lepidus,[c]
Volcatius,[c] Glabrio,[d] the two consuls designate, and
the praetors. We made quite a full house, being
about 200 altogether. Lupus[e] had roused our
expectations. He discussed the question of the
Campanian land with extreme particularity, and was
listened to in profound silence. You are well aware
what material it offers for a speech. He omitted

[e] Publius Rutilius Lupus, who was strongly opposed to
Caesar's law for the division of the Campanian land.

CICERO

Nihil ex nostris actionibus praetermisit. Fuerunt
nonnulli aculei in C. Caesarem, contumeliae in Gel-
lium, expostulationes cum absente Pompeio. Causa
sero perorata, sententias se rogaturum negavit, ne
quod onus simultatis nobis imponeret. Ex superiorum
temporum conviciis, et ex praesenti silentio, quid
senatus sentiret, se intellegere dixit. Ilico coepit
dimittere,[2] cum Marcellinus, noli, inquit, ex ta-
citurnitate nostra, Lupe, quid aut probemus hoc
tempore aut improbemus, iudicare. Ego, quod ad
me attinet, idemque arbitror ceteros, idcirco taceo,
quod non existimo, cum Pompeius absit, causam agri
Campani agi convenire. Tum ille se senatum negavit
2 tenere. Racilius surrexit, et de iudiciis referre coepit.
Marcellinum quidem primum rogavit. Is cum graviter
de Clodianis incendiis, trucidationibus, lapidationibus
questus esset, sententiam dixit, ut ipse iudices
praetor urbanus[1] sortiretur ; iudicum sortitione
facta, comitia haberentur ; qui iudicia impedivisset,
eum contra rempublicam esse facturum. Approbata
valde sententia, C. Cato contra dixit, et Cassius
maxima acclamatione senatus, cum comitia iudiciis
3 anteferret. Philippus assensit Lentulo. Postea

---

[1] *Manutius* : per praetorem urbanum *MSS.*
[2] *Orelli*: intellegere. Dixit Milo. Coepit dimittere.
Tum *MSS.*

---

[a] Gellius Poplicola, an adherent of Clodius.
[b] Cn. Cornelius Lentulus Marcellinus, consul designate
for the following year, 56.
[c] L. Racilius, a tribune and a staunch supporter of Cicero.
[d] As consul designate.
[e] *i.e.*, without the assistance of the quaestors.
[f] A tribune ; *cf. Q. Fr.* i. 2. 15.

478

nothing of the measures I had taken. There were some stinging references to C. Caesar, some abuse of Gellius,[a] some remonstrances with the absent Pompey. As he was late in bringing his speech to a conclusion, he said he would not ask for our votes, for fear of burdening us with a personal wrangle. He said that he clearly inferred the feelings of the Senate from the loud protests of earlier days and its present silence. He proceeds at once to dismiss the Senate, when Marcellinus[b] says, "You must not judge by our silence, Lupus, what we approve, or do not approve, at the present moment. As far as I am concerned, and I think it is the case with the rest of us, my reason for not speaking is, that I do not consider it right and proper that the question of the Campanian land should be discussed in Pompey's absence." Then Lupus said that he had no further business for the Senate.

Racilius[c] got up and began to raise the question of 2 the proposed prosecutions. Marcellinus was of course the first he called upon[d]; and he, after seriously protesting against the burnings, killings, and stonings of Clodius, proposed a resolution "that the *praetor urbanus* should himself[e] draw the lots for the jury, that the elections should not be held until after the allotment of the jurors, and that whoever obstructed the trials would be acting against the common-wealth." The proposal having met with hearty approval, C. Cato[f] spoke against it, and so did Cassius,[g] the Senate loudly protesting when he gave the elections precedence in time over the trials. Philippus agreed with Lentulus.[h]

[g] A tribune.
[h] *i.e.*, Marcellinus, the consul designate.

Racilius de privatis me primum sententiam rogavit.
Multa feci verba de toto furore latrocinioque P.
Clodi ; eum, tamquam reum, accusavi, multis et
secundis admurmurationibus cuncti senatus. Orationem meam collaudavit satis multis verbis, non
mehercule indiserte, Vetus Antistius ; isque iudi-
ciorum causam suscepit, antiquissimamque se habiturum dixit. Ibatur in eam sententiam. Tum
Clodius rogatus, diem dicendo eximere coepit. Fure-
bat, a Racilio se contumaciter inurbaneque[1] vexatum.
Deinde eius operae repente a Graecostasi et gradibus
clamorem satis magnum sustulerunt, opinor, in Q.
Sextilium et amicos Milonis incitatae. Eo metu
iniecto, repente magna querimonia omnium, discessimus. Habes acta unius diei. Reliqua, ut arbitror, in
mensem Ianuarium reicientur. De tribunis plebis
longe optimum Racilium habemus. Videtur etiam
Antistius amicus nobis fore. Nam Plancius totus
noster est. Fac, si me amas, ut considerate diligenterque naviges de mense Decembri.

[1] *Müller, following ed. Rom.* : urbaneque *Tyrrell,* " *with polished insolence.*"

[a] A tribune.
[b] A platform near the Curia Hostilia and the *Comitium* where Greek, and afterwards other, ambassadors listened to the debates in the Senate, a sort of " strangers' gallery."

After that Racilius called upon me first of the 3 unofficial senators for my opinion. I spoke at great length on all the insane and murderous acts of P. Clodius ; I arraigned him as though he were in the dock, amid the frequent approving murmurs of the whole Senate. My speech was praised at quite sufficient length and, I assure you, with no little eloquence, by Vetus Antistius,[a] who also took upon himself the defence of the priority of the trials—a priority he said he would regard as being of capital importance. The senators were crossing the floor in favour of this opinion, when Clodius, being called upon, set about talking out the sitting. He declared in a frenzy of rage that Racilius had worried him in an insulting and unmannerly way. Thereupon his hired ruffians on the Graecostasis[b] and the steps of the senate-house raised quite a fierce yell, incited, I suppose, to attack Q. Sextilius and Milo's friends. Under the cloud of that sudden alarm, we broke up, with strong protests on every side. So much for the transactions of a single day. What remains to be done will, I imagine, be put off to the month of January. Among the tribunes of the plebs by far the best man we have is Racilius. It seems likely that Antistius too will be friendly to us. As for Plancius,[c] he is with us heart and soul. As you love me, see to it that you are deliberate and careful about taking ship now that December is with us.

[c] Cn. Plancius who, as quaestor of Macedonia, showed great kindness to Cicero during his banishment.

CICERO

II

Romae, a.u.c. 698.

1 Non occupatione, qua eram sane impeditus, sed
parvula lippitudine adductus sum, ut dictarem hanc
epistulam et non, ut ad te soleo, ipse scriberem. Et
primum me tibi excuso in eo ipso, in quo te accuso.
Me enim adhuc nemo rogavit, " num quid in Sardiniam vellem " ; te puto saepe habere, qui, " num
quid Romam velis," quaerant. Quod ad me Lentuli
et Sesti nomine scripsisti, locutus sum cum Cincio.
Quoquo modo res se habet, non est facillima, sed
habet profecto quiddam Sardinia appositum ad re-
cordationem praeteritae memoriae. Nam, ut ille
Gracchus augur, posteaquam in istam provinciam
venit, recordatus est, quid sibi, in campo Martio
comitia consulum habenti, contra auspicia accidisset,
sic tu mihi videris in Sardinia de forma Numisiana et
de nominibus Pomponianis in otio recogitasse. Sed
ego adhuc emi nihil. Culleonis auctio facta est.
Tusculano emptor nemo fuit. Si condicio valde bona
2 fuerit, fortasse non omittam. De aedificatione tua
Cyrum urgere non cesso. Spero eum in officio fore.
Sed omnia sunt tardiora, propter furiosae aedilitatis
exspectationem. Nam comitia sine mora futura
videntur. Edicta sunt a. d. xi. Kal. Febr. Te tamen

---

^a An agent of Atticus.
^b The father of the Gracchi ; the story is told by Cicero
in *Nat. Deor.* ii. 11. ^c An architect.
^d Another architect. ^e *i.e.*, of P. Clodius.

II

It was not pressure of business (though I am sorely 1
hampered in that respect), but a slight inflammation
of the eyes that induced me to dictate this letter
instead of writing it, as I generally do when corre-
sponding with you, with my own hand. And first
of all I excuse myself to you on the very point on
which I accuse you. For nobody so far has asked me
whether I have any commands for Sardinia, while you,
I fancy, often have people inquiring whether you have
any commands for Rome. You wrote to me on
behalf of Lentulus and Sestius ; well, I have spoken
to Cincius.[a] However the matter stands, it is not
of the easiest. But assuredly there is something
in Sardinia peculiarly conducive to recalling past
memories ; for just as the great Gracchus,[b] the augur,
on his arrival in that province, recollected what had
happened to him when holding the consular elections
in the Campus Martius contrary to the auspices, so
it seems to me that you in your moments of leisure
in Sardinia have bethought yourself afresh of the
house-plan of Numisius[c] and your debts to Pomponius. So far I have bought nothing. Culleo's
auction is over and done with; my Tusculan property
found no purchaser. If I have a very favourable offer
for it, it is just possible I may not let it slip.

As regards your building, I never cease hurrying 2
on Cyrus.[d] I hope he will do his duty ; but everything hangs fire owing to the prospect of a madcap
aedileship[e] ; for the elections seem likely to be held
without delay. They are announced for January 20.

CICERO

sollicitum esse nolo. Omne genus a nobis cautionis
3 adhibebitur. De rege Alexandrino factum est senatus consultum, cum multitudine eum reduci periculosum reipublicae videri. Reliqua cum esset in senatu
contentio, Lentulusne an Pompeius reduceret, obtinere causam Lentulus videbatur. In ea nos et
officio erga Lentulum mirifice, et voluntati Pompei
praeclare satisfecimus. Sed per obtrectatores Lentuli res calumnia extracta est. Consecuti sunt dies
comitiales, per quos senatus haberi non poterat.
Quid futurum sit latrocinio tribunorum, non divino ;
sed tamen suspicor per vim rogationem Caninium
perlaturum. In ea re Pompeius quid velit, non dispicio. Familiares eius quid cupiant, omnes vident.
Creditores vero regis aperte pecunias suppeditant
contra Lentulum. Sine dubio res a Lentulo remota
videtur esse, cum magno meo dolore. Quamquam
multa fecit, quare, si fas esset, iure ei succensere
possemus. Tu, si ita expedit, velim quam primum
bona et certa tempestate conscendas ad meque venias.
Innumerabiles enim res sunt, in quibus te quotidie
in omni genere desiderem. Tui nostrique valent.
XIV. Kal. Febr.

---

[a] Ptolemy Auletes ; *cf. Fam.* i. 1 and 2, where the whole
story is told.
[b] Cicero blamel Lentulus for his indifference, if it was
not jealousy, in the matter of fixing Cicero's indemnity.

However I do not want you to be anxious. I shall exercise every kind of caution.

In the matter of the Alexandrine king,[a] a decree 3 of the Senate has been passed to the effect that his restoration by the employment of "*a host of men*" seems fraught with danger to the commonwealth. In what remained to be discussed in the Senate—the question whether he should be restored by Lentulus or Pompey—it seemed that Lentulus was making good his case, a case in which I was amazingly successful in discharging my obligations to Lentulus, and brilliantly so in satisfying the wishes of Pompey —but Lentulus's case was protracted by the spiteful obstruction of his detractors. Then followed the comitial days, during which a meeting of the Senate could not be held. What result the ruffianly conduct of the tribunes will have, I cannot predict; anyhow I suspect Caninius will force his bill through by violence. In all this I have no clear idea as to what Pompey wants; what his particular friends desire, nobody can fail to see. Those who are financing the king make no secret of supplying sums of money to fight Lentulus. It is beyond doubt that the business seems to have been taken out of Lentulus's hands, and it is a great grief to me. And yet he has done many things for which I might be justly angry with him,[b] were such a thing conceivable. If it suits your interests, I should like you to take ship when the weather is fair and settled, and join me as soon as possible. For there are numberless things in which I miss you daily in all sorts of ways. Your people and mine are well. January 17.

CICERO

III

M. CICERO S. D. Q. FRATRI

Romae, a.u.c. 698.

1 Scripsi ad te antea superiora ; nunc cognosce,
postea quae sint acta. A Kal. Febr. legationes in
Idus Febr. reiciebantur. Eo die res confecta non est.
A. d. iv. Non. Febr. Milo adfuit. Ei Pompeius ad-
vocatus venit. Dixit Marcellus, a me rogatus. Honeste discessimus. Producta dies est in viii. Id. Febr.
Interim reiectis legationibus in Idus, referebatur
de provinciis quaestorum et de ornandis praetoribus.
Sed res, multis querellis de republica interponendis,
nulla transacta est. Cato legem promulgavit de imperio Lentuli abrogando. Vestitum filius mutavit.
2 A. d. viii. Id. Febr. Milo adfuit. Dixit Pompeius,
sive voluit ; nam, ut surrexit, operae Clodianae clamorem sustulerunt ; idque ei perpetua oratione contigit, non modo ut acclamatione, sed ut convicio et
maledictis impediretur. Qui ut peroravit (nam in eo
sane fortis fuit, non est deterritus, dixit omnia ; atque interdum etiam silentio cum auctoritate per-
egerat) sed ut peroravit, surrexit Clodius. Ei tantus

<hr>

a i.e., of Cilicia. His son assumed mourning (as was often
done in such circumstances) to excite sympathy with his
father.

486

III

CICERO TO QUINTUS IN SARDINIA

Rome, February 12 and 15, 56 B.C.

I have already told you in my letter what occurred 1
earlier ; now let me inform you of what has been
done since that. On February 1, it was proposed to
postpone the reception of foreign deputations until
February 13. The postponement was not carried on
that day. On February 2, Milo appeared to stand
his trial. Pompey came to support him. Marcellus
was called upon by me, and spoke. We came off with
the honours of war. The trial was adjourned to the
6th. Meanwhile the deputations having been put off
until the 13th, the question of assigning provinces to
the quaestors and of supplying the praetors with the
proper officers and forces was brought before the
house ; but so many complaints of the state of public
affairs were interposed, that nothing was settled. C.
Cato gave notice of a proposal to remove Lentulus
from his government,[a] and Lentulus's son put on
mourning.

On the 6th Milo again appeared for trial. Pompey 2
spoke, or rather such was his intention ; for when he
got up, Clodius's hired gangs raised a yell, and that
is what he had to endure the whole time he was
speaking, being interrupted not only with shouts,
but with insults and abuse. When he had finished his
speech (he showed great fortitude in the circumstances ; he never quailed, he said all he had to say,
and now and then amid a silence compelled by his
impressive personality), but, as I say, when he had
finished his speech, up got Clodius. He was met with

487

CICERO

clamor a nostris (placuerat enim referre gratiam), ut neque mente neque lingua neque ore consisteret. Ea res acta est, cum hora vi. vix Pompeius perorasset, usque ad horam viii., cum omnia maledicta, versus etiam obscenissimi in Clodium et Clodiam dicerentur. Ille furens et exsanguis interrogabat suos, in clamore ipso, quis esset, qui plebem fame necaret. Respondebant operae, " Pompeius." Quis Alexandriam ire cuperet. Respondebant, " Pompeius." Quem ire vellent. Respondebant, " Crassum." Is aderat tum, Miloni animo non amico. Hora fere ix., quasi signo dato, Clodiani nostros consputare coeperunt. Exarsit dolor. Urgere illi, ut loco nos moverent. Factus est a nostris impetus ; fuga operarum. Eiectus de rostris Clodius ; ac nos quoque tum fugimus, ne quid in turba. Senatus vocatus in curiam ; Pompeius domum. Neque ego tamen in senatum, ne aut de tantis rebus tacerem, aut in Pompeio defendendo (nam is carpebatur a Bibulo, Curione, Favonio, Servilio filio) animos bonorum virorum offenderem. Res in posterum dilata est. Clodius in Quirinalia produxit 3 diem. A. d. vii. Id. Febr. senatus ad Apollinis fuit, ut Pompeius adesset. Acta res est graviter a Pompeio. Eo die nihil perfectum est. A. d. vi. Id. ad

---

a For this rendering (from *lost* to *countenance*) I am indebted to Tyrrell.

b February 17.

c He was probably afraid to enter Rome on account of the mobs. It was not because he held *imperium*, as he had already entered Rome to speak for Milo (§ 2).

such a deafening shout from our side (for we had determined to give him as good as he gave), that he lost all control over his faculties, his voice, and his countenance.[a] Such was the scene from the time when Pompey had barely finished his speech at noon, right up to two o'clock, when every kind of abuse, and even doggerel of the filthiest description, was vented upon Clodius and Clodia. Maddened and white with rage, he asked his partisans (and he was heard above the shouting) who the man was that starved the people to death ; his rowdies answered " Pompey." Who was bent upon going to Alexandria ? They answered " Pompey." Whom did they want to go ? They answered " Crassus." (Crassus was there at the time, but with no friendly feeling for Milo.) About three o'clock the Clodians, as if at a given signal, began to spit upon our men. We resented it in a paroxysm of rage. They tried to hustle us and get us out. Our men charged them, and the roughs took to their heels. Clodius was flung off the *rostra*, and then we too fled, for fear of something happening in the *mêlée*. The Senate was summoned to the Curia ; Pompey went home. I did not myself, however, attend the Senate, so as not, on the one hand, to keep silent on matters of such gravity, or, on the other, by defending Pompey (who was being attacked by Bibulus, Curio, Favonius, and Servilius junior) to hurt the feelings of the loyalists. The business was adjourned to the following day. Clodius got the trial postponed until the Quirinalia.[b]

On February 7 the Senate met in the temple of 3 Apollo, in order that Pompey might be present.[c] He dealt with the matter impressively, but on that day nothing was done. On the 8th in the temple of Apollo

CICERO

Apollinis senatus consultum factum est, EA, QUAE
FACTA ESSENT A. D. VIII. ID. Febr. CONTRA REMPUBLICAM
ESSE FACTA. Eo die Cato est vehementer in Pompeium invectus, et eum oratione perpetua tamquam
reum accusavit. De me multa, me invito, cum mea
summa laude dixit. Cum illius in me perfidiam in-
creparet, auditus est magno silentio malevolorum.
Respondit ei vehementer Pompeius Crassumque
descripsit, dixitque aperte, se munitiorem ad cus-
todiendam vitam suam fore, quam Africanus fuisset,
4 quem C. Carbo interemisset. Itaque magnae mihi res
iam moveri videbantur. Nam Pompeius haec intellegit, nobiscumque communicat, insidias vitae
suae fieri ; C. Catonem a Crasso sustentari ; Clodio
pecuniam suppeditari ; utrumque et ab eo, et a
Curione, Bibulo ceterisque suis obtrectatoribus con-
firmari ; vehementer esse providendum, ne opprima-
tur, contionario illo populo a se prope alienato, nobilitate inimica, non aequo senatu, iuventute improba.
Itaque se comparat, homines ex agris arcessit.
Operas autem suas Clodius confirmat. Manus ad
Quirinalia paratur ; in eo multo sumus superiores
ipsius copiis. Sed magna manus ex Piceno et Gallia
exspectatur, ut etiam Catonis rogationibus de Milone

---

^a They would not interrupt a speech likely to embroil
Cicero with Pompey.
^b C. Papirius Carbo, to whom Pompey compares Crassus,
was probably innocent of the murder of Africanus. See note
b to *Fam.* ix. 21. 3.

a decree of the Senate was carried, " that what had been done on the 6th was against the interests of the State." On that day Cato vehemently inveighed against Pompey, and throughout his speech arraigned him as though he were in the dock. He spoke a great deal about me, much against my will, though in highly laudatory terms. When he denounced Pompey's treacherous conduct to myself, he was listened to amid profound silence on the part of my ill-wishers.[a] Pompey replied to him in vehement terms, and made an obvious allusion to Crassus, openly declaring " that he himself would be better prepared to safeguard his own life than Africanus had been, who was murdered by C. Carbo."[b]

So it appears to me that issues of great importance 4 are developing. For Pompey clearly understands this, and talks to me about it—that plots are being hatched against his life ; that C. Cato is being backed up by Crassus ; that Clodius is being supplied with money, and that both of them are being encouraged, not only by Crassus, but by Curio and Bibulus and the rest of his detractors ; that he has to take strenuous measures to prevent being utterly crushed, with a speech-swallowing populace practically estranged from him, with a nobility hostile, a Senate unfairly prejudiced, and the youth of the country without principle. So he is making preparations, and calling up men from rural districts, while Clodius is strengthening his hired gangs. A regiment of them is being trained for the Quirinalia, to meet which date we are far superior in numbers, with Pompey's own forces ; besides, a large contingent is expected from Picenum and Gaul, so that we may also oppose Cato's motions about Milo and Lentulus.

CICERO

5 et Lentulo resistamus. A. d. IV. Id. Febr. Sestius ab
indice Cn. Nerio, Pupinia, de ambitu est postulatus,
et eodem die a quodam P. Tullio de vi. Is erat aeger.
Domum (ut debuimus) ad eum statim venimus, eique
nos totos tradidimus ; idque fecimus praeter hominum opinionem, qui nos ei iure succensere putabant ;
ut humanissimi, gratissimique et ipsi et omnibus
videremur ; itaque faciemus. Sed idem Nerius index
edidit ad allegatos Cn. Lentulum Vatiam et C.
Cornelium.[1] Eodem die senatus consultum factum
est, UT SODALITATES DECURIATIQUE DISCEDERENT ;
LEXQUE DE IIS FERRETUR, UT, QUI NON DISCESSISSENT,
6 EA POENA, QUAE EST DE VI, TENERENTUR. A. d. III. Id.
dixi pro Bestia de ambitu apud praetorem Cn. Domitium in foro medio maximo conventu, incidique
in eum locum in dicendo, cum Sestius, multis in
templo Castoris vulneribus acceptis, subsidio Bestiae
servatus esset. Hic προῳκονομησάμην quiddam
εὐκαίρως de his, quae in Sestium apparabantur
crimina, et eum ornavi veris laudibus, magno assensu
omnium. Res homini fuit vehementer grata. Quae
tibi eo scribo, quod me de retinenda Sesti gratia
7 litteris saepe monuisti. Prid. Id. Febr. haec scripsi

---

[1] Cornelium : †ista ei *Tyrrell*; *Warde Fowler thinks*
ista ei *may be a corruption of* testes, *a gloss explaining*
allegatos : *Madvig suggests* instare, *" were threatening
Sestius"*: *I follow Nobbe in omitting* ista ei *altogether*: *Prof.
R. Ellis conjectures* adalligatos, *"as being compromised as
well."*

[a] P. Tullius Albinovanus.
[b] Cicero was displeased with the bill Sestius drew up for
his restoration (*cf. Att.* iii. 23. 4). We know of no other
reason why Cicero should have been angry with Sestius.
[c] The text is here incurably corrupt. See critical note
above.

492

On February 10, Sestius was prosecuted by the 5 informer, Cn. Nerius of the Pupinian tribe, for bribery, and on the same day by one P. Tullius [a] for breaking the peace. He was ill. I immediately went to see him at his house, and put myself unreservedly at his disposal ; and what I did was more than most people expected, for they supposed that I was justly indignant with him,[b] with the result that both he himself and the world in general thought me the most kind-hearted and grateful of men ; and that is how I mean to act. But that same informer Nerius also gave in the names of Cn. Lentulus Vatia and C. Cornelius as additional intermediaries.[c] On the same day a decree of the Senate was passed " that political clubs and caucuses should be broken up, and that a law concerning them should be proposed whereby all who refused to disband should be liable to the penalty fixed for breaking the peace."

On the 11th I defended Bestia on a charge of 6 bribery before the praetor, Cn. Domitius, in the middle of the forum, before a vast assembly ; and in the course of my speech, I incidentally dwelt upon the time when Sestius, covered with wounds in the temple of Castor, was only saved by the help of Bestia. At this point I adroitly seized the opportunity to make a sort of anticipatory refutation of the charges which are being trumped up against Sestius, and I paid him some compliments he really deserved, with the hearty approval of all present. It gave the poor fellow the greatest pleasure. I tell you this because you have often advised me in your letters to keep on good terms with Sestius.

I am writing this on the 12th, before day-break ; 7

ante lucem. Eo die apud Pomponium in eius nuptiis
eram cenaturus. Cetera sunt in rebus nostris
huiusmodi (ut tu mihi fere diffidenti praedicabas)
plena dignitatis et gratiae ; quae quidem tua, mi
frater, patientia, virtute, pietate, suavitate etiam,
tibi mihique sunt restituta. Domus tibi ad lacum[1]
Pisonis Liciniana conducta est. Sed, ut spero,
paucis mensibus post Kalend. Quint. in tuam com-
migrabis. Tuam in Carinis mundi habitatores Lamiae
conduxerunt. A te post illam Olbiensem epistulam
nullas litteras accepi. Quid agas et ut te oblectes,
scire cupio, maximeque teipsum videre quam primum.
Cura, mi frater, ut valeas ; et quamquam est hiems,
tamen Sardiniam istam esse cogites. xv. Kalend.
Mart.

IV

M. CICERO Q. FRATRI S.

Romae, a.u.c. 698.

1 Sestius noster absolutus est a. d. iv. Id. Mart. ; et,
quod vehementer interfuit reipublicae, nullam videri in eiusmodi causa dissensionem esse, omnibus
sententiis absolutus est. Illud, quod tibi saepe curae
esse intellexeram, ne cui iniquo relinqueremus vitu-
perandi locum, qui nos ingratos esse diceret, nisi il-

---

[1] *Boot*: lucum *mss.*, *but* luci *were generally dedicated to
divinities.*

---

[a] Atticus's marriage to Pilia.
[b] The chief port of Sardinia.
[c] A notoriously unhealthy island in the summer months.
[d] Sestius had kept a band of armed men during his
tribunate in the preceding year to oppose P. Clodius and
his roughs. He had therefore been accused of *vis* (breaking
the peace), with the result here described. Cicero's speech
on the occasion is still extant.

494

this is the day on which I am going to dine with Pomponius to celebrate his marriage.[a]

In all other respects my position is just what you assured me it would be, though I could hardly believe it—a position of dignity and popularity ; and all this has been restored to you and me, brother mine, by your patience, courage, and brotherly devotion, and, I must also add, by your charm of manner. A house has been taken for you that belonged to Licinius, near Piso's pool, but in a few months' time, say after July 1, you will move into your own. Your house in the Carinae has been taken on lease by some genteel tenants, the Lamiae. I have received no letter from you since the one you sent from Olbia.[b] I am anxious to know how you are getting on, and how you amuse yourself, but most of all to see you in person as soon as possible. Take care of your health, my dear brother, and, although it is winter, yet bear in mind that the place you are living in is Sardinia.[c]

IV

CICERO TO QUINTUS IN SARDINIA

Rome, March, 56 B.C.

Our friend Sestius was acquitted [d] on March 11, 1 and, moreover (and it is a matter of paramount importance to the State that there should be no appearance of difference of opinion in a case of this sort)—he was acquitted unanimously. As to what I had often gathered to be a cause of anxiety to you, that I should not leave a loophole for fault-finding to any ill-natured critic who might charge me with ingrati-

CICERO

lius perversitatem quibusdam in rebus quam humanissime ferremus, scito hoc nos in eo iudicio con-
secutos esse, ut omnium gratissimi iudicaremur. Nam
in defendendo moroso homini cumulatissime satisfecimus, et (id quod ille maxime cupiebat) Vatinium,
a quo palam oppugnabatur, arbitratu nostro con-
cidimus, dis hominibusque plaudentibus. Quin etiam
Paullus noster cum testis productus esset in Sestium,
confirmavit se nomen Vatini delaturum, si Macer
Licinius cunctaretur; et Macer a Sesti subselliis
surrexit, ac se illi non defuturum affirmavit. Quid
quaeris? homo petulans et audax, Vatinius, valde
2 perturbatus debilitatusque discessit. Quintus tuus,
puer optimus, eruditur egregie. Hoc nunc magis
animadverto, quod Tyrannio docet apud me. Domus
utriusque nostrum aedificatur strenue. Redemptori
tuo dimidium pecuniae curavi. Spero nos ante hiemem contubernales fore. De nostra Tullia, tui mehercule amantissima, spero cum Crassipede nos confecisse. Dies erant duo, qui post Latinas habentur
3 religiosi; ceteroqui confectum Latiar erat. Ἀμφιλαφίαν autem illam, quam tu soles dicere, bono modo
desidero, sic prorsus, ut advenientem excipiam liben-

ᵃ For Vatinius see note *a* to *Fam.* i. 9. 4.
ᵇ L. Aemilius Paullus, consul in 50.
ᶜ C. Licinius Macer Calvus, orator and poet.
ᵈ The houses of the two brothers adjoined each other.
ᵉ ἀμφιλαφία (from ἀμφιλαφής, "taking in on either side,
or with both hands") was apparently the term Quintus had
used for the "unlimited means" required for his own and his
brother's building operations. *Cf. Ep.* 15*b.* 3 of this Book.
The metaphor in *excipere* is from a hunter who stands ready
to *welcome* the game when it breaks cover. *Cf.* Hor. *Od.*
iii. 12. 12 "latitantem fruticeto excipere aprum."

496

tude if I failed to put up with Sestius's wrong-headedness in certain matters as good-humouredly as possible, let me assure you that in this trial I succeeded in establishing my reputation as the most grateful man alive. For in my defence not only did I give immense satisfaction to a cross-grained man, but I also (and this was his dearest wish) made mince-meat of Vatinius,[a] who was openly attacking him, just as the fancy took me, with the applause of gods and men. Furthermore, when our friend Paullus[b] was brought forward as a witness against Sestius, he declared that he would lay information against Vatinius if Macer Licinius[c] was slow about doing so; and Macer rose from the benches where sat the friends of Sestius, and declared that he would not fail to do as Paullus wished. To cut the story short, that aggressive and impudent fellow Vatinius left the court in a state of confusion and nervous collapse.

That excellent boy, your son Quintus, is being 2 admirably taught, and I notice it all the more now, because Tyrannio gives him his lessons at my house. The building of both our houses is going on vigorously. I have seen to it that your contractor has had half his money paid to him. I hope that before winter we shall be under the same roof.[d] As to our daughter Tullia, who, I positively assure you, is very much attached to you, I hope we have settled her betrothal to Crassipes. There are two days which are reckoned as holidays after the Latin festival; otherwise the festival of Jupiter Latiaris has come to an end.

Now as to that "*opulence*"[e] you so often talk about, 3 I have a longing for it, but quite in moderation—just so far as gladly to welcome my quarry, if it comes my

ter latentem non excitem. Etiam nunc tribus locis
aedifico, reliqua reconcinno ; vivo paullo liberalius,
quam solebam ; opus erat. Si te haberem, paullisper
fabris locum darem. Sed et haec (ut spero) brevi
4 inter nos communicabimus. Res autem Romanae
sese sic habent. Consul est egregius Lentulus, non
impediente collega ; sic, inquam, bonus, ut meliorem
non viderim. Dies comitiales exemit omnes. Nam
etiam Latinae instaurantur ; nec tamen deerant
5 supplicationes. Sic legibus perniciosissimis obsistitur,
maxime Catonis ; cui tamen egregie imposuit Milo
noster. Nam ille vindex gladiatorum et bestiario-
rum emerat de Cosconio et Pomponio bestiarios ; nec
sine his armatis umquam in publico fuerat. Hos alere
non poterat. Itaque vix tenebat. Sensit Milo.
Dedit cuidam non familiari negotium, qui sine sus-
picione emeret eam familiam a Catone ; quae simul
atque abducta est, Racilius, qui unus est hoc tempore
tribunus plebis, rem patefecit, eosque homines sibi
emptos esse dixit (sic enim placuerat) et tabulam
proscripsit, SE FAMILIAM CATONIANAM VENDITURUM. In
eam tabulam magni risus consequebantur. Nunc
igitur Catonem Lentulus a legibus removit, et eos,
qui de Caesare monstra promulgarunt, quibus inter-

---

a Marcellinus, consul with Marcius Philippus. Acting in
concert, in order to prevent C. Cato and his friends from
bringing in bills to the prejudice of Lentulus Spinther and
Milo, the two consuls had recourse to every possible political
manœuvre to cause delay in the elections, *e.g.* the celebration
of the movable festival, the *feriae Latinae*, when they might
more justifiably have held the *supplicationes* that were
due, and would also have had the effect of delaying the
elections.

way, but not to hunt it out, if it keeps under cover. Even as it is, I am building in three different places, and refurbishing my other houses. I am living rather more generously than I used to ; I have to do so. If I had you with me, I should give the masons free scope for a while. But this too we shall shortly, I hope, talk over together.

The position at Rome is as follows : Lentulus [a] is 4 an excellent consul, and his colleague does not stand in his way—so good, I repeat, that I have never seen a better. He has cancelled all the comitial days. Why, even the Latin festival is being celebrated anew; and yet he had the *supplicationes* to fall back upon.

By these means the most ruinous bills are being 5 resisted, especially that of C. Cato ; but our friend Milo has played a splendid trick upon him. That champion of gladiators and beast-fighters had bought some beast-fighters from Cosconius and Pomponius, and had never appeared in public without them as an armed body-guard. He could not pay for their keep, so could hardly maintain his hold upon them. Milo got wind of it. He engaged a certain person, with whom he was not intimate, to buy the whole gang from Cato without exciting his suspicion. No sooner had they been marched off than Racilius, who just now stands alone as tribune of the plebs, divulged the whole affair, declared that the men had been bought for him (that is what they had agreed upon) and put up a notice "*that he had Cato's gang for sale.*" The result of that notice was laughter loud and long. So now Lentulus has prevented Cato, and those who promulgated outrageous proposals about Caesar, from carrying their laws, there being no

cederet nemo. Nam quod de Pompeio Caninius agit,
sanequam refrixit. Neque enim res probatur, et
Pompeius noster in amicitia P. Lentuli vituperatur,
et hercule non est idem. Nam apud illam perditis-
simam atque infimam faecem populi propter Milonem
suboffendit ; et boni multa ab eo desiderant, multa
reprehendunt. Marcellinus autem hoc uno mihi quidem non satisfacit, quod eum nimis aspere tractat ;
quamquam id senatu non invito facit ; quo ego me
libentius a curia et ab omni parte reipublicae sub-
6 traho. In iudiciis ii sumus, qui fuimus. Domus
celebratur ita, ut cum maxime. Unum accidit im-
prudentia Milonis incommode, de Sex. Clodio, quem
neque hoc tempore, neque ab imbecillis accusatoribus mihi placuit accusari. Ei tres sententiae teter-
rimo in consilio defuerunt. Itaque hominem populus
revocat et retrahatur necesse est. Non enim ferunt
homines. Et quia, cum apud suos diceret, paene
damnatus est, vident damnatum. Ea ipsa in re
Pompei offensio nobis obstitit. Senatorum enim urna
copiose absolvit, equitum adaequavit, tribuni aerarii
condemnarunt. Sed hoc incommodum consolantur
quotidianae damnationes inimicorum, in quibus me

---

[a] Probably a descendant of a freedman of the *gens Claudia*,
a man of low repute, and P. Clodius's chief instrument in
carrying out his schemes of violence and outrage.

[b] The *iudices* consisted of three *decuriae*, made up respectively of senators, knights, and *tribuni aerarii* (probably
persons of property, representing the classes below the
knights). Each of the three *decuriae* had its separate
balloting-urn.

tribune to intervene. For as to Caninius's proposal about Pompey, it has utterly collapsed. It is not a popular proposal in itself, and our friend Pompey is censured for his breach of friendship with Lentulus, and, upon my honour, he is not the man he was. For his support of Milo is not altogether agreeable to those who constitute the worst and lowest dregs of the people, while the patriotic party regret his sins of omission and blame him for his sins of commission, and there are plenty of both. Marcellinus, however, does not quite satisfy me in one regard—he treats him too harshly ; and yet he does so with no objection on the part of the Senate, which makes me all the more wishful to withdraw myself from the House and from all participation in politics.

In the courts I hold the same position as I did. My 6 house is as thronged as ever it was. There is one awkward incident due to Milo's lack of foresight in the matter of Sextus Clodius,[a] of whose prosecution at this particular juncture, and by a feeble lot of accusers, I did not approve. Before a most corrupt jury Milo only failed to obtain a condemnation by three votes. The populace, therefore, are for having the fellow up again, and he must be dragged back into court. People cannot tolerate it, and because he was all but condemned when pleading before a jury of his own partisans, they look upon him as already condemned. Even in this matter the feelings of dislike for Pompey stood in our way. For the votes of the senators acquitted him with a handsome margin, those of the knights were equally divided, those of the *tribuni aerarii* were against him.[b] But I am consoled for this misfortune by the daily condemnations of my enemies, among whom, to my

perlubente Servius allisus est, ceteri conciduntur.
C. Cato contionatus est, comitia haberi non siturum,
si sibi cum populo dies agendi essent exempti. Ap-
7 pius a Caesare nondum redierat. Tuas mirifice
litteras exspecto; atque adhuc clausum mare scio
fuisse; sed quosdam venisse tamen Ostia dicebant,
qui te unice laudarent, plurimique in provincia fieri
dicerent. Eosdem aiebant nuntiare, te prima navi-
gatione transmissurum. Id cupio; et, quamquam
teipsum scilicet maxime, tamen etiam litteras tuas
ante exspecto. Mi frater, vale.

V

MARCUS Q. FRATRI S.

Romae, A.U.C. 698.

1 Dederam ad te litteras antea, quibus erat scriptum, Tulliam nostram Crassipedi prid. Non. April.
esse desponsatam, ceteraque de re publica privata-
que perscripseram. Postea sunt haec acta. Non.
Apr. senatus consulto Pompeio pecunia decreta est
in rem frumentariam ad HS cccc. Sed eodem die
vehementer actum de agro Campano clamore senatus

---

a Probably Servius Pola; *cf. Fam.* viii. 12. 2.
b Quintus was now employed in Sardinia as Pompey's
legatus in the collection of corn-supplies.
c About £340,000.
502

great delight, Servius [a] has suffered shipwreck, and all the rest are being made mince-meat of. C. Cato announced at a public meeting that he would not permit the elections to be held should he have been deprived of the days for transacting business with the people. Appius has not yet returned from visiting Caesar.

It is wonderful how eagerly I await a letter from 7 you, and yet I know that the sea is still closed to navigation ; but for all that they tell me that certain persons have arrived at Ostia, who praised you above all men, and declared that you are most highly esteemed in the province.[b] They say that it is reported by the same persons that you intend to cross as soon as ever it is possible to sail. That is just what I desire ; and although, of course, I look forward to seeing you in the flesh more than anything, still even a letter from you in the meantime is something to look forward to. Brother mine, good-bye.

V

CICERO TO QUINTUS IN SARDINIA

Rome, April 11, 56 B.C.

I sent you a letter before in which I wrote that our 1 daughter Tullia had been betrothed to Crassipes on April 4, and gave you a full account of everything else concerning our public and private affairs. This is what has happened subsequently. On April 5 by a decree of the Senate money was voted to Pompey for the corn-supply, amounting to 40,000 *sestertia*.[c] But on the same day there was a heated debate on the Campanian land, when the Senate was nearly as

prope contionali. Acriorem causam inopia pecuniae
2 faciebat et annonae caritas. Non praetermittam ne
illud quidem—M. Furium Flaccum, equitem Romanum, hominem nequam, Capitolini et Mercuriales de
collegio eiecerunt, praesentem, ad pedes unius cuius-
3 que iacentem. Exiturus a. d. viii. Id. Apr. sponsalia
Crassipedi praebui. Huic convivio puer optimus,
Quintus tuus meusque, quod perleviter commotus
fuerat, defuit; a. d. vii. Id. April. veni ad Quintum,
eumque vidi plane integrum, multumque is mecum
sermonem habuit et perhumanum de discordiis
mulierum nostrarum. Quid quaeris ? nihil festivius.
Pomponia autem etiam de te questa est. Sed haec
4 coram agemus. A puero ut discessi, in aream tuam
veni. Res agebatur multis structoribus. Longilium
redemptorem cohortatus sum. Fidem mihi faciebat,
se velle nobis placere. Domus erit egregia. Magis
enim cerni iam poterat, quam quantum ex forma
iudicabamus. Itemque nostra celeriter aedificabatur.
Eo die cenavi apud Crassipedem. Cenatus in hortos
ad Pompeium lectica latus sum. Luci eum convenire
non potueram, quod abfuerat. Videre autem volebam, quod eram postridie Roma exiturus, et quod
ille in Sardiniam iter habebat. Hominem conveni
et ab eo petivi, ut quamprimum te nobis redderet.

---

a A college which had charge of the Capitoline games.
b A corporation of merchants; cf. Livy, ii. 27. 5.

noisy as a public meeting. The discussion of the question was embittered by the scarcity of money and the high price of provisions.

And even this is an incident I shall not omit ; the 2 Capitolini [a] and the Mercuriales [b] expelled from their respective colleges one M. Furius Flaccus, a Roman knight, but a rascal, he being present at the time, prostrating himself at the feet of each member of the college in turn.

On April 6, being about to leave Rome, I gave a 3 betrothal party to Crassipes. At that banquet that excellent boy Quintus (he is mine too) was not present, owing to his having been indisposed, though not at all seriously. On the 7th I went to see him and found him in perfect health, and he and I had a long and very affectionate talk about the squabbles of our women-folk ; to put it shortly, nothing could have been merrier. Pomponia, however, grumbled about you too ; but of this when we meet.

On leaving the boy I visited your building-site. 4 The work was being pressed on with a lot of builders. I urged Longilius the contractor to hasten. He convinced me that he was anxious to give every satis-faction. It will be a magnificent house ; we could now get a clearer idea of it than we could form from studying the plan. My own house, too, was being rapidly built. That day I dined with Crassipes. After dinner I rode in my litter to see Pompey at his pleasaunce. I had not been able to have an interview with him during the day, as he was not at home ; but I wanted to see him, because I am leaving Rome to-morrow, and he has to go to Sardinia. I had a talk with him, and begged of him to let us have you back as soon as possible. He said " without a moment's

5 Statim dixit. Erat autem iturus (ut aiebat) a. d. III.
Id. Apr., ut aut Labrone, aut Pisis conscenderet.
Tu, mi frater, simul ut ille venerit, primam naviga-
tionem (dummodo idonea tempestas sit) ne omiseris.
A. d. III. Id. April. ante lucem hanc epistulam conscripseram, eramque in itinere, ut eo die apud T.
Titium in Anagnino manerem. Postridie autem in
Laterio cogitabam ; inde, cum in Arpinati quinque
dies fuissem, ire in Pompeianum ; rediens aspicere
Cumanum, ut, quoniam in Non. Maias Miloni dies
prodita est, prid. Non. Romae essem, teque, mi carissime et suavissime frater, ad eam diem (ut sperabam)
viderem. Aedificationem Arcani ad tuum adventum
sustentari placebat. Fac, mi frater, ut valeas quam
primumque venias.

VIII *

M. CICERO S. D. Q. FRATRI

Romae, a.u.c. 698.

1 O litteras mihi tuas iucundissimas, exspectatas, ac
primo quidem cum desiderio, nunc vero etiam cum
timore ! Atque has scito litteras me solas accepisse

---

a Labro is unknown, but possibly we should read (as
Tyrrell suggests) Telamo, which, like Pisae, is on the coast of
Etruria.

b Titus Titius, a friend of Cicero's, who addressed to him
Fam. xiii. 75. He had a villa at Anagnia in Latium.

c The property of Quintus in Arpinum.

d Also the property of Quintus, between Arpinum and
Aquinum.

* The numbering of the Letters from this point (VIII.,
IX., etc., instead of VI., VII., etc.) is due to the adoption of
Mommsen's admirable rearrangement of Letters IV.-VII.

506

delay." He intends to start (so he told me) on April [5] 11, so as to take ship at Labro [a] or Pisae. See to it, my dear brother, that as soon as he arrives you do not miss the first opportunity you have of sailing, provided only that the weather be suitable. I am putting together this letter on April 11 before dawn, and am just about to start on my journey, so that I may stay to-day with T. Titius [b] at Anagnia; but to-morrow I intend to be at Laterium,[c] and from there, after spending five days in Arpinum, to visit my Pompeian house, having a peep at my Cuman villa on my return, so that (since Milo's trial has been fixed for May 7) I may be at Rome on the 6th, and see you, my dearest and sweetest of brothers, I hope, on that day. I thought it best that the building operations at Arcanum [d] should be held up until you return. Make a point of keeping well, my dear brother, and of joining me as soon as possible.

VIII *

CICERO TO QUINTUS, ON HIS WAY TO ROME FROM SARDINIA

Rome, middle of May, 56 B.C.

Oh! what an intense pleasure your letter was to [1] me, a letter long awaited, and at first with yearning only, but now with alarm also! And I would have you know that it was the only letter I had received

(sadly muddled together in the MSS.), which makes them coherent and intelligible. The numbering from this point retains the commonly accepted order of the rest of the Letters in this Book.

CICERO

post illas, quas tuus nauta attulit, Olbia datas. Sed
cetera (ut scribis) praesenti sermoni reserventur. Hoc
tamen non queo differre. Id. Maiis senatus frequens
divinus fuit in supplicatione Gabinio deneganda.
Adiurat Procilius hoc nemini accidisse. Foris valde
plauditur. Mihi cum sua sponte iucundum, tum
iucundius, quod me absente (est enim εἰλικρινὲς
iudicium) sine oppugnatione, sine gratia nostra.

2 Eram Anti.[1] Quod Idibus et postridie fuerat dictum,
de agro Campano actum iri, non est actum. In hac
causa mihi aqua haeret. Sed plura quam constitue-
ram. Coram enim. Vale, mi optime et optatissime
frater, et advola. Idem te nostri rogant pueri; illud[2]
scilicet, cenabis, cum veneris.

IX

M. CICERO S. D. Q. FRATRI

Romae, a.u.c. 699.

1 Placiturum tibi esse librum meum suspicabar; tam
valde placuisse, quam scribis, valde gaudeo. Quod
me admones de nostra Urania, suadesque, ut me-

---

[1] *Manutius*: gratia nostra erat. Quod ante *Mommsen*.
[2] pueri. Illud *Purser*.

---

[a] Now Governor of Syria. He had applied for a *supplicatio*
either for his success in Palestine against Aristobulus and
his son Alexander, or some previous victories over Arabs.

[b] A tribune.

[c] Literally "I have run dry," a metaphor from the
damming of a stream, or possibly from the running down of
the water allowance in the *clepsydra* (water-clock), meaning
that Cicero had to stop speaking on so dangerous a subject.

[d] Or, as Purser takes it, "Of course there is this—you
will, etc." (putting a full-stop after "request of you").

[e] His poem *De temporibus suis*.

508

since that which your sailor brought me, posted at Olbia. But, as you write, let everything else be kept back for personal conversation. This much, however, I cannot put off; on May 15 a full Senate acted gloriously in refusing a *supplicatio* to Gabinius.[a] Procilius [b] swears that this has never happened to anyone else. It is loudly applauded in the streets; to me it was not only delightful on its own account, but even more so because it was done in my absence (it was an unprejudiced decision) without any opposition or favour on my part. I was at Antium.

What, it has been alleged, was to be settled 2 on the 15th and the following day in the matter of the Campanian land, was never settled at all. In this business I am at a deadlock.[c] But I have said more than I had intended to say; for we will talk it over when we meet. Good-bye, my best and most desirable of brothers, and wing your way to me. Our two boys make the same request of you; of course it is this [d]—you will dine with us when you arrive.

IX

CICERO TO QUINTUS

Rome, February, 55 B.C.

I had an idea that my book [e] would please you, 1 but that it should have pleased you as greatly as you say in your letter is a great joy to me. As to your reminding me of my Urania,[f] and advising me to

[f] The reference is obscure. Possibly it refers to a passage in Cicero's poem *De consulatu suo*, recommending literature and philosophy as against politics. "*And yet*," he goes on, "in spite of what I then wrote, I went to see Pompey."

minerim Iovis orationem, quae est in extremo illo
libro, ego vero memini, et illa omnia mihi magis
2 scripsi, quam ceteris. Sed tamen postridie, quam tu
es profectus, multa nocte cum Vibullio veni ad Pompeium, cumque ego egissem de istis operibus atque
inscriptionibus, per mihi benigne respondit ; magnam
spem attulit. Cum Crasso se dixit loqui velle ;
mihique, ut idem facerem, suasit. Crassum consulem
ex senatu domum reduxi ; suscepit rem ; dixitque
esse, quod Clodius hoc tempore cuperet per se et per
Pompeium consequi ; putare se, si ego eum non impedirem, posse me adipisci sine contentione, quod
vellem. Totum ei negotium permisi, meque in eius
potestate dixi fore. Interfuit huic sermoni P. Crassus,
adulescens nostri (ut scis) studiosissimus. Illud autem,
quod cupit Clodius, est legatio aliqua—si minus per
senatum, per populum—libera, aut Byzantium aut
ad Brogitarum aut utrumque. Plena res nummorum.
Quod ego non nimium laboro, etiamsi minus assequor,
quod volo. Pompeius tamen cum Crasso locutus est.
Videntur negotium suscepisse. Si perficiunt, optime ;
3 sin minus, ad nostrum Iovem revertamur. A. d. iii.
Id. Febr. senatus consultum est factum de ambitu in
Afrani sententiam, quam ego dixeram, cum tu adesses ;
sed magno cum gemitu Senatus, consules non sunt

---

^a *Libera legatio* was an unofficial embassy, enabling a
senator to travel abroad on his own private affairs at the
expense of the State. *Cf. Fam.* xi. 1. 2.

^b Clodius, as tribune, had restored certain Byzantine
exiles, and he had made Brogitarus, a Galatian and son-in-
law of Deiotarus, priest of Cybele at Pessinus ; and he was
now going to those parts to raise the money for which he
held bonds from the exiles and Brogitarus. Tyrrell.

^c Apparently that the praetors should be elected and enter
upon office at once, and so evade the prosecution which
Cato desired.

510

remember Jupiter's speech at the end of that book,
I do indeed remember it, and I addressed all that to
myself rather than to the rest of the world.

And yet, the day after you started, late at night, 2
taking Vibullius with me, I paid Pompey a visit; and
when I pleaded with him about the works and inscriptions in your honour, he responded with remarkable
kindness, and greatly raised my hopes. He said he
wanted to have a talk with Crassus, and urged me
to do the same. I escorted Crassus as consul from
the Senate to his house ; he took the matter up, and
told me that there was something which Clodius was
anxious to get just now through his own and Pompey's
instrumentality ; and he thought that if I did not
thwart Clodius's scheme, I could secure what I wanted
without a fight. I put the whole business in his hands
and assured him that I would be at his disposal.
Publius Crassus, his young son, was present at this
interview, and he is, as you are aware, devotedly
attached to me. Now what Clodius is so anxious to
get is some honorary embassy,[a] if not by decree of the
Senate, then by popular vote, either to Byzantium
or to Brogitarus,[b] or to both. There is a lot of money
in it. I am not troubling myself unduly about the
matter, even if I fail to get what I want. The fact
remains that Pompey has spoken to Crassus, and it
seems to me that they have taken the matter up.
If they carry it through, nothing could be better ;
if not, let us return to my " Jupiter."

On February 11, a decree of the Senate was passed 3
concerning bribery, on the motion of Afranius,[c]
which I had explained to you when you were here
with me. But, though the Senate groaned aloud at it,
the consuls did not follow up the proposals of those

CICERO

persecuti eorum sententias qui, Afranio cum essent
assensi, addiderunt, ut praetores ita crearentur, ut
dies LX. privati essent. Eo die Catonem plane repudia-
runt. Quid multa? tenent omnia, idque ita omnes
intellegere volunt.

X

MARCUS Q. FRATRI S.

Cumani, A.U.C. 699.

1 Tu metuis, ne me interpelles? Primo, si in isto
essem, tu scis, quid sit interpellare? An te Ateius?
Mehercule mihi docere videbaris istius generis
humanitatem, qua quidem ego nihil utor abs te. Tu
vero, ut me et appelles et interpelles et obloquare et
colloquare, velim. Quid enim mihi suavius? Non
mehercule quisquam μουσοπάτακτος libentius sua recentia poemata legit, quam ego te audio quacumque
de re, publica, privata, rustica, urbana. Sed mea factum est insulsa verecundia, ut te proficiscens non
tollerem. Opposuisti semel ἀναντίλεκτον causam,
Ciceronis nostri valetudinem; conticui: iterum Ci-
2 cerones; quievi. Nunc mihi iucunditatis plena
epistula hoc aspersit molestiae, quod videris, ne mihi

---

[a] This would have suited Cato, since, as private citizens,
they could be proceeded against. But the consuls would have
none of it, and they were, as Cicero adds, " omnipotent."

[b] Or "has Ateius been interrupting you?" Ateius being
some notorious bore.

512

who, when they agreed to Afranius's motion, added a rider that the praetors should only be appointed with the proviso that they should remain private citizens for sixty days.[a] On that day the consuls' repudiation of Cato was uncompromising. Why should I waste words? They have everything in their hands, and they want everybody to know it.

X

CICERO TO QUINTUS

Cumanum, April or May, 55 B.C.

You afraid that you will interrupt *me* ? In the first 1 place, supposing I were as busy as you think, do you know what is meant by the term " *to interrupt* " ? Is Ateius [b] your informant ? Upon my word, it would seem that you are teaching me a form of courtesy peculiarly your own for which I have no use at all— coming as it does from *you*. Why, I should like to have you attract as well as distract my attention, talk *at* me as well as talk *to* me. What could delight me more ? I solemnly aver that no muse-smitten poetaster ever recites his latest effusions with greater pleasure than I listen to you holding forth on any topic, be it public or private, rural or urban. But it was all the fault of my stupid reserve that I did not take you with me when I set out. Once you put me off with an unanswerable excuse—the health of my boy Cicero ; I held my tongue ; the second time it was both the young Ciceros ; I raised no objection.

And now I have a letter as pleasant as could be, 2 with just this touch of annoyance—that you seem to

513

molestus esses, veritus esse atque etiam nunc vereri.
Litigarem tecum, fas si esset ; sed mehercule istuc
si umquam suspicatus ero, nihil dicam aliud, nisi vere-
bor, ne quando ego tibi, cum sum una, molestus sim.
Marium autem nostrum in lecticam mehercule con-
iecissem, non illam regis Ptolemaei Asicianam. Memini enim, cum hominem portarem ad Baias, Neapoli,
octophoro Asiciano, machaerophoris centum sequen-
tibus, miros risus nos edere, cum ille, ignarus sui
comitatus, repente aperuit lecticam, et paene ille
timore, ego risu corrui. Tunc, ut dico, certe sustulis-
sem, ut aliquando subtilitatem veteris urbanitatis
et humanissimi sermonis attingerem. Sed hominem
infirmum in villam apertam, ac ne rudem quidem
3 etiam nunc, invitare nolui. Hoc vero mihi peculiare
fuerit, hic etiam isto frui. Nam illorum praediorum
scito mihi vicinum Marium lumen esse. Apud Ani-
cium videbimus ut paratum sit. Nos enim ita philo-
logi sumus, ut vel cum fabris habitare possimus.
Habemus hanc philosophiam non ab Hymetto, sed ab
arce Ψυρίᾳ.[1] Marius et valetudine est et natura im-
4 becillior. De interpellatione tantum sumam a vobis
temporis ad scribendum, quantum dabitis. Utinam
nihil detis, ut potius vestra iniuria, quam ignavia mea

[1] *Tunstall* : Abdera *or* Gargetto *Dr. Reid* : ab arce *or*
arcula Cyrea *Tyrrell.*

---

[a] For Marius see note *a* on *Fam.* vii. 1. 1.
[b] Asicius seems to have been a close friend of Ptolemy
Auletes, who either gave or sold him his capacious litter
with its regular body-guard of a hundred swordsmen, the
sight of whom frightened the nervous valetudinarian Marius.
[c] Cicero elsewhere (*Att.* xvi. 13*a*. 2) refers to Arpinum as
νῆσος Ψυρίη. Psyria is an island in the Aegean sea mentioned
by Homer (*Od.* iii. 171). He means that he is no effeminate
valetudinarian, but a hardy hillman.

have been, and even now to be, afraid of being an annoyance to me. I should go to law with you, if such a thing were conceivable ; but I swear that if ever I suspect your harbouring such a thought—I'll say no more than this, that at any moment when I am in your company I shall be afraid of being a nuisance to you. As for our friend Marius,[a] I declare I should have bundled him into my litter—not the one that Asicius[b] got from King Ptolemy. For I remember how when I was giving the fellow a lift from Naples to Baiae in Asicius's eight-man litter, with a hundred swordsmen in our train, I can't tell you how I laughed when Marius, all unconscious of his escort, suddenly opened the litter and nearly collapsed with fright, and I with laughter. Well, as I say, I should certainly have picked him up then, so as to get into touch (better late than never) with that subtle charm of old-world courtesy and exquisitely refined conversation. But to invite a man in feeble health to a villa exposed to the weather and, up to the present, not even roughly finished—I simply hadn't the heart.

It would of course be a special treat to me to **3** enjoy his company here also ; for I would have you know that to have him for my neighbour is as the very light of the sun on that country seat of mine. I will see about his being put up at the house of Anicius. As for myself I am the sort of book-worm that can get along with workmen in the house. For that philosophy I have to thank, not Hymettus, but the heights of Arpinum.[c] Marius is somewhat feeble both in health and character.

As for my being interrupted, I shall take from you **4** just so much time for writing as you allow me. I pray that you may allow me none, so that my doing no

cessem! De republica nimium te laborare doleo;
(video te ingemuisse; sic fit εἰ δ᾽ ἐν αἷᾳ ἔζησας; nun-
quam enim dicam ἔα πάσας[1]) et meliorem civem
esse, quam Philoctetam, qui, accepta iniuria, illa
spectacula quaerebat, quae tibi acerba esse video.
Amabo te, advola; consolabor te et omnem ab-
stergebo dolorem; et adduc, si me amas, Marium.
Sed adproperate. Hortus domi est.

XI

M. CICERO S. D. Q. FRATRI

Romae, A.U.C. 700.

1   Epistulam hanc convicio efflagitarunt codicilli tui.
Nam res quidem ipsa et is dies, quo tu es profectus,
nihil mihi ad scribendum argumenti sane dabat. Sed
quemadmodum, coram cum sumus, sermo nobis
deesse non solet, sic epistulae nostrae debent inter-
2 dum alucinari. Tenediorum igitur libertas securi
Tenedia praecisa est, cum eos praeter me et Bibulum
3 et Calidium et Favonium nemo defenderet. De te a

[1] *sc.* μελεδώνας *Lambinus:* τὰς μεληδόνας *Ed. Crat.*

---

[a] The source of this quotation is unknown, but the
meaning seems to be " What would you have done, had
you been on the spot? And indeed there is much to be
anxious about."

[b] No such passage appears in Sophocles' play.

[c] *Codicilli* were tablets made of thin pieces of wood and
covered with wax, used in cases of urgency and haste.

[d] The inhabitants of Tenedos had petitioned the Senate
for some measure of independence, which the Senate refused.

[e] A proverbial expression for summary execution; Tenes,

work may be due to your wrong treatment of me rather than to my own indolence.

As to politics, I grieve that you are distressing yourself unduly (I notice you have groaned; well, there's no getting out of it, " Yet hadst thou but lived in the land "—I shall never add the words, " away with all sorrow and care "),[a] and that you are a better citizen than Philoctetes,[b] who, having suffered wrong, desired to see such sights as, I perceive, are painful to you.

I entreat you, wing your way here : I shall comfort you and wipe all sorrow from your eyes ; and, as you love me, bring Marius with you. But hurry up, both of you. There is a garden attached to my house.

XI

CICERO TO QUINTUS IN SOME SUBURBAN RESIDENCE

Rome, February 10 or 11, 54 B.C.

This letter has been elicited by the strong and im- 1 portunate language of your note.[c] As to the actual business, and what occurred the day you set out, it affords no material at all to write about. But just as when we are together it is not often that we are at a loss for something to talk about, so our letters ought occasionally to ramble at random.

Well, then, the liberty of the Tenedians [d] has been 2 cut short with a Tenedian axe,[e] since there was nobody to defend them except myself, Bibulus, Calidius, and Favonius.

" the fabled eponym " of the island, had established there an ultra-Draconian penal code.

Magnetibus ab Sipylo mentio est honorifica facta,
cum te unum dicerent postulationi L. Sextii Pansae
4 restitisse. Reliquis diebus, si quid erit, quod te scire
opus sit, aut etiamsi nihil erit, tamen scribam quotidie
aliquid. Prid. Id. neque tibi, neque Pomponio deero.
5 Lucreti poemata, ut scribis, ita sunt,—multis luminibus ingeni, multae tamen artis.[1] Sed cum veneris . . .
Virum te putabo, si Sallusti *Empedoclea* legeris, hominem non putabo. Vale.

XII

MARCUS Q. FRATRI S.

Romae, a.u.c. 700.

1 Gaudeo tibi iucundas esse meas litteras, nec tamen
habuissem scribendi nunc quidem ullum argumentum, nisi tuas accepissem. Nam prid. Id., cum Ap-

---

[1] *M*: multae etiam *Orelli*: multae tamen artis cum
inveneris virum te putabo; si Sallusti *etc. H. A. J. Munro*:
non multae tamen artis. Sed si ad umbilicum veneris, virum
te putabo. Si Sallusti *etc. Bergk*.

---

[a] Probably a *publicanus* against whose demands an appeal
had been made by the Magnesians of Lydia (*ab Sipylo*).
[b] Lucretius's *De Rerum Natura* had just been published,
a few months after the poet's death. That the text (that of
M) of this solitary and casual allusion by Cicero to Lucretius
is probably corrupt would appear from the use of *poemata*
for the singular, and the sudden change from the abl.
luminibus to the gen. *artis.*
The text as it stands probably means that Lucretius shows
the *genius* of the old school (*e.g.* Ennius, "ingenio maximus,
arte rudis," and Attius), surprisingly combined (*tamen*)
with much of the *ars*, the more polished craftsmanship, of the
New, or Alexandrine, School (*e.g.* Catullus). But is there
much of such *ars* in the *De Rerum Natura*?

The Magnesians from Sipylus made a compli- 3
mentary reference to you, to the effect that you were
the only man to stand up against the demand of L.
Sextius Pansa.[a] During the days that remain, if any- 4
thing occurs which it is necessary for you to know, or
even if nothing occurs, I shall nevertheless write something to you every day. On February 12, I shall not
fail either you or Pomponius.

The poems of Lucretius are just as you write— 5
with frequent flashes of genius, and yet exceedingly
artistic.[b] But when you come . . . .[c] If you get
through Sallust's *Empedoclea*, I shall think you a fine
fellow, but no ordinary mortal.

XII

CICERO TO QUINTUS IN THE COUNTRY

Rome, February 13, 54 B.C.

I am delighted that you were pleased with my 1
letter ; and yet I should not have had any material
for a letter even then, had I not received yours. For,

Munro suggests another reading, which may be rendered
"as for any great artistry, however, if you discover the
poems to possess it, I shall think you a hero"; and Bergk
yet another, meaning "They do *not*, however, show much
artistry. But if you read them to the last page, I shall
think you a hero." (See critical note.)
It is after all possible that the *ars* in our text may not
mean "artistic finish" at all, but simply "the scientific
treatment of a subject"—here *ars physica* (natural science),
as we have *ars metrica, grammatica, rhetorica*. In that case
the passage would mean "The poems contain 'purple patches'
of genius in plenty, but for all that they are extremely
technical,"—which is no unfair description of the *De Rerum
Natura*.
[c] Supply some such words as " we can discuss the matter."

519

pius senatum infrequentem coegisset, tantum fuit
2 frigus, ut pipulo[1] coactus sit nos dimittere. De Commageno, quod rem totam discusseram, mirifice mihî
et per se et per Pomponium blanditur Appius. Videt
enim, hoc genere dicendi si utar in ceteris, Februa-
rium sterilem futurum ; eumque lusi iocose satis,
neque solum illud extorsi oppidulum, quod erat
positum in Euphrati Zeugmate, sed praeterea togam
sum eius praetextam, quam erat adeptus Caesare
3 consule, magno hominum risu cavillatus. " Quod nos
vult," inquam, " renovare honores eosdem, quo minus
togam praetextam quotannis interpolet, decernendum nihil censeo. Vos autem homines nobiles, qui
Bostrenum praetextatum non ferebatis, Commagenum feretis ? " Genus vides et locum iocandi. Multa
dixi in ignobilem regem ; quibus totus est explosus.
Quo genere commotus (ut dixi) Appius totum me
amplexatur. Nihil est enim facilius, quam reliqua
discutere. Sed non faciam, ut illum offendam, ne

---

[1] *An emendation (for* populi convicio MSS.) *adopted by
Prof. Housman, who rejects* convicio *as a gloss on* pipulo.
Tyrrell reads pipulo, convicio *asyndetically.*

---

[a] Lit. " chirping of chickens," then used of demonstrations
of restlessness at public meetings.
[b] Antiochus, King of Commagene in Syria. He had
received the little kingdom from Pompey at the end of the
Mithridatic war.
[c] Which Antiochus had impudently claimed.
[d] Cicero's meaning is somewhat obscure, but, assuming
the text to be right, it seems to be this : " As far as I am
concerned, Antiochus is at liberty to have a clean *toga prae-*

on the 12th, after Appius had got together a sparsely attended Senate, the proceedings were so frosty, that he was forced by our whimperings [a] to dismiss us.

As to the Commagenian,[b] because I had exploded 2 the whole affair, it is amazing how Appius fawns upon me, both personally and through Pomponius ; for he sees that if I adopt the same style of speaking in all the other cases, February will be a barren month for him. And I made fun of Antiochus in quite a merry way, and not only made him take his hands off that tiny town situated in the territory of Zeugma on the Euphrates,[c] but I moreover excited much general laughter by jeering at the fellow's *toga praetexta* which he had obtained in the consulship of Caesar. "As to his wishing us (I said) to renew those same 3 honours, it is my opinion that no decree at all is needed to forbid his furbishing up his *toga praetexta* every year. But will you, my noble friends, who did not tolerate the wearing of the *toga praetexta* by the Bostran, tolerate it in the case of this Commagenian ? "[d] You see the style I adopted, and the opportunity I had for a bit of fun. I spoke a lot in condemnation of his scurvy majesty, with the result that he was hissed off the stage neck-and-crop. But that same style of mine greatly agitated Appius, and he embraces me like a mother. The rest of his proposals it is the easiest thing in the world to scatter to the winds. But I am not going so far as to offend him, for fear he implores the protection of Jupiter

texta as often as he pleases, but as for his wearing it in public you will not allow him to do so any more than you allowed the Bostran to do so." Bostra (the Bozrah of Isaiah) was in Arabia Petraea. The reference is to some unknown tetrarch of that district.

imploret fidem Iovis Hospitalis, Graios omnes con-
4 vocet, per quos mecum in gratiam rediit. Theopompo satisfaciemus. De Caesare fugerat me ad te
scribere. Video enim, quas tu litteras exspectaris.
Sed ille scripsit ad Balbum, fasciculum illum epistularum, in quo fuerat et mea et Balbi, totum sibi aqua
madidum redditum esse, ut ne illud quidem sciat,
meam fuisse aliquam epistulam. Sed ex Balbi epi-
stola pauca verba intellexerat, ad quae rescripsit his
verbis : " De Cicerone video te quiddam scripsisse,
quod ego non intellexi ; quantum autem coniectura
consequebar, id erat eiusmodi, ut magis optandum,
5 quam sperandum putarem." Itaque postea misi ad
Caesarem eodem illo exemplo litteras. Iocum autem
illius de sua egestate ne sis aspernatus. Ad quem ego
rescripsi, nihil esse, quod posthac arcae nostrae fiducia
conturbaret ; lusique in eo genere et familiariter et
cum dignitate. Amor autem eius erga nos perfertur
omnium nuntiis singularis. Litterae quidem ad id,
quod exspectas, fere cum tuo reditu iungentur ;
reliqua singulorum dierum scribemus ad te, si modo
tabellarios tu praebebis. Quamquam eiusmodi frigus
impendebat, ut summum periculum esset, ne Appio
suae aedes urerentur.

---

[a] *i.e.*, Ζεὺς Ξένιος. We can only conjecture that certain
Greeks helped to effect a reconciliation between Cicero and
Appius.

[b] *i.e.*, Quintus. What Caesar gathered from Balbus's
letter was probably that Quintus was prepared to desert
Pompey and come over to him. Caesar thought the news
was " too good to be true."

[c] This sentence may be paraphrased thus : " And yet
(there will be little to tell you because) Appius's proposals
are so *coldly* received that there may be a *hot* reaction
against him "—a pretty instance of παρὰ προσδοκίαν.

Hospitalis,[a] and rouses a rally of all the Greeks, for it was through them that we became reconciled.

I shall satisfy Theopompus. I forgot to write to 4 you about Caesar; for I see what sort of a letter you have been expecting. But he wrote to Balbus and told him that the whole packet of letters, in which were mine and Balbus's, was so soaked with water when he received it that he did not even know there was any letter from me. He had, however, made out a few words in Balbus's letter, to which he replied in the following words : " I see that you have written something about Cicero,[b] which I could not understand, but as far as I could conjecture, it was the sort of thing that I thought more to be desired than hoped for." So later on I sent Caesar an exact duplicate of 5 my letter.

You must not be put off with that little joke of Caesar's about his lack of means. My reply to it was that there was no reason why he should in future make a mess of his affairs by relying on my money-chest; and I kept up the joke with him in that sort of way, familiarly but without loss of dignity. His devotion to us, however, as reported by messages from all sides, is quite extraordinary. The letter bearing upon what you are waiting for will practically coincide with your return. Anything more that happens day by day I will let you know by letter, provided only that you furnish me with letter-carriers. And yet the political barometer is so near freezing-point that Appius is in extreme danger of having his house burnt about his ears.[c]

Tyrrell takes *suae aedes urerentur* as meaning " his house may be *frost-bitten*," *i.e.*, utterly deserted by *salutatores*, etc.

CICERO

XIII

M. CICERO S. D. Q. FRATRI

Romae, A.U.C. 700.

1 Risi "nivem atram," teque hilari animo esse et
prompto ad iocandum valde me iuvat. De Pompeio
assentior tibi, vel tu potius mihi. Nam, ut scis,
iampridem istum canto Caesarem. Mihi crede, in
2 sinu est, neque ego discingor. Cognosce nunc Idus.
Decimus erat Caelio dies. Domitius ad numerum
iudices non habuit. Vereor, ne homo teter et ferus,
Pola Servius, ad accusationem veniat. Nam noster
Caelius valde oppugnatur a gente Clodia. Certi nihil
est adhuc ; sed veremur. Eodem igitur die Syriis[1]
est senatus datus frequens ; frequentes contra Syriaci
publicani. Vehementer vexatus Gabinius ; exagitati
tamen a Domitio publicani, quod eum essent cum
equis prosecuti. L. noster Lamia paullo ferocius,
cum Domitius dixisset, Vestra culpa haec acciderunt,
equites Romani ; dissolute enim iudicatis, Nos iudi-
camus, vos laudatis, inquit. Actum est eo die nihil ;

[1] *M²*: Tyriis MSS.

---

[a] The tenth day after his arraignment, ten days having,
according to custom, to intervene between the arraignment
and the trial of a person accused, here M. Caelius Rufus,
Cicero's correspondent. This trial is referred to in *Fam.* viii.
12. 2.

[b] L. Domitius Ahenobarbus, the consul for the year (54).

[c] A sort of professional prosecutor. *Cf. Fam.* viii. 12. 2.

[d] Governor, as proconsul, of Syria ; but he had quitted
his province in order to restore Ptolemy Auletes to the
throne of Egypt, with the result that Syria was harassed
by pirates.

XIII

Rome, February 14, 54 B.C.

Your " black snow " tickled me, and I am highly 1
delighted that you are in a merry mood which
prompts you to joke. As to Pompey, I quite agree
with you, or rather you agree with me. For, as you
are aware, I have long been singing the praises of
your friend Caesar. Believe me, he is my bosom
friend, and I never try to unbind " the hoops of
steel."

Now let me tell you about the Ides. It was 2
Caelius's tenth day.ᵃ Domitiusᵇ failed to get the
requisite number of jurors. I am afraid that abomin-
able and ruffianly fellow, Pola Servius,ᶜ will turn up
for the prosecution. For our friend Caelius is being
bitterly attacked by the Clodian family. There is
nothing certain so far; but I am apprehensive. On the
same day then the Syrians were granted a full Senate;
on the other side the *publicani* of Syria appeared in full
force. Gabiniusᵈ was fiercely abused; but the *publicani*
on the other hand were denounced by Domitius for
having (as he said) honoured Gabinius with an escort
of cavalry. When Domitius said: " It is all your
fault, Knights of Rome, that this happened, since
your verdicts are lax," our friend L. Lamia ᵉ rather
too impetuously rejoined: " Yes, they are our verdicts, but it is you senators who vouch for a man's
character." On that day nothing was done, and
night broke off the discussion.

ᵉ An *eques* who had befriended Cicero during his exile.
Cf. Fam. xi. 16. 2 and xii. 29. 1.

CICERO

3 nox diremit. Comitialibus diebus, qui Quirinalia se-
quuntur, Appius interpretatur, non impediri se lege
Pupia, quo minus habeat senatum, et quod Gabinia
sanctum sit, etiam cogi, ex Kal. Febr. usque ad Kal.
Mart. legatis senatum quotidie dare. Ita putantur
detrudi comitia in mensem Martium. Sed tamen his
comitialibus tribuni plebis de Gabinio se acturos esse
dicunt. Omnia colligo, ut novi scribam aliquid ad te.
4 Sed, ut vides, res me ipsa deficit. Itaque ad Calli-
sthenem et ad Philistum redeo, in quibus te video vo-
lutatum. Callisthenes quidem vulgare et notum negotium, quemadmodum Graeci aliquot locuti sunt.
Siculus ille capitalis, creber, acutus, brevis, paene
pusillus Thucydides, sed utros eius habueris libros
(duo enim sunt corpora), an utrosque, nescio. Me
magis de Dionysio delectat. Ipse est enim veterator
magnus, et perfamiliaris Philisto Dionysius. Sed quod
ascribis, aggrederisne ad historiam ? me auctore
potes. Et, quoniam tabellarios subministras, hodierni
diei res gestas Lupercalibus habebis. Oblecta te
cum Cicerone nostro quam bellissime.

---

a For this and the Gabinian law see note *c* on *Fam.* i. 4. 1.

b *i.e.,* the legality of Gabinius's restoration of Ptolemy
Auletes.

c A native of Olynthus, who wrote a history of the Phocian
War, and the campaigns of Alexander the Great, whom he
accompanied to Asia. *Cf. Fam.* v. 12. 2. Callisthenes lived
387–327 B.C.

d A Syracusan, born about 435 B.C., a great favourite of
Dionysius the elder.

Appius takes the view that he is not prevented 3 by the Pupian law [a] from holding a Senate on the comitial days which follow the Quirinalia, and that by the provisions of the Gabinian law he is even compelled to grant a Senate to the emissaries every day from February 1 to March 1. So it is thought that the elections are being postponed till the month of March. For all that the tribunes of the plebs declare that they will settle the affair of Gabinius [b] in the course of these comitial days. I am collecting every scrap of news so that I may have something fresh to tell you. But, as you see, it is just material that fails me.

So I return to Callisthenes [c] and Philistus,[d] in both 4 of whom I see you have been wallowing. Callisthenes is a hackneyed and commonplace piece of goods, as several Greeks have remarked. The Sicilian is a first-class writer, pithy, pointed, and concise, almost a pocket-edition of Thucydides; but which of his books you have had in your hands (for there are two compilations), or whether you have had both, I don't know. The one on Dionysius gives me most pleasure; for Dionysius is a big rogue, and Philistus knows him thoroughly. But about your postscript—do you really intend taking up history? If I may say so, you have the ability. And now that you are supplying me with letter-carriers, you will hear to-day's achievements on the Lupercalia. Amuse yourself with our dear Cicero as agreeably as you can.

XIV

Cumis aut Pompeiis, A.U.C. 700.

1 Duas adhuc a te accepi epistulas; earum alteram in
ipso discessu nostro, alteram Arimino datam. Plures,
quas scribis te dedisse, non acceperam. Ego me in
Cumano et Pompeiano, praeterquam quod sine te,
ceterum satis commode oblectabam; et eram in iisdem locis usque ad Kal. Iun. futurus. Scribebam illa,
quae dixeram, πολιτικά; spissum sane opus et
operosum; sed si ex sententia successerit, bene erit
opera posita; sin minus, in illud ipsum mare deicie-
mus, quod spectantes scribimus. Aggrediemur alia,
2 quoniam quiescere non possumus. Tua mandata per-
sequar diligenter et adiungendis hominibus et quibusdam non alienandis. Maximae mihi vero curae
erit, ut Ciceronem tuum nostrumque videam, si licet[1],
quotidie; sed inspiciam, quid discat, quam saepissime; et, nisi ille contemnet, etiam magistrum me ei
profitebor; cuius rei nonnullam consuetudinem nactus sum in hoc horum dierum otio, Cicerone nostro
3 minore producendo.[2] Tu, quemadmodum scribis, quod
etiamsi non scriberes, facere te diligentissime tamen
sciebam, facies scilicet, ut mea mandata digeras,

---

[1] *Tyrrell*: scilicet *edd., which Purser thinks is right,*
"*of course*; *but (more than that I shall, etc.).*"
[2] *Boot*: perdocendo *Nobbe.*

528

XIV

CICERO TO QUINTUS IN GAUL

Cumae or Pompeii, middle of May, 54 B.C.

I have so far received two letters from you, one 1
of them at the very moment of my departure, the
other posted at Ariminum; the additional letters you
write that you have sent me I have not received. I am
enjoying myself quite comfortably, except that you
are not with me, at my Cuman and Pompeian resid-
ences, and I intend being in these same spots till
June 1. I am engaged upon the treatise I told you
about, on the *Republic*—a very stiff and toilsome
piece of work; but if it succeeds to my satisfaction,
the labour will have been well laid out; if not, I
shall hurl it down into that very sea I am gazing upon
as I write. I shall apply myself to something else,
since inactivity is more than I can stand.

I shall carry out your instructions to the letter, 2
both as regards conciliating certain people, and not
estranging certain others. My chief anxiety, however, will be to see your Cicero (he belongs to both
of us), if I may, every day, but I shall test his progress
as often as possible, and, unless he disdains me, I shall
even offer him my services as a teacher—a capacity
in which I have acquired some amount of experience
during these days of leisure in bringing on my own,
I mean the younger, Cicero.

You will, of course, do as you write you will (and 3
even if you did not put it down on paper, I am none
the less assured that you are most conscientious in
doing so), I mean that you will arrange, follow out,

persequare, conficias. Ego, cum Romam venero,
nullum praetermittam Caesaris tabellarium, cui
litteras ad te non dem. His diebus (ignosces) cui darem, fuit nemo ante hunc M. Orfium, equitem Romanum, nostrum et pernecessarium, et quod est ex municipio Atellano, quod scis esse in fide nostra. Itaque eum tibi commendo in maiorem modum, hominem domi splendidum, gratiosum etiam extra domum ; quem fac ut tua liberalitate tibi obliges. Est
tribunus militum in exercitu nostro. Gratum hominem observantemque cognosces. Trebatium ut valde
ames, vehementer te rogo.

XVA

M. CICERO S. D. Q. FRATRI

Romae, A.U.C. 700.

1 A. d. IV. Non. Iun., quo die Romam veni, accepi
tuas litteras, datas Placentiae : deinde alteras postridie, datas Blandenone, cum Caesaris litteris, re-
fertis omni officio, diligentia, suavitate. Sunt ista
quidem magna, vel potius maxima. Habent enim
vim magnam ad gloriam et ad summam dignitatem.

---

a See *Fam.* xiii. 7. 1.

b C. Trebatius Testa, Cicero's lawyer friend, to whom
he wrote *Fam.* vii. 6-22, who was now serving with Quintus,
under Caesar, in Gaul.

c A town near Placentia in Cisalpine Gaul.

and execute my instructions. For myself, when I arrive in Rome, I shall allow no letter-carrier of Caesar's to pass by without giving him a letter for you. During these last days (pray forgive me) there has been no one to whom I might entrust a letter, until the present bearer turned up—M. Orfius, a knight of Rome, one who is my friend, not only on account of his very close connexion with me, but also because he comes from the municipality of Atella, which, as you are aware, is under my patronage.[a] I accordingly commend him to you with more than ordinary warmth as a man of exalted position in his own town, and popular outside it too. Pray make a point of laying him under an obligation to you by treating him handsomely. He is a military tribune in your army. You will find him a grateful fellow, who will show you every attention. I earnestly beg of you to be a good friend to Trebatius.[b]

XVa

CICERO TO QUINTUS IN GAUL

Rome, early in June, 54 b.c.

I received your letter posted at Placentia on June 1 2, the day I arrived in Rome ; then, on the following day, I got another posted at Blandeno,[c] together with a letter from Caesar, brimming over with every sort of kindness, assiduous attention, and charm. These expressions of goodwill on his part are significant or rather *most* significant ; for they have a powerful influence in the direction of our honour and glory and exaltation in the State. But believe me (you know

Sed mihi crede, quem nosti, quod in istis rebus ego
plurimi aestimo, id iam habeo, te scilicet primum tam
inservientem communi dignitati ; deinde Caesaris
tantum in me amorem, quem omnibus his honoribus,
quos me a se exspectare vult, antepono. Litterae
vero eius una datae cum tuis (quarum initium est,
quam suavis ei tuus adventus fuerit, et recordatio
veteris amoris, deinde, se effecturum, ut ego in medio
dolore ac desiderio tui te, cum a me abesses, potissimum secum esse laetarer) incredibiliter delectarunt.
2 Quare facis tu quidem fraterne, quod me hortaris,
sed mehercule currentem nunc quidem, ut omnia mea
studia in istum unum conferam. Ego vero ardenti
quidem studio hoc fortasse efficiam, quod saepe viato-
ribus, cum properant, evenit, ut, si serius, quam
voluerunt, forte surrexerint, properando etiam citius,
quam si de multa nocte vigilassent, perveniant, quo
velint, sic ego, quoniam in isto homine colendo tam
indormivi diu, te mehercule saepe excitante, cursu
corrigam tarditatem, tum equis, tum vero (quoniam
scribis poema ab eo nostrum probari) quadrigis poe-
ticis. Modo mihi date Britanniam, quam pingam co-
loribus tuis penicillo meo. Sed quid ago ? quod mihi

---

a Probably one addressed to Caesar on his expedition to
Britain.

me by this time) when I say that I already possess what I value most of all in the whole situation—I mean, first of all, your own efficient service in support of our common position, and, secondly, Caesar's extraordinary affection for me, which I set above all those honours he wishes me to anticipate at his hands. In fact, his letter, delivered simultaneously with yours (which begins with his saying how delighted he was with your arrival and the renewal of the memory of your old affection, and he goes on to say that he will so manage matters that in the midst of my sorrow and yearning for you, I should be cheered by your being, though away from me, in *his* company more than any other), that letter, I say, gave me more pleasure than you could possibly believe.

You are therefore acting, indeed, like a brother in 2 urging me (though at the present moment, upon my honour, you are but spurring a willing horse) to concentrate all my energies upon him alone. Yes, verily, so hot is my zeal that I shall perhaps succeed in doing what often occurs in the case of travellers, when they are in a hurry—I mean that, if they happen to get up later than they intended, by making extra haste they arrive at their destination even sooner than if they had woke up at dead of night; so I, since I have been asleep so long over the matter of paying court to your friend (though you, heaven knows, repeatedly tried to rouse me), shall make up for my slowness by galloping, not only on a relay of horses, but also (since you write that my poem *a* meets with his approval) by driving a four-horsed chariot of poesy. Only you people must give me Britain for a subject, so that I may paint it in your colours, but with my own brush. But what am I about? What

CICERO

tempus, Romae praesertim, ut iste me rogat, manenti,
vacuum ostenditur ? Sed videro. Fortasse enim (ut
3 fit) vincet tuus amor omnes difficultates. Trebatium
quod ad se miserim, persalse et humaniter etiam
gratias mihi agit. Negat enim, in tanta multitudine
eorum, qui una essent, quemquam fuisse, qui vadi-
monium concipere posset. M. Curtio tribunatum ab
eo petivi (nam Domitius se derideri putasset, si esset
a me rogatus ; hoc enim est eius quotidianum, se ne
tribunum militum quidem facere ; etiam in senatu
lusit Appium collegam, propterea isse ad Caesarem,
ut aliquem tribunatum auferret), sed in alterum
4 annum. Id et Curtius ita volebat. Tu, quemadmodum me censes oportere esse in republica et in
nostris inimicitiis, ita et esse et fore auricula infima
5 scito molliorem. Res Romanae se sic habebant. Erat
nonnulla spes comitiorum, sed incerta ; erat aliqua
suspicio dictaturae, ne ea quidem certa ; summum
otium forense, sed senescentis magis civitatis, quam
acquiescentis. Sententia autem nostra in senatu
eiusmodi, magis ut alii nobis assentiantur, quam nos-
metipsi.

Τοιαῦθ᾽ ὁ τλήμων πόλεμος ἐξεργάζεται.

---

^a M. Curtius Postumus ; Cicero calls himself his *patronus*
in *Att.* ix. 6. 2.

^b Ahenobarbus, consul with Appius Claudius Pulcher
for 54.

^c Possibly borrowed from Catullus (*mollior imula oricilla*,
25. 2), but as Cicero never once mentions Catullus (*cf.* 9. 2
above), it may only be, as Tyrrell suggests, an ordinary

prospect have I of a moment's leisure, especially if I stay, as he asks me to, in Rome ? But I shall bear it in mind. Very likely, as usual, my love for you will surmount all difficulties.

For having sent him Trebatius he expresses his 3 gratitude to me very wittily and courteously too. He declares that in all that crowd who were on his staff there was not a single man who could draw up so much as a form of recognizance. I applied to him for a tribuneship for M. Curtius [a] (as for Domitius,[b] he would have suspected me of making fun of him had I asked him for it ; indeed his daily joke is that he has not even the appointment of a military tribune ; even in the Senate he twitted his colleague Appius with having gone to Caesar for the sole purpose of getting a tribuneship out of him), but for next year ; and that is just what Curtius wanted.

As to what you think my behaviour should be in 4 politics and in dealing with my enemies, I would have you know that I am, and always will be, " softer than the lobe of your ear." [c]

The position of affairs in Rome is as follows : there 5 is some hope of the elections being held, but it is a vague one ; there is also some suspicion of a dictatorship, but even that has no certain foundation ; the forum is profoundly tranquil, but that indicates senile decay, rather than acquiescence, on the part of the State, while the opinions I express in the Senate are such that others agree with them more than I do myself. " *Such is the havoc wrought by wretched war.*" [d]

proverb. For *oricilla = auricilla* *cf. plostrum = plaustrum. Polla = Paulla* and *Clodius = Claudius.*
  [d] Eur. *Suppl.* 119.

XVᴮ

Romae, a.u.c. 700.

1 Calamo bono et atramento temperato, charta etiam
dentata res agetur.ᵃ Scribis enim, te meas litteras
superiores vix legere potuisse ; in quo nihil eorum,
mi frater, fuit, quae putas. Neque enim occupatus
eram, neque perturbatus nec iratus alicui ; sed hoc
facio semper, ut, quicumque calamus in manus meas
2 venerit, eo sic utar, tamquam bono. Verum attende
nunc, mi optime et suavissime frater, ad ea dum re-
scribo, quae tu in hac eadem brevi epistula πραγμα-
τικῶς valde scripsisti. De quo petis, ut ad te, nihil
occultans, nihil dissimulans, nihil tibi indulgens, ger-
mane fraterneque rescribam, id est, utrum advoles,
ut dixerimus, an ad expediendum te, si causa sit,
commorere—si, mi Quinte, parva aliqua res esset, in
qua sciscitarere, quid vellem, tamen, cum tibi per-
missurus essem, ut faceres, quod velles, ego ipse, quid
vellem, ostenderem. In hac vero re hoc profecto
quaeris, cuiusmodi illum annum, qui sequitur, exspectem ; plane aut tranquillum nobis, aut certe
munitissimum ; quod quotidie domus, quod forum,

ᵃ Polished or smoothed with the *dens* (tusk) of the
elephant.

536

XVʙ

CICERO TO QUINTUS IN GAUL

Rome, July 27, 54 ʙ.ᴄ.

For this letter I shall use a good pen, well-mixed 1
ink, and ivory-polished *ᵃ* paper too. For you write
that you could hardly read my last, but for that
there were none of those reasons which you suspect,
my dear brother. I was not busy, nor upset, nor
angry with someone, but it is always my practice to
use whatever pen I find in my hand as if it were a
good one.

But now, my best and dearest of brothers, let me 2
have your attention while I reply to what you have
written in such a very business-like manner in this
short letter I have before me. As to the matter about
which you beg of me to write back to you, concealing
nothing, withholding nothing, not sparing your feelings, but frankly, and as a brother should—I mean
whether you are to wing your way home as we had
arranged, or to stay on to clear yourself of liabilities,
if there be any reason to do so—well, my dear
Quintus, if the matter in regard to which you in-
quired what I wished were a small one, yet, though
I should have allowed you to do what you wished, I
should have shown you what I myself wished. In this
matter, however, the real meaning of your inquiry is
—what sort of a year do I expect next year to be ?
I expect it to be either an entirely tranquil one for us
or, at any rate, an impregnable one in respect of my
position ; and this is clearly proved every day at my
house, in the forum, and by manifestations of feeling

537

quod theatri significationes declarant, nec laboramus
mea conscientia copiarum nostrarum, quod Caesaris,
quod Pompei gratiam tenemus. Haec me, ut con-
fidam, faciunt. Sin aliquis erumpet amentis hominis
furor, omnia sunt ad eum frangendum expedita.
3 Haec ita sentio, iudico, ad te explorate scribo. Dubitare te, non assentatorie, sed fraterne veto. Quare
suavitatis equidem nostrae fruendae causa cuperem
te ad id tempus venire, quod dixeras ; sed illud malo
tamen, quod putas magis e re tua ; nam illa etiam
magni aestimo—ἀμφιλαφίαν illam tuam, et explica-
tionem debitorum tuorum. Illud quidem sic habeto,
nihil nobis expeditis, si valebimus, fore fortunatius.
Parva sunt, quae desunt, pro nostris quidem moribus,
et ea sunt ad explicandum expeditissima, modo valea-
4 mus. Ambitus redit immanis. Numquam fuit par.
Idib. Quint. fenus fuit bessibus ex triente, coitione
Memmi et consulum cum Domitio ; hanc Scaurus
utinam vinceret ! Messalla flaccet. Non dico
ὑπερβολικῶς ; vel HS centies constituunt in praero-

---

in the theatre ; and I am in no anxiety, conscious as I am of my resources, seeing that I retain the favour of Caesar and that of Pompey. This gives me confidence. If, on the other hand, there is any outburst of frenzy on the part of our demented friend,[a] all preparations have been made to crush him.

These are my sentiments and my considered 3 opinions, and I send them to you with full assurance. I forbid you to have any doubt about it, not because I would tickle your ears, but because I am your brother. I should therefore desire you for my part to come at the time you mentioned, so that we may enjoy the pleasure of each other's society ; on the other hand, I prefer that other course even more— the course you consider more to your interest ; for I attach much importance to those other things also— the *" opulence "* [b] you talk about, and getting rid of your liabilities. You may take my word for it that, once we are free of debt, if only we keep well, we shall be better off than anybody in the world. Our wants are trifling, considering the way we live, and those wants we are perfectly free to get rid of, if only we keep our health.

There is a horrible recrudescence of bribery and 4 corruption. Never has there been anything equal to it. On July 15, interest rose from 4 to 8 per cent, in consequence of the coalition arranged by Memmius and the consuls with Domitius : [c] would that Scaurus could defeat it. Messalla has no backbone. I am not indulging in exaggerations ; they are contracting to distribute as much as 10,000 *sestertia* [d] among the

gained nothing thereby ; while Domitius Calvinus and the " flabby " Messalla were elected consuls for 53.

[d] About £88,000.

gativa pronuntiare. Res ardet invidia. Tribunicii
candidati compromiserunt, HS quingenis in singulos
apud M. Catonem depositis, petere eius arbitratu,
ut, qui contra fecisset, ab eo condemnaretur. Quae
quidem comitia gratuita si fuerint, ut putantur, plus
unus Cato fuerit, quam omnes leges omnesque iudices.

XVI

M. CICERO S. D. Q. FRATRI

Romae, A.U.C. 700.

1 Cum a me litteras librari manu acceperis, ne
paullum quidem oti me habuisse iudicato, cum autem
mea, paullum. Sic enim habeto, numquam me a
causis et iudiciis districtiorem fuisse, atque id anni
tempore gravissimo et caloribus maximis. Sed haec
(quoniam tu ita praescribis) ferenda sunt; neque com-
mittendum, ut aut spei aut cogitationi vestrae ego
videar defuisse; praesertim cum, tametsi id difficilius
fuerit, tamen ex hoc labore magnam gratiam magnamque dignitatem sim collecturus. Itaque, ut tibi
placet, damus operam, ne cuius animum offendamus,
atque ut etiam ab his ipsis, qui nos cum Caesare tam
coniunctos dolent, diligamur, ab aequis vero, aut
etiam a propensis in hanc partem, vehementer et

---

a The century voting first at the *comitia centuriata* was
called *centuria praerogativa*, and its vote would have a
great moral effect on the voting of the other centuries.

b More than £4000 each.

c This was a great compliment to Cato's integrity. He
was now praetor.

first century.*a* The business is a blaze of scandal. The candidates for the tribuneship, having agreed to abide by arbitration, have deposited 500 *sestertia* *b* apiece in the hands of M. Cato *c*—they to canvass according to his instructions, and any of them failing to do so to be condemned by him. And if that election proves free from all corruption, as it is supposed it will, Cato will have proved himself more powerful than all the laws and jurors put together.

XVI

CICERO TO QUINTUS IN GAUL

Rome, end of August, 54 B.C.

When you receive a letter from me in my secre- 1 tary's hand, you may be sure that I have not had even a moment's leisure ; if in my own, that I have had just a little. For you may take it from me that I have never been more distracted by cases and trials, and that in the most unhealthy season of the year, and when the heat is most oppressive. But, since it is you who so instruct me, I must put up with it all, and never make the mistake of seeming to have disappointed either the expectations or the ideas you and Caesar have of me, especially since, however difficult it may have proved, it is nevertheless likely that the result of my effort will be no little gain in popularity and prestige. And so, as you would have me do, I shall take every care not to hurt anyone's feelings, but to win the esteem of even those who resent my having become so closely attached to Caesar, and the sincere respect and affection of those who are impartial, or even inclined to our side.

541

2 colamur et amemur. De ambitu cum atrocissime
agereretur in senatu multos dies, quod ita erant pro-
gressi candidati consulares, ut non esset ferendum,
in senatu non fui. Statui ad nullam medicinam rei-
3 publicae sine magno praesidio accedere. Quo die
haec scripsi, Drusus erat de praevaricatione a tribunis
aerariis absolutus, in summa, quattuor sententiis,
cum senatores et equites damnassent. Ego eodem
die post meridiem Vatinium eram defensurus. Ea
res facilis est. Comitia in mensem Sept. reiecta sunt.
Scauri iudicium statim exercebitur, cui nos non
deerimus. Συνδείπνους Σοφοκλέους, quamquam a te
actam fabellam video esse festive, nullo modo probavi.
4 Venio nunc ad id, quod nescio an primum esse debuerit. O iucundas mihi tuas de Britannia litteras!
Timebam Oceanum, timebam litus insulae. Reliqua non equidem contemno, sed plus habent tamen
spei, quam timoris, magisque sum sollicitus exspectatione ea, quam metu. Te vero ὑπόθεσιν scribendi
egregiam habere video. Quos tu situs, quas naturas
rerum et locorum, quos mores, quas gentes, quas pug-
nas, quem vero ipsum imperatorem habes! Ego te
libenter, ut rogas, quibus rebus vis, adiuvabo et tibi

ᵃ See the preceding letter.
ᵇ Probably Livius Drusus Claudianus, father of Livia,
mother of the emperor Tiberius.
ᶜ *Praevaricatio*, a fraudulent mismanagement of the case
by collusion of the parties. *Cf. Fam.* viii. 8. 2.
ᵈ See note *b* on 4. 6 above.
ᵉ At Caesar's pressing request. For the whole story see
Fam. i. 9. 19.
ᶠ Sophocles wrote a satyric drama, entitled Σύνδειπνοι,
the theme being the anger of Achilles at being excluded
from a banquet in Tenedos. Some *contretemps* of the kind
had occurred in Caesar's camp in Gaul, and Cicero was

There were very heated discussions for several 2 days in the Senate on the question of bribery and corruption, the candidates for the consulship having gone to such lengths as could no longer be tolerated ; [a] but I was not in the House. I have made up my mind to make no move in the direction of remedying the ills of the State without a powerful backing.

On the day I am writing this, Drusus [b] has been 3 acquitted on a charge of *praevaricatio* [c] by the *tribuni aerarii* [d] by four votes in the final count, though the senators and knights had condemned him. This same afternoon I am going to defend Vatinius. [e] That will be an easy matter. The *comitia* have been postponed to the month of September. Scaurus's trial will be brought on forthwith, and I shall not fail to support him. Your *Sophoclean Banqueters* [f] I don't at all like, though I see that you played your part with *éclat*.

I now come to a topic which I should perhaps have 4 taken first. Oh ! what a delightful letter was yours to me about Britain ! I dreaded the ocean, I dreaded the coast of that island. What remains of your enterprise I do not underrate, but it is more hopeful than alarming, and it is just the eager anticipation of it rather than apprehension that makes me restless. I can see, however, that you have glorious subject matter for your pen. What encampments, what natural characteristics of things and places, what manners and customs, what tribes, and what battles you have to write about, and, finally, what a man in your commander-in-chief himself ! I shall willingly assist you, as you ask me, in any way you wish, and

perturbed at the incident, in which Quintus appears to have been involved.

CICERO

versus, quos rogas, γλαῦκ᾽ εἰς Ἀθήνας[1] mittam.
5 Sed heus tu, celari videor a te. Quomodonam, mi
frater, de nostris versibus Caesar? nam primum
librum se legisse scripsit ad me ante, et prima sic,
ut neget, se ne Graeca quidem meliora legisse. Reliqua ad quemdam locum ῥᾳθυμότερα. Hoc enim
utitur verbo. Dic mihi verum, num aut res eum, aut
χαρακτήρ non delectat? Nihil est, quod vereare. Ego
enim ne pilo quidem minus me amabo. Hac de re
φιλαλήθως et, ut soles, scribe fraterne.

---

[1] *Cratander*: Athenas noctuam *M.*

---

[a] Literally "an owl to Athens," where the owl, as the bird
sacred to Pallas Athene, was bred and protected.
[b] Or "easy-going," "lacking in elaboration."

shall send you the verses for which you ask—"coals to Newcastle." [a]

But look you here, it seems to me that you are [5] keeping something back from me. What, oh what, my dear brother, did Caesar think of my verses? He wrote to me some time ago that he had read my first book; and of the first part he declared that he had never read anything better, even in Greek; the rest of it, as far as a certain passage, was rather "happy-go-lucky" [b]—that is the term he uses. Tell me the truth—is it the subject or the style that does not please him? You needn't be afraid; I shall fancy myself not a whit the less. Write about this like a lover of truth and, as you always do, like a brother.

M. TULLI CICERONIS
EPISTULARUM AD QUINTUM FRATREM

LIBER TERTIUS

I

M. CICERO S. D. Q. FRATRI

Romae, a.u.c. 700.

1 I. Ego ex magnis caloribus (non enim meminimus
maiores) in Arpinati summa cum amoenitate fluminis
me refeci ludorum diebus, Philotimo tribulibus com-
mendatis. In Arcano a. d. iv. Idus Sept. fui. Ibi
Mescidium cum Philoxeno, aquamque, quam ii duce-
bant non longe a villa, belle sane fluentem vidi,
praesertim maxima siccitate, uberioremque aliquanto sese collecturos esse dicebant. Apud Herum recte
erat. In Maniliano offendi Diphilum Diphilo tardio-
rem. Sed tamen nihil ei restabat praeter balnearia
et ambulationem et aviarium. Villa mihi valde

---

a The Fibrenus.

b The *Ludi Romani*, held from 4th to 19th September.

c So that he might secure accommodation for them at the
games.

d Probably contractors. *e* A steward at Arcanum.

f Probably the estate of a neighbour. *g* An architect.

546

CICERO'S LETTERS TO HIS BROTHER QUINTUS

BOOK III

I

CICERO TO QUINTUS IN GAUL

Partly from Arpinum, and partly from Rome, September, 54 B.C.

I. After the great heat—indeed, I cannot remem- 1
ber greater—I have been recuperating at Arpinum,
and enjoying the lovely scenery of the river [a] while
the games [b] are on, having left my fellow-tribesmen
under the charge of Philotimus.[c] On September
10 I was at Arcanum. There I saw Mescidius along
with Philoxenus [d] and the water, which they were
bringing by a canal not far from your villa, flowing
quite beautifully, especially considering the intense
drought ; and they told me that they were going to
collect a much more abundant supply of it. Everything is all right with Herus.[e] On your Manilian
estate [f] I found Diphilus [g] out-doing himself in
dilatoriness ; and yet he had nothing left to do but
the baths and a promenade and an aviary. I was
extremely pleased with the villa, because the paved

placuit, propterea quod summam dignitatem pavi-
mentata porticus habebat, quod mihi nunc denique
apparuit, posteaquam et ipsa tota patet et columnae
politae sunt. Totum in eo est (quod mihi erit curae),
tectorium ut concinnum sit. Pavimenta recte fieri
videbantur. Cameras quasdam non probavi, mutari-
2 que iussi. Quo loco in porticu te scribere aiunt ut
atriolum fiat, mihi, ut est, magis placebat. Neque
enim satis loci esse videbatur atriolo ; neque fere
solet nisi in his aedificiis fieri, in quibus est atrium
maius ; nec habere poterat adiuncta cubicula et eiusmodi membra. Nunc hoc vel honestate testudinis,
valde bonum aestivum locum obtinebit. Tu tamen
si aliter sentis, rescribe quam primum. In balneariis
assa in alterum apodyteri angulum promovi, propterea
quod ita erant posita, ut eorum vaporarium, ex quo
ignis erumpit, esset subiectum cubiculis. Subgrande
cubiculum autem et hibernum altum valde probavi,
quod et ampla erant et loco posita ambulationis uno
latere, eo, quod est proximum balneariis. Columnas
neque rectas, neque e regione Diphilus collocarat.
Eas scilicet demolietur. Aliquando perpendiculo et
linea discet uti. Omnino spero paucis mensibus opus
Diphili perfectum fore. Curat enim diligentissime
3 Caesius, qui tum mecum fuit. II. Ex eo loco recta
548

colonnade gives it a dignity that cannot be surpassed, and that has only just struck me since the whole colonnade itself has come into view, and the columns have been polished. All depends upon the stuccoing being neatly done, and that I shall see to. It seemed to me that the pavements were being properly laid. There were some arched roofs which I did not care for, and I ordered them to be altered.

As regards the place in which they tell me that, according to your written instructions, the antechamber should be built, that is, in the colonnade, I liked it better as it is. For there did not seem to be room enough for the antechamber, nor is one usually built, except in those edifices which have a larger court, nor could it have bedrooms and apartments of that sort built in it. As it is, the handsome curve of its ceiling will of itself make it serve as an excellent summer-room. However, if you think otherwise, write back as soon as possible. In the bathroom I removed the stove to the other corner of the dressing-room, because it was so placed that its steam-pipe, from which flames break out, was exactly under the bedrooms. There was a fairly spacious bedroom and another lofty one for winter use, of which I heartily approved, because they were not only roomy, but situated in the right place, on one side of the promenade, that next the bathroom. The columns Diphilus had placed were neither perpendicular nor opposite each other. He will, of course, have to pull them down. Some day or other he will learn the use of the plumb-line and the tape. On the whole, I hope Diphilus's job will be completed in a few months, for Caesius, who was with me at the time, is keeping a very careful eye upon him.

Vitularia via profecti sumus in Fufidianum fundum,
quem tibi proximis nundinis Arpini de Fufidio HS
cccɪɔɔ. emeramus. Ego locum aestate umbrosiorem
vidi numquam, permultis locis aquam profluentem,
et eam uberem. Quid quaeris? Iugera ʟ. prati Caesius irrigaturum facile te arbitrabatur. Equidem hoc,
quod melius intellego, affirmo, mirifica suavitate te
villam habiturum, piscina et salientibus additis, palaestra, et silva vitium ridicata.[1] Fundum audio te
hunc Bovillanum velle retinere. De eo quid videatur,
ipse constitues. Cascellius[2] aiebat, aqua dempta,
et eius aquae iure constituto, et servitute fundo illi
imposita, tamen nos pretium servare posse, si vendere
vellemus. Mescidium mecum habui. Is se ternis
nummis in pedem tecum transegisse dicebat ; sese
autem mensum pedibus aiebat passuum ɪɪɪcɪɔ.
Mihi plus visum est. Sed praestabo, sumptum
nusquam melius posse poni. Cillonem arcessieram
Venafro. Sed eo ipso die quattuor eius conservos et
4 discipulos Venafri cuniculus oppresserat. Idibus
Sept. in Laterio fui. Viam perspexi, quae mihi ita

---

[1] *Kayser* : †viridicata *mss.* : viridicata *Nobbe.*
[2] *Reid* (cf. Att. xv. 26. 4) : Caesius *Manutius.*

---

[a] Along which cattle were driven to the Greek cities on
the coast.
[b] About £850.
[c] A *iugerum* was rather more than half an acre.
[d] It is not known where this was ; certainly not at
Bovillae in Latium.
[e] " As owner of the two estates (at Arpinum and Bovillae)
Quintus could deal with the water as he liked. But if he
sold the estate whence he took the water, he would have to
declare in the conveyance that he sold subject to this right.
That would be establishing for the dominant estate (where

II. From that spot I proceeded straight along the *via* 3 *Vitularia*[a] to your Fufidian estate, which we purchased for you in the last few weeks from Fufidius for 100,000 sesterces[b] at Arpinum. A more shady spot in summer I never saw, water also gushing out in lots of places, and a plentiful supply of it too. To put it shortly, Caesius thought that you would have no difficulty in irrigating fifty *jugera*[c] of meadow land. For my part, I can assure you of this, and it is a matter I know more about, that you will have a marvellously charming villa to live in, with the addition of a fish-pond with *jets d'eau*, an exercising-ground, and a plantation of vines ready staked. I am told that you wish to retain this Bovillan estate.[d] You will yourself decide to do what you think best about it. Cascellius often told me that even if the water were taken away, and the right of drawing it were established, and a servitude imposed on that estate, we could still keep our price, if we desired to sell it.[e] I have had Mescidius with me. He said that he had agreed with you to do the work for three sesterces a foot, and that he had paced the ground and found it to be 3000 paces. I should have thought it more. But I will guarantee that nowhere would the money be spent more profitably. I had summoned Cillo from Venafrum; but on that very day four of his fellow-workmen and pupils had been crushed by the falling in of a tunnel at Venafrum.

On September 13 I was at Laterium.[f] I thorough- 4 ly examined the road, which pleased me so much

he used the water) a *ius aquae ducendae*, and imposing on the servient estate the obligation to allow the water to be so taken." Roby, *Classical Review*, i. 67, quoted by Tyrrell.

[f] Another property of Quintus at Arpinum.

placuit, ut opus publicum videretur esse, praeter CL.
pass. Sum enim ipse mensus ab eo ponticulo, qui est
ad Furinae, Satricum versus. Eo loco pulvis, non
glarea iniecta est (id mutabitur), et ea viae pars valde
acclivis est, sed intellexi aliter duci non potuisse,
praesertim cum tu neque per Locustae, neque per
Varronis velles ducere. Varro ante suum fundum
prope munierat. Locusta non attigerat ; quem ego
Romae aggrediar et, ut arbitror, commovebo, et simul
M. Taurum, quem tibi audio promisisse, qui nunc
Romae erat, de aqua per fundum eius ducenda rogabo.
5 Nicephorum, villicum tuum, sane probavi ; quaesivi-
que ex eo, ecquid ei de illa aedificatiuncula Lateri, de
qua mecum locutus es, mandavisses. Tum is mihi
respondit, se ipsum eius operis HS xvi. conductorem
fuisse, sed te postea multa addidisse ad opus, nihil
ad pretium ; itaque id se omisisse. Mihi hercule
valde placet, te illa, ut constituebas, addere ; quamquam ea villa, quae nunc est, tamquam philosopha
videtur esse, quae obiurget ceterarum villarum in-
saniam. Verumtamen illud additum delectabit.
Topiarium laudavi ; ita omnia convestit hedera,
qua basim villae, qua intercolumnia ambulationis, ut

a Nothing much is known of this goddess.
b A village in the neighbourhood of Arpinum.
c " Quintus seems to have drawn the road in such a way
as not to trench on their property, and in return he expected
each proprietor to keep the road in repair where it skirted
his estate." Tyrrell.
d About £140.

I thought it might have been a public highway,
except for 150 paces,—for I measured it myself
from the little bridge near the temple of Furina,[a]
walking towards Satricum.[b] Just there it had a
surface of dry clay instead of gravel (that will have
to be altered), and that section of the road is a very
steep incline, but I understand that it could not
be taken in any other direction, especially as you
yourself objected to taking it through either Locusta's
property or Varro's. Varro had properly paved the
road in front of his own estate ; Locusta had not
touched it,[c] but I shall approach him in Rome, and
I fancy I shall make an impression upon him, and
at the same time I shall ask M. Taurus, who, I am
told, has made you a promise to that effect, and is
now in Rome, about bringing the water through his
property.

I highly approved of your steward Nicephorus, 5
and I asked him if you had given him any instructions
as to that little house which is being built at Laterium,
about which you spoke to me. Then he told me in
reply that he himself had contracted to do the work
for sixteen *sestertia*,[d] but that you had subsequently
made many additions to the work, but nothing to the
payment, in consequence of which he had thrown it
up. That you are making those additions as you
had resolved, is, I positively assure you, most gratifying to me ; and yet that villa, just as it stands, strikes
one as having such a philosophic air as to reprove
the craziness of all the other villas. And yet after
all the proposed addition will be charming. Your
landscape - gardener won my praise ; he has so
enveloped everything with ivy, not only the foundation wall of the villa, but also the spaces between the

denique illi palliati topiariam facere videantur et
hederam vendere. Iam ἀποδυτηρίῳ nihil alsius, nihil
6 muscosius. Habes fere de rebus rusticis. Urbanam
expolitionem urget ille quidem et Philotimus et
Cincius ; sed etiam ipse crebro interviso ; quod est
facile factu. Quamobrem ea te cura liberatum volo.
7 III. De Cicerone quod me semper rogas, ignosco
equidem tibi, sed tu quoque mihi velim ignoscas.
Non enim concedo tibi, plus ut illum ames, quam ipse
amo. Atque utinam his diebus in Arpinati, quod et
ipse cupierat, et ego non minus, mecum fuisset. Quod
ad Pomponiam, si tibi videtur, scribas velim, cum
aliquo exibimus, eat nobiscum, puerumque ducat.
Clamores efficiam, si eum mecum habuero otiosus.
Nam Romae respirandi non est locus. Id me scis
antea gratis tibi esse pollicitum ; quid nunc putas,
8 tanta abs te mihi mercede proposita? Venio nunc
ad tuas litteras ; quas pluribus epistulis accepi, dum
sum in Arpinati. Nam mihi uno die tres sunt
redditae, et quidem, ut videbantur, eodem abs te
datae tempore ; una pluribus verbis, in qua primum
erat, quod antiquior dies in tuis fuisset ascripta litteris, quam in Caesaris. Id facit Oppius nonnumquam

---

^a We should say, " bring down the house," by his success
as a teacher.
^b In your gratitude and affection.

columns of the promenade, that I declare the Greek statues seem to be in business as landscape-gardeners, and to be advertising their ivy. As it now is, the dressing-room is the coolest and mossiest retreat in the world.

That is about all as far as country matters are 6 concerned. It is true that the gardener and Philotimus, and Cincius also, are pressing forward the elaborate adornment of your town house, but I often drop in and I see them myself, too, and it is no trouble to me. I would therefore have you freed from any anxiety on that account.

III. You are always asking me about your son 7 Cicero ; well, I pardon your solicitude, of course, but I should be glad if you, too, would pardon me. For that you love him more than I do myself is a point on which I refuse to yield to you. And I only wish that he had been with me these last few days at Arpinum, as he had himself desired, and I no less ! As to Pomponia, I should like you, if you please, to write and tell her to come with me, whenever I go out of town anywhere, and bring the boy. If I have him with me when I am at leisure, I shall win loud applause ; *a* at Rome I have no time to breathe. You know I promised you this for nothing before : what do you expect now that you have offered me so great a reward *b* ?

I come now to your letters, which I received in 8 several packets when I was at Arpinum. In fact, three were delivered to me in one day, and indeed apparently despatched by you at the same time, one of them of considerable length, in which the first thing you noticed was that my letter to you bore an earlier date than that to Caesar. That is

necessario, ut, cum tabellarios constituerit mittere,
litterasque a nobis acceperit, aliqua re nova impedia-
tur, et necessario serius, quam constituerat, mittat,
neque nos datis iam epistulis diem commutari cure-
9 mus. Scribis de Caesaris summo in nos amore.
Hunc et tu fovebis et nos, quibuscumque poterimus
rebus, augebimus. De Pompeio et facio diligenter et
faciam quod mones. Quod tibi mea permissio man-
sionis tuae grata est, id ego, summo meo dolore et desiderio, tamen ex parte gaudeo. In Hippodamis et
nonnullis aliis arcessendis quid cogites, non intellego.
Nemo istorum est, quin abs te munus, fundi suburbani
instar, exspectet. Trebatium vero meum quod isto
admisceas, nihil est. Ego illum ad Caesarem misi,
qui mihi iam satisfecit ; si ipsi minus, praestare nihil
debeo, teque item ab eo vindico et libero. Quod
scribis te a Caesare quotidie plus diligi, immortaliter
gaudeo. Balbum vero, qui est istius rei (quemadmodum scribis) adiutor, in oculis fero. Trebonium meum
10 a te amari, teque ab illo, pergaudeo. De tribunatu
quod scribis, ego vero nominatim petivi Curtio, et
mihi ipse Caesar nominatim Curtio paratum esse

---

[a] Oppius and Balbus were Caesar's agents at Rome.
[b] *Cf.* § 21 of this letter.
[c] For C. Trebatius Testa, the lawyer, see *Fam.* vii. 6, note *e*.
[d] See note *a* on *Fam.* x. 28.
[e] *Cf. Q.F.* ii. 15a. 2.

what Oppius ^a occasionally cannot help doing—I mean that, when he has decided to send letter-carriers and has received a letter from me, something unexpected occurs to hinder him, and he is unavoidably later than he intended in sending the carriers ; while I, when once the letter has been handed to him, do not trouble about having the date altered.

You write of Caesar's extraordinary affection for 9 us. That affection not only will you encourage, but I, too, shall foster it in every possible way. As to Pompey, I am, and shall be, careful to do what you advise. That you are pleased with my permission to prolong your stay, though I shall grieve and miss you greatly, I am to some extent glad. What your intention is in sending for your Hippodamuses ^b and some others passes my comprehension. There is not one of that gang who does not expect something equivalent to a suburban estate as a *douceur* from you. But that you should lump up my friend Trebatius ^c with that lot is sheer nonsense. I have sent him to Caesar, and Caesar has already done quite enough for me ; if he has not done so much for Trebatius, it is no business of mine to guarantee him anything, and you, too, I deliver and release from all obligation to him. Your writing that Caesar's esteem for you increases daily is an undying joy to me. Balbus, indeed, who, as you write, is helping on that state of affairs, is the very apple of my eye. It is a great joy to me that you love my friend Trebonius, ^d and he you.

You write about the military tribuneship ; well, 10 I really did canvass for it in specific terms for Curtius, ^e and Caesar himself wrote back to me in specific terms that there was one ready for Curtius, and twitted

rescripsit, meamque in rogando verecundiam obiur-
gavit. Si cui praeterea petiero (id quod etiam Oppio
dixi, ut ad illum scriberet), facile patiar mihi negari,
quoniam illi, qui mihi molesti sunt, sibi negari a me
non facile patiuntur. Ego Curtium (id quod ipsi dixi)
non modo rogatione, sed etiam testimonio tuo diligo,
quod litteris tuis studium illius in salutem nostram
facile perspexi. De Britannicis rebus, cognovi ex
tuis litteris, nihil esse, nec quod metuamus, nec quod
gaudeamus. De publicis negotiis, quae vis ad te
Tironem scribere, neglegentius ad te ante scribebam,
quod omnia, minima maxima, ad Caesarem mitti
11 sciebam. IV. Rescripsi epistulae maximae. Audi
nunc de minuscula ; in qua primum est de Clodi ad
Caesarem litteris ; in quo Caesaris consilium probo,
quod tibi, amantissime petenti, veniam non dedit,
uti ullum ad illam Furiam verbum rescriberet. Alterum est de Calventi Mari oratione. Quod scribis,
miror, tibi placere, me ad eum rescribere, praesertim
cum illam nemo lecturus sit, si ego nihil rescripsero,
meam in illum pueri omnes, tamquam dictata, per-

---

[a] He means that, though he is obliged to grant such
requests, the ultimate success of such canvassing is a matter
of no concern to him ; "I canvass for them under pressure ;
if the canvass is of no avail, serve them right for pestering
me."

[b] Calventius (so called after his maternal grandfather) is
L. Calpurnius Piso Caesoninus, whom Cicero had attacked
the year before (55) for his misdeeds as governor of
Macedonia in 57 and 56. (That is the speech mentioned
just below.) Cicero here calls him *Marius*, because Piso
was now to him what Marius had once been to Metellus.
The story is as follows: In 100 B.C. Q. Metellus Numidicus
refused to take the oath of obedience to the agrarian laws
of Saturninus, the adherent of C. Marius. Metellus was

me with the shy way I made the request. If I canvass for anybody besides (as I told Oppius to write to Caesar) I shall have little objection to a refusal, since those who pester me with requests decidedly object to my refusing them.[a] I esteem Curtius (as I told him himself) not only because you ask me to do so, but also because of your testimony in his favour, since your letter enabled me easily to appreciate his enthusiasm for my restoration. As to the situation in Britain, your letter gives me to understand that we have no reason either for apprehension or for exultation. As to public affairs, about which you wish Tiro to write to you, I have hitherto been writing to you less minutely because I was aware that everything as of the least, so of the greatest, importance was being reported to Caesar.

IV. I have answered your longest letter; now 11 hear what I have to say about your very little one, which begins about Clodius's letter to Caesar; in regard to that incident, I think Caesar was quite right in not acceding to your request, prompted though it was by the friendliest feeling, that he should send a single word of reply to that arch-fiend. Your second point is about the speech of Calventius Marius.[b] I am surprised at your writing that my replying to him would give you pleasure, especially as nobody is likely to read his speech, if I make no reply to it, whereas every schoolboy learns mine

expelled from the Senate, and threatened with exile by Marius. He might have resisted Marius with success, but, to avoid civil dissension, he retired from Rome. Cicero here implies that he could have defied Piso, had he chosen to do so, as Metellus could have defied Marius, but decided to treat him with silent contempt. *Cf. Fam.* i. 9. 16, where Cicero again compares himself to Metellus.

discant. Libros meos, quos exspectas, inchoavi sed
conficere non possum his diebus. Orationes efflagi-
tatas pro Scauro et pro Plancio absolvi. Poema ad
Caesarem, quod composueram, incidi. Tibi quod
rogas, quoniam ipsi fontes iam sitiunt, si quid habebo
12 spati, scribam. Venio ad tertiam. Balbum quod ais
mature Romam bene comitatum esse venturum mecumque assidue usque ad Id. Maias futurum, id mihi
pergratum perque iucundum erit. Quod me in eadem
epistula, sicut saepe antea, cohortaris ad ambitionem
et ad laborem, faciam equidem ; sed quando vive-
13 mus ? Quarta epistula mihi reddita est Id. Sept.,
quam a d. iv. Id. Sext. ex Britannia dederas. In ea
nihil sane erat novi, praeter *Erigonam* ; quam si ab
Oppio accepero, scribam ad te, quid sentiam ; nec
dubito, quin mihi placitura sit. Et, quod praeterii,
de eo, quem scripsisti de Milonis plausu scripsisse ad
Caesarem, ego vero facile patior ita Caesarem existimare, illum quam maximum fuisse plausum. Et
prorsus ita fuit ; et tamen ille plausus, qui illi
14 datur, quodammodo nobis videtur dari. Reddita est
etiam mihi pervetus epistula, sed sero allata, in qua
de aede Telluris et de porticu Catuli me admones.
Fit utrumque diligenter. Ad Telluris quidem etiam

---

^a His treatise, *De Republica*, of which only portions have
come down to us.

^b *Cf. Ep.* 4. 4.

^c Some commentators take this as meaning " with plenty
of money in his purse." But it probably means " with a
large escort of Caesar's troops," to take part in the elections.

^d Adjoining Cicero's house in Rome, destroyed with the
house when he went into exile, but afterwards restored by
order of the Senate.

against him by rote as an exercise. My books,[a] all of which you are eagerly awaiting, I have begun, but cannot finish for the next few days. The speeches in defence of Scaurus and Plancius, which you so insistently demand, I have accomplished. The poem to Caesar, which I had put together for final arrangement, I have broken off. For *you*, since your own wells of poesy are now running dry,[b] if I have any spare time, I shall write what you request.

I come to your third letter. You say that Balbus 12 will come to Rome at an early date, handsomely attended,[c] and that he will be with me without a break till May 15 ; that will be very gratifying to me, and will give me much pleasure. In the same letter you urge me, as you often have before, to be ambitious and strenuous ; well, I certainly shall be so ; but when shall we begin to enjoy life ?

Your fourth letter I received on September 13 ; 13 you had posted it in Britain on August 10. There was nothing new in it except about your *Erigona* ; if I get it from Oppius, I'll write and tell you what I think of it ; but I have no doubt that I shall find it charming. And there is that bit, too (I forgot to mention it), about the man who, according to your letter, wrote to Caesar about the applause given to Milo ; well, I have not the least objection to Caesar's getting the impression that nothing could have been heartier; and such was undoubtedly the case. And yet the applause given to Milo seems in a sense to be given to me.

I have also received a very old letter, but late in 14 its delivery, in which you remind me of the temple of Tellus and the colonnade of Catulus.[d] Both works are being carefully executed. Indeed, I have even had a statue of you set up near the temple of Tellus.

tuam statuam locavi. Item de hortis quod me admones, nec fui umquam valde cupidus, et nunc domus
suppeditat mihi hortorum amoenitatem. Romam
cum venissem a. d. xiii. Kal. Octob., absolutum offendi
in aedibus tuis tectum ; quod supra conclavia non
placuerat tibi esse multorum fastigiorum, id nunc
honeste vergit in tectum inferioris porticus. Cicero
noster, dum ego absum, non cessavit apud rhetorem.
De eius eruditione quod labores, nihil est, quoniam
ingenium eius nosti ; studium ego video. Cetera
15 eius suscipio, ut me puto praestare debere. V. Gabinium tres adhuc factiones postulant ; L. Lentulus,
flaminis filius, qui iam de maiestate postulavit ; Ti.
Nero cum bonis subscriptoribus ; C. Memmius tribunus plebis cum L. Capitone. Ad Urbem accessit
a. d. xii. Kal. Octobr. Nihil turpius, nec desertius.
Sed his iudiciis nihil audeo confidere. Quod Cato
non valebat, adhuc de pecuniis repetundis non erat
postulatus. Pompeius a me valde contendit de reditu
in gratiam ; sed adhuc nihil profecit ; nec, si ullam
partem libertatis tenebo, proficiet. Tuas litteras
16 vehementer exspecto. Quod scribis te audisse in
candidatorum consularium coitione me interfuisse, id
falsum est. Eiusmodi enim pactiones in ea coitione

---

a *Maiestas* (in full *laesa* or *minuta maiestas*) was any act
derogatory to the dignity or prejudicial to the interests of
the Roman people. In this case it was Gabinius's unauthorized intervention (for the handsome fee of 10,000
talents) in the restoration of Ptolemy Auletes to the neglect
of his duties as Governor of Syria.
b Father of the emperor Tiberius.
c Not to be confused with C. Memmius Gemellus, one of
the candidates for the consulship.
d M. Cato, now praetor.
e For a fuller account of this see the next letter.

Also you remind me about the pleasure-gardens; well, I was never very keen on them, and, as it is, my town house supplies me with all the amenities of a pleasure-garden. When I arrived at Rome on September 18, I found the roof on your house completely finished; that part above the day-rooms, which you had not cared to be too heavily gabled, has now a noble slope down to the roof of the colonnade below.

Our boy Cicero had no holiday with his rhetoric-master while I was away. There is no reason why you should be anxious about his education, since you know his ability, and I see to his application. All else connected with him I take on my shoulders, as I think it my duty to make myself responsible.

V. So far Gabinius is being prosecuted by three 15 parties—by L. Lentulus, son of the *flamen*, who has now indicted him for *maiestas* [a]; Ti. Nero,[b] with sound men backing his indictment; and C. Memmius,[c] tribune of the plebs, in conjunction with L. Capito. He approached the walls of the city on September 19, the picture of disrepute and desolation. But with the present law-courts, I dare not be confident of anything. On account of Cato's [d] ill-health he has not yet been indicted for extortion. Pompey is making a strong effort to become reconciled with me, but as yet has met with no success, and, if I retain a particle of independence, he will never succeed. I await your letter with intense eagerness.

You write that you have been told that I took 16 part in the coalition of the candidates for the consulship; [e] well, that is not true. The compacts made in that coalition—compacts subsequently divulged by

563

factae sunt, quas postea Memmius patefecit, ut nemo
bonus interesse debuerit ; et simul mihi committen-
dum non fuit, ut his coitionibus interessem, quibus
Messalla excluderetur ; cui quidem vehementer satis-
facio rebus omnibus ; ut arbitror, etiam Memmio.
Domitio ipsi multa iam feci, quae voluit, quaeque a
me petivit. Scaurum beneficio defensionis valde
obligavi. Adhuc erat valde incertum, et quando
17 comitia, et qui consules futuri essent. Cum hanc iam
epistulam complicarem, tabellarii a vobis venerunt
a. d. xi. Kal. Oct. Septimo vicesimo die. O me sollicitum ! quantum ego dolui in Caesaris suavissimis
litteris ! sed quo erant suaviores, eo maiorem dolorem
illius ille casus afferebat. Sed ad tuas venio litteras.
Primum tuam remansionem etiam atque etiam probo,
praesertim cum, ut scribis, cum Caesare communi-
caris. Oppium miror quidquam cum Publio ; mihi
18 enim non placuerat. Quod interiore epistula scribis,
me Idib. Sept. Pompeio legatum iri, id ego non audivi,
scripsique ad Caesarem, neque Vibullium Caesaris
mandata de mea mansione ad Pompeium pertulisse,
neque Oppium. Quo consilio ? Quamquam Oppium ego tenui, quod priores partes Bibuli erant.
Cum eo enim coram Caesare egerat, ad Oppium

Memmius—were of such a kind that no honest man ought to have been party to them ; and, at the same time, it was not for me to make the mistake of being party to those coalitions from which Messalla was shut out. To him I am giving complete satisfaction in every respect, and also, I believe, to Memmius. To Domitius himself I have rendered many services, which he desired and requested of me. Scaurus I have laid under a great obligation by my kindness in defending him. So far it is extremely uncertain both when the elections will be held and who will be consuls.

Just as I was in the act of folding this letter, there 17 came letter-carriers from you and Caesar on September 20 ; they had been twenty-seven days on the road. How distressed I was ! And how I grieved over Caesar's most charming letter*a*! But the more charming it was, the greater the grief it caused me for his affliction. But I come to your letter. In the first place, I reiterate my approval of your staying on, especially after having had, as you write, an interview with Caesar. I am surprised at Oppius having anything to do with Publius*b* ; it was not what I advised.

As to what you say in the middle of your letter— 18 that I am going to be appointed *legatus* to Pompey on September 13—I have heard nothing about it, and I wrote to Caesar saying that neither Vibullius nor Oppius had conveyed his message to Pompey about my staying on in Rome. What their object was I don't know. And yet, in the case of Oppius, it was I who held him back, because it was Bibulus who had a prior claim ; for it was with him that Caesar had had an interview, while he had only

scripserat. Ego vero nullas δευτέρας φροντίδας habere
possum in Caesaris rebus. Ille mihi secundum te et
liberos nostros ita est, ut sit paene par. Videor id
iudicio facere. Iam enim debeo, sed tamen amore
sum incensus.

19 VI. Cum scripsissem haec infima, quae sunt mea
manu, venit ad nos Cicero tuus ad cenam, cum Pomponia foris cenaret. Dedit mihi epistulam legendam
tuam, quam paullo ante acceperat, Aristophaneo
modo valde mehercule et suavem et gravem ; qua
sum admodum delectatus. Dedit etiam alteram
illam mihi, qua iubes eum mihi esse affixum, tamquam magistro. Quam illum epistulae illae delectarunt ! quam me ! Nihil puero illo suavius, nihil nostri
amantius. Hoc inter cenam Tironi dictavi, ne mirere
20 alia manu esse. Annali litterae tuae pergratae
fuerunt, quod et curares de se diligenter, et tamen
consilio se verissimo iuvares. P. Servilius pater ex
litteris, quas sibi a Caesare missas esse dicebat, sig-
nificat valde te sibi gratum fecisse, quod de sua
voluntate erga Caesarem humanissime diligentissime-
21 que locutus esses. Cum Romam ex Arpinati rever-
tissem, dictum mihi est, Hippodamum ad te profectum
esse. Non possum scribere, me miratum esse, illum
tam inhumaniter fecisse, ut sine meis litteris ad te

ᵃ It is doubtful whether he means the great comic poet or
Aristophanes of Byzantium, the critic ; *suavem* would rather
indicate the former.

ᵇ L. Villius Annalis, a senator. *Cf. Fam.* viii. 8. 3.

ᶜ P. Servilius Isauricus, father of Cicero's correspondent,
the proconsul of Asia (*Fam.* xiii. 68, and 66-72).

written to Oppius. I assure you that, as for "second thoughts," I could have none in my relations with Caesar. He comes next to you and my children with me, and so closely next that he is almost on a par with them. It seems to me that such is my deliberate conviction (and it ought to be so by this time), and yet a strong predilection has its influence upon me.

VI. After I had written these last words, which 19 are in my own hand, your son Cicero came in and had dinner with me, as Pomponia was dining out. He gave me your letter to read, which he had only just received—and, upon my word, it was a clever mixture of grave and gay in the style of Aristophanes,[a] and I was highly delighted with it. He also gave me that other letter of yours in which you bid him cling to me as to a tutor. How delighted he was with those letters, and so was I ! He is the most charming boy in the world, and most devoted to me. I dictated this to Tiro during dinner, so do not be surprised at its being written in a different hand.

Annalis[b] was much pleased with your letter, 20 because, as he said, you took such pains about him, and at the same time helped him with your very frank advice. P. Servilius[c] senior, in consequence of a letter which he said Caesar had sent him, expresses his extreme gratitude to you for having spoken so very courteously and impressively of his kindly feeling for Caesar.

After my return to Rome from Arpinum I was 21 told that Hippodamus[d] had set out to join you. I cannot say that I was surprised at his having acted so unkindly as to have set out without any letter to

---

[a] Cf. § 9 of this letter.

proficisceretur ; illud scribo, mihi molestum fuisse.
Iam enim diu cogitaveram, ex eo, quod tu ad me
scripseras, ut, si quid esset, quod ad te diligentius
perferri vellem, illi darem ; quod mehercule hisce
litteris, quas vulgo ad te mitto, nihil fere scribo, quod
si in alicuius manus inciderit, moleste ferendum sit.
Minucio me et Salvio et Labeoni reservabam. Labeo
aut tarde proficiscetur aut hic manebit. Hippodamus
22 ne numquid vellem quidem rogavit. T. Pinarius
amabiles ad me de te litteras mittit ; se maxime
litteris, sermonibus, cenis denique tuis delectari. Is
homo semper me delectavit, fraterque eius mecum
est multum. Quare, ut instituisti, complectere adu-
23 lescentem. VII. Quod multos dies epistulam in
manibus habui, propter commorationem tabellario-
rum, ideo multa coniecta sunt, aliud alio tempore,
velut hoc : T. Anicius mihi saepe iam dixit, sese tibi,
suburbanum si quod invenisset, non dubitaturum
esse emere. In eius sermone ego utrumque soleo ad-
mirari, et te de suburbano emendo, cum ad illum
scribas, non modo ad me non scribere, sed etiam
aliam in sententiam scribere, et, cum ad illum scribas, nihil te recordari de se, de epistulis illis, quas
in Tusculano eius tu mihi ostendisti, nihil de praeceptis Epicharmi, γνῶθι πῶς ἄλλῳ κέχρηται ; totum

---

[a] Cicero's friend, whom he recommends to Cornificius in
Fam. xii. 24. 3.

[b] We know no more of him than that Cicero did not think
him a man to be trusted.

you from me; I simply remark that I was annoyed.
For I had long since resolved, after what you wrote
to me, to entrust to him whatever there might be
which I should like to be conveyed to you with
particular care; because I assure you that in these
letters, which I send you in an ordinary way, I hardly
write anything which would cause me annoyance if
it fell into anybody else's hands. I reserve myself
for Minucius and Salvius and Labeo. Labeo will
either be late in setting out, or will not set out at all.
Hippodamus never so much as asked me whether I
had any commission.

T. Pinarius *a* sends me an amiable letter about 22
you; he says he is highly delighted with your literary
taste, your conversation, and, last but not least, with
your dinners. I have always found pleasure in his
society, and I see a great deal of his brother. For
that reason you will, I am sure, continue, as you have
begun, to show the young man marked attention.

Because I have had a letter on my hands for 23
many days on account of delay on the part of the
letter-carriers, many things have been jumbled up
in it, written at various times, as, for instance, this:
T. Anicius *b* has repeatedly told me that if he found
a suburban property he would not hesitate to buy it
for you. In my conversations with him, I am surprised at two things—that when you write to him
about buying a suburban property, not only do you
fail to write to me about it, but even write as if you
had other intentions; and again, that when you write
to him, you recall nothing about himself, about those
letters of his which you showed me at Tusculum,
nothing about the precept of Epicharmus, " Find out
how he has treated another," in short, as far as I

denique vultum, animum, sermonem eius, quemadmodum conicio, quasi dedidicisse[1]; sed haec tu videris.
24 De suburbano, cura, ut sciam, quid velis ; et simul,
ne quid ille turbet, vide. Quid praeterea ? Quid ?
Etiam. Gabinius a. d. iv. Kal. Octobr. noctu in
Urbem introivit ; et hodie h. viii., cum edicto C.
Alfi de maiestate eum adesse oporteret, concursu
magno et odio universi populi paene afflictus est.
Nihil illo turpius. Proximus est tamen Piso. Itaque
mirificum ἐμβόλιον cogito in secundum librorum
meorum includere, dicentem Apollinem in concilio
deorum, qualis reditus duorum imperatorum futurus
esset ; quorum alter exercitum perdidisset, alter
25 vendidisset. Ex Britannia Caesar ad me Kal. Sept.
dedit litteras, quas ego accepi a. d. iv. Kalend.
Octobr. satis commodas de Britannicis rebus ; quibus,
ne admirer, quod a te nullas acceperim, scribit, se
sine te fuisse, quum ad mare accesserit. Ad eas ego
ei litteras nihil rescripsi, ne gratulandi quidem causa,
propter eius luctum. Te oro etiam atque etiam, mi
frater, ut valeas.

[1] *Added by Wesenberg.*

[a] C. Alfius was tribune of the plebs in 59. He was
quaesitor in the trial of Gabinius for *maiestas*.
[b] Piso had wasted his army in petty warfare with the
tribes on the borders of Macedonia, and Gabinius had
practically sold his by employing it to restore Ptolemy
Auletes for a bribe.

can make out, that you have entirely unlearnt, as it were, what you must have gathered from his looks, his disposition, and his conversation; but all this is for you to see to.

Take care to let me know your wishes as to the 24 suburban estate, and, incidentally, see that Anicius doesn't cause you any trouble. What else is there? What? Oh yes, Gabinius entered the city by night on September 27, and to-day, at two o'clock, when according to C. Alfius's [a] edict, he ought to have appeared to face the charge of *maiestas*, he was almost crushed to the ground by the enormous throng that proved the hatred of the whole people. He was the most ignominious sight in the world. Piso, however, is a good second. So I am thinking of inserting in the second of my books an amazing paragraph—Apollo holding forth at a council of the gods on what sort of a home-coming there would be in the case of two commanders, one of whom had lost, and the other sold, his army. [b]

Caesar posted me a letter from Britain on Septem- 25 ber 1, which I received on the 27th—a satisfactory letter enough as far as regards the situation in Britain; and in it, to prevent my being surprised at not getting a letter from you, he writes that you were not with him when he got down to the coast. To that letter I made no reply, not even by way of congratulation, because of his mourning.

I implore you again and again, my dear brother, to keep well.

CICERO

II

M. CICERO S. D. Q. FRATRI

Romae, A.U.C. 700.

1   A. d. vi. Id. Octob. Salvius Ostiam vesperi navi
profectus erat cum his rebus, quas tibi domo mitti
volueras. Eodem die Gabinium ad populum lucu-
lente calefecerat Memmius, sic, ut Calidio verbum
facere pro eo non licuerit. Postridie autem eius diei,
qui erat tum futurus, cum haec scribebam ante lucem,
apud Catonem erat divinatio in Gabinium futura
inter Memmium et Ti. Neronem et C. et L. Antonios,
M. F. Putabamus fore, ut Memmio daretur, etsi
erat Neronis mira contentio. Quid quaeris ? Probe
premitur, nisi noster Pompeius, dis hominibusque
2 invitis, negotium everterit. Cognosce nunc hominis
audaciam, et aliquid in republica perdita delectare.
Cum Gabinius, quacumque veniebat, triumphum se
postulare dixisset, subitoque, bonus imperator, noctu
in Urbem (hostium plane[1]) invasisset, in senatum se
non committebat. Interim ipso decimo die, quo
ipsum oportebat hostium caesorum numerum et
militum renuntiare, inrepsit, summa infrequentia.

---

[1] hostium plenam *Koch* : hostilem in modum *Wesenberg*.

---

[a] C. Memmius, the tribune.
[b] Counsel for Gabinius. There is no doubt a play in the
Latin on *calefecerat* and *Calidius* (*calidus*).
[c] *Divinatio* was the technical term for a formal inquiry
as to which of several accusers presenting themselves was
the proper person to conduct the prosecution.
[d] *i.e.*, the combination against Gabinius.
[e] It would seem that all governors on returning from their
provinces were called up to report to the Senate any losses

572

II

Rome, October 11, 54 B.C.

On October 10 in the evening, Salvius took ship 1
and started for Ostia, taking the things you wanted
sent to you from home. On the same day Mem-
mius ^a gave Gabinius such a blazing hot time of it
before the people, that Calidius ^b hadn't a chance of
saying a word for him. To-morrow (that is the day
after to-morrow, since I am writing before daybreak)
there is to be a trial ^c before Cato to decide who is to
conduct his prosecution, among Memmius, Tiberius
Nero, and C. and L. Antonius, the sons of Marcus.
I think it likely that Memmius will be appointed,
though Nero is making a wonderful effort. In short,
Gabinius is in a very tight corner, unless our friend
Pompey, to the disgust of gods and men, contrives
to upset the apple-cart.^d

Now mark the fellow's impudence, and find 2
something to amuse you amid the ruins of the
Republic. Gabinius, having declared wherever he
came, that he was demanding a triumph, and having suddenly changed his plans, and—consummate
commander that he is—entered the city (he knew
it was his enemies' city) by night, did not, however, trust himself to enter the Senate. Meantime,
exactly on the tenth day, on which it was his duty in
person to report the number of the slain among the
enemy and his own men,^e he crept into the Senate
when it was very thinly attended. When he wished

sustained by the Romans and the enemy in any actions
fought during the governorships.

Cum vellet exire, a consulibus retentus est ; introducti publicani.   Homo undique saucius[1] cum a me maxime vulneraretur, non tulit, et me trementi voce exsulem appellavit.   Hic (o di ! nihil umquam honorificentius nobis accidit) consurrexit senatus cum clamore ad unum, sic ut ad corpus eius accederet ; pari clamore atque impetu publicani.   Quid quaeris ? omnes, tamquam si tu esses, ita fuerunt.   Nihil hominum sermone foris clarius.   Ego tamen me teneo ab accusando, vix mehercule ; sed tamen teneo, vel quod nolo cum Pompeio pugnare (satis est, quod instat de Milone), vel quod iudices nullos habemus. Ἀπότευγμα formido ; addo etiam malevolentiam hominum, et timeo, ne illi, me accusante, aliquid accedat ; nec despero rem et sine me et nonnihil per 3 me confici posse.   De ambitu postulati sunt omnes, qui consulatum petunt ; a Memmio Domitius, a Q. Acutio, bono et erudito adulescente, Memmius, a Q. Pompeio Messalla, a Triario Scaurus.   Magna in motu res est, propterea quod aut hominum aut legum interitus ostenditur.   Opera datur, ut iudicia ne fiant. Res videtur spectare ad interregnum.   Consules comitia habere cupiunt ; rei nolunt, et maxime Mem-

a *sc.* of Syria, who had suffered from the depredations of pirates while Gabinius was otherwise engaged—restoring Ptolemy in Egypt.

b Cicero's enemies might support Gabinius to spite him.

c The tribune.

d The candidate for the consulship.

to leave, he was detained by the consuls, and the *publicani* [a] were brought in. Wounded on every side, and being most bitterly assailed by myself, the fellow could stand it no longer, and, in a voice trembling with rage, he called me an *exile*. Upon that (and, O ye gods, never was I paid a higher compliment) the Senate rose with a shout, every man of them, and even made a move to attack him, as did the *publicani*, shouting and making for him in like manner. To cut the story short, they all behaved exactly as you would have done yourself. Nothing can be more unmistakable than the general talk outside the House. Yet I refrain from prosecuting him ; it is difficult, upon my word ; but, still, I do refrain, whether because I do not wish to be at feud with Pompey (the near approach of Milo's affair is sufficient reason for that) or because we have no proper jurors. I am afraid of a *fiasco* ; and, besides, I have to consider the ill-will of certain folk, and fear that *my* being his prosecutor will be of some advantage to him ; [b] and I am not without hope that the business may be settled without me, and at the same time to some extent through my instrumentality.

All who are candidates for the consulship have 3 been indicted for bribery—Domitius by Memmius,[c] Memmius [d] by Q. Acutius, an excellent and learned young man, Messalla by Q. Pompeius, Scaurus by Triarius. There is great excitement over the affair, because it obviously means the destruction either of certain persons or of the laws. Every effort is being made to prevent the trials taking place. The situation seems to point to an interregnum. The consuls are anxious to hold the elections, but the defendants

mius, quod Caesaris adventu sperat se futurum
consulem. Sed mirum in modum iacet. Domitius
cum Messalla certus esse videbatur. Scaurus re-
frixerat. Appius sine lege curiata confirmat se
Lentulo nostro successurum : qui quidem mirificus
illo die (quod paene praeterii) fuit in Gabinium ;
accusavit maiestatis ; nomina data, quum ille verbum
nullum. Habes forensia. Domi recte, et ipsa domus
a redemptoribus tractatur non indiligenter. Vale.

III

M. CICERO S. D. Q. FRATRI

Romae, A.U.C. 700.

1 Occupationum mearum tibi signum sit librari
manus. Diem scito esse nullum, quo die non dicam
pro reo. Ita, quidquid conficio aut cogito, in ambulationis fere tempus confero. Negotia nostra sic se
habent ; domestica vero, ut volumus. Valent pueri,
studiose discunt, diligenter docentur ; et nos et inter se amant. Expolitiones utriusque nostrum sunt
in manibus ; sed tua ad perfectum iam res rustica
Arcani et Lateri. Praeterea de aqua et via nihil
praetermisi quadam epistula, quin enucleate ad te

---

^a Because as long as they were under an accusation, they
could not stand for the consulship.
^b See *Fam.* i. 9. 25, where the whole situation is explained.

don't want it,[a] and least of all Memmius, who hopes
that on Caesar's arrival he will be consul. But he is
" down and out "—surprisingly so. Domitius, with
Messalla as colleague, seems to be a certainty.
Scaurus is stale fish. Appius declares that he will
step into our friend Lentulus's shoes, even without
a *lex curiata*; [b] and on the great day (I nearly forgot
to mention it) he astonished everybody by his attack
on Gabinius; he accused him of *maiestas*, and gave
the names of his witnesses, while Gabinius spoke not
a word. Now you have all the news of the forum.
At home all is right, and your house itself is being
dealt with by the contractors with considerable
assiduity.

III

CICERO TO QUINTUS

Rome, October 21, 54 B.C.

The handwriting of my secretary should indicate 1
to you the pressure of my engagements. I assure
you that there is never a day on which I don't speak
on behalf of some defendant, with the result that
whatever I compose or think out, I generally pile on to
the time for my walks. So it stands with my business;
affairs at home, however, are just as I would have them
be. Our boys are well, they apply themselves to
their lessons, they are being carefully taught, and
they are devoted to us and to each other. The
elaborate finishing off of each of our houses is still
in hand; but your rural operations at Arcanum and
Laterium are now approaching completion. Again,
as to the water and the road, in a certain letter of
mine I omitted no single detail, so as not to fail to

perscriberem. Sed me illa cura sollicitat angitque
vehementer, quod dierum iam amplius L. intervallo
nihil a te, nihil a Caesare, nihil ex istis locis, non modo
litterarum, sed ne rumoris quidem affluxit. Me
autem iam et mare istuc et terra sollicitat; neque
desino (ut fit in amore) ea, quae minime volo, cogitare.
Quare non equidem iam te rogo, ut ad me de te, de
rebus istis scribas (numquam enim, cum potes, prae-
termittis), sed hoc te scire volo, nihil fere umquam
me sic exspectasse, ut, cum haec scribebam, litteras
2 tuas. Nunc cognosce ea, quae sunt in republica.
Comitiorum quotidie singuli dies tolluntur obnuntia-
tionibus, magna voluntate bonorum omnium ; tanta
invidia sunt consules propter suspicionem pactorum
a candidatis praemiorum. Candidati consulares quattuor, omnes rei ; causae sunt difficiles ; sed enitemur,
ut Messalla noster salvus sit, quod est etiam cum
reliquorum salute coniunctum. Gabinium de ambitu reum fecit P. Sulla, subscribente privigno Memmio, fratre Caecilio, Sulla filio. Contra dixit L.
Torquatus ; omnibusque libentibus non obtinuit.
3 Quaeris, quid fiat de Gabinio ? Sciemus de maiestate
triduo ; quo quidem in iudicio odio premitur omnium

---

a Who had prosecuted Sulla on a charge of "breaking the
peace" (*de vi*) in 62, when Sulla was defended by Cicero.

write fully and explicitly. But the anxiety that so
seriously disturbs and tortures me is that, for a period
of now over fifty days, nothing in the shape of a letter
or even of a rumour has trickled its way to me from you
or from Caesar, or from those parts where you are.
And now both the sea and the land, where you are,
cause me anxiety, and, as always happens when one's
affections are engaged, I never cease imagining what
I least desire to imagine. And for that reason I am
not now asking you to write to me about yourself
and all that concerns you (which you never omit to do
when you can), but I should like you to know this,
that I have hardly ever looked forward with such
eagerness to anything as I do to a letter from you
as I write these words.

Now let me tell you about the political situation. 2
One date after another for the holding of the elections is being daily cancelled by the announcement
of adverse omens, to the great satisfaction of all
sound citizens; so utterly unpopular are the consuls,
because they are suspected of having bargained for
a bribe from the candidates. All the four candidates
for the consulship are on their trial; their cases are
difficult to defend, but I shall make a strenuous effort
to secure the acquittal of our friend Messalla, and
that is closely bound up with the acquittal of the
rest. Gabinius has been accused of bribery by
P. Sulla, and the backers of Sulla's indictment are
his stepson Memmius, his cousin Caecilius, and his
son Sulla. L. Torquatus *a* opposed him, but, to
everybody's satisfaction, failed to establish his claim.

You ask what is being done about Gabinius. Well, 3
in three days' time we shall know about the charge
of *maiestas*; and in that trial he is handicapped by

CICERO

generum, maxime testibus laeditur[1]; accusatoribus
frigidissimis utitur; consilium varium; quaesitor
gravis et firmus Alfius; Pompeius vehemens in
iudicibus rogandis. Quid futurum sit, nescio; locum
tamen illi in civitate non video. Animum praebeo
ad illius perniciem moderatum, ad rerum eventum
4 lenissimum. Habes fere de omnibus rebus. Unum
illud addam. Cicero tuus nosterque summo studio
est Paeoni sui rhetoris, hominis, opinor, valde exer-
citati et boni. Sed nostrum instituendi genus esse
paullo eruditius et θετικώτερον, non ignoras. Quare
neque ego impediri Ciceronis iter atque illam disciplinam volo, et ipse puer magis illo declamatorio genere
duci et delectari videtur. In quo quoniam ipsi quoque fuimus, patiamur illum ire nostris itineribus;
eodem enim perventurum esse confidimus. Sed
tamen, si nobiscum eum rus aliquo eduxerimus, in
hanc nostram rationem consuetudinemque induce-
mus. Magna enim nobis a te proposita merces est,
quam certe nostra culpa numquam minus assseque-
mur. Quibus in locis et qua spe hiematurus sis, ad
me quam diligentissime scribas velim. Vale.

[1] *Madvig*: caeditur *M*.

---

[a] See *Q.F.* iii. 1. 24.
[b] θετικώτερον, belonging rather to the province of θέσις,
which Cicero defines (*Top.* 79) as a discussion of a general
or abstract principle, as opposed to ὑπόθεσις, the discussion
of a particular case.
[c] *i.e.*, Quintus's gratitude and enhanced affection.

the hatred all classes entertain for him; he is damaged most of all by witnesses; he has the most ineffective accusers; the panel of jurors is of a promiscuous kind; the presiding praetor, Alfius,[a] is a man of strong and sterling character; Pompey is very active in soliciting the jurors. What will happen I don't know, but I cannot see that there is any room for him in the State. My own feelings as regards his condemnation are under control, as regards the issue of events perfectly placid.

I have now told you about almost everything. 4 There is one thing I must add; your Cicero (and indeed he is our Cicero) is deeply devoted to his rhetoric master Paeonius, in my opinion, an exceedingly well-trained and excellent fellow. But, as you are well aware, my own system of instruction is somewhat more scholarly and argumentative.[b] I do not therefore desire that your Cicero's educational course should be interfered with, and the boy himself appears to be more attracted and charmed by that declamatory style; and since I myself once followed that line, let us allow him to proceed along the same paths as I did; for I feel sure that he will arrive at the same goal. But, all the same, if I take him with me into the country anywhere, I shall bring him over to this system and practice of my own. For the reward [c] you have set before me is a magnificent one, and it will certainly not be through any fault of mine that I shall forfeit it. I should like you to write and tell me as exactly as possible, where, and with what prospects in view, you are going to spend the winter. Good-bye.

IV

Romae, a.u.c. 700.

1 Gabinius absolutus est. Omnino nihil accusatore
Lentulo subscriptoribusque eius infantius, nihil illo
consilio sordidius. Sed tamen nisi incredibilis contentio et preces Pompei, dictaturae etiam rumor
plenus timoris fuisset, ipsi Lentulo non respondisset,
qui tamen illo accusatore, illoque consilio sententiis
condemnatus sit XXXII., cum LXX. tulissent. Est
omnino tam gravi fama hoc iudicium, ut videatur
reliquis iudiciis periturus, et maxime de pecuniis repetundis. Sed vides nullam esse rempublicam,
nullum senatum, nulla iudicia, nullam in ullo nostrum
dignitatem. Quid plura de iudicibus ? Duo prae-
torii sederunt, Domitius Calvinus,—is aperte absolvit,
ut omnes viderent, et Cato,—is, diribitis tabellis,
de circulo se subduxit et Pompeio primus nuntiavit.

2 Aiunt nonnulli, Sallustius item, me oportuisse accusare. Iis ego iudicibus committerem ? Quid
essem, si me agente esset elapsus ? Sed me alia
moverunt. Non putasset sibi Pompeius de illius

---

^a Cn. Sallustius, to whom Cicero addressed *Fam.* ii. 17.
He was quaestor to Bibulus in Syria ; Cicero seems to have
thought highly of him.

IV

CICERO TO QUINTUS IN GAUL

Rome, October 24, 54 B.C.

Gabinius has been acquitted ! Nothing on earth 1
could have been more puerile than his accuser
Lentulus, and those who endorsed his indictment ;
nothing more corrupt than that panel of jurors.
But still, had it not been for the strenuous efforts and
supplications of Pompey, and an alarming rumour
also of a dictatorship, even Lentulus would have
been more than a match for him, seeing that even
with such an accuser and such a jury he was condemned by no less than 32 votes out of 70 recorded.
This trial is so utterly discredited that it seems
likely that he will be convicted in the other trials,
and most of all in that for extortion. But you can
see that there is really no Republic in existence,
no Senate, no law-courts, no position of authority
held by any one of us. What more can I tell you
about the jurors ? Two praetorians took their seats,
Domitius Calvinus—he voted for acquittal quite
openly, for all to see—and Cato—he, as soon as the
voting-tablets had been counted, withdrew from the
surrounding throng and was the first to tell Pompey
the news.

There are some, Sallustius *a* among them, who say 2
that I ought to have undertaken the prosecution.
Was I to entrust myself to such jurors as that ?
What would have become of me, had I conducted
the case, and he had escaped ? But I was influenced
by other considerations. Pompey would not have

salute, sed de sua dignitate mecum esse certamen ;
in Urbem introisset : ad inimicitias res venisset ;
cum Aesernino Samnite Pacideianus comparatus
viderer ; auriculam fortasse mordicus abstulisset.
Cum Clodio quidem certe rediisset in gratiam. Ego
vero meum consilium (si praesertim tu non improbas)
vehementer approbo. Ille, cum a me singularibus
meis studiis ornatus esset, cumque ego illi nihil de-
berem, ille mihi omnia, tamen in republica me a se
dissentientem non tulit (nihil dicam gravius), et minus
potens eo tempore, quid in me florentem posset,
ostendit. Nunc, cum ego ne curem quidem multum
posse, res quidem publica certe nihil possit, unus
ille omnia possit, cum illo ipso contenderem ? Sic
enim faciendum fuisset. Non existimo te putare id
3 mihi suscipiendum fuisse. Alterutrum, inquit idem
Sallustius, defendisses idque Pompeio contendenti
dedisses. Etenim vehementer orabat. Lepidum
amicum Sallustium, qui mihi inimicitias putet peri-
culosas subeundas fuisse aut infamiam sempiternam ! Ego vero hac mediocritate delector ; ac mihi
illud iucundum est, quod, cum testimonium secundum
fidem et religionem gravissime dixissem, reus dixit,

---

[a] Pacideianus (*cf.* Hor. *Sat.* ii. 7. 97) was the most skilful
gladiator of the time, but Aeserninus was his superior in
courage and brute force.

[b] "Or else you should have prosecuted him" is obviously
understood.

thought he was having a struggle with me for
Gabinius's salvation, but for his own position ; he
would have entered the city ; it would have ended
in our becoming enemies ; I should have looked
like some Pacideianus pitted against the Samnite
Aeserninus,[a] and quite possibly he would have bitten
my ear off. He would certainly have effected a
reconciliation with Clodius. For my part, I warmly
approve (especially if you do not disapprove) of my
own decision. Although it was my unique oratorical
efforts on his behalf that had brought him distinction,
and although I owed him nothing, while he owed
me everything, for all that, my not agreeing with
him in politics was more than he could stand (I shall
use no stronger expression), and, though less powerful
than myself at the time, he showed me what power
he could wield against me, in the heyday of my
career. As things now are, when I don't even care
for much power, and the State has certainly no
power at all, while he stands alone in his omnipotence,
was I to enter upon a personal conflict with him ?
For that is what would have had to be done. I don't
believe you think I should have taken up the cudgels
in such a matter.

"One thing or the other," says that same Sallustius, 3
" you should have defended him, and made that
concession to Pompey's prayers ; he implored you
earnestly enough."[b] A pretty sort of friend Sallustius,
to think that I should have incurred either dangerous
enmities, or everlasting infamy. For my part, I rub
my hands over this middle course I have adopted,
and I am delighted that when, in accordance with
my honour and my oath I had given my evidence in
the most impressive manner, the defendant declared,

si in civitate licuisset sibi esse, mihi se satisfacturum,
4 neque me quidquam interrogavit. De versibus, quos
tibi a me scribi vis, deest mihi quidem opera, quae
non modo tempus, sed etiam animum vacuum ab
omni cura desiderat; sed abest etiam ἐνθουσιασμός;
non enim sumus omnino sine cura venientis anni,
etsi sumus sine timore. Simul et illud (sine ulla mehercule ironia loquor) : tibi istius generis in scribendo
5 priores partes tribuo, quam mihi. De bibliotheca
tua Graeca supplenda, libris commutandis, Latinis
comparandis, valde velim ista confici, praesertim cum
ad meum quoque usum spectent. Sed ego, mihi ipsi
ista per quem agam, non habeo. Neque enim venalia
sunt, quae quidem placeant, et confici, nisi per
hominem et peritum et diligentem, non possunt.
Chrysippo tamen imperabo, et cum Tyrannione
loquar. De fisco quid egerit Scipio, quaeram.
Quod videbitur rectum esse, curabo. De Ascanione,
tu vero, quod voles, facies ; me nihil interpono. De
suburbano, quod non properas, laudo ; ut tu habeas,
6 hortor. Haec scripsi a. d. ix. Kalend. Novemb.,
quo die ludi committebantur, in Tusculanum proficiscens, ducensque mecum Ciceronem meum in
ludum discendi, non lusionis ; ea re non longius

---

[a] Cf. Juv. Sat. vii. 53-58, " sed vatem egregium . . . |
anxietate carens animus facit, omnis acerbi | impatiens."
[b] Nothing is known of this transaction, but cf. Q.F. iii. 5. 6.
[c] Probably one of Quintus's slaves.

that if he were permitted to remain a member of the State, he would satisfy my claims to his gratitude; and he refrained from cross-examining me at all.

About the verses you wish me to write for you, as 4 a matter of fact, I lack the necessary energy, which requires not only leisure, but a mind free from all anxiety; [a] but the divine *afflatus* is also wanting; for I am not altogether without anxiety as regards the coming year, although I do not fear it. At the same time there is also the fact (and, on my oath, I am speaking without a touch of irony) that in this style of composition I assign a higher rank to you than I do to myself.

As to the replenishing of your Greek library, the 5 exchange of books, and the collection of Latin books, I should be very glad to see all that done, especially as it tends to my own advantage as well. But I have nobody whom I could employ as my own agent in the business. For such books as are really desirable are not for sale, and cannot be got together except through an agent who is both an expert and a man who takes pains. I shall send orders to Chrysippus, however, and have a talk with Tyrannio. I shall find out what Scipio has done as regards the treasury. [b] I shall see to it that what seems right is done. As to Ascanio [c] you will do as you please; I have no finger in the pie. As to a suburban property, I approve your being in no hurry, but I urge you to secure one.

I am writing this on October 24, the day on 6 which the games begin, just as I am starting for my Tusculan villa, taking my dear Cicero with me to a school for learning, not a school of gladiators, no farther away from Rome than I wished to be, the reason being that I wanted to be there on Novem-

quam vellem, quod Pomptino ad triumphum a. d. iii.
Non. Novemb. volebam adesse. Etenim erit nescio
quid negotioli. Nam Cato et Servilius praetores pro-
hibituros se minantur ; nec, quid possint, scio. Ille
enim et Appium consulem secum habebit, et praetores,
et tribunos plebis. Sed minantur tamen, in primis-
quo Ἀρη ιι ιέων Q. Scaevola. Cura, mi suavissime et
carissime frater, ut valeas.

V and VI

M. CICERO S. D. Q. FRATRI

Tusculani, a.u.c. 700.

1   Quod quaeris, quid de illis libris egerim, quos,
cum essem in Cumano, scribere institui, non cessavi
neque cesso ; sed saepe iam scribendi totum consilium rationemque mutavi. Nam iam duobus factis
libris, in quibus, novendialibus iis feriis, quae fuerunt
Tuditano et Aquilio consulibus, sermo est a me in-
stitutus Africani, paullo ante mortem, et Laeli,
Phili, Manili, P. Rutili, Q. Tuberonis et Laeli genero-
rum, Fanni et Scaevolae ; sermo autem in novem et
dies et libros distributus de optimo statu civitatis
et de optimo cive ; sane texebatur opus luculenter,

---

* He was one of Cicero's *legati* in Cilicia. He claimed a
triumph for his successful campaign against the Allobroges
in 61.

b De Republica.

c In 129 B.C. the Novendialia were a nine days' festival
held on the occasion of some inauspicious portent.

d For Scipio Africanus's supposed murder see note *b* on
Fam. ix. 21. 3.

ber 3 to support Pomptinus's[a] application for a triumph. As a matter of fact, there is going to be some little trouble about it. Cato and Servilius, the praetors, threaten to forbid it, and yet I don't know what they can do. He will have with him Appius the consul, the praetors, and the tribunes of the plebs. And yet they do threaten him, and in particular Q. Scaevola, "*breathing battle*." My most charming and dearest of brothers, take care of your health.

V AND VI

CICERO TO QUINTUS IN GAUL

Tusculanum, late in October, 54 B.C.

You ask me what I have done about those books[b] I began to write at my Cuman villa ; well, I have not been, and am not, idle, but I have often remodelled the whole plan and scheme of the composition. I had already completed two books, in which I had set going a conversation held during the festival of the Novendialia, which took place in the consulship of Tuditanus and Aquilius[c] between Africanus (shortly before his death[d]) and Laelius, Philus, Manilius, P. Rutilius, Q. Tubero,[e] and Laelius's sons-in-law, Fannius and Scaevola. Now that conversation, spread over nine days and taking nine books, was on "The ideal constitution of the State" and "The ideal citizen." The work was being composed excellently well, and the

[e] L. Furius Philus was consul in 136 ; Manilius was consul in 146 ; Q. Tubero was a nephew of Africanus and a strong opponent of the Gracchi.

hominumque dignitas aliquantum orationi ponderis
afferebat. Hi libri cum in Tusculano mihi legerentur
audiente Sallustio, admonitus sum ab illo, multo
maiore auctoritate illis de rebus dici posse, si ipse
loquerer de republica, praesertim cum essem non
Heraclides Ponticus, sed consularis et is, qui in
maximis versatus in republica rebus essem. Quae
tam antiquis hominibus attribuerem, ea visum iri
ficta esse ; oratorum sermonem in illis nostris libris,
qui essent[1] de ratione dicendi, belle a me removisse ;
ad eos tamen rettulisse, quos ipse vidissem ; Aristo-
telem denique, quae de republica et praestante viro

2 scribat, ipsum loqui. Commovit me, et eo magis,
quod maximos motus nostrae civitatis attingere non
poteram, quod erant inferiores, quam illorum aetas,
qui loquebantur. Ego autem id ipsum tum eram
secutus, ne, in nostra tempora incurrens, offenderem
quempiam. Nunc et id vitabo, et loquar ipse tecum,
et tamen illa, quae institueram, ad te, si Romam
venero, mittam. Puto enim te existimaturum a me
libros illos non sine aliquo meo stomacho esse relictos.

3 Caesaris amore, quem ad me perscripsti,[2] unice delector ; promissis his, quae ostendit, non valde
pendeo ; nec honores sitio nec desidero gloriam ;
magisque eius voluntatis perpetuitatem, quam pro-

[1] *Wesenberg :* quod esset *MSS.*
[2] *Bücheler, followed by Tyrrell :* perscripsit *M.*

---

[a] Who was no more than a theorist on politics.
[b] The three books *De oratore.*
[c] *i.e.,* in his *Politics* and *Ethics.*

speeches were given considerable weight by the high rank of the interlocutors. But when these books were being read out to me at my Tusculan villa, in the hearing of Sallustius, it was suggested to me by him that these subjects could be discussed with far greater authority if the speaker on the Republic were myself, especially as I was not a mere Heraclides Ponticus,[a] but a consular, and one who had been engaged in the most critical State affairs; that the words I attributed to men of such antiquity would surely be regarded as so much fiction; that in those books of mine, which dealt with the science of rhetoric,[b] I had shown good taste in dissociating myself from the conversation of the orators, and yet had assigned the speeches to men whom I had personally met; and, finally, that Aristotle speaks in the first person when he writes on " The Republic " and " The eminently good man." [c]

He impressed me, and all the more because of my 2 inability to touch upon the most important disturbances in our State, since they were of a later date than the age of my speakers. But that is the very plan I had adopted at the time, so as not to hurt somebody's feelings by encroaching upon our own days. As it is, I shall avoid doing that, and shall myself be the man speaking with you, and, all the same, when I come to Rome, I shall send you the original draft; for I am sure you will believe that I did not abandon the first draft of those books without something of a pang.

Caesar's affection for me, of which you write so 3 fully, gives me exceptional pleasure; I do not depend to any great extent upon the offers he holds out; I do not thirst for public offices, nor do I pine for glory; and I look forward more to the continu-

591

CICERO

missorum exitum exspecto. Vivo tamen in ea ambitione et labore, tamquam id, quod non postulo,
4 exspectem. Quod me de faciendis versibus rogas,
incredibile est, mi frater, quam egeam tempore ; nec
sane satis commoveor animo ad ea, quae vis, canenda.
Ὑποθέσεις¹ vero ad ea, quae ipse ego ne cogitando
quidem consequor, tu, qui omnes isto eloquendi et
exprimendi genere superasti, a me petis ? Facerem
tamen, ut possem ; sed (quod te minime fugit) opus
est ad poema quadam animi alacritate, quam plane
mihi tempora eripiunt. Abduco equidem me ab
omni reipublicae cura, dedoque litteris ; sed tamen
indicabo tibi, quod mehercule in primis te celatum
volebam. Angor, mi suavissime frater, angor, nullam
esse rempublicam, nulla iudicia ; nostrumque hoc
tempus aetatis, quod in illa auctoritate senatoria
florere debebat, aut forensi labore iactari, aut domesticis litteris sustentari ; illud vero, quod a puero
adamaram,

πολλὸν² ἀριστεύειν καὶ ὑπείροχον ἔμμεναι ἄλλων,

totum occidisse ; inimicos a me partim non oppugna-
tos, partim etiam esse defensos ; meum non modo
animum, sed ne odium quidem esse liberum ; unum-
que ex omnibus Caesarem esse inventum, qui me
tantum, quantum ego vellem, amaret, aut etiam (sicut

¹ most edd. : διατυπώσεις Bücheler ; possibly. as Tyrrell
suggests, ἐμπνεύσεις, "inspirations."
² mss. : but Homer has αἰὲν in Il. vi. 208 and xi. 784.

ance of his goodwill, than to the fulfilment of his promises. Yet my life is spent in such a laborious effort to please him, as if I were looking forward to what I do not ask for.

As to your asking me about writing some verses, 4 you couldn't believe, my dear brother, how pressed I am for time, and I really lack the necessary inclination to write the poetry you want. But come now, is it you who seek suggestions for what I myself do not succeed in attaining, even in imagination—you who have surpassed everybody in that kind of fluent and graphic expression ? I would do your bidding to the best of my ability, but (as you are the last man to forget) the composition of a poem demands a certain sprightliness of mind, of which I have been completely robbed by the times we live in. I withdraw myself, it is true, from all public cares, and devote myself to literature ; and yet, I will divulge to you what, on my oath, I especially wished to keep hidden from you. It is agony to me, my dearest brother, sheer agony, to think that there is no constitution, no administration of justice, and that during the period of my life when my proper influence in the Senate should have been at its zenith, I am either distracted by my forensic labours, or fortified only by my literary pursuits at home, while that aspiration to which I had been passionately devoted from my very boyhood, "*Far to excel, and alone to be leader of others,*" has completely vanished ; that my foes, in some cases, I have left unattacked, in others I have even defended ; that not only my inclinations, but my very dislikes are not free ; and that in all the world I have found in Caesar the one man to love me as I could wish, or even (as others think) the

alii putant) hunc unum esse, qui vellet. Quorum tamen nihil est eiusmodi, ut ego me non multa consolatione quotidie leniam ; sed illa erit consolatio maxima, si una erimus ; nunc ad illa vel gravissimum 5 accedit tui desiderium. Gabinium si, ut Pansa putat oportuisse, defendissem, concidissem ; qui illum oderunt (hi sunt toti ordines), propter quem oderunt,[1] meipsum odisse coepissent. Tenui me, ut puto, egregie, tantum ut facerem, quantum omnes viderent.[a] Et in omni summa, ut mones, valde me ad otium 6 pacemque converto. De libris Tyrannio est cessator. Chrysippo dicam. Sed res operosa est et hominis perdiligentis. Sentio ipse, qui in summo studio nihil assequor. De Latinis vero, quo vertam me, nescio, ita mendose et scribuntur et veneunt ; sed tamen, quod fieri poterit, non neglegam. Crebrius, ut ante ad te scripsi, Romae est ; et qui omnia se adiurat debere tibi, valde renuntiat.[2] De aerario puto confectum esse, dum absum.

7 Quattuor tragoedias XVI. diebus absolvisse cum scribas, tu quidquam ab alio mutuaris ? et πλείους[3]

---

[1] *The extraordinary construction of the phrase* propter quem oderunt, *in which* quem *is apparently governed by both the preposition and the verb, has escaped the notice of commentators. We must either suppose that* eum *has dropped out after* propter, *or accuse Cicero of a solecism.*

[2] valde te nunc iactat (*abuses you*) *Boot.*

[3] *Prof. Robinson Ellis :* †πλέος *MSS. :* κλέος *Nobbe :* πάθος *Usener.*

---

[a] I agree with Prichard and Bernard that some such words as " mihi faciendum esse " are understood after *viderent*.

one man who had any wish to do so. Still there is nothing in all this so bad but that I daily soothe myself with many a consolation; but the greatest consolation of all will be our being together; as it is, to my other sorrows is added my yearning for you, and that is the hardest to bear of all.

Had I defended Gabinius, as Pansa thinks I ought 5 to have done, I should have brought utter ruin upon myself; those who hate him (and that means the orders in their entirety) would have begun to hate me personally, because of him they hate. I have, I think, kept an admirable course, in confining myself to doing what the world saw I had to do.[a] And, to sum up the whole situation, I am taking your advice, and resolutely turning my face in the direction of tranquillity and peace.

In the matter of the books, Tyrannio is a sluggard. 6 I shall have a word with Chrysippus, but it is a laborious business, and one that needs a very energetic man. My own experience tells me that, for however strenuously I work, I have nothing to show for it. As for the Latin books, I don't know which way to turn; they are copied out and sold so full of mistakes. However I shall not omit to do all that can be done. Crebrius, as I wrote to you before, is at Rome, and, while he swears that he owes you everything, he stoutly refuses repayment. I fancy that business of the treasury was settled in my absence.[b]

Though you write that you had finished off four 7 tragedies in sixteen days, are you sure that you are not borrowing anything from someone else? And

[b] Cf. § 5 in Ep. 4 of this Book.

595

CICERO

quaeris, cum *Electram* et *Troada*[1] scripseris ? Cessator esse noli ; et illud γνῶθι σεαυτόν noli putare ad
arrogantiam minuendam solum esse dictum, verum
etiam ut bona nostra norimus. Sed et istas et
Erigonam mihi velim mittas. Habes ad duas epistulas
proximas.

VII

M. CICERO S. D. Q. FRATRI

Tusculani, a.u.c. 700.

1 Romae, et maxime Appia ad Martis, mira pro-
luvies. Crassipedis ambulatio ablata, horti, tabernae
plurimae ; magna vis aquae usque ad piscinam publicam. Viget illud Homeri :

ἤματ' ὀπωρινῷ, ὅτε λαβρότατον χέει ὕδωρ
Ζεύς, ὅτε δή γ' ἄνδρεσσι κοτεσσάμενος χαλεπαίνῃ,

cadit enim in absolutionem Gabini

οἳ βίῃ εἰν ἀγορῇ σκολιὰς κρίνωσι θέμιστας,
ἐκ δὲ δίκην ἐλάσωσι, θεῶν ὄπιν οὐκ ἀλέγοντες.

2 Sed haec non curare decrevi. Romam cum venero,

---

[1] *Prof. Robinson Ellis* : †Troadem MSS.

[a] Reading πλείους with Prof. Robinson Ellis, I append
an epitome of his ingenious explanation of this obscure
passage. "I believe this," he says, "to be a learned
mythological allusion to the *varying number of the Pleiades*,
which, according as Electra was visible or not, were reckoned
as six or seven alternately." And he takes Cicero to mean,
"Are you not content with the six tragedies you have
written, but still look for the seventh, or missing, Pleiad,
after showing such familiarity with Electra and her conduct
as a Trojan woman ? " *Hermathena*, xiii. (1887), p. 139,
quoted by Tyrrell.
[b] Hom. *Il.* xvi. 385-388.

596

after writing the *Electra* and the *Trojan Woman*, are you searching for one Pleiad more?[a] You must not rest on your oars, and you must not be under the idea that the well-known *nosce teipsum* was only meant to apply to the abatement of arrogance, but also means that we should recognize our own gifts. But I should like you to send me those tragedies and the *Erigona* also. You now have an answer to your last two letters.

VII

CICERO TO QUINTUS

Tusculanum, late in October or early in November, 54 B.C.

At Rome, and especially on the Appian Way, up 1 to the Temple of Mars, there is a tremendous flood. Crassipes' promenade has been carried away, pleasure-grounds too, and quite a number of shops. There is an immense quantity of water right up to the public fish-pond. That passage in Homer still holds true :

> As on a day in late autumn when down in a torrent resistless
> Zeus pours the rain, in resentment and wrath at the misdeeds of mortals

(for it exactly fits in with the acquittal of Gabinius)

> Who in the place of assembly distort without mercy their judgments,
> Banishing justice from earth, and the voice of the gods never heeding.[b]

But I am determined not to let these things trouble me.

When I return to Rome, I shall write and tell you 2

quae perspexero, scribam ad te, et maxime de dic-
tatura, et ad Labienum et ad Ligurium litteras dabo.
Hanc scripsi ante lucem, ad lychnuchum ligneolum,
qui mihi erat periucundus, quod eum te aiebant,
cum esses Sami, curasse faciendum. Vale, mi suavissime et optime frater.

VIII

M. CICERO S. D. Q. FRATRI

Romae, A.U.C. 700.

1 Superiori epistulae quod respondeam, nihil est,
quae plena stomachi et querellarum est; quo in
genere alteram quoque te scribis pridie Labieno
dedisse; qui adhuc non venerat. Delevit enim mihi
omnem molestiam recentior epistula. Tantum te et
moneo et rogo, ut in istis molestiis et laboribus et
desideriis recordere, consilium nostrum quod fuerit
profectionis tuae. Non enim commoda quaedam
sequebamur parva ac mediocria. Quid enim erat,
quod discessu nostro emendum putaremus? Praesidium firmissimum petebamus et optimi et poten-
tissimi viri benevolentia ad omnem statum nostrae
dignitatis. Plura ponuntur in spe, quam in pecuniis;
reliqua ad iacturam struantur.[1] Quare si crebro

---

[1] *Nobbe*: struentur *M*: reservantur *Cratander*.

---

[a] To join Caesar in Gaul.
[b] Just as in a storm it was usual to throw part of the cargo
overboard to lighten and save the ship, so now they must
sacrifice all prospect of immediate gain to secure this hope
for the future. For *iactura cf.* Acts, xxvii. 38.

the result of my observations, and send a letter to Labienus and to Ligurius also.

I am writing this before daybreak, by the light of a little wooden torch-stand, which has always been a great delight to me, because they told me that you had seen to its construction when you were in Samos.

Good-bye, my dearest and best of brothers.

VIII

CICERO TO QUINTUS

Rome, late in November, 54 B.C.

I have nothing to say in answer to your earlier 1 letter, which teems with resentment and dissatisfaction, and you write that on the preceding day you entrusted another letter also of the same sort to Labienus, who has not yet arrived. I do not answer your earlier letter, because all feeling of annoyance has been obliterated from my mind by your letter of more recent date. This much only I advise you, and indeed beg of you to do—in the midst of your troubles and toils and longings, to recall to mind the purpose we had in view when you left Rome.[a] It was not petty or paltry advantages that we were aiming at. What was it then, for which we thought that even our separation was a proper price to pay? Well, what we sought was the strongest possible reinforcement of our whole political position by enlisting the goodwill of a man of irreproachable character, and at the same time of unquestioned ascendancy. The investment is in hope rather than in cash; let all else be got ready for throwing overboard.[b] So

referes animum tuum ad rationem et veteris consili
nostri, et spei, facilius istos militiae labores ceteraque,
quae te offendunt, feres ; et tamen, cum voles,
depones. Sed eius rei maturitas nequedum venit,
2 et tamen iam appropinquat. Etiam illud te admoneo, ne quid ullis litteris committas, quod, si
prolatum sit, moleste feramus. Multa sunt, quae
ego nescire malo, quam cum aliquo periculo fieri
certior. Plura ad te vacuo animo scribam, cum (ut
spero) se Cicero meus belle habebit. Tu velim cures,
ut sciam, quibus nos dare oporteat eas, quas ad te
deinde litteras mittemus ;—Caesarisne tabellariis, ut
is ad te protinus mittat, an Labieni. Ubi enim isti
3 sint Nervii, et quam longe absint, nescio. De virtute
et gravitate Caesaris, quam in summo dolore ad-
hibuisset, magnam ex epistula tua accepi voluptatem.
Quod me institutum ad illum poema iubes perficere,
etsi distentus cum opera, tum animo sum multo
magis, quoniam tamen ex epistula, quam ad te
miseram, cognovit Caesar, me aliquid esse exorsum,
revertar ad institutum, idque perficiam his supplica-
tionum otiosis diebus ; quibus Messallam iam nostrum
reliquosque molestia levatos, vehementer gaudeo;
eumque quod certum consulem cum Domitio nume-

---

[a] It was in the winter of this year that Quintus so gallantly
defended his camp against an overwhelming force of Nervii.
Their territory in Gallia Belgica extended from the river
Sabis (*Sambre*) to the sea, and was partly covered by the
forest of Arduenna (*Ardennes*).

[b] For the loss of his daughter Julia (*cf. Ep.* 1. 25 above).

if you constantly throw your thoughts back to the purpose of our original policy, and what we then had in view, you will find less difficulty in enduring your military labours, and anything else that is obnoxious to you ; and, after all, you can give up those duties whenever you please ; but the hour for that has not arrived, though it is already approaching.

I give you this piece of advice also—not to commit 2 to any form of writing anything the publication of which may cause us annoyance. There are many things I would rather not know than be told of them at some considerable risk. I shall write to you at greater length with a mind free from care when my Cicero, as I hope he will be, is in comfortable health. Please be careful to let me know to whom I ought to entrust the letter I shall send you later on —to Caesar's letter-carriers, so that he may send them straight to you, or to Labienus's ; for I have no idea where those Nervii *a* of yours are, and how far off they are.

Your letter about the courage and dignity of 3 Caesar, which, as you tell me, he displayed in the midst of his intense sorrow,*b* was a source of great pleasure to me. You bid me finish the poem addressed to him which I have begun ; well, in spite of the distractions of work, and far more of my thoughts, still, now that Caesar has got to know from a letter which I sent you that I have something on the stocks, I shall return to what I have begun, and shall finish it during these leisure days of the *supplicationes* ; and I am greatly delighted that during those days our friend Messalla and the rest have at last been relieved from annoyance ; and in reckoning upon him as certain to be consul together with Domitius, you

CICERO

ratis, nihil a nostra opinione dissentitis. Ego Messallam Caesari praestabo. Sed Memmius in adventu
Caesaris habet spem ; in quo illum puto errare ; hic
quidem friget. Scaurum autem iampridem Pompeius
4 abiecit. Res prolatae. Ad interregnum comitia
adducta. Rumor dictatoris iniucundus bonis ; mihi
etiam magis, quae loquuntur. Sed tota res et
timetur et refrigescit. Pompeius plane se negat
velle ; antea ipse mihi non negabat. Hirrus auctor
fore videtur. O di, quam ineptus ! quam se ipse
amans sine rivali ! Caelium Vinicianum, hominem
mihi deditum, per me deterruit. Velit, nolit, scire
difficile est. Hirro tamen agente, nolle se non pro-
babit. Aliud hoc tempore de republica nihil loque-
5 bantur. Agebatur quidem certe nihil. Serrani
Domestici fili funus perluctuosum fuit a. d. VIII.
6 Kalend. Decemb. Laudavit pater scripto meo. Nunc
de Milone. Pompeius ei nihil tribuit, et omnia
Cottae, dicitque se perfecturum, ut illo Caesar in-
cumbat. Hoc horret Milo, nec iniuria, et, si ille
dictator factus sit, paene diffidit. Intercessorem dic-

ᵃ Strictly speaking, the *interregnum* would only become
necessary when the consuls left office at the end of the year.
. . . But Cicero was right, and the *interregnum* lasted till
July 53. W. W. How.

ᵇ Probably he means Pompey, and not Hirrus.

ᶜ Cf. *Fam.* viii. 4. 3, where he is mentioned as having
urged the dictatorship of Pompey with disastrous results
to himself.

ᵈ Nothing more is known of him.

ᵉ M. Aurelius Cotta held Sardinia for Pompey in 49.

602

are all of you in strict agreement with what I think myself. I will go bail to Caesar for Messalla's conduct. But Memmius pins his hopes on Caesar's arrival in Italy; in which I think he is mistaken; here there is no doubt that he is a back number. Scaurus has long since been thrown over by Pompey.

All business has been postponed, and the elections 4 so long deferred that there must be an interregnum.[a] The rumour of a dictatorship is not to the liking of the loyalists; still less to my liking is what people say. But the whole proposal is regarded with alarm, and falling into the background. Pompey flatly denies that he has any wish for it; previously he used to make no such denial in talking to me himself. It seems likely that Hirrus will be the proposer. Ye gods, what a fool he is![b] What a lover of himself, without a rival in the field! As for Caelius Vinicianus,[c] a man devoted to me, it was through me that Pompey managed to frighten him off. It is hard to be sure whether he does or does not desire it. If it is Hirrus, however, who proposes it, he will not convince people that he does not desire it. There is no other topic of political conversation at the present moment; nothing at any rate is being done.

The funeral of Serranus Domesticus's [d] son on 5 November 23 was a very sad incident. His father delivered a funeral oration over him which I had written.

And now about Milo. Pompey gives him no 6 encouragement, and gives it all to Cotta,[e] and says he will contrive that Caesar shall throw his weight on that side. Milo is alarmed at this, and rightly so, and if Pompey is made dictator, he almost gives up hope. If he helps anyone who vetoes the dictator-

taturae si iuverit manu et praesidio suo, Pompeium
metuit inimicum ; si non iuverit, timet, ne per vim
perferatur. Ludos apparat magnificentissimos : sic,
inquam, ut nemo sumptuosiores ; stulte bis terque,
non postulatus, vel quia munus magnificum dederat,
vel quia facultates non erant, vel quia potuerat magistrum se, non aedilem putare. Omnia fere scripsi.
Cura, mi carissime frater, ut valeas.

IX

M. CICERO S. D. Q. FRATRI

Romae, a.u.c. 700.

1   De Gabinio nihil fuit faciendum istorum, quae
amantissime cogitata sunt. Τότε μοι χάνοι. Feci
summa cum gravitate, ut omnes sentiunt, et summa
cum lenitate, quae feci. Illum neque ursi neque le-
vavi. Testis vehemens fui, praeterea quievi. Exitum iudici foedum et perniciosum levissime tuli.
Quod quidem bonum mihi nunc denique redundat,
ut his malis reipublicae licentiaque audacium, qua

ᵃ The death of a wealthy friend had given Milo, as his
executor, the opportunity of giving games on a lavish scale
in his honour. Such "funeral" games were not uncommon.
ᵇ Hom. *Il.* iv. 182, the end of the line being εὑρεῖα χθών.
Virgil has a similar expression in *Aen.* iv. 24 "sed mihi
vel tellus optem prius ima dehiscat."

ship with his bands and bodyguard, he fears he will make Pompey his enemy ; if he does not do so, he is afraid that the measure will be carried by force. He is preparing to give the most magnificent games, at a cost, I assure you, that has never been exceeded by anyone.[a] Considering that they are not demanded of him, he is acting like a fool for these two or three reasons at least—because he has already given a magnificent gladiatorial show, or because he has not the means, or because he might have remembered that he was only an executor, and no aedile. That is about all I have to write.

My dearest brother, be careful of your health.

IX

CICERO TO QUINTUS IN GAUL

Rome, December, 54 B.C.

In the matter of Gabinius, I was not obliged to adopt any of the measures, you, in the kindness of your heart, proposed. No, rather than that, " *may earth gape and swallow me.*" [b] In all I did, I acted with the utmost dignity, as everybody feels, and with the utmost tenderness too. I neither jumped upon him nor picked him up. I was a forcible witness, but beyond that I did and said nothing. The result of the trial, disgraceful and pernicious as it was, I bore with unruffled equanimity. And that was a blessing, which now, when all is done, redounds to my advantage, in that I am not in the least disturbed by these evils of the Republic, and the unbridled excesses of shameless men, which used previously

ante rumpebar, nunc ne movear quidem. Nihil est
2 enim perditius his hominibus, his temporibus. Itaque, ex republica quoniam nihil iam voluptatis capi
potest, cur stomacher, nescio. Litterae me, et studia
nostra et otium villaeque delectant, maximeque pueri
nostri. Angit unus Milo. Sed velim finem afferat
consulatus ; in quo enitar non minus, quam sum
enisus in nostro ; tuque istinc, quod facis, adiuvabis.
De quo cetera (nisi plane vis eripuerit) recte sunt ;
de re familiari timeo. Ὁ δὲ μαίνεται οὐκ ἔτ᾽ ἀνεκτῶς,
qui ludos HS. ccccɔɔɔɔ. comparet. Cuius in hoc uno
inconsiderantiam et ego sustinebo, ut potero, et, tu
3 ut possis, est tuorum nervorum. De motu temporum venientis anni, nihil te intellegere volueram
domestici timoris, sed de communi reipublicae statu ;
in quo etiamsi nihil procuro, tamen nihil curare vix
possum. Quam autem te velim cautum esse in
scribendo, ex hoc conicito, quod ego ad te ne haec
quidem scribo, quae palam in republica turbantur, ne
cuiusquam animum meae litterae interceptae offen-
dant. Quare domestica cura te levatum volo. In republica scio quam sollicitus esse soleas. Video Messallam nostrum consulem, si per interregem, sine

---

ᵃ Hom. *Il.* viii. 355.
ᵇ Or, as Schütz suggests, " I shall cover by aiding him
with money," or again, " I shall restrain."

to break my heart. For anything more corrupt than the men and the times of to-day cannot be conceived.

And so, since no pleasure can be got out of politics, 2 I don't see why I should fret myself; I find a joy in literature and my favourite pursuits, in the leisure of my country houses, but most of all in our boys. My one and only trouble is Milo. But I hope his being made consul will put an end to all that; in that matter I shall exert myself as much as I did in the case of my own consulship, and you will help, as indeed you do, from where you are. In his case everything else is in good train, unless all is lost by absolute violence; but it is his private estate that I am afraid of. "*And now is he beyond endurance mad,*" [a] since the games he is going to give will cost a million sesterces. His thoughtlessness in this one particular I shall bear [b] as well as I can, and it will require all your strength of mind to enable you to do so.

As regards the vicissitudes of fortune in the coming 3 year, I did not intend you to take me as implying any alarm concerning our domestic affairs, but only referring to the general political situation; and in that, though I have no official charge of anything, still I can scarcely have no charge at all upon me. But how cautious I should like you to be in writing, you must infer from the fact that I, in writing to you, avoid mentioning even those political irregularities which all may see, for fear my letter should be intercepted and hurt anybody's feelings. For that reason I would have you be relieved of all domestic anxiety. I know how deeply concerned you always are in public affairs. I foresee that our friend Messalla will be consul, if appointed by the *interrex*, without

iudicio ; si per dictatorem, tamen sine periculo.
Odi nihil habet. Hortensi calor multum valebit.
Gabini absolutio lex impunitatis putatur. Ἐν
παρέργῳ—de dictatore tamen actum adhuc nihil est.
Pompeius abest ; Appius miscet ; Hirrus parat ;
multi intercessores numerantur ; populus non curat ;
4 principes nolunt ; ego quiesco. De mancipiis quod
mihi polliceris, valde te amo ; et sum equidem, ut
scribis, et Romae et in praediis infrequens. Sed cave,
amabo, quidquam, quod ad meum commodum attineat, nisi maximo tuo commodo et maxima tua
5 facultate, mi frater, cogitaris. De epistula Vatini
risi. Sed me ab eo ita observari scio, ut eius ista odia
6 non sorbeam solum, sed etiam concoquam. Quod me
hortaris, ut absolvam, habeo absolutum suave, mihi
quidem uti videtur, ἔπος ad Caesarem ; sed quaero
locupletem tabellarium, ne accidat, quod *Erigonae*
tuae, cui soli, Caesare imperatore, iter ex Gallia
7 tutum non fuit. Quid ? si caementum[1] bonum non
haberem, deturbarem aedificium ? quod quidem
quotidie mihi magis placet, in primisque inferior
porticus et eius conclavia fiunt recte. De Arcano,

---

[1] *Editio Jensoniana*: canem tam *M*, *which Prof. Robinson
Ellis supports with an ingenious explanation which, however,
hardly tallies with what follows.*

---

[a] Because, in the former case, he would take up his office
at once, and so escape trial ; in the latter, even if brought
to trial (for which there would be time) he would certainly
be acquitted. Tyrrell.

[b] Or "keeps such a watchful eye upon me." It appears
that Vatinius (for an account of whom see *Fam.* i. 19. 4,
7, 19, 20 and v. 9. 1) had written a letter to Caesar about
Cicero which Quintus had seen.

[c] Quintus's tragedy, the *Erigona*, had been lost in transit
to Rome.

any trial at all,[a] if by a dictator, even then without risk of condemnation. There is no hatred of him, and Hortensius's warm defence will greatly strengthen his case. The acquittal of Gabinius is regarded as an Act of General Amnesty. *En passant*,—after all, nothing has yet been done about a dictator. Pompey is away ; Appius is making mischief ; Hirrus is on the warpath ; many tribunes are reckoned upon as ready to veto ; the people are apathetic ; the leading men object to it, and as for myself, I lie low.

For your promise about the slaves, I heartily bless 4 you ; and it is true that both at Rome and on my estates I am short-handed. But be sure, my dear brother, that you do not contemplate doing anything with a view to my convenience, unless it is entirely convenient to yourself, and quite within your means.

I laughed over Vatinius's letter. But I know he 5 has such a respect for me [b] that I swallow his bitter animosities without suffering indigestion.

As to your urging me to finish my job, I have now 6 finished my " epic " to Caesar, and a charming one it is, in my opinion ; but I am in search of a trust-worthy letter-carrier, so that it may not meet with the same mishap as your *Erigona* ; she is the only traveller who did not find the journey from Gaul a safe one since Caesar has been in chief command.[c]

What do you mean ? If the quarry-stone I had 7 was not good, was I to pull down the whole building ? and a building that pleases me more every day, and the lower arcade in particular and the chambers connected with it are being properly constructed. As for Arcanum,[d] it is an edifice worthy of Caesar,

[a] One of Quintus's two estates near Arpinum, the other being Laterium.

Caesaris[1] opus est vel mehercule etiam elegantioris
alicuius. Imagines enim istae, et palaestra, et piscina, et nilus, multorum Philotimorum est, non Diphi-
lorum. Sed et ipsi ea adibimus, et mittemus et
8 mandabimus. De Felicis testamento tum magis
querare, si scias. Quas enim tabulas se putavit ob-
signare, in quibus in unciis firmissimum locum
tenemus[2] (lapsus est per errorem et suum et Sicurae
servi), non obsignavit ; quas noluit, eas obsignavit.
9 Ἀλλ᾽ οἰμωζέτω ! nos modo valeamus. Ciceronem, et
ut rogas, amo, et ut meretur, et ut debeo. Dimitto
aut 1 a me, et ut a magistris ne abducam, et quod
mater a Porcia[3] non discedit, sine qua edacitatem
pueri pertimesco. Sed sumus una tamen valde
multum. Rescripsi ad omnia, mi suavissime et
optime frater. Vale.

---

[1] *Tyrrell is inclined to substitute* Caesi ; *for Caesius see*
iii. 1. 2 (ad fin.).

[2] *Wesenberg*: firmissimum tenes MSS.

[3] *Prof. R. Ellis*: in Porcianam (sc. domum) discedit, "*is
going to stay with Porcia*," *Wesenberg*.

---

[a] Philotimus was a satisfactory architect ; Diphilus, the
cessator ("lazy dog"), was not.

or, upon my word, of even some more fastidious connoisseur. For your statues, exercising-ground, fish-pond, and conduit are worthy of ever so many Philotimuses (not Diphiluses).[a] But I shall visit them myself, and send men there, and give them instructions.

About Felix's [b] will, you would complain still more 8 bitterly, if you only knew the facts. The document he thought he was sealing, in which we most certainly have a place as heirs to a twelfth of his estate (his slip was due to a mistake on his own part as much as on that of his slave Sicura), he did not seal; the document he didn't want to seal, he sealed! But let him go hang, so long as we keep our health.

I love your Cicero as you ask me to, and as he 9 deserves, and as I am bound to do. But I am letting him leave me for two reasons ;—so as not to take him away from his teachers, and because his mother never leaves Porcia's side, and when she is away the boy's voracity appals me. But for all that we have a great deal of each other's company. I have now answered all your inquiries, my dearest and best of brothers. Good-bye.

[b] We know no more than appears here of this Felix.

CICERO'S
LETTERS TO BRUTUS

WITH AN ENGLISH TRANSLATION BY
M. CARY, D.Litt.

FORMERLY PROFESSOR OF ANCIENT HISTORY
AT THE UNIVERSITY OF LONDON

PREFACE

THE letters written by Cicero to Brutus and by Brutus to Cicero were not included in the first issue of volume III of Cicero's correspondence in 1929. These letters have now been added with a translation by M. Cary.

26 June 1953

E. H. WARMINGTON
Editor

INTRODUCTION

I. THE TEXT OF THE LETTERS TO BRUTUS

THE 26 letters of which the text and translation are given below constituted in ancient times the IXth book of the published correspondence between Cicero and Marcus Brutus, falling within the last few months of Cicero's life (March or April to July, 43 B.C.). Four other letters of earlier date survive in the collection of Cicero's "Letters to his Friends" (xiii. 10-14); they will be found in the translation of that series by Mr. Glynn Williams.

Of the 26 letters that compose the present volume 21 (nos. VI-XXVI, forming Bk. I according to the traditional classification) are preserved in a number of MSS., mostly of the fourteenth and fifteenth centuries, of which the Codex Mediceus (M) is generally regarded as the most authoritative ; one main branch of this family also contains the letters to Atticus and to Quintus Cicero. The remaining five letters (nos. I-V, constituting Bk. II) remained unknown until 1528, when a scholar named Cratander transcribed them from a family of MSS. which has since disappeared.

In all the MSS. the letters are arranged out of their proper chronological order ; and certain small portions of the text are plainly not in their correct place —an error due to the transposition of several sheets in the archetype. In three cases (Bk. I. 2, 2a ; 3, 3a ; 4, 4a) two distinct letters have been amalgamated into one composite piece. Minor errors in the MSS. are neither numerous nor important.

The most recent editions by modern scholars are those of L. C. Purser (Clarendon Press, 1903) ; of H. Sjögren (Teubner, 1914) ; and of W. Y. Tyrrell and L. C. Purser (*The Correspondence of Cicero*, 2nd edition, vol. vi. : Dublin University Press and Longmans, Green ; 1933).

The text of Tyrrell and Purser, which closely follows that of Sjögren, has been adopted in the present volume, with a few alterations which are indicated in the footnotes.   The letters are printed in the chronological order established by Tyrrell and Purser. Like all students of Cicero's correspondence, the present translator has derived much assistance from the introduction and notes to Tyrrell and Purser's edition.

Further details about the MS. tradition will be found in the Introduction to Sjögren's text and in an article by H. Sternkopf (*Hermes*, 1911, pp. 355-375).

II. THE AUTHORSHIP OF THE LETTERS TO BRUTUS

The genuineness of the correspondence between Cicero and Brutus was not called into question until 1741, when a Cambridge scholar, Dr. James Tunstall,[a] declared it to be a forgery and thus gave rise to a controversy which lasted until the later years of the nineteenth century. The main reasons advanced against the genuineness of the letters were : (1) that

[a] The earliest defender of the letters was another Cambridge man, Dr. Conyers Middleton.

their language contained specimens of Silver Age
latinity ; (2) that they perpetrated errors of fact,
relating to the situation of 43 B.C., such as would have
been impossible to Cicero and Brutus ; (3) that they
were not in keeping with the characters and accomplishments of Cicero and of Brutus, as revealed to us
in the other works of Cicero and in Plutarch's " Life
of Brutus."

A closer examination of the " Letters to Brutus "
has shown to the general satisfaction of modern
scholars that most if not all of them are genuine.
For some of the alleged specimens of Silver Age latinity parallels have been adduced from undoubtedly
genuine works of Cicero ; and most of the apparent
historical errors have been disposed of by re-arranging
the pieces in their correct chronological order. The
only letters whose authenticity is not generally accepted are nos. XVII and XXV (I. 17 and 16),
addressed by Brutus to Atticus and to Cicero respectively.[a] These arouse suspicion by the poverty of
their argument and the abruptness, not to say incoher-
ence of their style, which would seem unworthy of a
well-educated man like Brutus. But the argument of
these letters turned on highly controversial questions
of public policy in which Brutus had a difficult case to
uphold ; and if we bear in mind that behind his Stoic
pose there lurked a hot and stubborn temper,[b] we
need not be surprised that he should in these two

---

[a] One of the chief defenders of the authenticity of the
letters, L. Gurlitt, maintains that no. XXIV (I. 15) is made up
of two authentic letters (§§ 1-2 and 12-13) and an interpolated
middle piece (§§ 3-11).

[b] See the excellent appreciation in Tyrrell and Purser,
vol. vi. pp. cix-cxxiv.

instances have lapsed into the sputtering and at times downright rude style which has shocked modern critics. In the absence of more compelling adverse evidence, letters XVII and XXV have been recognized as genuine in the present volume.

III. SUMMARY OF EVENTS, JANUARY–JULY, 43 B.C.

The period covered by the " Letters to Brutus " was one of renewed civil war after the uneasy truce which followed upon the murder of Caesar. The issues on which this war was fought were complex, and the various contending parties did not at first aline themselves on a common front.

The main seat of war was in North Italy, where Mark Antony claimed for himself the province of Gallia Cisalpina and sought to evict the governor in possession, Decimus Brutus. With the authorization of the Senate, which had rallied round Cicero against Antony, Decimus Brutus refused to quit his province and stood a siege in the town of Mutina (December, 44 B.C.). By April, 43 B.C., Brutus was being hard pressed ; but meanwhile the Senate had mobilized new armies under the command of the consuls A. Hirtius and C. Vibius Pansa (two old officers of Caesar), and at the instigation of Cicero it had enlisted in its service a force of Caesarian veterans which Caesar's adoptive son, C. Iulius Caesar Octavianus, had raised on his own responsibility, and had conferred upon him the rank of an independent commander. On April 14 the combined armies of the consuls and of Octavian beat off an attack by Antony at Forum Gallorum, and on the 21st they inflicted a severe defeat upon him near Mutina. The siege of the town was now raised, and Antony made a hasty retreat from Italy to Gallia Narbonensis (S.E. France).

At Rome it was at first assumed that the victorious armies would pursue Antony and make short work of him. But the deaths of Hirtius and Pansa, of whom the former was killed in the action of Mutina, and the latter died shortly afterwards of wounds, deprived the coalition forces of their best leaders ; and Octavian, the son of Caesar, refused to co-operate with Decimus Brutus, his father's murderer. Antony was thus able to extricate himself and to put pressure upon the governor of Gallia Narbonensis, M. Aemilius Lepidus, to join hands with him. Lepidus, who had previously assured the Senate of his loyalty, consented to put his powerful army at Antony's disposal ; and it was an insufficient offset to this success of Antony that L. Munatius Plancus, governor of Gallia Comata (Central and Northern France), remained loyal to the Republic for the time being (till July or August). Meanwhile Octavian showed signs of breaking with the Senate and coming to terms with Antony. By midsummer, 43 B.C., therefore, the situation had become critical for the senatorial forces in Italy, and the Senate's only chance now lay in the timely arrival of reinforcements from Marcus Brutus.

In August, 44 B.C., M. Brutus and C. Cassius ended a period of indecision, during which they had wandered somewhat aimlessly about Italy, by betaking themselves to the eastern provinces and raising armies there on their own authority. By March, 43 B.C., Cassius had rendered himself master of Syria ; but he still had to reckon with opposition from P. Cornelius Dolabella, Antony's colleague in the consulship of 44 B.C., who claimed Syria as his province and had gained possession of the province of Asia (W. Asia Minor) by a treacherous attack on its governor, C. Trebonius. Though Cassius eventually overcame Dolabella, he was not in a position to bring timely succour to the senatorial forces in Italy.

Meanwhile Brutus had gained possession of Macedonia and Illyria and had captured Antony's brother C. Antonius, who had sought to occupy this province for himself. During the spring and summer of 43 B.C., therefore, he was free to send an expeditionary force to Italy. In March or early April, while Decimus Brutus lay in great straits at Mutina, Cicero called for M. Brutus' intervention. After the battle of Mutina he offered M. Brutus a free hand and suggested his opening a campaign against Dolabella in Asia Minor. In June and July, when Antony was making his recovery, Cicero repeatedly summoned Brutus to Italy, but Brutus refused to budge. Though he, like Cicero, had quarrelled with Antony, he was less determined to resist Antony *à l'outrance*; he was allied with Lepidus by a marriage connexion; above all, he differed profoundly from Cicero in his estimate of Octavian. While Cicero had his suspicions about Octavian, he hoped against hope to retain him in the service of the Senate; Brutus could see nothing in Octavian but another usurper of monarchy, like his adoptive father. On long views Brutus was probably right; yet it may be debated whether in 43 B.C. he did not make a " great refusal " and throw away the last chance of a Republican victory, or at least of a peace by compromise.

M. TULLI CICERONIS EPISTULARUM
AD BRUTUM

I (II. 1)

M. CICERO S. D. M. BRUTO

Romae, a.u.c. 711

1 Cum haec scribebam, res existimabatur in extremum adducta discrimen : tristes enim de Bruto
nostro litterae nuntiique afferebantur : me quidem
non maxime conturbabant : his enim exercitibus duci-
busque, quos habemus, nullo modo poteram diffidere :
neque assentiebar maiori parti hominum : fidem
enim consulum non condemnabam, quae suspecta
vehementer erat. Desiderabam non nullis in rebus
prudentiam et celeritatem, qua si essent usi, iam
pridem rem publicam recuperassemus. Non enim
ignoras quanta momenta sint in re publica temporum
et quid intersit idem illud utrum ante an post de-
cernatur, suscipiatur, agatur. Omnia, quae severe
decreta sunt hoc tumultu, si aut, quo die dixi senten-

---

^a Decimus Brutus, who was being besieged by Mark
Antony in Mutina.

622

THE CORRESPONDENCE OF CICERO
AND BRUTUS

I (II. 1)

CICERO TO BRUTUS

Rome, end of March or beginning of April, 43 B.C.

As I write this letter, the war is considered to have 1
reached a highly critical stage. The news brought in
by letters and by couriers about our friend Brutus [a]
is discouraging. Yet for my part I am not greatly
disturbed; for I simply cannot lose confidence in the
armies and the generals now at our disposal, nor can
I fall in with the prevailing opinion. For I have
nothing to say against the loyalty of the consuls,
which has come under sharp suspicion; what I find
lacking is good judgement and promptitude in several
matters: had they shown this, we should have regained a free state long ago. For you do not need
to be told how much turns on time in politics, and
what a difference it makes to the selfsame policy,
whether one is beforehand or belated in laying it
down, taking it in hand, and carrying it into effect.
Take all the drastic resolutions which have been
voted in this emergency—if these had been imple-
mented on the date when I spoke to the motion,

623

tiam, perfecta essent et non in diem ex die dilata
aut, quo ex tempore suscepta sunt ut agerentur, non
tardata et procrastinata, bellum iam nullum habe-
2 remus. Omnia, Brute, praestiti rei publicae, quae
praestare debuit is, qui esset in eo, in quo ego sum,
gradu senatus populique iudicio collocatus, nec illa
modo, quae nimirum sola ab homine sunt postulanda,
fidem, vigilantiam, patriae caritatem : ea sunt enim,
quae nemo est qui non praestare debeat : ego autem
ei, qui sententiam dicat in principibus de re publica,
puto etiam prudentiam esse praestandam, nec me,
cum mihi tantum sumpserim, ut gubernacula rei
publicae prenderem, minus putarim reprehendendum, si inutiliter aliquid senatui suaserim quam si
3 infideliter. Acta quae sint quaeque agantur scio
perscribi ad te diligenter. Ex me autem illud est
quod te velim habere cognitum, meum quidem animum in acie esse neque respectum ullum quaerere,
nisi me utilitas civitatis forte converterit. Maioris
autem partis animi te Cassiumque respiciunt. Quam
ob rem ita te para, Brute, ut intellegas aut, si hoc
tempore bene res gesta sit, tibi meliorem rem publicam esse faciendam aut, si quid offensum sit, per te
esse eamdem recuperandam.

instead of being put off from day to day, or if they had not been held back and postponed ever since they were adopted for translation into action, we should by now have the war off our hands.

Brutus, I have displayed in the service of the state 2 all those qualities which should be shown by one who stands as I do in senatorial rank and popular estimation, and not merely those which should be demanded in a man as a matter of course, loyalty, watchfulness, love of country—for those are what no man may withhold. Now my view is that he who takes the lead in stating an opinion on public affairs should display sagacity into the bargain; and seeing that I have taken so much upon myself as to grasp the helm of state, I should consider myself no less worthy of censure if my advice to the Senate were unpractical than if it were disloyal.

I know that you receive full and accurate accounts 3 of past and present doings; but coming from me, this is what I would have you understand, that I for one am in spirit in the fighting line and am not looking for any line of retreat, unless by any chance the interest of the community should make me change my front. But most men regard you and Cassius as their standby. Therefore, Brutus, get yourself to realize that if the present campaign goes in our favour, the reform of the state will be incumbent upon you; or else, if we have a set-back, it will be for you to retrieve the state.

CICERO

II (II. 3)

M. BRUTUS S. D. M. CICERONI

Dyrrhachii, A.U.C. 711

1 Litteras tuas valde exspecto, quas scripsisti post
nuntios nostrarum rerum, et de morte Trebonii:
non enim dubito quin mihi consilium tuum explices.
Indigno scelere et civem optimum amisimus et provinciae possessione pulsi sumus, quam recuperari
facile est : neque minus turpe aut flagitiosum erit
2 post recuperari. Antonius adhuc est nobiscum, sed
me dius fidius et moveor hominis precibus et timeo
ne illum aliquorum furor excipiat. Plane aestuo.
Quod si scirem quid tibi placeret, sine sollicitudine
essem. Id enim optimum esse persuasum esset
mihi. Qua re quam primum fac me certiorem quid
3 tibi placeat. Cassius noster Syriam, legiones Syria-
cas habet, ultro quidem a Murco et a Marcio et
ab exercitu ipso arcessitus. Ego scripsi ad Tertiam
sororem et matrem, ne prius ederent hoc, quod
optime ac felicissime gessit Cassius, quam cum con-
4 silium cognovissent tibique visum esset. Legi orationes duas tuas, quarum altera Kal. Ian. usus es,
altera de litteris meis, quae habita est abs te contra

---

a C. Trebonius, one of Caesar's assassins, and governor
of the province of Asia. He was treacherously attacked and
killed by Dolabella.
b Gaius Antonius, brother of Mark Antony. Appointed
governor of Macedonia, he was defeated and captured by
Brutus.
c L. Statius Murcus and Q. Marcius Crispus were two
officers of Caesar whom he sent to quell disorders in Syria.
d A. Fufius Calenus, consul in 47 B.C. Antony's chief

626

II (II. 3)

Dyrrhachium, April 1, 43 B.C.

I anxiously await the letter which you wrote on 1
receipt of the news of our campaign and of the death
of Trebonius.[a] I feel sure it contains for me an orderly
statement of your policy. A foul crime has taken
from us an excellent citizen and has wrested from us
the control of a province. To retrieve it is no
trouble ; but it will be none the less a humiliation
and a scandal that we should be retrieving the loss
instead of preventing it.

Antonius [b] is still with me. But I'll take my oath 2
upon it, I am being impressed by the man's entreaties,
and I am afraid that the passionate pleadings of
several persons may snatch him away. I am in a
downright fever. If I but knew what you would
have me do, I should be free from worry, for I should
be convinced that you know best. Therefore let me
know as soon as possible what you think right.

Our friend Cassius holds Syria and the Syrian 3
legions : Murcus and Marcius [c] and the troops themselves actually called him in before he made a move.
I have written to my sister Tertia and my mother not
to publish the report of this splendid and most fortunate exploit of Cassius before ascertaining what you
would advise, and what you think of it.

I have read your two speeches, the one which you 4
delivered on January 1, and the other on my dispatches, when you spoke in opposition to Calenus.[d]

spokesman in the Senate. The two *Philippics* to which
Cicero refers here are the fifth and the seventh.

CICERO

Calenum. Nunc scilicet hoc exspectas, dum eas
laudem. Nescio animi an ingenii tui maior in his
libellis laus contineatur. Iam concedo ut vel Philip-
pici vocentur, quod tu quadam epistula iocans scrip-
5 sisti. Duabus rebus egemus, Cicero, pecunia et
supplemento : quarum altera potest abs te expediri,
ut aliqua pars militum istinc mittatur nobis, vel
secreto consilio adversus Pansam vel actione in
senatu, ab ipso senatu altera, quae magis est necessaria neque meo exercitui magis quam reliquorum.
Hoc magis doleo Asiam nos amisisse : quam sic vexari
a Dolabella audio, ut iam non videatur crudelissimum
eius facinus interfectio Trebonii. Vetus Antistius
6 me tamen pecunia sublevavit. Cicero, filius tuus,
sic mihi se probat industria, patientia, labore, animi
magnitudine, omni denique officio, ut prorsus numquam dimittere videatur cogitationem cuius sit filius.
Qua re quoniam efficere non possum, ut pluris facias
eum, qui tibi est carissimus, illud tribue iudicio meo,
ut tibi persuadeas non fore illi abutendum gloria tua,
ut adipiscatur honores paternos. Kalend. April.
Dyrrhachio.

C. Vibius Pansa, consul in 43 B.C. One of the com-
manders of the senatorial forces in the campaign of Mutina.
 The Roman province of Asia (W. Asia Minor).
 P. Cornelius Dolabella, son-in-law of Cicero, and consul
in 44 B.C. Appointed governor of Syria, he invaded Asia
without orders.
 See Letter XVI.
 M. Tullius Cicero, junior. He interrupted his studies at
Athens in order to join Brutus' army.

Now I'll warrant you are waiting for me to pay you compliments on them. I cannot say whether these pamphlets are a higher testimonial to your fine spirit or to your wealth of genius. I readily grant you that they should be dubbed " Philippics," if you like : that is the title you jestingly gave them in one of your letters.

We stand in want of two things, Cicero, money and 5 fresh drafts. The latter it is in your power to make available : you can send us a contingent from where you are, either by a private understanding with Pansa,[a] or by proceedings in the Senate ; the former could come from the Senate directly. The need for the former, which is just as great in the armies of the other generals as in mine, makes me regret so much the more the loss of Asia.[b] I hear that Dolabella [c] is harrying it to such effect that his murder of Trebonius no longer strikes me as his most fiendish atrocity. All the same, Vetus Antistius [d] has met part of my needs with a money contribution.

Your son Cicero [e] gives me such a good account of 6 himself in respect of his energy, power of endurance, application, high spirits, in a word, in every helpful quality, that he seems never for a moment to lose out of mind whose son he is. Therefore, seeing that I cannot contrive to make you hold him in still higher affection (for he is the apple of your eyes), I ask you, in deference to my considered opinion, to assure yourself that he will not need to poach on your renown in order to attain his father's high rank. Dyrrhachium, April 1.

III (II. 2)

Romae, a.u.c. 711

1 Planci animum in rem publicam egregium, legiones,
auxilia, copias ex litteris eius, quarum exemplum
tibi missum arbitror, perspicere potuisti. Lepidi,
tui necessarii, qui secundum fratrem affines habet
quos oderit proximos, levitatem et inconstantiam
animumque semper inimicum rei publicae iam credo
2 tibi ex tuorum litteris esse perspectum. Nos exspectatio sollicitat, quae est omnis iam in extremum
adducta discrimen. Est enim spes omnis in Bruto
3 expediendo, de quo vehementer timebamus. Ego
hic cum homine furioso satis habeo negotii, Servilio,
quem tuli diutius quam dignitas mea patiebatur, sed
tuli rei publicae causa, ne darem perditis civibus
hominem, parum sanum illum quidem, sed tamen
nobilem, quo concurrerent, quod faciunt nihilo minus,
sed eum alienandum a re publica non putabam.
Finem feci eius ferendi. Coeperat enim esse tanta
insolentia, ut neminem liberum duceret. In Planci
vero causa exarsit incredibili dolore, mecumque per
biduum ita contendit et a me ita fractus est, ut eum
in perpetuum modestiorem sperem fore. Atque in

ᵃ L. Munatius Plancus, governor of Gallia Comata. For
his relations to Cicero see *Epp. ad Fam.* x. 1-24.

ᵇ M. Aemilius Lepidus, the future triumvir. At this time
he was governor of Gallia Comata, and the husband of
Brutus' sister. He subsequently consented to his brother
being placed on the proscription lists.   ᶜ Decimus Brutus.

ᵈ P. Servilius Vatia Isauricus, consul 48 b.c. He advocated negotiation with Mark Antony.

ᵉ Antony's adherents.

III (II. 2)

Rome, April 11, 43 B.C.

Of Plancus' [a] splendid loyalty to the state, of his 1
legions, auxiliary forces and equipment, you have
been able to get a clear idea from his letter, of which
I think you received a copy. As for your bosom
friend Lepidus,[b] who hates his connexions by marriage only one degree less than he hates his brother,
I believe you will by now have realized from the
letters of your own family that he is lacking in
principle and consistency, and is chronically ill-
disposed to the free state.

We are haunted by a feeling of suspense, which is 2
now wholly centred on our extremely critical position;
for all our hopes are set on the relief of Brutus,[c] about
whom we are exceedingly anxious.

Here I am having trouble enough with that mad- 3
man Servilius.[d] I have put up with him longer than
my self-respect would allow ; yet I did put up with
him for the state's sake, for fear I should present him
to the desperadoes [e] as a rallying-point—a man, you
know, who is lacking in sense, but to offset that has
blue blood in his veins. Even so, they are rallying
round him ; but I think I ought not to provoke him
to disaffection.—I have done with my complaisance to
him, for he is becoming so rude as to treat us like so
many slaves. In the matter of Plancus, to be sure,
he blazed up with extraordinary bitterness, and for
two whole days he battled with me so fiercely and
received such a mauling from me, that I hope he will
mend his manners for once and all. Oh, and in the

hac contentione ipsa, cum maxime res ageretur, a. d.
v. Idus Apriles litterae mihi in senatu redditae sunt
a Lentulo nostro de Cassio, de legionibus, de Syria :
quas statim cum recitavissem, cecidit Servilius, complures praeterea : sunt enim insignes aliquot, qui
improbissime sentiunt, sed acerbissime tulit Servilius
assensum esse mihi de Planco.   Magnum illud mon-
strum in re publica est ; sed quomodo nunc est, mihi
crede, non erit, III. Id. April.[1]

IV (II. 4)

M. CICERO S. D. M. BRUTO

Romae, A.U.C. 711

1   Datis mane a. d. III. Id. April. Scaptio litteris,
eodem die tuas accepi Kal. April. Dyrrhachio datas
vesperi.   Itaque mane prid. Id. Apr. cum a Scaptio
certior factus essem non esse eos profectos, quibus
pridie dederam, et statim ire, hoc paullulum exaravi
2   ipsa in turba matutinae salutationis.   De Cassio
laetor et rei publicae gratulor, mihi etiam, qui re-
pugnante et irascente Pansa sententiam dixerim, ut
Dolabellam bello Cassius persequeretur.   Et quidem
audacter dicebam sine nostro senatus consulto iam

---

[1] *See Tyrrell and Purser.*

---

[a] P. Cornelius Lentulus Spinther, deputy-governor of
Asia after the death of Trebonius. See *Epp. ad Fam.* xii.
14-15.
[b] See Introduction.
[c] Letter III (II. 2).   Scaptius was an agent of Brutus
(perhaps to be identified with his bailiff in Cilicia—*Epp. ad
Att.* v. 21, vi. 2).

very middle of the duel, just while we were having it out, a letter dated April 9 was handed to me in the Senate ; it was from our friend Lentulus *a* and brought news of Cassius,*b* the legions, and of Syria. I had hardly finished reading it out, than Servilius collapsed, and a number of others with him ; for there are several persons of note whose attitude is quite unscrupulous. But what exasperated Servilius most of all was that I carried the House in the matter of Plancus. That is an impressive indication of the trend of politics. But take my word for it, the present mood won't last. April 11.

IV (II. 4)

CICERO TO BRUTUS

Rome, April 12, 43 B.C.

Early on April 11 I handed a letter *c* to Scaptius, 1 and on the same day received the note dispatched by you on the evening of April 1. On the morning of April 12, accordingly, having ascertained from Scaptius that the messengers to whom I had given my note on the previous day were not yet on the way, and were now on the point of starting out, I am jotting down this short postscript even while my morning callers are thronging round me.

I am glad about Cassius ; and my congratulations 2 go to the state, and also to myself, seeing that it was I who proposed in opposition to Pansa and in disregard of his anger, that Cassius should be charged with the operations against Dolabella. Yes, and I defiantly announced that he was already engaged on

633

illud eum bellum gerere. De te etiam dixi tum quae
dicenda putavi. Haec ad te oratio perferetur, quo-
3 niam te video delectari Philippicis nostris. Quod
me de Antonio[a] consulis, quoad Bruti exitum cog-
norimus, custodiendum puto. Ex iis litteris, quas
mihi misisti, Dolabella Asiam vexare videtur et in
ea se gerere taeterrime. Compluribus autem scripsisti Dolabellam a Rhodiis esse exclusum : qui si ad
Rhodum accessit, videtur mihi Asiam reliquisse. Id
si ita est, istic tibi censeo commorandum : sin eam
semel cepit, mihi crede, statim[1] in Asiam censeo per-
sequendum : nihil mihi videris hoc tempore melius
acturus.

4 Quod egere te duabus necessariis rebus scribis,
supplemento et pecunia, difficile consilium est. Non
enim mihi occurrunt facultates, quibus uti te posse
videam praeter illas, quas senatus decrevit, ut pecunias a civitatibus mutuas sumeres.[b] De supplemento autem non video quid fieri possit. Tantum
enim abest ut Pansa de exercitu suo aut dilectu tibi
aliquid tribuat, ut etiam moleste ferat tam multos
ad te ire voluntarios, quo modo equidem credo, quod
iis rebus, quae in Italia decernuntur, nullas copias
nimis magnas esse arbitretur, quo modo autem multi
suspicantur, quod ne te quidem nimis firmum esse
velit, quod ego non suspicor.

---

[1] statim *conj. by Tyrrell and Purser* : at.

[a] Gaius Antonius.
[b] See Letter II § 5.

that campaign without waiting for our commission from the Senate. In the same session I made such reference to you as seemed appropriate. My speech shall be communicated to you, for I observe that you take a delight in our " Philippics."

In answer to your inquiry about Antonius,[a] my 3 view is that he ought to be kept in detention until we know the result of Brutus' campaign. I gather from the letter which you sent me that Dolabella is harrying Asia and is behaving atrociously in it. And yet you have written to quite a number of people that Dolabella had been shut out from Rhodes ; but if he went as far as Rhodes, it looks to me as if he had left Asia. If that is a fact, I recommend that you should stay where you are ; but once he has captured Rhodes—if that happens, believe me, you must pursue him into Asia at once. It seems to me you could do nothing better at this time.

Touching upon your remark that you are short of 4 two necessaries, fresh drafts and money,[b] I am puzzled what to propose to you. I cannot think of any expedients to which in my view you could have recourse, except the resolutions which the Senate carried, that you should raise a loan among the free communities. But I do not see what can be done about reinforcements ; for Pansa is so little disposed to let you have any part of his army or of his new levies, that he even takes offence at the numbers which are joining you as volunteers. According to my own belief, he estimates that no force can be too large for the operations which are being decided on in Italy ; but the reason which many people surmise is that he wants no one, not even you, to make too firm a stand. This suspicion I do not share.

5 Quod scribis te ad Tertiam sororem et matrem
scripsisse, ut ne prius ederent ea, quae gesta a Cassio
essent, quam mihi visum esset, video te veritum esse
id, quod verendum fuit, ne animi partium Caesaris,
quomodo etiam nunc partes appellantur, vehementer
commoverentur. Sed ante quam tuas litteras accepimus, audita res erat et pervulgata, tui etiam
tabellarii ad multos familiares tuos litteras attulerant.
Qua re neque supprimenda res erat, praesertim cum
id fieri non posset, neque, si posset, non divulgandam
6 potius quam occultandam putaremus. De Cicerone
meo et, si tantum est in eo, quantum scribis, tantum
scilicet, quantum debeo, gaudeo, et si, quod amas
eum, eo maiora facis, id ipsum incredibiliter gaudeo,
a te eum diligi.

V (II. 5)

M. CICERO S. D. M. BRUTO

Romae, a.u.c. 711

1 Quae litterae tuo nomine recitatae sint Id. April.
in senatu eodemque tempore Antonii, credo ad te
scripsisse tuos, quorum ego nemini concedo ; sed
nihil necesse erat eadem omnes, illud necesse me ad
te scribere, quid sentirem tota de constitutione huius
belli et quo iudicio essem quaque sententia. Volun-

You say that you wrote to your sister and your 5
mother, not to make known the successes of Cassius
before I thought proper. I see you were afraid, as
you had a right to be, lest the Caesarian party, which
is the name still being given to that body, should be
badly upset. But before we received your note the
story was out and had become common property ;
your own couriers too had delivered correspondence
to many acquaintances of yours. To suppress the
news was therefore false policy, especially as that was
not practicable ; and we thought that, supposing it
were possible, we should all the same publish it
rather than keep it dark.

As for my son Cicero, if there is as much in him as 6
you tell me, I am of course as glad as I should be ;
or again, if your fondness for him makes you exagger-
ate, your very excess gives me immense pleasure at
the thought that you are his good friend.

V (II. 5)

CICERO TO BRUTUS

Rome, April 14, 43 b.c.

I believe you have heard from your family which 1
of your letters was read out in the Senate on April 13,
and of Antony's letter being read at the same time.
I yield to none of your folk in my concern for you ;
but there is no need for all of us to tell the same
story. My special duty is to inform you of my
impressions about the general condition of this
war, of my considered opinion and my personal
feeling on it. My ideals on the main political issue

tas mea, Brute, de summa re publica semper eadem
fuit, quae tua, ratio quibusdam in rebus—non enim
omnibus—paullo fortasse vehementior. Scis mihi
semper placuisse non rege solum, sed regno liberari
rem publicam : tu lenius, immortali omnino cum tua
laude, sed, quid melius fuerit, magno dolore sensimus,
magno periculo sentimus. Recenti illo tempore tu
omnia ad pacem, quae oratione confici non poterat,
ego omnia ad libertatem, quae sine pace nulla est,
pacem ipsam bello atque armis effici posse arbitrabar :
studio non deerant arma poscentium, quorum re-
2 pressimus impetum ardoremque restinximus. Itaque
res in eum locum venerat, ut, nisi Caesari Octaviano
deus quidam illam mentem dedisset, in potestatem
perditissimi hominis et turpissimi M. Antonii venien-
dum fuerit, quocum vides hoc tempore ipso quod sit
quantumque certamen : id profecto nullum esset,
nisi tum conservatus esset Antonius. Sed haec
omitto : res enim a te gesta memorabilis et paene
caelestis repellit omnes reprehensiones, quippe quae
ne laude quidem satis idonea affici possit. Exstitisti
nuper vultu severo ; exercitum, copias, legiones
idoneas per te brevi tempore comparasti : di immortales ! qui ille nuntius, quae illae litterae, quae
laetitia senatus, quae alacritas civitatis erat ! nihil
umquam vidi tam omnium consensione laudatum.

---

[a] This refers to the seduction of Antony's troops by
Octavian in November 44 B.C., which in Cicero's opinion
prevented a military dictatorship by Antony.

[b] Brutus had vetoed a suggestion by his fellow-conspira-
tors, that Antony too should be killed on the Ides of March.

have always been the same as yours, Brutus ; my way of thinking in certain matters (I do not say in all) was perhaps a little more drastic. You know that it was always my resolve that the state should be freed not merely of a monarch but of monarchy. You took a more lenient view, and this was altogether to your undying credit ; but which was the better policy we have been made to feel to our bitter sorrow, and are experiencing at our great peril. At that time, not so long ago, your supreme goal was peace, which could not be won by oratory ; mine was liberty, which without peace is an illusion. I considered that peace as well as liberty could be secured by force of arms. The party that called for arms was thoroughly in earnest ; yet we stifled their enthusiasm and damped down their ardour.

Consequently things came to such a pass, that but 2 for that divine inspiration which came to Caesar Octavianus,[a] we should have had to fall under the power of that utter desperado, that foul wretch, Marcus Antonius, and you can see what a struggle, and how hard-fought, we have even now with him. This conflict of course would be non-existent, if Antony's life had not then been spared.[b] But I say nothing of this, for your unforgettable and almost superhuman exploit disarms all criticism, indeed I cannot even match it with really adequate words of praise. In these last days you have asserted yourself with a grim visage ; by your own effort you have in a short time raised sufficient troops, supplies and legions. Heavens, what a piece of news that was, what a bulletin ! How gladdened was the Senate, and how elated the citizens ! I never saw such an unanimous expression of praise for anything.

Erat exspectatio reliquiarum Antonii, quem equitatu
legionibusque magna ex parte spoliaras : ea quoque
habuit exitum optabilem ; nam tuae litterae, quae
recitatae in senatu sunt, et imperatoris et militum
virtutem et industriam tuorum, in quibus Ciceronis
mei, declarant.   Quod si tuis placuisset de his litteris
referri et nisi in tempus turbulentissimum post discessum Pansae consulis incidissent, honos quoque
iustus et debitus dis immortalibus decretus esset.
3 Ecce tibi Idib. April. advolat mane Celer Pilius, qui
vir, di boni, quam gravis, quam constans, quam
bonarum in re publica partium ! hic epistulas affert
duas, unam tuo nomine, alteram Antonii ; dat Servilio tribuno plebis, ille Cornuto : recitantur in
senatu.   ANTONIUS PROCOS. : magna admiratio, ut si
esset recitatum DOLABELLA IMPERATOR, a quo quidem
venerant tabellarii, sed nemo Pili similis, qui proferre
litteras auderet aut magistratibus reddere.   Tuae
recitantur, breves illae quidem, sed in Antonium
admodum lenes : vehementer admiratus senatus ;
mihi autem non erat explicatum, quid agerem :
falsas dicerem ? quid, si tu eas approbasses ? con-
4 firmarem ? non erat dignitatis tuae.   Itaque ille dies
silentio ; postridie autem, cum sermo increbruisset

Probably to be identified with an obscure partisan of
Caesar.
   M. Caecilius Cornutus, praetor urbanus.   In the absence
of the consuls, he presided over the Senate.

Curiosity was rife concerning Antonius' remnant, after you had taken most of his cavalry and legions from him. In this case too it heard the result for which it had hoped ; for your dispatch, which was read out in the Senate, proclaims the gallantry of commander and soldiers alike, and the good work of your staff, including my son Cicero. If only your kinsfolk had agreed to a motion on this dispatch and had not been caught in a period of great disorder after the departure of the consul Pansa, a vote of homage to the immortal gods would also have been passed, as is usual and proper.

Now just imagine ! On the morning of April 13 **3** Celer Pilius [a] came scurrying in. Good lord, what a man ! What dignified bearing ! What aplomb ! What a fine figure he cuts on the political scene! This fellow brings two dispatches, one from you, the other from Antony ; he hands them to Servilius the tribune of the plebs, who passes them on to Cornutus.[b] They are read out in the Senate : " Antonius, proconsul." We were quite taken aback, as if we had heard the words " Dolabella, imperator." He too, to be sure, had sent couriers, but there was nobody of Pilius' kidney who had the face to exhibit them or hand them over to the magistrates. Your letter was read out—that note which had little indeed to say but was decidedly lenient to Antony. The Senate was greatly astonished. For my part, I had no idea what course I should take. Was I to denounce the note as a forgery ? But suppose you had guaranteed your authorship ! Was I to certify it ? But that would have let you down !

So this day passed with nothing said. But next **4** day, when everybody was talking about it, and the

CICERO

Piliusque oculos vehementius hominum offendisset,
natum omnino est principium a me : de proconsule
Antonio multa ; Sestius causae non defuit : post
mecum, quanto suum filium, quanto meum in periculo futurum duceret, si contra proconsulem arma
tulissent ; nosti hominem : causae tamen non defuit.
Dixerunt etiam alii ; Labeo vero noster nec signum
tuum in epistula nec diem appositum nec te scripsisse
ad tuos, ut soleres : hoc cogere volebat, falsas litteras
5 esse et, si quaeris, probabat. Nunc tuum est consilium, Brute, de toto genere belli. Video te lenitate
delectari et eum putare fructum esse maximum,
praeclare quidem, sed aliis rebus, aliis temporibus
locus esse solet debetque clementiae : nunc quid
agitur, Brute ? Templis deorum immortalium im-
minet hominum egentium et perditorum spes nec
quidquam aliud decernitur hoc bello, nisi utrum simus
necne. Cui parcimus aut quid agimus ? His ergo
consulimus, quibus victoribus vestigium nostrum
nullum relinquetur ? Nam quid interest inter Dolabellam et quemvis Antoniorum trium ? Quorum si
cui parcimus, duri fuimus in Dolabella. Haec ut ita
sentiret senatus populusque Romanus, etsi res ipsa
cogebat, tamen maxima ex parte nostro consilio

ᵃ P. Sestius, a former supporter of Cicero whom the
orator defended in the speech *Pro Sestio.*
ᵇ Pacuvius Antistius Labeo, one of the tyrannicides.
ᶜ The three brothers Marcus, Gaius and Lucius Antonius.
642

sight of Pilius gave people a bad shock, it was on my initiative that a discussion took place at all. I let myself go about the "proconsul Antonius." Sestius,[a] who came after me, backed up my case. He had a word with me afterwards and warned me in what danger his son and mine, he thought, would stand, if they had borne arms against a "proconsul." You know the man : he *did* back me up. Others spoke besides. But our friend Labeo[b] pointed out that the letter contained neither your signature nor a date-mark, and that you had not written as usual to your family. He offered this as certain evidence that the letter was a forgery and, if you care to know, he was carrying his point.

Now, Brutus, it is for you to advise me about the 5 general conduct of the war. I observe that you glory in leniency and think that it carries the richest reward. An excellent principle, no doubt ! But it is not conditions and times like these that give the usual and proper scope for a policy of pardon. At present, Brutus, what is afoot ? The hopes of down-at-heels and desperadoes are grimly set on the temples of the immortal gods, and the issue at stake in this war is nothing else than whether we are to exist or not. To whom are we showing mercy ? Or what are we about ? Are we then in this crisis having regard for men who, if theirs is the victory, will not leave a trace of us ? For what is the difference between Dolabella and any one of the Antonius trio ? [c] If we show indulgence to any of these, our treatment of Dolabella was harsh. Though the logic of facts compelled the Senate and people of Rome to adopt this view, yet it was mainly at my prompting and by the weight of my support that this result was

atque auctoritate perfectum est. Tu si hanc rationem non probas, tuam sententiam defendam, non
relinquam meam : neque dissolutum a te quidquam
homines exspectant nec crudele ; huius rei moderatio
facilis est, ut in duces vehemens sis, in milites liberalis.
6 Ciceronem meum, mi Brute, velim quam plurimum
tecum habeas : virtutis disciplinam meliorem re-
periet nullam quam contemplationem atque imita-
tionem tui. xviii. Kalend. Maias.

VI (I. 2 §§ 3-6)

M. CICERO S. D. M. BRUTO

Romae, a.u.c. 711

3 ... Te benevolentiam exercitus equitumque
4 expertum vehementer gaudeo. De Dolabella, ut
scribis, si quid habebis novi, facies me certiorem, in
quo delector me ante providisse, ut tuum iudicium
liberum esset cum Dolabella belli gerendi : id valde
pertinuit, ut ego tum intellegebam, ad rem publicam,
5 ut nunc iudico, ad dignitatem tuam. Quod scribis
me maximo otio egisse, ut insectarer Antonios, idque
laudas, credo ita videri tibi, sed illam distinctionem
tuam nullo pacto probo : scribis enim acrius pro-
hibenda bella civilia esse quam in superatos iracundiam exercendam. Vehementer a te, Brute, dissentio,
nec clementiae tuae concedo, sed salutaris severi-

achieved. If you reject this way of thinking I shall speak up for your view, but without abandoning mine. Men do not look for any behaviour on your part that is either lax or vindictive. You may easily strike a balance in this case by dealing drastically with the leaders and showing generosity to the troops.

I would like you, my dear Brutus, to have my son 6 Cicero at your side as much as possible. He will never obtain a better training in the manly arts than by studying and imitating you. April 14.

VI (I. 2 §§ 3-6)

CICERO TO BRUTUS

Rome, April 17, 43 B.C.

. . . I am delighted to hear that you found the 3 army and the mounted troops well disposed. If, as 4 you say, you have news of Dolabella, you will let me know. I rejoice that in his case I made timely provision, so that you should be free to decide whether to make war on Dolabella. As I perceived at the time, my action closely touched the interests of the state ; as I now judge matters, it touches your honour.

You remark that I took plenty of time before I 5 opened my attack on the Antonii, and you commend me for this. Well, I do believe that this is your point of view. But nothing could induce me to accept that distinction which you draw. You say that we should display more zeal in banning civil wars than in wreaking vengeance on the vanquished. I heartily disagree with you, Brutus, and I cannot defer to your leniency. No, a wholesome sternness carries the day

tas vincit inanem speciem clementiae ; quod si
clementes esse volumus, numquam deerunt bella
civilia. Sed de hoc tu videris : de me possum idem,
quod Plautinus pater in Trinummo :

Mihi quidem aetas acta ferme est : tua istuc refert maxime.

6 Opprimemini, mihi crede, Brute, nisi provideritis ;
neque enim populum semper eundem habebitis neque
senatum neque senati ducem. Haec ex oraculo
Apollinis Pythii edita tibi puta : nihil potest esse
verius. xv. Kal. Maias.

VII (I. 3 §§ 1-3)

M. CICERO S. D. M. BRUTO

Romae, a.u.c. 711

1 Nostrae res meliore loco videbantur ; scripta enim
ad te certo scio, quae gesta sunt. Quales tibi saepe
scripsi consules esse tales exstiterunt. Caesaris vero
pueri mirifica indoles virtutis : utinam tam facile eum
florentem et honoribus et gratia regere ac tenere
possimus, quam facile adhuc tenuimus ! est omnino
illud difficilius, sed tamen non diffidimus ; persuasum
est enim adulescenti, et maxime per me, eius opera

---

^a L. 219.
^b The battle of Forum Gallorum.
^c Octavian (C. Iulius Caesar Octavianus).

against the vain show of leniency ! Why, if we choose to be lenient, there will never be a lack of civil wars ! But this is for you to look into. To myself I can apply the same words as the father uses in Plautus' " Trinummus " [a] :

> My life is all but over; but for you
> This matter is of close concern.

Take my word for it, Brutus, you will all be over- **6** whelmed, if you will not look ahead ; for you will not find the people ever unchanging, nor the Senate, nor the leaders of the Senate. Take this utterance as voiced from the oracle of the Pythian Apollo; no- thing could be more true. April 17.

VII (I. 3 §§ 1-3)

CICERO TO BRUTUS

Rome, about April 21, 43 b.c.

Our cause seems in better circumstance ; for I **1** know for sure that you have been posted up about our achievements.[b] The consuls have shown up true to their character, as I have often described it to you. But the boy Caesar [c] is marvellously well endowed with manly character. If only I could direct and hold him, now that he is gathering strength from his official position and patronage, as easily as I have held him hitherto ! That is altogether a harder task, though I am not losing confidence for all that ; for the young man has made up his mind—and it was I who chiefly impressed it upon him—that we owe our safety

647

nos esse salvos, et certe, nisi is Antonium ab urbe
2 avertisset, perissent omnia. Triduo vero aut qua-
triduo ante hanc rem pulcherrimam timore quodam
perculsa civitas tota ad te se cum coniugibus et
liberis effundebat ; eadem recreata a. d. xii. Kal.
Maias te huc venire quam se ad te ire malebat : quo
quidem die magnorum meorum laborum multarumque vigiliarum fructum cepi maximum—si modo est
aliquis fructus ex solida veraque gloria ;—nam tantae
multitudinis, quantam capit urbs nostra, concursus
est ad me factus, a qua usque in Capitolium deductus
maximo clamore atque plausu in rostris collocatus
sum : nihil est in me inane—neque enim debet,—sed
tamen omnium ordinum consensus, gratiarum actio
gratulatioque me commovet propterea, quod popula-
rem me esse in populi salute praeclarum est. Sed
3 haec te malo ab aliis. Me velim de tuis rebus con-
siliisque facias diligentissime certiorem illudque
consideres, ne tua liberalitas dissolutior videatur : sic
sentit senatus, sic populus Romanus, nullos umquam
hostes digniores omni supplicio fuisse quam eos cives,
qui hoc bello contra patriam arma ceperunt, quos
quidem ego omnibus sententiis ulciscor et persequor
omnibus bonis approbantibus. Tu quid de hac re
sentias, tui iudicii est : ego sic sentio, trium fratrum
unam et eandem esse causam.

ᵃ The speaker's platform in the Forum.

to his efforts ; and to be sure, if he had not drawn Antony away from the city, all would have been lost.

And yet, three or four days before this glorious 2 event the entire citizen body, as if unnerved with fear, was fain to stream out to you with family and all ; yet on April 20 they had recovered their nerve and would rather that you should come here than that they should go to you. That was the day on which I gathered the full harvest of my hard toil and frequent vigils, if any substantial harvest can indeed accrue from a well-founded and genuine renown ; for the crowd that flocked round me was as vast as our city could contain. I was escorted by it right up to the Capitol and then was made to take my stand on the Rostra *a* amid huge acclamation and applause. I am not at all being vain ; there is no justification for that. But all the same, I am deeply impressed by the unanimity of all classes, by their thanksgivings and felicitations, and for this reason, that it is glorious to achieve popularity in the cause of the people's safety. But I would sooner you heard about this from others.

Please spare no pains to keep me informed of your 3 position and your policy, and bear in mind that your generosity must not give an impression of a loss of firm purpose. This is the Senate's, this is the people's conviction, that no enemy ever deserved more richly the utmost rigour of punishment than those citizens who took up arms against their country in this war. These are the men whom I castigate and pursue in all my pronouncements, with the approval of all loyal men. You must judge for yourself how you feel about this ; my feeling is that the three brothers are one and all in the same case.

CICERO

VIII (I. 3 § 4)

M. CICERO S. D. M. BRUTO

Romae, a.u.c. 711

4   Consules duos, bonos quidem, sed dumtaxat bonos
consules, amisimus : Hirtius quidem in ipsa victoria
occidit, cum paucis diebus ante magno proelio vicisset ; nam Pansa fugerat vulneribus acceptis, quae
ferre non potuit.   Reliquias hostium Brutus persequi-
tur et Caesar ; hostes autem omnes iudicati, qui
M. Antoni sectam secuti sunt, idque senatus consultum plerique interpretantur etiam ad tuos sive
captivos sive dediticios pertinere.   Equidem nihil
disserui durius, cum nominatim de C. Antonio de-
cernerem, quod ita statueram, a te cognoscere causam
eius senatum oportere.   v. Kal. Maias.

IX (I. 5)

M. CICERO S. D. M. BRUTO

Romae, a.u.c. 711

1   A. d. v. K. Maias, cum de iis, qui hostes iudicati
sunt, bello persequendis sententiae dicerentur, dixit
Servilius etiam de Ventidio et ut Cassius persequere-

ᵃ The consul A. Hirtius won successive victories over
Antony's forces at Forum Gallorum (April 14th) and Mutina
(April 21st).
ᵇ Decimus Brutus and Octavian.

VIII (I. 3 § 4)

CICERO TO BRUTUS

Rome, April 27, 43 B.C.

We have lost two consuls, loyal men both, but nothing more than loyal. Hirtius to be sure met his death in the hour of victory, after he had won another victory in a great battle a few days earlier.[a] They were his victories, for Pansa had taken to flight with wounds which he could not endure. The remnants of the enemy are being pursued by Brutus and Caesar.[b] Now all those who have attached themselves to Marcus Antonius' following have been declared public enemies, and according to the general construction put upon it this resolution of the Senate applies also to your captives or capitulants. For my part I used no specially harsh language when I pronounced on Gaius Antonius in person, because I had decided that the Senate must obtain the facts of the case from you. April 27.

IX (I. 5)

CICERO TO BRUTUS

Rome, May 5, 43 B.C.

On April 27, when the debate was on concerning measures of war against those who have been declared public enemies, Servilius went on to speak about Ventidius,[c] and proposed that Cassius should take

---

[c] P. Ventidius Bassus, an officer of Antony who brought him reinforcements after the battle of Mutina.

tur Dolabellam. Cui cum essem assensus, decrevi hoc
amplius, ut tu, si arbitrarere utile exque re publica
esse, persequerere bello Dolabellam, si minus id commodo rei publicae facere posses sive non existimares
ex re publica esse, ut in iisdem locis exercitum con-
tineres. Nihil honorificentius potuit facere senatus,
quam ut tuum esset iudicium, quid maxime conducere
rei publicae tibi videretur. Equidem sic sentio, si
manum habet, si castra, si ubi consistat uspiam Dolabella, ad fidem et ad dignitatem tuam pertinere eum
2 persequi. De Cassii nostri copiis nihil sciebamus—
neque enim ab ipso ullae litterae neque nuntiabatur
quidquam, quod pro certo haberemus— ; quanto
opere autem intersit opprimi Dollabellam, profecto
intellegis, cum ut sceleris poenas persolvat, tum ne
sit, quo se latronum duces ex Mutinensi fuga confer-
ant. Atque hoc mihi iam ante placuisse potes ex
superioribus meis litteris recordari : quamquam tum
et fugae portus erat in tuis castris et subsidium salutis
in tuo exercitu. Quo magis nunc liberati, ut spero,
periculis in Dolabella opprimendo occupati esse debemus. Sed hoc cogitabis diligentius, statues sapienter : facies nos, quid constitueris et quid agas, si tibi
3 videbitur, certiores. Ciceronem nostrum in vestrum
collegium cooptari volo. Existimo omnino absentium

ᵃ By a Lex Domitia of 104 B.C. the election of pontifices
was vested in a special electoral assembly of 17 tribes. The
collegium pontificum had the right of nomination and of a
formal *congé d'élire.*

the field against Dolabella. I gave him my support
and added this rider, that *you* should take the field
against Dolabella, if you should decide that this was
expedient and in the interests of the state ; but that
if you were not in a position to do so with advantage
to the state, or if you reckoned it bad policy, you
should keep your army in its present position. The
Senate could not have paid you a greater compliment
than to leave it to your discretion what you considered to be most in the public interest. My own
opinion is that if Dolabella has an armed band, a fortified position, any place where he can make a stand,
your cause and your high position demand that you
should go after him.

I know nothing about the forces of our friend Cas- **2**
sius, for I have no letter from him in person, and no
news in which I could have assurance has come in.
But you understand of course how important it is
that Dolabella should be overcome, partly that he may
pay the full penalty of his crime, but also to deprive
the robber-chiefs who have fled from Mutina of a
rallying-point. And indeed you may recall from my
previous correspondence that I favoured this course
for some time back, although your camp was then our
haven of refuge and your army the last guarantee of
our safety. Now that, as I hope, we are free from
danger, we ought all the more to be taken up with
the overthrow of Dolabella. But you will ponder
over this with particular care, and you will summon
wisdom to your resolve. You will, if you think fit,
let us know what decision you have reached, and
what measures you are taking.

I want my son Cicero to be co-opted into your **3**
college.[a] I reckon that it is quite possible to take

CICERO

rationem sacerdotum comitiis posse haberi ; nam
etiam factum est antea : Gaius enim Marius, cum in
Cappadocia esset, lege Domitia factus est augur, nec
quo minus id postea liceret, ulla lex sanxit ; est etiam
lege Iulia, quae lex est de sacerdotiis proxima, his
verbis, QVI PETET CVIVSVE RATIO HABEBITVR. Aperte
indicatum posse rationem haberi non petentis. Hac
de re scripsi ad eum, ut tuo iudicio uteretur, sicut in
rebus omnibus, tibi autem statuendum est de Domitio, de Catone nostro ; sed quamvis licet absentis
rationem haberi, tamen omnia sunt praesentibus fa-
ciliora. Quod si statueris in Asiam tibi eundum, nulla
4 erit ad comitia nostros arcessendi facultas. Omnino[1]
Pansa vivo celeriora omnia putabamus ; statim enim
collegam sibi subrogavisset, deinde ante praetoria
sacerdotum comitia fuissent : nunc per auspicia
longam moram video ; dum enim unus erit patricius
magistratus, auspicia ad patres redire non possunt :
magna sane perturbatio. Tu, tota de re quid sentias,
velim me facias certiorem. iii. Nonas Maias.

[1] facultas. Omnino Pansa *Purser.* facultas omnino.
Pansa *Tyrrell and Purser.*

---

[a] A law of Caesar, not otherwise known.
[b] Cn. Domitius Ahenobarbus, consul in 32 B.C.
[c] M. Porcius Cato, son of Cato of Utica, and brother-in-
law of Brutus.
[d] If this had happened, the corporate patricians would
at once have nominated an interrex, who would have con-
vened the electoral assembly in place of the deceased consul.

654

absent persons into consideration at the elections of priests. In fact, this has been done before now, for when Gaius Marius was in Cappadocia, he was made augur under the Domitian law, and no statute has ruled out this procedure for the future. There is also a phrase in the Julian law,[a] the latest measure to regulate the priesthoods : "whosoever shall make application or be taken into consideration." This plainly implies that a person not applying may also be taken into consideration. I have written to him, so that he may avail himself of your advice on this as on all other matters ; but it is for you to settle the case of Domitius [b] and our friend Cato.[c] And yet, although it may be lawful to take an absent person into consideration, everything is made easier all the same for those who are present ; and if you decide that you must go to Asia, there will be no opportunity of summoning our candidates to the polls.

If Pansa were still alive, I believe that everything 4 all round would have moved faster, for he would have held the by-election for his new colleague without loss of time, and then the elections for the priesthoods would have preceded those for the praetorships. Now I can see that the auspices will cause a long delay ; for so long as an individual patrician remains in the magistracy, the auspices cannot revert to the patriciate.[d] Quite an imbroglio, I do declare ! I wish you would let me know your opinion on the whole question. May 5.

X (I. 4 §§ 1-3)

M. BRUTUS S. D. M. CICERONI

Dyrrhachii, A.U.C. 711

1 Quanta sim laetitia affectus cognitis rebus Bruti
nostri et consulum, facilius est tibi existimare quam
mihi scribere : cum alia laudo et gaudeo accidisse,
tum quod Bruti eruptio non solum ipsi salutaris fuit,
2 sed etiam maximo ad victoriam adiumento. Quod
scribis mihi trium Antoniorum unam atque eandem
causam esse, quid ego sentiam mei iudicii esse, statuo
nihil nisi hoc, senatus aut populi Romani iudicium esse
de iis civibus, qui pugnantes non interierint. "At hoc
ipsum," inquies "inique facis, qui hostilis animi in
rem publicam homines cives appelles." Immo iustis-
sime ; quod enim nondum senatus censuit nec populus Romanus iussit, id arroganter non praeiudico
neque revoco ad arbitrium meum : illud quidem non
muto, quod ei, quem me occidere res non coegit,
neque crudeliter quidquam eripui neque dissolute
quidquam remisi habuique in mea potestate, quoad
bellum fuit. Multo equidem honestius iudico magisque quod concedere possit res publica miserorum
fortunam non insectari quam infinite tribuere po-

---

^a In answer to Letter VII.
^b Decimus Brutus, who had broken out of Mutina.
^c Gaius Antonius.

X (I. 4 §§ 1-3)

It is easier for you to imagine than for me to ex- 1
press in writing how delighted I was to be informed
of the doings of our friend Brutus [b] and of the consuls.
Of all the events, that which earns my highest praise
and gives me most satisfaction is that Brutus' sortie
not only secured his own safety, but contributed more
than anything to the victory.

You tell me that the case of the three Antonii is 2
one and the same, and that it is for me to form my
own conclusions. I have only this one rule to lay
down, that judgement on those citizens who escaped
death in battle belongs to the Senate and people of
Rome. " Ah," you will exclaim, " you are wrong in
what you just said, in that you give the name of
citizens to men who are enemies of the state in intention ! " No, no, I am absolutely right ! For I
will not presume to pass a premature judgement on
a case on which the Senate has not yet formulated
an opinion nor the people expressed its will, nor will
I call away the case for my private decision. In this
I stand firm : in dealing with a man [c] whom the force
of circumstances did not oblige me to kill, I have
not robbed him of anything in a spirit of vindictiveness, nor have I carelessly given anything away to
him, but I have retained him in my power for the
war's duration. Nay, I consider it far more honourable and more permissible under the state's authority
to refrain from pressing hard on the plight of the
stricken than to lavish without stint upon the power-

tentibus, quae cupiditatem et arrogantiam incendere
3 possint. Qua in re, Cicero, vir optime atque fortissime mihique merito et meo nomine et rei publicae
carissime, nimis credere videris spei tuae statimque,
ut quisque aliquid recte fecerit, omnia dare ac per-
mittere, quasi non liceat traduci ad mala consilia
corruptum largitionibus animum. Quae tua est
humanitas, aequo animo te moneri patieris, praesertim de communi salute : facies tamen, quod tibi
visum fuerit ; etiam ego, cum me docueris . . .

XI (I. 4 §§ 3-6)

M. BRUTUS S. D. M. CICERONI

In castris, A.U.C. 711

3 . . . Nunc, Cicero, nunc agendum est, ne frustra
oppressum esse Antonium gavisi simus neu semper
primi cuiusque mali excidendi causa sit, ut aliud re-
4 nascatur illo peius. Nihil iam neque opinantibus aut
patientibus nobis adversi evenire potest, in quo non
cum omnium culpa, tum praecipue tua futura sit,
cuius tantam auctoritatem senatus ac populus Romanus non solum esse patitur, sed etiam cupit, quanta
maxime in libera civitate unius esse potest : quam
tu non solum bene sentiendo, sed etiam prudenter

ful such gifts as may inflame their greed and insolence.

In this matter, Cicero, you best and bravest of 3 men, and deservedly dearest to me both on my own and on the public account, I think your hopes colour your beliefs overmuch, and as soon as any man has taken some right step, you are over-hasty in granting him everything and putting all at his disposal, as though it were against the laws of Nature that a man should have his head turned by immoderate favours and be perverted to wicked purposes. A man of your high culture will take my warning good-humouredly, the more so as it touches on our common safety. All the same, you will act on your own discretion. I too, when you have informed me, . . .

XI (I. 4 §§ 3-6)

BRUTUS TO CICERO

In camp, May 15, 43 B.C.

Now, Cicero, now we must so act, that our rejoicings 3 over the crushing of Antony shall not prove delusive, and that the agency by which we seek to remove each evil as it presents itself shall not always be the means of producing a worse evil in its stead. For no di- 4 saster which may befall us through lack of foresight or through supineness can fail to bring discredit on all of us, but especially on you, whom the Senate and people of Rome allow, nay desire to wield such a measure of plenary authority as a free state can commit to one man. This authority you must protect, not by your loyal sentiment alone, but by your

tueri debes. Prudentia porro, quae tibi superest, nulla
abs te desideratur nisi modus in tribuendis honoribus.
Alia omnia sic adsunt, ut cum quolibet antiquorum
comparari possint tuae virtutes : unum hoc a grato
animo liberalique profectum, cautiorem ac modera-
tiorem liberalitatem, desiderant ; nihil enim senatus
cuiquam dare debet, quod male cogitantibus exemplum aut praesidio sit. Itaque timeo de consulatu,
ne Caesar tuus altius se ascendisse putet decretis tuis,
5 quam inde, si consul factus sit, sit descensurum. Quod
si Antonius ab alio relictum regni instrumentum
occasionem regnandi habuit, quonam animo fore putas, si quis auctore non tyranno interfecto, sed ipso
senatu putet se imperia quaelibet concupiscere
posse ? quare tum et facilitatem et providentiam lau-
dabo tuam, cum exploratum habere coepero Caesarem honoribus, quos acceperit, extraordinariis fore
contentum. "Alienae igitur," inquies, "culpae me
reum subiicies ?" Prorsus alienae, si provideri potuit,
ne exsisteret : quod utinam inspectare possis timorem
de illo meum !
6   His litteris scriptis consulem te factum audivimus :
vero incipiam proponere mihi rem publicam iustam
660

sagacity. Moreover, your sagacity, of which you have enough and to spare, is all that we ask for—save for some moderation in the bestowal of high office.

You have everything else in such abundance, that your merits would bear comparison with any of the ancient worthies; they lack but one thing as the outcome of a grateful and generous disposition, that its generosity should be tempered by greater prudence and a keener sense of proportion. For the Senate should not bestow upon anyone such gifts as may provide a precedent or position of vantage to men with evil designs. That is why I feel alarmed about the consulship, lest your Caesar should think that your decrees had raised him to such a pinnacle that, once elected to a consulship, he should refuse to climb down from it.

Why, if Antony found in the equipment of mon-5 archy left by another man an opportunity of making himself a monarch, how do you think it will affect a man if he should imagine himself free to covet any sort of sovereign power, and this at the prompting, not of a slain tyrant, but of the Senate itself? Therefore I shall extol your readiness and your foresight on the day when I begin to feel convinced that Caesar will be content with such extraordinary honours as he may receive. "Then you will hold me to account for the failings of others?" you will say. Yes, for others' faults, no less, if they could have been prevented by a display of foresight! I say this, because I wish you could gain insight into my apprehensions about that man!

After writing this note I heard that you had been 6 made consul. If I see that come true, then indeed I shall begin to visualize a free state true to its name

et iam suis nitentem viribus, si istuc videro. Filius
valet et in Macedoniam cum equitatu praemissus
est. Idibus Maiis, ex castris.

XII (I. 6)

M. BRUTUS S. D. M. CICERONI

Candaviae, a.u.c. 711

1 Noli exspectare, dum tibi gratias agam : iampridem hoc ex nostra necessitudine, quae ad summam
benevolentiam pervenit, sublatum esse debet. Filius
tuus a me abest, in Macedonia congrediemur ; iussus
est enim Ambracia ducere equites per Thessaliam et
scripsi ad eum, ut mihi Heracleam occurreret : cum
eum videro, quoniam nobis permittis, communiter
constituemus de reditu eius ad petitionem aut com-
2 mendationem honoris.   Tibi Glycona, medicum
Pansae, qui sororem Achilleos nostri in matrimonio
habet, diligentissime commendo.   Audimus eum venisse in suspicionem Torquato de morte Pansae cus-
todirique ut parricidam.   Nihil minus credendum
est; quis enim maiorem calamitatem morte Pansae
accepit ?   praeterea est modestus homo et frugi,
quem ne utilitas quidem videatur impulsura fuisse ad
facinus.   Rogo te, et quidem valde rogo—nam Achilleus noster non minus, quam aequum est, laborat—,
eripias eum ex custodia conservesque : hoc ego ad

ᵃ In answer to Letter IX.
ᵇ A. Manlius Torquatus, Pansa's quaestor.

and standing firmly once more on its own feet. Your
son is well, and I have sent him in advance to Macedonia with a troop of horse. May 15, in camp.

XII (I. 6)

BRUTUS TO CICERO [a]

Candavia (in Epirus), May 19, 43 B.C.

Don't wait for me to express my thanks to you. 1
In view of our intimacy, which has risen to the highest
degree of friendliness, we ought long ago to have
dispensed with this formality. Your son has parted
company with me ; we are to meet again in Macedonia. He is under orders to conduct a troop of horse
from Ambracia by way of Thessaly. I have written
to him to rejoin me at Heraclea. When I see him,
we shall confer and come to an arrangement—since
you are leaving the matter in our hands—for him to
return for his suit or to obtain a recommendation.

To you I most earnestly recommend Glycon, the 2
physician of Pansa, who has the sister of our man
Achilles for his wife. I hear he has fallen under
Torquatus' [b] suspicion in connexion with the death
of Pansa, and is being kept in custody as a parricide.
Nothing could deserve less credence, for to whom
has Pansa's death dealt a worse disaster ? Besides,
he is steady and a worthy fellow who, you would
think, could not even be driven to crime by the prospect of gain. I beg you, yes, I beg you insistently
(for our man Achilles is as much perturbed as the
occasion demands), rescue him from detention and

meum officium privatarum rerum aeque atque ullam
3 aliam rem pertinere arbitror.   Cum has ad te scriberem litteras, a Satrio, legato C. Trebonii, reddita
est epistula mihi, a Tillio et Deiotaro Dolabellam
caesum fugatumque esse : Graecam epistulam tibi
4 misi Cicerei cuiusdam ad Satrium missam.   Flavius
noster de controversia, quam habet cum Dyrrhachi-
nis hereditariam, sumpsit te iudicem : rogo te, Cicero,
et Flavius rogat, rem conficias.   Quin ei, qui Flavium
fecit heredem, pecuniam debuerit civitas, non est
dubium, neque Dyrrhachini infitiantur, sed sibi dona-
tum aes alienum a Caesare dicunt : noli pati a
necessariis tuis necessario meo iniuriam fieri. XIIII.
K. Iunias ex castris ad imam Candaviam.

XIII (I. 1)

M. CICERO S. D. M. BRUTO

Romae, A.U.C. 711

1   L. Clodius, tribunus plebis designatus, valde me
diligit vel, ut ἐμφατικώτερον dicam, valde me amat :
quod cum mihi ita persuasum sit, non dubito—bene
enim me nosti—, quin illum quoque iudices a me
amari ; nihil enim mihi minus hominis videtur quam
non respondere in amore eis, a quibus provocere.   Is
mihi visus est suspicari, nec sine magno quidem

ᵃ L. Tillius Cimber, a tyrannicide ; governor of Bithynia.
  ᵇ King of the Galatians.
   ᶜ C. Flavius, Brutus' praefectus fabrum.

keep him safe. I consider that this is as clear a case as any of a call to duty in a private affair.

While I was writing this note, I was handed a 3 dispatch from Satrius, the legate of Trebonius, that Dolabella had been cut up and routed by Tillius *a* and Deiotarus.*b* I have sent you a letter in Greek from a certain Cicereius to Satrius.

Our friend Flavius *c* has chosen you umpire in a 4 dispute about a legacy which he has on hand with the people of Dyrrhachium. I beg you, Cicero, and Flavius begs you, to settle the matter. It is not in doubt that the person who appointed Flavius as his heir had the money owing to him by the city, and the people of Dyrrhachium do not deny it ; but they allege that the debt was remitted in their favour by Caesar. Do not suffer a wrong to be done to my close friend by yours. May 19, in camp, at the base of the Candavia valley.

XIII (I. 1)

CICERO TO BRUTUS

Rome, about May 20, 43 B.C.

L. Clodius, a tribune of the plebs elect, has a great 1 fondness or, to express myself with more verve, a great love for me. Having satisfied myself of this, I have no doubt you will conclude (for you can read me like a book) that I requite his love. For it seems to me that nothing less becomes a man than to make no response to those who would draw you out in mutual love. I have had the impression that he suspects (and does so indeed to his own great distress)

dolore, aliquid a suis vel per suos potius iniquos ad
te esse delatum, quo tuus animus a se esset alienior.
Non soleo, mi Brute, quod tibi notum esse arbitror,
temere affirmare de altero, est enim periculosum
propter occultas hominum voluntates multiplicesque
naturas : Clodi animum perspectum habeo, cognitum, iudicatum ; multa eius indicia, sed ad scribendum non necessaria, volo enim testimonium hoc tibi
videri potius quam epistulam. Auctus Antonii beneficio est—eius ipsius beneficii magna pars a te est— :
2 itaque eum salvis nobis vellet salvum. In eum autem
locum rem adductam intellegit—est enim, ut scis,
minime stultus—, ut utrique salvi esse non possint :
itaque nos mavult ; de te vero amicissime et loquitur
et sentit. Quare, si quis secus ad te de eo scripsit
aut si coram locutus est, peto a te etiam atque etiam,
mihi ut potius credas, qui et facilius iudicare possum
quam ille nescio quis et te plus diligo. Clodium tibi
amicissimum existima civemque talem, qualis et prudentissimus et fortuna optima esse debet.

that his personal enemies have originated or rather transmitted to you some piece of news, so as to make you less well-disposed to him. It is not my habit, my dear Brutus—and I think you need not be told so—to make haphazard assertions about another man : the hidden motives of men and their complex natures make that a rash proceeding ; but Clodius' mind I have probed and tried and weighed up judicially. There are many revelations of it, but these need not be set down on paper, for I want you to take this as a formal deposition rather than a letter of recommendation. He has obtained promotion by favour of Antony, and Antony's favour was actually inspired in large measure by you. So he would like Antony to come to no harm, provided that we suffer none.

But he realizes (for he is, as you know, anything but 2 dull-witted) that it has come to this, that *both* parties cannot be secure. For this reason he prefers us to be so, indeed his remarks and his feelings in regard to you are most friendly. Therefore if anyone has represented him otherwise to you in a letter or in conversation, I beg you insistently to take my word in preference, seeing that I have better means of judging than his traducer (whoever he may be), and I have a greater affection for you. Let Clodius rank in your esteem as a very good friend and as a citizen of such worth as his ample good sense and his abundant fortune ought to make him.

CICERO

XIV (I. 2)

M. CICERO S. D. M. BRUTO

Romae, A.U.C. 711

1 Scripta et obsignata iam epistula litterae mihi redditae sunt a te plenae rerum novarum, maximeque
mirabile Dolabellam quinque cohortes misisse in
Chersonesum. Adeone copiis abundat, ut is, qui ex
Asia fugere dicebatur, Europam appetere conetur?
quinque autem cohortibus quidnam se facturum arbitratus est, cum tu eo loco quinque legiones, optimum
equitatum, maxima auxilia haberes? quas quidem
cohortes spero iam tuas esse, quoniam latro ille tam
2 fuit demens. Tuum consilium vehementer laudo,
quod non, prius exercitum Apollonia Dyrrhachioque
movisti, quam de Antonii fuga audisti, Bruti erup-
tione, populi Romani victoria. Itaque, quod scribis
postea statuisse te ducere exercitum in Chersonesum
nec pati sceleratissimo hosti ludibrio esse imperium
populi Romani, facis ex tua dignitate et ex re publica.
3 Quod scribis de seditione, quae facta est in legione
quarta decima fraude C. Antonii—in bonam partem
accipies—magis mihi probatur militum severitas
quam tua clementia. . . .

ᵃ The Gallipoli peninsula.

XIV (I. 2)

Rome, about May 20, 43 b.c.

My note had already been written and sealed up 1
when your letter came to hand with its big budget
of news, and most astonishing of all, that Dolabella
had sent five cohorts to the Chersonese.[a] Is he so
over-provided with troops, that when reported in
flight from Asia he should make a dash at Europe?
But five cohorts! Whatever did he expect to achieve
with those, when you had five legions in the same
quarter, an excellent cavalry and very strong auxiliary forces? Indeed, seeing that the bandit has
committed such a mad act, I hope that by now those
cohorts are in your possession.

I heartily commend your strategy, in that you did 2
not move your army from Apollonia and Dyrrhachium until you had heard of the flight of Antony,
of Brutus' sortie, of the Roman people's victory.
Therefore when you decided (as you inform me) to
conduct your army to the Chersonese and not to
suffer that utter scoundrel of an enemy to insult the
sovereignty of Rome, your action is in keeping with
your high position and in the interests of the state.

As for the mutiny which was caused, so you say, by 3
the intrigues of C. Antonius among the fourteenth
legion, you will take it in good part—I think better
of the strong measures taken by the troops than of
your leniency. . . .

CICERO

XV (I. 8)

M. CICERO S. D. M. BRUTO

Romae, A.U.C. 711

1 Multos tibi commendabo et commendem necesse
est—optimus enim quisque vir et civis maxime sequitur tuum iudicium tibique omnes fortes viri navare
operam et studium volunt nec quisquam est, quin
ita existimet, meam apud te et auctoritatem et
2 gratiam valere plurimum—sed C. Nasennium, muni-
cipem Suessanum, tibi ita commendo, ut neminem
diligentius. Cretensi bello Metello imperatore oc-
tavum principem duxit ; postea in re familiari occupatus fuit : hoc tempore cum rei publicae partibus,
tum tua excellenti dignitate commotus vult per te
aliquid auctoritatis assumere. Fortem virum, Brute,
tibi commendo, frugi hominem et, si quid ad rem
pertinet, etiam locupletem : pergratum mihi erit, si
eum ita tractaris, ut merito tuo mihi gratias agere
possit.

XVI (I. 11)

M. BRUTUS S. D. M. CICERONI

In castris, A.U.C. 711

1 Veteris Antistii talis animus in rem publicam, ut
non dubitem, quin et in Caesare et in Antonio se

---

^a 69–67 B.C., against the Cretan pirates.
^b Q. Caecilius Metellus Creticus, consul 69 B.C.
^c C. Antistius Vetus, a former officer of Caesar ; perhaps
to be identified with the consul suffectus of 30 B.C.

XV (I. 8)

CICERO TO BRUTUS

Rome, end of May or early June, 43 B.C.

I shall recommend large numbers of men to you, 1
and recommend them I must needs. For all the
worthiest men and citizens pay the highest regard to
your judgement, and all stout-hearted men want
to work heart and soul for you, and there is none but
holds the view that my claim to your deference and
gratitude carry great weight with you.

But C. Nasennius, from the borough of Suessa, I 2
recommend to you with special earnestness. In the
Cretan war,[a] under the command of Metellus,[b] he was
first centurion of the eighth cohort. In the years
to follow he attended to his family affairs. At
the present time, under the compelling influence of
party loyalty and of your pre-eminent high rank,
he wants to obtain through you some position of
authority. I recommend him to you, Brutus, as a
gallant man, a man of distinction and, if this is
relevant to the case, of ample means. I shall be
deeply obliged, if you give him such treatment that
he may be able to thank me on the strength of your
good deed.

XVI (I. 11)

BRUTUS TO CICERO

In camp, first half of June, 43 B.C.

Vetus Antistius [c] is so good a patriot that he would, 1
I doubt not, have stood forth as an enthusiastic

praestaturus fuerit acerrimum propugnatorem communis liberatis, si occasioni potuisset occurrere ; nam,
qui in Achaia congressus cum P. Dolabella milites
atque equites habente quodvis adire periculum ex
insidiis paratissimi ad omnia latronis maluerit quam
videri aut coactus esse pecuniam dare aut libenter
dedisse homini nequissimo atque improbissimo, is no-
bis ultro et pollicitus est et dedit HS. |XX| ex sua pe-
cunia et, quod multo carius est, se ipsum obtulit et
2 coniunxit. Huic persuadere cupiimus, ut imperator
in castris remaneret remque publicam defenderet :
sed[1] statuit id sibi non licere,[2] quoniam exercitum
dimisisset ; statim vero rediturum ad nos confirmavit
legatione suscepta, nisi praetorum comitia habituri
essent consules—nam illi ita sentienti de re publica
magno opere auctor fui, ne differret tempus petitionis
suae— : cuius factum omnibus gratum esse debet,
qui modo iudicant hunc exercitum esse utilem[3] rei
publicae, tibi tanto gratius, quanto maiore et animo
gloriaque libertatem nostram defendis et dignitate, si
contigerit nostris consiliis exitus, quem optamus,
perfuncturus es. Ego etiam, mi Cicero, proprie fa-
miliariterque te rogo, ut Veterem ames velisque esse
quam amplissimum, qui etsi nulla re deterreri a
proposito potest, tamen excitari tuis laudibus indul-

---

[1] sed *added by Tyrrell and Purser.*
[2] non licere *added by Gurlitt.*
[3] utilem *A² Crat. :* debet *or* debere.

champion of the common liberty in the face of Caesar
and Antony, if he had been able to meet the emergency. When he came across Dolabella with in-
fantry and mounted troops in Achaia, he preferred
to brave any danger from a covert attack by a bandit
who is quite prepared for any trick, than to offer the
appearance of having given money, whether under
duress or of his own free will, to an utterly villainous
and unscrupulous fellow ; and the same man has
offered and actually made us a free gift of 2,000,000
sesterces out of his funds and has presented himself
in person and come to my side—a service which I
prize far more highly.

We were anxious to induce him to stay with the 2
colours as an independent commander and defend the
free state. He has decided that this course is not
open to him, seeing that he has disbanded his forces.
But he assured us that he would return to me with
a legate's commission, were it not that the consuls
were about to hold elections for the praetorships. I
mention this, for since this was what he felt about
his political career, I strongly urged him not to put
off the time of his candidature. What he has done
should earn the gratitude of all men, if they but
recognize that this army of mine is of service to the
state ; but you should feel all the more obliged to
him, as you have shown more spirit and won more
renown in defence of our liberty, and will crown your
career with a higher honour, if our policy should be
favoured with the result for which we hope. I too,
my dear Cicero, beg you particularly and as a close
friend to be kind to Vetus and to wish him all possible distinction. Though nothing could deter him
from his resolve, yet encouragement and generous

gentiaque poterit, quo magis amplexetur ac tueatur
iudicium suum : et mihi gratissimum erit.

XVII (I. 17)

M. BRUTUS S. D. ATTICO

In castris, A.U.C. 711

1   Scribis mihi mirari Ciceronem, quod nihil significem
umquam de suis actis : quoniam me flagitas, coactu
tuo scribam, quae sentio.   Omnia fecisse Ciceronem
optimo animo scio ; quid enim mihi exploratius esse
potest quam illius animus in rem publicam ? sed
quaedam mihi videtur, quid dicam ? " imperite," vir
omnium prudentissimus, an " ambitiose " fecisse, qui
valentissimum Antonium suscipere pro re publica
non dubitarit inimicum ? Nescio, quid scribam tibi,
nisi unum : pueri et cupiditatem et licentiam potius
esse irritatam quam repressam a Cicerone, tantumque
eum tribuere huic indulgentiae, ut se maledictis non
abstineat, iis quidem, quae in ipsum dupliciter reci-
dunt, quod et plures occidit uno seque prius oportet
fateatur sicarium, quam obiiciat Cascae quod obiicit,
et imitatur in Casca Bestiam. An, quia non omnibus horis iactamus Idus Martias similiter atque ille
Nonas Decembres suas in ore habet, eo meliore con-

---

^a Octavian.

^b P. Servilius Casca, one of the leading tyrannicides.

^c L. Calpurnius Casca, one of Cicero's principal opponents
at the time of the Catilinarian conspiracy.

^d December 5th, 63 B.C., was the date on which Cicero
executed Catiline's accomplices, after a debate in the Senate.

treatment from you may stimulate him to adhere
to his decision and persist in it all the more firmly.
And you will do me a great favour.

XVII (I. 17)

BRUTUS TO ATTICUS

In camp, early June, 43 B.C.

You write to me that Cicero is surprised that 1
I never refer to any of his activities. In view of
your insistence, I shall record my opinions under
duress from you. I know that Cicero has always
acted with the best intentions ; for what could be
better approved in my eyes than his high spirit in
matters of politics ? But I have the impression that
this most sagacious of men has acted on some
occasions—how shall I put it ?—unskilfully, or in his
personal interest, seeing that he has not hesitated,
" for the state's sake," to incur a feud with Antony
when at the height of his power. I know not what to
write to you, save just this, that Cicero has inflamed
rather than checked the boy's [a] greed and lawlessness
and is lavishing upon him so many signs of obsequi-
ousness, that he cannot refrain from making malicious
remarks, which recoil upon him in a double sense, in
that he has more than one man's blood on his hands
and so must own up to murder on his own part,
before he can reproach Casca [b] as he does ; and again,
when he attacks Casca he follows in Bestia's [c] wake.
Granted that we do not boast at all hours of the Ides
of March, in the same way as he carries the Nones
of December on his tongue,[d] does that give Cicero a

dicione Cicero pulcherrimum factum vituperabit,
quam Bestia et Clodius reprehendere illius consula-
2 tum soliti sunt? Sustinuisse mihi gloriatur bellum
Antoni togatus Cicero noster: quid hoc mihi prodest,
si merces Antoni oppressi poscitur in Antoni locum
successio et si vindex illius mali auctor exstitit alterius
fundamentum et radices habituri altiores. Sic patiamur, ut iam ista, quae facit, dominationem an dominum an Antonium timentis sint? Ego autem gratiam
non habeo, si quis, dum ne irato serviat, rem ipsam
non deprecatur. Immo triumphus et stipendium
et omnibus decretis hortatio, ne eius pudeat concupiscere fortunam, cuius nomen susceperit : consu-
3 laris hoc aut Ciceronis est ? Quoniam mihi tacere
non licuit, leges, quae tibi necesse est molesta esse ;
etenim ipse sentio, quanto cum dolore haec ad te
scripserim, noc ignoro, quid sentias in re publica et
quam desperatum quoque sanari putes posse, nec
mehercule te, Attice, reprehendo, aetas enim, mores,
liberi segnem efficiunt, quod quidem etiam ex Flavio
4 nostro perspexi. Sed redeo ad Ciceronem : quid
inter Salvidienum et eum interest ? quid autem
amplius ille decerneret ? " Timet," inquies, " etiam
nunc reliquias belli civilis." Quisquam ergo ita timet

---

^a Q. Salvidienus Rufus, a man of obscure origin who had
bound up his fortune with that of Octavian.

better warrant to cast abuse on our magnificent deed
than Bestia and Clodius possessed when they made
a habit of carping at his consulship?

Our Cicero boasts to me, that in civilian garb he 2
bore the brunt of Antony's armed assault. Of what
benefit is this to me, if the reward claimed for the
overthrow of Antony is to be the reversion to Antony's
position, and if he who championed us against that
evil has taken the lead in raising up another evil
which will be more firmly based and more deeply
rooted? Are we to humour him, on the theory that
his present doings are inspired by fear of despotism,
or of a despot—or of Antony in person? I for my
part can feel no obligation to a man who draws the
line at serving an *angry* despot, but does not protest
against despotism as such. Nay more, a triumph, pay
for the army, an incitation in every decree to brazen
it out and scramble for the position of the man whose
name he has assumed—is that what one expects of a
consular or of Cicero?

Since you would not let me remain silent, you will 3
read things which are bound to annoy you. To be
sure I also can feel how much it hurts me to write to
you in this strain, and I am well aware what are your
views about the state, and how desperate too, though
not incurable, you consider its condition. And I
swear, Atticus, I do not blame you! Your age, your
habits, your family dull your spirit; yes, and our
friend Flavius too made me realize this!

But to return to Cicero. What is the difference 4
between Salvidienus[a] and him? Why, what more
fullsome honours could the former propose? You
say, "he fears even now the aftermath of the civil
war." Does anyone hold a war that is as good as

profligatum, ut neque potentiam eius, qui exercitum
victorem habet, neque temeritatem pueri putet ex-
timescendam esse ? an hoc ipsum ea re facit, quod
illi propter amplitudinem omnia iam ultroque de-
ferenda putat ? O magnam stultitiam timoris, id
ipsum, quod verearis, ita cavere, ut, cum vitare fortasse potueris, ultro arcessas et attrahas ! Nimium
timemus mortem et exsilium et paupertatem : haec
nimirum[1] videntur Ciceroni ultima esse in malis, et
dum habeat a quibus impetret, quae velit, et a quibus
colatur ac laudetur, servitutem, honorificam modo,
non aspernatur—si quidquam in extrema ac miser-
5 rima contumelia potest honorificum esse.   Licet ergo
patrem appellet Octavius Ciceronem, referat omnia,
laudet, gratias agat, tamen illud apparebit, verba
rebus esse contraria : quid enim tam alienum ab
humanis sensibus est quam eum patris habere loco,
qui ne liberi quidem hominis numero sit ? atqui eo
tendit, id agit, ad eum exitum properat vir optimus,
ut sit illi Octavius propitius. Ego vero iam iis artibus
nihil tribuo, quibus Ciceronem scio instructissimum
esse ; quid enim illi prosunt, quae pro libertate
patriae, quae de dignitate, quae de morte, exsilio,
paupertate scripsit copiosissime ? quanto autem magis

---

[1] *Stangl* : mihi.

won in such dread, as not to give a thought to the power of the man who disposes of the victorious army, nor for the adventurousness of the boy, that these give occasion for the utmost alarm? Is this the reason for his particular line of action, that he thinks that everything should be laid at that man's feet, in anticipation of his demands, as a tribute to his greatness? What fools fear makes of men, that your precautions against the object of your dread should actually have the effect of drawing it on and bringing it over you, when there was a chance of steering clear of it! We carry our fear of death and exile and poverty too far. These of course appear to Cicero as the extremes of misfortune, and so long as he can find people who will give him what he wants and will cultivate and compliment him, he does not disdain servitude, so long as it is servitude with honour—if there can be any honour in suffering the deepest and most ignominious affronts.

Let Octavius then call Cicero "father," submit 5 everything to him, compliment him, and express his gratitude, all the same the fact will show through, that his words are belied by his deeds. For what can be so inconsistent with decent human feeling as to treat like a parent a person who does not even count as a free man? Yet this is the object and proceeding of that worthy fellow, this the goal to which he is driving, that Octavius may be gracious to him. For my part I no longer pay any homage to those arts in which I know that Cicero is a virtuoso. For of what use to him are those extremely voluminous writings of his *In Defence of our Country's Freedom, On Dignified Conduct, On Death, On Exile, On Poverty*? Aye, how much surer a touch in those matters has

illa callere videtur Philippus, qui privigno minus
tribuerit, quam Cicero, qui alieno tribuat ! Desinat
igitur gloriando etiam insectari dolores nostros : quid
enim nostra victum esse Antonium, si victus est, ut
6 alii vacaret, quod ille obtinuit ? Tametsi tuae litterae
dubia etiam nunc significant. Vivat hercule Cicero,
qui potest, supplex et obnoxius, si neque aetatis
neque honorum neque rerum gestarum pudet : ego
certe, quin cum ipsa re bellum geram, hoc est cum
regno et imperiis extraordinariis et dominatione et
potentia, quae supra leges se esse velit, nulla erit tam
bona condicio serviendi, qua deterrear, quamvis sit
vir bonus, ut scribis, Octavius,[1] quod ego numquam
existimavi ; sed dominum ne parentem quidem maiores nostri voluerunt. Te nisi tantum amarem, quantum Ciceroni persuasum est diligi se ab Octavio, haec
ad te non scripsissem : dolet mihi, quod tu nunc
stomacharis amantissimus cum tuorum omnium, tum
Ciceronis ; sed persuade tibi de voluntate propria mea
nihil esse remissum, de iudicio largiter, neque enim
impetrari potest, quin, quale quidque videatur ei, ta-
7 lem quisque de illo opinionem habeat. Vellem mihi
scripsisses, quae condiciones essent Atticae nostrae :
potuissem aliquid tibi de meo sensu perscribere.
Valetudinem Porciae meae tibi curae esse non miror.
Denique, quod petis, faciam libenter, nam etiam

[1] *Tunstall* : Antonius.

---

[a] L. Marcius Philippus, consul in 56 B.C., and stepfather
of Octavian. He favoured a compromise between Antony
and the Senate.

[b] The daughter of Atticus, eventually betrothed to
M. Vipsanius Agrippa. (She was only seven years old at
the time.)

[c] Brutus' wife, daughter of Cato of Utica.

Philippus,[a] seeing that he has given away less to his stepson than Cicero gives away to a stranger. So let him cease positively to pursue us with his boastings and inflame our sores! For what advantage is it to us that Antony has suffered defeat, if his defeat merely serves to put the place which he held at another's disposal?

And yet your letter implies a doubt even now. 6 Very well then! Let Cicero live on as a suppliant and an underling, since he is capable of such things, if he has no respect for his age or high rank or his achievements. For me, I am sure, no terms of servitude will ever be so attractive, but I shall wage war against the real enemy, that is, with monarchy and irregular commands and despotism and a power that presumes to set itself above the laws, no matter how good a man (as you say) Octavius is, though I never took him for that. Nay, our ancestors would not tolerate despotism even in a parent.

If my affection for you were not as great as is Octavius' fondness for Cicero in Cicero's own conviction, I should not have written to you in this tone. I am sorry that your abundant love for your own folk, aye, and for Cicero, is causing you vexation; but assure yourself of this, that my personal goodwill is unabated, though my judgement of him is greatly impaired : for you cannot prevent a man from seeing things in that particular light in which they present themselves to him.

I wish you had informed me of the terms for our 7 dear Attica's [b] betrothal; I should then have been able to give you something of my views. I am not surprised that Porcia's [c] health is causing you anxiety. Finally, I shall be glad to do what you ask me, for

sorores me rogant : et hominem noro et quid sibi
voluerit.

XVIII (I. 10)

M. CICERO S. D. M. BRUTO

Romae, a.u.c. 711

1   Nullas adhuc a te litteras habebamus, ne famam
quidem, quae declararet te cognita senatus auctoritate in Italiam adducere exercitum ; quod ut faceres
idque maturares, magno opere desiderabat res publica, ingravescit enim in dies intestinum malum nec
externis hostibus magis quam domesticis laboramus,
qui erant omnino ab initio belli, sed facilius frange-
bantur : erectior senatus erat non sententiis solum
nostris, sed etiam cohortationibus excitatus : erat in
senatu satis vehemens et acer Pansa cum in ceteros
huius generis, tum maxime in socerum, cui consuli
non animus ab initio, non fides ad extremum defuit.

2 Bellum ad Mutinam ita gerebatur, nihil ut in Caesare reprehenderes, nonnulla in Hirtio ; huius belli
fortuna,

> ut in secundis, fluxa, ut in adversis, bona :

erat victrix res publica caesis Antonii copiis, ipso

ᵃ Fufius Calenus (Letter II § 4).

your sisters are making the same request. I shall get to know the man and find out his intentions.

XVIII (I. 10)

CICERO TO BRUTUS

Rome, middle of June, 43 B.C.

I have so far received no letter from you, no, nor 1 even a rumour to notify me that you were acquainted with the Senate's resolution and were bringing an army to Italy. The free state is most anxious that you should do so, and that quickly, for our home troubles are growing more serious every day, and our difficulties with our enemies in the field are no greater than with those inside the gate. These enemies were present since the very beginning of the war, but it used to be easier to suppress them. The Senate had been encouraged, not only by our formal statements of opinion, but also by our calls to action, to take up a stiffer attitude. In the Senate Pansa displayed sufficient energy and zeal in dealing with the others of this sort and especially with his father-in-law [a]; in his consulship he showed no lack of spirit from the outset, and no lack of loyalty at the end.

The operations at Mutina were being conducted 2 in such a manner that no fault could be found with Caesar, albeit a certain amount with Hirtius. The luck of this war was

Frail for prosperous times, but good for times of woe.

Victory was the free state's when Antony's forces

683

expulso. Bruti deinde ita multa peccata, ut quodam
modo victoria excideret e manibus : perterritos, in-
ermes, saucios non sunt nostri duces persecuti datum-
que Lepido tempus est, in quo levitatem eius saepe
perspectam maioribus in malis experiremur. Sunt
exercitus boni, sed rudes Bruti et Planci, sunt fide-
3 lissma et maxima auxilia Gallorum. Sed Caesarem
meis consiliis adhuc gubernatum, praeclara ipsum
indole admirabilique constantia improbissimis litteris quidam fallacibusque interpretibus ac nuntiis
impulerunt in spem certissimam consulatus : quod
simul atque sensi, neque ego illum absentem litteris
monere destiti nec accusare praesentes eius necessarios, qui eius cupiditati suffragari videbantur. Nec
in senatu sceleratissimorum consiliorum fontes aperire dubitavi, nec vero ulla in re memini aut senatum meliorem aut magistratus ; numquam enim in
honore extraordinario potentis hominis vel potentis-
simi potius—quandoquidem potentia iam in vi posita
est et armis—accidit ut nemo tribunus plebis, nemo
alio in magistratu, nemo privatus auctor exsisteret.
Sed in hac constantia atque virtute erat tamen sol-
licita civitas : illudimur enim, Brute, tum militum
deliciis, tum imperatoris insolentia : tantum quisque

ª Antony.   See the eighth *Philippic*.

were cut up and himself driven off. After that Brutus committed so many blunders that victory, as it were, slipped out of his grasp. Our leaders failed to pursue a demoralized, disarmed and badly mauled army, and time was given to Lepidus to exhibit that fickleness of his, which has often shown through in worse disasters. The troops of Brutus and Plancus are sound, but lacking in experience ; the Gallic auxiliaries are entirely loyal, and strong in numbers.

But Caesar, who had hitherto been guided by my 3 advice, and is a man of splendid natural endowment and remarkable firmness of character, has been instigated by some utterly unscrupulous letters from certain quarters, and by deceitful agents and messengers, to reckon with complete certainty on a consulship. As soon as I became aware of this, I neither ceased to send him warning letters in his absence, nor to upbraid to their face his intimates who appeared to be pandering to his greed, and in the Senate I never hesitated to disclose the sources of those most criminal suggestions. And yet, to be sure, I cannot remember on any occasion a more patriotic Senate or boards of magistrates ; for it has never yet happened that when an irregular office was being claimed by a powerful, or rather by an overwhelmingly strong personage [a] (for to be sure power now rests on physical force and armed might), that not a tribune of the plebs, not a magistrate of any other rank, not a private member came forward with a motion to that effect. But in the face of this firmness and manly bearing the citizens felt none the less uneasy ; for, Brutus, the troops with their fastidious attitude and the general with his brazen demands, both of them are making play with us. Every man

CICERO

se in re publica posse postulat, quantum habet virium;
non ratio, non modus, non lex, non mos, non officium
valet, non iudicium, non existimatio civium, non
4 posteritatis verecundia. Haec ego multo ante pro-
spiciens fugiebam ex Italia tum, cum me vestrorum
edictorum fama revocavit; incitavisti vero tu me,
Brute, Veliae. Quamquam enim dolebam in eam me
urbem ire, quam tu fugeres, qui eam liberavisses,
quod mihi quoque quondam acciderat periculo simili,
casu tristiore, perrexi tamen Romamque perveni nul-
loque praesidio quatefeci Antonium contraque eius
arma nefanda praesidia, quae oblata sunt Caesaris,
consilio et auctoritate firmavi: qui si steterit fide
mihique paruerit, satis videmur habituri praesidii;
sin autem impiorum consilia plus valuerint quam
nostra aut imbecillitas aetatis non potuerit gravita-
tem rerum sustinere, spes omnis est in te. Quam
ob rem advola, obsecro, atque eam rem publicam,
quam virtute atque animi magnitudine magis quam
eventis rerum liberavisti, exitu libera: omnis om-
5 nium concursus ad te futurus est. Hortare idem per
litteras Cassium: spes libertatis nusquam nisi in
vestrorum castrorum principiis est. Firmos omnino
et duces habemus ab occidente et exercitus; hoc

claims for himself a power in the state proportionate to his military strength; reason, moderation, legality, tradition, loyalty carry no weight; trained judgement, public opinion, respect for posterity go for nothing.

Foreseeing this a long time in advance, I was 4 making my escape from Italy at the moment when the stir which was caused by your proclamations called me back; but it was you at Velia, Brutus, that roused me to action. For although I was loth to set foot in a city from which you were fleeing after you had set it free—an experience which had once befallen me under similar conditions of danger, but by a more distressing turn of events—I held my course all the same and made my way to Rome and without any military protection I shook up Antony, and in defiance of his armed ruffians, by my guidance and influence I strengthened the forces of defence that offered themselves under Caesar. If he will stand immutable and follow my lead, I believe that we can count on adequate protection; but if the promptings of those villains carry more weight with him than my advice, or if the infirmity of my old age falters under the weight of my commitments, all our hopes reside in you. Therefore come flying, I implore you, and definitely set free the state which hitherto you have freed by your manly bearing and highmindedness rather than by the actual outcome of events. All the world is ready to cast itself upon you.

Write to Cassius to urge him to the same course. 5 Our hope of freedom dwells nowhere but in the headquarters of your camp. In the West our generals and our troops are absolutely steadfast. I feel con-

adulescentis praesidium equidem adhuc firmum esse
confido, sed ita multi labefactant, ut, ne moveatur,
interdum extimescam. Habes totum rei publicae
statum, qui quidem tum erat, cum has litteras
dabam. Velim deinceps meliora sint: sin aliter fuerit
—quod di omen avertant!—rei publicae vicem dolebo,
quae immortalis esse debebat, mihi quidem quantu-
lum reliqui est ?

XIX (I. 9)

M. CICERO S. D. M. BRUTO

Romae, a.u.c. 711

1 Fungerer officio, quo tu functus es in meo luctu,
teque per litteras consolarer, nisi scirem iis remediis,
quibus meum dolorem tu levasses, te in tuo non egere,
ac velim facilius, quam tunc mihi, nunc tibi tute
medeare. Est autem alienum tanto viro, quantus es
tu, quod alteri praeceperit, id ipsum facere non posse.
Me quidem cum rationes, quas collegeras, tum auctoritas tua a nimio maerore deterruit ; cum enim
mollius tibi ferre viderer, quam deceret virum, praesertim eum, qui alios consolari soleret, accusasti me

---

ᵃ By the death of his wife Porcia. See Letter XVII § 7.
688

fident indeed that the defence which the young man provides here stands firm ; but so many hands are causing it to reel that I am sometimes filled with alarm lest it should give ground.

You have the whole political situation, just as it is at the time of my sending off this letter. I could wish that it should improve with the march of events. But should it be otherwise (may heaven forfend what this betokens !), my sorrow will go to the free state, for this by rights should be immune from death. As for myself, how little have I left to me !

XIX (I. 9)

CICERO TO BRUTUS

Rome, about the 18th of June, 43 b.c.

I should discharge the friendly duty which you [1] performed on the occasion of my bereavement, and should send you a letter of condolence, did I not know that you do not require for your bereavement [a] those solaces with which you mitigated my grief, and I hope you will now effect an easier cure in your own case than you did then in mine. A man of your strength of character would indeed be untrue to himself, if he were not able to accomplish in his own case what he had enjoined upon some other person. For my part, the arguments which you had mustered, and also your moral influence, deterred me from extravagant mourning ; for when I appeared to you to bear up with less resoluteness than befitted a man, especially one who was in the habit of consoling others,

689

CICERO

per litteras gravioribus verbis quam tua consuetudo
2 ferebat. Itaque iudicium tuum magni aestimans
idque veritus me ipse collegi et ea, quae didiceram,
legeram, acceperam, graviora duxi tua auctoritate
addita. Ac mihi tum, Brute, officio solum erat et
naturae, tibi nunc populo et scenae, ut dicitur, serviendum est ; nam, cum in te non solum exercitus tui,
sed omnium civium ac paene gentium coniecti oculi
sint, minime decet, propter quem fortiores ceteri
sumus, eum ipsum animo debilitatum videri. Quam
ob rem accepisti tu quidem dolorem—id enim ami-
sisti, cui simile in terris nihil fuit,—et est dolendum
in tam gravi vulnere, ne id ipsum, carere omni sensu
doloris, sit miserius quam dolere ; sed, ut modice, ce-
3 teris utile est, tibi necesse est. Scriberem plura, nisi
ad te haec ipsa nimis multa essent. Nos te tuumque exercitum exspectamus, sine quo, ut reliqua
ex sententia succedant, vix satis liberi videmur fore.
De tota re publica plura scribam et fortasse iam
certiora iis litteris, quas Veteri nostro cogitabam
dare.

you wrote me a reproving letter in terms more severe than your usual style would admit.

Therefore, as I attached great value to your judge- **2** ment and feared your reproof, I pulled myself together and took the lessons which I had taught and studied and assimilated the more to heart, when you reinforced them with your moral weight. Yes, and I, Brutus, was at that time under no obligation save to the social code and the law of Nature ; but *you* must now play up to the public and the stage you hold, as the saying goes. For when the gaze of your soldiers, and not only of them, but of all citizens and of almost the entire world is centred upon you, it would be scandalous for a man who inspires the rest of us with greater courage to exhibit in his own case an enfeebled spirit. For this reason you opened your heart to your sorrow (for what you lost never had its like on earth), and under such a heavy blow you must needs sorrow, lest your very anodyne, complete imperviousness to pain, should afflict you worse than the sense of pain ; but whereas moderation in grief is expedient in others, it is indispensable for you.

I should write more, were it not that what I *have* **3** written is too long, when addressed to you. We are waiting for you and your army ; without it we think we shall scarcely attain sufficient freedom, even though all else should fall out as we have planned. I shall write more about the general political situation and perhaps shall give you more certain news in the letter which I propose to give to our friend Vetus.

CICERO

XX (I. 7)

M. BRUTUS S. D. M. CICERONI

In castris, A.U.C. 711

1 L. Bibulus quam carus mihi esse debeat, nemo
melius iudicare potest quam tu, cuius tantae pro re
publica contentiones sollicitudinesque fuerunt: itaque
vel ipsius virtus vel nostra necessitudo debet conciliare
te illi ; quo minus multa mihi scribenda esse arbitror,
voluntas enim te movere debet nostra, si modo iusta
est aut pro officio necessario suscipitur. Is in Pansae
locum petere constituit ; eam nominationem a te
petimus : neque coniunctiori dare beneficium, quam
nos tibi sumus, neque digniorem nominare potes
2 quam Bibulum. De Domitio et Apuleio quid attinet
me scribere, cum ipsi per se tibi commendatissimi
sint ? Apuleium vero tu tua auctoritate sustinere
debes ; sed Apuleius in sua epistula celebrabitur,
Bibulum noli dimittere e sinu tuo, tantum iam virum,
ex quanto, crede mihi, potest evadere, qui vestris
paucorum respondeat laudibus.

ᵃ L. Calpurnius Bibulus, son of Caesar's old opponent,
and stepson of Brutus. He was an officer in Brutus' army.
  ᵇ In the collegium pontificum.
  ᶜ See Letter IX § 3.
  ᵈ M. Apuleius, quaestor in 43 B.C., and one of Brutus'
paymasters.

692

XX (I. 7)

In camp, about June 22, 43 B.C.

You have been such a stout champion of the state, **1** and have shown such anxious care for it, that no one can appraise better than you how fond I ought to be of L. Bibulus.[a] In view of this, either consideration ought to win your interest in him, his own merits or my intimacy with him. That is all the more reason, I think, for my not writing at length ; for my wish ought to carry weight with you, granted that it is reasonable, and that I am seeking to realize it as in duty bound to oblige a friend. He has decided to sue for Pansa's place.[b] ; we beg you to nominate him for it. You could not bestow a favour on a closer friend than I am to you, nor nominate a more worthy candidate than Bibulus.

As for Domitius [c] and Apuleius,[d] what concern of **2** mine is it to write, since they stand high in your favour by virtue of their own personalities ? Apuleius, you know, has a claim to be supported by your influence. But Apuleius will receive a testimonial in his own letter. Do not deprive Bibulus of your fostering care : he is already a man of such calibre that, believe me, he may in the course of his development rise equal to the eulogies of your élite.

XXI (I. 13)

M. BRUTUS S. D. M. CICERONI

In castris, A.U.C. 711

1   De M. Lepido vereri me cogit reliquorum timor :
qui si eripuerit se nobis, quod velim temere atque
iniuriose de illo suspicati sint homines, oro atque obsecro te, Cicero, necessitudinem nostram tuamque
in me benevolentiam obtestans, sororis meae liberos
obliviscaris esse Lepidi filios meque eis in patris locum
successisse existimes : hoc si a te impetro, nihil profecto dubitabis pro eis suscipere.   Aliter alii cum suis
vivunt, nihil ego possum in sororis meae liberis facere,
quo possit expleri voluntas mea aut officium.   Quid
vero aut mihi tribuere boni possunt—si modo digni
sumus, quibus aliquid tribuatur—aut ego matri ac
sorori puerisque illis praestaturus sum, si nihil valuerit
apud te reliquumque senatum contra patrem Lepi-
2   dum Brutus avunculus ?   Scribere multa ad te neque
possum prae sollicitudine ac stomacho neque debeo ;
nam, si in tanta re tamque necessaria verbis mihi
opus est ad te excitandum et confirmandum, nulla spes
est facturum te, quod volo et quod oportet : quare
noli exspectare longas preces ; intuere me ipsum,
qui hoc a te, vel a Cicerone, coniunctissimo homine,
privatim, vel a consulari tali viro remota necessitudine

XXI (I. 13)

BRUTUS TO CICERO

In camp, July 1, 43 B.C.

My fear of what is to follow makes me feel alarmed **1** about M. Lepidus. If he has bolted from us—and I would fain hope that people's suspicions about him are unfounded and do him injustice—I beg and entreat you, Cicero, in the name of our close friendship and your kindly feelings towards me, forget that the children of my sister are the sons of Lepidus, and imagine that I now stand in the position of father to them. If I can obtain this request of you, there is nothing, I am sure, that you will hesitate to undertake on their behalf. Each man orders his family life differently ; in the case of my sister's children nothing that I can do could give full expression to my goodwill and sense of duty towards them. What gift indeed can I accept from loyal citizens—supposing that I am worthy of any gifts—or what assistance am I to offer to my mother or sister or those boys, if in your eyes and those of the Senate their uncle Brutus carries no weight against their father Lepidus?

I am too much worried and chagrined to write to **2** you at length, nor is that my duty. For if in such an important and intimate matter I must expend words in order to rouse your interest and make up your mind, there is no hope of your doing what I wish and what duty bids. Therefore don't expect a long supplication. Look into my heart : it is I who have a right to this favour from you, either on private considerations, because you are Cicero, my intimate friend, or, personal ties apart, because of your

privata, debeo impetrare. Quid sis facturus, velim
mihi quam primum rescribas. Kal. Quinctilibus ex
castris.

XXII (I. 12)

1   Etsi daturus eram Messallae Corvino continuo litteras, tamen Veterem nostrum ad te sine litteris meis
venire nolui.   Maximo in discrimine res publica,
Brute, versatur victoresque rursus decertare cogimur :
id accidit M. Lepidi scelere et amentia.   Quo tempore
cum multa propter eam curam, quam pro re publica
suscepi, graviter ferrem, tum nihil tuli gravius quam
me non posse matris tuae precibus cedere, non sororis,
nam tibi, quod mihi plurimi est, facile me satisfacturum arbitrabar.   Nullo enim modo poterat causa
Lepidi distingui ab Antonio omniumque iudicio etiam
durior erat, quod, cum honoribus amplissimis a senatu
esset Lepidus ornatus, tum etiam paucis ante diebus praeclaras litteras ad senatum misisset, repente
non solum recepit reliquias hostium, sed bellum
acerrime terra marique gerit, cuius exitus qui futurus sit, incertum est : ita, cum rogamur, ut miseri-

---

ᵃ M. Valerius Messalla Corvinus, a former associate of
Brutus at Athens.   Subsequently one of Augustus' right-
hand men.

consular rank and record. Please inform me as soon as possible in a return letter what you intend to do. July 1, in camp.

XXII (I. 12)

CICERO TO BRUTUS

Rome, early July, 43 B.C.

Although I shall be handing a letter to Messalla 1 Corvinus [a] directly, all the same I do not want our friend Vetus to come to you without a note from me. Brutus, the state is in a highly dangerous situation, and we who won the day are obliged to stake our whole fortunes once more. This has befallen us through the wickedness and sheer folly of Lepidus. In a time like this the task which I have shouldered on the state's behalf is causing me much vexation, but nothing vexes me more than that I cannot yield to the entreaties of your mother and your sister ; as for yourself, I believe it will be an easy matter to meet your wishes, and that is what matters most. The case of Lepidus cannot possibly be considered apart from that of Antony ; indeed the general opinion is that he was the more hardened villain, in that Lepidus had been honoured by the Senate with the highest marks of distinction, yes, and a few days before he had sent to the Senate an admirable dispatch ; yet all of a sudden he has not only given refuge to the remnant of the enemy, but is conducting a campaign by land and sea with the utmost vigour ; and how the issue of this campaign will fall out cannot be foreseen. Therefore when we are asked to show

697

cordiam liberis eius impertiamus, nihil affertur, quo
minus summa supplicia, si—quod Iuppiter omen aver-
tat !—pater puerorum vicerit, subeunda nobis sint.
2 Nec vero me fugit, quam sit acerbum parentum
scelera filiorum poenis lui, sed hoc praeclare legibus
comparatum est, ut caritas liberorum amiciores par-
entes rei publicae redderet ; itaque Lepidus crudelis
in liberos, non is, qui Lepidum hostem iudicat. Atque
ille si armis positis de vi damnatus esset, quo in iudicio
certe defensionem non haberet, eandem calamitatem
subirent liberi bonis publicatis. Quamquam, quod
tua mater et soror deprecatur pro pueris, id ipsum et
multa alia crudeliora nobis omnibus Lepidus, Antonius et reliqui hostes denuntiant; itaque maximam
spem hoc tempore habemus in te atque exercitu tuo :
cum ad rei publicae summam, tum ad gloriam et
dignitatem tuam vehementer pertinet te, ut ante
scripsi, in Italiam venire quam primum : eget enim
vehementer cum viribus tuis, tum etiam consilio res
3 publica. Veterem pro eius erga te benevolentia singularique officio libenter ex tuis litteris complexus
sum eumque cum tui, tum rei publicae studiosissimum amantissimumque cognovi. Ciceronem meum
propediem, ut spero, videbo ; tecum enim illum
698

some measure of pity for his children, there is no effective guarantee that we may not have to endure the most cruel punishment, if the father of the boys should be the winner (and I pray to Heaven that my foreboding may not come true).

Of course I am well aware how harsh it is that the 2 sins of the parents should be expiated by punishment of the sons ; but this is an excellent provision of our laws, so that affection for their children should make parents hold the state more dear. Thus it is Lepidus who is cruel towards his children, not the man who pronounces Lepidus a public enemy. And again, suppose that after laying down his arms he had been sentenced by court on a charge of breaking the peace —and on such a count he certainly could not offer a defence—his children would suffer the same injury through the confiscation of their estate. And yet the very treatment which your mother and sister wish to spare the boys, Lepidus, Antonius and the other public enemies proclaim that this and many other and harsher penalties shall be inflicted on us. Therefore in this crisis our chief hope resides in you and your army. It is of the most urgent importance for the whole future of the state, aye, and for your reputation and prestige, that you should come to Italy without losing a moment, as I have told you before ; for the state urgently needs both your strong forces, and your advice as well.

In consideration of his goodwill and his outstand- 3 ing sense of duty towards you, I have given Vetus a hearty welcome, as you asked me in your letter ; and I recognized that he had a great enthusiasm and affection for you and for the free state. I hope to see my son Cicero before long ; for I am

CICERO

et te in Italiam celeriter esse venturum confido.

XXIII (I. 14)

M. CICERO S. D. M. BRUTO

Romae, a.u.c. 711

1 Breves litterae tuae, breves dico? immo nullae: tri-
busne versiculis his temporibus Brutus ad me? nihil
scripsissem potius. Et requiris meas: quis umquam
ad te tuorum sine meis venit? quae autem epistula
non pondus habuit? quae si ad te perlatae non
sunt, ne domesticas quidem tuas perlatas arbitror.
Ciceroni scribis te longiorem daturum epistolam: recte id quidem, sed haec quoque debuit esse plenior.
Ego autem, cum ad me de Ciceronis abs te discessu
scripsisses, statim extrusi tabellarios litterasque ad
Ciceronem, ut, etiamsi in Italiam venisset, ad te rediret; nihil enim mihi iucundius, nihil illi honestius.
Quamquam aliquoties ei scripseram sacerdotum
comitia mea summa contentione in alterum annum
esse reiecta—quod ego cum Ciceronis causa elabo-
ravi, tum Domitii, Catonis, Lentuli, Bibulorum,
quod ad te etiam scripseram—: sed videlicet, cum
illam pusillam epistulam tuam ad me dabas, nondum

ᵃ See Letters III § 3, IX § 3, XX.

confident that he will be coming with you to Italy, and coming quickly.

XXIII (I. 14)

CICERO TO BRUTUS

Rome, July 14, 43 B.C.

That is a brief note of yours ; brief, I say : nay rather, it amounts to nothing. Can Brutus address me in days like these in three short lines ? Had I been in your place, I should rather not have written at all. And you ask for a note from me ! What courier of yours ever reached you without a letter of mine ? And which letter did not contain a heavy budget ? If these haven't been delivered to you, I conclude that not even your home correspondence has come to hand. You say you will give a longer letter to my son Cicero. Good so far, but this one too should be more substantial. For my part, as soon as you informed me that Cicero had parted company with you, I at once bundled off a courier and a note to Cicero, bidding him return to you, even if he had arrived in Italy ; for nothing could give me more satisfaction or give him more credit. And yet I had told him in several letters that the election for the priesthoods had been postponed to another year— a result for which I fought tooth and nail. I went to these pains both for the sake of Cicero and of Domitius, Cato, Lentulus, and the Bibuli [a] ; this I notified to you also. But obviously you had not yet received word of it when you sent off that tiny note of yours to me.

701

2 erat tibi id notum. Quare omni studio a te, mi
Brute, contendo, ut Ciceronem meum ne dimittas
tecumque deducas, quod ipsum, si rem publicam, cui
susceptus es, respicis, tibi iam iamque faciendum est.
Renatum enim bellum est, idque non parvum scelere
Lepidi ; exercitus autem Caesaris, qui erat optimus,
non modo nihil prodest, sed etiam cogit exercitum
tuum flagitari, qui si Italiam attigerit, erit civis nemo,
quem quidem civem appellari fas sit, qui se non in
tua castra conferat. Etsi Brutum praeclare cum
Planco coniunctum habemus, sed non ignoras, quam
sint incerti et animi hominum infecti partibus et exitus proeliorum. Quin etiam, si, ut spero, vicerimus,
tamen magnam gubernationem tui consilii tuae-
que auctoritatis res desiderabit : subveni igitur, per
deos, idque quam primum, tibique persuade non te
Idibus Martiis, quibus servitutem a tuis civibus de-
pulisti, plus profuisse patriae quam, si mature veneris, profuturum. II. Idus Quinctiles.

XXIV (I. 15)

M. CICERO S. D. M. BRUTO

Romae, a.u.c. 711

1 Messallam habes : quibus igitur litteris tam accurate scriptis assequi possum, subtilius ut explicem,
quae gerantur quaeque sint in re publica, quam tibi

---

^a These two commanders temporarily joined hands near
Grenoble.

Therefore, dear Brutus, I urge you most emphati- **2** cally not to let my son Cicero leave you, but to bring him back with you ; and your own return, if you have any regard for the free state to which you are dedicated, must take place now and at once.   For the war has re-started, and this on a large scale, thanks to the criminal act of Lepidus.   And the forces of Caesar, which were excellent, are not merely of no use but even compel me to clamour for your army.   If this is landed in Italy, no citizen worth the name will fail to betake himself to your camp.   We have in our favour, it is true, the junction of Brutus with Plancus [a] —a splendid achievement ; but you know well how uncertain are the minds of men when corrupted by party intrigue, and the issues of battles.   Moreover if, as I hope, victory is ours, even so the situation will require the strong guidance of your counsel and your moral influence.   In Heaven's name, then, come to our rescue, and that with all possible speed, and be convinced that you did your country no greater service on the Ides of March, when you struck away the chains of servitude from your fellow-citizens, than you will yet render it, if you arrive betimes.   July 14.

XXIV (I. 15)

CICERO TO BRUTUS

Rome, between July 11 and 27, 43 B.C.

You have Messalla at your side.   No matter how **1** carefully I indite my letters, how can I contrive to explain with greater finesse what is happening and how the state stands, than he will report it ?   He is

CICERO

is exponet, qui et optime omnia novit et elegantissime
expedire et deferre ad te potest ? cave enim existimes, Brute—quamquam non necesse est ea me ad
te, quae tibi nota sunt, scribere, sed tamen tantam omnium laudum excellentiam non queo silentio
praeterire—, cave putes probitate constantia, cura
studio rei publicae quidquam illi esse simile, ut elo-
quentia qua mirabiliter excellit, vix in eo locum ad
laudandum habere videatur, quamquam in hac ipsa
sapientia plus apparet : ita gravi iudicio multaque arte
se exercuit in verissimo genere dicendi. Tanta autem
industria est tantumque evigilat in studio, ut non
maxima ingenio, quod in eo summum est, gratia ha-
2 benda videatur.   Sed provehor amore : non enim id
propositum est huic epistulae, Messallam ut laudem,
praesertim ad Brutum, cui et virtus illius non minus
quam mihi nota est et haec ipsa studia, quae laudo,
notiora ; quem cum a me dimittens graviter ferrem,
hoc levabar uno, quod ad te tamquam ad alterum
me proficiscens et officio fungebatur et laudem maxi-
3 mam sequebatur.   Sed haec hactenus.   Venio nunc
longo sane intervallo ad quandam epistulam, qua
mihi multa tribuens unum reprehendebas, quod in
honoribus decernendis essem nimius et tamquam pro-
digus.   Tu hoc : alius fortasse, quod in animadver-
sione poenaque durior, nisi forte utrumque tu ; quod

---

^a Letter XI.

excellently posted up about everything and can explain and convey it to you in the most accomplished style. You must not suppose, Brutus—though I need not tell you what you know already; yet for all that I cannot pass over in silence his high pre-eminence in all noble pursuits—you must not imagine that in the matter of good character, firmness of purpose, conscientiousness, and zeal for the free state there is anything to approach him; so much so that methinks the art of oratory, in which he holds a wonderful supremacy, scarcely finds scope for eulogy in such a man! And yet his merit stands out all the more in this very expertness of knowledge : so severe was the judgement, so exacting the technique, with which he has trained himself in the soundest style of oratory. And his application is so great, he spends so many hours of the night in study, that most of the credit does not go to his natural endowment, which in his case is consummate!

But my affection is carrying me away; for it is not 2 the purpose of this letter to sing Messalla's praises, especially not to Brutus, who knows his merits as well as I, and knows even better these particular accomplishments which I am extolling. As I was bidding him a sorrowful good-bye, I had this one consolation, that in passing over to you—to my second self, as it were—he was performing a friendly duty and treading the path of high distinction. But enough of this!

I now come, at long last, to a certain letter,[a] in 3 which amid a mass of compliments you find one fault, that I am immoderate and as it were a spendthrift in votes of honour. That is what you say; some one else perhaps will say that I am too harsh in the matter of censure and punishment—but maybe *you* say this

si ita est, utriusque rei meum iudicium studeo tibi
esse notissimum, neque solum, ut Solonis dictum
usurpem, qui et sapiens unus fuit ex septem et
legum scriptor solus ex septem : is rem publicam
contineri duabus rebus dixit, praemio et poena. Est
scilicet utriusque modus, sicut reliquarum, et quae-
4 dam in utroque genere mediocritas. Sed non tanta
de re propositum est hoc loco disputare. Quid ego
autem secutus hoc bello sim in sententiis dicendis,
aperire non alienum puto. Post interitum Caesaris
et vestras memorabiles Idus Mart., Brute, quid ego
praetermissum a vobis quantamque impendere rei
publicae tempestatem dixerim, non es oblitus : magna pestis erat depulsa per vos, magna populi Romani
macula deleta, vobis vero parta divina gloria, sed
instrumentum regni delatum ad Lepidum et Antonium, quorum alter inconstantior, alter impurior, uterque pacem metuens, inimicus otio. His ardentibus
perturbandae rei publicae cupiditate quod opponi
posset praesidium, non habebamus—erexerat enim
se civitas in retinenda libertate consentiens, nos tum
nimis acres, vos fortasse sapientius excessistis urbe
ea, quam liberaratis, Italiae sua vobis studia profi-
5 tenti remisistis. Itaque, cum teneri urbem a parrici-
dis viderem nec te in ea nec Cassium tuto esse posse
706

as well. If that is the case, I am anxious to make quite clear to you my opinion on either point, and this not only that I may appropriate a saying of Solon, who was the sage *par excellence* among the Seven, and the only legislator of their number. He said that two things held a state together, reward and punishment. In either case of course a certain adherence to the mean is involved, as in all other things, and a certain moderation should be observed under both heads.

But this is not the place for a dissertation on so **4** large a subject. Yet I do not think it amiss to set forth what principles I followed during this war in my formal statements of opinion.

You have not forgotten, Brutus, what I said after the death of Caesar and your memorable Ides of March, about your lost opportunities and the storm which was about to break over the state. A great pestilence had been driven off, thanks to you, a great stain on the Roman people had been wiped out, aye, and for yourselves you had achieved undying fame ; but the apparatus of monarchy had been transferred to Lepidus and Antony ; one of these was more of a turncoat, the other more of a ruffian, either of them dreaded peace and disliked tranquillity. While these men were burning with eagerness to plunge the state into chaos, we had no means of defence to set against them ; for while the citizens braced themselves up in a united resolve to retain their freedom, and I at that time showed an excess of zeal, you quitted the city which you had set free and dispensed with the devoted service which Italy was offering—and this was perhaps the more discreet course.

So when I saw that the city was in the power of **5** cutthroats, and that neither you nor Cassius could

eamque armis oppressam ab Antonio, mihi quoque
ipsi esse excedendum putavi—tetrum enim spectacu-
lum oppressa ab impiis civitas opitulandi potestate
praecisa— ; sed animus idem, qui semper infixus in
patriae caritate, discessum ab eius periculis ferre non
potuit. Itaque in medio Achaico cursu, cum etesia-
rum diebus Auster me in Italiam quasi dissuasor mei
consilii rettulisset, te vidi Veliae doluique vehementer; cedebas enim, Brute, cedebas—quoniam Stoici
6 nostri negant fugere sapientes. Romam ut veni,
statim me obtuli Antonii sceleri atque dementiae,
quem cum in me incitavissem, consilia inire coepi Bru-
tina plane—vestri enim haec sunt propria sanguinis—
rei publicae liberandae. Longa sunt, quae restant,
et praetereunda, sunt enim de me : tantum dico,
Caesarem hunc adulescentem, per quem adhuc sumus,
si verum fateri volumus, fluxisse ex fonte consiliorum
7 meorum. Huic habiti a me honores, nulli quidem,
Brute, nisi debiti, nulli nisi necessarii ; ut enim primum
libertatem revocare coepimus, cum se nondum ne
Decimi quidem Bruti divina virtus ita commovisset, ut
iam id scire possemus, atque omne praesidium esset in
puero, qui a cervicibus nostris avertisset Antonium,
quis honos ei non fuit decernendus ? quamquam ego
illi tum verborum laudem tribui, eamque modicam ;

live there in safety while it was being held down by
Antony with armed force, I decided that I also ought
to leave it; for a community under the heel of
scoundrels, with all possibility of relief cut off, was a
shocking sight. But my spirit, which is immutably
and for ever rooted in my country, could not endure
that I should leave it in its hour of peril. Thus it
was that midway on my course to Achaia, when a
south wind in the season of the trades bore me back
to Italy, as if in protest against my plan, I saw you at
Velia, to my deep distress: for you were backing out,
Brutus,—I say "backing out," since our Stoic teachers
declare that the sage never "takes to flight."

On my arrival in Rome I at once took a stand **6**
against Antony's lawlessness and insanity. When I
had drawn his anger upon me, I began to entertain
plans in Brutus' own vein (for these plans are inbred
in your family's blood) for the liberation of the state.
What followed is a long story and need not be retold,
for it is about me. I merely mention that this young
Caesar, to whom we owe our survival (if we are willing to admit the truth), derived from the headspring
of my mentorship.

I obtained for him marks of honour, Brutus, but **7**
none that were unearned or superfluous. For as we
made a first beginning of recovering our liberty at
a time when not even the heroic courage of Decimus
Brutus had yet been roused to action so far as to give
us an assurance of freedom regained, and our entire
defence rested in the hands of the boy who had
removed Antony off our necks, what honour should
have been withheld from him? Though the compliments which *I* then bestowed upon him were votes
of thanks couched in moderate terms, I also had a

decrevi etiam imperium, quod quamquam videbatur
illi aetati honorificum, tamen erat exercitum habenti
necessarium, quid enim est sine imperio exercitus ?
Statuam Philippus decrevit, celeritatem petitionis
primo Servius, post maiorem etiam Servilius : nihil
8 tum nimium videbatur. Sed nescio quo modo homines facilius in timore benigni quam in victoria grati
reperiuntur : ego enim, D. Bruto liberato cum lae-
tissimus ille civitati dies illuxisset idemque casu Bruti natalis esset, decrevi, ut in fastis ad eum diem
Bruti nomen ascriberetur, in eoque sum maiorum exemplum secutus, qui hunc honorem mulieri Larentiae
tribuerunt, cuius vos pontifices ad aram in Velabro
sacrificium facere soletis : quod ego cum dabam Bruto,
notam esse in fastis gratissimae victoriae sempiternam volebam ; atqui illo die cognovi paullo plures in
senatu malevolos esse quam gratos. Eos per ipsos
dies effudi—si ita vis—honores in mortuos, Hirtium
et Pansam, Aquilam etiam ; quod quis reprehendit,
nisi qui deposito metu praeteriti periculi fuerit ob-
9 litus ? Accedebat ad beneficii memoriam gratam
ratio illa, quae etiam posteris esset salutaris : exstare
enim volebam in crudelissimos hostes monumenta

---

a For Servius Sulpicus Rufus see *Epp. ad Fam.* iv. 1-6.
Like Philippus and Servilius, he was prepared to negotiate
with Antony.

b Acca Larentia, a mysterious personage of early Roman
legend.

c L. Pontius Aquila, a tyrannicide. He was killed in the
action at Mutina.

high command conferred upon him ; though this might appear honour indeed for a man of his age, it was none the less indispensable for one at the head of an army—for what is an army without a high command ? Philippus carried a motion for a statue, Servius *a* made a first proposal for earlier acceptance as a candidate, Servilius followed this up with still higher priority. Nothing at that time appeared excessive.

But for some strange reason you will sooner find **8** benevolence in the hour of fear than gratitude in the hour of victory. For after the relief of Brutus, when that most joyful day had dawned upon the community, and by a coincidence that day too was Brutus' anniversary, I carried a motion that the name of Brutus be entered under date in the state calendar, and therein I followed the example of our forefathers, who bestowed this honour upon the lady Larentia,*b* at whose altar in the Velabrum you pontiffs are wont to make sacrifice. In paying this tribute to Brutus I wanted to insert in the calendar a permanent record of a most welcome victory. Yes, on that day I discovered that in the Senate ill-will commanded somewhat larger numbers than gratitude. At that particular time I showered honours—if you like to put it so—on dead men, Hirtius and Pansa, and even on Aquila.*c* Who will find fault with this, except a man who has forgotten his past peril now that his fear is no longer on him ?

My grateful recollection of a service rendered was **9** reinforced by a consideration which posterity too might do well to bear in mind ; for it was my wish that everlasting monuments of the public loathing for a most brutal enemy should be raised up in the

odii publici sempiterna. Suspicor illud tibi minus
probari, quod a tuis familiaribus, optimis illis quidem
viris, sed in re publica rudibus, non probabatur, quod
ut ovanti introire Caesari liceret decreverim ; ego
autem—sed erro fortasse, nec tamen is sum, ut mea
me maxime delectent—nihil mihi videor hoc bello
sensisse prudentius ; cur autem ita sit, aperiendum
non est, ne magis videar providus fuisse quam gratus.
Hoc ipsum nimium, quare alia videamus. D. Bruto
decrevi honores, decrevi L. Planco : praeclara illa
quidem ingenia, quae gloria invitantur, sed senatus
etiam sapiens, qui, qua quemque re putat, modo honesta, ad rem publicam iuvandam posse adduci, hac
utitur. At in Lepido reprehendimur, cui cum statuam in rostris statuissemus, iidem illam evertimus :
nos illum honore studuimus a furore revocare ; vicit
amentia levissimi hominis nostram prudentiam, nec
tamen tantum in statuenda Lepidi statua factum est
10 mali, quantum in evertenda boni. Satis multa de
honoribus : nunc de poena pauca dicenda sunt ; intellexi enim ex tuis saepe litteris te in eis, quos bello
devicisti, clementiam tuam velle laudari. Existimo
equidem nihil a te nisi sapienter ; sed sceleris poenam praetermittere—id enim est, quod vocatur ignoscere—, etiamsi in ceteris rebus tolerabile est, in hoc
bello perniciosum puto : nullum enim bellum civile

---

a An *ovatio* was a triumphal procession on a smaller
scale.

sight of all. I suspect that you did not altogether approve what was disapproved by your intimates (excellent men, I admit, but unversed in politics), that I carried a resolution conferring upon Caesar the right of a Joyous Entry.[a] For myself—but perhaps I am at fault, only I am not the man to take the highest pleasure in my own achievements—I do not think that in this war I ever had a sounder idea ; the reason for this I must not disclose, lest I should make an impression of foresight rather than of grati- tude.—I am labouring this point too much ; so let us turn to something else. I had honours conferred upon D. Brutus and upon L. Plancus. Theirs are indeed noble natures that heed the call of glory ; but the Senate too shows discretion, in that it offers whatever inducement (consistent with honour) it thinks will serve in each particular case to win a man to the service of the state. But you take me to task about Lepidus : we first set up a statue in his honour on the Speakers' Platform, then we cast it down. We made an effort to recall him from his madness by honouring him. The infatuation of that fluffiest of fellows proved too strong for our precau- tions ; even so, less harm was done in setting up Lepidus' statue than good in casting it down.

Enough has been said about honours. Now I must make a few remarks about punishment ; for I have often discerned from your letters that you wish to be given credit for leniency in regard to those whom you have overmastered in war. I consider indeed that your wisdom is unfailing ; yet I believe that to remit punishment for crime (for that is what " pardoning " amounts to), however passable it may be on another occasion, is utterly ruinous in this war.

fuit in nostra re publica omnium, quae memoria mea
fuerunt, in quo bello non, utracumque pars vicisset, tamen aliqua forma esset futura rei publicae ;
hoc bello victores quam rem publicam simus habituri,
non facile affirmarim, victis certe nulla umquam erit.
Dixi igitur sententias in Antonium, dixi in Lepidum severas, neque tam ulciscendi causa, quam ut
et in praesens sceleratos cives timore ab impugnanda
patria deterrerem et in posterum documentum statu-
11 erem, ne quis talem amentiam vellet imitari. Quamquam haec quidem sententia non magis mea fuit
quam omnium : in qua videtur illud esse crudele, quod
ad liberos, qui nihil meruerunt, poena pervenit ; sed
id et antiquum est et omnium civitatum, si quidem
etiam Themistocli liberi eguerunt, et, si iudicio
damnatos eadam poena sequitur cives, qui potuimus
leniores esse in hostes ? quid autem queri quisquam
potest de me, qui, si vicisset, acerbiorem se in me
futurum fuisse confiteatur necesse est ? Habes rationem mearum sententiarum de hoc genere dumtaxat honoris et poenae ; nam, de ceteris rebus quid
senserim quidque censuerim, audisse te arbitror.
12 Sed haec quidem non ita necessaria : illud valde necessarium, Brute, te in Italiam cum exercitu venire
quam primum. Summa est exspectatio tui ; quod si
Italiam attigeris, ad te concursus fiet omnium. Sive
enim vicerimus—qui quidem pulcherrime viceramus

For of all the civil wars in our state which I can recall, none were waged on such terms but that whichever side won, at all events some form of free state would have survived. In the present war I should not find it easy to lay down what manner of free state we shall have, if we are to be the winners; if we lose, the free state will certainly disappear for ever. I therefore advocated severe measures against Antony and against Lepidus, not so much for retribution's sake, as to discourage and deter evil-minded citizens from attacking their country at the present time, and to set up a warning example for the future, so that none should feel inclined to repeat such acts of madness.

And yet this particular measure did not reflect 11 mine any more than the universal opinion. You see vindictiveness in this, that the penalty extends to the innocent children. But that is an ancient usage and common to all states, if it be true that even Themistocles' children were left destitute; and if the same punishment falls upon citizens condemned by a court, how could we be more lenient towards public enemies? And what complaint can any man make about me, if he cannot help confessing that if victory had been his he would have treated me more harshly? You have the reasoned statement of my views on this particular subject of honour and punishment; I believe you have heard my opinions and pronouncements on other matters.

But of course this is not so urgent; what *is* highly 12 urgent, Brutus, is that you should come to Italy with your army at the earliest possible moment. We are awaiting you most anxiously. Why, if you land in Italy there will be a general rush to meet you! For suppose we win, and a very handsome victory

nisi Lepidus perdere omnia et perire ipse cum
suis concupivisset—, tua nobis auctoritate opus est
ad collocandum aliquem civitatis statum ; sive etiam
nunc certamen reliquum est, maxima spes est cum
in auctoritate tua, tum in exercitus tui viribus. Sed
propera, per deos ! scis, quantum sit in temporibus,
13 quantum in celeritate. Sororis tuae filiis quam diligenter consulam, spero te ex matris et ex sororis
litteris cogniturum : qua in causa maiorem habeo
rationem tuae voluntatis, quae mihi carissima est,
quam, ut quibusdam videor, constantiae meae ; sed
ego nulla in re malo quam in te amando constans
et esse et videri.

XXV (I. 16)

M. BRUTUS S. D. M. CICERONI

In castris, A.U.C. 711

1 Particulam litterarum tuarum, quas misisti Octavio,
legi missam ab Attico mihi. Studium tuum curaque
de salute mea nulla me nova voluptate affecit ; non
solum enim usitatum, sed etiam cotidianum est aliquid
audire de te, quod pro nostra dignitate fideliter atque
honorifice dixeris aut feceris. At dolore, quantum
maximum capere animo possum, eadem illa pars epistulae scripta ad Octavium de nobis affecit. Sic enim
illi gratias agis de re publica, tam suppliciter ac
716

was ours, had not Lepidus insisted on undoing every-thing and undoing himself with his own associates, we need your moral influence in order to effect some sort of political settlement ; but if we have even now a stiff fight before us, our chief hope rests both in your influence and especially in the might of your army. But make haste, for Heaven's sake ! You know how much depends on correct timing and on speed.

I hope you will perceive from your mother's and sister's letters what an earnest interest I take in your nephews. In their case my chief consideration is to fulfil your desire, which I hold most dear, rather than to be consistent with myself, as some people imagine. But there is nothing in which I would rather be consistent, and show it, than in my affec-tion for you.

XXV (I. 16)

BRUTUS TO CICERO

In camp, mid-July, 43 B.C.

I have read the short extract from the note which you sent to Octavius : Atticus sent it to me. Your devotion and concern about my safety brought no fresh pleasure to me, for it is not only a usual but a daily experience for me to hear about you, of some loyal or complimentary words or deeds with which you protected my honour. But that part of the letter in which you wrote to Octavius about me brought upon me the most acute distress that I could possibly endure in my mind. For this is how you offer him thanks in matters of state, in such a

demisse—quid scribam ? pudet condicionis ac fortunae, sed tamen scribendum est—commendas nostram salutem illi—quae morte qua non perniciosior ?
—, ut prorsus prae te feras non sublatam dominationem, sed dominum commutatum esse. Verba tua
recognosce et aude negare servientis adversus regem
istas esse preces. Unum ais esse, quod ab eo postu-
letur et exspectetur, ut eos cives, de quibus viri boni
populusque Romanus bene existimet, salvos velit :
quid ? si nolit, non erimus ? atqui non esse quam
2 esse per illum praestat. Ego medius fidius non existimo tam omnes deos aversos esse a salute populi
Romani, ut Octavius orandus sit pro salute cuiusquam
civis, non dicam pro liberatoribus orbis terrarum—
iuvat enim magnifice loqui et certe decet adversus
ignorantes, quid pro quoque timendum aut a quoque
petendum sit—. Hoc tu, Cicero, posse fateris Octavium et illi amicus es ? aut, si me carum habes, vis
Romae videri, cum, ut ibi esse possem, commen-
dandus puero illi fuerim ? cui quid agis gratias, si, ut
nos salvos esse velit et patiatur, rogandum putas ?
an hoc pro beneficio habendum est, quod se quam

suppliant and humble tone! What am I to write?
I'm ashamed at being in such a position—I'm ashamed
of my lot—and yet, write I must. You entrust him
with our protection : is that not more disastrous than
no matter what sort of death? Just in order that you
may plume yourself, not on the overthrow of autocracy but on a change of autocrat! Consider your
own words, and dare to deny that those are the entreaties of a person of servile estate in the presence
of a king! There is, so you affirm, one demand and
one claim to be made upon him, that he should agree
to the safety of those citizens of whom good patriots
and the Roman people have a high opinion. Well!
Suppose he refuses : will that put an end to our existence? Ah, but I would rather not exist than owe my
existence to him!

I'll take an oath upon it, I cannot believe that all 2
Heaven has so little regard for the safety of the
Roman people that we must beg Octavius for the
safety of any citizen whatsoever—I shall not say for
the liberators of the whole world. You see, I take
pleasure in high-flown language, and this is clearly
appropriate in the face of men who do not know what
fears we should harbour, what requests we should
make in this case and that. Can you, Cicero, admit
that Octavius holds such power, and give him
your friendship? Or, if you have any affection for
me, do you want me to show myself in Rome, on the
condition that this boy's favour must first be obtained
for me, so that I can have my existence there? Why
do you offer thanks to him, if you think that application must be made to him, so that our safety shall
depend on his consent and sufferance? Or is this
to count as a favour, that he chose to be the person,

Antonium esse maluerit, a quo ista petenda essent ?
Vindici quidem alienae dominationis, non vicario, ec-
quis supplicat, ut optime meritis de re publica liceat
3 esse salvis ? Ista vero imbecillitas et desperatio,
cuius culpa non magis in te residet quam in omnibus
aliis, et Caesarem in cupiditatem regni impulit et
Antonio post interitum illius persuasit, ut interfecti
locum occupare conaretur, et nunc puerum istum ita
extulit, ut tu iudicares precibus esse impetrandam
salutem talibus viris misericordiaque unius vix etiam
nunc viri tutos fore nos, haud ulla[1] alia re. Quod si
Romanos nos esse meminissemus, non audacius dominari cuperent postremi homines, quam id nos pro-
hiberemus, neque magis irritatus esset Antonius
regno Caesaris quam ob eiusdem mortem deterritus.
4 Tu quidem, consularis et tantorum scelerum vindex—
quibus oppressis vereor ne in breve tempus dilata
sit abs te pernicies—, qui potes intueri, quae gesseris,
simul et ista vel probare vel ita demisse ac facile pati,
ut probantis specimen habeas ? quod autem tibi cum
Antonio privatim odium ? nempe, quia postulabat
haec, salutem ab se peti, precariam nos incolumitatem habere, a quibus ipse libertatem accepisset, esse

---

[1] *Var. lect.* aut nulla.

rather than Antony, from whom those favours would
have to be begged ?   Given a true champion against
a despotism imposed from outside, not a substitute
despot, does any man make humble request to him,
that he should permit those who have deserved nobly
of the state to live in safety ?

It was your faint-heartedness, your abandonment of 3
hope (the blame for which rests no more upon you
than upon everyone else), that prompted Caesar to
aspire to kingship, and induced Antony after his death
to try to usurp the place of him who was slain ; and
now it has exalted that boy of yours, leading you to
the conclusion that men with a record like ours must
obtain security by supplication, and that our safety
should even now depend precariously on the merciful-
ness of one person hardly yet a man, not on anything
else.   Yet if we had borne in mind that we were
Romans, the dregs of mankind would not be more
forward in their scramble for despotism than we in
making a stand against it, nor would Caesar's
monarchy have been more of an incitement to Antony
than his death has proved a deterrent.

As for you, who have been consul and have avenged 4
crimes of such magnitude—yet I fear that by their
suppression you have merely gained a short respite
from ruin—how can you contemplate your past
achievements and at the same time approve of your
friend's actions, or acquiesce in them in such a
humble and pliant spirit as to offer a semblance of
approval ?   And what means this privately conducted
feud of yours with Antony ?   Why, because he made
these demands, that our lives should be in his gift,
that we should hold our position by his leave, though
he had received his freedom at our hands, that he

arbitrium suum de re publica, quaerenda esse arma
putasti, quibus dominari prohiberetur: scilicet, ut illo
prohibito rogaremus alterum, qui se in eius locum
reponi pateretur, an ut esset sui iuris ac mancipii
res publica? nisi forte non de servitute, sed de condicione serviendi recusatum est a nobis. Atqui non
solum bono domino potuimus Antonio tolerare nostram fortunam, sed etiam beneficiis atque honoribus ut participes frui, quantis vellemus; quid enim
negaret eis, quorum patientiam videret maximum
dominationis suae praesidium esse? Sed nihil tanti
fuit, quo venderemus fidem nostram et libertatem.
5 Hic ipse puer, quem Caesaris nomen incitare videtur
in Caesaris interfectores, quanti aestimet, si sit com-
mercio locus, posse nobis auctoribus tantum, quantum
profecto poterit, quoniam vivere per se et pecunias
habere et dici consulares volumus! Ceterum ne
nequidquam perierit ille (cuius interitu quid gavisi
sumus, si mortuo eo nihilo minus servituri eramus?),
nulla cura adhibetur? Sed mihi prius omnia di deae-
que eripuerint quam illud iudicium, quo non modo
heredi eius, quem occidi, id non concesserim, quod
in illo non tuli, sed ne patri quidem meo, si reviviscat,
ut patiente me plus legibus ac senatu possit: an hoc
722

should have the last word in the state, was it for this that you thought we should have recourse to arms as a means of beating off despotism—with this result, mark you!, that after beating off one despot we should solicit another to let himself be installed in the former man's place, or that he should be vested with a full title of property in the state? Unless maybe we made our protest, not against slavery, but against the particular terms of our bondage. And yet under Antony's benevolent tyranny we could not only have endured our own lot, but we could have enjoyed the greatest preferments and high positions of state that we might have asked for, on a basis of partnership; for what would he deny to the men in whose passivity he could see a bulwark of his own autocracy? But no favour carried so high a price as to induce us to sell our loyalty and liberty.

This boy in particular, whom the name of Caesar **5** seems to spur on against Caesar's slayers, what price would he offer (suppose this were a matter of haggling), that we should procure him such power as he will of course obtain, seeing that by his goodwill we want to remain alive, and to keep our estates, and to be styled consulars! Besides, are we taking no precautions lest our old enemy should have perished to no purpose? How could we rejoice at his death, if now that he is gone we were to remain none the less in bondage? But may the host of heaven strip me of all else rather than of my settled resolve not to give away, I shall not say to the heir of the man whom I slew, but not even to my own father, should he come to life again, what I could not brook in the slain man, a power superior to the Laws and Senate, with my connivance! Do you really believe that the rest of

tibi persuasum est, fore ceteros ab eo liberos, quo
invito nobis in ista civitate locus non sit ? Qui porro
id, quod petis, fieri potest ut impetres ? Rogas enim,
velit nos salvos esse : videmur ergo tibi salutem ac-
cepturi, cum vitam acceperimus ? quam, si prius
dimittimus dignitatem et libertatem, qui possumus
6 accipere ? An tu Romae habitare, id putas incolumem esse ? res, non locus oportet praestet istuc
mihi : neque incolumis Caesare vivo fui, nisi posteaquam illud conscivi facinus, neque usquam exsul esse
possum, dum servire et pati contumelias peius odero
malis omnibus aliis. Nonne hoc est in easdem tene-
bras recidisse, si ab eo, qui tyranni nomen ascivit
sibi,—cum in Graecis civitatibus liberi tyrannorum
oppressis illis eodem supplicio afficiantur,—petitur,
ut vindices atque oppressores dominationis salvi sint ?
Hanc ego civitatem videre velim aut putem ullam,
quae ne traditam quidem atque inculcatam libertatem recipere possit plusque timeat in puero nomen
sublati regis, quam confidat sibi, cum illum ipsum,
qui maximas opes habuerit, paucorum virtute sublatum videat ? Me vero posthac ne commendaveris
Caesari tuo, ne te quidem ipsum, si me audies : valde
care aestimas tot annos, quot ista aetas recipit, si prop-
7 ter eam causam puero isti supplicaturus es. Deinde,

the people will be free from the man whose favour we must win before we can hold a place within that citizen body ? Moreover, how can you possibly obtain what you are after ? You ask that he should consent to our security. Do you think, then, that when we have been given our lives we shall be given our security ? How can we be in receipt of this, if to begin with we divest ourselves of our high rank and liberty ?

To have your residence in Rome, is that your idea 6 of civic security ? The facts, not the place, must be my guarantee. Neither could I enjoy my full civic rights in Caesar's lifetime, until after I had resolved upon my great deed, nor can I be an exile in any place, so long as I hold slavery and the suffering of indignities in deeper loathing than all other misfortunes. Is this not a relapse into our former Dark Age, if I must beg the man who took for himself the name of tyrant, that those who avenged and overthrew a despotism should come to no harm, whereas in the Greek states the children of tyrants suffer the same punishment when the tyranny is overthrown ? Could I wish to set eyes on a state, or regard it as a state at all, if it cannot even recover the freedom handed down to it and driven home into it, and feels more alarm at the name of a fallen king, when assumed by a boy, than confidence in itself, though it can see that the monarch himself in the plenitude of his power owed his fall to the firm action of a mere handful ? No, don't you hereafter commend me to your Caesar, do not commend yourself either, if you will listen to me ! You must attach a rare value to those years of life which your present age allows you, if for that reason you are going to fall on your knees before that boy !

CICERO

quod pulcherrime fecisti ac facis in Antonio, vide
ne convertatur a laude maximi animi ad opinionem
formidinis ; nam, si Octavius tibi placet, a quo de
nostra salute petendum sit, non dominum fugisse,
sed amiciorem dominum quaesisse videberis. Quem
quod laudas ob ea, quae adhuc fecit, plane probo; sunt
enim laudanda, si modo contra alienam potentiam,
non pro sua suscepit eas actiones ; cum vero iudicas
tantum illi non modo licere, sed etiam a te ipso tribu-
endum esse, ut rogandus sit, ne nolit esse nos salvos,
nimium magnam mercedem statuis—id enim ipsum
illi largiris, quod per illum habere videbatur res publica—, neque hoc tibi in mentem venit, si Octavius
illis dignus sit honoribus, quia cum Antonio bellum
gerat, iis qui illud malum exciderint, cuius istae reli-
quiae sunt, nihil, quo expleri possit eorum meritum,
tributurum umquam populum Romanum, si omnia
8 simul congesserit. Ac vide, quanto diligentius homines metuant, quam meminerint: quia Antonius vivat
atque in armis sit, de Caesare vero, quod fieri potuit
ac debuit, transactum est neque iam revocari in
integrum potest, Octavius is est, qui quid de nobis
iudicaturus sit exspectet populus Romanus, nos ii
sumus, de quorum salute unus homo rogandus videatur. Ego vero, ut istoc revertar, is sum, qui non

726

Furthermore, see to it that your splendid achieve- 7
ments, past and present, in Antony's case, be not
transformed from a source of honour for a heroic spirit
into one of a reputation for timidity. For if Octavius
takes your fancy, the man to whom you would have
me apply for security, people will think that you were
not shunning a master, but were seeking a more
friendly master. Your praise for what he has hitherto
done has my unfeigned approval; for his actions call for
praise, provided always that he has undertaken them
to break another man's power, not to further his own.
But when you conclude that so much power should
not only be for him to take, but should be presented
to him by yourself, so that one must ask him not to
declare himself against our safety, you fix the price
of the bargain too high (for you lavish upon him that
very authority which he was thought to have pro-
cured for the state), and this does not enter your
mind, that if Octavius is worthy of any high office
because he is waging a war with Antony, the Roman
people will never be able to bestow a full measure
of recompense upon those who removed the bane of
which this is the residue, if in one act it heaps all it
has on the shoulders of one man.

And observe how much more insistent is men's 8
sense of fear than their memory: seeing that Antony
is still alive and in arms, but in Caesar's case, what
could and should have been done has been accomplished once for all and cannot now be reversed,
Octavius is the man on whose decisions what to do
with us the Roman people must wait, and we are the
men for whose safety, it would seem, application
must be made to one individual! No—to return to
what you said—, I am the sort of man who would

modo non supplicem, sed etiam coërceam postulantes,
ut sibi supplicetur, aut longe a servientibus abero
mihique esse iudicabo Romam, ubicumque liberum
esse licebit, ac vestri miserebor, quibus nec aetas
neque honores nec virtus aliena dulcedinem vivendi
9 minuere potuerit.   Mihi quidem ita beatus esse videbor, si modo constanter ac perpetuo placebit hoc
consilium, ut relatam putem gratiam pietati meae ;
quid enim est melius quam memoria recte factorum
et libertate contentum neglegere humana ? Sed certe
non succumbam succumbentibus nec vincar ab eis,
qui se vinci volunt, experiarque et tentabo omnia
neque desistam abstrahere a servitio civitatem nostram. Si secuta fuerit quae debet fortuna, gaude-
bimus omnes ; si minus, ego tamen gaudebo. Quibus
enim potius haec vita factis aut cogitationibus
traducatur quam iis, quae pertinuerint ad liberandos
10 cives meos ? Te, Cicero, rogo atque hortor, ne de-
fatigere neu diffidas, semper in praesentibus malis
prohibendis futura quoque, nisi ante sit occursum,
explores, ne se insinuent, fortem et liberum animum,
quo et consul et nunc consularis rem publicam vindi-
casti, sine constantia et aequabilitate nullum esse
putaris. Fateor enim duriorem esse condicionem
spectatae virtutis quam incognitae : bene facta pro

not merely refuse to make entreaty, but would put under restraint those who demand that entreaty be made to them. Or else I shall hold myself far aloof from those who accept servitide, and shall find Rome for myself wherever a man may still be free ; and I shall feel sorry for you, whose love of sweet life neither your age nor your high position, nor the example of courage which others set you, will be able to curtail.

For my part I shall be happy in my own eyes if 9 only I hold firmly and without a break to this resolve, that I shall deem myself repaid in gratitude for my devotion to my country. For what is better than the memory of righteous deeds and disregard of human exigencies in the pure enjoyment of liberty ? But assuredly I shall not submit myself to the submissive, nor take defeat from those who court defeat ; and I shall essay and adventure everything, and shall never cease to draw our community out of the reach of servitude. If our efforts meet with the fortune which they deserve, we shall all be glad ; if otherwise, *I* shall be glad even so. For what actions or reflections could better occupy this life of ours than those relating to the liberty of my fellow-citizens ?

Cicero, I beg and admonish you, do not flag or lose 10 heart ; and while you ward off present evils always cast a searching glance upon future ones too, lest they steal in upon you while there is none to cope with them in advance. Understand once for all that the courageous and free spirit with which you championed the state as consul, and now as a consular, goes for nothing without a firm purpose and an even temperament. I grant you that merit well-tried has a more exacting task than merit undiscovered. We

729

debitis exigimus, quae aliter veniunt, ut decepti ab
iis, infesto animo reprehendimus. Itaque resistere
Antonio Ciceronem, etsi maxima laude dignum est,
tamen, quia ille consul hunc consularem merito prae-
11 stare videtur, nemo admiratur. Idem Cicero, si
flexerit adversus alios iudicium suum, quod tanta
firmitate ac magnitudinine animi direxit in extur-
bando Antonio, non modo reliqui temporis gloriam
eripuerit sibi, sed etiam praeterita evanescere coget
—nihil enim per se amplum est, nisi in quo iudicii
ratio extat—, quia neminem magis decet rem publicam amare libertatisque defensorem esse vel ingenio vel rebus gestis vel studio atque efflagitatione
omnium. Quare non Octavius est rogandus, ut velit
nos salvos esse : magis tute te exsuscita, ut eam
civitatem, in qua maxima gessisti, liberam atque
honestam fore putes, si modo sint populo duces ad
resistendum improborum consiliis.

XXVI (I. 18)

M. CICERO S. D. M. BRUTO

Romae, A.U.C. 711

1 Cum saepe te litteris hortatus essem, ut quam
primum rei publicae subvenires in Italiamque exer-
730

require of it a high performance as of right, and when things fall out otherwise we assail men with reproaches for the deception they have practised on us. Therefore Cicero's defiance of Antony calls for the highest praise, yet because it is assumed that the historic consul is morally bound to set the standard for to-day's consular, no one is impressed.

But if the same Cicero should defer to others in **11** his convictions, which he applied so resolutely and in such a grand manner when he bundled Antony out, he will find that he not only has thrown away his reputation for the future, but will also ensure that his past achievements shall be blotted out—for nothing is great in itself that does not bear the plain mark of reasoned judgement—; because no one man is better fitted to be a patriot and to champion liberty with wise thoughts or brave deeds, or with the devotion and the imperious call to leadership of the entire community. For these reasons we must *not* beg Octavius to deign to keep us safe. No, no ! You must rouse yourself up, and realize that the state which was the scene of your greatest achievements will enjoy its freedom and honour on these terms alone, if leaders are forthcoming for the people in making a stand against the policies of reprobates.

XXVI (I. 18)

CICERO TO BRUTUS

Rome, July 27, 43 B.C.

Having repeatedly urged you in my letters to come **1** to the rescue of the state as soon as possible, and to

citum adduceres, neque id arbitrarer dubitare tuos
necessarios, rogatus sum a prudentissima et diligentissima femina, matre tua, cuius omnes curae ad te
referuntur et in te consumuntur, ut venirem ad se
a. d. VIII. Kal. Sextiles : quod ego, ut debui, sine
mora feci. Cum autem venissem, Casca aderat et Labeo et Scaptius. At illa rettulit quaesivitque, quidnam mihi videretur, arcesseremusne te atque id tibi
conducere putaremus, an tardare ac commorari te
2 melius esset. Respondi id, quod sentiebam, et dignitati et existimationi tuae maxime conducere te primo
quoque tempore ferre praesidium labenti et inclinatae
paene rei publicae ; quid enim abesse censes mali in
eo bello, in quo victores exercitus fugientem hostem
persequi noluerint et in quo incolumis imperator,
honoribus amplissimis fortunisque maximis, coniuge,
liberis, vobis affinibus ornatus, bellum rei publicae
indixerit ? Quid dicam " in tanto senatus populique
consensu," cum tantum resideat intra muros mali ?
3 Maximo autem, cum haec scribebam, officiebar dolore, quod, cum me pro adulescentulo ac paene puero
res publica accepisset vadem, vix videbar, quod pro-
miseram, praestare posse. Est autem gravior et
difficilior animi et sententiae, maximis praesertim
in rebus, pro altero quam pecuniae obligatio : haec
enim solvi potest et est rei familiaris iactura tolera-

---

^a Lepidus.

bring your army to Italy, and believing as I did that your intimates were in full agreement with me, I was asked by a woman of great capacity and energy, your mother, whose every care centres on you and is wholly exercised on your behalf, to meet her on July 25. This I promptly did, as in duty bound. On my arrival I found Casca there and Labeo and Scaptius. But *she* put the question and invited my opinion : were we to give you a call, and were we to decide that this was in your interests, or was it better for you to hold back and make no move ?

I told her in reply what I felt, that it was in the 2 highest interests of your exalted rank and reputation to bring support at the earliest possible moment to the free state, which is losing its foothold and on the verge of collapse. For what calamity, think you, is lacking in a war in which the victorious armies have refused to pursue a fleeing enemy, and a general [a] with his forces intact, endowed with the highest public distinctions and with an ample fortune, with a wife and children and a marriage connexion with you, has declared war upon the state ? Why should I say " with such unanimity among Senate and people," seeing that so much evil disposition still lurks within the walls ?

But what grieves me most sorely at the time of 3 writing is that when the state accepted me as surety for this stripling—one might almost call him a boy— I hardly seemed in a position to make good my promise. You see, it is a more serious and arduous risk, especially on an issue of paramount importance, to engage on behalf of another one's soul and one's sentiment than to pledge one's money ; for a money pledge can be redeemed, and the forfeiture of one's

bilis ; rei publicae quod spoponderis, quemadmodum
solvas, si is dependi facile patitur, pro quo spopon-
4 deris ? Quamquam et hunc, ut spero, tenebo multis
repugnantibus : videtur enim esse in eo indoles, sed
flexibilis aetas multique ad depravandum parati, qui
splendore falsi honoris obiecto aciem boni ingenii
praestringi posse confidunt. Itaque ad reliquos hic
quoque labor mihi accessit, ut omnes adhibeam
machinas ad tenendum adulescentem, ne famam sub-
eam temeritatis : quamquam quae temeritas est ?
Magis enim illum, pro quo spopondi, quam me ipsum
obligavi, nec vero paenitere potest rem publicam
me pro eo spopondisse, qui fuit in rebus gerundis cum
5 suo ingenio, tum mea promissione constantior. Maximus autem, nisi me forte fallit, in re publica nodus est
inopia rei pecuniariae : obdurescunt enim magis co-
tidie boni viri ad vocem tributi, quod ex centesima
collatum impudenti censu locupletium in duarum
legionum praemiis omne consumitur ; impendent
autem infiniti sumptus cum in hos exercitus, quibus
nunc defendimur, tum vero in tuum—nam Cassius
noster videtur posse satis ornatus venire. Sed et

family property is to be borne, but political obligations, how are you to discharge them, if the person
on whose behalf you went bail is ready and willing
to make a call on you for full payment?

And yet, so I hope, I shall keep my hold even on 4
him, in spite of opposition from many quarters. For
he seems to have good natural qualities, but he is
pliable at his age, and many are prepared to pervert
him : they are confident that the keen edge of his
sound character can be blunted by dangling before
him the glitter of high office falsely won. So this task
has been imposed upon me on top of all the others,
that I must bring to bear every device by which I
may hold back the young man, lest I be saddled with
a reputation for rashness. And yet wherein does the
rashness lie? For the obligation rested rather upon
the person for whom I stood surety than upon myself; and indeed the state cannot regret that I
pledged myself on behalf of a man who owes it as
much to my guarantee as to his own character that
in the campaign he has been comparatively steadfast.

But, unless I happen to be mistaken, the most 5
knotty problem in affairs of state is the lack of financial resources. For men of goodwill shut their ears
more and more each day to the call of taxation ; because of brazen under-valuations by the well-to-do,
the proceeds of the one-per-cent are being entirely
swallowed up by the bonuses for two legions. Moreover we are confronted with unlimited expenditure,
both on the armies here, by which we are defended
for the present, and also on your forces ; for it seems
as if our friend Cassius could arrive here with a
sufficient equipment. But these and many other

haec et multa alia coram cupio, idque quam primum.
6 De sororis tuae filiis non exspectavi, Brute, dum
scriberes: omnino ipsa tempora—bellum enim ducetur
—integram tibi causam reservant; sed ego a principio, cum divinare de belli diuturnitate non possem,
ita causam egi puerorum in senatu, ut te arbitror e
matris litteris potuisse cognoscere, nec vero ulla res
erit umquam, in qua ego non vel vitae periculo ea
dicam eaque faciam, quam te velle quaeque ad te
pertinere arbitrer. vi. Kal. Sextiles.

matters I want to talk over with you face to face, and that at the earliest possible moment.

I did not wait for you, Brutus, to write about your 6 sister's children. Altogether, the mere state of the times (for the war will be a long one) is keeping their case open against your return. But from the outset, when I could not foretell the long duration of the war, I pleaded the case of the boys in the Senate with such force as I believe you may have been able to ascertain from your mother's letters. Indeed there will never be any affair in which I shall not, even at the risk of my life, speak and act in the way which I shall judge to be in accord with your wishes and in your interest. July 27.

matters I want to talk over with you face to face,
and that at the earliest possible moment.

I did not want for you, Brutus, to write about your
sister's children. Altogether, the mere state of the
times (for the war will be a long one) is keeping their
case open against your return. But from the outset,
when I could not foretell the long duration of the
war, I pleaded the case of the boys in the Senate with
such force as I believe you may have been able to
ascertain from your mother's letters. Indeed there
will never be any affair in which I shall not, even at
the risk of my life, speak and act in the way which
I shall judge to be in accord with your wishes and in
your interest. July 27.

CHRONOLOGICAL ORDER OF THE LETTERS
based on the order fixed in R. Y. Tyrrell and
L. C. Purser, *The Correspondence of M. Tullius
Cicero*, vol. vii., Dublin, 1901 (by kind permission
of the Board of Trinity College, Dublin).

ABBREVIATIONS

A = *Epistulae ad Atticum.*
F = *Epistulae ad Familiares.*
Q.Fr. = *Epistulae ad Quintum Fratrem.*
Br. = *Epistulae ad M. Brutum.*

B.C.

68 A i. 5, 6, 7 ?
67 A i. 9, 8, 10, 11
66 A i. 3, 4
65 A i. 1, 2
64 [*Q. Cic. de petit. consul.*]
63 F xiii. 76 ?
62 F v. 7, 1, 2, 6
61 A i. 12, F v. 5, A i. 13, 14, 15, 16, 17
60 A i. 18, 19, 20, ii. 1, 2, 3, Q.Fr. i. 1
59 A ii. 4, 5, 6, 7, 8, 9, 12, 10, 11, 13, 14, 15, 16, 17, 18, 19,
     20, 21, 22, 23, 24, 25, Q.Fr. i. 2, F xiii. 42, 41 ; also
     43 ? (before 58 B.C. ; so also xiii. 44, 45, 46)
58 A iii. 3, 2, 4, 1, 5, 6, F xiv. 4, A iii. 7, 8, 9, Q.Fr. i. 3,
     A iii. 10, 11, 12, 14, 13, Q.Fr. i. 4, A iii. 15, 16, 17,
     18, 19, 20, F xiv. 2, A iii. 21, 22, F xiv. 1, A iii. 23,
     F xiv. 3, A iii. 24, 25
57 A iii. 26, 27, F v. 4, A iv. 1, 2, 3, Q.Fr. ii. 1, F vii. 26 ;
     also xiii. 51 ?
56 F i. 1, 2, 3, 4, 5a, Q.Fr. ii. 2, A iv. 4, Q.Fr. ii. 3, F i. 5b, 6,
     Q.Fr. ii. 4, 5, A iv. 4a, 5, F v. 12, A iv. 6, 7, 8, F v. 3,
     i. 7, xiii. 6a, 6b, Q.Fr. ii. 8 (= 6), A iv. 8a

ORDER OF THE LETTERS

B.C.

55 F i. 8, Q.Fr. ii. 9 (=7), A iv. 10, 9, Q.Fr. ii. 10 (=8),
A iv. 11, 12, F vii. 2, 3, 1, xiii. 74, 40, A iv. 13

54 F v. 8, Q.Fr. ii. 11 (=9), 12 (=10), F vii. 5, Q.Fr. ii.
13 (=11), F vii. 6, 7, A iv. 14, Q.Fr. ii. 14 (=12),
F vii. 8, Q.Fr. ii. 15a (=13), 15b (=14), A iv. 15, 16,
Q.Fr. ii. 16 (=15), iii. 1, A iv. 17 (part) plus 18
(part), F vii. 9, 17, Q.Fr. iii. 2, 3, 4, A iv. 18 (part),
Q.Fr. iii. 5 plus 6, 7, F vii. 16, Q.Fr. iii. 8, A iv. 19
(part), 17 (part), Q.Fr. iii. 9, F i. 9, vii. 10, i. 10,
xiii. 49, 60, 73

53 F ii. 1, vii. 11, ii. 2, 3, vii. 12, 13, 14, 18, 15, ii. 4, 5, 6,
xiii. 75 ; also xvi. 13 ?, 14 ?, 15 ?, 10 ?, 16 ?

52 F v. 17, 18, iii. 1, vii. 2

51 F iii. 2, A v. 1, 2, 3, 4, 5, 6, 7, F iii. 3, viii. 1, A v. 8,
F iii. 4, A v. 9, F viii. 2, 3, A v. 10, F xiii. 1, A v. 11,
F ii. 8, A v. 12, 13, 14, F iii. 5, viii. 4, A v. 15, 16, 17,
F viii. 5, 9, xv. 3, iii. 6, xv. 7, 8, 9, 12, A v. 18, F xv. 2,
A v. 19, F xv. 1, iii. 8, viii. 8, ii. 9, 10, viii. 10, ii. 7,
A v. 20, F vii. 32, xiii. 53, 56, 55, 61, 62, 64, 65, 9 ;
also 47 ?

50 F xv. 4, 10, 13, 14, viii. 6, 7, iii. 7, ii. 14, ix. 25, xiii. 59,
58, iii. 9, A v. 21, F xiii. 63, A vi. 1, F xiii. 54, 57,
ii. 11, A vi. 2, F ii. 13, 18, xiii. 2, 3, iii. 10, ii. 19, 12,
A vi. 3, F iii. 11, xv. 5, viii. 11, A vi. 4, 5, 7, F viii. 13,
ii. 17, 15, xv. 11, iii. 12, A vi. 6, F iii. 13, xv. 6,
viii. 12, 14, A vi. 8, 9, F xiv. 5, A vii. 1, F xvi. 1, 2,
3, 4, 5, 6, 7, 9, A vii. 3, 4, 5, 6, 7, 8, 9

49 F xvi. 11, v. 20, A vii. 10, 11, 12, F xiv. 18, A vii. 13,
13a, F xiv. 14, A vii. 14, 15, F xvi. 12, A vii. 16,
F xvi. 8, A vii. 17, 18, 19, 20, 21, 22, 23, 24, viii. 11a,
vii. 25, viii. 12b, vii. 26, viii. 1, 11b, 12c, 12d, 2, 12a,
3, 11c, 6, 4, 5, 7, 8, 9, 10, 11, 11d, 12, F viii. 15,
A viii. 15a, 13, 14, 15, 16, ix. 1, 2, 12a, 3, 5, 7a, 6, 6a,
7c, 7b, 4, 7, 8, 9, 10, 11a, 11, 12, 13a, 13, 14, 15, 16,
17, 18, 19, x. 1, 2, 3, 3a, 4, 9a (= F viii. 16),
A x. 5, 8a, 8b, 6, F iv. 1, A x. 7, F iv. 2, 19, A x. 8, 9,
F ii. 16, A x. 10, 11, 12, 12a, 13, 14, 15, 16, 17, 18,
F xiv. 7

48 A xv. 1, 2, F viii. 17, ix. 9, xiv. 8, A xi. 3, F xiv. 21,
A xi. 4, F xiv. 6, 12, A xi. 5, F xiv. 19, A xi. 6, F xiv.
9, A xi. 7, F xiv. 17, A xi. 8

47 A xi. 9, F xiv. 6, A xi. 10, 11, 12, 13, 14, 15, 16, 17,

B.C.

F xiv. 11, A xi. 18, F xiv. 15, A xi. 25, 23, F xiv. 10,
13, A xi. 19, 24, F xiv. 24, 23, A xi. 20, 21, 22, F xiv.
22, xv. 15, xiv. 20, 21 ; also xiii. 48 ?

46 F xiii. 10, 11, 12, 13, 14, xi. 1, xiii. 29, v. 21, A xii. 2,
F ix. 3, 2, 7, 5, vii. 3, vi. 22, ix. 4, A xii. 5c, 3, 4,
F ix. 6, A xii. 5, F ix. 16, 18, vii. 33, ix. 20, vii. 27,
28, ix. 19, 26, 17, 15, xiii. 68, iv. 13, 15, 8, 7, 9, vi. 6,
13, 12, 10a, 10b, xii. 17, iv. 3, 4, 11, ix. 21, vi. 14,
A xii. 6a, 6b, 7, 8, 11, F vii. 4, ix. 23, A xii. 1, F xiii.
66, 67, 69, 70, 71, 72, 17, 18, 19, 20, 21, 22, 23, 24,
25, 26, 27, 28a, 28b, 78, 79, vi. 8, 9, v. 16, xv. 18 ;
also xii. 20 ?, xiii. 52 ?

45 F xv. 16, vi. 7, 5, 18, iv. 14, 10, ix. 10, vi. 1, 3, 4, xv. 17,
19, ix. 13, xiii. 16, A xii. 13, 14, 15, 16, 18, 17, 18a,
19, 20, xiii. 6, F iv. 5, A xii. 12, 21, 22, 23, 24, 25,
26, 27, 28, 29, 33, 30, 32, 31, 34, 35 ?, F xiii. 15,
v. 13, vi. 21, iv. 6, vi. 2, ix. 11, 36, 37, 37a, 38, 38a,
39, 40, F v. 14, A xii. 42, F v. 15, A xii. 41, 43, 44,
45 ?, xiii. 26, xii. 46, 47, 48, 50, 49, 51, 52, 53, xiii. 1,
2, 27, 28, 29, 2a, 30, 31, 32, xii. 5a, F iv. 12, A xiii. 4,
5, 33, 6a, 8, 7, 7a, xii. 5b, F vi. 11, A xiii. 9, 10,
11, 12, 13, 14, 15, 16, 17, 18, 19, 21a, F ix. 22, A xiii.
20, 22, 33a, 23, F xiii. 77, v. 9, A xiii. 24, 25, F ix. 8,
A xiii. 35, 36, 43, F. vi. 20, A xiii. 44, 34, F vi. 19, A
xii. 9, F xvi. 22, A xii. 10, xiii. 21, F xvi. 17, A xiii.
47a, F xvi. 19, A xiii. 48, 37, 38, 39, 40, 41, 45, 46,
47, F vii. 24, A xiii. 49, 50, F vii. 35, A xiii. 51, F xii.
18, 19, xiii. 4, 5, 7, 8, v. 11, vii. 29, v. 10b, A xiii.
52, F ix. 12, A xiii. 42, F xiii. 30, 31, 32, 33, 34, 35,
36, 37, 38, 39, xvi. 18, 20

44 F vii. 30, viii. 50, v. 10a, vii. 31, xii. 21, vi. 15, xi. 1,
vi. 16, xv. 20, A xiv. 1, 2, 3, 4, 5, 6, 7, 8, F vi. 17,
A xiv. 9, 10, 11, 12, 13a, 13b, 13, 14, 15, 16, 17a
(= F ix. 14), F xii. 1, A xiv. 17, 19, 18, 20, 21, 22,
xv. 1, 1a, 2, 3, 4, 4a, F xii. 16, A xv. 6, 5, 7, F xi. 2,
A xv. 8, 9, 10, 11, 12, 16, 16a, 15, 17, 18, 19, 20, 21,
F xvi. 23, A xv. 22, 23, 24, 14, 25, F vii. 21, 22, xi. 29,
A xv. 26, 27, 28, xvi. 16, 16a, xv. 29, xvi. 1, 5, 4,
2, 3, F vii. 20, A xvi. 6, F vii. 19, A xvi. 16b, 16c,
16d, 16e, 16f, F xi. 3, A xvi. 7, F xi. 27, 28, xvi. 21,
x. 1, 2, xii. 22 (1-2), 2, xvi. 25, xi. 4, 6 (1), xii. 3,
23, A xv. 13, xvi. 8, 9, 11, 12, 10, 13a, 13b, 13c, 14,

ORDER OF THE LETTERS

F xvi. 24, A xvi. 15, F xi. 5, x. 3, xi. 7, 6 (2-3), ii. 22 (3-4), xvi. 26, 27, x. 4

43 F x. 5, xi. 8, xii. 24, 4, x. 28, ix. 24, xii. 5, 11, 7, x. 31, xii. 25a, x. 6, 27, xii. 28, 26, 27, 29, x. 7, 8, 10, xii. 6, Br. ii. 1, 3, 2, F x. 12, Br. ii. 4, F x. 30, Br. ii. 5, i. 2, sects. 4-6, i. 3, sects. 1-3, F x. 9, Br. i. 3, sect. 4, F xi. 9, 11, 13b, xii. 25b, Br. i. 5, F x. 14, xi. 10, 11, xii. 12, x. 13, xi. 13a, 15, 21, sects. 1-6, Br. i. 4, sects. 1-3, F x. 21, Br. i. 4, sects. 4-6, F xi. 12, x. 34a, 18, xi. 18, Br. i. 6, 1, 2, sects. 1-3, F x. 17, xi. 19, x. 34, sects. 3-4, xi. 20, 23, x. 19, 25, 16, xii. 15, sects. 1-6, 14, x. 20, 35, Br. i. 8, F xi. 16, 17, x. 33, Br. i. 11, 17, F xii. 15, xi. 26, 21, 24, x. 23, 32, Br. i. 10, F xii. 8, 30, xi. 13, sects. 4-5, xii. 13, Br. i. 9, F xi. 25, xii. 9, Br. i. 7, F xi. 15, x. 22, 26, Br. i. 13, F xii. 10, x. 29, xi. 32, Br. i. 12, 14, 15, 16, 18, F x. 24

INDEX OF NAMES I.

CICERO'S LETTERS TO HIS FRIENDS, BOOKS XIII–XVI

(The references are to the Book, Letter, and Section or Sections)

Acastus, xiv. 5. 1; xvi. 5. 2; 10. 2; 14. 2

Achaia, xiii. 26. 2; 27. 3; 28a. 2; 78. 1; xv. 15. 2

Acilius Glabrio (M'.), Cicero's letters to, xiii. 30-39; 50

Actium, xvi. 6. 2; 9. 1

Aegypta, xvi. 15. 1, 2

Aelius Lamia (L.), xiii. 62

Aemilius Avianius (M.), xiii. 2; 21. 1; 27. 2

Aemilius Lepidus (M.), xiii. 26. 3

Aesculapius, xiv. 7. 1

Afranius (L.), xvi. 12. 4

Africa, xiii. 6. 2; xv. 15. 2

Agusius (T.), xiii. 71

Ἀλαβανδεῖς, xiii. 56. 1

Alabandinensis, xiii. 56. 2; 64. 1

Albinius (C.), xiii. 8. 1-3

Alexandrinum bellum, xiii. 16. 2; xv. 15. 2

Allienus (A.), Cicero's letters to, xiii. 78; 79

Alyzia, xvi. 2; 3. 1

Amafinii, xv. 19. 2

Amanus (Mt.), xv. 4. 4, 7, 8, 9

Ampius Balbus (T.), xiii. 70

Ampius Menander (T.), xiii. 70

Ancharius (Q.), Cicero's letter to, xiii. 40

Anchialus, xiii. 45

Ancona, xvi. 12. 2

Andricus, xvi. 14. 1

Andro, xiii. 67. 1

Anneius (M.), xiii. 55. 1, 2; 57. 1, 2; xv. 4. 2, 8

Annius Milo (T.), xv. 4. 12

Anterus, xvi. 21. 8

Antigonus, xiii. 33

Antiochia, xv. 4. 7

Antiochus (Commagenus), xv. 1. 2; 3. 1; 4. 3

Antipater (Derbes), xiii. 73. 2

Antistius (T.), xiii. 29. 3

Antonius (M.), xvi. 11. 2; 23. 1, 2; 24. 2

Apamea (Phrygias), xv. 4. 2

Apollo, xiv. 7. 1

Apollonia, xiii. 29. 4

Apollonius, xiii. 16. 1

Appuleius, Cicero's letters to, xiii. 45, 46

Aquinum, xvi. 24. 2

Arabes, xv. 1, 2; 4. 7

Arae Alexandri, xv. 4. 9

Areopagitae, xiii. 1. 5

Ariarathes, xv. 2. 6

Ariminum, xvi. 12. 2

Ariobarzanes, xv. 2. 4-8; 4. 6; 5. 1

Aristocritus, xiv. 3. 1, 4

Armenius Rex, xv. 2. 2; 3. 1

Arpinas (fundus) xiv. 7. 3

Arpinates, xiii. 11. 1; 12. 1

Arretium, xvi. 12. 2

Artavasdes, xv. 2. 2

Artemo, xiii. 67. 1

Asclapo, xiii. 20; xvi. 9. 2, 4

Asia, xiii. 68. 2; 69. 1; xv. 1. 5 4. 4; 15. 2

Asiaticae διοικήσεις, xiii. 72. 1

Ateius Capito (C.), xiii. 29. 2-8

Atellanum municipium, xiii. 7. 1

INDEX OF NAMES I.

Athenae, xiii. 1. 1, 3; xiv. 5. 1, 2; xv. 19. 1

Athenaeus, xv. 4. 6

Athenais, xv. 4. 6

Athenienses, xvi. 21. 5

Atilius, xiii. 62

Attius pigmentarius, xv. 17. 2

Aufidianum nomen, xvi. 19

Aurelius, xvi. 24. 1

Aurelius (C.), xiii. 40. 1

Aurelius (L.), xiii. 40. 1

Avianius Evander (C.), xiii. 2

Avianius Flaccus (C.), xiii. 35. 1; 75. 1, 2; 79; Gaius filius, 79; Marcus filius, *ib.*

Avianius Hammonius (C.), xiii. 21. 2; 27. 2

Avianius Philoxenus, xiii. 35. 1

Bargylietae, xiii. 56. 2

Bibulus. See Calpurnius

Billienus, xvi. 22. 2

Bithynia, xiii. 9. 1, 3; 29. 4

Bithynica societas, xiii. 9. 2

Bolanus (M.), xiii. 77. 2, 3

Britannia, xv. 16. 2

Brundisium, xiii. 10. 3; 50. 1, 2; 12; xiv. 4. 2, 3, 5, 6; xv. 17. 4; 21. 2 : xvi. 9. 2, 3

Bruttius, xvi. 21. 4, 5

Bruttius (L.), xiii. 38

Brutus. See Junius Brutus

Bulliones, xiii. 42. 1

Buthrotum, xvi. 7

Caecina (A.), xlii. 66. 1, 2

Caerellia, xiii. 72. 1, 2

Caesar. See Julius *or* Octavius

Caesena, xvi. 27. 2

Caesius (M.), xiii. 11. 3 ; 12. 1

Caesius (P.), Cicero's letter to, xiii. 51

Calactini, xiii. 37

Calpurnius Bibulus (M.), xv. 1. 1, 5 ; 3. 2 ; 4. 7

Calpurnius Piso Caesoninus (L.), xiv. 14. 2

Calpurnius Piso Frugi (C.), xiii. 31. 1 ; xiv. 1, 3, 4 ; 2. 2 ; 4. 4

Calvus. See Licinius

Camillus (C.), xiv. 5. 2 ; 14. 2

Cappadocia, xv. 1. 2, 6 ; 2. 1, 2, 8 ; 3. 1 ; 4. 4, 6, 7, 15

Capua, xvi. 11. 3 ; 12. 6

Cassiope, xvi. 9. 1

Cassius, philologus, xvi. 21. 5

Cassius Longinus (C.), Cicero's letters to, xv. 14-18; his to Cicero, xv. 19

Cassius (Q.), xvi. 11. 2

Castrinius Paetus (L.), xiii. 13

Catiana spectra, xv. 16. 1 ; 19. 1

Catii, xv. 19. 2

Catina, xiii. 30. 1

Catinenses, xiii. 30. 1

Catius, Insubar, xv. 16. 1 ; 19. 1, 2

Cato. See Porcius

Catones, xv. 6. 1

Caunii, xiii. 56. 3

Cibyra, xiii. 21. 1

Cicero. See Tullius

Cilices, xv. 1. 3

Cilicia, xiii. 12. 1 ; 16. 2 ; 57. 1 ; xv. 1. 2, 3 ; 2. 2, 3, 7, 8 ; 4. 3, 4, 7, 8

Ciliciensis provincia, xiii. 67. 1

Claudius Marcellus (C.), Cicero's letters to, xv. 7 ; 10 ; 11.—xiii. 29. 4

Claudius Marcellus (C.), father of the above, Cicero's letter to, xv. 8

Claudius Nero (Ti.), xiii. 64. 1, 2

Clodius Archagathus (M.), xiii. 32. 1

Clodius Philhetaerus, xiv. 4. 6

Clodius Philo (C.), xiii. 32. 1

Cluvius, Cicero's letter to, xiii. 7

Cluvius (M.), xiii. 56. 1, 2, 3

Colophonius, xiii. 69. 2

Commagenus, xv. 1. 2 ; 3. 1, 2 ; 4. 3

Commoris, xv. 4. 9

Considius Nonianus, xvi. 12. 3

Corcyra, xiii. 29. 4 ; xvi. 7 ; 9. 1

Corcyraei, xvi. 9. 1

Cornelius (P.), negotiator, xiii. 6*a* ; 14. 1

Cornelius Balbus (L.), xvi. 23. 1 ; 24. 2

Cornelius Dolabella (P.), xiii. 36. 1 ; xiv. 9 ; 14. 1 ; 18. 1 ; xvi. 12. 5 ; 24. 2

Cornelius Lentulus (L.), consul in 49 B.C., xvi. 11. 3

Cornelius Lentulus Spinther (P.), consul in 57 B.C., xiii. 48 ; xiv. 1. 2

Cornelius Sulla (P.), xv. 17. 2 ; 19. 3

Cossinius (L.), xiii. 23. 1

Cossutianae tabernae, xvi. 27. 2

Crabra (Aqua), xvi. 18. 3

Crassipes. See Furius

INDEX OF NAMES I.

Crassus. See Licinius Crassus
Cratippus, xvi. 21. 3, 5
Culleolus, Cicero's letters to, xiii. 41. 42
Cumanum, xvi. 10. 1
Cures, xv. 20. 1
Curius, Cicero's letter to, xiii. 49
Curius (M'.), xiii. 17. 1, 3; 50. 1, 2; xvi. 4. 2; 5. 1, 2; 9. 3, 4; 11. 1
Curtius Mithres (C.), xiii. 69. 1
Curtius Peducaeanus (C.), Cicero's letter to, xiii. 59
Curtius Postumus (C.), xiii. 5. 2, 3; 69. 1
Cuspiana, xiii. 6. 2
Cuspius (P.), xiii. 6. 1-4; 6a; xvi. 17. 2
Custidius (L.), xiii. 58
Cybistra, xv. 2. 2, 5; 4. 4, 6
Cyprii, xiii. 48
Cyprus, xv. 4. 15
Cyzicus, xiv. 4. 3

Deiotarus, xv. 1. 6; 2. 2 sqq.; 4. 5, 7, 15
Demetrius, xvi. 17. 2; 19; 22. 2
Demetrius Megas, xiii. 36. 1
Demetrius Phalereus, xvi. 22. 2
Democritus, xv. 16. 1
Democritus of Sicyon, xiii. 78. 1
Demostratus, xiii. 33.
Derbes, xiii. 73. 2. Cf. Antipater
Dexippus, xiv. 3. 3, 4
Diodotus, xiii. 16. 4
Dionysius, anagnostes, xiii. 77. 3
Dolabella. See Cornelius Dolabella
Domitius Ahenobarbus (L.), xvi. 12. 3
Dyrrachium, xiv. 1. 6, 7; 3. 4

Egnatius Rufus (L.), xiii. 43. 1; 44 45; 47; 73. 1; 74
Eleutherocilices, xv. 4. 10
Elis, xiii. 26. 2
Ephesii, xiii. 65. 1
Ephesus, xiii. 55; 56. 1; 57. 2; 65. 1; 69. 1; xv. 3. 2
Epicrates, xvi. 21. 5
Epicurus, xiii. 1. 3, 4; xv. 19. 2
Epiphanea, xv. 4. 7, 8
Epiroticae res, xiii. 18. 2
Epirus, xiv. 1. 3; 3. 4
Erana, xv. 4. 9
Euphrates, xv. 1. 1, 9; 3. 1

Euripides, xiii. 15. 2; xvi. 8. 2
Euthydemus, xiii. 56. 1

Fadius Gallus (M.), xiii. 59; xv. 14. 1, 2
Faucius (M.), xiii. 11. 1
Flaminius Flamma (T.), xvi. 24. 1
Flavius (C.), xiii. 31. 1, 2
Flavius (L.), xiii. 31. 1
Formiae, xiv. 18. 2; xvi. 12. 5
Formianum, xvi. 10. 1; 12. 6
Fregellanus ager, xiii. 76. 2
Fufidius (Q.), xiii. 11. 1; 12. 1
Fufius (A.), xiii. 3
Furius Crassipes, Cicero's letter to, xiii. 9
Furnius (C.), xv. 14. 5

Galli, xvi. 27. 2
Gallia, xiii. 7. 1; 11. 1; 14. 1
Galliae, xvi. 12. 3, 4
Gargettius (Epicurus), xv. 16. 1
Genucilius Curvus (L.), xiii. 53. 1, 2
Gorgias, xvi. 21. 6
Graeca scripta, xv. 4. 12
Graecae litterae, xiii. 16. 4
Graece declamitare, xvi. 21. 5
Graeci, xvi. 4. 2; 24. 1
Graecus, xvi. 21. 8

Halesina civitas, xiii. 32. 1
Harpalus, xvi. 24. 1
Hector (Naevianus), xv. 6. 1
Hegesaretus of Larissa, xiii. 25
Helico, xvi. 18. 2
Hellespontus, xiii. 53. 2
Helvia, Cicero's mother, xvi. 26. 2
Heracleotae, xiii. 56. 2
Hermia, xvi. 15. 1, 2
Hilarus, xiii. 33
Hippias of Calacte, xiii. 37
Hippius (Q.), xiii. 76. 1
Hirtius (A.), xvi. 24. 2; 27. 1, 2
Hispania, xiii. 16. 3; xv. 17. 3; xvi. 12. 3, 4
Hispaniae, xv. 19. 4
Homerus, xiii. 15. 1, 2
Hydruns, xvi. 9. 2

Iamblichus, phylarchus, xv. 1. 2
Iconium, xv. 3. 1; 4. 2
Isauri, xv. 2. 1
Italia, xiv. 1. 3, 7; 5. 2; 12; xv. 15. 3; xvi. 6. 2; 9. 2; 11. 3

INDEX OF NAMES I.

Julius (L.), xiii. 6. 3
Julius Caesar (C.), Cicero's letters to, xiii. 15. 16.—xiii. 4. 2; 5. 1, 2; **7.** 1, 3, 5; 8. 2; 13. 3; 19. 1; 29. 3-7; 36. 1; 68. 2; xiv. 1. 2; 8; 11; 15; 23; 24; xv. 15. 3; 19. 3, 4; xvi. 11. 2, 3; 12. 2, 3; 18. 3
Junia, xv. 8
Junius Brutus (M.), Cicero's letters to, xiii. 10-14.—xv. 14. 6; 20. 3

Laberiana praedia, xiii. 8. 3
Laberius (M.), xiii. 8. 2
Labienus (T.), xiv. 14. 2; xvi. 12. 4
Lacedaemonii, xiii. 28a. 1, 2
Laenus Flaccus (M.), xiii. 63. 1; xiv. 4. 2
Laodicea, xiii. 54; xv. 4. 2
Laodicensis, xiii. 67. 1
Latina scripta, xv. 4. 12
Latine (declamitare), xvi. 21. 5
Latini, xiii. 30. 1
Leonidas, xvi. 21. 5
Lepta (Q.), xiv. 17; xvi. 4. 4; 23. 2
Leucas, xv. 1. 2; 2; 4. 4; 5. 1, 2; 9. 1
Licinius Aristoteles (A.), xiii. 52
Licinius Calvus (C.), xv. 21. 4
Licinius Crassus (M.), xiii. 16. 1, 3; xiv. 2. 2
Licinius Crassus (P.), son of the above, xiii. 16. 1
Ligurius (A.), xvi. 18. 3
Lilybitanus, xiii. 34
Livineius Regulus (L.), xiii. 60. 1
Livineius Trypho (L.), xiii. 60. 1
Lucceius (L.), xiii. 41. 1, 2; 42. 1, 2
Lucense municipium, xiii. 13
Luceria, xv. 15. 4
Lycaonia, xv. 1. 2; 2. 1; 4. 2
Lyso Lilybitanus, xiii. 34
Lyso of Patrae, xiii. 19. 1-3; 24. 1, 2; xvi. 4. 1, 2; 5. 1; 9. 3, 4

Macedonia, xiii. 29. 3, 4; xiv. 4. 3
Maenius Gemellus (C.), xiii. 19. 2
Mamercus (Q.), xiii. 11. 1
Manlius (T.), xiii. 22. 1, 2
Manlius Sosis (L.), xiii. 30. 1
Marcelli, xv. 10. 1
Marcellini, xv. 10. 1
Marcellus. See Claudius Marcellus
Marcilius (M.), xiii. 54

Marcius Philippus (Q.), Cicero's letters to, xiii. 73, 74
Mario, xvi. 1. 1, 2; 2; 3. 2; 5. 1
Melitensis, xiii. 52
Memmius (C.), Cicero's letters to, xiii. 1-3
Menandrus, xvi. 13
Mescinius Rufus (L.), xiii. 26. 1, 4 28. 1-3; xvi. 4. 3; 9. 4
Messienus (P.), xiii. 51
Metras, xv. 4. 6
Metrodorus, xvi. 20
Mindius (M.), xiii. 26. 2; 28. 2
Mindius (Macellarius), xv. 17. 2
Minturnae, xiv. 14. 2
Minucius Thermus (Q.), Cicero's letters to, xiii. 53-57
Mitylenae, xvi. 21. 5
Motho, xvi. 18. 2
Μυλασεῖς, xiii. 56. 1
Munatius (C.), Cicero's letter to, xiii. 60
Munatius Plancus (L.), Cicero's letter to, xiii. 29
Musae=litterae, xvi. 10. 2
Mylasini, xiii. 56. 1

Naevius (Cn.), the poet, xv. 6. 1
Narona, xiii. 77. 3
Neapolis, xiii. 30. 1
Neapolitanus, xiii. 30. 1
Nicaeenses, xiii. 61
Nostius Zoilus, xiii. 46
Nysaei, xiii. 44. 1

Octavius (Octavianus) Caesar, xvi. 24. 2
Ofilius (A.), xvi. 24. 1
Oppia, xiii. 28. 2
Oppius (L.), xiii. 43. 1, 2; 44; 73. 1; 74
Orator, Cicero's book, xv. 20. 1
Orodes, xv. 1; 2
Orpheus, a slave, xiv. 4. 4
Otacilius Naso (Cn.), xiii. 33

Pacorus, xv. 1. 2
Pansa. See Vibius Pansa
Paphii, xiii. 48
Papia, xvi. 24. 2
Paredrus, xvi. 18. 2
Pariana civitas, xiii. 53. 2
Parthi, xv. 1. 1, 2; 2. 1; 3. 1; **4. 3,** 4, 7, 10; 9. 3
Parthicus equitatus, xv. **1. 2**

INDEX OF NAMES I.

Patrae, xiii. 17. 1; xvi. 1. 2; 5. 2; 6. 2

Patrenses, xiii. 19. 2

Patro, the Epicurean, xiii. 1. 2-5

Paulus (L.), Cicero's letters to, xv. 12, 13. — xiii. 29, 4; xv. 13. 3; 14. 5

Pausanias, xiii. 64. 1

Pescennius, xiv. 4. 6

Petreius (M.), xvi. 12. 4

Phaedrus, the philosopher, xiii. 1. 2, 4, 5

Pharnaces, xv. 16. 2

Philippus of Lacedaemon, xiii. 28a. 1

Philo of Larissa, xiii. 1. 2

Philocles, xiii. 56. 2

Philomelium, xiii. 43. 1; xv. 4. 2

Philotimus, xiv. 18. 2; 24

Philoxenus, xiii. 37

Pindenissus, xv. 4. 10

Pinnius (T.), xiii. 61

Pisaurum, xvi. 12. 2

Plancius (Cn.), xiv. 1. 3; xvi. 9. 2

Plancus. See Munatius Plancus

Plato, xv. 18. 1

Plautius (A.), xiii. 29. 4

Plotiana bona, xiii. 8. 2

Pollex, xiv. 6

Pompeius (Q.), xiii. 49

Pompeius Bithynicus (A.), xvi. 23. 1

Pompeius Magnus (Cn.), xiii. 29. 3; 41. 2; 42. 1; 56. 3; 75. 2; xiv. 1. 2; 2. 1; xvi. 10. 2, 3; 11. 3; 12. 3

Pompeius (Cn.), son of the above, xv. 19. 4

Pomponius Atticus (T.), xiii. 1. 5; 17. 1; 18. 1, 2; 23. 1; xiv. 5. 2; 10; 14. 2; 19; xvi. 23. 2

Porcius Cato (M.), Uticensis, Cicero's letters to, xv. 3. 4; 6; his to Cicero, xv. 5.—xv. 4. 16; xvi. 22. 1

Preciana hereditas, xiv. 5. 2

Precilius, xiii. 15. 1, 2, 3

Publius, xvi. 22. 1

Pupius (Cn.), xiii. 9. 3

Quintius Gallus, Cicero's letters to, xiii. 43, 44

Regienses (Lepidi), xiii. 7. 4

Regulus. See Livineius

Rex, Cicero's letter to, xiii. 52

Roma, xiii. 1. 2, 3; 14. 1; 19. 1; 24. 1; 26. 3; 28. 2; 29. 4; 38; 56. 1; 56. 2; 67. 1; 73. 1; xiv. 5. 2; 14. 1; 18. 1; xv. 13. 1; 14. 4, 6; 20. 2; xvi. 9. 3; 12. 3, 6

Romanus civis, xiii. 30. 1; 36. 2

Romanus eques, xiii. 14. 1; 31. 1; 38; 43. 1; 45; 51; 62

Romanus populus, xiii. 4. 1, 2, 3; xv. 1. 1, 2, 3, 5; 2. 2, 5, 7; 4. 5, 13; 9. 1; 12. 1

Romanus rusticus, xvi. 21. 7

Rufus. See Caelius Rufus Mescinius Rufus, unknown, xiv. 14. 2

Rupilius (P.), xiii. 9. 2

Rutilius (M.), Cicero's letter to, xiii. 8

Sabinus, xv. 20. 1; xvi. 16. 2

Sallustius (Cn.), xiv. 4. 6; 11

Sardiani, xiii. 55. 1; 57. 2

Scribonius Curio (C.), xv. 14. 5 xvi. 11. 2

Senate and Magistrates, Cicero's letters to, xv. 1, 2

Sepyra, xv. 4. 9

Servilius Strato, xiii. 64. 1

Servilius Vatia Isauricus, xvi. 23. 2

Sestius (P.), xiii. 8. 1, 3

Sestius (L.), son of the above, xiii. 8. 1

Sextilius Rufus (C.), Cicero's letter to, xiii. 48

Sicca, xiv. 4. 6; 15

Sicilia, xiii. 30. 1, 2; 79

Siciliensis quaestura, xiii. 38

Siculus, xiii. 36. 1

Sicyon, xiii. 21. 1, 2

Sicyonius, xiii. 78. 1

Silius Nerva (C.), Cicero's letter to, xiii. 47; 61-65

Sophocleum aliquid, xvi. 18. 3

Statius (Q.), xvi. 16. 2

Stoici, xv. 19. 1

Sullani venditiones, xiii. 8. 2

Sullanum tempus, xiii. 4. 1; 5. 2

Sulpicius Rufus (P.), Cicero's letter to, xiii. 77

Sulpicius Rufus (Servius), Cicero's letters to, xiii. 17-27a

Sulpicius Rufus (Servius), son of the above, xiii. 27. 4

Synnada, xv. 4. 2

INDEX OF NAMES I.

Syria, xiii. 57. 1; xv. 1. 1-3; 2. 1, 3, 7; 3. 2; 4. 3, 4

Tarcondimotus, xv. 1. 2

Tebarani, xv. 4. 10

Terentia, Cicero's letters to her and children, xiv. 1-4; 6; 14; 18; to her alone, xiv. 5; 7-13; 15-17; 19-24.—xiv. 1. 5; 2. 1; 3. 1, 5; 4. 5, 6; 5. 2; xvi. 9. 2; 12. 6

Terentius Hispo, xiii. 65. 1, 2

Terentius Varro Gibba (M.), xiii. 10. 1, 2, 4

Terentius Varro Murena (A.), xiii. 22. 1; xvi. 12. 6

Tertia, xvi. 22. 1

Theophrastus, xvi. 17. 1

Thermus. See Mincius Thermus

Thespias, xiii. 22. 1

Thessalonica, xiv. 2. 4

Thyrreum, xvi. 5. 1

Tiro. See Tullius Tiro

Titius (T.), Cicero's letter to, xiii. 75

Titius Rufus (C.), Cicero's letter to, xiii. 58

Titius Strabo (L.), xiii. 14. 1, 2

Titurnia familia, xiii. 39

Titurnius Rufus (M.), xiii. 39

Transpadani, xvi. 12. 4

Trebatius Testa (C.), xiv. 17

Trebonius (C.), xv. 20. 2

Tullia (or Tulliola), Cicero's letters to her and her brother and mother, xiv. 1-4; 6; 14; 18.—xiv. 1. 1, 6; 2. 1; 4. 3; 5. 1; 7. 1, 2; 9; 11; 15; 17; 19; xvi. 12. 6; 16. 1

Tullius (L.), xv. 4. 8

Tullius Cicero (M.), xv. 16. 1; 26. 1

Tullius Cicero (M.), son of the above, Cicero's letters to him

and his sister and mother, **xiv.** 1-4; 6; 14; 18.—xiv. 1. 1, 6; 4. 3, 6; 5. 1; 7. 3; 11; 15; xvi. 12. 6; 16. 1

Tullius Cicero (Q.), his letters to Tiro, xvi. 8; 26; 27: to his brother Marcus, xvi. 16.—xiii. 62; xiv. 1. 4; 14. 2; xv. 4. 8, 10; xvi. 3. 1; 7

Tullius Cicero (Q.), son of the above, xiv. 14. 2; xvi. 8. 2; 16. 1

Tullius Tiro (M.), Cicero and his family's letters to, xvi. 1; 3; 4; 5-7; 9; 11; Cicero's alone. xvi. 2; 10; xii.-xv. ; 17-20; 22-24; Quintus's letters to him, xvi. 8; 26; 27: Cicero's son Marcus's letter to him, xvi. 21; 25.—xvi. 1. 2; 3. 2; 4. 2-4; 6. 2; 7; 9. 4; 10. 1; 16. 1; 20; 21. 2, 7; 22. 2

Tusculanum praedium. xiv. 20; xvi. 18. 1

Tyba, xv. 1. 2

Ummius, xvi. 14. 1

Valeria tabula, xiv. 2. 2

Valerius (P.), xiv. 2. 2

Valerius Orca (Q.), Cicero's letters to, xiii. 4-6a

Valgius Hippianus (C.), xiii. 76. 2

Vennonius (C.), xiii. 72. 2

Venusinum praedium, xiv. 20

Vesta, xiv. 2. 2

Vibius Pansa (C.), xv. 17. 3; 19 2, 3; xvi. 27. 1, 2

Volaterranae, xiii. 4. 1, 3, 4

Volaterranus ager, xiii. 4. 2; 5. 2

Volcatius Tullus (L.), xiii. 14. 1

Volumnia, xiv. 16

Volusius (M.), xvi. 12. 6

Xenomenes, xvi. 5. 1

INDEX OF NAMES II.

CICERO'S LETTERS TO QUINTUS

(The references are to the Book, Letter, and Section or Sections)

Acutius (Q.), iii. 2. 3
Aeserninus, iii. 4. 2
Aesopus, i. 2. 14
Afranius (L.), ii. 9. 3
Afri, i. 1. 27
Africanus (P. Cornelius Scipio), i. 1. 23 ; ii. 3. 3 ; iii. 5 and 6. 1
Agesilaus, i. 2. 7
Alexandria, ii. 3. 2
Alexandrinus, rex, ii. 2. 3
Alfius (C.), iii. 1. 24 ; 3. 3
Allienus, i. 1. 10
Anagninum, ii. 5. 5
Anicius (T.), ii. 10. 3 ; iii. 1. 23
Annalis, iii. 1. 20
Antandrius, i. 2. 4
Antistius Vetus, ii. 1. 3
Antium, ii. 8. 1
Antonii (C. and L.), sons of Marcus, iii. 2. 1
Antonius (M.), i. 2. 13 ; 3. 7
Apameensis, i. 2. 4
Apollo, ii. 3. 3 ; iii. 1. 24
Apollonidensis, i. 2. 10, 11
Appia, via, i. 1. 17 ; iii. 7. 1
Appius Claudius Pulcher, ii. 4. 6 ; 12. 1, 2, 3, 5 ; 13. 3 ; 15*a*. 3 ; iii. 2. 3 ; 4. 6 ; 9. 3
Aquilius (M.), cons. 129 B.C., iii. 5 and 6. 1
Arcanum, ii. 5. 5 ; iii. 1. 1 ; 3. 1 ; 9. 7
Ἀρης, iii. 4. 6
Ariminum, ii. 14. 1
Aristophaneus, modus, iii. 1. 19
Aristoteles, iii. 5 and 6. 1

Arpinas, ii. 5. 5 ; iii. 1. 1 ; 7. 8, 20
Arpinum, iii. 1. 3
Arrius (Q.), i. 3. 8
Ascanio, iii. 4. 5
Asia, i. 1. 8, 9, 20, 24, 26, 30, 31, 34, 45 ; 2. 14
Asiatici, i. 1. 17
Asiciana, lectica, ii. 10. 2
Asicianus, octophorus, ii. 10. 2
Asicius, ii. 10. 2
Ateius, ii. 10. 1
Atellanum, municipium, ii. 14. 2
Athenae, i. 2. 14 ; ii. 16. 4
Attalus, i. 2. 14
Atticus. See Pomponius
Aurelia (lex), i. 3. 8

Baiae, ii. 10. 2
Balbus (L. Cornelius), ii. 12. 4 ; iii 1. 9, 12
Bestia (Calpurnius), ii. 3. 6
Bibulus (Calpurnius), ii. 3. 2, 4 ; ii. 2 ; 16. 4 ; iii. 1. 18
Bostrenus, ii. 12. 2
Bovillanus, fundus, iii. 1. 3
Britannia, ii. 15*a*. 2 ; iii. i. 13, 25
Britannicae, res, iii. 1. 10, 25
Brogitarus, ii. 9. 2
Byzantium, ii. 9. 2

Caecilius, cousin of P. Sulla, iii. 3. 2
Caecilius (L.), i. 2. 6
Caelius Rufus (M.), ii. 13. 2
Caelius Vinicianus, ii. 8. 4
Caepio (Q. Servilius), i. 8. 7

INDEX OF NAMES II.

Caesar (C. Julius), i. 2. 11, 16; ii. 1.
  1; 4. 5, 6; 12. 2, 4, 5; 13. 1; 15a.
  1, 3; 15b. 2, 4; 16. 15; iii. 1. 8,
  9, 10, 11, 13, 17, 18, 20, 25; 2. 3;
  3. 1; 5 and 6. 3, 4; 8. 2, 3, 6; 9.
  6, 7
Caesius, i. 1. 14; 2. 4; iii. 1. 2, 3
Calidius (M.), i. 3. 7; ii. 11. 2; iii.
  2. 1
Calisthenes, ii. 13. 4
Calpurnius Piso Caesoninus (L.),
  iii. 1. 24
Calpurnius Piso Frugi (C.), i. 4. 2;
  ii. 3. 7
Calventius Marius, iii. 1. 11
Campanus, ager, ii. 1. 1; 5. 1; 8. 1
Caninius, ii. 2. 3; 4. 5
Capito (L.), iii. 1. 15
Capitolini, ii. 5. 2
Carbo, Papirius (C.), ii. 3. 3
Caria, i. 1. 25
Carinae, ii. 3. 7
Cascellius, i. 1. 5; iii. 1. 3
Cassii, i. 2. 3
Cassius (C.), ii. 1. 2
Castor (C.), ii. 3. 6
Catienus, i. 2. 6
Cato (C. Porcius), i. 2. 15; ii. 1. 2;
  3. 1, 4; 6. 5, 6; 9. 3
Cato (M. Porcius), ii. 3. 3; 15. 4;
  iii. 1. 15; 2. 1; 4. 1, 6
Catoniana, familia, ii. 4. 5
Catuli, porticus, iii. 1. 14
Caunii, i. 1. 33
Censorinus, i. 2. 13
Chaerippus, i. 1. 14; iii. 2. 1
Chrysippus, iii. 4. 5; 5 and 6, 6
Cicero, son of Marcus, i. 3. 3, 10;
  ii. 13. 4; 14. 1; iii. 3. 4; 4. 6; 8. 2
Cicero, son of Quintus, iii. 1. 7, 14,
  19; 9. 8
Cicerones pueri, ii. 10. 1
Ciliciensis, i. 2. 7
Cillo, iii. 1. 3
Cincius, ii. 2. 1; iii. 1. 6
Clodia, sister of P. Clodius, ii. 3. 2
Clodia, gens, ii. 13. 1
Clodiana, incendia, ii. 1. 2
Clodianae, operae, ii. 3. 2
Clodiani, ii. 3. 2
Clodius (P.), ii. 1. 3; 3. 2, 4; 9. 2;
  iii. 1. 11; 4. 2
Clodius (Sextus), ii. 4. 6
Commagenus, rex, ii. 12. 2

Cornelius (C.), ii. 3. 5
Cosconius, ii. 4. 5
Crassipes ii. 4. 2; 5. 1; 6. 1, 2;
  iii. 7. 1
Crassus (P. Licinius), i. 3. 7; ii. 3.
  2, 3, 4; 9. 2. 3
Crassus (P. Licinius), son of above.
  ii. 9. 2
Crebius, iii. 5 and 6. 6
Culleo, ii. 2. 1
Cumanum, ii. 5. 5; 14. 1; iii. 5 and
  6. 1
Curio (C. Scribonius), ii. 3. 2, 4
Curius (M.), i. 4. 3
Curtius (M.), ii. 15a. 3; iii. 1. 10
Cyrus the Great, i. 1. 23; 2. 7
Cyrus the architect, ii. 2. 2

Diodotus, i. 2. 12
Dionysius the Elder (of Syracuse),
  ii. 13. 4
Dionysopolitae, i. 2. 4
Diphilus, iii. 1. 1, 2; 9. 7
Domitius (Cn. Calvinus), i. 2. 16;
  ii. 3. 6; 13. 2; 15a. 3; iii. 1. 16;
  4. 1
Drusus (Livius Claudianus), ii.
  16. 3

Electra, iii. 5 and 6. 7
Empedoclea, ii. 11. 5
Ephesus, i. 2. 14
Epicharmus, iii. 1. 23
Erigona, iii. 1. 13; 5 and 6. 7; 9. 6
Euphrates, ii. 12. 2

Fabius (C.), i. 2. 6
Fabricius, i. 4. 3
Fadius Gallus (M.), i. 4. 3
Fannius (C.), iii. 5 and 6. 1
Favonius (M.), ii. 3. 2; 11. 2
Felix, iii. 9. 8
Flaccus (M.), Furius, ii. 5. 2
Flavius (L.), i. 2. 10, 11
Formiae, i. 1. 17
Fufidianus, fundus, iii. 1. 3
Fundanius (C.), i. 2. 10
Furina, iii. 1. 4

Gabinia, lex, ii. 13. 3
Gabinius (A.), ii. 8. 1; 13. 2, 3; iii.
  1. 15, 24; 2. 1, 2, 3; 3. 2, 3; 4. 1;
  5 and 6. 5; 7. 1; 9. 1, 3
Galli, i. 1. 27

750

INDEX OF NAMES II.

Gellius, Poplicola, ii. 1. 1
Glabrio (M'. Acilius), ii. 1.
Gracchus, ii. 2. 1
Graeca, ii. 16. 5
Graeca, bibliotheca, iii. 4. 5
Graeci, i. 1. 7, 16, 18, 19, 33, 35, 36; 2. 4, 6; ii. 13. 4
Graecia, i. 1. 28
Graecostasis, ii. 1. 3
Graii, ii. 12. 3
Gratidius, i. 1. 10

Halicarnassus, i. 1. 25
Hephaestus, i. 2. 4
Heraclides Ponticus, iii. 5 and 6. 1
Hermia, i. 2. 12
Hermippus, i. 2. 4
Herus, iii. 1. 1
Hippodamus, iii. 1. 9, 21
Hirrus, iii. 8. 4; 9. 3
Hispani, i. 1. 27
Homerus, iii. 7. 1
Hortensius (Q.) Hortatus, i. 3. 8; iii. 9. 3
Hymettus, ii. 10. 3
Hypaepenus, i. 2. 14

Juppiter Hospitalis, ii. 9. 1; 12. 3

Labeo, i. 1. 14; iii. 1. 21
Labienus, iii. 7. 2; 8. 1, 2
Labro, ii. 4. 2
Laelius (C.), iii. 5 and 6. 1
Lamia (L.), ii. 13. 2
Lamiae, ii. 3. 7
Latorium, ii. 5. 5; iii. 1. 4, 5; 3. 1
Latiar, ii. 4. 2
Latinae, feriae, ii. 4. 2; 6. 4
Latini, libri, iii. 4. 5; 5 and 6. 6
Lentulus (L.), iii. 1. 15
Lentulus (P. Cornelius Vatia), ii. 3. 5
Lentulus (P. Cornelius Spinther), i. 2. 16; 4. 5; ii. 1. 2; 2. 1, 3; 5, 4
Lepidus (M. Aemilius), ii. 1. 1
Liciniana, domus, ii. 3. 7
Licinius plagiarius, i 2. 6
Licinius, servus, i. 2. 14
Ligurius, iii. 7. 2
Locusta, iii. 1. 4
Longilius, ii. 4. 2
Lucretius (T.), ii. 11. 5

Lucullus (Licinius), i. 2. 12
Lucullus (M. Terentius Varro), ii. 1. 1
Lupercalia, ii. 13. 4
Lupus (P. Rutilius), ii. 1. 1

Macer (Licinius), ii. 4. 1
Magnetes, ii. 11. 2
Manilius (M'.) Nepos, iii. 5 and 6. 1
Manilianus (fundus), iii. 1. 1
Marcellinus (Cn. Cornelius Lentulus), ii. 1. 1, 2; 6. 5
Marcellus, Claudius, ii. 3. 1
Marius (M.), ii. 10. 2, 3, 4
Martis, templum, iii. 7. 1
Martius, campus, ii. 2. 1
Megaristus, i. 2. 4
Memmius (C.), i. 2. 16; 2. 1; 8. 3; iii. 1. 15, 16; 2. 3
Memmius (C.), tribune, iii. 2. 1
Mercuriales, ii. 5. 2
Mescidius, ii. 1. 1, 3
Messalla (M. Valerius), i. 3. 9; ii. 15b. 4; iii. 1. 16; 2. 3; 3. 2; 8. 3; 9. 3
Milo, Annius (T.), i. 4. 3; ii. 1. 3; 3. 1, 2; 4. 5, 7; iii. 1. 13: 2. 2, 8. 6; 9. 2
Mysi, i. 2. 5
Mysius, i. 1. 19

Naso (L. Octavius), i. 2. 10
Neapolis, ii. 10. 2
Nerius (Cn.), ii. 3. 5
Nero. See Tiberius
Nervii, iii. 8. 2
Nicephorus, iii. 1. 5
Nicias Smyrnaeus, i. 2. 4
Nigidius Figulus (P.), i. 2
Numisiana, forma, ii. 2. 1
Nympho Colophonius, i. 2. 4

Oceanus, ii. 16. 4
Octavius (C.), i. 1. 2, 21; 2. 7
Olbia, ii. 8. 1
Olbiensis epistula, ii. 3. 7
Oppius (C.), iii. 1. 8, 10, 13, 17, 18
Orfius, ii. 14. 2
Ostia, ii. 4. 5; iii. 2. 1

Pacideianus Samnis, iii. 4. 2
Paconius, i. 1. 19

INDEX OF NAMES II.

Paeonius, iii. 3. 4
Pansa (C. Vibius), iii. 5 and 6. 5
Petro Epicureus, i. 2. 4
Phaethon, i. 4. 4
Philippus (L. Marcius), ii. 1. 2
Philistus, ii. 13. 4
Philoctetes, ii. 10. 4
Philogonus, i. 3. 4
Philoxenus, iii. 1. 1
Philotimus, iii. 1. 1, 6; 9. 7
Philus (L. Furius), iii. 5 and 6. 1
Phrygius, i. 1. 19
Picenum, ii. 3. 4
Pinarius (T.), iii. 1. 22
Pisae, ii. 5. 5
Piso. See Calpurnius
Placentia, ii. 15a. 1
Plancius, ii. 1. 3; iii. 1. 11
Plato, i. 1. 29
Plato Sardinius, i. 2. 14
Pompeianum, ii. 5. 5; 14. 1
Pompeius Magnus (Cn.), i. 2. 16; 3.
  9; 4. 4; ii. 1. 1; 2. 3; 3. 1, 2, 3,
  4; 4. 2, 5, 6; 5. 1; 9. 2; 15b. 2;
  iii. 19. 15, 18; 2. 1, 2, 3; 3. 3; 4.
  1, 2, 3; 8. 3, 4, 6, 9, 3
Pompeius (Q. Rufus), iii. 2. 3
Pomponia, ii. 5. 2; iii. 1. 7, 19
Pomponiana, nomina, ii. 2. 1
Pomponius Atticus, i. 3. 8; 4. 1;
  ii. 3. 6; 4. 5; 11. 3; 12. 2
Pomptinus (C.), iii. 4. 6
Porcia, sister of Cato, wife of L.
  Domitius Ahenobarbus, iii. 9. 8
Procilius, ii. 8. 1
Psyria (Ψυρία) arx, ii. 10. 3
Ptolemaeus, rex, ii. 10. 2
Publicius (Q.), i. 2. 14
Publius, iii. 1. 17
Pupinia, lex, ii. 3. 5

Quintus Cicero (P.), ii. 12. 4
Quintus, son of above, ii. 4. 2;
  4. 2
Quirinalia, ii. 3. 2, 4; 13. 3

Racilius, ii. 1. 2, 3; 4. 5
Rhodii, i. 1. 33
Roma, i. 1. 22, 42; 2. 15; 3. 4; ii.
  2. 1; 4. 2; 5. 5; 14. 1; 15a. 2;
  iii. 1. 4, 7, 11, 14, 21, 26; 5 and 6.
  2, 6; 7. 1, 2; 9. 4
Romanae, res, ii. 4. 4; 15a. 5

Romanus populns, i. 1. 26, 33
Rutilius (P.), iii. 5 and 6. 1

Salvius, iii. 1. 21
Samos, i. 1. 25; iii. 7. 2
Sallustius, poet, ii. 11. 5
Sallustius (Cn.), iii. 4. 2, 3; 5 and
  6. 1
Sardinia, ii. 2. 1; 3. 7; 5. 4
Satricum, iii. 1. 4
Scaevola (Q. Mucius), the jurist,
  iii. 5 and 6. 1
Scaevola (Q. Mucius), the tribune,
  i. 2. 13; iii. 4. 6
Scaurus (M. Aemilius), ii. 15b. 4;
  16. 3; iii. 1. 11; 2. 3; 8. 3
Scipio, iii. 4. 5
Serranus Domesticus, iii. 8. 5
Servilius (P.), ii. 1. 1; iii. 1. 20; 4. 6
Servilius Isauricus (P.), son of
  above, ii. 3. 2, 7
Servius Pola, ii. 4. 6; 13. 2
Sestius (P.), i. 4. 1, 2, 3, 5; ii. 2. 1;
  3. 5, 6; 4. 1
Sextilius (Q.), ii. 1. 3
Siculus, ii. 13. 4
Sicura, iii. 9. 8
Siphylus, ii. 11. 2
Smyrna, i. 2. 5
Sophocles, ii. 16. 3
Statius, i. 2. 1, 2, 3
Sulla (P.), i. 1. 33; 2. 9; iii. 3. 2
Sulla (P.), son of above, iii. 3. 2
Sullani homines, i. 1. 21
Syriaci publicani, ii. 13. 2
Syriacus, i. 2. 7

Taurus (M.), iii. 1. 4
Tellus, iii. 1. 14
Tenedius, ii. 11. 2
Terentia, i. 3. 10
Theopompus, i. 2. 9; ii. 12. 4
Thessalonica, i. 3. 10; 4. 1
Thucydides, ii. 13. 4
Tiberius Nero, iii. 1. 15; 2. 1
Tiro, iii. 1. 19
Titius (T.), ii. 5. 5
Torquatus (L.), iii. 3. 2
Tralles, i. 1. 17
Trebatius, iii. 1. 9; ii. 14. 2; 15a. 3
Trebonius, iii. 1. 9
Triarius, iii. 2. 3
Troas, iii. 5 and 6. 1
Tubero Aelius (Q.), iii. 5 and 6. 1

INDEX OF NAMES II.

Tubero (T.), i. 1. 10
Tullia, ii. 4. 2; 5. 1
Tullius Albinovensis, ii. 3. 5
Tuditanus (C. Sempronius), consul in 129 B.C., iii. 5 and 6. 1
Tuscenius, i. 1. 19; 2. 6
Tusculanum, ii. 2. 1; iii. 1. 23; 4. 6; 5 and 6. 1
Tyrannio, ii. 4. 2; iii. 4. 5; 5 and 6. 6
Tyrii, ii. 13. 2

Urania, ii. 9. 1

Varro, iii. 1. 4
Vatia. See Lentulus
Vatinius, ii. 4. 1; 16. 3; iii. 9. 5
Venafrum, iii. 1. 3
Vergilius, i. 2. 7
Volcatius Tullus (L.), ii. 1. 1
Vibullius, ii. 9. 2
Vitularia (via), iii. 1. 3

Xenophon, i. 1. 23; 2. 7

Zeugma, ii. 12. 2
Ζεύς, iii. 7. 1
Zeuxis, i. 2. 4, 5

INDEX OF NAMES III.

CICERO'S LETTERS TO BRUTUS

(The serial number of the letters follows that of the text)

Achaia, xvi. 1 ; **xxiv. 5**

Achilleus, xii. 2

Ambracia, xii. 1

Antonii, x. 2

Antonius, C., ii. 2 ; iv. 3 ; viii. ; xiv. 3

Antonius, M., v. 1-4 ; vii. 1 ; viii. ; xi. 3, 5 ; xiii. 1 ; xiv. 2 ; xvi. 1 ; xvii. 1, 2, 5 ; xviii. 2, 4 ; xxii. 1, 2 ; xxiv. 4, 7, 8, 10 ; xxv. 2-4, 7, 8

Apollo, vi. 6

Apollonia, xix. 2

Appuleius, xx. 2

Aquila, xxiv. 8

Asia, ii. 5 ; iv. 3 ; ix. 3 ; xiv. 1

Attica, xvii. 7

Atticus, xvii. 3 ; **xxv. 1**

Bestia, xvii. 1

Bibuli, xxiii. 1

Bibulus, L., xx. 1-2 ; xxiii. 1

Brutus (Dec.), i. 1 ; iii. 2 ; iv. 3 ; viii. ; x. 1 ; xiv. 2 ; xviii. 2 ; xxiii. 2 ; xxiv. 7-9

Brutus (M.), i. 2, 3 ; v. 1, 5, 6 ; vi. 5, 6 ; xiii. 1 ; xv. 1 ; xviii. 3, 4 ; xix. 2 ; xxi. 1 ; xxii. 1 ; xxiii. 1, 2 ; xxiv. 1, 2, 4, 5, 7, 12

Caesar (C. Iulius, the dictator), xii. 4 ; xvi. 1 ; xxiv. 1, 4 ; xxv. 3-6, 8

Caesar (C. Iulius Octavianus), iv. 5 ; v. 2 ; vii. 1 ; viii. ; xi. 4 ; xviii. 3, 4 ; xxiii. 2 ; xxiv. 6, 9 ; xxv. 6

Calenus, ii. 4

Candavia, xii. 4

Capitolium, vii. 1

Cappadocia, ix. 3

Casca, xvii. 1 ; xxvi. 1

Cassius i. 3 ; ii. 3 ; iii. 3 ; iv. 2, 5 ; ix. 1, 2 ; xvii. 1, 2, 4-6 ; xviii. 5 ; xxiv. 5

Cato, ix. 3 ; xxiii. 1

Celer Pilius, v. 3, 4

Chersonesus, xiv. **1, 2**

Cicereius, xii. 3

Cicero, M., ii. 4 ; x. 3 ; **xi. 3** ; xii. 4 ; xvi. 1 ; xvii. 1, 2, 4-6 ; xxi. 1, 2 ; xxv. 2, 10, 11

Cicero, M. (son of the above), ii. 6 ; iv. 6 ; v. 2, 6 ; ix. 3 ; xxii. 3 ; xxiii. 1, 2

Clodius, L., xiii. 1, 2

Clodius, P., xvii. 1

Cornutus, v. 3

Cretense Bellum, xv. 2

Deiotarus, xii. 3

Dolabella, ii. 5 ; iv. 2, 3 ; v. 3, 5 ; vi. 4 ; ix. 1, 2 ; xii. 3 ; xiv. 1 ; xvi. 1

Domitia lex, ix. 3

Domitius, ix. 3 ; xv. 2 ; xxiii. 1

Dyrrhachium, ii. 6 ; iv. 1 ; xii. 4 ; xiv. 2

Europa, xiv. 1

Flavius, xii. 4 ; xvii. **3**

Glycon, xii. 2

INDEX OF NAMES III.

Heraclea, **xii.** 1
Hirtius, viii. ; **xxiv.** 8

Italia, iv. 4 ; xviii. 1, 4 ; **xxii.** 2,
   3 ; xxiii. 2 ; xxiv. 5, 12
Iulia lex, ix. 3
Iuppiter, xxii. 1

Labeo, v. 4 ; **xxvi.** 1
Larentia, xxiv. 8
Lentulus, iii. 3 ; xviii. 1
Lepidus, iii. 1 ; xviii. 2 ; **xxi.** 1 ;
   xxii. 1, 2 ; xxiii. 2 ; **xxiv.** 4, 9,
   10, 12

Macedonia, xi. 6 ; **xii.** 1, 4
Marcius, ii. 3
Marius, ix. 3
Messalla Corvinus, **xxii.** 1 ; xxiv.
   1, 2
Metellus, **xv.** 2
Murcus, ii. 3
Mutina, **ix.** 2 ; **xviii.** 2

Nasennius, xv. 2

Octavianus, v. 2
Octavius, xvii. 5, 6 ; **xxv.** 1, 2, 7,
   8, 11

Pansa, ii. 5 ; iv. 2, 4 ; v. 2 ; **viii.** ;

   ix. 4 ; **xii.** 2 ; **xviii.** 1 ; **xx.** 1 ;
   xxiv. 8
Pnilippus, ii. 4 ; xvii. 5 ; xxiv. 7
Plancus, iii. 1, 3 ; xviii. 2 ; xxiii.
   2 ; xxiv. 9
Porcia, xvii. 7

Rhodes, iv. 3
Roma, xviii. 4 ; **xxv.** 8

Salvidienus, xvii. 4
Satrius, xii. 3
Scaptius, iv. 1 ; **xxvi.** 1
Servilius, M., v. 3
Servilius, P., iii. 3 ; **ix.** 1 ; **xxiv.** 7
Servius, xxiv. 7
Sestius, v. 4
Suessa, **xv.** 2
Syria, ii. 3 ; **iii.** 3

Tertia, **ii.** 3 ; iv. 5
Themistocles, xxiv. 11
Thessalia, xii. 1
Tillius, xii. 3
Torquatus, xii. 2
Trebonius, ii. 1, 5 ; **xii.** 3

Velabrum, **xxiv.** 8
Velia, xviii. **4** ; **xxiv.** 5
Ventidius, ix. 1
Vetus, C. Antistius, ii. 5 ; **xvi.** 1,
   2 ; **xix.** 3 ; **xxii.** 1, 3

Printed in Great Britain by R. & R. CLARK, LIMITED, *Edinburgh*

THE LOEB CLASSICAL LIBRARY

THE LOEB CLASSICAL LIBRARY

VOLUMES ALREADY PUBLISHED

LATIN AUTHORS

AMMIANUS MARCELLINUS. J. C. Rolfe. 3 Vols.

APULEIUS : THE GOLDEN ASS (METAMORPHOSES). W. Adlington (1566). Revised by S. Gaselee.

ST. AUGUSTINE : CITY OF GOD. 7 Vols. Vol. I. G. E. McCracken.

ST. AUGUSTINE, CONFESSIONS OF. W. Watts (1631). 2 Vols.

ST. AUGUSTINE : SELECT LETTERS. J. H. Baxter.

AUSONIUS. H. G. Evelyn White. 2 Vols.

BEDE. J. E. King. 2 Vols.

BOETHIUS : TRACTS AND DE CONSOLATIONE PHILOSOPHIAE. Rev. H. F. Stewart and E. K. Rand.

CAESAR : ALEXANDRIAN, AFRICAN AND SPANISH WARS. A. G. Way.

CAESAR : CIVIL WARS. A. G. Peskett.

CAESAR : GALLIC WAR. H. J. Edwards.

CATO AND VARRO : DE RE RUSTICA. H. B. Ash and W. D. Hooper.

CATULLUS. F. W. Cornish ; TIBULLUS. J. B. Postgate ; and PERVIGILIUM VENERIS. J. W. Mackail.

CELSUS : DE MEDICINA. W. G. Spencer. 3 Vols.

CICERO : BRUTUS AND ORATOR. G. L. Hendrickson and H. M. Hubbell.

CICERO : DE FINIBUS. H. Rackham.

CICERO : DE INVENTIONE, etc. H. M. Hubbell.

CICERO : DE NATURA DEORUM AND ACADEMICA. H. Rackham.

CICERO : DE OFFICIIS. Walter Miller.

1

THE LOEB CLASSICAL LIBRARY

CICERO: DE ORATORE, etc. 2 Vols. Vol. I: DE ORATORE, Books I and II. E. W. Sutton and H. Rackham. Vol. II: DE ORATORE, Book III; DE FATO; PARADOXA STOICORUM; DE PARTITIONE ORATORIA. H. Rackham.

CICERO: DE REPUBLICA, DE LEGIBUS, SOMNIUM SCIPIONIS. Clinton W. Keyes.

CICERO: DE SENECTUTE, DE AMICITIA, DE DIVINATIONE. W. A. Falconer.

CICERO: IN CATILINAM, PRO MURENA, PRO SULLA, PRO FLACCO. Louis E. Lord.

CICERO: LETTERS TO ATTICUS. E. O. Winstedt. 3 Vols.

CICERO: LETTERS TO HIS FRIENDS. W. Glynn Williams. 3 Vols.

CICERO: PHILIPPICS. W. C. A. Ker.

CICERO: PRO ARCHIA, POST REDITUM, DE DOMO, DE HARUSPICUM RESPONSIS, PRO PLANCIO. N. H. Watts.

CICERO: PRO CAECINA, PRO LEGE MANILIA, PRO CLUENTIO, PRO RABIRIO. H. Grose Hodge.

CICERO: PRO CAELIO, DE PROVINCIIS CONSULARIBUS, PRO BALBO. R. Gardner.

CICERO: PRO MILONE, IN PISONEM, PRO SCAURO, PRO FONTEIO, PRO RABIRIO POSTUMO, PRO MARCELLO, PRO LIGARIO, PRO REGE DEIOTARO. N. H. Watts.

CICERO: PRO QUINCTIO, PRO ROSCIO AMERINO, PRO ROSCIO COMOEDO, CONTRA RULLUM. J. H. Freese.

CICERO: PRO SESTIO, IN VATINIUM. R. Gardner.

[CICERO]: RHETORICA AD HERENNIUM. H. Caplan.

CICERO: TUSCULAN DISPUTATIONS. J. E. King.

CICERO: VERRINE ORATIONS. L. H. G. Greenwood. 2 Vols.

CLAUDIAN. M. Platnauer. 2 Vols.

COLUMELLA: DE RE RUSTICA; DE ARBORIBUS. H. B. Ash, E. S. Forster, E. Heffner. 3 Vols.

CURTIUS, Q.: HISTORY OF ALEXANDER. J. C. Rolfe. 2 Vols.

FLORUS. E. S. Forster; and CORNELIUS NEPOS. J. C. Rolfe.

FRONTINUS: STRATAGEMS AND AQUEDUCTS. C. E. Bennett and M. B. McElwain.

FRONTO: CORRESPONDENCE. C. R. Haines. 2 Vols.

GELLIUS. J. C. Rolfe. 3 Vols.

HORACE: ODES AND EPODES. C. E. Bennett.

HORACE: SATIRES, EPISTLES, ARS POETICA. H. R. Fairclough.

JEROME: SELECT LETTERS. F. A. Wright.

JUVENAL AND PERSIUS. G. G. Ramsay.

2

LIVY. B. O. Foster, F. G. Moore, Evan T. Sage, A. C. Schlesinger and R. M. Geer (General Index). 14 Vols.

LUCAN. J. D. Duff.

LUCRETIUS. W. H. D. Rouse.

MARTIAL. W. C. A. Ker. 2 Vols.

MINOR LATIN POETS: from PUBLILIUS SYRUS to RUTILIUS NAMATIANUS, including GRATTIUS, CALPURNIUS SICULUS, NEMESIANUS, AVIANUS, with " Aetna," " Phoenix " and other poems. J. Wight Duff and Arnold M. Duff.

OVID: THE ART OF LOVE AND OTHER POEMS. J. H. Mozley.

OVID: FASTI. Sir James G. Frazer.

OVID: HEROIDES AND AMORES. Grant Showerman.

OVID: METAMORPHOSES. F. J. Miller. 2 Vols.

OVID: TRISTIA AND EX PONTO. A. L. Wheeler.

PETRONIUS. M. Heseltine; SENECA: APOCOLOCYNTOSIS. W. H. D. Rouse.

PLAUTUS. Paul Nixon. 5 Vols.

PLINY: LETTERS. Melmoth's translation revised by W. M. L. Hutchinson. 2 Vols.

PLINY: NATURAL HISTORY. 10 Vols. Vols. I-V and IX. H. Rackham. Vols. VI and VII. W. H. S. Jones.

PROPERTIUS. H. E. Butler.

PRUDENTIUS. H. J. Thomson. 2 Vols.

QUINTILIAN. H. E. Butler. 4 Vols.

REMAINS OF OLD LATIN. E. H. Warmington. 4 Vols. Vol. I (Ennius and Caecilius). Vol. II (Livius, Naevius, Pacuvius, Accius). Vol. III (Lucilius, Laws of the XII Tables). Vol. IV (Archaic Inscriptions).

SALLUST. J. C. Rolfe.

SCRIPTORES HISTORIAE AUGUSTAE. D. Magie. 3 Vols.

SENECA: APOCOLOCYNTOSIS. Cf. PETRONIUS.

SENECA: EPISTULAE MORALES. R. M. Gummere. 3 Vols.

SENECA: MORAL ESSAYS. J. W. Basore. 3 Vols.

SENECA: TRAGEDIES. F. J. Miller. 2 Vols.

SIDONIUS: POEMS AND LETTERS. W. B. Anderson. 2 Vols.

SILIUS ITALICUS. J. D. Duff. 2 Vols.

STATIUS. J. H. Mozley. 2 Vols.

SUETONIUS. J. C. Rolfe. 2 Vols.

TACITUS: DIALOGUS. Sir Wm. Peterson; and AGRICOLA AND GERMANIA. Maurice Hutton.

TACITUS: HISTORIES AND ANNALS. C. H. Moore and J. Jackson. 4 Vols.

THE LOEB CLASSICAL LIBRARY

TERENCE. John Sargeaunt. 2 Vols.
TERTULLIAN: APOLOGIA AND DE SPECTACULIS. T. R. Glover;
Minucius Felix. G. H. Rendall.
VALERIUS FLACCUS. J. H. Mozley.
VARRO: DE LINGUA LATINA. R. G. Kent. 2 Vols.
VELLEIUS PATERCULUS AND RES GESTAE DIVI AUGUSTI.
F. W. Shipley.
VIRGIL. H. R. Fairclough. 2 Vols.
VITRUVIUS: DE ARCHITECTURA. F Granger. 2 Vols.

GREEK AUTHORS

ACHILLES TATIUS. S. Gaselee. (2nd Imp.)
AELIAN: ON THE NATURE OF ANIMALS. A. F. Scholfield.
3 Vols. Vols. I and II.
AENEAS TACTICUS, ASCLEPIODOTUS AND ONASANDER. The
Illinois Greek Club.
AESCHINES. C. D. Adams.
AESCHYLUS. H. Weir Smyth. 2 Vols.
ALCIPHRON, AELIAN AND PHILOSTRATUS: LETTERS. A. R.
Benner and F. H. Fobes.
APOLLODORUS. Sir James G. Frazer. 2 Vols.
APOLLONIUS RHODIUS. R. C. Seaton.
THE APOSTOLIC FATHERS. Kirsopp Lake. 2 Vols.
APPIAN'S ROMAN HISTORY. Horace White. 4 Vols.
ARATUS. Cf. CALLIMACHUS.
ARISTOPHANES. Benjamin Bickley Rogers. 3 Vols. Verse
trans.
ARISTOTLE: ART OF RHETORIC. J. H. Freese.
ARISTOTLE: ATHENIAN CONSTITUTION, EUDEMIAN ETHICS,
VIRTUES AND VICES. H. Rackham.
ARISTOTLE: GENERATION OF ANIMALS. A. L. Peck.
ARISTOTLE: METAPHYSICS. H. Tredennick. 2 Vols.
ARISTOTLE: METEOROLOGICA. H. D. P. Lee.
ARISTOTLE: MINOR WORKS. W. S. Hett. "On Colours,"
"On Things Heard," "Physiognomics," "On Plants,"
"On Marvellous Things Heard,""Mechanical Problems,"
"On Indivisible Lines," "Situations and Names of
Winds," "On Melissus, Xenophanes, and Gorgias."
ARISTOTLE: NICOMACHEAN ETHICS. H. Rackham.

4

THE LOEB CLASSICAL LIBRARY

ARISTOTLE: OECONOMICA AND MAGNA MORALIA. G. C. Armstrong. (With Metaphysics, Vol. II.)

ARISTOTLE: ON THE HEAVENS. W. K. C. Guthrie.

ARISTOTLE: ON THE SOUL, PARVA NATURALIA, ON BREATH. W. S. Hett.

ARISTOTLE: ORGANON—THE CATEGORIES. ON INTERPRETATION. H. P. Cooke; PRIOR ANALYTICS. H. Tredennick.

ARISTOTLE: ORGANON—POSTERIOR ANALYTICS. H. Tredennick; TOPICS. E. S. Forster.

ARISTOTLE: ORGANON—SOPHISTICAL REFUTATIONS. COMING-TO-BE AND PASSING-AWAY. E. S. Forster. ON THE COSMOS. D. J. Furley.

ARISTOTLE: PARTS OF ANIMALS. A. L. Peck; MOTION AND PROGRESSION OF ANIMALS. E. S. Forster.

ARISTOTLE: PHYSICS. Rev. P. Wicksteed and F. M. Cornford. 2 Vols.

ARISTOTLE: POETICS; LONGINUS ON THE SUBLIME. W. Hamilton Fyfe; DEMETRIUS ON STYLE. W. Rhys Roberts.

ARISTOTLE: POLITICS. H. Rackham.

ARISTOTLE: PROBLEMS. W. S. Hett. 2 Vols.

ARISTOTLE: RHETORICA AD ALEXANDRUM. H. Rackham. (With Problems, Vol. II.)

ARRIAN: HISTORY OF ALEXANDER AND INDICA. Rev. E. Iliffe Robson. 2 Vols.

ATHENAEUS: DEIPNOSOPHISTAE. C. B. Gulick. 7 Vols.

ST. BASIL: LETTERS. R. J. Deferrari. 4 Vols.

CALLIMACHUS: FRAGMENTS. C. A. Trypanis.

CALLIMACHUS: HYMNS AND EPIGRAMS, AND LYCOPHRON. A. W. Mair; ARATUS. G. R. Mair.

CLEMENT OF ALEXANDRIA. Rev. G. W. Butterworth.

COLLUTHUS. Cf. OPPIAN.

DAPHNIS AND CHLOE. Cf. LONGUS.

DEMOSTHENES I: OLYNTHIACS, PHILIPPICS AND MINOR ORATIONS: I-XVII AND XX. J. H. Vince.

DEMOSTHENES II: DE CORONA AND DE FALSA LEGATIONE. C. A. Vince and J. H. Vince.

DEMOSTHENES III: MEIDIAS, ANDROTION, ARISTOCRATES, TIMOCRATES, ARISTOGEITON. J. H. Vince.

DEMOSTHENES IV-VI: PRIVATE ORATIONS AND IN NEAERAM. A. T. Murray.

DEMOSTHENES VII: FUNERAL SPEECH, EROTIC ESSAY, EXORDIA AND LETTERS. N. W. and N. J. DeWitt.

THE LOEB CLASSICAL LIBRARY

Dio Cassius : Roman History. E. Cary. 9 Vols.
Dio Chrysostom. 5 Vols. Vols. I and II. J. W. Cohoon.
Vol. III. J. W. Cohoon and H. Lamar Crosby. Vols. IV
and V. H. Lamar Crosby.
Diodorus Siculus. 12 Vols. Vols. I-VI. C. H. Oldfather.
Vol. VII. C. L. Sherman. Vols. IX and X. Russel M.
Geer. Vol. XI. F. R. Walton.
Diogenes Laertius. R. D. Hicks. 2 Vols.
Dionysius of Halicarnassus : Roman Antiquities. Spel-
man's translation revised by E. Cary. 7 Vols.
Epictetus. W. A. Oldfather. 2 Vols.
Euripides. A. S. Way. 4 Vols. Verse trans.
Eusebius : Ecclesiastical History. Kirsopp Lake and
J. E. L. Oulton. 2 Vols.
Galen : On the Natural Faculties. A. J. Brock.
The Greek Anthology. W. R. Paton. 5 Vols.
The Greek Bucolic Poets (Theocritus, Bion, Moschus).
J. M. Edmonds.
Greek Elegy and Iambus with the Anacreontea. J. M.
Edmonds. 2 Vols.
Greek Mathematical Works. Ivor Thomas. 2 Vols.
Herodes. Cf. Theophrastus : Characters.
Herodotus. A. D. Godley. 4 Vols.
Hesiod and the Homeric Hymns. H. G. Evelyn White.
Hippocrates and the Fragments of Heracleitus. W. H. S.
Jones and E. T. Withington. 4 Vols.
Homer : Iliad. A. T. Murray. 2 Vols.
Homer : Odyssey. A. T. Murray. 2 Vols.
Isaeus. E. S. Forster.
Isocrates. George Norlin and LaRue Van Hook. 3 Vols.
St. John Damascene : Barlaam and Ioasaph. Rev. G. R.
Woodward and Harold Mattingly.
Josephus. H. St. J. Thackeray and Ralph Marcus. 9 Vols.
Vols. I-VII.
Julian. Wilmer Cave Wright. 3 Vols.
Longus : Daphnis and Chloe. Thornley's translation
revised by J. M. Edmonds ; and Parthenius. S. Gase-
lee.
Lucian. A. M. Harmon. 8 Vols. Vols. I-V.
Lycophron. Cf. Callimachus.
Lyra Graeca. J. M. Edmonds. 3 Vols.
Lysias. W. R. M. Lamb.

THE LOEB CLASSICAL LIBRARY

MANETHO. W. G. Waddell; PTOLEMY: TETRABIBLOS. F. E. Robbins.

MARCUS AURELIUS. C. R. Haines.

MENANDER. F. G. Allinson.

MINOR ATTIC ORATORS. 2 Vols. K. J. Maidment and J. O. Burtt.

NONNOS: DIONYSIACA. W. H. D. Rouse. 3 Vols.

OPPIAN, COLLUTHUS, TRYPHIODORUS. A. W. Mair.

PAPYRI. NON-LITERARY SELECTIONS. A. S. Hunt and C. C. Edgar. 2 Vols. LITERARY SELECTIONS (Poetry). D. L. Page.

PARTHENIUS. *Cf.* LONGUS.

PAUSANIAS: DESCRIPTION OF GREECE. W. H. S. Jones. 5 Vols. and Companion Vol. arranged by R. E. Wycherley.

PHILO. 10 Vols. Vols. I-V. F. H. Colson and Rev. G. H. Whitaker; Vols. VI-IX. F. H. Colson.
Two Supplementary Vols. Translation only from an Armenian Text. Ralph Marcus.

PHILOSTRATUS: THE LIFE OF APOLLONIUS OF TYANA. F. C. Conybeare. 2 Vols.

PHILOSTRATUS: IMAGINES; CALLISTRATUS: DESCRIPTIONS. A. Fairbanks.

PHILOSTRATUS AND EUNAPIUS: LIVES OF THE SOPHISTS. Wilmer Cave Wright.

PINDAR. Sir J. E. Sandys.

PLATO I: EUTHYPHRO, APOLOGY, CRITO, PHAEDO, PHAEDRUS. H. N. Fowler.

PLATO II: THEAETETUS AND SOPHIST. H. N. Fowler.

PLATO III: STATESMAN, PHILEBUS. H. N. Fowler; ION. W. R. M. Lamb.

PLATO IV: LACHES, PROTAGORAS, MENO, EUTHYDEMUS. W. R. M. Lamb.

PLATO V: LYSIS, SYMPOSIUM, GORGIAS. W. R. M. Lamb.

PLATO VI: CRATYLUS, PARMENIDES, GREATER HIPPIAS, LESSER HIPPIAS. H. N. Fowler.

PLATO VII: TIMAEUS, CRITIAS, CLITOPHO, MENEXENUS, EPI-STULAE. Rev. R. G. Bury.

PLATO VIII: CHARMIDES, ALCIBIADES, HIPPARCHUS, THE LOVERS, THEAGES, MINOS AND EPINOMIS. W. R. M. Lamb.

PLATO: LAWS. Rev. R. G. Bury. 2 Vols.

PLATO: REPUBLIC. Paul Shorey. 2 Vols.

PLUTARCH: MORALIA. 15 Vols. Vols. I-V. F. C. Babbitt;

THE LOEB CLASSICAL LIBRARY

Vol. VI. W. C. Helmbold; Vol. VII. P. H. De Lacy and B. Einarson; Vol. X. H. N. Fowler; Vol. XII. H. Cherniss and W. C. Helmbold.

PLUTARCH : THE PARALLEL LIVES. B. Perrin. 11 Vols.

POLYBIUS. W. R. Paton. 6 Vols.

PROCOPIUS : HISTORY OF THE WARS. H. B. Dewing. 7 Vols.

PTOLEMY : TETRABIBLOS. *Cf.* MANETHO.

QUINTUS SMYRNAEUS. A. S. Way. Verse trans.

SEXTUS EMPIRICUS. Rev. R. G. Bury. 4 Vols.

SOPHOCLES. F. Storr. 2 Vols. Verse trans.

STRABO : GEOGRAPHY. Horace L. Jones. 8 Vols.

THEOPHRASTUS : CHARACTERS. J. M. Edmonds; HERODES, etc. A. D. Knox.

THEOPHRASTUS : ENQUIRY INTO PLANTS. Sir Arthur Hort. 2 Vols.

THUCYDIDES. C. F. Smith. 4 Vols.

TRYPHIODORUS. *Cf.* OPPIAN.

XENOPHON : CYROPAEDIA. Walter Miller. 2 Vols.

XENOPHON : HELLENICA, ANABASIS, APOLOGY, AND SYMPOSIUM. C. L. Brownson and O. J. Todd. 3 Vols.

XENOPHON : MEMORABILIA AND OECONOMICUS. E. C. Marchant.

XENOPHON : SCRIPTA MINORA. E. C. Marchant.

VOLUMES IN PREPARATION

GREEK AUTHORS

ARISTOTLE : HISTORY OF ANIMALS. A. L. Peck.

PLOTINUS. A. H. Armstrong.

LATIN AUTHORS

BABRIUS AND PHAEDRUS. B. E. Perry.

DESCRIPTIVE PROSPECTUS ON APPLICATION

LONDON   CAMBRIDGE, MASS.

WILLIAM HEINEMANN LTD   HARVARD UNIV. PRESS